METHODS THAT WORK

Ideas for Literacy and Language Teachers

Edited by

John W. Oller, Jr.
University of New Mexico

Heinle & Heinle Publishers
A Division of Wadsworth, Inc.
Boston, Massachusetts 02116 USA

The publication of *Methods That Work, Second Edition* was directed by the members of the Heinle & Heinle ESL Publishing Team:

David C. Lee, *Editorial Director*
Susan Mraz, *Marketing Manager*
Kristin Thalheimer, *Production Editor*

Also participating in the publication of this program were:

Publisher: Stanley J. Galek
Editorial Production Manager: Elizabeth Holthaus
Assistant Editor: Kenneth Mattsson
Project Manager: Margaret Cleveland
Manufacturing Coordinator: Mary Beth Lynch
Interior Design and Composition: Greg Johnson
Cover Design: Susan Schon

Heinle & Heinle Publishers is a division of Wadsworth, Inc.

Manufactured in the United States of America

ISBN 0-8384-4271-4

10 9 8 7 6 5 4 3 2

"I had a teacher, once . . ."

Mary Finnochiaro, TESOL Address, 1984

Contents

ACKNOWLEDGEMENTS

For the second edition of this book, the persons to be thanked are more numerous than for the first. This one owes its existence to tens of thousands of users who made the first edition successful. Therefore, at the very first, on behalf of myself and my coworker on that edition, Dr. Patricia Richard-Amato, I want to thank those users. In addition, I must also thank the Modern Language Association for the honor of the Mildenberger Medal that Pat and I shared in 1984 along with one of our coauthors, Sandra Savignon (who was honored for another book of her own, *Communicative Competence: Theory and Classroom Practice,* 1983).

For my own part, relative to this new edition, there are many people to whom I personally owe a debt of gratitude. Foremost among them is my former student, collaborator, and distinguished colleague, Dr. Richard-Amato. Her book, *Making It Happen: Interaction in the Second Language Classroom,* according to a survey by Grosse (1991: 39), had surpassed all but two of its competitors and was reported as the main coursebook in more methods courses for ESL teachers than the first edition of *Methods That Work.* When I first saw Dr. Richard-Amato's manuscript, I knew that it was destined to be a book that language teachers would gladly receive. I was correctly quoted by her publishers as saying that people who liked *Methods That Work* would love *Making It Happen.* While Dr. Richard-Amato is no longer an editor of this volume, her influence is still felt, and I personally want to thank her for the help and inspiration that she has afforded, not only to me as her teacher and friend, but also, I believe, to the profession at large. On a more personal note, I will never forget that it was Pat's idea to dedicate the first edition of *Methods That Work* to the memory of my Dad, whose Spanish program Pat had studied in a Colorado high school.

In addition, I am glad to thank all of the contributors to the first volume, some of whom, sad to say (Tracy Terrell, Robert J. Di Pietro, Caleb Gattegno, and Jonathan de Berkeley Wykes) have died in the interim—a poignant reminder that all of us really are mortal, just as Aristotle noted with special reference to Socrates. With respect to the first edition, I also want to personally thank the reviewers, fellow teachers, colleagues, students, and all the users who made it one of the most widely used methods books in the history of language teaching. Of them I hope that someone may say in future days, as Mary Finocchiaro told us back in 1984 in her plenary address to the TESOL organization, "I had a teacher once. . . ." In fact, this is my hope for all those old friends and new collaborators associated with this present edition. Thanks especially go out to those who responded enthusiastically and in many cases nearly instantaneously to my mass mailing asking for input to the new edition (or who responded to our request for input in the Preface to the first edition). The help was invaluable—and an uplifting encouragement for this new venture. I am especially grateful to the following (in alphabetical order): Diane Fagin Adler, Jim Alatis, Neil Anderson, J. J. Asher, Leila Barbara, Benoît Behnan, Dean Brodkey, Pat Carrell, Tetsuro Chihara, Andrew D. Cohen, Jim Cummins, Jack Damico, Fred Davidson, John Edwards, Judy Gladden, Tomás Graman, Else Hamayan, Sue Hirschmann, Javad Jafarhpur, Dorothy James, Otto Johnston, Dimitri Katsareas, Stephen Krashen, Gladys Lipton, Harold Madsen, Kathleen M. Marcos, Gladis E. Maresma, I. Fernando Maresma, Miriam Met, Joan Morley, Leonard Newmark, Donald Omark, Tahereh Paribakt, Christina Bratt Paulston, Kyle Perkins, Gail Povey, Kanchana Prapphal, John Rassias, Nancy Rhodes, Ellen Rintell, Mario Rinvolucri, John Schumann, Tom Scovel, V. D. Singh, Charles Stansfield, Shirley Stapleton, Susan Stern, Earl Stevick, Nina Wallerstein, Mari Wesche, and Phyllis Wilcox. And what can I say that could even come close to expressing the gratitude owed those many users of the first edition who went the second mile by implementing and testing its ideas? All of them helped to produce this second edition.

It is a pleasure also to thank my long-time friend, Rupert Ingram, founder of Newbury House Publishers, for the encouragement to pursue the first edition, along with the present publishers, their staff, the contributors to this volume, and all those who allowed their work to be used here in the second edition. I am grateful for permission to reprint from the following publishers, authors, and photographers for each of the named items:

The American Council of Teachers of Foreign Languages for materials from the *Foreign Language Annals*, including:

Theodore B. Kalivoda, Genelle Morain, and Robert J. Elkins (1971). The audio-motor unit: A listening comprehension strategy that works. *Foreign Language Annals, 4,* 392–400;

Eileen W. Glisan (1986). Total physical response: A technique for teaching all skills in Spanish. *Foreign Language Annals, 19,* 419–427;

Steven Sternfeld (1989). The University of Utah's Immersion/Multiliteracy Program: An example of an area studies approach to the design of first-year college foreign language instruction. *Foreign Language Annals, 22(4),* 341–352;

Ben Christensen (1990). Teenage novels of adventure as a source of authentic material. *Foreign Language Annals, 23(6),* 531–537;

Ann Masters Salomone (1991). Immersion teachers: What can we learn from them? *Foreign Language Annals, 24(1),* 57–63;

Helena Curtain (1991). Methods in elementary school foreign language teaching. *Foreign Language Annals, 24(4),* 323–328;

Jane Tucker Mitchell and Mary Lynn Redmond (1991). The FLES course: Key to K–12 certification. *Foreign Language Annals, 24(6),* 507–510;

Wendy Allen, Keith Anderson, and León Narvaréz (1992). Foreign languages across the curriculum: The applied foreign language component. *Foreign Language Annals, 25(1),* 11–19;

Paul W. Seaver, Jr. (1992). Pantomime as an L2 classroom strategy. *Foreign Language Annals, 25*(1), 21–31.

The American Forum at 45 John Street, Suite 1200, New York, NY 10038 for:

Carolyn Andrade, Richard R. Kretschmer, Jr., and Laura W. Kretschmer (1989). Two languages for all children: Expanding to low achievers and the handicapped. In Kurt E. Müller (Ed.), *Languages in elementary schools* (pp. 177–199). New York: The American Forum.

The *Beijing Review: A Chinese Weekly of News and Views* for:

Ma Baolin (1987). Teaching language by using theater. *Beijing Review, 30*(29), I–III.

Cambridge University Press for:

John Morgan and Mario Rinvolucri (1983). *Once upon a time: Using stories in the language classroom* (pp. 1–3, 8–12, 18, 36–37). London: Cambridge University, as excerpted and revised.

The journal *Cross Currents: An International Journal of Language Teaching and Cross-Cultural Communication* for:

Stephen D. Krashen (1991). Sheltered subject matter teaching. *Cross Currents, 28* (Winter), 183–188;

Kanchana Prapphal (1991). Cooperative learning in a humanistic English class. *Cross Currents, 28*(Summer), 37–40.

ERIC and the National Council of Teachers of English for:

Robert H. White and Raymond J. Rodrigues (1981). Appendix C: The open language experience, and Appendix D: Sample plan for an open language experience—shopping at the supermarket, in *Mainstreaming the Non-English Student* (pp. 32–40). Chicago: ERIC (ED 197 382) and NCTE.

The journal *Language Learning* for:

Tetsuro Chihara, John W. Oller, Jr., Kelley Weaver, and Mary Anne Chávez-Oller (1977). Are cloze items sensitive to constraints across sentences? *Language Learning, 27, 63*–73.

Susan L. Stern (1980). Drama in second language learning from a psycholinguistic perspective, *Language Learning, 30*(1), 77–100;

Patricia L. Carrell (1984). Evidence of a formal schema in second language comprehension. *Language Learning, 34*(2), 87–112.

The Modern Language Association, the *Modern Language Journal,* and the University of Wisconsin Press for:

J. J. Asher, Jo Anne Kusudo, and Rita de la Torre (1974). Learning a second language through commands: The second field test. *Modern Language Journal, 58,* 24–32;

Maureen Weissenrieder (1987). Listening to the news in Spanish. *Modern Language Journal, 71*(1), 18–27;

Fred Genesee, Naomi E. Holobow, Wallace E. Lambert, and Louise Chartrand (1989). Three elementary school alternatives for learning through a second language. *Modern Language Journal, 73*(3), 250–263;

Yukie Horiba (1990). Narrative comprehension processes: A study of native and non-native readers of Japanese. *Modern Language Journal, 74*(2), 188–202.

The National Clearinghouse for Bilingual Education for:

Stephen D. Krashen (1991). Bilingual education: A focus on current research. *Focus: Occasional Papers in Bilingual Education,* Number 3, 1–15.

Newbury House Publishers for:
  Donna M. Brinton, Marguerite Ann Snow, and Marjorie Bingham Wesche (1989). Putting content-based second language instruction in context. In *Content-based second language instruction* (pp. 1–13). Philadelphia: Newbury House.
The Open University Press for excerpts from:
  Richard F. Walker, Saowalak Rattanavich, and John W. Oller, Jr. (1992). *Teaching all the children to read* (pp. 1–9, 12–35, 114, 122). Philadelphia: Open University.
Oxford University Press in New York for:
  Carolyn Graham (1978). *Jazz Chants*. New York: Oxford University Press, as excerpted;
  Wendy Assinder (1991). Peer teaching, peer learning: One model. *English Language Teaching, 45*(3), 218–228;
  Charlyn Wessels (1991). From improvisation to publication on an English through Drama course. *English Language Teaching, 45*(3), 230–236;
  Helen Johnson (1992). Defossilizing. *English Language Teaching, 46*(2), 180–189.
The Rassias Foundation of Dartmouth College and *The Ram's Horn* for:
  Joel D. Goldfield (1992). Educational technology: Sharing the experience. *The Ram's Horn, 6,* 48–51.
The Regional Language Center and the *RELC Journal* for:
  Subramaniyan Nambiar (1985). The use of pop songs in language learning. *Guidelines: A Periodical for Language Teaching, 7*(1), 79–84;
  Supot Arevart and Paul Nation (1991). Fluency improvement in a second language. *RELC Journal, 22*(1), 84–94, as excerpted;
  Supot Arevart (1989). Grammatical change through repetition. *RELC Journal, 20*(2), 42–60, as excerpted;
  Ian Tudor and Richard Tuffs (1991). Formal and content schemata activation in L2 viewing comprehension. *RELC Journal, 22*(2), 79–97.
Yankee for:
  Richard M. Bacon with photographs by Russell Schleipman (1977). The thunder and lightning professor. September, 108–113, 200, 201, 205.

Any materials included in the book but not named in the above list were prepared especially for this volume.

Finally, I thank the staff of the Reference Department of the University of New Mexico Zimmerman Library, who helped to track down more than a few wayward titles, dates, and page numbers. My friend and colleague, Angus Linney, who read and critiqued the manuscript in its final phases of development, helped me and the publishers make some difficult editorial decisions in order to keep the book at a manageable length. He also helped me improve the Discussion Questions. In addition, I thank my various collaborators and co-authors whose names and affiliations follow: (For what errors remain, of course, I alone am responsible.)

Allen, Wendy W., Department of French, St. Olaf College, Northfield, MN

Anderson, Keith O., Department of German, St. Olaf College, Northfield, MN

Andrade, Carolyn, Supervisor of Elementary Education, Cincinnati Public Schools, Cincinnati, OH

Arevart, Supot, Policy and Planning Division, Office of the National Primary Education Commission, Ministry of Education, Bangkok, Thailand

Asher, James J., Department of Psychology, California State University at San Jose

Assinder, Wendy, Australian College of English, Bondi Junction, NSW, Australia

Bacon, Richard M., author for Yankee

Baolin, Ma, staff correspondent for *The Beijing Review*

Brinton, Donna M., TESL/Applied Linguistics, UCLA, Los Angeles, CA

Carrell, Patricia L., Dean of the Graduate School, University of Akron, Akron, OH

Chávez-Oller, Mary Anne, Director of Testing and Employment, City of Albuquerque, Department of Personnel

Chihara, Tetsuro, Department of English, Osaka Jogakuin Junior College, Osaka, Japan

Christensen, Ben, Department of Spanish, CSU at San Diego, San Diego, CA

Curtain, Helena, Foreign Language Curriculum Specialist, Milwaukee Public Schools, Milwaukee

Damico, Jack S., Doris B. Hawthorne Professor of Communicative Disorders, Southwestern Louisiana University, Lafayette

Damico, Sandra K., Department of Communicative Disorders, LSU, Baton Rouge

de Berkeley-Wykes, Jonathan, formerly a teacher in Oman, Turkey, deceased

de la Torre, Rita, Department of Psychology, California State University at San Jose

Elkins, Robert J., Department of Foreign Languages, University of West Virginia, Morgantown

Glisan, Eileen W., Department of Spanish and Classical Languages, Indiana University of Pennsylvania, Indiana, PA

Goldfield, Joel D., Department of Foreign Languages, Plymouth State College, Plymouth, NH

Graham, Carolyn, Department of English, NYU, New York, NY

Greenberg, Liza A., Department of Educational Foundations, University of New Mexico, Albuquerque

Horiba, Yukie, Asian Languages and Literatures, Amherst, MA

Hurtado de Vivas, Romelia, Department of CIMTE, University of New Mexico, Albuquerque

Johnson, Helen, Britannia Royal Naval College, Dartmouth, England

Kalivoda, Theodore B., Department of Spanish Education, University of Georgia, Athens

Krashen, Stephen D., College of Education, University of Southern California

Kretschmer, Laura W., Department of Communications, University of Cincinnati, Cincinnati, OH

Kretschmer, Richard R., Jr., Department of Special Education, University of Cincinnati, Cincinnati, OH

Kusudo, Jo Anne, Department of Psychology, California State University at San Jose

Mitchell, Jane Tucker, Department of Pedagogical Studies and Supervision, University of North Carolina at Greensboro

Morain, Genelle, Department of Foreign Languages, University of Georgia, Athens

Morgan, John, Pilgrims, Endcliffe, Eden Mount, Grange-over-Sands, Cumbria, England

Nambiar, Subramaniyan A., Federal Inspectorate of Schools, Taipin, Perak, Malaysia

Narvaéz, León, Department of Spanish, St. Olaf College, Northfield, MN

Nation, Paul, Department of Communication, Victoria University of Wellington, New Zealand

Oller, John W., Sr. author of *La familia Fernández,* deceased

Prapphal, Kanchana, Chulalongkorn University Language Institute, Bangkok, Thailand

Rattanavich, Saowalak, Department of Instruction, Srinakarinwirot University, Bangkok, Thailand

Redmond, Mary Lynn, Department of Education, Wake Forest University, Winston-Salem, NC

Rinvolucri, Mario, Pilgrims, 8 Vernon Place, Canterbury, Kent, England

Rodrigues, Raymond J., Department of Curriculum and Instruction, New Mexico State University, Las Cruces, NM

Salomone, Ann Masters, Department of French, Ohio State University, Chillicothe, OH

Schleipman, Russell, photographer for *Yankee*

Seaver, Paul W., Jr., Department of Spanish, Bloomsburg University, Bloomsburg, PA

Snow, Marguerite Ann, English as a Second Language, California State University at Los Angeles

Stern, Susan L., Department of TESL/Applied Linguistics, UCLA

Sternfeld, Steven, Department of Languages, University of Utah, Salt Lake City, UT

Taira, Tatsuo, Department of English, University of the Ryukyus, Okinawa, Japan

Tudor, Ian, Institut de Phonétique, Université Libre de Bruxelles, Belgium

Tuffs, Richard, Institut de Phonétique, Université Libre de Bruxelles, Belgium

Walker, Richard F., Literacy Specialist for Rotary Foundation, Jindalee, Queensland, Australia

Weissenrieder, Maureen, Department of Hispanic Linguistics, Ohio University, Athens, OH

Wesche, Mari Bingham, Centre for Second Language Learning, University of Ottawa, Ottawa, Ontario (Canada)

Wessels, Charlyn, Stevenson College, Edinburgh England, UK

White, Robert H., Department of CIMTE, Univeristy of New Mexico, Albuquerque

Yü, Grover K. H., Department of Languages and Linguistics, CSU at Fresno, CA

FOREWORD TO THE SECOND EDITION

Like the first edition, the second volume of *Methods That Work* is still a book of success stories for language teachers. However, it's not just for language teachers, but for *all* the teachers in the schools. The reason for the increased scope is that all teachers are bound to find communication a richer challenge in years to come because of the rapid growth of minority language populations around the world (see Scarcella, 1990). Of course, as teachers know, teaching means communicating effectively—that is, caring for students (Moskowitz, 1978) and sharing a community of knowledge and experience with them (Little & Sanders, 1989). The focus here is often on the teaching of foreign languages, English as a second language, and curricula for students from minority language backgrounds, but because of the changing demographics in today's world—with minority language students rapidly becoming the majority in many urban settings around the world and especially here in the U.S. (Ortiz & Yates, 1983; Cummins, 1986; Hamayan & Damico, 1991; Kagan, 1992)—all content-area teachers will find useful material in this book. Reading teachers as well as speech-language pathologists are addressed specifically and will find much that is applicable to their work.

In addition to being somewhat thicker, the book has also been internationalized. The present version contains entries not only from the U.S. and Canada, but also from Belgium, Thailand, Singapore, Malaysia, China, Japan, Australia, and New Zealand. In addition, in order to cope with the exponential growth of knowledge, a wider range of topics is covered in this volume than in the previous one. It now includes more information on elementary schools, bilingual education, literacy, schema theory (episodic organization) and grammar, speech-language pathology, special education, and computer technology. I admit that all this is a lot for one book, but I believe teachers in the classrooms will see a greater relevance and coherence in this volume than in any that has been available up till now. The problems dealt with here are fundamentally related and are, I believe, the central core of what education will be about in the twenty-first century.

We are learning, I believe, even as we are being catapulted towards a new century and even a whole new millennium, to value differences more than we used to. At the same time we are growing more aware that education depends on communication and on a sense of community (Little & Sanders, 1989). And all of it depends on acquiring and developing common language systems. We must love our students enough to want to talk with them in a language that both we and they can understand. We need to care about them and to share with them not only what comes from our own experience, but also what comes from theirs, and we need to respect and appreciate the differences. In such a context, a book like Gertrude Moskowitz's *Caring and Sharing in the Foreign Language Class* (1978) makes a lot of sense, but as Eugene Nida once observed in a talk I heard back in graduate school days (about 1967), "If we agreed perfectly on everything, one of us wouldn't need to be here." And, as Moskowitz would probably point out, even differences require a common ground in order to be noticed, and even more commonality if they are to be understood. Therefore, in the hope of achieving a richer sense of community and a deeper appreciation of our differences, as in the Introduction to the first edition of *Methods That Work* (pp. xi-xii), I will reflect briefly on a challenging and fulfilling conversation (because it has already become a public one) that has developed with my esteemed friend and colleague (Earl Stevick, 1990: 71-98) since the first edition of *Methods That Work* appeared back in 1983. His remarks were, in part, a defense and commentary on the late Charles Curran's "counseling learning" approach (1961, 1976, 1983). As I said back then, we language teachers are a fairly close professional family, and for that reason I feel free to speak here (as I did back then) somewhat intimately. For those dear readers who might find the exercise too quaint or poignant, I will ask them to just skip over the next paragraph. (Better that than we should part company so early in our journey. And thanks for the indulgence, either way!)

As I noted in the previous volume, I still believe that *redemption* in its Judeo-Christian theological sense (a term Curran applied as a description of what happens when we acquire a new language) is too big a job for language learners or teachers to take upon themselves. In my humble view, redemption is still the work of Christ dying on the cross for my sins and everyone else's, being buried, and rising again from the dead. While my much loved senior colleague Earl Stevick (1990) in his substantial, sensitive, and kindly commentary, *Humanism in Language Teaching* (especially pp. 71-98), has thoughtfully and appealingly explained some of the subtler aspects of Curran's theological approach, with respect to language teaching I take a more pragmatic view than I perceive Curran's to be. Of course, I agree that personal wholeness (of which *wellness, holiness, wealth,* and *health* are all cognates) is a desirable state to strive for, but *if* it could be achieved by acquiring languages (as I understood Curran to be suggesting), or by any other form of willful effort, then, as the apostle Paul put it, "Christ died for nothing" (Galatians 2:20). At any rate, as far as redemption in the profound Judeo-Christian sense is concerned, I have more confidence in a rough wooden cross that thudded into the ground at Golgotha some 2,000 years ago (McDowell, 1979) and a tomb guarded by Roman soldiers that turned up empty three days later (McDowell, 1981) than in any pure abstraction. Even when it comes to the most mundane aspects of day-to-day language teaching, I want to see the evidence—the present and historical facts of the material world. Therefore, in this book, I have sought to eliminate any merely speculative philosophy in favor of hard evidence. The only kind of theory that I want to appear here is the kind that can be expressed in a method that works. In any case, this has been my goal.

Returning to the main thread, Jim Cummins (1981, 1983, 1986, 1989) has stressed that educators are in a position to help preserve the rich linguistic resources (the language heritage) that children bring with them as they walk into our classrooms (also see McKay & Wong, 1988). It is already clear and will become even more so in the next few decades that all the teachers in the schools, more than many of us have been inclined to realize, are, and ought to be, language acquisition specialists and language teachers—over and above whatever else we may be. Therefore, because of the special challenges that lie ahead, I believe that many teachers will value the help that the second edition of *Methods That Work* offers. There is no doubt that the first edition succeeded because of its emphasis on what works. Even ten years ago, Pat and I predicted that the naysayers would be quick to complain that a book full of success stories was out of touch. They did, but their voices were few and uncertain. They said that language acquisition is laced with mysteries, and, of course, they were right in this much. It is true that our still unanswered questions can be added to, divided into a thousand more, and multiplied to infinity and gone. But merely saying that language acquisition is complex is no theory. Every conceivable aspect of human experience and every bit of the material world is complex, so a theory that merely extols such a multitude of complexities gets nowhere. What we teachers need to know is what works, and we need to know now (cf. Kalivoda et al., Chapter 3). As practitioners, we can't afford the luxury of waiting for someone in some ivory-tower to sort through an endless agenda of theoretical complexities. We can't wait for a distant tomorrow to find out how to do best what *has* to be done *today*.

As Patricia Richard-Amato and I said in the first edition, we'd have loved to have had *Methods That Work* in our hands when we set out to become language teachers. Today I can say with equal conviction that I'd have picked the second edition of *Methods That Work* off any seller's bookshelf in a twinkling, and I'd have been glad to get it into my mind and my heart even more than in my hands. If we look first to cases in which language acquisition—learning to read, to write, to speak, etc.—all actually *do* occur, particularly where these successes are achieved against the odds and in difficult sociocultural contexts, and if we seek to understand how such things could happen, we will be in an excellent position to formulate a satisfactory understanding (theory) of how they do in fact happen, and even to figure out ways (methods) to make them keep on happening (cf. Richard-Amato, 1988—*Making It Happen*).

I still believe that the experience of teachers is a *valid* source of evidence concerning what works in classrooms. In fact, I think that the *best* educational research *has* to take place in classrooms. I still think that nothing is more practical than a theory tested through a method that works. By the same token, there can be no better theory than the sort that can be shown by some method to actually work in practice, until some other can be shown in practice to work better. In the final analysis, I still agree with Stevick, Krashen, Richard-Amato, and all those others who have said that the classroom *can be* an *optimal* setting for language acquisition. After all, classrooms are real places, and it just ain't so that language acquisition is *necessarily* more likely to occur on a noisy bus or in a restaurant than in a classroom. There is no moment in time more real than the present moment, and there is no place more real than the place we are in. Classrooms are real places, and real learning can occur in them. The point of this book is to say that our job *can be done*. Languages can be taught and learned. Communication is possible. Cross-cultural understanding can be achieved, and teachers *can* help a great deal to make it happen.

The book is still a "smorgasbord," and users are not expected to consume every item on the menu. Readers are invited to make a selection. If there is to be a future for this book, surely the credit will go to those teachers out there in the real classrooms who are making it happen. As in the first edition, all the articles have been selected or specially prepared because of the methods they suggest, and/or for the experimental testing of methods against actual experience, and/or for the explanations they offer of how and why certain methods work. I hope teachers and teacher trainers who used the first edition will agree that the present version offers an enriched fare, and I hope that language teachers everywhere will enjoy it. Bon appetit! I believe some of the ideas contained here will work for you. And, again, thank you. THANK you! THANK YOU!!!

John W. Oller, Jr.
Albuquerque, New Mexico
January 3, 1993

CHAPTER 1

Introducing the Second Edition

EDITOR'S INTRODUCTION

*T*hose who can't wait to sink their teeth into some serious nourishment may want to skip directly to whatever part most appeals to them. Those who like to enjoy a leisurely meal of multiple courses may want to review the menu with us in this chapter before proceeding. This first chapter discusses what appears in this book and why. Chapter 1 gives a definition of "methods that work," but a thoroughgoing theoretical exposition is saved for Chapter 37, which appears at the end of the book. The intention is to put the most comprehensible material first and work up to the more difficult material. The overall goal is to introduce users to a wide range of programs, principles, curricula, and materials that work. Nobody is expected to consume everything. Users are invited to pick and choose. Throughout the book, but especially in Part 1, the emphasis is on scaffolding—providing learners with information through multiple sensory modalities so they will be able to connect targeted language material successfully with their own experience (and vice versa, to connect their experience with the targeted language material). Everywhere the emphasis is on making sense of the connection between language forms and meaningful subject matter. This holds for literacy as much as for language teaching in all its aspects. It holds for language arts in the primary language of the students as much as it does for second or foreign language teaching, or for the kinds of therapeutic interventions that speech-language pathologists and special education teachers do.

The criteria for inclusion of material in this new edition had to be made more stringent than for the previous one. One reason is that a good deal has been learned in ten years. Owing to results from practice, research, and theory, we really do know more these days about what works and why. We also see some of the connections between acquiring a language and becoming literate, and between normal developments and abnormal ones more clearly now than we did a decade ago. As a result, a lot of good material had to be excluded to keep the length within bounds. But, I suppose, this should not be regretted. We should be glad that there is so much good material to choose from. To have included all that was recommended or offered by various authors would have required several volumes thicker than this one. Of course, there is no guarantee that the absolute best choices have been made, and there is no way to determine what those might be. But the choices on the menu represent my best effort, with a lot of help from

many wonderful friends and colleagues around the world. I have tried to select tested methods, powerful evidences, and theories that fit the data.

THE PRAGMATIC ORIENTATION

If anything, the book is more pragmatically oriented than before. As Swain and Lapkin (1989: 153) have put it regarding the well-known successes of the Canadian immersion programs,

> We have learned that grammar should not be taught in isolation from content. But then, neither should content be taught without regard to the language involved. A carefully planned *integration* of language and content, however, holds promise [italics theirs].

In this book, the stress is on the integration—*content linked with language through meaningful experience in many different ways*. The theory of pragmatic mapping (illustrated in many ways throughout the book but discussed especially in Chapter 37), I believe, offers the most succinct and most comprehensive explanation of all of the different methods that do work and in showing why they work. The basics of the theory are not difficult, and readers who know the literature will recognize a number of elements common to less comprehensive theories. The difference, as discussed in Chapter 37, is that the theory of pragmatic mapping, though simple in principle, offers some completely abstract and therefore entirely general insights into the processes of comprehension, communication, language acquisition, and literacy.

Based on experience with the first edition, I suppose that most users of this book will prefer to get straight at the methods of language instruction. That is why Part 1, concerning ways to make input both comprehensible and palatable, appears first.[1] The theoretical discussion is held till the very last chapter. However, we may as well note up front that sound theory is essential for anyone who wants to reach beyond a working acquaintance with any method to see *how* and *why* it works. For a small minority of graduate students and researchers, the theoretical discussion will be the very part that they cannot wait to get into. They will appreciate without a moment's hesitation that the logical consequences of the theory to be presented in Chapter 37 are critical to the coherence of the whole story that is about to unfold. Therefore, some of them may want to skip to the last chapter and read it without delay. At any rate, the logical basis that appears there is foundational, even though the story is told throughout the book by a large cast of teachers who are also researchers and theoreticians. They come from a wide variety of backgrounds and pursue many different educational objectives. To see the profound coherence of the whole effort, therefore, I believe Chapter 37 will be helpful.

ON THE TERM *METHODS*

Over the years, ever since Ed Anthony (1963) proposed to distinguish between *approach* (something akin to a theory), *method* (a curriculum, program, or procedure), and *technique* (any action in the classroom to implement the method), there have been too many refinements and other ways of slicing up the instructional pie even to sum them up. A fine-grained, hairsplitting, historical analysis has been offered by Strain (1986), in which such terms as *Method* (note the upper case M), *method* (spelled with a lower case m), and *methodology* (spelled anyway you like) are distinguished in subtle ways along with *method-procedure, method-technique, design, procedure, presentation, implementation, activity, syllabus, materials, evaluation, tactics, strategies, curriculum,* and so on. All of these terms and various arrangements and choreographies were used in one way or another by Anthony and Norris (1969), Strevens (1980), Richards and Rodgers (1982), Richards (1983), and Strain (1986). Strain claims that "increasingly broader varieties and forms of instruction" were called "methods" in the first edition of *Methods That Work* (Oller & Richard-Amato, 1983).

Well, what *should* be understood by the term *methods* in the title of this book? In this volume, as in the previous one, a method is a way to put a theory into practice. A language teaching method (that works) must be one that enables learners to connect the particular facts of their own experience with the forms of the target language. This is what is meant by the term *pragmatic mapping* (Oller, 1975b, 1983b, 1990, and Chapter 37). There is an inevitable normative (sociocultural) aspect to this process, because really acquiring a language means becoming able to use it the way people who know it use it. There is, therefore, as C. S. Peirce noted long ago (1868, in Moore et al., 1984: 239) an inevitable community aspect to the process of acquiring any language (Little & Sanders, 1989). In this very practical sense, *method* includes anything and everything from classroom realia and props to curriculum, games, activities, tests, and whatever else it takes to move a class full of people (or a single individual) from not knowing a language very well to knowing it a good deal better. Method connects theory with practice, and vice versa.

Of course, there are some things that a method (at least one that works) is not. Suppose a man, who is not even a regular golfer goes out, tees up, and makes a hole-in-one on the first try (thereby qualifying to win a new car—as my friend Steve Wilson did recently). Would we attribute his success to a method? Hardly. We'd call it "luck." Dumb luck. Especially if we know that when this guy hits the ball, it usually goes almost anywhere but the general direction of the flag. But suppose my lucky friend were to say that the reason he made his hole-in-one that day was because he kept silent for exactly six weeks before hitting the ball. Or maybe he'd say it was because of a vigorous little jig he danced while the ball was hurtling toward the hole. Or what if he said he'd been reincarnated as a golfer while stepping up to the tee? He might have imagined a primal forest and swung the club exactly like some imagined ancestor reaching down after a fallen coconut, naturally. Or he might have done some deep breathing, listened to baroque music on his Walkman for fifteen or twenty minutes, and then visualized himself as a cloud floating directly over the flag. We would be reluctant, I suppose, to regard the silence, the jig, the return to nature, or the out-of-body experience as methods. We might call them coincidences or even superstitions, but not methods. But suppose the golfer were Nancy López and could describe the manner of addressing the ball to provide the right power and follow-through, the precise positioning and management of the wrists, hands, feet, eyes, and head, so as to ensure just the right arc of the swing, contact between the ball and the sweet spot, and the best trajectory from the tee to the flag. And suppose, furthermore, that she could consistently drop the ball within a few feet of the flag on, say, 80 out of a 100 tries. Now *that* we might call a method.

OVERVIEWING THE SECOND EDITION

In this book a **method that works** is *one that is backed up by sensible theory and consistent with practical evidence.* It ought to be redundant to add the clause *that works* because a method that doesn't work (a failure?) ought not to be called a method at all. It should also be superfluous to say that working methods must be backed up by sensible theory and consistent practical evidence. Approaches that lack theoretical support ought to be regarded as lucky accidents if they work at all and as unlucky ones if they don't, and methods that lack consistent practical evidence ought to be regarded as hypothetical (i.e., purely theoretical)

possibilities. Here, as in the previous edition, the term **methods** is deliberately applied to whatever is involved in bringing to life the connection between language and experience. It includes programs, curricula, procedures, demonstrations, modes of presentation, research findings, tests, manners of interaction, materials, texts, films, videos, computers, and more. Research, some of it, that shows how or why certain methods work is also included, in addition to reports from teachers and students.

In Part 1 (and to a great extent throughout the book) we consider how scaffolding can be constructed to enable learners to understand language forms that are, as Krashen (1981, 1982, 1985a-c, 1989b) urges in his "input hypothesis," a little beyond the learner's current level of development. For language acquirers, the new target language forms are in a language different from the primary language of the student. For preliterate students, who are just learning to read and write, the target language forms are just the unfamiliar forms of the written language. And for many children of third-world or minority language backgrounds, both problems are confronted simultaneously: these children need to acquire literacy, and they need to do it in a language that is also relatively new to them.

It turns out that language acquirers do not really have to lift themselves by their bootstraps (as Spolsky, 1985, 1989, and others feared they might, owing to misinterpretations of Krashen, 1981, 1982, 1985a-c), but they do need to climb up on a scaffolding (in a different meaning system) so they can reach up to negotiate new forms of the target language (Oller, 1970, 1988). The scaffolding may be of a sensory-motor type, as in a film or student activity. Or it may involve any sort of other representational medium such as gesture, mime, dramatization, responding to commands, prior knowledge of the content, familiar forms in the target language, etc. Sometimes, owing to translation of target language material into a known language, scaffolding may be provided through that known linguistic system (by translating the target language forms into the student's primary language), but most likely the scaffolding will consist of some combination of sensory-motor, gestural, and linguistic representations in the target language. Usually, in the language teaching programs that achieve the greatest degree of success, the native language is diligently avoided in favor of the target language until the target language is well-established. On the other hand, where content teaching is needed, it is nearly always best to use a known language if one is available (Krashen, Chapter 9). Besides, as both theory and the research shows (cf. Cummins, 1984; Hakuta, 1986; Oller et al., 1991), furthering the development of the primary language ensures long-term dividends to any child, and acquiring more than one language is also quite generally beneficial, even for children identified as low achievers or handicapped learners (Andrade, Kretschmer & Kretschmer, Chapter 10; Damico & Damico, Chapter 29).

Parts 2 and 4 in this edition also address the expressed need for more information on elementary programs.[2] Part 2 deals mainly with immersion and content-based instruction in the lower grades, and Part 4 (especially Chapter 17) is concerned with enabling children to become literate as well as some of the remarkable dividends to be gained from episodic organization. Part 3 deals with the extension to adults of the benefits of immersion-type programs. The Canadian immersion experiments in elementary schools are probably the best known, owing to work that Wallace Lambert started together with some of his students and colleagues in the suburb of St. Lambert in Montreal back in 1965.[3] What is not so well-known is that before the First World War produced a wave of xenophobia in the good old U.S.A., a variety of bilingual immersion programs flourished here during the latter part of the nineteenth century. The most widespread were the English-German bilingual programs, as Dimitri Katsareas shows in his 1993 dissertation (also see Schlossman, 1983, and Toth, 1990). In "immersion-type" programs, students who do not yet know the target language are nevertheless instructed through it. They are immersed in the language. Of course, immersion in any target language devoid of determinate (comprehensible and comprehended) content will not work. That approach is closer to what is called "submersion." In order for language acquisition to occur, content-laden representations of the true narrative type (see Chapter 37) and a supportive environment in which to negotiate meanings are crucial.

Mouthing surface forms or listening to them by the truckload won't produce much language acquisition at all. Harlan Lane (1964) called "submersion-type" approaches the "sunburn" or "language bath" methods. He pointed out that drenching people in target language forms doesn't necessarily accomplish very much toward teaching them to understand and speak that language. Approaches to language teaching that have students hearing and mouthing utterances in the target language without necessarily understanding them are like trying to teach math by getting students to recite numbers and equations or by having them listen to others performing such recitations. Even if the students write the numbers and read the equations out loud, they're not doing mathematics. What is missing is the sort of reasoning—the comprehension—that would articulately connect the target language forms (or numbers and equations, if you like) with some meaningful content. That connecting, the pragmatic linking of target language forms with the actual experience of the student, is the part that cannot be left out.

Therefore, the key to the success of all immersion-type programs (Parts 2 and 3) is the integration of the target language forms with content. Furthermore, as we will see in Part 4, even children in severely oppressed minority-language situations (e.g., Aborigines in Australia and the Hill Tribes of Thailand) can acquire both literacy and a new language at the same time. In fact, contrary to a lot of speculative theorizing about why such a feat ought to be impossible, it really is possible for traditional low-achievers to acquire a target language while they are also learning to read it. How is this possible? The answer is scaffolding (Part 1). Climbing up on a scaffold effectively makes us taller than we were. It extends our reach. All teaching can be characterized as providing students with the means to create and use appropriate scaffolds. In fact, human beings are able to benefit from multiple kinds of scaffolding all at the same time. While some have argued for top-down processing and others for bottom-up, it is abundantly clear that language users, even in early stages of acquisition, normally benefit not only from top-down *and* bottom-up processing, but that we also work the top, bottom, and sides against the middle simultaneously. Or, putting the whole equation in terms of the theory in Chapter 37, we are able to use a rich variety of semiotic (meaningful) forms to enable us to solve comprehension problems. We are often able, for instance, to translate what we see into gestures and linguistic forms (heard and/or spoken and/or read and/or written) while at the same time achieving a deeper level of conceptual understanding of what we see (Jackendoff, 1987).

In fact, every form of comprehension is ultimately dependent on the articulate mapping of representations of different kinds into each other as we relate them all the while to our experience (Peirce, 1868; Einstein, 1936, 1941, 1944; Oller, 1989). The backbone of experience itself, as is proved logically in Chapter 37, is episodic organization—the arrangement of facts into the shape of a true narrative. This sort of arrangement comes with certain logical benefits including relative determinacy (meanings that are made relatively certain), connectedness (inferential links of the meanings at hand with other meanings), and generalizability (relevance to a potentially infinite range of possible experiences). All of this is spelled out in detail in Chapter 37 and is amply evidenced in Part 4.

Part 5 includes a miscellany of reports about old resources such as newscasts, cooperative learning, novels, and repetition, and new technologies involving VCR's and computers. It's an old and new idea (Clarke, 1989) to use existing resources rather than trying to do everything ourselves by creating every scrap of material for our classes. Why not use existing media presentations such as newscasts (Weissenrieder, Chapter 23)? Or why not get some help from able students through cooperative learning and peer teaching (Assinder, Chapter 24)? And what about good old grammar? It hasn't been forgotten. Johnson (Chapter 25) helps us see how to "defossilize" students with terminal "intermediate-itis." Or, to achieve a rich episodic connectedness between the language of one lesson and the next, how about using novels of adventure written at a reasonably low level of difficulty (Christensen, Chapter 26)? Even repetition (Arevart & Nation, Chapter 27) helps to

improve fluency and accuracy. Episodic organization can also, of course, be put to good use in computer-assisted interactions (Taira, Chapter 28). Finally, Part 5 concludes with some ideas about how speech-language pathologies and special education-type handicaps can be dealt with through the same methods recommended throughout the book (Damico & Damico, Chapter 29).

Part 6 offers a dessert tray that should tempt many a teacher's palate. Choices range from pop songs, jazz chants, pantomime, storytelling, games and drills to jigsaw reading and drama. Users should not allow themselves to be fooled into thinking that this last section is only fun and games, because in this section there are also some interesting theoretical arguments and some persuasive demonstrations of methods that really do work. Seaver, for instance, in Chapter 32, gives a substantial treatment of mime and gesture, and Wessels (Chapter 36) comes very close to summing up the best from all the foregoing chapters. Finally, Chapter 37 caps off the whole argument with a comprehensive theoretical perspective. The intent of that chapter is to say why some methods work so much better than others.

NOTES

1 Dr. Dean Brodkey of the College of Education at the University of New Mexico is to be thanked for giving me a sharp rap on the chin, thus helping me to bite the bullet in postponing the abstract theoretical discussion to the end of the book. Thanks, Dean, from me and, I expect, most of the users of this edition!

2 Special thanks are owed to Gladys Lipton, Else Hamayan, and to the Damicos for pointing out the need to beef up the material for teachers and other educators who work with children in the lower grades.

3 At a Georgetown Round Table meeting in 1978, Einar Haugen quipped that Wallace Lambert, the principal investigator in that initial immersion experiment, had thus achieved "minor sainthood."

DISCUSSION QUESTIONS

1. Why should we expect experience that is accessible through more than one modality—e.g., seeing, hearing, feeling, moving—to be easier to understand, to recall, and, in general, to make sense of?

2. Why is it essential for students to make sense of what happens at school?

3. How can a scaffolding of accessible meaning help students climb up to levels that would have been inaccessible without the scaffolding? What kinds of scaffolding have helped you to solve one or another kind of discourse processing problem? Can you think of comprehension problems that cannot be solved without certain kinds of scaffolding?

PART 1

SCAFFOLDING IN LANGUAGE TEACHING

To a greater extent than is usually realized (but see Enright & McCloskey, 1988), in second language teaching and literacy instruction the fundamental objective is to enable students to make the connection between certain language forms and their own experience. Asher's method (Chapter 2), known as Total Physical Response (TPR), makes the connection initially through commands. These are modeled at first by the instructor. Later they will be carried out by the students along with the instructor and then by the students without modeling by the instructor. Of course, Asher is among the first to admit that TPR works best at the beginning. It is a way to get the fledgling student up and flying. After that, the sky is the limit. TPR is not the end of anything. It is just one of the best starting points that has ever been discovered. The proof that the target language forms have been comprehended, in the beginning stages of language instruction, is that the students can perform what is required by the commands.

Because Asher's TPR method is so simple, it has been criticized, plenty. For instance, one of the world's leading authorities on the psychology of language teaching and testing, John B. Carroll, complained that the TPR approach is limited merely to commands (Carroll, 1970). But to argue this is to fail to see the natural connections between "Jump!" "The teacher said, 'Jump!'" "She said to jump." "I jumped when the teacher said, 'Jump!'" "Jane and I jumped when the teacher said to jump." "The whole class jumped when the teacher told us to." "We jumped because the teacher said to." "When the teacher tells us to jump, we will all jump." "Watch the teacher, and when she says to jump, just do what I do." "If the teacher should say anything, like maybe 'Jump!' for instance? Whatever I do, you do. Okay?" Etc., etc., *ad infinitum*.

The research shows that even *imagining* carrying out commands in one's native language produces a substantial amount of recall (47% of 35 commands in a study by Lieberman & Altschul, 1971). Seeing the commands executed yields higher recall (53%). And performing the commands gets even better results (62%). But critics who fail to see the relatedness between a command such as "Jump!" and declaratives such as "I will jump" or "She said to jump" or questions such as "What did you say?" "Are you talking to me?" "Let me see if I've got this straight: *You* want *ME* to jump?"—those same critics are also apt to fail to see that memory and learning are intimately connected. To them it will seem odd to say that what helps us remember a series of commands in our native language may help us even more in doing something more difficult, such as acquiring a new language or becoming literate. Then, there are also a few really irrational critics. There are some people, even a few educators, who would rather absorb a new language, or have children learn to read by osmosis. They imagine that putting a tape recorder under their pillow or just listening to baroque music while their spirits float up into the clouds will take all the work out of language acquisition. Those people find Asher's TPR approach altogether unappealing. Still, it has this one small advantage. The evidence is in. It works. It works with different age groups, with different instructors, and with languages as far apart as the east is from the west.

Chapter 3 by Kalivoda, Morain, and Elkins shows how the TPR approach can be adapted to the connectedness characteristic of narratives and of experience in general (see Part 4 for elaboration). Their article begins with a plaintive note that I believe will strike a chord in the hearts of language teachers everywhere. While the ivory-tower theoreticians worship at the shrine of complexity, where they multiply, divide, and exponentiate the "complexities of language acquisition that no one really understands," and sociopolitical, economic, and other factors beyond number, the lonely language teacher still has to face classes "Monday through Friday from September to June," as Kalivoda et al. note. But why is education so slow to change? Eileen Glisan (Chapter 4) faces these questions head-on. For one thing, there is always a lag between the research and its dissemination. For another, teachers have generally understood that TPR works in the beginning stages of language instruction but have been unclear about how to proceed from there. Glisan has some suggestions for those teachers. In keeping with the philosophy underlying TPR itself and with the old Chinese proverb ("Tell me and I will forget . . . involve me and I will learn"), Glisan gives plenty of hands-on suggestions that teachers can apply from Monday to Friday. Glisan shows how TPR can be developed towards a whole language curriculum by leading us through a series of sensible activities step-by-step.

Next we come to the famous and much loved "maniac" of Dartmouth College, Professor John Rassias, the best-known language teacher in the world. He is a one-man traveling stage show and a language-teaching phenomenon from hip to jowl. Rassias has been featured on such major network programs in the U.S. as *60 Minutes, Good Morning America, The David Brinkley Evening Magazine, The Charles Kuralt Show,* and in Australia on *Four Corners.* In September 1992, a documentary film titled *Rassias in China* was aired on PBS. Known for antics such as breaking eggs on students' heads and begging on bended knee for some response or other, he has been written up in photo features in places as far removed from Dartmouth College as Paris, Berlin, and Beijing. His techniques are being used in North America, Europe, Asia, and Africa in languages as diverse as Arabic, ASL, Chinese, French, Italian, Spanish, German, Russian, Japanese, Swahili, and Modern Greek, to name only a few. The Rassias methods have been used with such diverse audiences as the New York City Transit Police, border patrol officers, Citibank and IBM Execs, and grad students in French medical schools.

How can such madness even be relevant to language teaching? Simple. Rassias makes the target language meanings interesting and gets them across through acting—and he does it with an inexhaustible and contagious supply of unselfish enthusiasm. The students are soon caught up in the acting, even shy ones, and before they know it, they're speaking French or Italian and loving every second of it. I smile to think of the teacher in the Kalivoda, Morain, and Elkins study (Chapter 3) who thought he might "look foolish" doing an "audio-motor" mini-drama by pretending to take an onion out of a refrigerator drawn on the blackboard. I expect he might have died straight away if someone had suggested he ought to try "The Rassias Madness."

Even John Rassias admits that his style is not for everyone, but I don't think there is a teacher alive who could not benefit from the uninhibited, peerless *joie de vivre* that is spelled R-A-S-S-I-A-S. But there is another reason, beyond humor and entertainment, that I wanted the "thunder and lightning" professor in this book. I think he is right when he urges students to try to sound like they're speaking French when they speak French (though he once bit his own French teacher for depressing his tongue to get him to produce a French sounding *r*; cf. Wolkomir, 1980). Surface form and grammar, as Rassias has correctly insisted all along, really do count for something, and they do deserve serious attention and concerted effort in the language classroom. It's fine to say with a wave of the hand that students will just naturally overcome their pidginized versions of the target language, but the research shows (see Parts 2 and 3) that we calibrate our expectations for our Italian (or whatever language) according to what we need to accomplish in communication (see Johnson, Chapter 25).

The unparalleled brilliance of "The Rassias Method" is to get students to aim a great deal higher than the run-of-the-mill foreign language course that serves up a couple of tacos, teaches students the words to "Las Mañanitas," and dubs them "bilingual." Rassias makes sense. He gets his students to make the meaning connection through dramatic contortions that frighten the pants off most language teachers, and then he gets them to act and sound like people who really speak French, or Italian, or whatever. And, by the way, his method works (cf. Byrd, 1980; Johnston, 1980, 1983; Stansfield & Horner, 1987; Lein, 1992). Even the Dartmouth-based journal of the Rassias method, *The Ram's Horn*, suggests its vitality: The editors say on the title page that just as "the long blasts of the ram's horn blew down the walls of Jericho" (before Joshua's advancing army), the purpose of the journal of the Rassias Foundation is "to blow down the walls of inhibition, to go beyond boundaries and restrictions—toward a new understanding of human communication." Or as Rassias was quoted by Robert Wolkomir as saying (1980: 100), "We want to aim some big educational ray guns at these stupid language barriers and vaporize them, poof!"

Ahora, querido amigo o amiga (si es posible tutearte), quiero cambiar la ropa de la lengua para decirte una cosa. Hace muchos años que decidí hacerme profesor de lenguas. Por una parte era porque me dí cuenta que el apellido «Oller» era de Cataluña. Supe también que mis antepasados vinieron de allá y que soy español (o sea catalán). Sí, es verdad. Por eso quisiera aprender la lengua natal de mis antepasados por el lado de mi papá. Y por otra parte quisiera hacerme maestro de español porque esa fue la carrera de mi padre. At any rate, that's the way I began my pilgrimage as a language student and, later, a language teacher, more years ago than I'd like to admit. And, all of that, is just part of the reason I include Chapter 6, which I coauthored with my Dad. Another reason is that I want language teachers who use this book to realize that I am one of them. Ever since Tillie C'de Baca, my fifth-grade teacher in Las Vegas, New Mexico, pointed out that acquiring another language was like opening a new window through which to see the world, I have known what I would do. Or, as John Rassias put it to Pierre

Laforet for an article that appeared in the popular French magazine, *Figaro du Samedi* (1984: 158), *«la connaisance totale de plusieurs langues peut donner á l'être humain une autre vision du monde»*.

Chapter 6 also offers an alternative route for the teacher who is not a one-person acting troop or who is not yet ready to invent an entire curriculum. If the truth must be known, I'm just like that teacher who didn't want to pretend to take a knife out of a drawer sketched on the blackboard! The plan of *El español por el mundo* enables even the relatively unproficient speaker of the target language to move with the students toward native-like proficiency. Through full-scale dramatization of lifelike episodes on film, native language models, and a fully developed curriculum, the ideas in Chapter 6 embody the essence of the theory throughout this book. Though *El español por el mundo* (Oller, Sr., 1963; Oller, Sr., & González, 1965) could benefit from technological updating (along the lines of Goldfield, Chapter 5, and Taira, Chapter 28), it is still more complete than any language teaching curriculum that I know of. It easily accommodates key recommendations of Asher, Rassias, Krashen, and others, but its most distinctive aspect is the respect paid to meaningful sequence (see Part 4 on this theme). Instead of time-warping to a new universe each time the class convenes (or whenever we turn a page)—from one disjointed activity, concept, or meaning to another through a jerky series of underdetermined and almost unrelated worlds—the pragmatic approach of Chapter 6 is structured around a developing story line. It consists of a series of episodes in which the central characters are consistently, continuously, and naturally involved. The result (see Chapters 20 and 28) is superior comprehension, internalization, retention, recall, and acquisition of the target language material. Years after exposure, students can still recall whole episodes of the story line as well as the attendant language forms. The method works chiefly because a story line makes a real difference.

In Chapter 7, Raymond J. Rodrigues and Robert H. White—esteemed colleagues in the Land of Enchantment—show how to prepare students for real-life contexts. Their methods are uniquely appropriate to "second" language teaching (such as ESL) provided the classroom is located in a community where the target language (in their case, English) is commonly used for everyday purposes outside the classroom. Their example, a trip to a grocery store, is one that language teachers in almost any context will easily be able to extend to many other everyday contexts that can be role played in the classroom. In fact, teachers working at the elementary levels will probably have plenty of firsthand experience with re-creations of the grocery store context in an activity center in their own classrooms. The benefit to be gained from Rodrigues and White (Chapter 7) is to see how the language that is connected to everyday experiences can be developed so students internalize the relevant language forms and can access them whenever they are actually in the appropriate context.

Finally, concluding Part 1, Susan L. Stern (Chapter 8) explores reasons "Why Drama Works." She concentrates on psychological or "psycholinguistic" aspects of the effects of drama, but the implications for sociological effects are not neglected. It seems, among other things, that through drama, which by definition is a kind of fictional role-playing with a return ticket to the real world, students are enabled to step into new personalities and situations with reduced threat to their egos and ethnic identities. As a result, they can acquire the language relevant to real contexts without being exposed to all the risks of those contexts in the outside world. They are able to benefit more fully from the sheltered environment afforded to them by the classroom. Another benefit of Stern's contribution is to show the natural connection of many of the methods discussed in other chapters of Part 1 and throughout the book to language-related disabilities such as various forms of aphasia, dyslexia, and other disorders. Looking ahead, we may note that Damico and Damico (Chapter 29) return to this topic and show why and how many of the methods that work with normal students can also be used to good advantage with persons traditionally designated as "language disordered" or "learning disabled."

CHAPTER 2

Learning a Second Language Through Commands: The Second Field Test

James J. Asher, Jo Anne Kusudo, and Rita de la Torre

EDITOR'S INTRODUCTION

Imperative drills in a target language consist of commands issued and/or modeled by an instructor and then carried out by students. The emphasis is on comprehension first as demonstrated and established in appropriate active responses, moving eventually through a series of gentle steps at the student's own pace into productive control of the language. Participating in such drills ensures the successful linking of utterances in the target language with the student's own experience. The whole person gets into the act. First, there is the auditory stimulus accompanied by a demonstrated action. The input is always at least partly comprehended on the first presentation because the student can see what the instructor is doing as well as hear the command. Later, the student demonstrates comprehension by carrying out the command. The sensory-motor accompaniments of such responsive actions provide a whole fabric of meaningful experience into which the utterances of the target language are woven. Unlike many methods that jump right into speaking, Asher's approach, also known as the Total Physical Response or TPR, provides a listening period during which the student is not expected to produce any utterances in the target language. Asher and his collaborators contend that contrary to the claims of certain critics, the transition from TPR drills into the full scope of target language functions can be effected smoothly. They demonstrate here (and see also Chapter 3 by Kalivoda et al. and Chapter 4 by Glisan) that the TPR method is not limited to the teaching of imperatives, as some critics had contended. The starting point is simple, and the principle is comprehensible, but this does not mean for a second that it cannot embrace the full complexities of natural language systems. On the contrary, it can be proved logically that imperatives are inevitably connected with all the natural complexities of language systems. What is more, Asher's method works, and we know why (cf. Chapter 37).

Figure 2.1 on page 12 is a still picture from a documentary film[1] produced in 1964 that showed the complexity of Japanese understood by American children after 20 minutes of training.[2] The instructional strategy was based on asking the students to be silent, listen carefully to a command in Japanese, then act immediately. The approach was called the learning strategy of the "total physical response."

Since that time, the effectiveness of commands to achieve listening skill in a second language has been confirmed in a series of experimental studies in Russian, Japanese, French, Spanish, and German.[3]

The imperative drill can be traced back to 1925, when Harold E. and Dorothée Palmer (1970) observed that physically responding to verbal stimuli is "one of the simplest and most primitive forms of stimulus and reaction in the whole range of speech-activities" (p. 38). This may be the first pattern of responses by the young child to language uttered by his mother. For example,

FIGURE 2.1

mother may say, "Look at that little cat in the garden!" and the baby turns his head and looks in the appropriate direction. Still later, mother directs the child to "fetch things or to pick things up or to put things in various places, and the baby performs all these actions so accurately and so naturally that one is almost tempted to believe that the child has an instinct for understanding his native language" (p. 39).

The Palmers then suggested in their classic book, *English Through Actions,* that executing orders is a prerequisite to achieving the power of expression in a second language. Even further, they advocated that no approach to teaching foreign speech is likely to be economical or successful if it does not include in the first stage an extensive period of time for classroom work involving students carrying out orders by the teacher. Twenty-five years later, in 1950, Tan Gwan and Robert Gauthier introduced in Canada the Tan Gau approach, which was based in large part upon the imperative drill.

Currently, the *total physical response,* the *audio-motor approach,* and the *silent way* all have in common the imperative drill. In Tan Gau, the

total physical response, and the audiomotor formats, production is delayed until listening comprehension has been developed to a considerable extent through commands by the instructor. In the silent way, there is an immediate switch from listening to production, and from the beginning an attempt is made to "fine tune" the student's pronunciation.

With few learning trials, physically responding to commands seems to produce long-term memory. This phenomenon can be generalized beyond second language learning because it has been shown that even in one's native language, responding to commands has an impact on retention. For instance, Lieberman and Altschul (1971) conducted a study in which a list of 35 simple commands (such as stand on one foot, fold your arms, and put your hands on your hips) were played on a tape recorder to groups of college students. One group ($N = 50$) was instructed to close their eyes, relax, and imagine themselves performing the commands. Another group ($N = 53$) watched a model perform, and still a third group ($N = 46$) performed when they heard the commands.

After the list of commands was played, each student had 5 minutes to write the commands he could recall. The recall of each group was significantly different. The one-way analysis of variance yielded an F of 25.6 ($p < .01$). Specifically, the mean recall for the "imagine" group was 47 percent (SD = 12 percent); for the "see" group, the mean was 53 percent (SD = 10 percent); and the group that performed the commands had a mean recall of 62 percent (SD = 8 percent).

The study by Lieberman and Altschul demonstrated short-term memory for commands. James H. Humphrey of the University of Maryland showed in 1972 that even 3 months after science concepts were learned through motor activities, the mean recall of the experimental group was 73 percent (SD = 6 percent) and the control was 50 percent (SD = 5 percent), which yielded a matched group t of 4.33 with df = 9 ($p < .01$). Humphrey published studies (1960, 1962, 1965, 1967, 1968, 1970) which indicated that a learning format based on motor activity by children enhanced the assimilation of a wide range of academic concepts and skills.[4]

After viewing the motion picture of children learning a sample of Japanese, many FL teachers have commented, "Commands are fine, but what happens next? How does the student learn other linguistic features such as the verb tenses, function words, and especially abstractions, which are difficult to manipulate, such as, for instance, 'honor,' 'justice,' and 'government'? How does the student make the transition from the physical and action-oriented imperative to linguistic features that seem to be nonphysical?"

In an effort to answer these important questions, experimental training programs have been developed with the intention of exploring three questions:

1. Can the entire linguistic code of the target language be learned with a format in which the students physically respond to commands?
2. Can listening fluency for the target language be achieved without using the student's native language?
3. Will there be a large amount of positive transfer of learning from listening comprehension to other skills such as speaking, reading, and writing? This transfer should vary depending upon the fit between orthography and phonology. In Spanish, for instance, there should be a large amount of positive transfer because Spanish utterances are written the way they sound.

Since the independent variable was long-term training with a complex instructional program, there was not the experimental control that is possible with a laboratory problem such as eyelid conditioning. Our research strategy has been to explore the parameters of the complex instructional program in a series of field tests. By trying the program in a range of situations which included different languages, different age groups, and different instructors, the expectation was that the instructional format would consistently produce significant gains in learning. The intent was to move by successive approximations in which each field test was better controlled than the previous one.

THE FIRST FIELD TEST

The first field test was reported by Asher in the March 1972 issue of *The Modern Language Journal*. Adults between the ages of 30 and 60 experienced about 32 hours of training in German with an instructor who used commands to achieve listening comprehension.

First, we found that most grammatical features of German could be nested into the imperative form. With imagination, almost any aspect of the linguistic code for the target language could be communicated using commands. For example, the *future tense* can be embedded into a command such as, "When Luke walks to the window, *Marie will* write Luke's name on the blackboard!" The *past tense* can be incorporated into the command structure. For instance, say: "Abner, run to the blackboard!" After Abner has completed the action, say: "Josephine, if *Abner ran* to the blackboard, run after him and hit him with your book." As to the *present tense* these were nested in the imperative —for instance, "When *Luke walks* to the window, Mary will write Luke's name on the blackboard!"

Our second finding was that basic listening fluency could be achieved in German without using the students' native language. For certain abstractions however, the German was written on one side of a cardboard card and English on the other. Then such abstractions as "honor," "justice," and "government" were manipulated as objects. For instance, the instructor said in German "Luke, pick up 'justice' and give it to Josephine." "Abner, throw 'government' to me."

As to the level of listening skill, the experimental group with only 32 hours of training had significantly better listening comprehension than college students completing either 75 or 150 hours of college instruction in German.

The third finding was that listening skill in German had a large amount of positive transfer to reading. Even though the experimental group had no systematic training in reading, their skill was comparable with a control group that did receive systematic instruction in reading and writing.

Concerning speaking, there was positive transfer from listening comprehension to production, as may be seen in the documentary color film, *Strategy for Second Language Learning* (see footnote 1). At the climax of 60 hours, most of which was directed to listening skill, students invented skits and acted them out. The spoken German was flowing, spontaneous, and uninhibited, but there were many errors in pronunciation and grammar. Our tolerance for production errors was similar to the tolerance adults have for production errors by children learning their first language. If the students were willing to talk and talk and talk in German without anxiety about making mistakes, eventually, when their confidence was extremely high, they could be "fine tuned" to produce the subtleties of speech that approximate the native speaker. Our goal was a spontaneous shift from listening to a level of production in which the student's vocal output was intelligible to a native speaker.

Of course we are aware that all instructional problems in teaching a second language cannot be solved with one approach. Variety is essential to maintaining the student's attention and continued interest.

It seems clear, however, that most students (about 80 percent) can rapidly internalize the linguistic code—the structure of the language and vocabulary—when language is synchronized with actual movements of the student's body. In this context, "internalization" means that the linguistic input into the student has these three properties:

(1) short-term memory, (2) long-term memory, and (3) the ability to transpose linguistic elements to comprehend novelty (Asher, 1965, 1966, 1969a, 1969b; and Kunihira & Asher, 1965).

Theoretically, if the student can internalize listening comprehension of a second language, he or she can more gracefully make the transition to production, reading, and writing. If this transition is attempted too abruptly or too prematurely, before the individual student is ready, learning difficulties can be expected.

As listening comprehension is internalized, the student should eventually progress to the "naming stage" (Carroll, 1964), in which the student is able to ask questions such as, "What's that?" "What's that called?" and "What does it mean?" The important feature of the naming stage is not that the student can ask questions but that he or she is able to comprehend and internalize the information received from the answers.

One misconception (Carroll, 1970) is that when language is synchronized with movements of the body, the semantic content is limited to certain kinds of physical activity such as jumping, running, and sitting. This is a literal interpretation which does not accurately represent the parameters of instructional possibilities.

We have found that with a creative application, nonphysical vocabulary items and nonphysical structural features can be embedded in motor responses. Consider, as an illustration, these commands:

Marie, pick up the picture of the ugly old man and put it next to the picture of the government building!

Gregory, find the picture of the beautiful woman with green eyes, long black hair and wearing a sun hat that has red stripes. When you find the picture, show it to the class and describe the woman!

THE SECOND FIELD TEST

Procedure

Undergraduate college students, mostly psychology majors, enrolled in an experimental course for people without prior training in Spanish. The students (N = 27) received college credit for attending the class 3 hours one evening per week for two consecutive semesters.

When each experimental-course student was given the long form of the Modern Language Aptitude Test (MLAT), the mean was 114.4 with a standard deviation of 31.3. These students on the average were quite similar to the average language aptitude of college men and women reported in the MLAT test manual. After testing, the subjects were divided randomly into two separate groups that met on a different evening once each week.

Unfortunately, because of time limitations, no pretests were administered to the control groups. An ideal procedure would be to use standardized pretests with established norms for all groups so that baselines can be determined for prior language skills and aptitude.

Listening Training

The students sat in a semicircle around the instructor. The students adjacent to her were asked to be silent, listen carefully to each command in Spanish, and do exactly what the instructor did. The students were encouraged to respond rapidly without hesitation and to make a distinct, robust response with their bodies. For example, if the command was "Corran!" the students were to run with gusto. A distinct response was an unambiguous signal that the student understood the command. Then the first routine was commands in Spanish such as, "Stand up! Walk! Stop! Turn! Walk! Stop! Turn! Sit down!"

The instructor spoke the commands and acted together with two students on either side of her. This routine was repeated for three of four times until individual students indicated that they were ready to try it alone without the instructor as a model. Each repetition of the routine was not an exact duplication because we did not want memorization of a fixed sequence of behavior. One variation was, for instance: Stand up! Sit down! Stand up! Sit down! Stand up! Walk! Stop! Turn! Walk! Stop! Turn! Walk! Stop! Turn! Walk! Stop! Turn! Sit down!

The next step was to invite other members of the group to perform individually. Experiments have shown (Asher, 1969a) that students can observe a model act, but for long-term memory, each student should then perform alone.

In the next routine, the commands were expanded to: Walk to the door! Walk to the window! Walk to the table! Then "point" and "touch" were introduced. At this juncture in training, the students had enough elements so that constituents could be recombined to move the student with unexpected novel commands as: Eugene, stand up, walk to Claudine and touch her. Claudine walk to Norman, and touch his chair.

In manipulating the individual student, Spanish utterances were constantly recombined to present surprises and novelty, which delighted the students because they realized that they usually had perfect understanding for Spanish utterances they had never heard before. As training progressed, the instructor used playful, zany, and bizarre commands that maintained an extremely high interest level in students. Here are three samples:

> When Henry runs to the blackboard and draws a funny picture of Molly, Molly will throw her purse at Henry.
>
> Henry, would you prefer to serve a cold drink to Molly, or would you rather have Eugene kick you in the leg?
>
> Rosemary, dance with Samuel, and stick your tongue out at Hilda. Hilda, run to Rosemary, hit her on the arm, pull her to her chair and you dance with Samuel!

Production

After about 10 hours of training in listening comprehension, the students were invited but not pressured to reverse roles with the instructor. Those students who felt ready to try speaking uttered commands in Spanish to the instructor, who performed as directed by the students.

From this time on, about 20 percent of class time was role reversal, in which the students spoke Spanish to move the instructor or peers, and later on there were skits created by the students and performed in Spanish, and still later in training there was problem solving in which students, presented with an unexpected difficulty while in a Latin country, had to talk their way through to a solution.[5]

Reading and Writing

There was no systematic training in reading and writing. For a few minutes at the end of each class meeting, the instructor wrote on the blackboard any structure or vocabulary item requested by the students. These items in Spanish, with no English translations, were almost always utterances the students had heard during the class. As the instructor wrote on the blackboard, the students wrote in their notebooks.

Results (Midway Through Training)

The midpoint in training represented about 45 hours of instruction in which class time was 70 percent listening training through commands, 20 percent speaking, and 10 percent reading and writing. There were no homework assignments.

There was one experimental group and three control groups. The first control was a group of high school students with one year of Spanish, the second control group consisted of college students finishing their first semester of Spanish, and the third was college students completing their second semester of Spanish.

One measure of proficiency was stories in Spanish which had the appropriate vocabulary used in the training of experimental and control subjects. None of the students had heard, during training, the exact utterances in the stories.

After listening to a story, each student answered 10 true-false statements about the story as described in the March 1972 issue of *The Modern Language Journal* (Asher, 1972). The listening measure for a set of stories was followed by reading the stories in a printed booklet and answering the identical true-false questions.

Listening and Reading Skill for Stories

First, as may be seen in Table 2.1, the experimental group with about 45 hours of training and no homework assignments had a keener level of listening skill for stories than high school students with about 200 hours of classroom training not including homework (The t of 2.66 was significant beyond the .01 level for 39 df.)

Second, in listening skill for stories the experimental group vastly outperformed college students who were completing their first semester in Spanish, which was about 75 hours of classroom instruction not including homework. (As seen in Table 2.2, the t of 6.75 was significant beyond the .001 level for 69 df.) Surprisingly, the experimen-

TABLE 2.1   The Experimental Group with 45 Hours of Training Compared with Control Group I (High School Students Who Had 200 Hours of Training)—Listening Comprehension of Stories 1 and 2

	Mean	Standard Deviation	t	p
Experimental Group (45 hours) ($n = 27$)	16.63	2.15	2.66	.01
High School Group (200 hours) ($n = 14$)	14.43	3.37		

TABLE 2.2   The Experimental Group with 45 Hours of Training Compared with Control Group II (College Students Who Had 75 Hours of Training)—Total Score for Four Stories

	Mean		Standard Deviation			
	Experimental Group	Control II	Experimental Group	Control II	t	p
Listening	($n = 27$)	($n = 44$)				
	34.00	27.25	3.96	4.65	6.55	.001
Reading	($n = 21$)	($n = 44$)				
	34.86	33.09	1.75	2.66	3.22	.005

TABLE 2.3 The Experimental Group with 45 Hours of Training Compared with Control Group III (College Students Who Had 150 Hours of Training)—Total Score for Four Stories

| | Mean | | Standard Deviation | | | |
	Experimental Group	Control III	Experimental Group	Control III	t	p
Listening	(n = 27)	(n = 28)				
	34.00	29.57	3.96	6.11	3.21	.005
Reading	(n = 21)	(n = 28)				
	34.86	35.29	1.75	3.24	0.60	NS

TABLE 2.4 The Factor of Transitivity—Total Score for Four Stories

| | Mean | | Standard Deviation | | | |
	Control II	Control III	Control II	Control III	t	p
Listening	27.25	29.57	4.65	6.11	1.72	.05
Reading	33.09	35.29	2.66	3.24	3.01	.005

Control II = College Students (n = 44) in Control Group II with 75 hours of instruction
Control III = College Students (n = 28) in Control Group III with 150 hours of instruction

tal subjects also excelled in reading skills for stories. (The t of 3.22 was significant beyond the .001 level for 63 df.)

The third finding was rather extraordinary. The experimental group had a higher level of listening skill for stories than students finishing the second semester of Spanish, which is 150 hours of classroom instruction not including homework. (As seen in Table 2.3, the t of 3.21 was significant beyond the .01 level for 53 df.) It was also surprising that the reading skill of the second semester students did not surpass the experimental group. (The t of 0.60 was not significant for 47 df.)

The Transitivity Factor

It may be argued that an artifact of measurement accounts for the striking differences between groups. Since the stories were developed especially for this project, there may have been an unintentional bias in favor of the experimental training.

One test of the bias hypothesis is to compare the beginning and advanced college students for transitivity. For instance, if the stories were a reasonable measure, the second semester college students should perform with higher listening and reading skill than first semester college students. Table 2.4 confirms transitivity, since the advanced students performed significantly better in both listening and reading.

Standard Proficiency Tests

Midway through training, the experimental group took the Pimsleur Spanish Proficiency Tests—Form A (first level). Since the Pimsleur tests were designed for students in the typical audio-lingual program, they may underestimate the skills acquired by the experimental subjects.

As seen in Table 2.5, the average student performance in the experimental group was the 70th percentile rank for listening, the 85th percentile rank for reading, and the 76th percentile rank for writing. Speaking skill is assessed on the Pimsleur in three categories of "good," "fair," and "poor." The average student in the experimental group was in the "good" category.

TABLE 2.5 Mean and Median Percentile Rank of Experimental Subjects on the Pimsleur Spanish Proficiency Tests Form A (First Level)

	n	Mean	Median
Listening	18	70	70
Reading	17	85	85
Writing	16	76	74
Speaking	15	Good[a]	Good[b]

[a]Raw score of 70   [b]Raw score of 71

TABLE 2.6 Mean and Median Percentile Rank of Experimental Subjects on the Pimsleur Spanish Proficiency Tests Form C (Second Level)

	n	Mean	Median
Listening	16	49	55
Reading	16	69	66
Writing	17	67	60
Speaking	17	Fair[a]	Good[b]

[a]Raw score of 66   [b]Raw score of 68

Results (At the End of Training)

After 90 hours of training, proficiency was assessed with the Pimsleur Spanish Proficiency Tests—Form C (second level). This measurement was stringent because (1) it was designed exclusively for audio-lingual training, and (2) it was meant for students who had completed the second level, which is 150 hours of college instruction. Nevertheless, the experimental group performed beyond the 50th percentile rank for most skills, as may be seen in Table 2.6.

As with the first field test, a documentary motion picture has been prepared to show samples of student behavior during training and at the end of the second field test (see footnote 1).

Conclusions

Motivation

Most linguistic features can be nested into the imperative form, and if the approach is used creatively by the instructor, high student interest can be maintained for a long-term training program.

This experimental program started with 27 students but was reduced to 16 after the first semester. Most of those who left the program said that extrinsic reasons forced them to discontinue.

Transfer from Listening to Other Skills

Perhaps the most important finding was the large magnitude of transfer from listening to other skills. For instance, with almost no direct instruction in reading and writing, the students were on the average beyond the 75th percentile for level I and beyond the 65th percentile for level II. The results are even more significant when one considers that the total time in training was about one-half the instructional hours usually allocated for college instruction in levels I and II.

Future Plans

When language input is organized to synchronize with the student's body movement, the second language can be internalized in chunks rather than word by word. The chunking phenomenon means more rapid assimilation of a cognitive map about the linguistic code of the target language. As the code is internalized, it acts as an "advanced organizer" to facilitate the storage of information as, for instance, in the naming stage when the student begins to ask questions (i.e., "What is that called?").

The movement of the body seems to be a powerful mediator for the understanding, organization, and storage of macro-details of linguistic input. Language can be internalized in chunks, but alternate strategies must be developed for fine-tuning to micro-details.

One way to achieve this fine-tuning is to use a strategy developed by Winitz and Reeds (1973a and b) at the University of Missouri in Kansas City. In the Winitz-Reeds approach, the individual student views four pictures at a time and is directed in the target language to make a choice—for instance, select the picture of "the men" from among these possibilities: a man, a boy, women, and men.

In a step-by-step progression through hundreds of picture sets, the student is fine-tuned for phonologic, morphologic, and syntactic features in a target language.

Future plans call for experimental training in which the student can internalize chunks of language with body movements and fine-tune in a progression of decision making with pictures.

NOTES

1 Information on the availability of the three motion-picture films mentioned in this chapter may be obtained from James J. Asher, Psychology Department, San Jose State University, San Jose, California 95192.

2 The research here was performed under a contract with the United States Department of Health, Education, and Welfare, Office of Education, under PL85-964, title VI, Section 602, as amended.

3 The references are as follows: Russian (Asher 1965, 1966, 1969a; Asher & Price 1967; Postovsky 1974, 1975, 1977), Japanese (Asher 1964; Kunihira & Asher 1965; Kanoi 1970), French (Mear 1969, Pimsleur 1972), Spanish (Kalivoda, Morain, & Elkins, Chapter 3), and German (Asher 1972).

4 Also see the work of Bryant J. Cratty (1966, 1967, 1969, 1970) and a book by George O. Cureton (1973), in which motor learning was used to teach beginning reading to inner-city students.

5 Here are three sample problems: (1) You are taking a shower in your hotel bathroom, and a repairman has just come in the bathroom to fix the light. (2) You have just knocked on the door of the hotel room next door to complain about loud singing and dancing that is keeping you from sleeping. (3) You have a toothache and it is necessary to extract the tooth, but you want to explain to the dentist that you are allergic to drugs used in local anesthetics.

DISCUSSION QUESTIONS

1. John Carroll once objected that TPR is limited to actions such as jumping. How can we use TPR to teach tenses, declaratives, questions, and the connections that run through a story line?

2. If students do link target utterances with their experience during a listening period, what kinds of skills and knowledge will remain to be developed through practice in speech production?

3. How can TPR be integrated with and enriched by other approaches?

CHAPTER 3

The Audio-Motor Unit: A Listening Comprehension Strategy that Works

Theodore B. Kalivoda, Genelle Morain, and Robert J. Elkins

EDITOR'S INTRODUCTION

Kalivoda, Morain, and Elkins apply Asher's thinking (Chapter 2) with a couple of differences. For one, they insist (p. 24) on "meaningful sequence" (also see Oller, Sr. & Oller, Chapter 6, p. 57). By doing so, it is possible to take greater advantage of the prior knowledge and expectancies of students concerning whole sequences of events in their experience (also see Chapter 37). The imperative drills of Kalivoda, Morain, and Elkins are miniature dramas in which the teacher functions somewhat like a stage director. The teacher shows by actions what the tape recorder (or the teacher) says to do. The series of distinct commands is pragmatically linked to a series of even more distinct actions that are delicately coordinated with the commands. Later, the teacher can invite students to participate either in acting out the commands or in telling other actors what to do as they act out the series. Kalivoda, Morain, and Elkins show how vocabulary is naturally enriched through such supercharged imperative drills and how to incorporate subtleties of cultural difference so that they really become obvious to the students, e.g., how to eat steak the European way. Their recommendations work in French, Spanish, and German, so why not in Thai, Russian, Navajo, American Sign Language, or, in any language? Reactions of students and teachers are generally positive and confirm Asher's claims for transfer from listening to speaking to reading and writing. Those teachers who were not native speakers of the target language found that directing the drama drills tended to result in significant gains in their own skills. In fact, it is difficult to see how any foreign language user could fail to benefit from the sort of activities recommended by Kalivoda, Morain, and Elkins. For instance, do you know how to say "Don't smack your lips!" in more than one language? How many teachers can use the foreign language to tell their students how to eat politely in the culture of the language that they teach? Come on. Admit it. Eating is pretty basic in any culture.

The classroom teacher is not indifferent to the theorist. We listen attentively to the grammarian, the audiolingualist, the cognitive-coder, and the eclecticist. But while we wait for the Revelation, we have to go on teaching the language Monday through Friday from September to June. The question we ask most fervently when two or three gather together is, "What are you doing that works?"

Teachers who are searching for a way to improve students' listening skills may want to investigate the "audio-motor" unit, a supplementary device that seems to "work." Simply, it is a daily 10-minute activity designed to develop the listening skill (*audio-*) by requiring an immediate physical response (*motor*).

James J. Asher (1969b) has pioneered research in the area of listening skill coupled with physical activity. He attributes the current failure to produce students fluent in the language to the fact that most language teaching is multiple in dimension—involving the simultaneous presentation of different skills. Asher advocates a change to "serial learning" of the four skills, with "listening fluency" the first to be acquired. His experiments with the "total physical response technique," which combines listening with enacting, showed that students who learned by this strategy were superior in retention of the foreign languages to those of control groups.

However, Asher's "total physical response technique" is conceived as the sole learning activity for an extended period. Its use in the classroom would require a radical restructuring of the first-level language program and would render obsolete many of the materials now in use across the land. In addition, those students who leave the program after one year would have little or no contact with speaking, reading, and writing skills. Furthermore, it is questionable whether a unidimensional approach could be satisfying to students for an extended period of time.

The audio-motor unit described in this paper is indebted to Asher's work but varies markedly in approach. It is designed as a supplementary, not an exclusive, learning activity, and thus is immediately applicable to any classroom. It provides one answer to Wilga M. Rivers' call in 1966 for increased use of listening comprehension materials at regular intervals in the language learning program.

THE AUDIO-MOTOR UNIT

Format

The average length of the audio-motor unit is 10 minutes. This may be shortened or extended as class needs change from day to day.

To begin the unit, the teacher walks to a tape recorder and activates the voice of a native speaker. The voice, speaking at a comfortable speed that retains natural rhythm and intonation patterns, gives a series of some 20 commands, structured around a central theme.

The teacher acts out the appropriate responses to the commands, making use of gesture, pantomime, and facial expression. Sometimes a simple prop (a billfold, an eraser, an apple) may be used to illustrate meaning. The students listen to the tape and observe the actions of the teacher.

An audio-motor unit involving activities in the kitchen might include the following fragment. (The imaginary drawer might be one which has been sketched on the blackboard. The onion, knife, and spoon may also be sketched for the teacher to "pick off" the board on command.)

Tape: Open the drawer. (Teacher pulls out imaginary drawer.)
Tape: Take out a knife. (Teacher pantomimes.)
Tape: Place the onion on the table. (Pantomime)
Tape: Chop the onion. (Pantomime)
Tape: Your eyes are watering. Wipe them. (Pantomime)
Tape: Add the onion to the stew. (Pantomime)
Tape: Pick up the spoon. (Pantomime)
Tape: Stir the stew. (Pantomime)
Tape: Take a spoonful. Blow on it. (Pantomime)
Tape: Taste it. (Pantomime)
Tape: It's good. Smack your lips. (Pantomime)

Childish? Maybe. But how many students (and teachers for that matter) know how to say: "Your eyes are watering," "Blow on it," "Taste it," and "Smack your lips"? Teachers should not misinterpret the purpose behind such commands. It is recognized that the student may never be in a situation where he or she will give the direct command, "Smack your lips." He or she may, however, eventually encounter such forms as "Don't smack your lips'" or "He smacked his lips." The value of the command, then, lies in learning the vocabulary and in the transfer to other situations.

When the taped lesson is finished (2 to 3 minutes), the teacher replays it. This time he invites the students to join him in acting out the appropriate responses. If the activity does not require extensive movement, all students participate simultaneously, standing in the aisle by their desks. If a great deal of action is called for, the teacher may designate several students to represent the class, although once the class acquires the feel of pantomime they can simulate at the side of their desk even the actions required by such commands as, "Climb the ladder" and "Run to the window."

The taped sequence is repeated on ensuing days until the teacher is satisfied that most of the students can associate the proper physical response with a given command. To test this, the teacher takes over the giving of the commands and presents them in scrambled order. The entire class may respond, or individuals may be designated to demonstrate the responses. This portion of the unit offers opportunities for a competitive game situation which makes testing a positive activity.

In summary, then, the format of the audio-motor unit is simple: (1) the teacher acts out responses to taped commands; (2) students listen and observe; (3) the tape (or the teacher) repeats the commands; (4) the students respond physically.

As John B. Carroll (1965) has pointed out, "The more kinds of association that are made to an item, the better is learning and retention" (p. 280). With the audio-motor technique, the student first *sees* meaning as he *hears* sound; then he himself supplies the *muscular response* which fulfills meaning. Thus visual, auditory, and motor sense combine in this listening comprehension strategy.

Subject Matter

The content of each audio-motor unit is organized around a central theme. The prosaic world of the classroom is a logical starting place, but the nature of the activity required need not be humdrum. The familiar requests to "Open your books" and "Hand in your papers" are valid, but so are "Plug in the projector" and "Don't scribble on the desk."

The activities as initially presented on tape are given in a meaningful sequence. The student may be told to take out a piece of paper, draw an outline map of France, take it to the bulletin board, pick up a thumbtack, pin the map to the board, stand back and look at it, shake his head, remove the map, crumple it up, and throw it in the wastebasket.

Once the students grasp the audio-motor technique, there is no need to limit lesson horizons to the classroom. The teacher can set the scene by holding up a single picture or making a rapid sketch on the blackboard. Students play the game

with alacrity. There is no limit to the imaginative setting they seem willing to accept—as long as it lies within the normal scope of experience. A lesson on "How to Wind the Maypole" would lack the relevance that today's students demand.

Vocabulary Acquisition

Audiolingualists once minimized the importance of vocabulary learning in the early stages of language study. Valid though their urgings may have been, our students were left with a rather pallid lexicon. They knew the equivalent of "book," "window," "door," "sweater," and "record." They could "go," "come," "take a walk," "play tennis," and "drive a car." But in a world where involvement means perception on many levels, this is not enough. It is a distortion of culture to strip the physical and emotional content from language learning.

The audio-motor unit can teach recognition of a rich supply of nouns in the affective domain: the sneer, the sigh, the giggle, the guffaw, the shrug, the wink, the frown. It can provide a powerhouse of verbs to be assimilated with vigor and humor. There is no reason to limit today's bright students to "standing up" and "sitting down." They also want to wince, twist, squat, lurch, spit, stoop, and clutch. The audio-motor unit is an exceptionally efficient way to teach kinesics. By presenting the vocabulary of movement and emotion, it can restore life to an anemic lexicon.

Reentry of Materials

Careful structuring of the audio-motor units provides for reentry of materials at regular intervals. In a discussion of listening comprehension, Rivers (1966) emphasized reentry and suggested that it is effective when presented through the use of games:

> Games imaginatively devised give the students comprehension practice in a situation where interest is heightened by the competitive element . . . A few minutes of listening comprehension games at regular intervals, usually at the end of class lessons, will enable the teacher to reintroduce systematically material which is not currently being actively practiced. In this way, retention of material from earlier lessons will be constantly reinforced by active recapitulation without tedium.

The audio-motor unit provides a palatable form of reentry in which physical involvement and the spirit of competition reinforce the learning experience.

Cultural Concepts

Audio-motor lessons have the advantage of linking culture to language in a way that makes the cultural phenomena immediately obvious. Simply talking about an aspect of culture or looking at pictures that illustrate it cannot provide the learning impact that results from physical involvement.

An example of cultural learning may be seen in the following Spanish lesson:

You are at a restaurant	Estás en un restaurante.
Pick up your napkin.	Coge la servilleta.
Unfold it.	Desdóblala.
Put it on your lap.	Ponla sobre las piernas.
Pick up your fork in your left hand.	Coge el tenedor con la mano izquierda.
Pick up your knife in your right hand.	Coge el cuchillo con la mano derecha.
Cut a piece of meat.	Corta un trozo de carne.
Put it in your mouth.	Ponlo en la boca.
Chew it.	Mastícalo.
Swallow it.	Trágalo.
Put down your knife and fork.	Deja en el plato el tenedor y el cuchillo.
Leave your hands on the table.	Deja las manos en la mesa.
Pour a glass of wine.	Sírvete un vaso de vino.
Take a sip.	Bebe un poco.
You want some bread. Break off a piece.	Quieres pan. Parte un trozo.
Eat it.	Cómelo.
Pick up the bill.	Coge la cuenta.
Look at it.	Mírala.
Take out your wallet.	Saca tu billetera.
Pay the bill.	Paga la cuenta.
Leave a tip.	Deja una propina.
Leave the restaurant.	Sal del restaurante.

At least four significant cultural points are illustrated in this unit, each reinforced through physical enactment:

1. Techniques of eating meat: holding knife and fork in right and left hands, respectively, cutting one piece of meat at a time, lifting the cut piece to the mouth with the fork still in the left hand.
2. Leaving both hands resting lightly on the edge of the table when not in use.
3. Using wine as the common beverage at mealtime for young people as well as adults.
4. Eating bread by tearing off small pieces from the larger individual portion, instead of biting them off.

These four Spanish eating habits differ markedly from those commonly practiced in the United States and could serve as a springboard for a discussion of cross-cultural differences at a later moment.

Such cultural differences come to light unexpectedly in the preparation of audio-motor units. The authors, working French, Spanish, and German to create a unit involving activities in the kitchen, wanted to set up the sequence:

Go to the refrigerator.
Open the door.

At this point the German writer suggested that a command was missing. He insisted that "Bend over" should follow immediately after "Go to the refrigerator." His French and Spanish colleagues were mystified, until the resultant discussion brought out the fact that the typical German refrigerator is a low unit which falls far short of the height of an American refrigerator. One must "bend over" to open the door and look inside. Absorbing a tiny fragment of culture such as this may not seem important, but it might prevent an American student from blurting, "Oh, what a funny little refrigerator!" to a sensitive German host.

Variation in Routine

The inclusion of the audio-motor unit within the regular classroom session has another value. It provides a salutary relief from the pattern drill and directed dialogue. With instant physical involvement, the student "comes alive" in every sense—muscular as well as intellectual.

The nature of the activity ranges from the relatively mild act of entering a phone booth, consulting the directory, and placing a call, to the really gymnastic efforts of a lesson in calisthenics, where students, participating simultaneously, are required to bend, stretch, jump rope, and do knee bends.

The chance to get up and move around the room is appealing to students. Not only does it offer rest from the sedentary pursuit of knowledge, but it also represents meaningful activity in terms of the language learning that students are seeking.

THE AUDIO-MOTOR UNIT IN PRACTICE

Small-scale pilot programs using the audio-motor unit have been conducted in high schools in Florida and Georgia. The first large-scale use of the audio-motor strategy look place at the Southeastern Language Center on the University of Georgia campus during an intensive six-week course for high school students in the summer of 1970.

Procedure

Coordinate lessons were used in French, Spanish, and German classes. The language background of the students ranged from 1 to 6 years of language study. Six different audio-motor units, each composed of 20 commands, were presented at the rate of one unit per week. Classes with 1 and 2 years of language study participated in the audio-motor lesson daily, allocating the last 10 minutes of the hour to this activity. Advanced classes required only one or two 10-minute intervals to master the designated unit for any given week.

The teachers who conducted the audio-motor lessons received only the minimal instruction necessary to ensure similarity of presentation. There was no discussion concerning possible drawbacks to or benefits from such a program. One instructor asked to be excused from participating, explaining that he would "feel foolish" during the teacher-modeling phase of the unit. A total of eight teachers took part in the audio-motor program.

Results

At the end of the six-week period, students were asked to fill out a questionnaire (see Figure 3.1) giving their attitude toward the audio-motor units at the beginning and at the end of the six weeks, as

FIGURE 3.1 Student Questionnaire: Audio-Motor Units

Language Studied: _____   Please circle one: Male   Female

	Very positive	Positive	Somewhat positive	Somewhat negative	Negative	Very negative
1. What was your attitude toward this activity at the beginning of the 6 weeks?						
2. What was your attitude toward this activity at the end of the 6 weeks?						
3. What was your instructor's attitude toward this activity at the beginning of the 6 weeks?						
4. What was your instructor's attitude toward this activity at the end of the 6 weeks?						

5. Which lesson did you like most? _____

6. Which lesson did you like least? _____

7. Give your positive reactions to the audio-motor units.

8. Give your negative reactions to the audio-motor units.

FIGURE 3.2 Student Questionnaire

Items	Number of students rating items by categories					
	Very positive	Positive	Somewhat positive	Somewhat negative	Negative	Very negative
1. What was your attitude toward this activity at the beginning of the 6 weeks?	29	55	47	34	10	5
2. What was your attitude toward this activity at the end of the 6 weeks?	54	76	32	5	11	2
3. What was your instructor's attitude toward this activity at the beginning of the 6 weeks?	71	71	26	6	5	1
4. What was your instructor's attitude toward this activity at the end of the 6 weeks?	84	63	20	5	4	4

well as their perception of their instructors' attitude at the same intervals. Students were also asked to enumerate their positive and negative criticisms of the audio-motor strategy (see Figure 3.2).

A total of 180 students took part in the study. The response of 90 percent of these (162) students was positive. Neither the sex of the respondent nor the language studied proved to be significant in analyzing the questionnaire results.

Students indicated strongest approval for the following aspects of the audio-motor unit:

1. They felt it increased their language learning in terms of listening comprehension and vocabulary building.
2. They appreciated the change of pace it gave to classroom procedure.
3. They found it stimulating and entertaining.

On the other hand, negative reactions included such comments as, "too easy," "boring," "silly." Nine students expressed dissatisfaction in being unable to see the written form of the commands. Two students indicated a desire to participate orally in the lesson. It is interesting to note that a total of fifty six students did not list a negative reaction of any kind.

Instructors who had worked with the audio-motor units filled out a different questionnaire, evaluating their own reaction to the technique, as well as their students' reaction as perceived by the professors. They were also asked to list strengths and weaknesses of the audio-motor strategy. (See Figure 3.3.)

Of the eight teachers involved, six responded with positive reasons. They were principally impressed with four benefits derived from the use of the units:

1. Lexical and structural items and their syntactic arrangements that were being practiced through other classroom activities were reinforced by the physical response lesson. This subjective reaction would tend to uphold Asher's assertion (1969a) that "listening skill seems to have a large positive transfer to reading and writing depending upon the fit between phonology and orthography of a specific language" (p. 4).
2. Cultural learnings illustrated by the lessons and strengthened through physical enactment caused strong interest on the part of students.
3. Although the lessons were designed to facilitate development of the listening skill, evidence of their impact on student oral expression was seen in the students' spontaneous use of the commands both in and out of the classroom. Idioms and individual words seemed to become a part of the students' system of expression. Some teachers felt

FIGURE 3.3 Instructor Questionnaire: Audio-Motor Units

Language Studied: _____   Please circle one: Male   Female

	Very positive	Positive	Somewhat positive	Somewhat negative	Negative	Very negative
1. What was your attitude toward this activity at the beginning of the 6 weeks?						
2. What was your attitude toward this activity at the end of the 6 weeks?						
3. What was the attitude of your class toward this activity at the beginning of the program?						
4. What was the attitude of your class toward this activity at the end of the program?						

5. With which group did you use the AMU; students of beginning, medium, or advanced language ability?

6. How many minutes each day did you use this activity? _____

7. How many days per week did you use it? _____

8. At what time slot during the class hour did you use this activity? Beginning? Middle? End? At varying times?

9. Why did you present the activity at this time?

10. Please evaluate the activity in terms of the following areas:
   a. Vocabulary enrichment _____
   b. Grammatical reinforcement _____
   c. Carry-over into students' pronunciation _____
   d. Cultural learnings _____
   e. Your own acquisition of knowledge (if nonnative speaker) _____

11. Please add any further comments or suggestions you would care to make.

---

that there was an accompanying improvement in pronunciation, although they added that "this is hard to verify." Asher does cite evidence that "the skill of listening comprehension has high positive transfer especially to speaking a foreign language" (p. 4).

4. Nonnative speakers of the staff indicated that the lessons helped them with their own ability to say certain things in the foreign language. It is possible that teachers in secondary schools often fail to use the foreign language in the classroom because they are not sure how to say what the situation demands. Audio-motor lessons contain high-frequency situations found throughout the language hour and thus provide the teacher with useful expressions for greater communication in the foreign language.

Objections from the teachers who participated in the audio-motor lessons included two principal criticisms:

1. Some felt that the exclusion of the written word narrowed the benefits to be derived. They wanted the students to read and speak the commands as well as hear and enact them.

2. One would have preferred more explicit orientation to the procedures to be used and a chance to meet with other staff members to evaluate the program at its conclusion.

Analysis

In generalizing from the results of the questionnaires, it should be remembered that participants in this program were not "typical." Students who enroll at the Southeastern Language Center must have at least a B average in prior language study. Furthermore, students who are willing to devote six weeks of summer vacation to intensive language study are obviously highly motivated. It should also be kept in mind that participants at the Language Center attend class at least five hours per day. They might be more receptive, therefore, to a 10-minute departure from usual classroom activity than would students whose contact time with a foreign language consists of 50 minutes per day. On the other hand, one might speculate that students with average or lower grades, and students with weak motivation, would be even more responsive to an audio-motor unit than their more favored peers.

It is to be regretted that no controlled attempt was made to evaluate the effect of the audio-motor strategy upon retention. However, instructors did reenter materials from past units at frequent intervals, and reported that student response was highly accurate.

At the conclusion of the six-week period, videotapes were made of the audio-motor units in action. In an attempt to more nearly approximate the "beginning language" stage, German students were taught a French unit, French students learned Spanish, and Spanish students received instruction in German. The videotapes did capture the sense of concentration, the release that comes with physical involvement, the spontaneity and the learning satisfaction that characterize the audio-motor technique.

SUMMARY

The audio-motor unit as a device for teaching listening comprehension has met with an overwhelmingly positive response in a large-scale operation.

Using a visual and an audible stimulus initially to elicit a physical response, this strategy brings sight, hearing, and kinesic participation into interplay. Later the visible stimulus is dropped and the student relies only upon the oral command to motivate his or her physical response.

It is suggested that regular use of carefully prepared audio-motor units can provide listening comprehension activities which increase knowledge of lexical and structural items, add dimension to cultural understanding, and enliven the learning situation with zest and humor.

DISCUSSION QUESTIONS

1. What advantages are offered by drills with a "meaningful sequence" (alias "episodic organization")? For instance, how does such organization help students acquire new vocabulary?

2. One teacher says the activities recommended in this chapter would make him "feel foolish." How might this teacher be helped to become less self-conscious and a more expressive actor?

3. Another teacher says that students should see the imperatives written down as well as hear them and see them acted out, and that students should be required to say and read the commands. What consequences could be expected, and what measurement procedures could be used to assess them?

4. What kinds of reform are needed in foreign language teaching, literacy programs, and education in general to bring about a much higher success rate than we currently see? Why do schools tend to stick with familiar books and materials (e.g., the "Dick and Jane" basals) even when we admit, as Kalivoda, Morain, and Elkins do, that those materials don't work very well?

CHAPTER 4

Total Physical Response: A Technique for Teaching All Skills in Spanish

Eileen W. Glisan

EDITOR'S INTRODUCTION

Glisan says that TPR "is still in its infancy" (p. 38) and that much additional research is needed. Nevertheless, what we already know about the method confirms that it works in a wide variety of languages and contexts. It works well with nearly all children, and it works well with the large majority (about 90% judging from Kalivoda, Morain, and Elkins, Chapter 3) of adults. No language has proved unsusceptible to the method, and pure logic tells us that none ever will. Commands are as universal as transitive verbs of action. Glisan offers more than a plethora of concrete suggestions about how to extend TPR way beyond the initial stages of language instruction. She also gives a good and comprehensible review of relevant research and an accessible explanation of some of the best theoretical thinking available. Especially ápropos is the observation that with TPR, "like infants, students also begin to map language structure onto meaning, that is, to internalize language, by responding physically to stimuli" (p. 33). Moreover, as Asher himself (in press) has argued in his most recent writing on TPR, Glisan too contends that through TPR strategies, the left-brain specialty of taking things apart (analysis) is greatly assisted by the right-brain superiority of holistic comprehension (synthesis). In fact, both of these ideas can be seen as paraphrases of the theory of pragmatic mapping in Chapter 37 (also see the remarks by Jonathan de Berkeley-Wykes in Chapter 35). Finally, what makes Glisan's article so appropriate for this collection is that her guidelines are applicable to any foreign language program and also have fairly obvious extensions to literacy programs and education in general, as we will see with greater clarity below.

Tell me and I will forget;
Teach me and I will remember;
Involve me and I will learn.
— *Ancient Chinese Proverb*

INTRODUCTION

An issue that continues to be examined in foreign language teaching is the effect of initially delaying oral production through a period of extensive listening. Research findings (Winitz & Reeds, 1973b; Asher, 1982) have revealed that allotting a period of time for speech readiness can result in great benefits in terms of both linguistic and affective development.

Total Physical Response, a technique in which students respond physically to oral commands, presents an interesting, effective vehicle for applying this theory to the classroom. Yet why isn't the technique a component of most language programs? Why are teachers interested in learning about TPR but hesitant to implement it in their classrooms? First, we must allow for the usual lag between dissemination of research findings and their actual application in terms of teaching approaches. Second, research findings have been quite thorough in describing the first several lessons of TPR, but they are less than clear in explaining subsequent procedures. Third, proponents have marketed TPR as a strategy for teaching listening comprehension that offers optimal use during the first few weeks of exposure to the language. Fourth, the average teacher feels uncertain about adopting such a heretofore "unorthodox" method and fitting it into a conventional language curriculum. Finally, explicit curricular guidelines and teaching materials for utilizing TPR remain to be developed.

The purpose of this paper is to present a strategy for using TPR as one technique for teaching not only listening, but also speaking, reading, and writing in Spanish. It presupposes a teaching methodology based on communicative or functional skill acquisition. A plan is suggested for its implementation within the language curriculum. Specific examples are provided for Spanish, although the guidelines can be applied to the teaching programs of any foreign language.

RESEARCH IMPLICATIONS

Studies in Second Language Learning

Recent theories provide a basis for the Total Physical Response Method. Krashen's extensive work with the Input Hypothesis and Monitor Model in second language learning/acquisition has had far-reaching claims for language teaching. According to his theories, learners "acquire" language by being exposed to large quantities of meaningful input. Acquisition provides the means for second-language fluency while conscious rule learning serves as a "monitor" in editing speech output (Krashen, 1981, 1982; Krashen et al., 1984). Applied to classroom instruction, these claims imply that teachers need to provide maximum opportunities for students to hear the target language in interesting, real-life, communicative contexts.

Much research has examined the learner's role in attending to language input. Evidence suggests that learners participate in different types of communication at different times during the learning process. Burt and Dulay (1983) maintain that learners begin with "one-way communication" by

listening or reading the target language, progress to "partial two-way communication" by responding physically or orally in the native language, and finally arrive at "full two-way communication." This typology of learner interaction is similar to the three stages described in Krashen et al. (1984) as "comprehension," "early speech," and "speech emergence." For Terrell (1986), during these first two stages, learners "bind" or mentally associate a new word or form with meaning by reacting in a meaningful and physical manner.

Some experimentation suggests that students exposed to an initial "silent period" during which they respond without being forced to use the target language, perform better on both listening and speaking tasks than do students required to speak the language from the beginning (Winitz & Reeds, 1973b; Postovsky, 1974, 1977; Gary, 1975; Asher, 1972, 1982). Linguistic input is paramount to comprehension, which not only precedes oral production but "appears to be the basic mechanism through which the rules of language are internalized" (Winitz, 1981: 130). Research has shown that adults spend 40-50% of their communication time listening, 25-30% speaking, 11-16% reading, and 9% writing (Rivers, 1981). Input to trigger acquisition should contain some grammar and vocabulary items somewhat beyond ($i + 1$) the student's production level (Krashen, 1981). Some researchers, however, maintain that learners must be active conversational partners in order to internalize language input (Hatch, 1983). Although more experimentation is needed to explain learner interaction more conclusively, it seems safe to assume that "matching the type of communicative interaction with the learners' level of language development maximizes students' likelihood for success" (Burt & Dulay, 1983: 43). These findings suggest that teachers should provide sequenced activities that take into account the language readiness factor and that facilitate progression from one learning stage to the next.

While it is apparent that learners experience stages in their development of speech readiness, evidence also suggests that they acquire grammatical structures in a predictable order. Research dealing with the "Natural Order Hypothesis" has been done in English by Brown (1973), Dulay and Burt (1974), and Dulay et al. (1982), among others. Results of recent work by VanPatten (1985) and

VanPatten et al. (in progress) have identified a series of stages experienced by learners of Spanish in their internationalization of the copulas and *gustar*. Because the development of language skill may well be a natural process similar to that of first-language acquisition, teachers should provide ample opportunities for "real" linguistic and non-linguistic communication, should allow the various stages in speech production to occur, and should not be overly preoccupied with grammatical accuracy.

Much has been written recently about the shift in emphasis from overt grammar teaching to the development of functional proficiency. Information about this approach has by now been universally disseminated, with the development of the oral proficiency interview and curricular guidelines by ACTFL/ETS (American Council of Teachers of Foreign Languages/Educational Testing Services). Research in this area has evidenced the need for teachers to provide classroom opportunities for maximum linguistic input and authentic language use in all skill areas.

Many research findings have pointed to the importance of affective variables in the language learning process; that is, student success may be related to motivation, anxiety, and self-confidence factors. According to the Affective Filter hypothesis of Dulay and Burt (1977), as well as Krashen (1981), language learners experiencing anxiety or lack of motivation will have a filter or block that prevents them from internalizing input. Lambert (1972) and others, through extensive research and borrowing from social psychology theory, found motivation and attitude toward learning a language to be very important for effective learning. Indeed, several teaching methodologies have been proposed during the past decade that claim to lessen students' anxiety by creating a relaxed classroom atmosphere. Such methods as Silent Way (Gattegno, 1972); Suggestopedia (Lozanov, 1978), and Counseling Learning (Curran, 1976) attempt to tap into student individuality while removing psychic tensions and student limitations.

TPR STUDIES

The Total Physical Response, as developed by James J. Asher over the past twenty years, is founded on the implications discussed above. This theory emphasizes comprehension through an initial listening period during which students connect speech utterances with meaningful contexts. As in first-language acquisition, students first respond physically to oral commands and progress gradually to productive language use. Experimental results show that TPR, which advocates an "acquisition-rich" environment (Asher, 1982), increases student motivation and contributes to positive attitudes toward foreign language learning.

The significance of the imperative exercise was identified as early as 1925 by Harold E. and Dorothée Palmer (1972) who much later advocated its use as part of an extensive listening period in order to foster successful language skills.

Much experimental data exist from Asher and others in support of TPR. In the first field test reported by Asher (1972), adults between the ages of 30 and 60 received 32 hours of TPR training in German. Results indicated that these students had better listening comprehension skills than college students with 75 and 150 hours of German instruction and, further, that their listening ability had positive transfer to reading and speaking in German. Similar results occurred in using TPR to teach Japanese to college students (Kunihira and Asher, 1965), as well as in teaching Russian to children and adults (Asher & Price,1967; Ingram et al., 1975). Data from a field test with college students learning Spanish revealed that, after 90 hours of training in listening to and producing commands, students performed beyond the 50th percentile rank for listening, speaking, reading, and writing on the Pimsleur Spanish Proficiency Tests (Form C) (Asher et al., Chapter 2). Extensive documentation exists to support the benefits of TPR for children and adults acquiring French (Davies, 1976); German (Swaffar & Woodruff, 1978); Spanish (Kalivoda et al., Chapter 3, this volume). English as a Second Language (Asher, 1978); and even sign language (Murphy, 1979). Other findings indicate that TPR can facilitate grammatical understanding (Schessler, 1985; Cabello, 1985).

In addition to research examining TPR and skill acquisition, many studies have documented student attrition rates, student attitudes, and student evaluation of faculty. Swaffer and Woodruff's experiment (1978) with college students learning German showed that 78% of the first-semester

TPR students chose to continue their study of German, while only 55% of the "traditionally" taught students elected to continue. Experimentation also reveals that TPR students report increased interest in the target language and rate their teachers' effectiveness much higher (Asher, 1983).

What psycholinguistic phenomena account for why TPR works? Evidence from first-language acquisition studies indicate that infants acquire language by "constructing reality" through motor responses such as touching, crawling, and crying (Piaget, 1926). Like infants, students also begin to map language structure onto meaning, that is, to internalize language, by responding physically to stimuli. Research in brain lateralization indicates that the left hemisphere is responsible for language production, while the right hemisphere enables physical responses to occur. This suggests that infants use their right hemisphere to "decode" speech until the left brain is ready to orally produce language. The aim of the TPR strategy is to activate the right brain and give the left brain an opportunity to become ready for language production. In addition to TPR, other right-hemisphere teaching strategies have been formulated, such as the Winitz-Reeds comprehension strategy (1975) and the Nord Sensit Cell Model (1981), both of which make use of pictures during the listening period.

TPR PROGRAMS AND MATERIALS

TPR programs have been reported in elementary schools, high schools, and universities in Delaware, Texas, California, and Tennessee. The many projects undertaken by James J. Asher and Berty Segal in California have been widely publicized (Vetter, 1983).

Graduate students at the University of Tennessee recently developed a TPR program ("FLEX") for local kindergarten and first-grade students; the results have been so favorable that the program may be expanded (Wiley, 1985). In the Loara Elementary School in Anaheim, CA, TPR is utilized along with the "Language Experience Approach" in which students express thoughts through action and the sensory channels (Elenbaas, 1983). The results of a German TPR program at the University of Texas proved more

favorable than those of the non-TPR classes (Woodruff, 1976). Vetter (1983) has described a program that combines TPR, the Natural Approach, and English for Special Purposes: the "High Intensity Language Training" (HILT) focuses on the communicative functions (content and area-specific), which students need to succeed in the language. Similarly, Kestelman and Maiztegui (1980) have reported the "HILT—plus Program in Spanish for Educators."

Many materials for teaching TPR lessons have become available during the past few years. Asher has developed some twenty lesson plans and student picture kits for teaching vocabulary and grammar. Lesson plans and guidelines are available for English, Spanish, French, and German.[1] The materials developed at present, however, provide limited guidelines for implementing TPR lessons in a traditional language curriculum.

TPR AS A STRATEGY WITHIN THE CURRICULUM

Although the research has shown the positive results to be gained by utilizing TPR, many teachers consider it unfeasible to adopt the entire method at all levels of language. Moreover, TPR cannot easily be used to teach the abstract, and the exact techniques for presenting reading and writing are still unclear.

Indeed, recent research has advocated the implementation of an "active" listening period as an element of the language methodology. Nord (1981) previously established a four-phase listening period to include TPR activities and semantic decoding practice. Wipf (1984) has proposed the challenging of learners to progress more rapidly in listening and reading, since native language receptive skills surpass those of the generative skills. In the comprehension-based Spanish program of Long, et al. (1985), students acquire understanding through listening exercises and thematic visuals. In Terrell's (1986) "pre-textbook comprehension stage," beginning Spanish students internalize meaning through three to fifteen hours of extended listening activity. Although the development of these techniques has contributed a great deal to the teaching of effective listening comprehension, the well-defined use of TPR and guidelines for curricular modification have been lacking.

Variations of TPR can easily be adopted for use in a proficiency-based curriculum. TPR in this context means the response by students to various types of oral stimuli, not only to commands, during a pre-production stage. These responses include organizing classroom realia, drawing pictures, and silently interacting with classmates. Several pedagogical principles must first be established:

1. Language should be presented as real communication in meaningful, interesting contexts.
2. A maximum amount of comprehensible target-language input should be provided in the classroom.
3. Opportunities for comprehension should be provided before production is expected.
4. For each function[2] to be taught (with its inherent grammar and vocabulary), students should be exposed to a minimum of two fifteen-minute listening experiences (including some reading) before oral production is elicited.
5. In order for students to internalize the meaning of new language forms, these initial listening experiences should allow students to respond in some way (TPR) to oral stimuli.
6. Grammar should be taught indirectly for the purpose of developing communicative skill.
7. Error-free speech should not be given undue emphasis, especially before comprehension is achieved.
8. The teaching of every function should include activities for listening, reading, speaking, and writing.

LISTENING PERIODS

The two listening periods are designed to help students internalize meaning in stages. The first 15-minute listening experience could be provided two class periods prior to language production. Procedures characteristic of the first listening period (LP1) are the following:

LP1

1. Teacher provides oral input in the target language; students do not see written correspondences.
2. Meaning is conveyed through action/gestures by the teacher, as well as via pictures and realia.

3. Students respond to oral stimuli in various ways: physically acting out stimuli; identifying/organizing realia or pictures; responding in English.

The second 15-minute listening experience could occur one class period preceding language production. The following activities are done in the second listening period:

LP2

1. Teacher provides oral input in the target language, again conveying meaning through action/gestures.
2. Students again demonstrate comprehension by responding physically to oral stimuli.
3. Students do oral listening exercises in the target language, which may be multiple choice, yes/no questions, or true/false statements.
4. Teacher presents language in written form to give students reading practice; exercises and activities are done, such as skimming/scanning, vocabulary matching, and physical responses to written stimuli.

For the activities in which students react with "total physical responses" the following systematic phases are suggested:

1. Teacher gives oral stimuli several times and demonstrates action;
2. Small group of students (4–6) acts out oral stimuli with teacher;
3. The same small group of students acts out stimuli without teacher;
4. Individual students from the group physically respond to stimuli;
5. Individual students from the entire class physically respond to stimuli.

TPR AND LANGUAGE FUNCTIONS

The following is a list, by no means exhaustive, of TPR activities that are effective for practice of many language functions and contexts.[3] Many grammatical structures (as listed below in parentheses) can be "taught" indirectly by means of each activity's practice.

1. Drawing pictures, maps, portraits, floor plans:
   Functions:
   Indicating locations, conditions (*ser, estar,* prepositions) Identifying and describing people, places, things (adjectives, past participles used as adjectives)
2. Charting directions on maps:
   Functions:
   Getting around in the city (command forms)
   Reporting action impersonally (passive with *ser*)
   Vocabulary internalization: road signs, names of business establishments
3. Setting table with food items or using pictures on blackboard:
   Functions:
   Indicating locations (prepositions)
   Vocabulary internalization (culture): foods, meals, eating utensils
4. Organizing pictures/photos in order of occurrence in a story:
   Functions:
   Talking about what happens (present, imperfect, preterite, perfect tenses, future, conditional, subjunctive progressive, subject pronouns)
   Telling time (*ser* with time expressions)
   Expressing time relationships (subjunctive after adverbial conjunctions)
5. Organizing realia or pictures in semantic groups:
   Functions:
   Vocabulary internalization: adjectives, stores, medicines, travel terms (lodging, transportation, travel agency, etc.), banking, diversion activities, occupations, education, animals, mail, and many more
6. Taking inventory of items in class, school, home and making lists:
   Functions:
   Vocabulary internalization
   Expressing likes and dislikes (*gustar,* definite articles)
   Indicating ownership (possessive forms)
7. Passing objects around among classmates:
   Functions:
   Referring to people and things (object pronouns)
   Making comparisons (comparatives and superlatives)
8. Looking for hidden objects/people with specific characteristics in room:

Functions:
Indicating purposes, uses, destinations (*para,* personal *a*)
Describing things (adjective agreement)
Indicating the presence and absence of things (indefinite and negative words)
Expressing indefinite and unknown things (subjunctive)

9. Making food/crafts by following instructions:
   Functions:
   Giving advice or orders (commands, object pronouns, demonstratives)
   Expressing uses for things (noun + *de/para*)
   Expressing wishes/requests (subjunctive)
10. Acting out actions or skits individually or using doll or puppet:
    Functions:
    Describing how we get ready for the day (reflexive verbs and pronouns)
    Expressing physical and emotional needs (*tener* expressions)
    Expressing feelings (subjunctive after expressions of emotions)
    Expressing cultural gestures
11. Silent interaction with classmates—matching questions to answers, occupations to persons, stores to items sold:
    Functions:
    Getting information (asking questions)
    Vocabulary internalization
12. Filling in phone messages, charts, time schedules, advertisements based on oral input:
    Functions:
    Vocabulary internalization
13. Selecting pictures to describe oral language:
    Functions:
    Speculating about present and past (future and conditional)
    Indicating doubt and denial (subjunctive after expression of uncertainty)

TPR AND SPEAKING, READING, AND WRITING

After the second listening period, students begin speaking by narrating orally the stimuli to which they had attended. Students describe activities done in class, using the grammar and vocabulary practiced. The TPR scenarios provide the basis for initial speaking practice. Students then respond to a progression of oral questions: yes-no questions; questions with one-word answers; completion-type statements; personal questions; questions to classmates; interviews with teacher/classmates. Other oral communicative activities can also be done, such as role plays, mini debates, and small-group discussion. Subsequent oral work can include recombinations of other structures and vocabulary for review as well as presentation of more abstract concepts. Since the TPR practice results in a good understanding of the concrete, acquisition of the abstract should not be difficult.

As early as the second listening period, students can begin reading by responding physically to written stimuli. They can develop reading strategies quite early by responding to written language, which contains some unfamiliar structures and which recombines other forms previously learned. After they have progressed to speaking, students can do more extensive reading activities, such as identifying main ideas from a passage, selecting specific pieces of information, summarizing reading, giving opinions of statements or articles, and guessing meaning in context.

Writing can also be done very early by means of guided writing exercises that progress to more creative writing. Students begin by describing in written form the TPR activities done in class. Oral interviews done with classmates as well as personal stories can also be reported. Writing assignments can become increasingly complex as other structures and vocabulary are included in the activities; for example, students might be asked to explain which classroom physical activities they like or dislike, which activities will be done tomorrow, or even which activities they would do if they were the teacher. A daily log, in which class activities and other experiences are reported, is another effective exercise in developing writing skill.

Because of time constraints, allowing more time for the listening phase and TPR activities must entail teaching less grammar at the beginning level. Although more research is needed in this area, the author's personal experience has shown that more effective learning results when students know well a small core of the most important, high-frequency structures. Indeed, including the TPR component in the lesson presentation is not only a useful tool for effecting meaning internalization, but is also an excellent strategy for beginning speaking, reading, and writing.

SAMPLE LESSON OUTLINE:

"How We Get Ready for the Day"

The following plan is designed to teach students how to discuss their personal daily routines, particularly their morning preparations. Although students probably would have been exposed to telling time and describing people (with *ser, estar, tener*) prior to this lesson, practice of those functions does not necessarily have to precede the lesson. The sample function presented here would appropriately be followed by a lesson on describing daily activities, in which students would learn to discuss their day, evening, and weekend schedules and activities.

Since the lesson is proficiency-based, a variety of verb forms, pronouns, and vocabulary is practiced indirectly throughout the sequenced function-oriented activities. Two listening periods, in which students "bind" meaning, precede speaking, reading, and writing activities.

Function: Description of Personal Daily Routine
Context: Narration about Personal Activities in Present time
Grammar/Vocabulary Subsumed:

> despertarse
> levantarse   } + time expression
> bañarese/ducharse
> lavarse los dientes
> afeitarse las piernas/la cara
> peinarse
> sacarse el pelo
> rizarse el pelo
> maquillarse
> ponerse + articles of clothing
> desayunar con su familia
> recoger sus libros
> salir de su casa
> esperar el autobús
> caminar a la escuela
> asistir a una clase

I. *LP1:*

1. Teacher demonstrates the morning routine of María Elena, the class doll, manipulating the doll to respond to oral descriptions. The use of realia further clarifies the meaning. (This activity can be preceded by a description of María Elena

and a brief discussion: ¿Cómo es ella? ¿De dónde es? ¿Cuántos años tiene? ¿Dónde estudia? etc.)

Oral Stimuli:

María Elena se despierta a las siete. (Alarm clock sounds and indicates time.)
Se levanta a las siete y diez. (clock)
Se ducha por diez minutos. (clock, soap)
Se afeita las piernas. (shaver)
Se lava los dientes con Aim. (tube of toothpaste, toothbrush)
Se peina. (comb)
Se seca el pelo. (hairdryer)
Se riza el pelo. (curling iron)
Se maquilla. (bottle of makeup)
Se pone una falda negra y una blusa blanca. (other articles of clothing possible)
Desayuna con su familia. (coffee cup, breakfast roll)
Recoge sus libros.
Sale de la casa.
Espera el autobús. (bus stop sign)
Asiste a la clase de inglés.

Teacher repeats oral stimuli several times, changing the order and acting out responses with the doll.

2. While the teacher gives oral sentences, students act out responses with the doll. In large classes, two or three dolls might be used with students in groups. All students should be given the chance to respond. If it is not feasible to bring in realia, magazine pictures of items can be used.

II. *LP2:*
1. Teacher repeats oral stimuli from LP1, and students again respond physically with the doll.
2. Teacher describes his/her own daily routine, using a similar format in the first person with the help of realia.
3. Teacher presents same oral stimuli with pictures:

Marcos se afeita.
El señor Gómez sale de su casa.
Berta se maquilla.

The third person plural verb forms can also easily be integrated:

Los hermanos desayunan a las siete.
Ellas recogen sus libros.

Stimuli are repeated several times. Students respond by identifying the appropriate picture for each statement.
4. Students do listening exercises:
   a. Multiple choice: teacher gives 3 oral statements and then either mimes action, uses doll, or holds up a picture; students choose the correct verbal description (a, b, c).
   b. True-False: students identify as true or false oral descriptions of physical actions/pictures.
5. Students see written forms and practice reading:
   a. Students respond to written statements by miming actions or manipulating doll.
   b. Matching: students match verb form to related vocabulary (e.g., Recoge—los libros; sale—de la casa; se afeita—las piernas); verbs can also be matched to pictures of vocabulary items.

III. *Speaking Phase:*
1. Students narrate orally the actions as performed by the doll.
2. Students pretend to be the doll and narrate in first person.
3. Students respond to oral questions:
   a. Yes—no questions: ¿Se levanta ella? ¿Se peina? ¿Se lava los dientes?
   b. Questions with one-word answers: ¿A qué hora se despierta?
      ¿Con quiénes desayuna?
4. Students describe their daily routines and answer personal questions.
5. Students interview each other. They need to be given examples of the *tu* verb forms.

During subsequent classes, students can practice narrating daily routines in present, progressive, and past time.

IV. *Reading Phase:*
1. Students respond physically to written sentences, as prepared by teacher and classmates.
2. Students do other types of reading activities, for example:
   a. finding specific pieces of information in a chart or passage (e.g., ¿A qué hora se despierta?);

b. giving opinions of written statements (e.g., Yo prefiero levantarme temprano.—¿Estás de acuerdo?)

c. identifying most important ideas in a reading (e.g., How does Pedro's daily schedule differ from yours?)

V. *Writing Phase:*

1. Students describe in written form the TPR activities done in class. For example, one possible assignment is "Describe all activities that María Elena (the doll) did in class today."

2. Students write descriptions while physical responses are being done in class.

3. Students report in written form oral interviews with classmates as well as personal accounts. Teacher can assign paragraphs in which students express activities in future, progressive, or past. For example, an effective assignment is: "Make a list of 8 activities you did yesterday morning. Then form sentences and combine them into a paragraph using the following transitional words: *primero, segundo, entonces, antes de, después de, finalmente.*"

4. Students expand in written form results of oral survey done with classmates, explaining times students wake up and go to bed, what they eat for breakfast, whether they prefer to shower in the morning or evening, what kind of toothpaste they prefer, etc.

TPR AND UPPER LEVELS OF LANGUAGE

TPR can probably be utilized in upper-level language classes to review grammatical functions and vocabulary and to introduce more subtle structural concepts. The teacher can use the technique for strengthening listening comprehension skills and as a basis for speaking, reading, and writing practice. Assignments and activities can be made increasingly complex by using new vocabulary and more complex grammar. A continuous recombination of language elements and TPR activities throughout all levels will provide optimal opportunities for internalization of meaning to occur.

CONCLUSION

This essay has presented a plan for implementing the Total Physical Response technique into a proficiency-based foreign language program for Spanish and other languages. Research findings in support of an initial speaking period and the use of TPR were reviewed. The various phases of TPR with listening, speaking, reading, and writing practice were outlined together with an outline for teaching students how to discuss their daily preparation routines. Included were suggestions for utilizing TPR in all levels of language as a basis for review and internalization of meaning and structure.

Future experimentation should examine the effect of teaching receptive skills via TPR before speaking and writing. Since the use of TPR is in essence still in its infancy, further research is also needed in developing innovative strategies for its implementation as well as curricular guidelines and teaching materials.

NOTES

1 A complete list of materials is available from Sky Oaks Productions, Inc., P.O. Box 1102, Los Gatos, CA 95031.

2 The term *function* here is used to refer to the oral communicative task being accomplished, e.g., expressing likes/dislikes, getting information, expressing wishes/requests, etc.

3 The functions listed are taken from a recently published proficiency-based textbook: James M. Hendrickson, *Poco a Poco—Spanish for Proficiency.* Boston, MA: Heinle and Heinle, 1986.

DISCUSSION QUESTIONS

1. Does affect and the "affective filter" (of Krashen and others) justify the delay of oral production for some or all students during the early stages of language acquisition?

2. Glisan suggests incorporating reading and writing tasks and advancing from concrete to abstract language use through TPR. What other applications can you see for her suggestions? For instance, could they be applied in the teaching of reading? (See Chapter 17.)

3. A starting caveat is that language teachers should rely on "real communication in meaningful, interesting contexts" (p. 34). What happens when this caveat is neglected? What evidence is available?

4. How can "oral interviews" and "personal stories" (p. 36) be used to relate developing target language structures to the actual experience of students? Compare these ideas with the kinds of things that "whole language" and "experience-based" reading teachers do. (Again, see Chapter 17, and the rest of Part 4.)

CHAPTER 5

The Thunder and Lightning Professor: Teaching Language by Using Theater Plus Up-to-the-Minute Technology

Richard M. Bacon
Photography by Russell Schliepman
with updates by Ma Baolin
and Joel D. Goldfield

EDITOR'S INTRODUCTION

*T*his chapter is a collage of materials authored by professional journalists (Bacon and Baolin) and a language teacher (Goldfield), with the help of a professional photographer (Schleipman). Unlike many of the other entries, the material presented here is not from the usual "war" journals or anthologies. Originally, it appeared in a popular magazine, Yankee (1977), in the Beijing Review (1987), and in The Ram's Horn (1992). It's all about John A. Rassias, Greek-American and Director of Language Outreach Education at Dartmouth College. Rassias holds the distinguished William R. Kenan Chair as Professor of French and Italian at Dartmouth and has served on presidents' commissions and been honored again and again for teaching excellence at a national and international level, e.g., as recipient of the «Palmes Académiques» of France. But, despite his academic credits, Rassias is best known as the beloved maniac of the language classroom. His method has been affectionately referred to as "The Rassias Madness." Can teachers learn anything from it? Rassias thinks so, and many agree. All teachers must have some "affinity for the spotlight" (as Robert Wolkomir said in the 1983 edition of Methods That Work), and, as a result, all of us, I believe, can learn something worthwhile from someone who has an overdose of that affliction. But there really is a method in the Rassias Madness. John Rassias has the genius of understanding how to motivate communicative events through acting. Even as a child he was an action kind of guy. When his French teacher depressed his tongue with a pencil to get him to sound French, he bit her. Sound primitive? Not necessarily. Joel D. Goldfield shows that the radical appeal to the senses of the Rassias method can be incorporated to good effect in audio and video material through computer-assisted language learning.

"Acting and life are inseparable from effective teaching," says John A. Rassias. *Faithful to this philosophy are his astonishing methods which have proven so successful that his name—and Rassias-type language courses—have exploded from the hills of New Hampshire to national acclaim....*

Underlying the muted pause at ten minutes past eleven on a Tuesday morning in a basement room of Dartmouth Hall, was an electric mood of expectation. No one seemed exactly sure of what was about to happen, yet there was no apparent discomfort. Spotted among the black-upholstered rows of seats, knots of students whispered; others still clustered at the exits, their class break about over.

The next hour would culminate in bloodied hands, exhortations, splattered eggs, and cries of rage. Even on such a calm morning there would be thunder and lightning.

The formal half of the lecture on French literature was over. It had left its barely decipherable scrawl of notes across the triple-layered, electronically operated chalk boards that spanned the width of the high wall behind the dais. Twin television screens, mounted halfway up each side of the proscenium, stared back blankly in the uneasy stillness of the beige-walled, red-carpeted, windowless lecture hall in one of the oldest buildings at Dartmouth College in Hanover, New Hampshire.

Professor John A. Rassias entered almost unobtrusively. Member of the Department of Romance Languages and Literatures, Director of the Foreign Language Program, originator of the Dartmouth Intensive Language Model, he was laden with the paraphernalia of his lecture, the last act of Jean Paul Sartre's play, *Le Diable et le Bon Dieu*. Preoccupied, he nodded to the students as they drifted to their seats.

A graying man now in his early fifties and a onetime Marine, Professor Rassias is a revolutionist. Over recent years his thoughts and actions have recruited an army of dedicated intellectual loyalists.

He has been a controversial figure on the campus for a dozen years. Solidly built and of medium height, he tends today (despite a nodding acquaintance with weight-watching, numerous cups of coffee, cigarettes, and an abundance of nervous and physical energy) towards professorial paunchiness.

Professor Rassias, a Greek-American native of New Hampshire who is comfortably trilingual (English, Greek, French) but who can communicate in all the Romance languages as well as a handful of dialects spoken on the coast of West Africa and in Micronesia, is a man of substantial academic credentials (B.A., University of Bridgeport; Doctorat d'Université de Dijon, France; Certificat d'Institut de Phonétique; a sometime student at the Sorbonne in Paris), the recipient of teaching honors (Distinguished Teacher of the Year Award, 1962, University of Bridgeport; Outstanding Teacher of the Year, 1968, Dartmouth College; The Harbison Award from the Danforth Foundation for the ten outstanding teachers of America, 1970; nominated to Outstanding Educators of America, 1973), and a language consultant (M.A.T. program at Experiment in International Living; member of the Board of Directors of the Committee of International Medical Exchange; Peace Corps Language Programs).

He is also the author of innumerable pamphlets and books in the fields of his primary interests (modern Greek, French literature, and language teaching). In 1977, technically on sabbatical from Dartmouth, he was working to complete two more French grammar books as well as his autobiography, all of which were contracted with Harper & Row, publishers. Between times he has a full schedule of speaking engagements at colleges across the country (during a "normal" academic year he speaks on the average of once a week off-campus to conventions of language teachers, Dartmouth alumni meetings, corporations which are investing heavily now in his teaching theories), and he will return to Hanover periodically for language workshops, and fly to West Africa to resume an active consultant role with the Peace Corps there.

"You may think this is a put-on," an unidentified student whispered in the dusky hall as he wedged his way past to find a seat, "but every class is like this. Believe me, it makes a difference."

The professor had reached the dais. He leaned the base of a crudely made, three-foot-tall crucifix against the chalk tray, and struggled for a minute with a cuirass and medieval helmet he carried

If "all the world is a stage," then every classroom is a theater and every teacher is an actor. So it is, in any case, with Dartmouth Professor John A. Rassias. Here we see him in action on a lecture tour in mainland China.

"In the traditional classroom passivity reigns," says Professor Rassias. "The extremes I use are for awakening." What extremes? Well, kissing students as positive reinforcement for correct responses, and occasionally pleading on his knees with a student to demonstrate "We're all in this together; we're equals."

under his arm. During the break he had strapped on leather shin guards over his dark blue pants. As he adjusted the breast plate, he carried on a rapid-fire monologue in French, motioning the students to move closer.

These pieces of equipment and three or four straight wooden chairs scattered across the dais were his only props.

For most of the next hour John Rassias had the stage to himself. Occasionally he called up one student or another to assist as he focused his dramatic abilities on interpreting the characters of the final act of the Sartre play. The lecture room—however wall-to-wall carpeted and acoustically perfect it had been an hour before—had not until now seemed a place for intimacy.

John Rassias changes that. Without raising his voice above a hoarse whisper or a guttural, sensual pleading, he wills each character into life. Sometimes with a hunch-backed stoop or an ingratiating bow, often with wringing hands and rolling eyes, these characters parade across the stage one by one just as the emotions troop across Rassias's facile, contorting face. He strides from one side of the stage to the other in torment, in supplication, crashing chairs, pounding his leather-clad breast or ripping off his helmet to go down on his knees and plead directly with his audience who, by the very power of his emotionally charged voice and suggestive gestures, have themselves become participants with him in this moment of exposure.

In a mad climax he spins to address the crucifix. Then, uttering a hopeless scream, he whirls on the audience, his palms dripping blood. As peals of thunder reverberate and lights flash on cue, this devil-like ogre heaves handfuls of eggs into the darkness. His diabolical laughter is the only echoing sound in the student hush.

An article in *Time* magazine in 1978 said, "In a large sense, language study is thriving at Dartmouth because of the ebullient personality and unique teaching method of John Rassias."

The professor is an unselfconscious actor. He has studied drama, not as the basis for a career, but as a tool for more effective teaching. He wants all teachers to do the same, no matter what their chosen discipline may be.

"Camus summed it all up in his play *Caligula*," Rassias says now over coffee, the stage blood washed from his hands, props out of sight, but still sweaty in the aftermath of his exertions. "One of his characters says..." In the pause his mind races through the text to find an appropriate translation. "...'You don't believe enough in the theater.'" He lights another cigarette. "Communication is the key."

He is also fond of saying, "Nothing is real unless it touches something in me and I am aware of it."

The Rassias use of dramatic technique comes only after an exhaustive literary analysis of the work under discussion. It brings a further dimension to the literature. However, it is sometimes hard to separate the method from the man himself.

John Rassias is naturally outgoing, intense, and emotive. He frequently uses flamboyant gestures to press a point, and a range of facial expressions to reinforce his enthusiasm for what he is doing. He is constantly reaching out to touch his students in class, making them reel with a French embrace and a loud, smacking kiss on each cheek to complement a response.

"You know," Rassias says in a moment of calm, "the student has got to be made to stretch his powers, his capacities. Isn't that what teaching's all about? The extremes I use are for awakening. In the traditional classroom, passivity reigns. All you see is a bald head and a book propped in front of it. It makes you question if anything vital can be going on. The theater is an arena of action in which capacities are immediately tested and stretched."

He knows there is more to an understanding of literature and of human beings than a discussion of their parts. He tries to convey the emotions which compelled an author to write the work in the first place. Sometimes he appears in class dressed as the author (the Marquis de Sade, for example, bewigged and in eighteenth-century costume) and talks with his students, criticizing "my" works. On examinations students have been known inadvertently to address him as the Marquis, rather than the professor. Once, in presenting several classical Greek themes as seen by modern French playwrights, he arrived with a homemade clay head as a stage prop ("It was no work of art but it served its purpose.") that became his unspeaking companion for the French dramatic monologue that followed.

He had stuffed the head with raw chopped liver, hamburger, and plenty of ketchup direct from the local supermarket. In the eye sockets, behind a thin wall of hardened clay, he had inserted two uncooked eggs. When the appropriate time came to demonstrate the blinding of Oedipus, Rassias plunged a knife into each eye for a remarkably realistic bit of stage gore. Before the shock waves had subsided, he deftly severed the top of the clay cranium, disgorged its ruddy, putrid contents by the handful, and hurled them into the audience.

Startling? Of course. Bizarre? Perhaps, but what student can forget such a fanciful technique to reinforce learning? Certainly the staff of the Buildings and Grounds Department at Dartmouth can't, although everyone pitches in to try to set things to rights after each class.

Histrionics aside, are there enough tangible results to justify such shock methods to tuition-paying parents and old-guard graduates?

First, take a look at the Intensive Language Model he organized and runs as an outgrowth of the crash course he initiated at Dartmouth for Peace Corps volunteers in 1964.

His goal is to teach students to function in a foreign language as sensitive human beings after only ten weeks of instruction. Class sections are small and, during drill work that follows, get even smaller. From the first minute no English is spoken. The dialogue is meaningful. There is choral speaking in unison, constant rapid-fire repetition, individual oral application, and then a quick testing in which each student makes 65 responses per hour. Rassias contends his students speak more in a week with his method than they would in a year with the traditional approach.

It is not a one-man show. To organize this massive dose of learning, Rassias has master teachers in his department and relies heavily on upperclass apprentice teachers. It is they who take over class drills after the material has been presented by the master teacher.

There are three-day workshops to train each of them in what Rassias terms the "choreography of teaching." This involves the use of body language, finger-snapping, plentiful supportive gestures, and constant movement among those being taught.

"Never let a student doubt that you want him to learn the language and are confounded when he does poorly," Rassias instructs his teacher corps. All mistakes are immediately righted, and the student must repeat it correctly. Acceptable responses are reinforced with embraces, pats, clucking noises, and smiles.

In the final week of the semester his students are tested by other faculty members in the five areas of grammar, comprehension, vocabulary, fluency, and accent. They also must present dramatic skits which they conceive and produce before other members of the class.

Then, off to France. Since 1968 more than 1,000 Dartmouth students have had this experience. It is no "grand tour." Students are boarded with French families and immediately immersed in French life and culture. They have classes from nine until noon, then study French civilization and culture from two to five. There have been only two complaints to date from the foster families: one student with indigestion but not the proper technical vocabulary, swallowed a suppository: another let his thirst rule his manners and astounded his French hosts by guzzling his wine.

Every second year Rassias himself takes his family to France for the ten-week semester of instruction. At the end of that time, he throws the names of unknown French villages in a hat and pairs the students off.

"I drop them in a village without money, extra clothing, connections—nothing—and tell them to come back after three days with all the political, economic, social, cultural workings of that village at their fingertips. It's amazing what adventures they have, and how appreciative they become of hospitality and friendliness. When they come back to the campus they are ready for an analysis of French literature and ideas."

The Exxon Education Foundation sees in Professor Rassias's method an "educational innovation of demonstrated merit." It has already invested about $100,000 to disseminate the program. In 1970 Rassias completed a documentary film, *Effective Language Teaching,* which Exxon funded and which is the genesis of the Impact Program, again sponsored by Exxon, on the Hanover campus to which qualified faculty from other colleges and universities are invited for an intensive, four-day blitz workshop twice a year.

It was this film Rassias recently showed to a meeting of Dartmouth College alumni in Pittsfield,

Massachusetts. Having left Dartmouth late after one of his usual active lectures, several meetings, and unscheduled student appointments, he arrived a little breathless just as dinner was being served. He sat at a table with many of his recently graduated students, who had acted, in the social preliminaries, as a kind of advance party to propagate the faith. One woman, not at his table, said, "My daughter says I might not like him. He might make me feel uncomfortable. But she raves about him."

The film was shown after a sparsely sung college song. In it Rassias, master teachers, apprentices, and students demonstrated the Intensive Language Program. Besides tracing the routine Rassias uses, it offered interviews with participating students ("Exhilarating." "It makes me lose my inhibitions, and I can make mistakes.").

When the lights came on, Rassias got down to business. It was not the usual after dinner talk. He pulled off his tie and jacket, rolled up his sleeves, let the sweat bead on his forehead unnoticed, and reverting now to Greek so no one was likely to have an advantage—demonstrated to the accompaniment of finger-snapping, cajoling, loud smacking embraces, and body language that learning can be a stimulating activity.

"You know it's all a part of being alive," Rassias contended, "and making others feel alive. The teacher must make eye-to-eye contact with his students. This says, 'We're all in this together. We're all equals.'" Rassias must even drop to his knees occasionally—below the student—which suggests, "We all make errors."

"I've always maintained that the teacher is not one person in one place and another somewhere else. He's human, too. Acting and life are inseparable from effective teaching." At home, just across the river in Vermont, Rassias has recently built a barn-like post and beam structure that is his own miniature theater. It is a place where he has done some filming, where students can come at any hour of the day or night to practice their language skills, rehearse skits, or just get away from the campus. It is also where Rassias can prepare the next bit of bizarre stage business that he hopes will cement the lesson for tomorrow's student.

His wife, a tall, thin woman of Slavic background, has learned to speak Greek so she can converse with her mother-in-law who lives with

them and their three children. She relays the day's telephone messages with a light touch of humor, the same she had evidently expressed at her husband's announcement that he had been asked to write his autobiography. Life is sometimes a bit frenetic in the Rassias household.

John Rassias admittedly has no hobbies. He wanders off across the unmowed lawn towards his theater. He is practicing palming a sharp knife and hopes it will be more professional than the last time he attempted it before an audience. Then, dazzled students were treated to more than stage blood.

"But it made a good effect," Rassias says smiling.

TEACHING LANGUAGE BY USING THEATER

by Ma Baolin

Westerners sometimes find it off-putting, or even feel offended, when they learn that Chinese people refer to them as "big noses." But it is true that many foreigners do have big noses, at least compared to the relatively small, flat noses on the faces of many Han Chinese.

Take language teacher John A. Rassias as an example—he really does have a big nose. He also has big, burly shoulders, a rough hewn face, unruly hair, and, especially, a big personality.

But the 50 Chinese schoolteachers who sat waiting for him in a Beijing University classroom one day this spring had no way of knowing that they were about to meet a whirlwind. So when Rassias flung open the door and shouted an exuberant "Ni hao! I'm Luo Liyan!" it was no wonder that they were slightly stunned.

Rassias had made yet another of his grand entrances, all in the service of his unique method of language teaching. But seeing the teachers' perplexity at his calling himself by a Chinese rather than an English name, he took some time to explain. He said one of his Chinese colleagues in America had given him the name, which means "devoted to language teaching," and that he was very fond of it.

The teacher-students probably expected Rassias to pull out a grammar book and begin writing examples on the blackboard, but instead they soon found themselves embroiled in playing games and acting out skits. For example, Rassias would ask a group of students to pretend they were waking up in the morning and to go through all the motions—looking at the alarm clock, getting dressed, washing, eating breakfast—while one student would describe the actions verbally.

The exercise was one of hundreds Rassias has developed as part of his approach to teaching language, which is based on his philosophy that the most effective technique is to put students into real, living situations.

Rassias, a professor of French and director of the Language Outreach Program at Dartmouth College in New Hampshire, came to China in the spring of 1987 at the invitation of Beijing University and Beijing Normal University to offer three months of workshops on his method of teaching languages. IBM and the Rockefeller Foundation underwrote part of the trip.

With him was David Parry, a Dartmouth colleague and a flamboyant character in his own right. Parry, a prizewinning documentary filmmaker whose earlier films include *Yukon Journal, Music Child,* and *Premature,* was shooting footage on Rassias's visit to China.

Rassias gave three workshops to more than 150 language teachers—middle-school teachers, college teachers, teachers who teach English to Chinese students, and teachers who teach Chinese to foreigners—selected from all across China. Although he was in China for such a short time, it was long enough for him to demonstrate his whole array of teaching skills and techniques, to share his ideas about teaching with his Chinese colleagues, and to come to understand Chinese society and culture better.

"No Bad Students"

Rassias, a second-generation American whose first language was Greek, stresses the importance of drama and emotions in his teaching: "If you get the students involved and make them do what you want them to, they'll never forget what you teach them."

Paradoxically, he said, he became attuned to language as an outgrowth of tragedy when, while still a small child, he suffered third-degree burns from head to foot in an explosion in his home. At first it was feared that he had been blinded, but after nine months in bandages, he regained his sight.

"It was like being born twice," he recalled. "Because of the accident, my ear became very alert, not only to words, but to feelings. So when a person says something and doesn't mean it, I can almost hear it. That's why I stress the senses so much."

After graduating from the University of Bridgeport in Connecticut, Rassias went to France to study literature. There, he became involved in both teaching and acting.

"I reached a point where I had to choose between the theater and the classroom," he recalled. "And I had a revelation: why not do both? So I just take the essence of acting—the ability to touch an audience—and the essence of teaching—communication—and fuse them."

Regarding this point, Rassias admitted that he had been inspired by the Chinese philosopher Confucius, whose most famous maxim about teaching says, "If I hear something, I forget it; if you show me something, I remember it, but if you make me do something, I will never forget it because I will understand it."

Rassias believes that, for both actors and teachers, the best way to be effective is to keep the audience's, or the students', attention. He does so by using surprise and spontaneity.

He recounted that in one workshop, when he was talking about being spontaneous, he suddenly began coughing. The students got frightened, and some ran to get him water because they thought he was choking. Even Parry thought something was seriously wrong. Rassias reached into his pocket and pulled out some pills, actually bits of chalk, and popped them into his mouth while continuing to talk. He also kept on coughing, and every time he coughed he would spit out some of the chalk pieces. The students were confused, but also watched and listened spellbound.

"I did this just for the sake of spontaneity, to make them realize I might do anything, anytime, to make the lesson more interesting," he explained.

Rassias developed his approach to teaching language as a revolt against traditional methodologies. He says it is bad to make students memorize, because language "is always living, fleeting, changing, and growing."

He also believes that students should learn about the cultural features linked with the language they are studying.

"For instance, when an American says 'hello,' he says it from a completely different cultural background than when a Chinese says, *'Ni hao,'*" he said. "In my workshops, we discuss the cultural framework, for example, body language. People should know such things as how you shake hands, how close you stand, whether you meet the other person's eyes, and whether you touch."

Rassias also objects to teaching approaches which set teachers above their students. "I want people to develop their own personalities and resources," he said. "I believe there is no such thing as a bad student. There are only bad teachers. And they're bad because they don't care enough. They don't put enough energy into it, they don't show respect for their students, and they don't prepare their lessons."

A Personality Change

One woman from Xiamen University who teaches Chinese to foreigners said she liked Rassias's emphasis on acting as well as teaching because it made the classes lively and interesting for students. "Rassias's methods won't frighten students or make them nervous," she said. She added that her experience in the workshop had convinced her that Rassias's approach would "let students relax and help them concentrate."

Another teacher, a member of Beijing University's English department who served as Rassias's assistant during his stay, said her students had become much more interested in studying English after she adopted some of Rassias's methods.

One student in the workshop underwent a real transformation. A teacher of English from one of Beijing's middle schools was so tall, heavyset, and ungainly that the other students dubbed him *shamao* (fool). He became so self-conscious that he would hide in a corner of the classroom. He was too intimidated to answer questions or take part in any of the skits.

But as time went on and Rassias's kindness and empathy became evident, the man started feeling less and less nervous, and before long he was dashing up to the front of the classroom, answering questions, and acting in the skits. His classmates and Rassias as well began calling him "Mr. Volunteer."

Later, when the man went back to his school, he wrote a letter to Beijing University praising Rassias's methods. "Rassias not only taught me how to teach, he changed my personality," he wrote.

Rassias believes that the workshops succeeded because he tried to bridge the cultural gap between China and the United States by showing his students his weaknesses as well as his strengths.

"I'm not trying to be phony," he said. "I say, 'I've come to China to respect you 100 percent and with an open heart. I respect your culture and I won't do anything to offend you. But I'm always open and honest and direct, and I just hope you'll understand what I'm trying to do. So it doesn't matter if you're Chinese or American, because we're speaking without prejudices.'

"What I've been doing is trying to blow away all the crusts that cover the human heart so we can communicate heart to heart. As a teacher of language and culture, I believe that there are many similarities among all peoples and that we have to learn about these similarities. Where there are differences, we have to respect them, because if we don't do that, we are not going to survive on this globe."

EDUCATIONAL TECHNOLOGY: SHARING THE EXPERIENCE

by Joel D. Goldfield

The experiential, sensorial core of the Rassias Method makes special demands on educational technology, for as many of the senses as possible should be appealed to and skillfully integrated into the language learning process to encourage, enhance, and facilitate learning. Although the language and culture experience will often be vicarious in the language lab and classroom, it can be engaged or enhanced through the skillful use or selection of CALL, audio, and video materials. Recent research summarized in *Modern Media in Foreign Language Education: Theory and Practice* shows that students using computer software, for example, often learn better in "dyads" (pairs) than individually, depending on the material, time span, social context, and other factors, and one could make a reasonable extension to other small groups. Students in dyads devote a significant amount of time speaking in the foreign language about the materials on screen or at least *talking about* the lesson, if only in the native language with foreign language quotations or references interspersed. Thus, the parents or teachers with an eye for their children's or students' linguistic success can be encouraged to involve one or even two others in the activity on many occasions where independent study might otherwise be expected. I offer this thumbnail sketch of research on small-group interaction with various media to break through ostensible prejudices to a language-learning mode that can easily exist in harmony with the Rassias Method. Solitary confinement is not implicit in educational technology used outside the classroom. The senses are key, and a judicious, often self-guided proportion of individual and small-group experiences should provide for a successful language learning process outside the regular classroom.

After eighteen years of teaching experience, I can only encourage the discovery of small-group learning activities to replace some of the independent studying time, at least in the case of language learning. The use of Assistant ("Apprentice" or "Peer") Teachers in the Dartmouth Intensive Language Model was a natural outgrowth of structural, psychological, and pedagogical needs in the Peace Corps and at Dartmouth College, where the Rassias Method originated. The AT's efficiently structure what might otherwise be passive study time. It never ceases to amaze me how much undergraduates and high school students need to be encouraged to study together, to work together on projects, to test each other before a major examination, as though to discover *together* were some sort of cheating (undoubtedly because some teaching colleagues put such ominous emphasis on individual testing). Language is such a social convention, such a social skill, such a social entity, that the language-learning field should be the first to break through this mind-limiting isolationism.

Given the social and strategic suggestion made earlier regarding small-group language learning with various media, one might wonder if there are any foreign language videos which engage the senses (at least two of them) and provide opportunities for learner response. Starting close to home, I would suggest one video series that we have used at Plymouth State College as well as in tutorial evenings for the 10-day, French ALPS immersion program at Dartmouth College during the past eight summers. Students ranging in age from 17 to 70 and beyond have used *Contact French* episodes and interviews conceived and created by John A. Rassias as a videotape series in 1983 for CBS Fox's Educational Division.

These videotapes include a wide variety of situations which assist the students in addressing oral and cultural proficiency guidelines specified by ACTFL: social ones, such as apologizing, excusing, humoring, introducing people, etc., and topos-based ones, such as the airport, the hotel, shopping, wine-tasting, traveling by taxi, evening entertainment, diplomatic dealings, cooking, and many more. There is also a wealth of usually spontaneous interviews with various blue-and-white-collar workers. These exchanges are particularly useful at the intermediate and advanced levels. Advance organizers can be prepared for the less-skilled levels to help them focus on certain images, words and ideas. To allow students to practice with these cultural materials and receive instant feedback on their comprehension, for example, even at the word-by-word level, this author has prepared, with Prof. Rassias's permission, a videodisc including most of the interviews plus new audio tracks and original photos for appropriate encouragement and reward for student progress. Reports on the development of these materials and their testing in language center and classroom situations will appear periodically in *The Ram's Horn*.

One obvious and immediate advantage that both videotape and videodisc have over language-laboratory-style audiotapes is the video contextualization plus what I will call "read my lips." The viewer can follow the pronunciation somewhat more easily by repeatedly observing facial and lip movements and slowing down the video speed, if the VCR offers this feature. As if in a Dartmouth-style, fast-paced drill, the viewer is one of the students, occupying an invisible chair within the drill (practice) group. The attractively attired actors of the French-based "Rassias Repertory Theater" flank the viewer, and cajole and encourage replies by the Rassias whirlwind. And all this "in the safety of one's own home." While some of the procedures that Rassias Method practitioners use to diminish inhibitions (Krashen's *affective filter*)—pace, humor, verbal, gestural, and tactile encouragement, change of eye level and position in the room—are not available in this situation, viewers could use the videos privately or pick their learning companions for minimal anxiety.

As one reads in "The 'New Generation' Language Laboratory": "*Contact French*, John Rassias's series . . . is one of the most technically sophisticated yet least known video programs; our students are highly enthusiastic about Rassias's energetic presentation." The range of material and captivating nature of the small-group exercises probably struck the author's West Los Angeles College classes as innovative. Pacing, energy, pedagogical technique, humanity, and the involvement of other "students" in the video help defocus the laser light of individual questioning, just as they do in the regular practice sessions. Key words that often recur among observers of Rassias Method practitioners are *enthusiastic* and *enthusiasm*. Along with preparation, dramatization (role-playing, etc.), and specific pedagogical techniques defined elsewhere, the instructor's enthusiasm, in whatever style it is expressed, should affect students positively and further motivate language learning, reflecting Hillel's teaching: "If I am not for myself, who will be for me? And if I am only for myself, what am I? And if not now, when?" Indeed, by extension, a shared truth is that if we are "for" our subjects and our students, our students will be for them as well.

DISCUSSION QUESTIONS

1. Is the typical foreign language classroom a "Valium Valley"? What can be done to reduce the soporific stupor? What impact, for instance, can be expected from episodic organization and the infusion of high-voltage energy that Rassias demonstrates?

2. Rassias says that all communication ought to take place in the target language. To realize this difficult objective, he uses drama. Can any teacher get by without it? Is any communication altogether devoid of acting? (See Chapter 32 by Seaver.) What are some of the effects of such dramatizations on comprehension, communication, and interpersonal relationships in the classroom?

3. What's the difference between the drills that Rassias uses and those of the audio-lingual era? Rassias doesn't just pull unrelated sentences out of a strained brain or a magic hat. Notice what he does, and discuss the difference between that and practicing a list of sentences that merely illustrate some grammatical structure.

4. If an upturn in foreign language enrollments did accompany the introduction of the Rassias method (as has been claimed; Johnston, 1980, 1983; Lein, 1992), what would it mean? Or why, do you suppose, a student who had just had an egg broken on his head would describe the event as "an intense, loving experience" (*60 Minutes,* 1982)?

CHAPTER 6

An Integrated Pragmatic Curriculum: A Spanish Program

John W. Oller[1] and John W. Oller, Jr.

EDITOR'S INTRODUCTION

When it began to take shape back in the late 1950s and early 1960s, the pragmatic program described here did not fit the popular theories of the time. The wave of structural linguistics with its emphasis on contrastive analysis and syntactically motivated drills was just cresting. Consequently, when the first level of El español por el mundo *appeared, it met with stiff resistance. Objections included the fact that it ignored any contrastive analysis of the target language (Spanish) and the native language of most learners (English). Newmark (1966) would answer this criticism later by showing that we don't really have to fight off our native language in order to acquire another one. Contrastive analysis was an interesting sideshow, but barely relevant to language teaching. Another objection was that structural sequencing had been made light of. Irregular verbs were used from the very beginning, as well as imperatives with attached pronominals. And subjunctive forms (egads!) were used in the first semester. Krashen's "net hypothesis" and his concept of stage "i + 1" (not to mention the abundance of research evidence; especially see Part 4) would later counter the objection concerning structural sequencing, but those arguments and evidences were not yet available. Some said that* El español por el mundo *merely added a visual dimension to the audio-lingual standard of the day. What was different about* El español por el mundo, *and the key to its success, was immersing students in the world of the target language. But what the critics overlooked, students and teachers who used the program could see. The plan could produce native-like acquisition of Spanish, even in a formal classroom setting. This chapter shows how. It also contrasts pragmatics (of the sort discussed in greater depth in Chapter 37) with the erstwhile "notional/functional" syllabus.*

EL ESPAÑOL POR EL MUNDO: THE PRAGMATIC BASIS

The first level of *El español por el mundo—La familia Fernández*—was published in 1963 by Encyclopaedia Britannica Films. The second level, *Emilio en España*, appeared in 1965 (coauthored with Angel González). Both levels were dedicated to the belief that:

language on the useful everyday level is situational and sequential and that the moment a student can react automatically...to a given situation identified with his own experience, he "knows" the foreign language used in that situation. The proper procedure then is to immerse the student in the world in which this language is used, a world inhabited by people about whom he knows and cares (Oller, Sr., 1963: ix).

However, *El español por el mundo* did not merely bathe students in a flood of target language utterances (as in an unstructured "direct method"). Nor did it merely expose them to a series of situations or a list of examples of communicative functions in the target language (as in some applications of the "notional functional syllabus"). Rather, *El español por el mundo* put the students into the *world* of the target language, beginning with brief and simple episodes of experience and progressing to more complex ones. The objective was "immersion," not into a sea of utterances, but into full-fledged contexts of living where utterances have values and meanings by virtue of their integration into the purposes, the conflicts, and the relationships of people. *El español por el mundo* was committed to the thesis that utterances do not arise *in vacuo,* but in the course of ordinary experience in a rich and varied world of people and events, with purposes, goals, conflicts, and relationships. Thus, it was argued in the Teacher's Manual for *La familia Fernández* that the

> sharing of everyday experiences with people of a foreign tongue creates the climate of sympathy necessary and establishes the *sine qua non* for the teaching of the language, the *desire* of the students *to learn* to communicate with the people of that language . . . (Oller, Sr., 1963: ix).

Parallels and Contrasts with the "Notional/Functional Syllabus"

About ten years later, British theorists, notably Wilkins, Widdowson, and their disciples, would offer a theoretical distinction between "synthetic" teaching and "analytic" teaching. Later Johnson would capsulize this distinction as follows:

> In a synthetic approach the teacher isolates and orders the forms of the linguistic system, systematically presents them to the student one by one.... In analytic teaching it is the student who does the analysis from data presented to him in the form of "natural chunks." Wilkins associates the synthetic approach with structural syllabuses, and the analytic approach with notional specifications (1979: 195).

"Notional specifications" were characterizations of language use based on semantic or pragmatic analyses. More specifically, the term *notional* came from the traditional "notional" definitions of grammatical categories (e.g., "a 'noun' is the name of a person, place, or thing").

Wilkins' distinction between "synthetic" and "analytic" approaches paralleled the dichotomies of "discrete-point" versus "integrative" teaching as well as Krashen's distinction between "learning" and "acquisition" (1981, 1982). While "discrete-point" teaching tries to get students to synthesize a whole language system out of thousands of isolated bits and pieces presented one at a time, "integrative" teaching presents holistic communicative events and allows students to resolve them analytically into usable elements.

Therefore, in some respects, the British recommendations for a "notional/functional syllabus" would parallel the pragmatic approach. However, Johnson, who is himself a proponent of the "notional/functional approach" (1979), notes that the contrast between such an approach and a "structural" (i.e., "discrete-point" or "synthetic") approach is not entirely clear. He claims that "certainly many of the materials which have been produced following notional syllabuses indicate that this type of specification *can* lead to synthetic teaching" (1979: 196).

The problem is that in listing "notions and functions" one merely arrives at another set of isolated bits and pieces of language cut loose from their moorings in experience. In the words of Widdowson, the goal of the applied linguist should be to "specify the nature of different communicative acts, the way they are realized, the way they combine in different varieties of language use" (1979: 59), or in another place, he urges that the key is "the understanding of what conditions must obtain for an utterance to count as a particular communicative act" (p. 57). The aim is to become "able to describe a type of discourse in terms of the kind of communicative acts it represents, and the manner in which they are given linguistic expression" (p. 57). He apparently sees the goal as teaching "the rules of use" instead of "the rules of grammar" (p. 50). Similarly, Wilkins advocates a syllabus which will "cover all kinds of language functions" (1976: 19).

As a result, teaching such lists (e.g., teaching a variety of ways to apologize, or to accept an invitation, or to disagree politely with a superior) puts the student in much the same position as the old school structural approach. Students must synthesize the contexts which would motivate each notional/functional segment (i.e., type of communicative act), and they are right back in the same old boat as with the earlier discrete-point approaches, with the exception that the segments, the points to be manipulated, are now longer.

A Pragmatic Approach Begins with the World of Experience

A pragmatic approach goes considerably further than a "notional/functional syllabus." Instead of merely analyzing "concepts and functions" (Wilkins, 1976: 19), and then attempting to plan a syllabus around the "semantic demands of the learner" (p. 19), a pragmatic approach goes directly to the *world* of experience. However, this is not the same as going to isolated and unrelated "situations," which taken as separate incidents, may be as unmotivated as isolated utterances or grammatical elements. Nor is it the same as characterizations of different communicative acts or notional/functional uses of language.

A pragmatic approach assumes that the world is a spatio/temporal reality with the properties of wholeness and continuity. This is not only taken for granted by language users but is relied upon in order to make sense of experience. A pragmatic approach begins by placing the student in such a world. A distinctive and necessary characteristic, therefore, of *El español por el mundo* was the sequentiality of its episodes—the continuity of the life experiences which it depicted, and of which it consisted. In this respect, the program anticipated, agreed with, and responded to Widdowson's observation that "language teachers have paid little attention to the way sentences are used in combination to form stretches of connected discourse" (1979: 49).

LEVEL I: LA FAMILIA FERNÁNDEZ

In *La familia Fernández,* and in fact throughout both levels of *El español por el mundo,* the events of lesson 1 led into those of lesson 2, which led into lesson 3, and so forth. The idea behind this sequentiality was an appreciation of the impor-

tance of episodic organization in both its motivational and structural aspects (see Oller, 1983b). The idea was for students to go *with* speakers of the target language through ordinary experiences and thus to learn the language of those experiences:

> In *La familia Fernández. . .*we follow through film the daily multi-situational lives of a typical family of Mexico City. Their experiences are common to those of all civilized families, and the language, carefully checked for authenticity by many Spanish language experts, both lay and professional, is that used by the middle class people of Mexico. . . (Oller, Sr., 1963: ix).

In fact, *La familia Fernández* consisted of:

1. 54 filmed lessons
2. Each lesson accompanied by a filmstrip
3. Recorded exercises and drills
4. Recorded tests (two per lesson)
5. One student book containing over 1600 still photographs and cartoons
6. A teacher's manual with a word index—indicating initial usage of lexical items, plus the first three reentries. Initial entry of vocabulary in the exercises is in boldface type (Oller, Sr., 1963: ix).

From the outset, the pragmatic approach in question assumed that the input in the target language would have to be made comprehensible. This assumption would later be clarified by Krashen (1982, 1985c, 1991). However, it was also supposed that comprehensibility alone would not be sufficient. More than that, the language of common experiences would have to be actively operated on by the students so that the experiences of the characters in *La familia Fernández* would become personalized and appropriated by the students themselves:

> Simple "exposure" is not enough to teach a language to large groups of students.... Until a language becomes an integral part of the student's experience, until he can react to and activate automatically language which has been made part of his experience, he cannot communicate effectively in that language (Oller, Sr., 1963: ix).

The object of *El español por el mundo,* therefore, was to facilitate the student's own entrance into the world of experience of the target language—to get the student to "be there." This, it will be appreciated, is substantially more than mere exposure to discourse. Even more obviously it is more than mere practice with lists of sentences illustrating syntactic patterns, or lists of communicative acts illustrating notional/functional categories.

Even in the "structure drills" of *La familia Fernández* the goal of comprehension and incorporation of the language into one's own personal world of experience remained intact:

> Believing that all language experience should be psychologically motivated and should revolve around known facts within high frequency situations, we have structured all exercises to this end. Even the structure drills. . . are either based upon the known facts of the story or are cued by means of cartoons so as to render comprehension automatic without translation (Oller, Sr., 1963: x).

Multiple Cycles and the Communication Net

Another critical element was a systematic plan for developing facility in the language of each episode of experience. To accomplish this, the principle of multiple cycles was used (see the sixth recommendation in Chapter 1). The initial exposure to each new episode in the target language was achieved through a sound-motion film and followed by a film strip of still pictures capsulizing the events of the film and the meaning of each utterance at its point of occurrence. On the first exposure to each new lesson, the objective was comprehension. On each subsequent exposure, the objective remained the same, but the ante was upped. The progression from cycle to cycle was always intended to move the student from i to i + 1, i + 2, and so forth, in manageable steps. From the beginning, the intent was to throw the communication "net" (Krashen, 1980) so as to cover the student's present capacity (the "*i*th stage") and a little beyond (the "i + 1 stage").

The whole plan could be understood as a series of cycles spiraling outward to a greater expanse and a higher level of comprehension on each pass. In this series of broadening steps, the first step in each new lesson (from the beginning onward) was to show the film introducing the new material:

It is recommended that the teacher show the film at least three times and then by means of the "stills" go through the language with the students. During this activity overall general comprehension is obtained. It is not necessary, however, to achieve at this stage absolute and complete comprehension of each lexical item. Understanding grows from exercise to exercise (Oller, Sr., 1963: x).

Within each lesson the syllabus was designed so that many passes would be made through the target language utterances and expansions of them. The first objective, in keeping with the "input hypothesis" (Krashen, 1983, 1985b, 1991, 1992), was to establish comprehension of the facts of the story line. This was achieved largely through the film.

Anchoring Utterances in Facts of Experience

For instance, in the first episode (lesson 1 of *La familia Fernández*) the scene opens on a bright summer day with a little terrier disappearing around the corner of the house. The front door opens, and out walks 5-year-old Pepito Fernández. He's looking around and wondering out loud, "¿Dónde está Imán?" He calls, "¡Imán! ¡Imán!" As Pepito comes down the front steps into the enclosed courtyard, Imán (the same little white dog we saw running off moments earlier) comes running back in response to Pepito's call. The boy sees him coming, and announces, "Aquí viene Imán." He bends down and pets the dog. About that time, the gardener walks by with a hoe. He says, "Buenos días, Pepito." Pepito looks up and answers, "Buenos días, Señor." Then, Enrique, a teenager, arrives, entering the courtyard from the street. Pepito announces to the gardener, "Aquí viene Enrique." The gardener goes on about his business and Enrique approaches and greets Pepito. Then, Enrique asks, "¿Dónde está Emilio?" Pepito hears the door opening behind him and looks around over his shoulder. Gesturing toward the door, he answers, "Aquí viene Emilio." Then Enrique and Emilio exchange greetings. Enrique asks Emilio, "¿Estás listo?" Emilio answers, "Sí. Estoy listo." Enrique gestures toward the gate and says, "Vámonos." Emilio answers, "Sí. Vámonos." As the two older boys head for the gate leading to the street, Pepito takes up pursuit. At this point, lesson 1 ends.

After the first showing of the film (while the film was being rewound for a second pass), the teacher would ask questions to begin to establish the facts of the story in the minds of the students. This is an important step in comprehending the target language utterances that occur in the film. For instance, on the first showing the teacher might ask in English (the native language of the students) such questions as the following:

What is the little boy looking for when he comes out of the house?
What's the dog's name?
Who does the dog belong to?
What are the names of the two older boys?
What do you think is the relationship between Pepito and Emilio?
Where do you think the older boys are going?
What does Pepito do at the end of the film?

If any of the questions were not answered correctly after the first showing, they could be asked again after the second. For instance, it would be easy for a novice *not* to catch names like "Emilio" and "Enrique" on the first showing. So the students would be advised to see if they could catch the names of the older boys on the second viewing. Also, they might not have understood that Emilio and Enrique were going swimming on the first pass through the film, but both of these facts would probably be picked up on the second showing and certainly on the third. By then the "wh-" questions would have been answered. For example, "Who is Emilio?" The older brother of Pepito. "Who is Imán?" Pepito's dog. "Who is Enrique?" Emilio's friend. "Who is the man?" The gardener who takes care of the Fernández's yard. "What is Pepito doing when he comes out of the house?" Looking for his dog. "What does the gardener say to Pepito?" He says, "Buenos días." "Why does Enrique stop by?" He and Emilio are going swimming. "Why does Pepito run after them?" He probably wants to go with them.

The next step is to begin to establish familiarity with each utterance and its meaning. This probably could have been achieved in a variety of ways, and perhaps without plunging immediately into the production of utterances in Spanish, but firsthand experience with this program shows that students are quite capable of handling the challenge at this point. Moreover, launching production at this stage is critical to advancing the student's *i* and progressing to deeper levels of comprehension.

Incorporating the Utterances Themselves

In the Teacher's Manual for *La familia Fernández* backward buildup imitation drills were recommended—e.g., the student would hear, "¿Dónde está Imán?" on tape, or live from the teacher. Then the utterance would be broken down into manageable (i.e., repeatable) units. On the tape the student would hear "Imán" (student repeats, "Imán"). Again, "Imán" ("Imán"). Then "está" (students: "está"), "está Imán" (students: "está Imán"), "Dónde" (students: "Dónde"), "¿Dónde está Imán?"

By this method, each line of the dialogue was presented and then repeated by the student in small segments until the whole line could be uttered with some fluency. Throughout this phase students were reminded of meaning through the use of still pictures portraying the relevant events of the story. Granted, some lines of dialogue were more easily pictured than others, but throughout *La familia Fernández* virtually every line was such that its comprehension could be visually aided. From the opening imitation phase of lesson 1 and onward, it was possible (and recommended) for all the talk in the classroom to take place in the target language.

In a single 50-minute class period at the middle school or high school level it would be possible to progress through three showings of the film and through the imitation drill for the first lesson. In the second class meeting a quick review of the film would help to refresh the students' memories.

Questions and Answers

Then, during the second meeting the teacher would progress to the question/answer cycle. By this point the students have already begun to produce the utterances of the basic dialogue with some fluency and with accurate pronunciation, and they also have a good solid understanding of the meaning of each utterance. The meaning has been developed and enriched from the first showing of the film until now. At this point the students have been through the facts of the story until they are familiar. Now the central focus shifts back to the facts again as viewed through the utterances of the dialogue.

The questions at this stage are asked in the target language and concern the familiar facts of the story. For instance, students are shown a picture of Pepito coming out of the house, and they are asked, "¿Qué pregunta Pepito?" (What is Pepito asking?) By now they know that at this point in the story (the opening of lesson 1), Pepito is looking for Imán, and he is wondering aloud, "¿Dónde está Imán?" In the next picture Pepito is shown calling, "Imán. Imán." The question is "¿Qué grita Pepito?" Since new words are introduced in the questions (e.g., *pregunta* and *grita* in these cases), it takes some inferencing on the part of students to determine what is being asked. This element of uncertainty prevents the possibility of "parroting in repetition without comprehension" (Oller, Sr., 1963: x) and ensures that *some* genuine communication must take place during the execution of this exercise. Also, each response required of students is consistently linked "to a visual representation of its meaning" (Oller, Sr., 1963: *x*).

Linking of Form to Meaning and Vice Versa: Pragmatic Mapping

The emphasis on establishing the connection between meaning and form is one that is shared by proponents of the notional/functional or communicative approach. As Johnson (1979) points out, "There is a crucial difference between practice involving the linking of expression to actual meaning—and practice in which the student's attention is focused on achieving correctness of expression" (p. 200). He goes on to point out that this difference is essential to Krashen's distinction between "acquisition" and "learning." Also, he notes Savignon's caveat that students need "practice in linking expression to actual meaning" (1972; also see Savignon, 1983).

From beginning to end it is always the linking of form and meaning that motivates the activities of teacher and students in working through the material of *La familia Fernández*. First, the facts are established; then the students are familiarized further with the meaning and form of each utterance; then the utterances are used to express the

facts in significant but manageable ways through questions and answers. Subsequently, by graduating from talk about the facts in the film to talk (in the target language) about the talk of the film, a higher level of abstraction is achieved and a deeper level of comprehension is ensured. For instance, as the question-answer exercises proceed, it is possible for the instructor to help students understand specific grammatical elements (i.e., to establish the pragmatic mapping of utterance to meaningful context more precisely) by focusing attention on them through questions in the target language. To illustrate, consider the statement "Pepito pregunta, '¿Dónde está Imán?'" as a response to the question "¿Qué pregunta Pepito?" By producing the former utterance the student demonstrates at least some comprehension of the question. To push the comprehension still deeper, the teacher may ask, "¿Quién pregunta, '¿Dónde está Imán?' " ("Who asks, 'Where is Imán?'") to which the answer is, "Pepito." Then the teacher may ask, "¿Qué hace Pepito?" ("What does Pepito do?") to which the correct response is "Pregunta, '¿Dónde está Imán?'" Probing still further, the teacher may ask, "¿Por quién pregunta Pepito?" to which the answer is "Pregunta por Imán" ("He asks about Imán"), and so forth throughout the elements of the entire episode.

Structure Drills as Paradigms of Demonstrable Meaning Changes

At about this same level of development, say during the second or third class meeting, a simple high-frequency syntactic paradigm is developed and illustrated through the facts and meanings already established in the story and the communication that has already taken place in previous exercises concerning the story. A structure drill is introduced where each change in form has demonstrable consequences in terms of demonstrable meanings. For instance, students see a picture of Emilio pointing toward himself, saying, "Aquí estoy." Next, in the structure drill for lesson 1, is a picture of Enrique pointing toward Emilio. Enrique is saying, "Aquí está Emilio." In the following frame, Emilio and Enrique are shown together, and a third voice says, "Aquí están Emilio y Enrique." Finally in the fourth frame,

Emilio and Enrique are shown together, and Emilio is saying, "Aquí estámos Enrique y yo."

The objective of each structure drill is to expand some element already introduced in the story line and to show how changes in meaning result in changes in its form and vice versa. The result of these drills and expansions of them along the lines of the other exercises throughout the program is a progressive internalization of the grammar of Spanish and development of the sorts of intuitions concerning meaning and form that native speakers of Spanish possess.

So the students have events of experience accompanied by dialogue. Then they have questions about the events. Next, the focus shifts to the dialogue and its meaning. Students learn to reproduce the utterances of the dialogue. Then they talk about the dialogue and there are structure drills that expand on elements that arise in the dialogue, and questions about the utterances of those structure drills. (e.g., "Oye Emilio, ¿dónde estás?"—"Hey Emilio. Where are you?"—to which a student impersonating Emilio responds, "Aquí estoy." Or the student's own name may be used.) Then we have questions regarding the talk about the dialogue (e.g., Pepito is shown coming out of the house looking for Imán, and the teacher asks, "Por quién pregunta Pepito?" to which the student must respond, "Por Imán").

Communication Taking Place Throughout

At each phase, comprehension is necessary. Even though the exercises are repetitive and cyclic, it is generally impossible to give a correct answer at any point without understanding. Correct performance cannot be had by mere memorization of responses. Thus, the critical element of choice, something stressed by our British colleagues, is ensured. As Johnson puts it, quoting Colin Cherry, "information can be received only when there is doubt; and doubt implies the existence of alternatives—where choice, selection, or discrimination is called for" (1979: 202). Or in another place, Johnson says, "language teaching may be seen as the provision to students of sets of options from which selection can be made. It must also provide practice in the process of selecting from these options in real time" (p. 202).

Narrative: Same Facts and Story, More Complex Language

Beyond the level of talk about talk there is narrative. Each lesson consists first of the dialogue itself, presented through the film, and then talk about the dialogue in imitation drill, question-answer exercises, structure expansion exercises, and question-answer expansions of those exercises. In addition to all these methods of cycling through the material, there is full fledged narrative. For instance, instead of saying, "Pepito pregunta, '¿Dónde está Imán?'" we may say, "Pepito pregunta por su perro. Dice, '¿Dónde está Imán?'" ("Pepito asks about his dog. He says, 'Where is Imán?'").

Obviously it is easier to say "¿Dónde está Imán?" than it is to say "Pepito pregunta por su perro. Dice, '¿Dónde está Imán?'" However, by the time students are able to do the more advanced question-answer exercises of lesson 1, they will be ready to progress to the dialogue of lesson 2, and by the time they can do the question-answer drills of lesson 3, they will be able to handle lesson 1 in narrative form. Thus in the Teacher's Manual for *La familia Fernández* it was recommended that teachers work on a minimum of three lessons at a time. This gives a greater sense of progress, provides a built-in review, enhances the sense of continuity, and reduces boredom. (And by the way, can anyone truthfully claim that language acquisition by any method will not have its moments of tedium? But for some relief, see Part 6 of this book.)

Reading and Writing Activities

Also, by the time students have reached the dialogue of lesson 3, provided the material has been adequately covered, they will have begun to stabilize an authentic pronunciation of all the material covered and will therefore be ready to encounter it in written form. Hence, from about the third week on students will be doing reading and writing exercises over the material previously covered. Normally, at the beginning, reading and writing activities would lag about three lessons behind the current new material introduced first through the listening/viewing exercises of the film. In other words, the sequence was planned so that by the time the articulatory/productive exercises of imitation, question-answer, indirect restatement, and finally narrative were reached for lesson 1, the student would be about halfway through the same exercises for lesson 2, and would be working on listening comprehension of the film for lesson 3.

In the meantime, reading and writing activities would be introduced for lesson 1. It was assumed that there would be a good deal of positive transfer across modalities and that, therefore, all four of the traditionally recognized skills should be carried forward more or less simultaneously, with listening comprehension leading the way, followed by imitative production, then question-answer production, and so forth up to fuller productive use, followed by reading and writing activities in that order. However, as the students' facilities in the language progressed, it was assumed that the time lag between listening, speaking, reading, and writing could eventually be reduced and finally done away with between the intermediate and advanced level.

Meaningful Sequence Prevails Throughout

The critical factor that makes possible an integrated development of all four skills and that maximizes the positive benefits of transfer across modalities is the sequentiality of the lessons. That is, the facts of the story line in lesson 1 continue into lesson 2 and throughout. This is not to say that the characters are always doing the same things from one lesson to the next. On the contrary, they are never doing exactly the same thing from one lesson to the next, but the normal continuity of the world of experience is respected. For instance, in lesson 1, Enrique comes over to meet Emilio to go swimming. When it ends, Pepito takes up pursuit. At the beginning of lesson 2 Pepito catches up with them. He demands to know where they are going, "¿A dónde van ustedes?" With a look of exasperation, Emilio tells him, "¡No te importa!" ("It's none of your business.") Pepito starts yelling for mother. Emilio begs him to be quiet. ("Cállate, Pepito. Cállate.") Emilio concedes that he and Enrique are going swimming. Enrique agrees, "Sí. Vamos a nadar." Pepito's eyebrows rise and he asks, "Puedo ir con ustedes?" ("Can I go with you?") Emilio frowns, "No. No puedes." Pepito starts yelling for mother again. Again Emilio urges him to be quiet. "Bueno.

Bueno. Vamos." ("All right, all right, come on.") Pepito has won, but now that the victory is his, he loses interest. He says, "No. No quiero ir. Voy a jugar con Imán." ("No. I don't want to go. I'm gonna play with Imán.")

And so on it goes. One episode leads into the next. As students follow the characters through the various episodes, they also learn the language of those episodes. At the beginning, things seem to go along slowly and each utterance requires considerable effort. By lesson 3 students are beginning to achieve some fluency, and by lesson 54 (the end of *La familia Fernández*) students will have achieved a considerable facility and breadth in the language. At the midschool level it takes approximately 3 years to complete *La familia Fernández*. At the high school level the same material can be completed in 2 years, and at the college level in two semesters.

By the time lesson 54 is completed, the student will have mastered many elements of standard Mexican Spanish (a vocabulary of over 3,000 words, and all the basic syntax and morphology of the language). The student will have learned to read and write all the material of all the lessons and will be able to use the language creatively well beyond the confines of the particular elements practiced in exercise contexts.

LEVEL II: *EMILIO EN ESPAÑA*

In the second level of the program, *Emilio en España* (intended for use in the third and fourth semesters of college Spanish or the third and fourth years of high school Spanish), the students go with Emilio to Spain where he travels to visit his grandparents. As in the case of level I, level II continues to use the principle of multiple exposures to episodes of experience through multiple modalities of processing:

> We reiterate that all the necessary skills for effective communication should be taught at all levels of study.... Comprehension, speaking, reading, and writing should not be approached as separate and conflicting objectives but as logical, systematic and harmonious components of learning (Oller, Sr., & González, 1965: 7).

Acquisition Stressed Rather Than Learning

Level II also continues to stress the inductive approach to the teaching of grammatical rules. The objective is to get students to internalize (in Krashen's terms, to "acquire" rather than to "learn") grammatical rules (and a great deal more than mere grammatical rules) through use. However, in level II an appendix of explicitly stated grammatical rules is provided. The authors point out that:

> The specific rules which are printed in the appendix. . .and cross-referenced to *Generalizaciones, Lecturas Gramaticales,* and *Prácticas Sistemáticas,* provide opportunity for students who may profit from the concise definition of grammatical phenomena.... [However], the authors wish to caution teachers and students alike [that] this appendix is not designed for use in initial presentations. Study and discussions of grammatical principles per se are profitable in our opinion only when such study and discussion provide within themselves linguistic experience (Oller, Sr., & González, 1965: 7–8).

That is to say, explicit grammatical rules (*Generalizaciones*) were believed to be useful only when discussion of them could take place in the target language. In that way it would be possible for students to profit not only from the rule per se but also from the comprehensible input provided through discussion of the rule in the target language. Although *Emilio en España* was published in 1965, a thorough rationale for this approach would have to wait for Krashen's *Principles*. . .not to be published until 17 years later in 1982.

Concerning the expansion of vocabulary and structural patterns, the authors wrote:

> Presentation of new vocabulary and of structural patterns in a manner designed to secure comprehension by context, a technique used in Level I, assumes an increasingly important role in Level II. It is our belief that the student who has been immersed in the language, to the extent that his automatic reaction to new words and phrases is to search for meanings through mental image and situational context, is prepared to experience an explosion in comprehension (Oller, Sr., & González, 1965: 8).

Although a glossary was provided at the end of the textbook both for *La familia Fernández* and for *Emilio en España* indicating the initial entry and two subsequent entries of each new vocabulary item or grammatical form, the authors recommended that, at level II, students be encouraged to use one of several Spanish-to-Spanish dictionaries for checking meanings and usages of unfamiliar words.

Greater Creativity Allowed at Level II

There were also some significant contrasts between level I, *La familia Fernández,* and level II, *Emilio en España,* in terms of approach. In the early stages of level I emphasis had to be placed on deciphering utterances and gaining productive control of a whole new phonology, lexicon, and grammatical system. At level II, because of the development that had already taken place through level I, it was possible to move more rapidly and to allow the student greater creativity from the beginning.

Still, the principle of multiple cycles through discourse anchored in experience was used throughout. As in level I, lesson 1 of level II (and all subsequent lessons) began with a filmed episode.

In the first lesson of *Emilio en España* an elderly man, whom we will later discover is Santiago Fernández, grandfather to Emilio, and his plump wife, Rosario, are seated in the patio of their home in Sevilla. He's reading a magazine, and she's knitting. The maid enters with their customary hot chocolate. She asks, "¿Quieren ustedes su chocolate ahora?"

The old man answers, "¡Ah! Gracias."

At just that moment the doorbell rings. The old man speaks to the maid, "Ve a ver quién es, Rocío."

The maid leaves, and the old man, returning to his reading with the cup in his hand, takes a sip of the hot chocolate. With a mild look of surprise he almost drops the cup, sucking air over his burned lips and tongue. He says, "Cuidado, Rosario, que está muy caliente."

His wife tests her hot chocolate carefully and answers, "Sí que lo está. Dame el azúcar por favor."

He passes the sugar.

The maid returns, and the old man asks, "¡Ah! ¿Quién era?"

She says, "Es un telegrama, señor," as she hands it to him.

"¿De quién será?" he mumbles as he opens it and begins to read. His eyes widen. "¡Por fin! Va a llegar Emilio." (At last, Emilio is going to arrive.)

"¿Mi nieto?" asks Rosario with a look of incredulity.

"¿Qué otro va a ser?" (Who else would it be?) the old man retorts.

"¿Y vendrá aquí?" she persists undaunted.

"Primero va a Madrid," he answers patiently. "El telegrama es de tu hijo, Adolfo.[2] Emilio is arriving on Tuesday."

"¡Qué alegría!" exclaims Rosario; then she asks as an afterthought, "Pero, ¿por qué no vendrá aquí primero?" The old man answers that she knows there is no flight from Mexico City direct to Sevilla. "You're right," she answers, "we'll have to call Ignacio and tell him the good news."

"Buena idea," Santiago answers "¿Qué número de área tiene Salamanca?"

She doesn't remember and sends him frowning to the telephone directory a few steps away from the table. He finds the number finally and dials, "dos—uno—cinco—siete . . . ¡Hola! ¿Ignacio? . . . Sí, soy yo . . . Tenemos telegrama de Adolfo . . . Que llega Emilio dentro de una semana . . . ¿A Sevilla? No; a Madrid . . . Voy a ir a recibirle con Rosario . . . ¿Vas tú también? Bueno; nos vemos en Madrid . . . Saludos a todos. Adiós."

He hangs up the phone and comes back to the table.

"¿Entonces Ignacio va a estar a recibirle también?" Rosario asks.

"Yes," Santiago answers, "he's going to be in Madrid for a few days on business."

"¿Y Esperanza?" she asks.

"No," he says, "Esperanza is not coming, but Paco will arrive in the capital a couple of days later."

"¡Qué bien!" she says. "I need to buy some things in Madrid."

"Shall we fly?" he asks.

"I wouldn't think of it!" she answers with a look of horror. "For me it will have to be by train. Get on the telephone and make reservations immediately."

"Right now?" he sighs.

"Of course," she says matter-of-factly. "There are only five days till Emilio arrives."

Thus ends the opening episode.

Establishing the Facts

As in level I, the first step is to establish the facts of the film. What happens? Who is there? Who is coming to visit? Where will he arrive? etc. However, unlike the opening lesson of *La familia Fernández,* at level II it is possible to carry out all of the talk (with very rare exceptions) in Spanish.[3]

Since the language of the dialogue is now considerably more challenging than was possible in level I, the first step is to summarize the events of the story at the outset. For example, "Los abuelos están en el patio. Van a tomar chocolate caliente. Suena el timbre y la doncella va a ver quién es..." (Oller, Sr., & González, 1965: 36). Also, to make the transition from level I to II smoother for students who may have considerably varied backgrounds, all the tenses of the indicative are reviewed in the first few lessons.

As before, the next exercise poses questions relevant to what happened in the film. Here the vocabulary is expanded, and additional information may be filled in. For example, as this exercise progresses the students learn that Esperanza is the wife of Ignacio. Of course, this should be inferred from the telephone conversation between Santiago and his son Ignacio, but in the first question-answer exercise it is made explicit. The teacher, of course, is encouraged to expand upon this question-answer format *ad libitum* within the facts of the story. For instance, the teacher might ask who Paco is, to which there is a variety of correct responses. A student might answer correctly: "Es el hijo de Ignacio." Or "Es el primo de Emilio." Or the teacher might ask, "¿Quién es Ignacio?" to which a student might answer, "Es el hermano del padre de Emilio," or "El padre de Paco, el esposo de Esperanza, el hijo de Santiago y Rosario Fernández, y el tío de Emilio," and so forth.

After the question-answer exercises (accounting for a minimum of three passes per lesson through the facts of the story), there follows an expanded narrative recounting the facts of the film plus interpolations that expand upon the explicit happenings of the film. For instance, in the initial narrative (*La Primera Lectura*) for lesson 1 we learn that in addition to Adolfo, Emilio's father, and Ignacio, Paco's father, Santiago and Rosario have another son named Rodrigo who lives in Barcelona, Spain. This is information introduced for the first time. However, there are also new bits of information that were implied in the film and in previous exercises which are now made explicit. For instance, "A la abuela no le gustan las aviones." (Emilio's grandmother doesn't like airplanes.)

Grammar

Following *La Primera Lectura,* for each lesson there are several (as many as 12) structure review exercises which refer to facts in the film and certain logical expansions of the facts. For instance, in these exercises both regular and irregular verbs are reviewed, as well as many aspects of Spanish grammar. The technique at first is inductive acquisition of rules and patterns which are made more explicit in the grammatical *Generalizaciones* that follow. For example, in the opening lesson the authors discuss:

Los usos principales del presente en español . . .
a. Presente real. El verbo se refiere a una acción que está en progreso en el momento en que hablamos. Este es el presente verdadero. La acción del verbo se realiza ahora "¿Qué haces? Tomo chocolate. . ." (Oller, Sr., & González, 1965: 43).

In addition to the explicit statement of grammatical rules and principles, there are brief narratives called *Lecturas Gramaticales,* which illustrate certain subtleties of Spanish grammar in action. These readings are topically relevant to what has taken place or is about to take place in the main story line, but they are not limited to that story line. Also, they follow grammatical themes that arise in the main dialogue and related narrative versions. For instance, in lesson 1 there are readings that illustrate inductively certain facts about uses of the present indicative, also articles, and there is the following grammatical narrative (*Lectura Gramatical,* c.) illustrating nearly all the idiosyncratic masculine and feminine nouns ending in *-ma:*

El telegrama plantea *el problema* de cambiar *el programa*. Los abuelos discuten *el tema* de la visita y deciden usar *el sistema* ferroviario y llegar a Madrid a recibirle. No habrá dificultad en eso, a

pesar de *la fama* que tiene *el sistema* de Europa. *La suma* que tendrán que pagar es pequeña. De noche *la cama* les será muy cómoda e igual el asiento de día. *La goma* que usan para cubrir *las camas* y los asientos se llama goma espuma, y resulta muy bien para el caballero or para *la dama*. Podrán contemplar *el panorama,* o entretenerse escuchando y hablando en *el idioma* del país con los pasajeros. *El esquema* que tienen parece muy bueno, ¿verdad? (Oller, Sr., & González, 1965: 44).

Following the grammatical narratives in each lesson are writing exercises that provide an opening in Spanish to be completed by the students according to instructions of the teacher. Also, the dialogue from the film is given in its entirety.

Handling Cultural Information

Then follows another narrative version of the filmed story. This one is called *Expansión del Tema.* Whereas *La Primera Lectura* stayed closely within the facts and experiences of characters in the film, the *Expansión* deliberately ranges beyond to incorporate relevant geographical, historical, and cultural information. For instance, in the *Expansión del Tema* for lesson 1, some details are offered concerning the city of Sevilla, where the grandparents live. In addition, forecasting concerning future lessons is given:

Sevilla es la ciudad más representativa de Andalucía. Es la capital de la provincia de Sevilla, que es una de las ocho provincias de Andalucía. Más tarde vamos a visitar toda esta región con Emilio y sus parientes. . . (Oller, Sr., & González, 1965: 45).

Cultural similarities and contrasts are discussed in Spanish:

Los abuelos no son muy diferentes de los abuelos de cualquiera de nosotros. Los vemos por la tarde tomando chocolate. En España las horas de comer son distintas de las de los Estados Unidos. Los españoles, por lo general, no desayunan fuerte al levantarse por la mañana. Toman café, chocolate, o, especialmente los niños, leche caliente. A veces también comen panecillos o bollos. Más tarde, a eso de las diez y media de la mañana, toman el *bocadillo* con una bebida. El bocadillo consiste en un sandwich o un panecillo o cosas por el estilo.... Almuerzan entre la una y las tres de la tarde... (Oller, Sr., & González, 1965: 45).

Finally, following the *Expansión del Tema* for each lesson there are summary questions, which again may be supplemented by the teacher. As in *La familia Fernández,* the second lesson follows the experiential content of the first, and so forth throughout.

Varieties of Spanish

Because of the diversity of dialects of Spanish, the taped exercises for lessons 1 to 27 of *Emilio en España* include speakers representing a wide variety of regional variants. The authors observed:

Contrasts between cultures (foreign and native) tend to command a disproportionate share of classtime. This danger is minimized if discussions are conducted completely in the target language and thereby afford true linguistic experience [i.e., in Krashen's 1980 term "comprehensible input"] (Oller, Sr., & González 1965: 9).

Concerning the development of cultural understanding the authors wrote:

The direct objective of foreign language study in high school and lower division college classes should always be the attainment of communication skills. Where the setting is entirely different within the culture of the target language, as is the case, with . . . *El español por el mundo,* the indirect benefit of cultural appreciation is a natural outcome (Oller, Sr., & González 1965: 9).

CONCLUSION

When *El español por el mundo* first came on the market three decades ago, one of the common complaints was that it was too expensive for many small school districts to obtain. Even back in those days of single-digit inflation, it cost something over $3,000 to place *La familia Fernández* in a classroom. Although many critics were willing to concede that the program did achieve its aim of bringing the world of the foreign language into the classroom and of making communicative competence in the language accessible to students (and even to teachers), they contended that the price tag was too high. In spite of this objection, many school districts and a couple of state boards opted to buy it anyway.

Now, we live in a whole new era of technology. The cost effectiveness of video recording and playback equipment has made pragmatic language teaching with a sound-motion-picture component more accessible than at any point in history. For this reason it may be hoped that some of the concepts embodied in the foreign language program discussed in this chapter will continue to contribute in a small way to more-effective classroom language teaching.

NOTES

1 My father, John Oller, Sr. died in September 1980. Therefore, this chapter is put together from introductory remarks which he had written years earlier for the two levels of *El español por el mundo* and from the experience I had in using *El español por el mundo* at midschool, high school, and university levels. I would like to think that what is said here is entirely consistent with the theory and practice behind the programs, but for any discrepancies I must take full responsibility. Thanks are expressed to the publisher (Encyclopaedia Britannica Films, now Encyclopaedia Britannica Educational Corporation) and to Dr. Angel González, the coauthor of level II, *Emilio en España.*

2 English is used here to ensure comprehension, but, of course, in the actual lessons only Spanish was used.

3 It should be noted that all the dialogue and material in the films and written exercises throughout level II is in Spanish. The material is graded so as to become progressively more complex, and vocabulary entry is still controlled carefully as it was in *La familia Fernández,* but the rapidity of introduction of new vocabulary and a diversity of forms of expression is accelerated.

DISCUSSION QUESTIONS

1. What's the difference between bathing foreign language students in surface forms of a target language and immersing them in the world where that language is used for communication?

2. Foreign language teaching sometimes gets students to attend too exclusively to the surface form of target language utterances (e.g., their phonology, morphology, and syntax). However, in a "pragmatic" approach, students must still master the surface forms of target language utterances, so what's the difference?

3. What are some of the ways that the student's "*i + 1*" is systematically advanced as he or she progresses through the episodes and exercises of *El español por el mundo?*

4. How do the structure drills of this Spanish program differ from those in traditional audio-lingual programs? How are grammatical rules taught at the beginning of this Spanish program, and how does the philosophy of explicit rule presentation change as the student progresses to level II?

CHAPTER 7

From Role Play to the Real World

Raymond J. Rodrigues and Robert H. White

EDITOR'S INTRODUCTION

Many theoreticians speak of the "real" world as if classrooms were not in it. But any classroom, in any place at any time, is just as real as Grand Central Station in New York or the zoo in Albuquerque. However, what is often missing from the fictionalized material taught in the classroom is a comprehensible connection to the classroom or anything else in the real world. The key to making the connection between the sheltered fictions of the "class womb" (as an unintending punster once called it) and the less forgiving real world (to which those fictions must relate if they are to relate to anything at all) is to base the classroom fictions (the role playing, the storytelling, the acting, the dramatization, the films, books, etc.) in the real world to start with. For instance, if the supermarket role playing fits real-life contexts, students who master the fictional cases will be able to handle the real ones. "Pig simple" as Robert Newton Peck (1980) would say, but true. The only real bridge from vicarious experience in film, acting, role play, etc. that can get us across the gulf of imagination into the hard and real world must be created by using materials in the classroom that are grounded in real experience in the first place. We don't really have to invent the world. God already did that. All we have to do is relate the target language to the world in a way that our students can comprehend. Here, as in the previous chapter, the principle of multiple passes through a given text is apparent. The initial phase involves a simple dialog which is eventually committed to memory. Subsequent role playing and dramatizations lead to deeper saturation to be followed by open-ended activities with improvisation, culminating in a field trip where the student encounters the ultimate challenge of facing off with one or more untutored natives. Later, even deeper comprehension of the target language material is ensured by debriefing back in the classroom with expanded narratives and additional enactments or embellishments of the field-trip experience.

It has become evident to many teachers of ESL students that most of the available texts and materials are based on artificial sequencing of grammatical structures and stilted, often irrelevant, dialogues and topics. Only recently, with the stimulation of current research in second language learning and teaching, have new materials appeared based on the communicative needs of students. These new research insights and materials have finally accepted a principle often discovered in the past by classroom teachers: that effective ESL teaching must be based on helping students learn the language they need to function successfully in everyday situations and in future settings where they will be using English.

Another principle derived from current research concerns the comparison of first and second language learning in children *and* older learners and the possibility of patterning second language learning experiences on the model of natural first language learning. Just as children, in learning the first language, are exposed to a variety of experiences and accompanying language in a supportive environment to which they creatively respond, the second language learner may also be capable of responding to natural open language experiences based on communication needs.

In a plan based on those principles, students would be placed in a variety of experiences with accompanying language such as a trip to the zoo, lunch at a cafeteria, learning to play soccer, or going to the supermarket. In experiences such as these, learners are exposed to language in meaningful contexts. As beginners, their task is simply to attend to the sights and sounds of the experience, listen to the language which is part of the experience, and attempt to understand what they see and hear. Language presented in this situation can become meaningful to the student because of the many audiovisual clues which accompany it. The student can then begin to comprehend some of the language appropriate to the objects and actions in the setting. Since frequent field experiences may not be possible in school settings, simulated or vicarious experiences may be provided in the regular classroom. Appropriate films, videotapes, sound filmstrips, and dramatic presentations may be used to stimulate student attention and provide the meaningful contexts in which the language is best learned.

Although it may be possible for ESL students to learn English naturally through a curriculum made up of a long series of open language experiences, it is obvious that such a program would require years of student involvement. In practice, ESL classes for children, teenagers, and adults are limited to a fraction of the school day, or the students are in mixed classes and regular teachers are asked to provide some special ESL activities for students who need it. With the limited time available, it is necessary to follow open language experiences with more intensive structured situations, dialogues, and role-playing activities.

In the structured situation phase of this model, students are presented with simple but natural narratives or long dialogues of no more than 100 words based on the language of segments of the open language experience. These are accompanied by visual clues through use of pictures, objects, silent films, or filmstrips taken from the larger experience and used again to provide a meaningful context for the language presentation. Material of about 100 words in length has been found to be too long for quick memorization by students; thus the emphasis in this phase is for the student to concentrate on the meaning of the material. In addition, at least ten guide questions are presented to the student following the narration. These are constructed from the material in the narration and are designed to be answered by students with some of the language they have heard. What is encouraged here is the beginning of full responses using language understood from meaningful presentations.

In beginning classes a large difference in the ability of students to respond to the guide questions will exist. Many students will be too timid or unable to attempt responses in English, although their listening comprehension may be good. For most students, therefore, an additional phase involving the learning of short dialogues will be helpful and will give beginning students the confidence of actually using the language. The dialogues should be taken from the language of the structured situations, presented in no more than eight lines but using the natural yet simple language appropriate to the experience. Dialogues can be presented orally by the teacher or other students with repetition and guided memorizing, again with visual clues. Reading and writing can also begin in the dialogue phase with the teacher using charts containing the dialogue sentences and students learning to print their own word cards from the dialogues and arranging them in sentences as they memorize. These word cards can then be used for reviewing dialogues, constructing new sentences with the same and new words, and phonics activities based on these sight words, which will help the student make the transition to reading other relevant text materials and stories. Two or three students may be assigned to practice the dialogue until they feel confident enough to present it orally to the class.

Building of confidence through these memorized presentations will lead to students' participation in role playing and dramatic activities. After being involved in several structured situations and mastering related dialogues, students will have internalized enough of the basic language associated with the open language experience that they will be able to respond to role-playing situations planned by the teacher. These should be directly related to segments of the original open language experience. Students will be given short descriptions of a situation and asked to act out the roles of the people in these settings without looking at the printed dialogue material previously memorized. The role-playing activities should be similar to the narratives and dialogues, but sufficiently different to encourage freer use of the language.

Throughout the structured situation, dialogue, and role-playing phases, the teachers become diagnosticians, noting errors as the students attempt to respond, present dialogues, or act out role-playing situations. The teacher can categorize the errors, noting phonological (pronunciation), grammatical, and semantic errors made by a large number of class members, a small group, or an individual student. It is from these errors that the teacher plans appropriate practice activities. Recent second language learning research has indicated that making errors is a positive illustration of the students' attempts to internalize language forms by developing hypotheses based on the language material they hear. For example, students may have hypothesized from many examples and contexts that the *-ed* ending indicates past tense. As a result, they may overextend this hypothesis and apply it inappropriately to an irregular verb and make an error such as eat*ed* instead of *ate*. Errors such as this may disappear after the student has been exposed to the language for a longer period of time, but the teacher must eventually judge that a persistent error continues to interfere with meaning and provide practice activities for correction or prevention of this error. A valuable use of published ESL text material is to provide the teacher with ready-made practice activities for most predictable errors. These texts are usually organized with tables of contents and indexes that make it possible for the teacher to select quickly the practices needed for phonological, grammatical, and semantic errors. In this phase, the teacher and other students may work with individuals or small groups, guiding them through the appropriate practice activities. After ESL students have learned to read and write at basic levels, they may work at these materials individually or in pairs.

The evaluation phase of this model is based on a reality principle: the effectiveness of language instruction is best tested by assessing the student's use of the language in the actual experience. Thus, the students completing the phases of the unit are asked to repeat the open language experience to which they were first exposed and during which

they may have only been able to listen. For example, in an experience involving shopping at a supermarket, students are given a shopping list and a sum of money and asked to bring back a report on their activity and evidence of a successful shopping trip. If the actual field experience cannot be undertaken, a simulation of the experience may be arranged in a classroom.

Students who are unsuccessful in their performance would then be assigned repeated dialogues, role playing, and error-based activities followed by repetitions of the open-language experience. This recycling of some students need not prevent the introduction of another open language experience unit for the whole class.

Although some publishers are attempting to produce textbooks based on the communicative needs of ESL students with related phonological, grammatical, and vocabulary activities, they are unable to predict completely the needs of thousands of ESL students representing all ages and backgrounds. Only teachers struggling to meet the needs of their students can use interview techniques and interaction with students to determine and predict student communication needs and build practice activities related to the actual language errors of students.

The following outline for an open language experience unit plan and sample unit is offered as a possible model for teachers to use in their efforts to create more meaningful materials for their ESL students.

MODEL OPEN LANGUAGE EXPERIENCE UNIT OUTLINE

I. Determining needs and interests
   A. List the communication needs and interests of the target group.
   B. In what settings *will* they be using English?
   C. In what settings are they *currently* needing English?

II. Planning open language experience activities
   A. Select one of these needs or interests, and develop an open language experience activity in which the students can use their natural language learning abilities.

B. The meaning and language in this experience will be acquired by the student's *listening* and *observing* in the context.
C. Examples:
   1. Plan a field trip to a supermarket.
   2. Show a relevant sound film.
   3. Plan to bring in a group of native speakers of English to act out a situation, e.g., eating lunch at an American restaurant.
D. Write your plan for the open language experience activity in enough detail so that another ESL teacher can follow it.

III. Structured situations
   A. Select three parts of the open language experience. Example: checking out at the supermarket.
   B. Write three narratives of about 100 words each to be presented by the teacher or another student that describe or discuss three parts of the open language experience activity.
      1. Keep the language natural and appropriate to the situation.
      2. Keep vocabulary as simple as possible.
      3. Keep sentences as short as possible.
   C. Prepare visual cues to meaning to accompany the structured situation. Examples: pictures, objects, silent film, or filmstrip.
   D. Prepare at least 10 guide questions for each structured situation that can be answered by the students directly from the structured situation presentation.
   E. Have students role play what they remember.
   F. Note student errors as they attempt to answer the questions.

IV. Short dialogues
   A. Write at least six short dialogues (about eight lines each) based on the structured situations.
   B. Present each dialogue orally to the group.
   C. Have students practice each dialogue in pairs (or threes) and in front of the class.
   D. Note student errors as they present dialogues.

V. Drama and role playing in activities
   A. Plan additional activities based on the structured situation and dialogues.
   B. Note student errors.

VI. Error analysis
   A. Analyze student phonological (pronunciation), gramatical, and semantic error from the structured situations, dialogues, and other activities.
   B. Categorize the errors:
      1. Common class
      2. Small group
      3. Individual

VII. Planned practice—plan practice activities for the class, small groups, and individuals that focus on their particular errors and their developmental needs.

VIII. Repeated open language experience—ask students to repeat the open language experience and report the results.

IX. Recycling—have students who were unsuccessful in the open language experience repeat dialogues and practice activities.

X. Plan and present a new open language experience unit.

SAMPLE PLAN FOR AN OPEN LANGUAGE EXPERIENCE: SHOPPING AT THE SUPERMARKET

This is a report on the open language experience and materials used with an ESL class of Vietnamese refugees living in Albuquerque, New Mexico.

Needs Assessment

A translator was present at the first session, and through him the students were asked questions about the nature of their English needs. For instance, each student was asked how long he or she had been in the United States and whether or not he or she had had any formal schooling in his or her native country. Students were also asked what kinds of places—bank, post office, grocery store, airport, bakery—they had been to in the United States, and what they felt to be their most essential English language needs.

Planning the Open Language Experience Activity

Everyone had been to a grocery store in the United States, and each student expressed a need to learn the American system of money; hence, a grocery store setting was chosen for the open language experience, the need and current use of English in this setting having been established.

After the translator explained the purpose of the activity, the class was taken on a field trip to a small neighborhood grocery store. We took a grocery list with us and empty pop bottles to return. At the store the class was videotaped observing and listening to the teacher. The teacher asked the grocer about prices, compared prices of items and made choices of what items to buy, went through the checkout stand, got change, said goodbye to the grocer, went home, and put the groceries into the refrigerator and cupboards. The videotape of this experience, as well as the actual objects purchased, were used as vehicles or props for later lessons on various phases of grocery shopping.

The videotape was also used as a basis for discussion in class, for error analysis and correction, and for the amusement and motivation of the students. In testing, the final stage of the open language experience, when the students went to a large supermarket with a grocery list and purchased groceries "on their own," another videotape was made and used in class for error analysis and for assessment of teaching success.

The three phases of grocery shopping dealt with in this report include making a grocery list, choosing groceries, and going through the checkout stand.

Structured Situations

Narrative A

I want to make a grocery list. I get a pencil and a piece of paper to write down what I need. Let's see. What do I need? I open my refrigerator. I need milk. I need eggs. I need butter. I write down milk, eggs, butter. Also, I need orange juice. I have plenty of vegetables—onions, carrots, celery, and tomatoes. So I don't need to buy any vegetables. Do I have any fruit? I have oranges. But I don't have any apples. I need apples. So here is my grocery list: milk, eggs, butter, orange juice, apples.

Guide Questions

1. What is a grocery list?
2. How do I make a grocery list?
3. What do I open to see what I need?
4. Which vegetables do I have?
5. What vegetables do I need to buy?
6. What fruit do I have?
7. What fruit do I need to buy?
8. Which three dairy products do I need to buy?
9. What kind of fruit juice do I need to buy?
10. What items are on my grocery list?

Narrative B

At the grocery store I get a grocery cart. I look at my grocery list. It says: milk, eggs, butter, orange juice, apples. I find the *dairy* aisle. I put a quart of skimmed milk and a dozen eggs in my cart. I see that a pound (lb.) of butter costs $1.99. I see that a pound (lb.) of margarine costs $0.97. I put the margarine, not the butter, in my cart. I go to the produce aisle. I see red apples and green apples. I choose six green apples. I find the canned orange juice. I put one can of pure, unsweetened orange juice into my cart.

Guide Questions

1. What is a grocery cart?
2. What is on my grocery list?
3. How much milk do I choose?
4. How many eggs do I buy? How many eggs are there in a dozen?
5. Why do I choose margarine instead of butter?
6. In what aisle do I find apples?
7. What kinds of apples do I see?
8. Which apples do I choose?
9. How many apples do I buy?
10. What kind of orange juice do I put into my cart?

Narrative C

At the checkout register I put my groceries on the counter. The quart of milk costs $0.59, the pound of margarine costs $0.97, the dozen eggs cost $0.68. The clerk says, "The apples are $0.59 a pound; that will be $0.74." The can of juice costs $0.79. The total is $3.77 plus tax. Tax is $0.15. The total bill is $3.92. I give the clerk a five dollar bill. He gives me a penny, "$3.93," another penny, "$3.94," another penny, "$3.95," a nickel, "$4.00," a dollar bill, "$5.00." He puts my groceries in a bag and says, "Thank you." I say, "Thank you and goodbye."

Guide Questions

1. At the checkout stand where do I put my groceries?
2. How much does the milk cost?
3. How much does the margarine cost?
4. How much are the apples?
5. How much money do I give the clerk?
6. How many pennies does the clerk give me in change?
7. How many nickels does the clerk give me in change?
8. How many dollar bills does the clerk give me in change?
9. Where does the clerk put my groceries?
10. What is the last thing I say to the clerk?

Dialogues

Making a Grocery List

A: What do you need at the grocery store?
B: I don't know. Let me see.
A: Do you need any vegetables?
B: No, I have plenty.
A: Do you need some fruit?
B: Well, I have oranges, but I don't have apples.
A: Then you need some apples.
B: Yes, I need some apples.
A: I'm going to make out my grocery list.
B: Here's a pencil and paper. Let me write it for you.
A: Okay. Write down milk, eggs, and butter.
B: Okay. Milk, eggs, and butter. What else?
A: Write down apples.
B: Okay. Apples.
A: Write down orange juice. That's all.
B: Okay. I've got milk, eggs, butter, apples, and orange juice.

Choosing Groceries

A: Where do I find the dairy products?
B: Over there. You'll see the milk, butter, and eggs.
A: How much does the butter cost?
B: It's $1.99 a pound. The margarine is cheaper.
A: Where do I find the apples?
B: Over there in the produce section.
A: Excuse me. Where can I find the orange juice?

B: Over there. It says "Canned Juice."
A: Excuse me. Where is the dairy aisle?
B: Over there.
A: Thank you.
B: You're welcome.
A: Excuse me. Where is the produce?
B: There. See the carrots and lettuce?
A: Oh, yes. Thank you.
B: You're welcome.

Going Through the Checkout Line

A: Hello.
B: Hello.
A: How much were the eggs?
B: A dozen cost $0.79.
A: Fine.
B: That will be $3.92.
A: Here's a five dollar bill.
B: Thank you. Here's your change. Have a nice day.
A: Thank you. Goodbye.
A: Hello. How are you?
B: Hello. I'm fine, thank you.
A: That will be $3.92.
B: How much was the tax on that? A: $0.15.
B: Thanks. Here's a five dollar bill.
A: Your change is $1.08. Thank you. Have a nice day.
B: Thank you. Goodbye.

Role-playing Activities

Between the open language field experience of the trip to a small neighborhood grocery store and the test situation of having students purchase groceries at a large supermarket, we had several lessons that focused on role playing. We used an actual grocery cart and props of vegetables, milk cartons, margarine and butter cartons, and various other grocery items.

Role playing seemed to be the most successful phase of the open language experience. Students enjoyed and joked and created language to fit the situation. Given the dialogues, which they hadn't completely memorized but which they had understood, the students played with the possibilities of language. Given "Excuse me," to mean "let me pass with my grocery cart," one student elaborated, "I want to go by you." Given "Where is the produce?" another student elaborated, "I want to find the celery." Given the format, "I want to buy a gallon of milk," a student, seeing a knife on the kitchen counter, expanded the form to say, "Excuse me. I want to buy a knife."

ERROR ANALYSIS

With this particular group of Vietnamese the consensus of native speakers dealing with the students seemed to be that pronunciation was a serious problem. Vietnamese native speakers have difficulty with the pronunciation of English to such an extent that it is not advisable to ignore it.

In particular, this group of students tended to omit the final consonants of all English words. The word for book [bʊk] became [bu]; the word for cap [kæp] became [kæ]. First person, singular, present tense verbs invariably were pronounced without the final -s. The final -s in plurals was rarely pronounced. Hence a question such as "What does she eat?" elicited the response, "She eat apple and cookie." Since this response is easily understood by a native speaker, in a "real" conversation between a native speaker and a native Vietnamese speaker using English, there was no great effort to correct pronunciation; however, when we were doing drills and patterns, we felt it was very appropriate to concentrate on the pronunciation of the final consonants of words, especially the final -s with the plurals and the final consonant on common words such as *book* and *ship*. We focused attention on this problem through a translator, explaining that in English the final consonants and especially the pronunciation of -s's was important. This explanation seemed to help; certainly it facilitated our corrections and their being understood by the students.

DISCUSSION QUESTIONS

1. How can the teacher serve as "diagnostician" (or learning counselor) during role-play activities? In creating drills for difficult points, why is it essential to link every element of every drill to actual facts known in some way by the students?

2. The authors say that "the effectiveness of language instruction is best tested by assessing the student's use of the language in the actual experience" (p. 65). How should classroom testing be adjusted to meet this end?

3. Why does surface form matter so much? How will it relate to the success or failure of the supermarket trip? How do you react to the clerk you ask about the napkins, when you can't understand what he or she is saying? Role play it. See what you would do.

4. How does role play set up the "open language experience"?

CHAPTER 8

Why Drama Works:
A Psycholinguistic Perspective

Susan L. Stern

EDITOR'S INTRODUCTION

Stern notes that dramatizing communicative events leads to bodily and emotional involvement which results in the motivation to make meanings and intentions clear in the target language. Acting as if the context were real leads to competence in the language (also see Scarcella, 1983). I once heard an interview with an actor, I think it was Omar Shariff, who said that memorizing and acting out the lines to one movie script was sufficient to move him from not knowing English to being a speaker of the language. Another advantage of acting is that it removes some of the risks of genuine acts of communication, yet retains the texture. The student has the opportunity to gain the necessary skills to handle the higher stakes later. The fact is that pretend (dramatized) acts of communication are not unreal. Just like any other real act, dramatizations inevitably occur in some place, at some time. Nor are dramatizations without risk. Ask John Rassias, who is so used to being called a maniac that it no longer stings. Or recall the teacher (see Chapter 3) who didn't want to act out peeling an onion because he didn't want to "look foolish." Acting is not a zero-risk enterprise, but the fictionalizing of scenarios can reduce the stakes a great deal and, as Stern points out, enable the students to build "specific self-esteem" and "self-confidence" sufficient to enable them to perform real tasks in the target language that they would, otherwise, never have dared to attempt. In the meantime, critical adjustments in utterance forms in the target language may be made with less personal threat because they are directed toward the portrayal of a character, someone other than the student. In addition to dealing with a broad range of practice in fields as diverse as mental health, language teaching, and speech-language pathology, Stern takes her ideas a step further: she asks students to react to the merits of drama in the classroom. They agree. Drama works.

Drama is commonly used in ESL and foreign language classes for developing communicative competence, especially oral language skills.[1] Whether or not they use it themselves, most instructors would agree that drama, particularly role play, is a standard classroom technique which "has long been recognized as a valuable and valid means of mastering a language" (Hines, 1973: introduction).

It is not the purpose of this paper, however, to discuss dramatic techniques or argue for their usefulness. The intuitive assumption that drama in the ESL/foreign language classroom improves oral communication is taken as a given for this study, which approaches drama in L2 learning from a psycholinguistic perspective. The question to be explored is: Presuming that participation in dramatic activities helps L2 learners improve their communicative competence, how can this be explained in psycholinguistic terms; i.e., which psychological factors can explain why dramatic activities appear to improve the oral competence of L2 learners?

In answering this question, practical applications of drama in education and related fields were explored, beginning with ESL and foreign language classes. Any area that could illustrate the psychological basis of drama as a means of achieving a personal goal was investigated. Research revealed three such areas: drama in education, specifically in language classes; psychodrama, as practiced in the mental health field and in professional training programs; and role playing in speech therapy.

The objectives for using drama are different for each of these disciplines. In ESL and foreign language classes, drama is directed toward language acquisition. In child development, creative dramatics encourages the maturation and growth of creative capacity, with particular reference to verbal skills. Psychodrama helps restore a patient's mental health and trains individuals for new social roles. Speech therapy employs drama to help patients achieve or regain normal speech behavior and patterns.

Despite their differing aims, each of these disciplines appears to use drama for the same fundamental reason. It facilitates communication by bringing certain psychological factors into play which elicit the desired behavior in the individual. The common factors are motivation, empathy, sensitivity to rejection, self-esteem, and spontaneity. All but spontaneity are currently being investigated within the context of L2 acquisition (Schumann, 1975). The focus of the present study is the insight these factors provide into the psychological effects of drama. The goal is to understand how and why participation in dramatic activities helps L2 learners achieve communicative competence.

The chapter begins with a discussion of the relationship between drama and each of these psychological factors within the frameworks of the three disciplines mentioned above. Implications for L2 learners are suggested throughout the discussion, leading to a statement of the hypothesis. The report of an informal exploratory study designed to find support for the claims made by the hypothesis concludes the chapter.

DRAMA IN EDUCATION: ESL AND FOREIGN LANGUAGE CLASSES

Motivation

Motivation is the most frequently cited reason for using drama in ESL and foreign language classes. Dramatic activities inspire students to want to learn another language. They are a curative for the frustration and lagging interest which often occur during L2 learning, and they facilitate acquisition of the target language as a result (Hsu, 1975; Via, 1976; Moulding, 1978).

The purposefulness of dramatic activity can provide a strong instrumental motivation for language learning. In an intermediate-level class in spoken Chinese for American university students, for example, Hsu (1975) conducted an experiment in drama to develop the students' conversational ability and boost their sinking morale. She structured the entire course around presentation of a play, making it a group project that required students to communicate in Chinese throughout each aspect of preparation. Hsu found the activity to be highly motivating to her students, reactivating a high degree of interest in learning Chinese. Via (1976) also found play production as the culmination of a language course to be highly motivating to students when teaching English in Japan. Functioning as an end in itself as well as a topic for discussion and analysis, play production created a genuine communication need where students had to use natural conversational English in a meaningful context.

Play production can also be a source of integrative motivation by fostering cultural proximity. A play allows language learners to participate in the new culture, helping them develop a sensitivity as to how speakers of the target language interact with each other. It familiarizes them with the cultural appropriateness of words and expressions to specific settings and social situations. Ideally, this integrative experience should motivate learners to want to achieve a higher degree of language proficiency.

Moulding (1978) emphasized that drama provides the context for a meaningful exchange in which participants see a reason to communicate, and focuses on "how to do things" with the language rather than merely on "how to describe things. As Seaver shows in Chapter 32, language teaching has tended to kill motivation by divorcing the intellectual aspects of language (vocabulary + structures) from its body and emotions, limiting instruction to the former. Dramatic techniques restore the body and emotions to language learning, thereby restoring motivation.

Self-Esteem

Self-esteem is an evaluation we make of ourselves and our abilities in terms of worthiness, and "specific self-esteem" is a self-evaluation particular to a specific life situation (Heyde, 1977). Although this term rarely appears in TESL literature in reference to drama, the frequently cited concept of "self-confidence" seems to have the same meaning. Thus, for purpose of this study, "self-confidence" in L2 learning is synonymous with specific self-esteem—the learner's self-esteem as a speaker of the second language.

Heyde (1979) found that there appears to be a predictive quality to the correlation between self-esteem and the ability to orally produce a second language. Results indicate that students with high self-esteem received higher teacher oral production ratings than low self-esteem students. This implies that increased specific self-esteem should improve the language learner's oral proficiency. Advocates of drama in L2 learning support this hypothesis and believe that an effective way of raising self-esteem is through drama.

An analogy between acting and the martial arts suggested by Via (1976) explains one way in which drama helps self-confidence. Just as a yell accompanies the strike in order to build the confidence and increase the energy of the attacker, so a strong and clear voice (necessary when performing) gives the language learner confidence. Drama also raises self-esteem by demonstrating to L2 learners that they are indeed capable of expressing themselves in realistic communicative situations.

Sensitivity to Rejection

L2 learners who are afraid of what others may think of their less-than-perfect command of the language will be inhibited in using it. This is especially true of adults. Several educators have found that drama creates a nonthreatening situation, which can reduce and even eliminate sensitivity to rejection (Hines, 1973; Via, 1976; Early, 1977; Crookall, 1978; and Rassias in Chapter 5).

There are a number of possible explanations for the safety of the role-play situation. One is that it is only make-believe, and the learner needn't fear "the consequences of a lapse or miscalculation" (Early, 1977: 34). The role shields learners against the less desirable consequences of their assertions, and their assertions thereby become freer (Crookall, 1978: 2). A second explanation is that drama functions as a group effort, giving safety through numbers. A third is that critical judgment of what the participants say—and even how they say it—may be perceived by them as being directed toward the characters they are portraying rather than toward them personally. Consequently, they lose their normal inhibitions about speaking, "relax, forget, *become* the characters they are portraying, and language flows" (Hines, 1973: introduction).

According to Via (1976), playacting is a natural activity of children, and their lack of inhibition allows them when unobserved to engage in award-winning performances. For the adult, to revive this innate ability is just a matter of rediscovery. S. Peck (1977) observed that children immersed in an L2 situation with native-speaking children will join them in play. Unfamiliarity with the second language does not seem to inhibit their involvement; on the contrary, they begin to use it themselves.

These observations, coupled with the generally accepted belief that children have the natural ability to acquire a second language, lead to some exciting speculations about drama as a strategy in adult L2 learning. If role-play can temporarily revive "the child" in adult L2 learners, then the child's natural ability to acquire a second language might also be revived to some extent.

Empathy

The empathic act is "a temporary suspension of ego functions in favor of an immediate precognitive experience of another's emotional state as one's own;...a process of comprehending in which a temporary fusion of self-object boundaries... permits an immediate emotional apprehension of the affective experience of another" (Guiora,1972: 142). Guiora explains that empathic capacity is dependent upon the ability to partially and temporarily suspend the functions that maintain one's separateness from others (usually called ego boundaries); i.e., to partially and temporarily give up one's separateness of identity. Flexibility, or permeability of ego boundaries, is the index of one's ability to take on a new identity.

Guiora et al. (1972) hypothesized that the ability to approximate nativelike pronunciation in a second language is related to the flexibility or permeability of one's ego boundaries. His experiment with alcohol, in which subjects' pronunciation in a second language was improved after their having ingested small amounts of alcohol, seemed to uphold this hypothesis. This led Schumann (1975: 226) to suggest that "if artificial agents such as alcohol can foster permeability of ego boundaries and reduce inhibitions, then it would not be unreasonable to assume that given the right concatenation of natural psychological factors, permeability of ego boundaries might be possible for everyone."

Actors must achieve empathy, or ego permeability, in order to give a convincing and meaningful performance. Stanislavski believed that they must pretend to live out the lives of their characters in ways that transcend the play. They must enter their characters' consciousness by temporarily giving up their own identity to take on a new dimension. A common training procedure for actors is to identify with their characters or wish they were there, and then imagine what they would do (Beutler, 1976). Supporting the notion that drama fosters empathy in the participants, educators such as Shaftel and Shaftel (1952) have found that role play is a successful approach for forming positive intergroup relations because it permits the individual to understand and relate to the feelings of others.

It is therefore hypothesized that dramatic activities are an effective way of creating within the classroom setting that "concatenation of natural factors" which could make permeability of ego boundaries possible for everyone. If "the natural factors which induce ego flexibility and lower inhibitions are those conditions which make the learner less anxious, make him feel accepted and make him form positive identification with speakers of the target language" (Schumann, 1975: 227) and if drama is one of those natural factors that

induce flexibility and lower inhibitions, then one more explanation as to why drama is an effective technique in L2 learning will have been found.

DRAMA IN EDUCATION: ENGLISH FOR NATIVE SPEAKERS

A dramatic approach to the teaching of English has been practiced for a number of years in the British educational system. Instructors do not use drama to teach *about* language or the structure of the subject, or to teach *about* literature. Influenced by psychologists such as Piaget and Vygotsky, the theory of communication guiding the English curriculum focuses on personal and emotional experiences, imagination, intuition, and sensibility rather than subject matter. The question is not "how drama helps English nor how English helps drama, but how drama, English, movement and the other arts help the child" (Hoetker, 1969: 12). Drama has also found its way into the English curricula of American schools, especially at the elementary levels as *creative dramatics*. This includes a wide range of activities, from mimic play to improvisations and from dramatizations of stories to the eventual enactment of formal plays among older children (Hoetker, 1969).

The British and Americans share common assumptions about drama and employ similar techniques. It appears, however, that the goal of using drama in the British system is the total development of the child, whereas the goal of using drama among American educators more directly and specifically focuses on development of the language skills. As a strong advocate of dramatics in the American English curriculum, Moffett (1967: vii) sees drama as the matrix of all language activities, subsuming speech and engendering the varieties of writing and reading. Rogosheske (1972) cites a number of dedicated supporters of creative dramatics who claim it to be the most effective approach to instruction in the language skills.

Motivation

Drama can be especially effective with speakers whose skills are considered lower than average. Lazier (1969), for example, tried an experimental 12-week program in drama with a junior high school adjustment class composed of "disruptive" 13- to 15-year-olds classified as functional illiterates. Under his guidance, the students developed and staged an updated version of *West Side Story*. They rewrote the script by improvising the dialogue and recording their improvisations on paper. They then edited and refined to achieve clear and interesting communication. Although this task was extremely difficult for them, their motivation usually overcame lack of writing skill, and these students essentially formed a team of scriptwriters.

PSYCHODRAMA

Psychodrama is a general term referring to a group action technique used in psychotherapy and education, in which individuals act out roles involving social or psychological problems. Psychodrama typically begins with a warm-up period and discussion in which a theme (role, situation, problem) is agreed upon. The group members take roles and improvise a drama based upon the selected theme, then react to and analyze the performance. A scene might be dramatized a second or third time with different actors in the role, or the same actors reversing roles, followed by further reaction and analysis. There are several kinds of psychodrama, their primary difference being a matter of focus.

Sociodrama is an educational technique to train people for specific social roles, e.g., nursing, teaching. Its primary aim is the clarification of group themes, and it focuses on social problems. It involves acting out imaginary situations for purposes of self-understanding, improvement of skills, analyses of behavior, or to demonstrate how the participant operates or should operate (Corsini, 1966). Sociodrama has been used effectively in ESL classes to develop vocabulary, grammar, discourse strategies, and strategies for social interaction; to promote cultural understanding; and to elicit oral production (Scarcella, 1983).

Role playing is often used interchangeably with sociodrama. Blatner (1973) suggests, however, that most professionals would consider it to be more superficial and problem-oriented. The expression of deep feelings is not usually part of role playing. Rather, the goal tends to be the working out of alternative and more effective approaches to a general problem.

Psychodrama in the specific sense refers to the techniques employed in psychotherapy. A psychodrama is an enactment involving emotional problem solving in terms of one person's conflict. It is protagonist-centered, and moves toward relatively deep emotional issues. (*Note:* Unless specified as "*psychodrama* in psychotherapy," the term psychodrama will refer to the more general meaning.)

Empathy

Psychodramatic techniques reinforce empathic perceptions by developing interpersonal skills and sensitivity to others. For example, in a postgraduate development program for nursery school teachers conducted in a psychiatric clinic, the teachers were exploring grief due to death and bereavement when one of them asked how to deal with a child's question about death. This caused another teacher to enact the loss of a spouse, which catalyzed a dramatic and emotion-filled catharsis among the rest of the group in which they shared their own experiences of mourning. Thus, they touched their own deep feelings and related to the hypothetical child and to each other with greater authenticity (Blatner, 1973).

Role playing helps the individual become more flexible, i.e., develop a sense of mastery in many different role situations. "In turn, the components of each role can be applied more easily, in new situations, when syntheses must be developed" (Blatner, 1973: 126). This suggests that through role play, L2 learners can experience many kinds of situations in which they will use the language; and as they develop a sense of mastery in them, they should be able to apply the language more easily to new situations.

Sensitivity to Rejection/Self-Esteem

The idea that role playing is safe is frequently expressed in psychodramatic literature. Corsini (1966) explained that in real life, patients may not attempt new ways of doing things; if they fail, the results can be harmful. In therapeutic role playing, however, the very fact that they have the courage to demonstrate their functioning, no matter how inadequately, is a success. Consequently, patients are not embarrassed by a poor performance.

The same holds true for L2 learners. If they fail to communicate outside of class, the results can be embarrassing or even harmful. But in role play, having the courage to demonstrate the ability to use the second language is in itself a success, and they should therefore not be embarrassed by a poor performance. It follows that they should be less inhibited using the language in role play than in real life, and therefore function better than they thought they could. This in turn should raise their self-esteem.

Spontaneity

Analyses of people who have been through intensive psychodramas suggest a number of recurrent patterns which collectively might be described as "the spontaneity state" (Mann, 1970). It is proposed that this state, or spontaneity, be added to the list of psychological factors currently being investigated in L2 acquisition.

Mann explains that persons in the spontaneity state completely forget about the existence of the audience or cease to be concerned about its reactions. Their temporal sense alters, and they come to view time as an "eternal now," where past, present, and future are all enfolded in a dreamlike experience. Of most significance to L2 learning is that "the usual gap between thought and expression ceases to exist. Expression becomes an integrated whole" (Mann, 1970: 7-8). Also of relevance is the free-flowing creativity that is unleashed. "In varying degrees the person in such a state acts as though inspired. He draws on resources which neither he nor his friends may have thought he had at his disposal" (Mann, 1970: 7-8).

If this state can be induced in L2 learners via drama, the usual gap between thought and expression which ceases to exist in the native language might cease to exist in the second language as well. Equally relevant to L2 learning is the "free-flowing creativity" and the ability of the person to draw upon heretofore untapped resources. This might explain the following observation of an ESL student engaged in role play: "The transformation in his manner was unbelievable. He really 'hammed it up' during the phone conversation and everyone in the audience noticed" (Hinofotis & Bailey, 1978: 15).

Corsini defined *spontaneity* as "natural, rapid, enforced self-generated behavior to new situations." He explained that people are frequently placed in new situations in which they have to improvise, to do something, to react. To the degree that the response is good, it is satisfying, helps one adjust, and tends to become part of one's repertoire. It is hypothesized that L2 learners undergo the same psychological process when they confront new linguistic situations in role play. To the degree that they succeed in communicating, the experience is satisfying. It helps them adjust to becoming a speaker of the second language and tends to become part of their linguistic repertoire.

DRAMATICS IN SPEECH THERAPY

Psychodramatic methods and role playing, when adapted to a particular setting, can be remarkably effective for children with relatively poor cognitive and verbal skills (Blatner, 1973). Creative dramatics techniques are used as psychotherapy, as diagnostic observation, and as auditory training. Although children with speech handicaps must be individually examined and evaluated, they benefit from the group interaction central to creative dramatics.

The value of creative dramatics as an adjunct to speech therapy was demonstrated in a cooperative program offered by the creative dramatics classes and speech clinic of the University of Pittsburgh (McIntyre and McWilliams, 1959). Several children with articulation and stuttering disorders were enrolled in creative dramatics classes along with children whose speech was considered normal. The program was initiated to bridge the gap between therapy at the clinic and everyday speech. The successful results of this program served to illustrate the correlation of creative dynamics to speech correction. Similarly positive results using creative dramatics to improve articulation were reported by Ludwig (1955), McIntyre (1958), McIntyre and McWilliams (1959), and Wessels (Chapter 36). Role-playing techniques have also been adapted for adult aphasics to help them recover normal speech (Schlanger & Schlanger, 1971, also see Damico & Damico, Chapter 29).

Psychological Factors

The psychological factors contributing to the effectiveness of creative dramatics in speech therapy appear to be the same as those in operation in education and psychodrama. *Motivation* is a key factor. Schlanger and Schlanger (1971) claimed that the great psychological advantage of using role play with aphasics was that it helped them get closer to communicative intercourse so that they no longer felt that they were restricted to speaking isolated and often seemingly meaningless words in a rote manner. McIntyre and McWilliams (1959) commented on the enjoyment of the role-play experience and the happy and relaxed atmosphere that it created.

Loss of *sensitivity to rejection* and heightened *self-esteem,* which also appear to be significant factors in speech improvement, are fostered by dramatics. Schlanger and Schlanger (1971) report that role playing is used to reduce aphasic patients' anxieties about communicating. In the role of another person, they can act the way they want rather than the way they are expected to act. Moreover, their attempts to communicate are reinforced by reactions of fellow aphasics, approbation of participating clinicians, and the self-satisfaction engendered by successful spontaneous communication (which brings in the factor of *spontaneity*).

Over the several years that they worked with role play, Schlanger and Schlanger noticed the following changes in their patients: (1) some relief of frustration and anxiety concerning deficient communication, (2) loss of inhibition, (3) a strong sense of accomplishment, and (4) insight into the problems of self and the feelings and actions of others. The first three changes are indicative of lowered sensitivity to rejection and heightened self-esteem. The fourth suggests that increased empathy was in operation.

THE HYPOTHESIS

This brief investigation into the use of drama in language education, psychology, and speech therapy reveals that despite their differing aims, each employs drama because it facilitates communication. For language learning and speech therapy,

communication is the desired end in itself. For psychotherapy and child development, communicative ability is a prerequisite behavior that must be acquired before other behaviors, such as social adjustment and overall development of the child, can occur. But it appears to be the common assumption that drama can develop and/or elicit communicative competence in the individual.

The application of this assumption to L2 learning is the basis for the hypothesis of this study: Drama facilitates communication in L2 learners by encouraging the following psychological factors to operate: heightened self-esteem, motivation, and spontaneity; increased capacity for empathy; lowered sensitivity to rejection.

AN EXPLORATORY STUDY OF THE PSYCHOLOGICAL BASIS FOR USING DRAMA IN LANGUAGE TEACHING

Although formal empirical investigation of the hypothesis will be reserved for future research, a questionnaire was designed to explore the issue informally. The questionnaire had both a student and a teacher component. It was administered to three ESL instructors at the University of California, Los Angeles, who had recently used dramatic activities in their classes, and to the 24 advanced-level students who had participated in them. Class A was the regular university section of a course in oral communication. Class B was the university extension section of the same course. Class C was a course in phonetics also offered by university extension. The dramatic activities in which the students participated were *scenes from plays* and *improvisations*.

Dramatizing scenes from plays involved performing short scenes (about 8 to 10 minutes each), which involved two or three characters. The students were not asked to memorize lines but were told to look up and say them to the other character(s) with meaning and feeling. Both the scenes and the improvisations were videotaped, and the students viewed and discussed their performances afterward.

For classes A and C, improvisations consisted of interviews of the characters and improvisations based upon the scenes. The interview took place directly after the scene. The students had to imagine that they were still the characters they had just portrayed, and respond accordingly to questions posed by the instructor and the other students. The improvisation followed immediately afterward. The instructor described a situation to the students, similar to the scene they had just enacted, but with a significant twist in character or plot. They were given 5 minutes to consult with one another, and then performed. Class B participated in the same kind of interview, but for them improvisations were a separate activity based upon a role-play game. The students were assigned character roles in pairs and were presented with a dramatic situation to improvise in front of the class.

The Student Questionnaire

There were 24 respondents to the student component of the questionnaire: the 13 students enrolled in class A, 6 of the 10 students enrolled in class B, and all 5 students enrolled in class C. The ques-

tionnaire was designed to elicit their subjective responses to the psychological aspects of drama being investigated. In order to avoid making this purpose known to the students, it was presented to them as part of the final course evaluation, and distractor items were included which focused on concrete objectives for using drama, e.g., improving pronunciation and expression. (*Note:* See Appendix 8.1 for the student component of the questionnaire. Each item is labeled with the psychological factor it was designed to test, and the distractor items are identified.)

Part I asked the students to evaluate the usefulness of participating in (1) scenes from plays and (2) improvisations. Table 8.1 summarizes the results by collapsing the data from these two sections according to the areas of usefulness being evaluated. The items were evaluated on a five-point Likert scale. The mean scores for each class were calculated separately in order to capture any differences that might appear between the oral

TABLE 8.1 Usefulness of Drama as Perceived by Students[a]

Item on questionnaire Part I	Potential area of usefulness	Class A mean ($n = 13$)	Class B mean ($n = 6$)	Class C mean ($n = 5$)	Overall mean ($N = 24$)
	Improving pronunciation				
1a	Scenes from plays	3.5[b]	3.2	3.6	3.4
2a	Improvisations	2.7	3.2	3.4	2.95
	Improving intonation and expression				
1b	Scenes from plays	4.6	3.2	4.2	4.1
2b	Improvisations	3.6	4.0	3.6	3.7
	Gaining self-confidence				
1c	Scenes from plays	3.9	4.2	4.0	4.0
2c	Improvisations	4.3	4.2	4.2	4.25
	Becoming less inhibited or less embarrassed when speaking in front of a group				
1d	Scenes from plays	4.3	4.0	3.6	4.1
2d	Improvisations	4.4	4.7	4.2	4.33
	Increasing/enriching vocabulary				
1e	Scenes from plays	3.0	3.4	3.4	3.0
	Learning more about American Culture				
1f	Scenes from plays	3.0	3.0	4.2	3.2

[a]The data in Table 8.1 corresponds to the items on Part I of the questionnaire.
[b]The figures are based on the following Likert scale responses: 1 = not useful; 2 = a little useful; 3 = somewhat useful; 4 = quite useful; 5 = very useful.

communication classes and the pronunciation class, and between the university and extension classes. The "Overall $\overline{X}$" indicates the response of all 24 students as one group rather than the average of the three classes in order to give a truer reading due to the differences in class size.

Part II consisted of questions relating to the students' feelings about themselves during and after performance. The results may be found in Table 8.2. As in Table 8.1, the mean scores for classes A, B, and C were first calculated separately, and the Overall $\overline{X}$ represents the average of all 24 students as one group. Three different five-point Likert scales were used, corresponding to question 1, questions 2 through 6, and question 7.

Part III asked the students whether or not they would like to participate in more dramatic activities and solicited their comments as to why or why not. Their responses to the yes/no question are summarized in Table 8.3. The students' open-ended comments are incorporated into the discussion that follows, which synthesizes and summarizes the results reported in the three tables in terms of the psychological factors under study.

Motivation

Motivation was measured in terms of the degree of enjoyment students experienced while participating in dramatic activities, and by their desire to participate in more. Responses to items

TABLE 8.2 Student Reactions to Drama[a]

Item on questionnaire Part II	Topic	Class A mean ($n = 13$)	Class B mean ($n = 6$)	Class C mean ($n = 5$)	Overall mean ($N = 24$)
1	Ability to express self in English during performance	3.2[b]	3.2	4.0	3.3
2	Difficulty in understanding character	1.5[c]	1.7	2.2	1.7
3	Nervousness when participating in dramatic activities	2.5	3.2	2.0	2.6
4	Difficulty in identifying with or stepping into role of character	2.4	2.8	1.8	2.4
5	Embarrassment when acting	2.45	3.3	2.2	2.6
6a	Enjoyment when acting scenes from plays	4.1	3.8	4.0	4.0
6b	Enjoyment when acting improvisations	4.2	4.2	4.0	4.1
7	Evaluation of own performance	3.6[d]	3.2	4.0	3.8

[a] The data in Table 8.2 correspond to the items on Part II of the questionnaire.

[b] The figures in the first section are based on the following Likert scale:

1	2	3	4	5
Overall I was displeased with my ability. I felt very frustrated				Overall I was pleased with my ability. I felt I was able to express myself with ease.

[c] The figures in the second section are based on the following Likert scale:

1	2	3	4	5
not at all	a little	somewhat	quite	very much

[d] The figures in the third section are based on the following Likert scale:

1	2	3	4	5
I didn't like it. It was worse than I thought it would be.		about average		I liked it very much. It was better than I thought it would be.

TABLE 8.3 Desire to Participate in More Dramatic Activities[a]

Item on questionnaire Part III	Dramatic activity	Class A % (n = 13)		Class B % (n = 6)		Class C % (n = 5)		Overall % (N = 24)	
		Yes	No	Yes	No	Yes	No	Yes	No
1a	Scenes from plays (with script)	92	8	50	50	80	20	79	21
1b	Improvisations (without script)	92	8	83	17	100	0	92	8

[a]The data in Table 8.3 correspond to the items on Part III of the questionnaire.

6a and 6b (Table 8.2) indicate that students enjoyed both activities "quite a bit." (Scenes = 4.0; improvisations = 4.1.) Seventy-nine percent expressed the desire to participate in more scenes and 92 percent indicated that they would like to do more improvisations (Table 8.3).

In explaining why they would or would not like to participate in more dramatic activities (Part III), students commented on the following: the enjoyment or "fun" of drama; ways in which drama had helped them achieve the objectives of the course they were taking, e.g., improved pronunciation and intonation; learning more about American culture and becoming acquainted with works of American writers. Some students commented on psychological issues, such as drama helped them "loosen up," and improvisations helped them express themselves and their feelings. A number commented on how drama helped them feel more confident when speaking in front of a group. There were four negative comments, three of which referred to the scripted scenes from plays. Only one student was negative about drama in general, explaining, "I just don't like to act."

Self-Esteem

As Table 8.2 indicates (items 1 and 7), the students' post-evaluation of their performance (3.8) was higher than their recollection of how they felt they had expressed themselves in English at the time (3.3). This suggests that while their feelings about their ability at the time of performance had been mildly positive, the postviewing raised their self-esteem. It might explain why overall the students felt that scenes (4.0) and especially improvisations (4.25) had been quite useful in helping

them gain self-confidence in speaking English (Table 8.1, items lc and 2c).

Empathy

Empathy was evaluated in terms of the degree of difficulty students experienced in understanding and identifying with the characters they portrayed. As Table 8.2 reveals (items 2 and 4), they experienced very little difficulty in understanding their characters (1.7) and only slightly more difficulty in identifying with them (2.4).

Sensitivity to Rejection

Feelings of nervousness and embarrassment were the criteria used for determining sensitivity to rejection. The overall responses reported in Table 8.2 (items 3 and 5) indicate that the students had been slightly less than "somewhat" nervous (2.6) and embarrassed (2.6). In spite of this moderate degree of uneasiness, their overall responses to how useful scenes and improvisations had been in helping them become less inhibited or less embarrassed when speaking in front of a group (Table 8.1, items 1d and 2d) were 4.1 and 4.33, respectively.

Spontaneity

None of the items specifically evaluated spontaneity. However, in response to the open-ended questions which asked if participating in scenes from plays and improvisations had helped students communicate more effectively in any other way (Part I, 1g and 2e), five students commented either that drama had helped them respond "off the top of their heads" or that it had helped them respond more quickly to unexpected questions and/or situations.

Summary of Student Responses

Although no generalizations may be derived from the results of this informal survey, several impressionistic observations can be made. The students did feel that dramatic activities had helped them gain self-confidence in speaking English and become less embarrassed when speaking in front of a group. Along with improving intonation and expression (the instructors' primary objective for using drama), these two areas were perceived by the students as being the greatest benefits of participating in drama. They also felt that drama had helped them develop spontaneity in English. The students had felt positive about their ability to express themselves in English during the improvisations, and even more positive after seeing themselves on videotape. They had enjoyed participating in these activities and were motivated to participate in more. No comments can be made about a causal relationship between drama and empathy, but it can at least be said that the students did not appear to have any problems understanding, identifying with, or stepping into the roles of the characters.

The Teacher Questionnaire

The teacher questionnaire was open-ended, with no reference whatsoever to the psychological factors under study. This was to guarantee that any comments about the psychological effects of drama would be completely spontaneous. The questions were:

1. What were your specific objectives for using dramatic activities in your class? What did you hope to accomplish?
2. Why did you choose drama to meet these objectives, or what was it particularly about drama/role playing that lent itself to meeting these objectives?
3. Which, if any, of these objectives were met? Please comment on why you think they were successful.

The following discussion is a synthesis of the teachers' observations. The instructors are referred to as T-A, teacher of class A, the university course in oral communication; T-B, teacher of class B, the university extension course in oral communica-

tion; and T-C, teacher of class C, the university extension course in pronunciation. (*Note:* The author was the instructor of class A and felt it inappropriate to respond to her own questionnaire. Therefore, the instructor who had taught the university section of the same course the previous quarter, and used the same dramatic activities with her students, responded instead. The author's comments are included separately at the end of the discussion.)

T-B and T-C found that drama relaxed their students. T-A commented, "I do think the use of drama early in the term helped to lessen the nervousness the students felt about speaking in English in front of a group." She also discovered that drama appeared to create a safe classroom environment. "The students benefited from the activities almost as they would if they were interacting with Americans, but they were not under pressure to be themselves." T-B commented that drama enhanced the class atmosphere and relaxed the students' anxiety about speaking in front of each other and making oral presentations. She added that "the scenes from plays provided structure where students could 'loosen up' [their words]. We progressed from this to role-play."

T-C found drama to be a really welcome relief from the normal classroom activity, and to be highly motivating: "Affectively the implementation of drama in the classroom was very positive, in that not only the more outgoing students participated, but also (and surprisingly very willingly) the normally very passive ones." She also noted that dramatic activities helped her students lose their normal inhibitions and enabled them to assume personalities very much in contrast to their own. Another reference to empathy was made by T-B, who explained that drama facilitates adoption of a different identity.

The author's own experience with class A strongly supports the observations of these students and teachers. The students seemed to undergo a transformation when they "stepped out" of the classroom into an imaginary setting and situation, especially the shy students who normally spoke only when called upon—and then in a quiet and hesitant voice. They became more extroverted, initiating as well as responding to dialogue. Role playing seemed to stimulate them to activate their passive competence of the language. The more verbal and extroverted students were also transformed. Their speech became more fluent, and their intonation and inflection more nativelike, particularly during improvisations.

CONCLUSION

This paper has taken a speculative and theoretical approach to drama in L2 learning, with the intent of laying the groundwork and providing the inspiration for further investigation into the area. Its purpose was to present the hypothesis that drama positively affects L2 learning by encouraging the operation of certain psychological factors which facilitate oral communication, i.e., heightened self-esteem, motivation, and spontaneity; increased capacity for empathy; lowered sensitivity to rejection. This hypothesis was based upon logic, analogy, experience, and intuition. It was founded upon a literature review and was informally tested via the student/teacher questionnaire.

If the responses to the questionnaire can be taken as valid indicators, there may be some justification for the hypothesis, and drama in L2 learning is a promising area for further research. This study suggests several research possibilities. One would be a formal test of the hypothesis, i.e., to examine the psychological factors individually to determine if they are positively correlated with drama and if drama acts as a causal variable in fostering them in the participant. Related research would include further investigation into the relationship between each of the psychological factors and L2 acquisition. Another project would be to test the assumption behind the hypothesis: that dramatic activities in the ESL/foreign language classroom improve oral communication skills. Along these lines, Wesche (1977) has already found that role play correlates highly with a number of learning variables.

It is hoped that these suggestions will stimulate further research and that this theoretical study will lead to additional investigations of drama in second language learning from a psycholinguistic perspective.

APPENDIX 8.1

Student Questionnaire—Evaluation of Dramatic Activities

Your reactions to the dramatic activities that you participated in this quarter would be very much appreciated. Please answer as thoughtfully and accurately as possible.

PART I: Circle the number that most closely reflects your opinion.

1. SCENES FROM PLAYS (using script)
   How useful was acting out a scene from a play for you in each of the following areas?

		Not useful	A little useful	Somewhat useful	Quite useful	Very useful
D[a]	a) Improving pronunciation	1	2	3	4	5
D	b) Improving intonation and expression	1	2	3	4	5
Self-esteem	c) Gaining self-confidence in speaking English	1	2	3	4	5
Sensitivity to rejection	d) Becoming less inhibited, or less embarrassed when speaking in front of a group	1	2	3	4	5
D	e) Increasing/enriching your vocabulary	1	2	3	4	5
D	f) Learning more about American culture	1	2	3	4	5
	g) Did acting out scenes help you communicate more effectively in any other way? Please explain.					

2. IMPROVISATIONS BASED ON SCENES FROM PLAYS (without script)

How useful was participating in an improvisation for you in each of the following areas?

		Not useful	A little useful	Somewhat useful	Quite useful	Very useful
D	a) Improving pronunciation	1	2	3	4	5
D	b) Improving intonation and expression	1	2	3	4	5
Self-esteem	c) Gaining self-confidence in speaking English	1	2	3	4	5
Sensitivity to rejection	d) Becoming less inhibited, or less embarrassed when speaking in front of a group	1	2	3	4	5
D	e) Did it help you communicate more effectively in any other way? Please explain.					

PART II

Self-esteem

1. Think back to when you were performing the improvisations, and try to remember how you felt about your ability to express yourself in English at that time.

Overall I was displeased with my ability. I felt very frustrated.			Overall I was pleased with my ability. I felt I was able to express myself with ease.	
1	2	3	4	5

Empathy

2. How difficult did you find it to understand the character you were playing?

	Not at all difficult	A little	Somewhat	Quite	Very difficult
	1	2	3	4	5

Sensitivity to rejection

3. How nervous did you feel when participating in dramatic activities?

	Not at all nervous	A little	Somewhat	Quite	Very nervous
	1	2	3	4	5

Empathy

4. How difficult did you find it to identify with, or step into the role of the character you were playing

	Not at all difficult	A little	Somewhat	Quite	Very difficult
	1	2	3	4	5

Sensitivity to rejection

5. How embarrassed did you feel when acting in front of the class?

	Not at all	A little	Somewhat	Quite a bit	Very much
	1	2	3	4	5

Motivation

6. How much did you enjoy participating in the following activities?

	Not at all	A little	Somewhat	Quite a bit	Very much
a. scenes from plays (with script)	1	2	3	4	5
b. improvisation (without script)	1	2	3	4	5

Self-esteem

7. How did you evaluate your own performance?

I didn't like it. It was worse than I thought it would be.		About average	I liked it very much. It was better than I thought it would be	
1	2	3	4	5

PART III

1. Would you like to participate in more dramatic activities?
   a. scenes from plays (with script)   YES   NO
   b. improvisations (without script)   YES   NO
2. Why or why not? (Please use back of sheet to explain your answer, and to add any other comments you may have about the dramatic activities you participated in this quarter.)

---

[a]D = distractor items

NOTES

1 I wish to gratefully acknowledge the valuable and constructive comments and suggestions of Frances Hinofotis and John Schumann. I would also like to thank Donna Brinton and Meredith Pike for their contributions to the empirical study.

DISCUSSION QUESTIONS

1. How does Guiora's "ego permeability" idea figure in drama? Why does drama, assuming that Stern, Schumann, Guiora, and others are correct, have the effect of lowering inhibitions and the affective filter?

2. Besides the motivating aspect of preparing for a part in a drama or a role play, how can acting help students acquire the target language?

3. Is drama "the matrix of all language activities" (p. 73)? Consider a difficult job interview, checking into a motel where the cockroaches shake the building when they walk, taking out the garbage or cleaning a latrine, handing in an assignment to a teacher you want to impress, saying hello to a special person. . . .

4. What do you make of the fact that 79% of Stern's respondents say they are willing to participate in additional contrived scenes while 92% want to do more improvisations?

PART 2

IMMERSION AND ELEMENTARY SCHOOL LANGUAGE INSTRUCTION

What, after all, is immersion? In a recent article, Genesee, Holobow, Lambert, and Chartrand (1989) explain:[1]

In 1965, a group of English-speaking parents, educators, and researchers from a suburb of Montreal instituted a new approach to second language teaching in the public school system (Lambert & Tucker, 1972). This approach, called immersion, entailed the use of the second language (French in this case) as the medium of regular curriculum instruction. The students, none of whom spoke French upon entry to school, received instruction in their core subjects (e.g., math, science) from teachers who were native French speakers. The rationale was that the second language would be acquired incidentally as part of the students' general cognitive, academic, and social development in school. In other words, the students would acquire the target language in order to get on with their education. This approach was consistent with theories of first language development which argue that children acquire their first language, without direct or systematic tuition, in the context of significant and meaningful communication with mature speakers of the language (Genesee, 1984).

The immersion approach differs from traditional second language teaching alternatives in that the latter focus on direct language instruction so that classroom activities are taken up with learning vocabulary lists, verb forms, and grammar rules (Richards & Rodgers, 1986). There is an emphasis on correct language usage in the absence of real communication and, in fact, such courses often leave students with knowledge of the grammar of the language but with little ability to communicate in it. Their children's inability to communicate in French outside the classroom prompted the Montreal parents to seek alternative strategies to teach French (Lambert & Tucker, 1972). Interestingly, recent trends in second and foreign language teaching emphasize "integrated" or "content-based" second language approaches which reflect the same underlying rationale as immersion although on a more limited scale (see Snow, Met, & Genesee, 1989).

Since its inception in Quebec some 25 years ago, a variety of immersion programs have been developed (Genesee, 1987). They vary primarily in terms of the

---

1 The following quotation is used by permission of the authors cited and the *Modern Language Journal.*

starting point; that is, the grades in which the target language is used as the principal medium of communication (early, delayed, and late alternatives) and in terms of the amount of time devoted to the target language for regular curriculum instruction (total and partial immersion). Immersion is also now available in a variety of languages including French, Mohawk, Ukrainian, Hebrew, Spanish, and Chinese. There are even programs in which two second languages are used for curriculum instruction (Genesee & Lambert, 1983). Immersion programs are now offered in many different countries (see Genesee, 1981, for some examples in the U.S.A.).

Evaluations of these alternatives attest to the effectiveness of immersion in its various forms (Genesee, 1987). The effectiveness of immersion has been attributed to both its instructional features (Genesee, 1984) and to the fact that the participating students are members of majority ethnolinguistic groups. Lambert has argued that immersion programs are an additive bilingual education experience for majority language children because they provide such children with opportunities to acquire an additional language at no expense to the home language and culture. Thus, English-speaking children in North America are able to participate successfully in immersion programs because their English-language skills and their "Anglo" identity are not threatened by immersion in a second language and culture. One would expect that immersion programs in European nations would be equally successful (e.g., French students in German or Japanese immersion; Spanish children in English, Catalán, or Arabic immersion). At the same time, researchers have cautioned against the simple application of immersion in a second language for the education of minority language children; for example, Spanish-speaking American students in all-English immersion, or Turkish-speaking German students in all-German immersion (Genesee, 1984; Lambert, 1980). In this case, second language acquisition might pose a threat to the students' home language and culture and thereby impede both their linguistic and academic development—a situation Lambert has referred to as "subtractive bilingualism" (pp. 250-251).

Another term for the approaches that are apt to lead to "subtractive bilingualism" is *submersion*. No professional language teacher or researcher, as Krashen points out in Chapter 9, recommends *that* kind of "immersion." However, there are a surprising diversity of immersion-type approaches that get good results consistently and for reasons that are becoming increasingly well understood (Campbell, Gray, Rhodes, & Snow, 1985). This section offers a variety of choices for teachers who want to explore those approaches. It begins by examining elementary programs and works upward toward secondary and post-secondary education.

In his dissertation, Dimitri Katsareas (1993) has shown that immersion in American elementary schools is not as new as it might have seemed to be back in the mid-1960s. In fact, German-English bilingual schools were well known in the U.S. from the middle of the 19th century until about World War I (also see Schlossman, 1983, and Toth, 1990). At about that time, they disappeared, not to re-emerge with any vitality in the U.S. until about the time of the Bilingual Education Act of 1971. In Chapter 9 Krashen reviews the research on U.S. bilingual education programs since then. He shows that, when they are done right, according to what is known of language acquisition, they work well. And, even when they are not done according to any particularly well-developed plan, bilingual programs do not seem to do any harm. They do not work any less well than traditional monolingual programs. At any rate, because of the changing demographic picture in the U.S. and around the world, it is certain that much greater attention will be afforded all sorts of bilingual and immersion-type programs in the twenty-first century. The reason is explained succinctly by Spencer Kagan (1990: Chapter 2, p. 7):

> Our population is shifting in three ways: First, an increasing percentage of students are living in urban centers. Second, racial diversity is increasing. Third, in many key cities and states, we are about to hear loud and clear from a "new majority." . . . The rate of urbanization, world-wide is increasing logarithmically. In 1800 only 2.4% of the world lived in urban centers; by 1900 the number was about 10%. By 1950 the figure was 25% . . . .

In fact, by 1990 in California (the most populous state in the U.S.), the percentage of Anglo students had already slipped beneath the 50% mark. Ethnic minorities had already become the majority. A large number of these minority children, who are now in our schools in ever-increasing numbers, also have as their primary language some system other than English. They are apt to be classed, in the new alphabet soup, as LEPs (students of "limited English proficiency").

Scarcella (1990) has recommended that we get to know our minority language populations and conserve our minority language resources (also see Cummins, 1986). Not only is it important to empower minority students, as Scarcella has emphasized along with Cummins and others, by giving them full access to the majority language system and all its benefits, but wouldn't every schoolchild be enriched if "being educated" (especially in the U.S.) would come to mean "knowing more than one language"? For one thing, it would help to rid the U.S. of the epidemic of what I call "monoglottosis"—a terminal case of monolingualism (also see Simon, 1980, *The Tongue-Tied American*). It's an insidious, debilitating disease that captures its victims so completely that they remain altogether unaware of their handicapped condition. To those afflicted, the symptoms are imperceptible. They are captured in a monolingual prison whose walls are invisible to them but thick enough to keep the worlds of other peoples out of view.

Here I am inevitably reminded of the eloquent statement of my colleagues Sherman and Phyllis Wilcox in their book *Learning to See* (1991: 1-2) where they recommend in the continuation of their title, *American Sign Language as a Second Language*. In their Preface they say:

> Foreign language teachers often tell us that the goal of teaching a second language is to propel students beyond the limits of their own world, to encourage them to see through the language and culture of another people (Bugos, 1980). Such a goal is entirely appropriate for teachers of American Sign Language (ASL). In the best language classrooms, students are treated to an extended voyage into a new and exciting world. They learn to talk about the familiar in unfamiliar ways, to consider values that may seem questionable.
>
> ASL students, too, are exposed to a different world. They are learning a new language, one that is unlike any they are likely to have experienced before. ASL is, in every sense of the word, a foreign language. ASL students are also encouraged to view the world though the eyes of a different culture. The Deaf way of looking at the world is . . . a foreign culture to second language students . . . .
>
> Entry into a foreign land is never easy. The first step must be to learn the language and culture of the people who live there. For students who wish to visit the world of Deaf people, ASL classes are the door—learning to see is the key.

In their crusade to see ASL accepted as a basis for fulfilling the foreign language requirement in U.S. schools, the Wilcoxes have been joined by people like

Victoria Fromkin (1988), Harlan Lane (1984, 1988), and others (see Wilcox, 1988). A greater awareness of the important languages of the Deaf world can, as Marianne Erickson (1992: 14) puts it, "allow us, finally, to see the voices of a long-silent minority—who hear with their eyes and write with their heart."

In the final analysis, why shouldn't all school children be guaranteed a high degree of proficiency in at least two languages? Surely Deaf children ought to be provided with the opportunity not only to extend and develop fully their skills in ASL (or outside the U.S., in the Deaf norm for their situation), but they also ought to be enabled to acquire Signed English, which is an entirely different system (or some other signed variant of a spoken language) that will be of great use to them. According to Andrade, Kretschmer, and Kretschmer (Chapter 10), all school children are capable of acquiring a high degree of proficiency in more than one language. In accord with findings from Canadian-style immersion programs (Bruck, 1982, 1987; Genesee, 1992), Andrade and the Kretschmers contend that even children traditionally diagnosed as "language disordered" or "learning disabled" can benefit from bilingual programming. More reasons why this is so are given by the Damicos (Chapter 29) in Part 5.

Relative to the goal of enabling all our children to become bilingual, Chapter 11, by Jane Tucker Mitchell and Mary Lynn Redmond, is pertinent and encouraging. It is interesting that a southern state, North Carolina, has taken the lead in mandating a minimum of six years (kindergarten through grade five) of foreign language education for all children. In addition, the plan, adopted in 1985, also provides the option to all students who choose to do so of continuing work in their second language through grade 12. Chapter 12, by Helena Curtain, goes a long way toward showing how methods that work can be weaved into a tapestry of curricular alternatives for the elementary school. Her thoughts take us all the way from the developing phases of listening comprehension to literacy in the target language.

CHAPTER 9

Bilingual Education Works

Stephen D. Krashen

EDITOR'S INTRODUCTION

*D*oes study of subject matter and the acquisition of literacy in the child's primary language, when it is not English, retard the later acquisition of English? The research is reviewed here by Krashen. The answer is clear. Growth in the primary language is not a threat to subsequent acquisition of English. In fact, it appears that there are some definite advantages to be had by promoting development in the child's strongest language. But, of course, the term bilingual suggests proficiency in at least two languages. Furthermore, empowerment in any sociopolitical context generally requires access to the main language (or languages) of that context. Therefore, in the U.S., bilingual programs that work inevitably promote (rather than discourage) the acquisition of English. What may come as a surprise to the critics of bilingual programming is that it can greatly enrich majority language children as well as minority children. Krashen's readable review of the research prepares the ground for the argument in Chapter 10 (Andrade et al.) suggesting that all our children ought to have the privilege of knowing at least two languages. Bilingualism, rather than invoking fear or mistrust, ought to engender hope and respect across cultures. The aim of bilingualism for the twenty-first century, or preferably multilingualism for the majority of our schoolchildren, is an objective much to be preferred over the prevailing monolingualism of the United States in the twentieth century.

THE RESEARCH SUPPORTING BILINGUAL EDUCATION

The core of the case for bilingual education is that the principles underlying successful bilingual education are the same principles that underlie successful language acquisition in general. These principles are:

1. We acquire a second language by understanding messages, by obtaining comprehensible input.

2. Background knowledge can help make second language input more comprehensible, and can thus assist in the acquisition of the second language.

3. The development of literacy occurs in the same way as second language acquisition does. As Goodman (1982) and Smith (1982) have put it, "we learn to read by reading," by making sense of what is on the page. In turn, reading is the major source of our competence in vocabulary, spelling, writing style, and grammar. (For research evidence supporting these principles, see Goodman, 1982; Smith, 1982; Krashen, 1985a, 1985b, 1989a.)

The Importance of the First Language

One of the most salient features of a bilingual education program is the use of the first language as the medium of instruction. The first language can help in the following ways:

1. It supplies background knowledge, which can make English input more comprehensible.

2. It enhances the development of basic literacy. This is a two-step argument:

   a. If we, in fact, learn to read by reading, it will be much easier to learn to read in a language one already knows, since written material in that language will be more comprehensible.

   b. Once you can read, you can read. This ability transfers to other languages that may be acquired.

3. It helps in what we call "advanced literacy"—the ability to use language, oral and written, to solve problems. If students understand the composing process in one language, for example, they will be able to utilize it in other languages they acquire. (For supporting data and detail, see Cummins, 1981; Krashen, 1985a, 1985b, 1990.)

There are other ways the first language can help. Research evidence suggests that advanced first language development has cognitive advantages (see, e.g., Hakuta, 1986), practical advantages (Simon, 1980), and promotes a healthy sense of biculturalism (Cummins, 1981).

Explaining Bilingual Education: "The Paris Argument"

It is not easy to explain the theory underlying bilingual education to the public. I have had some success, however, with the following explanation, which I call "The Paris Argument." Pretend that you have just received, and accepted, an attractive job offer in Paris. Your French, however, is limited (you had two years of French in high school and one semester in college, and it was quite a while ago). Before your departure, the company that is hiring you will send you the following information, in English: What to do when you arrive in Paris, how to get to your hotel, where and how to find a place to live, where to shop, what kinds of schools are available for your children, how French companies function (how people dress in the office, what time work starts and ends, etc.), and specific information about the functioning of the company and your responsibilities.

It would be very useful to get this information right away in English, rather than getting it gradually, as you acquire French. If you get it right away, the world around you will be much more comprehensible, and you will thus acquire French more quickly.

Anyone who agrees with this, in my opinion, agrees with the philosophy underlying bilingual education.

CRITICISMS OF BILINGUAL EDUCATION

The arguments most often heard against bilingual education are: (1) it doesn't work— research on bilingual programs is inconsistent and contradictory, and (2) there is a better option—immersion.

There is a widespread perception that research shows bilingual education is a failure and that students in bilingual education programs do not acquire proficiency in English. What are the facts?

Comparing Bilingual Education and All-English Medium Programs

First, when "unexamined" bilingual programs are compared to "submersion" programs (programs using English as the medium of instruction with no special modification for meeting the linguistic needs of limited English proficient (LEP) students), or submersion with pullout English as a Second Language (where LEP students are separated from English proficient students for some part of the school day in order to receive English as a Second Language [ESL] instruction), there is typically no difference in terms of English language achievement. (An "unexamined" program is simply one that investigators have labeled "bilingual" without providing additional detail about how the program was organized. Such programs may or may not be fully consistent with the principles discussed earlier.)

Unfortunately, the results of these comparisons have been interpreted as negative, as showing that bilingual education doesn't work. Some of the problem is how the results are expressed. Rossell and Ross (1986), for example, reported the following results for English language achievement when transitional bilingual education and submersion programs are compared:

	Number of Studies
Transitional bilingual education better	8
No difference	14
Submersion better	6

Rossell and Ross concluded that "seventy-one percent of the studies show transitional bilingual education (TBE) programs to be no different or worse" than submersion (p. 399). This is, of course, true—in 20 out of 28 cases, TBE is no better or worse. But one could also conclude that TBE is just as good, if not better, than submersion programs 79 percent of the time (22 out of 28 cases).

Several scholars have pointed out that when bilingual education is shown to be just as effective as all-English programs, this is a remarkable result since it means that the children have acquired just as much English with significantly less exposure to English. This confirms the underlying theory of bilingual education. Some of the critics—but not all—have missed this point entirely (see Rossell and Ross, 1986: 407, for this discussion).

A recent study (Rossell, 1990) merits detailed discussion because of the importance attached to its conclusions in the popular press. Rossell compared a program labeled bilingual education and a pull-out ESL program in the Berkeley (California) Unified School District. No description of Berkeley's bilingual education program was provided, other than the fact that it was labeled "bilingual education" and that instruction was in Spanish 30 to 50 percent of the time. Rossell concluded, after a series of regression analyses, that there was no difference between the two programs. Interestingly, there is evidence of a slight superiority for bilingual education. In her Table 1 (IDEA Proficiency Test scores for students in grades K-12), the regression coefficient for participation in bilingual education is positive and reaches the .10 level for a one-tailed test (Rossell would probably call for a two-tailed test here, however).

In another analysis Rossell compared California Test of Basic Skills (CTBS) scores for bilingual and ESL pull-out students after "reclassification." Rossell concluded that these data show no difference between the two groups. For each subtest of the CTBS, however, the regression coefficient for participation in bilingual education was positive, and in the case of math, it reached the .05 level for a two-tailed test, which Rossell did not indicate.

Rossell also compared Berkeley LEP children's performance on California Assessment for Progress (CAP) tests to performance by LEP children in two districts considered to have "exemplary" bilingual programs, Fremont and San Jose (Krashen & Biber, 1988). Rossell reported no significant difference among the children in the three districts in reading, and reported that the Berkeley students excelled in math.

There are several problems with this conclusion. First, this analysis does not compare gain scores nor does it show how rapidly children reach norms. It considers LEP children as a group. This comparison is only valid if, in fact, LEP children in all three districts entered their respective systems at the same level of competence, and if all three districts used similar criteria for exiting children. This may not be the case. According to Rossell's analysis of reclassified children in Berkeley, many children scored very well on CTBS long before they were exited—in CTBS Reading, for example, children in ESL pull-out scored at the 33rd percentile two years before reclassification and at the 54th percentile one year before, while children in bilingual education who were reclassified scored at the 35th percentile two years before reclassification and near the 60th percentile one year before. CTBS Language data are similar, and scores in CTBS Math are even higher, with LEP children in Berkeley scoring above the 50th percentile four years before reclassification. Thus, Berkeley scores may look higher because some high-scoring children were retained in these programs longer.

Even if the analysis were a valid one—if children in all three districts entered at the same level and all three districts had equal reclassification criteria—Rossell's results would not necessarily reflect the quality of bilingual education in the Berkeley district. The comparison districts were chosen because their *bilingual* programs were exemplary. Yet the cross-district comparison performed by Rossell is of *all* LEP children in each district, taken as a group. A minority of the children in the sample were in bilingual education. According to Rossell's data, only 31 percent of the

108 schools studied had a bilingual education program (33 schools). Moreover, it is quite likely that not all of the LEP children in these 33 schools were in the bilingual program. (Interestingly, according to Rossell's analysis, schools that had bilingual education reported slightly higher CAP scores; the regression coefficient, however, was not significant.)

Several studies have shown that bilingual education programs can be as effective as all English programs. For example, Willig (1985) performed a meta-analysis on bilingual education evaluations originally studied by Baker and de Kanter (1983), and concluded that there was a modest overall positive effect for bilingual education, despite the fact that many of the studies (65 percent) were short-term, lasting one year or less. Willig also found that bilingual education looked better when the research designs used in the studies were better. Here are some examples:

■ When the comparison group had elements of bilingual education, there was no difference. But when the comparison group did not have elements of bilingual education, the bilingual group was superior.

■ When the bilingual program was "unstable" (frequent teacher turnover, disorganization), the comparison group was better. When the bilingual group was stable, it was superior.

■ When the comparison group contained graduates of bilingual education, there was no difference. When the comparison group did not contain graduates of bilingual education the bilingual group was better. As Crawford (1989) put it, Willig showed that on a level playing field, bilingual education could outscore the competition.

Recent research shows that when bilingual programs are set up correctly, they work very well. In our survey of successful programs in California (Krashen & Biber, 1988), we found that students in well-designed bilingual programs consistently outperformed comparison students, and did very well compared to local and national norms, often reaching national norms between grades three to six. According to the view of language acquisition presented earlier in this paper, we defined a "well-designed" program as one that had the following characteristics:

1. Comprehensible input in English, in the form of high quality ESL classes, and sheltered subject matter teaching (comprehensible subject matter teaching in the second language; see below).

2. Subject matter teaching in the first language, without translation. This provides background knowledge that will make English input more comprehensible.

3. Literacy development in the first language, which will transfer to the second language.

Our report has been criticized. Imhoff (1990) maintains that the programs in Krashen and Biber (1988) worked because they were in "exemplary schools that are well-funded, staffed by highly trained and dedicated teachers, and composed of small classes of selected students" (p. 52). To my knowledge, not all the schools described in our monograph were well-funded. The teachers did receive some extra in-service training in current theory and methodology, but to say that they were more dedicated is not only unfounded but is also an insult to teachers in the comparison groups. Nearly all of the students in the programs were unselected; there is no reason to suspect they were different than students in comparison groups, and there is no reason to suspect differences in class size.

Rossell has also criticized Krashen and Biber (1988), pointing out that one of the districts we studied, Fremont, took other positive action for LEP children in their bilingual program in addition to bilingual education (preschool, extra English reading, more parental involvement). While this could mean that these additional efforts were responsible for the Fremont children's outstanding performance, it is certainly not counter evidence to the hypothesis that bilingual education is effective, a hypothesis that has a great deal of additional supporting evidence.

Porter (1990a, 1990b), who repeatedly insists that bilingual education "just doesn't work" (Porter, 1990: 223), presents several kinds of arguments. In some cases, she is simply anti-bad-bilingual-education, attacking practices that many supporters of bilingual education would agree are questionable. These include delaying exposure to written English until students reach grade level in Spanish (Porter, 1990: 22), and programs in which teachers are encouraged to code-switch in class (Porter, 1990a: 31).

Other attacks are simply unfounded and are not supported by the data she presents. Porter claims, for example, that in Boston "several hundred" bilingual education students had not learned enough English to be exited by grade seven (Porter, 1990a: 60). Porter does not tell us, however, whether this is a small or large percentage of the total number of students served (if it is a small percentage, the data would indicate that the program was successful), what kind of bilingual education was used, or what the characteristics of these students were.

Another example is her report that only 4,000 out of 7,000 applicants passed an "English-language aptitude test" given by New York's Consolidated Edison company in 1988. None of those who passed, according to Porter, was a graduate of New York City's bilingual education program (Porter, 1990b: 24). Without more details, however, it is impossible to draw any conclusions from such a statement. Porter does not tell us, for example, how many of those who took the test were ever limited English proficient students or how many had even had bilingual education.

The Immersion Argument

Another popular argument against bilingual education is the claim that there is a better way—immersion. Imhoff (1990) supports this view: "The language teaching method that is generally the fastest, most efficient, and most effective is the Berlitz or immersion method. . ." (p. 50). Imhoff does not present evidence supporting his view, but could have cited Rossell and Ross (1986), who claim that immersion students outperformed students in bilingual education in English language proficiency in six out of seven studies. Before reviewing this claim we need to define the term *immersion*. There are, to my knowledge, at least four definitions:

1. *Submersion,* or "sink or swim." There is no support among language education professionals for submersion for LEP children today.
2. *Canadian-style immersion* (CSI). As is well-known, CSI is a program in which middle class children receive much of their subject matter

instruction through a second language. Efforts are made to make sure the language they hear is comprehensible. Children in these programs learn subject matter successfully, and acquire a great deal of the second language.

Consideration of the principles of bilingual education presented earlier leads to the conclusion that CSI is similar, if not identical, to bilingual education. Children in CSI receive comprehensible input in the second language and develop literacy and subject matter knowledge in their first language, both outside of school and in school. As noted earlier, children in CSI are typically middle class, and do a considerable amount of reading in English outside of school (suggested by Cummins, 1977 and confirmed by Eagon & Cashion, 1988). Even in early total immersion programs, a great deal of the curriculum is in English, with English language arts introduced around grade two. By grade six, half the curriculum of early total immersion is in English. Most important, the goal of CSI is bilingualism, not the replacement of one language with another.

3. *Sheltered subject matter teaching.* Sheltered subject matter teaching was inspired by the success of CSI. It is subject matter teaching done in a second language but made comprehensible. Research at the university level has confirmed that students in sheltered subject matter classes acquire impressive amounts of the second language and learn subject matter as well (Edwards, Wesche, Krashen, Clément, & Kruidenier, 1984; Lafayette, & Buscaglia, 1985; Hauptman, Wesche, & Ready, 1988; Sternfeld, Chapter 18).

Sheltered subject matter teaching is not a competitor to instruction delivered in the first language, but makes its contribution in a different way. As indicated earlier, both sheltered subject matter teaching and ESL provide comprehensible input directly, while teaching in the first language makes an indirect but powerful contribution by providing background knowledge and literacy.

Porter (1990a) approves of sheltered subject matter teaching ("content-based language teaching"), but feels that it cannot be used in bilingual programs that require subjects to be taught in their native language for several years (p. 125). Subject matter instruction and sheltered subject matter teaching can be sensibly combined, however. In what has been called the "Eastman Plan" (Krashen, 1985a, 1985b; Krashen & Biber, 1988), beginning limited English proficient students study core subject matter subjects in the primary language. When the students reach the intermediate level, subjects such as math and science are given as sheltered subject matter in English, since these subjects do not require as high a level of English language proficiency as social studies or language arts. Subjects requiring more abstract use of language are still taught in the first language at this stage, which will provide additional subject matter knowledge and literacy development.

Children with more competence in academic English study math and science in the mainstream. At this stage, social studies is taught in English using sheltered techniques, with continuing literacy development in the first language. Eventually, all core subjects are taught in English. An example of such a plan is presented in Table 9.1.

Such a plan provides comprehensible instruction at every step. It is superior to an all-English program, because it provides continuing development in the first language, which means continuous growth in subject matter knowledge and literacy development. It is better than a program that forces a child to jump from the first language class directly to the mainstream; with the sheltered class as a transition, the child will acquire a substantial amount of the English academic language needed.

Note that according to the plan in Table 9.1, children continue on to do advanced study in their first language—social studies, language arts, or related topics (enrichment). The advantages of advanced first language development were listed earlier. This part of the program can take the place of the foreign language study option for the former LEP student.

4. *Structured immersion.* Also inspired by the success of CSI, structured immersion (SI) is similar to sheltered subject matter teaching in some ways, but differs in other ways. As described by Gersten and Woodward (1985), SI has these four characteristics:

1. Comprehensible subject matter instruction to second language acquirers.
2. Use of the first language when necessary for explanation, but this is kept to a minimum.
3. Direct instruction of grammar.
4. Pre-teaching of vocabulary.

While the first two characteristics have support in the research literature, there is little evidence supporting the efficacy of direct grammar instruction (for reviews, see Krashen, 1984b; Hillocks, 1986), and pre-teaching vocabulary has not been found to be consistently effective (Mezynski, 1983).

Only a few studies of SI have been done. Gersten and Woodward (1985) report that children in SI in Uvalde (Texas) reached the 30th percentile of the reading comprehension subtest of the Metropolitan Achievement Test at the end of grade three. After leaving SI, however, they dropped to the 15th and 16th percentile in grades five and six (Becker & Gersten, 1982). While this

TABLE 9.1 Plan Combining ESL, Sheltered Subject Matter Teaching, and Instruction in the First (Home) Language

Level	Mainstream	Sheltered/ESL	First Language
Beginning	art, music, PE	ESL	all core subjects
Intermediate	art, music, PE	ESL, math, science	language arts, social studies
Advanced	art, music, PE, math, science	ESL, social studies	language arts
Mainstream	all core subjects		enrichment

performance was better than a comparison group, it is still dismal. Children at this grade level who have had proper bilingual education do much better (Krashen & Biber, 1988). (Uvalde children did somewhat better on the WRAT reading test, which emphasizes "decoding skills.")

In a second study of SI, Gersten and Woodward (1985) claimed that more LEP children in a California school district in SI performed at or above grade level than comparison children in bilingual education. There were several serious problems with this study, however. First, no details were provided about the bilingual education program. Second, the sample size was small (28 children in bilingual education, 16 in SI). If performance of just a few children had varied slightly, the results of this study would have looked very different. Third, the study only followed children until grade two.

Gersten and Woodward reported that the SI children did extremely well in a follow-up study, achieving high levels of performance (65th percentile) two years later, but only two groups of nine children each were studied, and no comparison with bilingual education was made. Similarly, SI students studied in Gersten (1985) showed very good gains over the one year they were followed, but no comparison group was used.

Effectiveness of Immersion Programs for LEP Children

We are now ready to return to the claim made by Rossell and Ross (1986) that immersion was more effective than bilingual education in English language development in six out of seven studies. As listed in Rossell and Ross's Table 1 (p. 398), the six studies in which immersion was considered superior were:

1. Gersten, 1985;
2. Peña-Hughes and Solís, 1980;
3. Barik and Swain, 1978;
4. Barik, Swain, and Nwanunobi, 1977;
5. Bruck, Lambert, and Tucker, 1977; and
6. Genesee Tucker, and Lambert, 1978.

Study 1 (Gersten, 1985) is the SI study described previously. As noted earlier, it suffers from a very small sample size, and no description

is given of the kind of "bilingual education" used for the comparison group.

Study 2 (Peña-Hughes & Solís, 1980) is unpublished, but it is discussed in several published papers. It is a comparison of two programs in McAllen, Texas. While Rossell and Ross label these "Immersion" and "bilingual education," Willig (1985,1987) classified the immersion group as bilingual education, noting that the "immersion" group had instruction in English in the morning and instruction in Spanish reading in the afternoon. In addition, the explicit goal of the immersion program was bilingualism—development of both languages.

Also, the group Rossell and Ross label "bilingual education" did not, apparently, have an ideal program. According to an article in the *Wall Street Journal* (Schorr, 1983), classes "were conducted partly in Spanish and partly in English," suggesting concurrent translation, a method shown to be ineffective (Legarreta, 1979). What apparently happened in McAllen is that children in a good bilingual program outperformed children in a poor bilingual program.

The remaining four studies are all studies of Canadian French immersion. Studies 3 and 4 (Barik & Swain, 1978; Barik, Swain, & Nwanunobi, 1977) are studies in which early total immersion is compared to partial immersion. In partial immersion, there is less teaching in French; from the beginning, some subjects are taught in English and some in French.

Rossell and Ross are not explicit concerning why these studies were included, but the idea seems to be that early total immersion is similar to all-English "immersion" for LEP Children, while partial immersion is similar to bilingual education. Since Barik et al. and Barik and Swain show that children in early total immersion acquire more French than children in partial immersion programs, "immersion," it is concluded, is better than bilingual education.

But Canadian early total immersion is not the same as an all-English immersion program for LEP children. In fact, both versions of CSI under consideration here, early total and partial immersion, are quite similar to bilingual education. As noted earlier, much of the CSI curriculum is in the first language, English, and children in these programs come to school with a great deal of literacy development in the primary language. Since children in both programs come to school so well-prepared, it is reasonable to expect that more exposure to the second language, French, will result in more acquisition of French.

Many LEP students in the United States, however, do not come to school with these advantages. An all-second language curriculum will be much less comprehensible to them, even if carefully "sheltered." While sheltering will clearly help, supplying background knowledge and literacy in the primary language is a sure way to ensure that instruction in English will be comprehensible. Rossell and Ross are clearly aware of this argument. They point out, in defense of their position, that CSI programs have worked for working class students as well as middle class students. A few reports of immersion programs for working class children have been published (e.g., Holobow, Genesee, Lambert, Gastright, & Met, 1987). While these children have done well, evaluations have so far been limited to grade two and below. Also, as Genesee (1983) notes, none of these children "can be said to come from destitute or 'hardcore' inner-city areas" (p. 30).

We thus know very little about how well working class children do in second language immersion programs and nothing about how well under-class children would do. What we do know is that children of lower socioeconomic background experience less print outside of school (e.g., Feitelson & Goldstein, 1986), and that the richness of the print environment is related to literacy development (Krashen, 1985a). We also know that these children do quite well in well-designed bilingual programs—programs that provide literacy development in the primary language.

Study 5 (Bruck, Lambert, & Tucker, 1977) compares children in total immersion (CSI) to native speakers of French, and thus has no bearing at all on the question of bilingual education versus immersion. Study 6 (Genesee, Lambert, & Tucker, 1977) is listed as an unpublished manuscript. The same authors, however, have published several reports comparing CSI to "Core French" (see, for example, Genesee, Tucker, & Lambert, 1978). Core French is simply "foreign language in the elementary school," standard foreign language instruction for about one period per day. If Rossell and Ross are indeed referring to these compar-

isons, they are, I assume, arguing once again that early total immersion is similar to an all-English "immersion" program for LEP children in the United States, and, apparently, that core French is similar to bilingual education. Once again, early total immersion is similar to bilingual education, not all-English "immersion." Also, it is not hard to see why Canadian children in early total immersion acquire more French than children in core French. Children in both programs are equally well-prepared for school, and children in early total immersion receive vastly more comprehensible input in the second language.

There is one more case that warrants discussion since it has caused some confusion. This is a report that students in the "bilingual immersion" program in El Paso, Texas, out-performed transitional bilingual education (TBE) students. According to Porter (1990a), in El Paso's bilingual immersion program, "all subjects are taught in English, although Spanish is used occasionally to reinforce a new concept" (p. 68). Porter, in fact, in a *Washington Post* article (Porter, 1990b: 24), refers to bilingual immersion as an "English-language 'immersion' program." El Paso's bilingual immersion, however, like the McAllen "immersion" program, is clearly bilingual. It contains a "native language cognitive development" component (NLCD), described by the El Paso Independent School District (1989b) as follows:

> NLCD is taught for 60 to 90 minutes per day. The objective of this component is to develop concepts, literacy, cognition, and critical thinking skills in Spanish. It is during this period that instruction and student-teacher interaction are entirely in Spanish. The more demanding content area concepts are also introduced during NLCD, particularly in first grade (p. 54).

The two programs differed not only in amount of first language use, but also in other important ways. The bilingual immersion program employed the Natural Approach for ESL, a whole language approach to language arts, and sheltered subject matter teaching, while TBE in El Paso (referred to in the El Paso reports as SB 477) used a skills-oriented approach, as described by the El Paso Independent School District (1987):

It must be understood that BIP (bilingual immersion program) is not an English version of the SB 477 instructional program. SB 477 is built on a philosophy that advocates traditional concepts of teaching language. . . . SB 477 focuses the child's attention on the details of language such as phonetic sounds and grammar rules (p. 9).

While TBE used some whole language and Natural Approach activities, the most commonly used materials in TBE were basal texts and workbooks (El Paso Independent School District, 1987: 18). According to a 1989 report, whole language and comprehensible input-based methodology had been gradually introduced into SB 477 from 1985 to 1987, but "observations indicate that the changes have not been fully implemented by SB 477 teachers" (El Paso Independent School District, 1989a: 10).

To summarize, "immersion" in El Paso combined instruction in the first language with comprehensible-input based methodology, similar to the Eastman plan described earlier in the text. The "bilingual" program (SB 477) used more instruction in the first language, but focused more on skill-building. It appears that the bilingual immersion program was more consistent with the principles of language and literacy development and first language use presented in this paper.

STRENGTHENING BILINGUAL EDUCATION BY READING IN THE PRIMARY LANGUAGE

Before concluding, I wish to add my own criticism of bilingual education. In my opinion, bilingual programs will not realize their the potential unless they do a much better job of providing a print-rich environment in the primary language. Research indicates that reading, especially free voluntary reading, is a major source of both language and literacy development, as well as knowledge. Reading in the primary language will thus provide much of the "common underlying proficiency" (Cummins, 1981) that helps ensure English language development. In addition, a reading habit in the first language will, most likely, transfer to the second language. Finally, reading contributes a great deal to advanced first language development.

The current situation is not good. The following excerpt, from informal notes made by Sandra Pucci of the University of Southern California, illustrates the point.

Ms. Pucci visited a book fair at a bilingual elementary school:

The book fair, an annual event at the school, was going on when I was there, and the kids were fairly excited, at least the ones whose parents had given them money to buy a book or two. I went in to check out the situation, and after receiving an enthusiastic "yes" as to whether they were selling books in Spanish, had a look at just what there was. The display consisted of eight cases of books of four shelves each. There was one shelf of Spanish books among them. On this shelf were 12 different titles, but only two . . . appeared to be above a third grade reading level. There were around five copies of each book. . . . At that given moment, there were about 20 kids milling about, mostly looking at the English shelves . . . the Spanish books were placed at the bottom, and were actually quite hard to get to.

Unfortunately, the situation at this school is typical. The good news is that the solution is straightforward—a print-rich environment.

CONCLUSIONS

Criticisms of bilingual education, as noted earlier, rest on two assertions: First, it has been claimed that bilingual programs don't work and that the evidence for them is inconsistent and contradictory. The research, however, is remarkably consistent. Properly organized bilingual programs do work, and even "unanalyzed" bilingual programs appear to work at least as well as all-English programs.

Second, it has been asserted that "immersion" is superior to bilingual education. This has not been demonstrated. As we have seen, there are several definitions of the term *immersion*. One of them, submersion, is rejected by all professionals as an option for LEP children. Canadian-style immersion is quite similar to bilingual education. Sheltered subject matter teaching makes a different kind of contribution to second language development and is a valuable part of bilingual education. The research support for structured immersion is, at best, mixed. Finally, much of the research claiming to show that immersion is superior to bilingual education actually consists of comparisons of different kinds of bilingual programs or comparisons of different varieties of Canadian-style immersion.

Bilingual education can be improved. But there is little doubt that bilingual education works.

DISCUSSION QUESTIONS

1. What sociocultural factors in the United States today help to promote the view that bilingual education is apt to diminish or retard the acquisition of English?

2. Suppose the child of an English-speaking visitor abroad in a foreign nation must receive schooling during the sojourn. Should that child receive instruction exclusively in Japanese, Arabic, or Thai? What factors would a parent of the child want school personnel to take into consideration?

3. What is the normal response to a situation in which repeated attempts to get an idea across are greeted with confusion or misunderstanding? What do you do? What implications follow for the schooling of minority language children? Compare "immersion" versus "submersion" contexts.

CHAPTER 10

Two Languages for All Children: Expanding to Low Achievers and the Handicapped

Carolyn Andrade, Richard R. Kretschmer, Jr., and Laura W. Kretschmer

EDITOR'S INTRODUCTION

Is it possible for all children to acquire more than one language? Can it be done in a school setting? The history of foreign language education in the U.S. would not seem to support such expectations, but Andrade, Kretschmer, and Kretschmer contend that the historical failure of foreign language teaching in America has been due largely to false assumptions and inappropriate methods of teaching. If the right sorts of adjustments are made in the methods, they contend, foreign language acquisition is a realistic possibility for all the children in our schools. What justifies this seemingly rosy optimism? A considerable amount of research, actually. There is ample evidence that even children who have traditionally been regarded as "at risk" or "handicapped" are able to benefit from appropriate foreign language instruction. The key here, as in every other approach that gets results, is enabling the students to make the connection between the unfamiliar forms of the target language and their own day-to-day experience.

From the earliest days of formal education in the United States, learning a foreign language has been considered a painful, albeit necessary, discipline which must be endured if one is to become an "educated" individual. With its rigid emphasis on learning through translation, memorization of grammar rules, and endless verb conjugation drills, generations of Americans gave up on other languages and came to believe that foreign language fluency was a realistic goal only for the intellectually gifted elite and the economically advantaged.

A slow but steadily growing awareness in this country of the importance of fluency in two languages, coupled with a greater understanding of both first and second language acquisition and a generation of children who have painlessly and successfully acquired two languages, has led educators and researchers to take a close look at the participants of elementary school foreign language programs.

The general public and foreign language professionals would agree that there is one group of children most likely to be successful language learners. Programs for these children, the academically talented or "gifted," often include a foreign language component. Perhaps since little time and energy has been devoted in the literature to average, below-average, and handicapped children, some segments of society believe that foreign language in the elementary school works counter to concept and skill development of below-average and handicapped children. For that reason, this paper will focus on the role of foreign language in the lives of children in "at risk" and "special" populations.

Part I examines the achievement and attitudes of students in a large, urban, midwestern public school district who participate in a foreign language magnet program. The thrust of Part II is the assessment and educational programming efforts with special-education students from non-English-speaking homes.

PART I. TWO LANGUAGES FOR CHILDREN IN CINCINNATI

Multiple advantages of providing young children with experiences in more than one language have often been cited. Landry (1973) reports greater divergent thinking skills and figural creativity among students in FLES programs when compared to their monolingual peers. Cultural activities related to language learning in the early elementary grades contribute to making children more tolerant of differences among people (Carpenter & Torney, 1974). Two languages enhance the cognitive development of children (Genesee, 1987; Rafferty, 1986; Hakuta & Diaz, 1984; Lambert & Tucker, 1972), as well as their listening skills (Ratte, 1968) and their self concept.

Despite these advantages, in this country most foreign language instruction still begins with teenagers. The proficiency movement notwithstanding, in most secondary schools, foreign language classes stress "learning about" language in order to pass computer-graded tests to measure students' ability to apply grammar rules, conjugate verbs, and understand the printed form of the language. Using the language for communication has not been a priority.

In the elementary school, however, communication is of primary concern because through communication children not only get information but make sense of the world around them. Especially in immersion programs, children use language as a tool to access information from "regular" subject areas such as math, music, science, social studies, and art. A focus on content within a clearly defined context aids children in acquiring the meaning of language (Cummins, 1984).

In his ten-year study of first-language acquisition, Gordon Wells (1986) demonstrates that children are simultaneously involved in learning language and gaining knowledge of the world around them. They are actively involved in both processes. Parents and care-givers are most likely to clarify, extend, and encourage conversation, thus fostering both language and cognitive development. Parents are willing to follow the direction of the child's language to understand the child's needs and wants.

In contrast, traditional foreign language teachers have a predetermined set of objectives which must be transmitted to students according to a schedule. They are less likely to allow the students to establish the direction of language or cognitive development. It is into this scenario that most foreign language education in the United States fits. Moreover, and quite unfortunately, most foreign language classes at the high-school level are filled with only the college-bound students, so teachers have relatively homogeneous groups with which to work. The homogeneity increases in upper-level language classes as it probably does in courses in other academic areas, e.g., organic chemistry or calculus, and results in a narrow range of teaching strategies and techniques.

In the elementary school, however, foreign language experiences can be incorporated into the curriculum before that "selection" process begins. All children can participate, and teachers can be expected to teach all children.

It is hard to imagine a third grade teacher saying, "Mary Lou just can't seem to learn her multiplication tables. She has had trouble with math ever since first grade. She'll probably never be any good in math, so I'm going to recommend that we pull her out of the math program. She can have an extra art class or maybe go to the gym instead." Of course, this scenario is not likely to be played out in any elementary school—public, private, or parochial. Not only will Mary Lou continue in math class for at least another five to seven years, but that third-grade teacher will use every strategy she knows and perhaps seek the aid of other teachers or paraprofessionals to ensure that Mary Lou proceeds to the next level with the skills she needs. Mathematics is considered an essential component of the elementary school curriculum. Like mathematics, other disciplines have developed strategies, techniques, methods—call them what you will—to ensure that every child learns. Why should foreign languages be any different?

Ever so slowly, professionals in business, government, and education are not only realizing the importance of learning other languages, but stating so publicly. At its annual convention in 1987, the National Association of Elementary School Principals adopted the following platform statement dealing with curriculum and instruction:

> NAESP believes that foreign language proficiency is important for students who will live in the 21st Century. NAESP therefore urges principals to consider the inclusion of instruction in a foreign language as a regular component of the school's instructional program.

The rationale for that platform statement was further explained in terms of the ethnic and linguistic diversity of our nation, the growing economic interdependence of world trading partners, and the contribution foreign language study makes to the understanding of one's own language.

The Task Force on International Education of the National Governors' Association (1989) has listed several objectives for action. Among those are "More of our students need to gain proficiency in foreign languages." To achieve that objective, the task force further recommends that individual states "offer opportunities to elementary school students for foreign language instruction beginning as early as first grade. All students should have the opportunity to learn to speak a second language in their early years."

In none of these documents do the authors suggest that foreign language education be limited to the academically talented or the "gifted" students. There is no better time than the present to focus increased attention on elementary school foreign language programs for all children.

The experience of the Cincinnatti Public Schools can be very helpful in understanding the effects, on students of varying academic abilities and from diverse socioeconomic groups, of participation in elementary school foreign language programs. From its humble beginnings with a little more than 150 students in 1974, ever growing community support and increased pressure to reduce racial isolation throughout the district have fostered the continued expansion of the Foreign Language Magnet Program. By the 1988-89 school year, over 4,000 students in 12 schools (ten elementary, one middle, and one high school) were receiving instruction in seven different languages (Arabic, Chinese, French, German, Japanese, Russian, and Spanish).

While the Cincinnatti Public Schools provides a wide variety of magnet Programs for its students, from Montessori to computers and from Paideia to fine arts, nearly one quarter of all magnet school participants are in foreign language magnets.

Regardless of the language of concentration, children are accepted into the Foreign Language Magnet Program only at kindergarten or grade one. Applications are processed by the Central Office on a first-come, first-served basis, with racial balance being the sole factor in placement decisions. No academic screening takes place in any of the elementary school foreign language programs. Students, therefore, come from a broad cross-section of the community.

Because children represent all racial and socioeconomic levels of the community, one would expect the academic achievement of these children to be consistent with national norms. The California Achievement Test is administered annually to all students in grades 1–11. Contrary to expectations, however, achievement among foreign language magnet children continues to be well above the anticipated national norms in both reading and mathematics. Furthermore, foreign language magnet participants score, on the average, higher than the average of all magnet school participants.

Table 10.1 shows the percentages of students in the Foreign Language Magnet Program scoring at or above the 50th percentile in reading and mathematics during the six-year period 1981-87.

TABLE 10.1 Language Magnet Students Scoring at or above 50th Percentile on CAT

Year	Reading	Mathematics
1981–82	61.2%	59.9%
1982–83	61.3%	62.8%
1983–84	70.1%	76.4%
1984–85	68.4%	74.2%
1985–86	72.3%	77.4%
1986–87	72.0%	77.7%

At the same time, the percentage of students in the above average stanine range (7-8-9) also continues to increase, thus remaining well above the

23% norm for the high stanine range, as shown in Table 10.2.

TABLE 10.2 Language Magnet Students Scoring in Stanines 7–9

Year	Reading	Mathematics
1981–82	26.2%	21.3%
1982–83	23.7%	26.9%
1983–84	37.5%	39.7%
1984–85	33.2%	36.8%
1985–86	33.7%	40.8%

During the six-year period noted above, the racial balance of the district remained relatively stable at 57% black and 43% white. The percentage of children in the low socioeconomic range, as evidenced by the numbers of children receiving free or reduced-cost lunches has been about 52% of the total district population.

Several reasons for the high student achievement have been suggested. It is possible that parents who choose magnet school programs for their children already have high academic expectations which are communicated to the children, who then come to school more likely to succeed. Motivation and parent involvement are, of course, two important factors which influence student performance in school.

Even though children come from a broad cross-section of the Cincinnati community, some would suggest that a greater percentage of academically capable children are attracted to the program in the first place. Another possible answer is that foreign language study enhances the academic performance of children of all ability levels. As a corollary which has yet to be explored, it is possible that the longer students participate in the foreign language experience, the greater the potential benefit to their academic achievement

Studying pupils in grades 3-6 in a French immersion program, Fraser-Child (1989) focused on achievement in language and reading. Among the purposes of the study was a determination of significant differences among low-achieving children who transferred out of the immersion program, low-achieving children who remained in the immersion program, and low-achieving children who never participated in an immersion program. Although the sample was small (57 children),

Fraser-Child's findings indicated that:

> the French immersion program did not appear to cause or contribute to the reading difficulties these children experience. . . . The concerns of many teachers and parents that French immersion is too challenging or too confusing for the child who is experiencing reading difficulties appear to lack empirical support.

In response to the question of possible negative consequences of program participation among Cincinnati children of varying achievement levels, the Foreign Language Magnet Office decided to chart academic performance of two groups of children through their elementary school years. The first cohort consisted of first graders in the 1981-82 school year ($n = 329$). The second cohort included first graders in the 1982-83 school year ($n = 449$). As children in each of those two cohorts exited the Foreign Language Magnet Program, they formed two additional groups so that by the end of grade, five two groups of participants and two groups of non-participants could be examined.

Historically, the attrition rate of the Foreign Language Magnet Program has ranged from 30% to 40% between grades one and six. Sometimes families who change residence prefer a new school rather than have their children transported to the former school. Some families move out of the district. Others may choose a different magnet program or perhaps a neighborhood program.

One might expect that poor academic performance would be a high indicator of program attrition. It must be noted, however, that classroom performance and achievement on standardized tests are not always parallel. For the two groups studied, the rate at which children were retained in grade (i.e., not promoted) was approximately 8% over the five-year period. And indeed, of the children who were retained at a particular grade level, a high percentage of them (53%) exited the program at the end of the repeated year. There is some evidence (Bruck, 1985) switching from a language program to an all-English program may damage the child's self-esteem and contribute to a sense of failure for the child.

In our experience the greatest percentage of students (approximately 30%) exiting the program came from the average stanine group (4-5-6).

Throughout the elementary school years, students who remained in the program consistently scored better in both reading and mathematics than did students who left the program. Grade 5 scores for each cohort are listed in Table 10.3.

TABLE 10.3 Grade 5 CAT Scores

| | Participants | | Non-Participants | |
	Mean	SD	Mean	SD
Reading				
1981–82	64.17	17.77	59.30	19.05
1982–83	63.33	16.22	57.19	16.69
Mathematics				
1981–82	63.40	17.27	59.85	21.42
1982–83	63.93	15.66	57.37	16.70

Interestingly enough, however, no significant upward or downward mobility was found in the low, average, or high stanines in either cohort of children regardless of program participation. In other words, children who tested in the low stanine range (1–2–3) in grade one and who exited the program remained in the low stanine range through grade five. The same was true for the middle (4–5–6) and high range (7–8–9). By the same token, children who scored in the low stanine range in grade one and remained in the program through grade five continued to score in the below average stanines. Of course, the latter group of children had the benefit of acquiring communication skills in two languages.

Although the number of children in the low stanine group was too small to make any far-reaching generalizations, it is fair to say that exiting the language magnet program did not increase achievement nor did remaining in the program hinder achievement.

When children from the two cohorts were matched by race and sex, interesting differences appeared. While program participation favorably influenced achievement among both blacks and whites and both males and females, the greatest ranges seem to occur among whites. Socioeconomic differences among children from both racial groups were not considered in Table 10.4, but could have a significant impact.

TABLE 10.4 CAT Scores by Race and Sex

| | Participants | | Non-Participants | |
	Mean	SD	Mean	SD
Reading				
1981–82				
BF	52.56	14.35	53.88	13.77
BM	62.42	14.09	55.54	14.23
WF	75.03	15.23	67.39	24.03
WM	71.31	18.62	59.07	19.97
1982–83				
BF	59.37	14.86	54.16	15.73
BM	58.72	14.53	53.12	13.39
WF	71.26	16.27	67.62	17.45
WM	66.69	16.82	58.64	19.70
Mathematics				
1981–82				
BF	56.07	16.03	55.82	18.31
BM	59.03	15.90	52.96	20.74
WF	72.03	14.85	67.83	22.95
WM	69.31	17.02	63.43	20.42
1982–83				
BF	62.26	17.19	50.06	14.10
BM	58.77	14.45	57.72	17.87
WF	68.47	12.42	63.23	8.56
WM	68.74	16.45	60.71	21.01

While many factors contribute to success in school, the Cincinnati experience points to the following:

- participation in elementary school foreign language programs does not hamper achievement in reading and mathematics, even among low stanine children;

- students who exit foreign language programs do not demonstrate higher achievement in an all-English program;

- students who remain in language programs, on the average, achieve at higher levels than children who exit the program.

Further evidence of the appropriateness of foreign language programs for all children comes from a four-year study, "The Effectiveness of a Partial French Immersion Program for Students from Different Ethnic and Social Class

Backgrounds" (Holobow et al., 1988), conducted by the Department of Psychology, McGill University. Two French Partial Immersion elementary schools participated in this study along with two control schools offering a regular English program. With the Partial Immersion model, students spend half their instructional day in French and half in English. They receive instruction in science and social studies exclusively in French. In addition, the French teacher reinforces and enriches math skills and concepts which were introduced by the English teacher. Reading/Language arts is taught in both French and English by the respective teachers.

The McGill study adds important information on the suitability of immersion education for children from lower socioeconomic backgrounds. The following section quotes heavily from the report of year four as prepared by Naomi Holobow of McGill University.

Questions addressed by the McGill Study were:

Will the positive results that have been obtained in previous evaluations of middle-class children participating in immersion programs generalize to working class children participating in an American setting?

Will such results generalize to a group of children for whom the standard English spoken at school may be a second dialect (the case for both black and white working class children)?

The research design included eight groups of children in both the pilot group (kindergarten, grades 1, 2, and 3) and the follow-up group one year later (kindergarten, grades 1 and 2) as shown in Figure 10.1.

Testing materials included the reading, mathematics, and science subtests of the California Achievement Test; French Comprehension Test; *Test linguistique maternelle;* a reading test devised by the Language Research Group of McGill University; and an oral interview. The conclusions of the McGill researchers include the following:

- The immersion students in both pilot and follow-up groups demonstrated the same levels of achievement in English phonetic analysis, structural analysis, vocabulary, and reading comprehension as their peers in the regular English program.

FIGURE 10.1

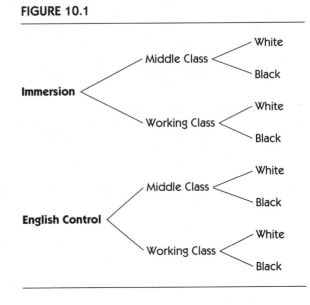

- The immersion students also scored comparably to the control students on standardized tests of mathematical computations, mathematical concepts and applications.

- The immersion students scored comparably to control students on standardized tests of science. This is particularly noteworthy since immersion students received science instruction exclusively in French during their entire school experience.

The researchers found no evidence of detrimental effects in the development of English reading, mathematics, or science skills of the working-class or middle-class children who spent half their school day in a language other than English (the Partial Immersion Program).

Furthermore, there was no evidence to suggest that black students in the Partial Immersion Program experienced any setbacks in their English language development, in spite of the fact that many were being schooled in a second dialect (standard English) as well as in a foreign language (French).

Interestingly, working-class immersion students, both black and white, scored as well as their middle-class peers on the French *Test linguistique maternelle,* which measures listening comprehension and oral production. This seems reasonable since both middle-class and working-class immersion students have the same role models during the school day and the same access to French.

The McGill University researchers concluded that "children from lower socioeconomic backgrounds as well as those from ethnic minority backgrounds can benefit from second language immersion programs." They were cautious to note, however, that these results should be applied only to minority-group children whose first language is English, albeit a non-standard dialect of English.

While the Cincinnatti experience is a significant beginning in opening the doors of foreign language classrooms to children of varying socioeconomic backgrounds and academic abilities, further longitudinal research in this area is essential.

PART II. SECOND LANGUAGE TEACHING AND THE HANDICAPPED CHILD

In this section we explore the issues involved in teaching multiple languages to a unique group of learners, namely, handicapped children. It has been documented that many handicapped children in the United States already have access to at least two languages; these children come from homes where the language spoken in the home is not English (Garrison & Hammill, 1971; Mercer, 1971; Grubb, 1974; Chan, 1983; Omark & Erickson, 1983; Ortiz & Yates, 1983; Delgado, 1984; Dew, 1984). The dominant language for them is most commonly Spanish or a Native American language, followed, in recent years, by a wide variety of Asian languages. However, the majority of handicapped children continue to come from homes where some form of English is the dominant language. Because of this diversity in population, the focus of bilingual efforts in special education has tended to be on identification of handicapping conditions in the bilingual population and on appropriate educational placement for these identified children (DeAvila & Havassey, 1974; Oakland, 1979; Mowder, 1980; Samuda & Crawford, 1980; Erickson & Omark, 1981; Luetke-Stahlman & Weiner, 1982; Plata, 1982; Damico et al., 1983; Leonard & Weiss, 1983; Mercer, 1983; Cummins, 1984; Mattes & Omark, 1984; Nutell et al., 1984; Barona & Barona, 1987). Until awareness of home language environ-

ments emerged, it was common for many children to be classified as handicapped because they were unable to successfully complete test batteries in English, test batteries that were biased toward standard anglophone cultural and social values and against the cultural and linguistic variations actually occurring in American society (Altus, 1953; Johnson & Sikes, 1965; Lesser et al., 1965; Christiansen & Livermore, 1970; Cole & Bruner, 1971; Garrison & Hammill, 1971; Killian, 1971; Mercer, 1971, 1973; Sabatino et al., 1972; Silverstein, 1973; Hallahan & Kauffman, 1977; McCreary & Padilla, 1977; Coles, 1978; Gerkein, 1978; Reschly, 1978; Gutkin, 1979; Tucker, 1980; Cole, 1981; Olmedo, 1981; Teeter et al., 1982; Terrell & Terrell, 1983). Fortunately, special education has made substantial strides toward non-biased assessment and toward special education instruction for limited English-proficient children (Omark & Erickson, 1983). This body of literature will not be considered further since the focus of this section is not on assessment or placement issues, but rather on how handicapped children can and/or should be exposed to languages other than English.

Definition of Handicap

Within the area of special education, there are a variety of handicapping conditions that can and do exist, both from an educational and legal point of view. For this discussion handicapped children are considered in three groups with regard to problems of language learning. Although children may have more than one handicap, for our discussion we will assume only one.

The first group of children to be considered generally have normal potential for language learning, but are deprived of normal and/or adequate exposure to language or communication. The second group of children have adequate sensory and cognitive abilities, but lack the motor control to display their knowledge of language through conventional means such as speech. The third group of children possess less potential for language learning, not because of a lack of input, but because of cognitive deficits of mild to profound degree that prevent them from mastering the linguistic/communicative regularities of formal symbol systems.

The first group referred to above is composed of hearing-impaired children ranging from mildly hard-of-hearing to profoundly Deaf, of visually impaired children ranging from partially sighted to Blind, and of children with severe social or emotional disturbance. Most of these handicapped children have normal potential for language acquisition and development, but their sensory and/or psycho-social handicaps prevent them from experiencing the full range of communicative/linguistic interactions needed to develop even a single, mature language.

Since languages are normally conveyed in a spoken mode, it is not surprising that hearing-impaired children have difficulty learning auditorily based language. Given the fact that many hearing-impaired persons learn distinct, but visually based language systems (Wilbur, 1987), it is clear that Deaf children can develop language, but fail to learn spoken language because of a lack of adequate exposure. Indeed, many Deaf or severely hearing-impaired children do develop excellent mastery of one or more languages, both in spoken and printed form, attesting to the realization of their normal potential, given adequate samples and appropriate learning opportunities.

Partially sighted and Blind children have a sensory handicap as well. As a consequence, they often fail to understand fully how language forms and language functions interact with communicative use (Urwin, 1978; Mills, 1979; Kekelis & Andersen, 1984; Bigelow, 1987). In other words, visually impaired children may learn the linguistic system, but they may not learn how or when to use their knowledge. Visually impaired children should be seen as having communication rather than linguistic difficulties. In addition to the communicative aspects of language, some semantic problems may emerge for visually impaired children such as failing to extend lexical items as fully normally sighted children (Andersen et al., 1984) or demonstrating problems with adjective constructions (Dunlea, 1984). Since these aspects of language are closely linked with visual experiences, it is not surprising that such difficulties would develop. Finally, visually impaired persons often do not have access to print without modifications such as enlarged print or tactile systems, e.g., braille. Like the hearing impaired, the problems of visually impaired children emerge not

because of an inability to learn language, but because of a lack of full access to the communicative act.

By definition, social or emotional disturbance yields behavior patterns that prevent normal social intercourse with others. In other words, socially or behaviorally disturbed children may actively resist meaningful contact with others. As a consequence, such children often have problems with the communicative functions of language, even though they may have acquired normal commands over the form aspects of language (Yudkovitz et al., 1976). It is also common for socially or behaviorally disturbed children to display difficulties with the semantic aspects of language. They formulate associations between language and its referents in a manner that reflects their distancing from other members of their society (Labov & Fanshel, 1977). Again, these problems reflect not an inability to acquire language but a lack of normal experiences from which to formulate hypotheses about language functions, functions commensurate with those of their own speech community.

The second group of children to be considered are those with orthopedic handicaps, that is, children who have severe motor involvements, due to conditions such as cerebral palsy, that leave them physically incapacitated. Many of these children lack sufficient motor control to generate intelligent speech, yet they may understand the language of others. If they have linguistic mastery, all that is often required is the provision of alternative or augmentive systems that can supplement or replace speech as the primary means of expression. Such systems can be sign language; communication boards with pictures, letters, words, or phrases to be indicated by the child through some form of pointing; or electronic devices that print or produce artificial speech. There is no reason why these alternative means could not be programmed for languages other than English. For instance, a communication board could be organized using a Spanish or Chinese lexicon. Likewise, microcomputer keyboards can be set easily to produce a wide variety of characters.

In contrast to the first two groups of children, there is also a group that seems to have adequate sensory function, environmental exposure, and speech motor control but who have distinct difficulties learning language. These children range from those described as language or learning disabled to children who display substantial deficits in all areas of development including language learning. This latter sub-group of children may be said to be developmentally disabled, or to have moderate to severe mental retardation. Finally, in this group are children with profound disruptions not only to language or communication development, but to all aspects of self-care: those classified as having severe to profound developmental delays and/or severe autism. All these sub-sets of children share a common problem in language learning although the degree of that problem varies according to the degree of handicap. Children with otherwise normal intelligence and a specific language learning problem display difficulties in many areas of primary language acquisition and development, including the acquisition of the sound system, the linguistic form, the meaning system, and the communicative functions of their primary language (Fey, 1986). Although there is some disagreement in the literature, there is sufficient evidence that children with specific language learning problems do have adequate environmental interaction for language learning (Cramblit & Siegel, 1977; Lasky & Klopp 1982; Conti-Ramsden & Friel-Patti, 1983), yet these children display difficulties in both interpersonal uses of language and in literacy acquisition. Thus, unlike the two previous groups, this third group's problem is not a lack of language experience or an inability to produce speech, but rather difficulty in understanding how language is formed and how it works in communication exchanges.

In summary, then, when discussing the learning of more than one language by handicapped children, we have to distinguish among those groups of children who have sensory, motor, or social/behavioral barriers to the learning of any language, that is, children who have the ability to acquire or express symbol systems once these barriers are overcome, and those children whose main problem is not a lack of adequate sensory input or motor expression, but rather a mild to moderate specific language learning problem or more pervasive developmental delay. Each of these groups of children has different needs and abilities, and we must consider different solutions for them with regard to the issue of second-language learning.

Bilingualism in the Handicapped Population

A search for recent literature on teaching second languages to handicapped children revealed only one set of reports on the development of more than one language in handicapped children. Bruck (1985b) studied the effects of a French immersion program on English-speaking children who could be described as having specific language-learning problems with their primary language. Bruck's studies indicate that these children's mastery of French was on par with their acquisition of English. The reports do not provide specific information on the second language acquisition process itself, however. This sparse literature would make it appear that there is little incidence of handicapped persons being exposed to or learning a second language. However, our personal experiences suggest this is not the case. A brief review of these experiences will demonstrate the capacity of a variety of so-called handicapped persons to master more than one language.

In the course of a party in New York City where most of the guests were hearing impaired, the authors met a congenitally, profoundly hearing-impaired woman who introduced us to her new husband (a Bulgarian whose hearing was normal). She spoke to him in French, translating our comments to him and his to us.

While working as part of a school intake team, Laura Kretschmer interviewed a young hearing-impaired man, Dominic, and his mother. Assessment of Dominic's mastery of signed and spoken English indicated relatively standard English acquisition patterns found in many hearing-impaired high-school-aged students. As the interviewer communicated with Dominic, the young man turned to his mother, who spoke only Italian, and interpreted what was said. Because the interviewer did not want to use Dominic as an interpreter, the services of an Italian-speaking team member were obtained. By using this additional team member, it was also possible to obtain an informal assessment of Dominic's use of Italian. Dominic's spoken Italian was described as being as functional as his English.

On a visit to Los Angeles, we visited a mainstreamed program for primary-aged hearing-impaired students, a program that contained many children with Spanish surnames. During lunch break, we noted a conversation among four hearing-impaired boys, ages 6 and 7. It was clear that they were using Spanish in play although we heard them all use English in the classroom. We commented on this, and the teacher walked over to the four boys to ask them a question. Immediately all four changed to English and carried on a conversational exchange that was intelligible and appropriate. Once the teacher departed and the boys began playing among themselves, they reverted to Spanish.

We are acquainted with a profoundly hearing-impaired man who, in order to earn a doctorate from a prestigious Canadian university, needed to pass a foreign language examination. Since he had studied French in high school, he pursued and passed the language requirement in French. His mastery of conversational French was demonstrated when he was observed to carry on a conversation with a French-speaking waitress at a Vietnamese restaurant.

Laura Kretschmer worked with a child with a specific language-learning disability whose Chinese-speaking family had moved to the United States from Taiwan. Although the family members did speak English, communication at home was usually in Chinese. At two-and-one-half the child did not speak any language. It was decided that speech/language therapy would center on the acquisition of English, a decision in which the parents concurred. The home language was also to be English, when it was natural for this to occur. Likely, however, many exchanges at home continued to be in Chinese. With therapy this child's English began to develop, as did her comprehension and use of Chinese. Her acquisition of English seemed to outdistance her use of Chinese. Unfortunately, her family left the program before she had developed complex language, so it is not clear how acquisition of two languages would have progressed.

We are acquainted with a program for a child with severe physical handicaps that necessitates using an augmentive communication system: a communication board on which pictures and words are displayed so that the child can point for conversation. This child's parents also wanted their son to be able to communicate with his Greek-speaking grandparents. In cooperation with a teacher of Greek from a nearby Greek Orthodox Church, his teacher introduced the child to Greek, and subsequently, to a second communication board developed for Greek.

A teacher from an Indian reservation reported on moderately to severely mentally retarded children, many with Down's Syndrome, who could carry on limited conversation both in English and in their Native American language. Impressively, many of the children recognized without prompting when to shift from English to their Native American language and vice-versa.

Although these examples are isolated, it is clear that there are handicapped persons who can and do learn more than one language, persons with a range of abilities and socio-economic backgrounds, as well as a variety of handicaps.

Why a Second Language for Handicapped Children?

Why should we provide handicapped children who can learn language with experience in more than one language? As is true with non-handicapped children, there are a variety of positive social and intellectual reasons for learning more than one language. A salient reason for handicapped children is that learning a second language provides an opportunity to think about language itself. This is particularly true, if as Krashen (1981) suggests, the child comes to monitor his use of the second language, that is, the child realizes he or she is using linguistic principles to generate utterances, principles different from those of his or her native language. The ability to think about language as language has been referred to as metalinguistic knowledge (McLaughlin, 1984; Cummins, 1987). It seems possible that if a handicapped child is having difficulty mastering aspects of his or her primary language that the metalinguistic knowledge gained from learning a second language would be beneficial to the child in enhancing mastery of the native language.

Secondly, exposure to a second language, particularly when presented as part of a program of bicultural exposure, increases the child's awareness of differences among individuals (Lambert, 1987). This should be true for both normally developing and handicapped children. Many handicapped children live restricted lives, often not of their own choosing; exposure to other languages and cultures can only enhance their communicative and intellectual abilities while simultaneously exposing them to the cultural diversity of life in the United States.

Second Language Programming with the Handicapped

Since it is established that handicapped persons can learn more than one language and that there are good reasons to consider including them in second language programs, we turn to issues of programming. As is true of so many issues relating to bilingual special education, there has been little research into when and how a second language should be introduced to these children. The literature on bilingualism in special education generally consists of position papers which favor bilingualism for the handicapped but provide little specific information on how this should be accomplished (Murphy, 1974; Chan, 1983).

From literature on regular bilingual education come the concepts of coordinate and compound bilingualism (Weinreich, 1953). Coordinate bilingualism refers to the simultaneous acquisition of two or more languages, while compound bilingualism refers to the acquisition of a mother tongue first and then the acquisition of additional languages. Keeping in mind that many handicapped children have some primary language-learning problems even if limited problems in communication use, the most reasonable recommendation for most handicapped children is compound bilingualism rather than coordinate bilingualism. That is, given the difficulty that many handicapped children have learning any language, it seems reasonable to establish a primary or dominant language first and then begin instruction in a second language. Which language should be learned first should be dictated by the language used in the child's household or by consensus with the educational facility. Thus, for many handicapped children, the first language developed may not be English. This position has been assumed by a number of special educators working with bilingual populations (Bolen, 1987; Luetke-Stahlman & Weiner, 1982; Pacheco, 1983; McMenamin, 1984; Miller & Abudarham, 1984; Blackwell & Fischgrund, 1985; Christensen, 1986). Of course, we still do not know how much mastery of the

mother tongue should be achieved before exposure to a second language begins. It seems that mastery of the basic components of the mother tongue is sufficient. For instance, we encouraged introducing a six-year-old hearing-impaired child to French, once she could express the basic word order of transitive sentences in English and had shown both understanding and use of the three basic operations yielding complex English sentences, namely, coordination, complementation, and relativization. Since her mother and grandparents were French speakers, the environment and motivation were supportive of such a move. Rondal (1984) points out that for some handicapped children bilingualism may be an unattainable goal. For severely or profoundly developmentally delayed children, the likelihood of learning even one language is so remote and the results so limited that to add a second language would be almost impossible. Additional program considerations are issues such as the potential for interference from one language to then other, which it has been argued may be greater for persons who have difficulty learning one language in the first place (Omark & Erickson, 1983; Cheng, 1987). Interference is thought to be particularly likely with regard to learning communication strategies, that is, how to conduct conversations. Omark and Erickson argue that for many special children who speak a language other than English, communication behavior appropriate to one language is often imported into their communication efforts in English. Unfortunately, such behavior is often perceived by others as atypical or pathological communication rather than as genuine language interference. It would seem reasonable that a similar effect would appear in the opposite direction, namely, for an English-speaking handicapped child learning another language. As noted previously, in reporting on a French immersion program in Canada for anglophone, language-delayed children, Bruck (1985b) noted that the children were able to master both languages slowly, but steadily. The level of attainment in French was significantly below that achieved by children without language-learning difficulties. Unfortunately, her reports do not comment on potential effects of phonological, syntactic, semantic or communicative interference. Research on interference issues awaits completion but should include examination of interference in handicapped children when English-dominant or non-English-dominant conditions are present.

In planning an instructional program, a number of practitioners have suggested that bilingualism should not be taught apart from biculturalism even for handicapped children. Exposure to a particular language should include exposure to the cultures from which that language comes (Pickering, 1976; Chinn, 1979; Almanza & Mosley, 1980; Omark & Erickson, 1983; Blackwell & Fischgrund, 1985; Lerman & Vila, 1985; Wallace & Fischgrund, 1985; Fradd & Tikunoff, 1987). This cultural exposure should be extended to the home language of limited-English-proficient children as a means of preserving the cultural heritage of the child. For the English-speaking handicapped child, it is a means by which the child can learn about the cultural diversity of American society as well as the larger world.

The degree of bilingualism to be attained is another programming issue. Bilingualism for handicapped learners can be seen as a continuum from mastery of two languages for academic purposes to development of a second language to a functional level. It may be reasonable for some children to be able to read and write on academic matters, or for pleasure and self-fulfillment. For other children, the ability to hold conversations on functional topics pertinent to them and their environment may be a more realistic goal. That is, bilingual programs need not be tied only to academic settings but can include vocational and avocational settings as well. Plata and Jones (1982) reported on a program where vocationally oriented tasks were used to help slow learning children become proficient in two languages.

It has been shown with normally learning children that if certain conditions are met, second language learning is more easily achieved. It is of paramount importance that the target language be presented as naturally as possible, in a communicative context (Krashen, 1987; Long, 1983; McLaughlin, 1984; Hakuta, 1986; Terrell, 1986; Taylor, 1987). Long and Porter (1985) emphasized that when students interact with one another in a second language while trying to jointly solve a problem, the likelihood of mastery of the second language is significantly increased.

Certain personal characteristics also need to be considered in program development. Motivation is critical. It has been suggested that motivation for language learning can be of two varieties, namely, instrumental and integrative (Gardner & Lambert, 1959; Wong-Fillmore, 1982; Oller et al., 1977: Hermann, 1980; Genesee et al., 1983; Strong, 1984; Horwitz & Young, 1990). Instrumental motivation refers to the child's desire to master the code itself because it is an intrinsically interesting activity; integrative motivation is thought to be derived from the desire of the child to participate in social activities in his or her environment where a different language is being used. Integrative motivation can be the result of activities both inside and outside the classroom. If a handicapped child has some primary language learning difficulty, his or her motivation for learning an additional language will be diminished. To help in counteracting this problem, the child might be motivated to learn a second language by exposing him to outside activities where a knowledge of a second language would be useful and/or by creating interesting activities within the classroom where knowledge of a second language allows the child to enter into social interactions. Within the classroom, children might be given exercises that stress whole-sentence (formulaic) productions that allows for interesting and successful mastery of the language (Wong-Fillmore, 1976), or problem-solving situations requiring the use of a second language (Long and Porter, 1985).

It has also been shown that a tolerance for ambiguity and a willingness to take risks are important personal characteristics for successful second language learning (Chapelle & Roberts, 1986; Ely, 1986). Many handicapped children do not tolerate ambiguity well and are frequently unwilling to take risks. So, it is possible that even though a child may have sufficient exposure to language and sufficient ability to learn a second language, he or she may be deterred from doing so because of these personal characteristics. Westby and Rouse (1985) have suggested an approach that might overcome a variety of personal issues and increase handicapped children's willingness to try to learn a second language. They suggested that a second language should be introduced initially in highly meaningful contexts that are familiar and comfortable for the child based on his or her personal experiences. Such activities could be cooking and preparing meals, pretending, board games, TV programs and so on. Children should progress to less familiar contexts such as group discussions, say Westby and Rouse, but the conversational topics should be familiar even though a less familiar context is used. From this, then, teaching can progress to the last stage, namely, using unfamiliar topics in new contexts. In other words, Westby and Rouse advocate teaching a second language by progressing from familiar topics in familiar contexts, to using familiar topics in unfamiliar contexts, leading finally to using unfamiliar topics in unfamiliar contexts, from the known to the unknown. Such a program should aid in developing risk taking behavior while simultaneously controlling ambiguity in second language learning experiences.

Summary Recommendation

In conclusion, we would recommend the introduction of second languages to most handicapped children, once a mother tongue has been developed. We would recommend second language introduction as an active context supported experience rather than a structured passive learning. It is clear that not every handicapped child can master a second language. Some will have difficulty because of severe cognitive deficits, some because of personal characteristics that reduce their aptitude for learning language. Many can acquire only a basic, functional use of a second language, while others may develop literacy in more than one language. When appropriate, especially for mainstreamed special children, we feel that introduction of a second language should be explored as part of the educational experience. Furthering the handicapped child's understanding of language learning in general, and increasing his or her awareness of cultural/linguistic differences in particular, argues for consideration of this special population when second language instruction is being planned.

CONCLUSION

The path into the twenty-first century is one filled with unknowns. Yet, as educators, we must pre-

pare young people for the political, economic, and cultural realities they will face. Basic to that preparation is a healthy self-concept, a sensitivity to similarities and differences among peoples, a willingness to adapt to changes, a familiarity with technology, and an ability to communicate in more than one language.

In order to realize that preparation for the adults of the next generation, we must draw secondary and post-secondary foreign language colleagues closer to an awareness of the potential of elementary school foreign language programs.

We must explore ways to extend the foreign language experience to more children by working collaboratively with parents, elementary educators and special educators.

We must establish a research agenda which includes examining the techniques used by teachers to make additional languages available to all children as tools for understanding rather than barriers preventing it.

We must prepare teachers to work with children of varying academic abilities and with varying degrees of motivation.

We must develop instructional materials in many different languages and disseminate them so that districts do not have to "reinvent the wheel."

We must encourage student-exchange programs to provide the day-to-day communication opportunities that contribute to language fluency and cultural sensitivity.

We must convince funding agencies to give foreign language programs top priority, stressing both the short-term and the long-term benefits of such programs.

We must collaborate with business and industry to develop career-oriented programs to demonstrate the utility of other languages in a wide variety of employment opportunities.

The list could be much longer. But, although priorities change from year to year and decade to decade in many professions, let us hope that the resolve of parents and foreign language educators strengthens the place of elementary school foreign language programs for all children so that by the year 2000 we do not have to include monolingualism among the list of handicapping conditions.

DISCUSSION QUESTIONS

1. If you are one of those many Americans who endured a traditional course or two in some "foreign" language, what kind of success did you enjoy? Did you get so you could understand conversations, jokes, and bon mots in the language? Or did you remain mostly unable to move beyond a rudimentary appreciation of a few words and phrases? If you experienced any noticeable success, to what would you attribute it?

2. It is commonly noted by linguists that even mentally retarded persons typically acquire some basic primary language skills. Should we expect non-primary language acquisition to be any harder for such persons?

3. What are some of the factors likely to make knowing more than one language a desirable attribute of educated persons in the twenty-first century? What drawbacks, if any, would such knowledge have?

CHAPTER 11

The FLES Methods Course: The Key to K–12 Certification

Jane Tucker Mitchell and Mary Lynn Redmond

EDITOR'S INTRODUCTION

This brief article covers a lot of ground. It anticipates much of the work that remains to be done in states where the elementary school language curriculum, teacher certification, and state requirements lag behind what is happening in leading states such as North Carolina. Gerard Toussaint and many of his coworkers in that state are to be congratulated as are support teams at colleges of education in institutions such as the University of North Carolina and Wake Forest University. In this chapter, Jane Tucker Mitchell and Mary Lynn Redmond outline the sort of content that they feel is essential to the preparation of teachers to supply the needs of North Carolina as the Basic Education Plan, adopted in 1985, is implemented in successive stages. Sensibly, these farsighted authors anticipate the increasing integration of foreign language teaching with other content areas such as language arts, social studies, science, math, physical education, health, and the fine arts. They assert flatly that "play, games, and drama are essential to any FLES program" (p. 114), and they offer specific suggestions about how the FLES element of the curriculum can be used to enrich and at the same time capitalize on concepts and skills from other content areas. TPR, storytelling, and drama figure largely among the recommended methods. Demonstration classes offered to elementary school children in conjunction with the methods course afford an invaluable hands-on experience to all the children and the teachers-in-training alike. Evaluations, on the whole, are positive and constructive, and, as expected with any sensible ongoing program, the evaluations from participants have led to improvements in the approach as it continues to develop.

In 1985 the state of North Carolina initiated a Basic Education Plan that mandated a kindergarten-grade 5 second language program for all public school children and required that a kindergarten-grade 12 second language program be available for students who wanted to achieve greater language proficiency. Administrators, parents, and even language teachers wondered where all the qualified teachers would be found. The consultants in the State Department of Public Instruction set the wheels in motion by naming a committee of teachers and teacher educators to formulate the competencies necessary for a K-12 certification program. As members of that committee and as teacher educators, we realized that we needed to prepare for the new requirements. It soon became apparent that the main addition to our current secondary certification would be more coursework in child psychology and a FLES (Foreign Language in the Elementary School) methods course.

We had both taught foreign language in the elementary school in the past and were aware that many changes had come about as a result of the renewed interest in FLES programs nationally. As we began researching the current literature on FLES, we became aware that the FLES teacher would need knowledge, not only of methods, but of program models, the elementary curriculum, second language acquisition, articulation, evaluation, and materials, to mention only the principal areas of expertise.

PROGRAM MODELS

We begin with the topic of program models since there is some confusion as to which program type produces pupils with the greatest proficiency. Often teachers do not know the difference between partial and total immersion or that FLES is a general term for all second language instruction in the elementary school as well as a particular program type. Knowledge of the different program models enables teachers to make better decisions for the right program to meet the needs of their local school systems. The program type we selected for primary focus is Integrated FLES, or what Curtain and Pesola call Content-enriched FLES (1988: 25). This is accompanied by an overview of the history of FLES in the United States so that teachers and program planners will be aware of and sensitive to past mistakes, such as inadequate planning and nonsequential programs. We also study the evolution of the recent Basic Education Plan in North Carolina—its funding, its implementation, and its curricula. FLES teachers must know what the state mandate means for local school districts as they strive to begin effective second language programs in their elementary schools.

If teachers are to implement an Integrated FLES program, they must be thoroughly familiar with the curriculum of all the content areas in the elementary school. An integral part of the FLES methods course centers around the North Carolina curriculum guides for the K-6 content areas, especially language arts, social studies, science, and math. We do not exclude healthful living (physical education and health) and the fine arts since play, games, and drama are essential to any FLES program, but they are given less emphasis, as past FLES programs were often criticized for taking time away from the "basic" areas. It is in these core areas that FLES plays a major role. For example, in the area of science, the FLES teacher can reinforce the work of the classroom teacher dealing with the five senses by incorporating hands-on activities that allow the children to see, hear, taste, touch, and smell. Repeating similar activities in a second language strengthens the child's understanding of the concepts by awakening other processes of thinking. To ensure that participants in the methods class know how to integrate these areas into their classes, they are required to prepare several activities from the various content areas that may be adapted for use at various levels of the second language curriculum.

METHODS

Participants in our methods classes are familiarized with Total Physical Response, the Natural Approach, and Krashen and his hypotheses about second language acquisition as well as storytelling and using drama in teaching the elementary child. As expected, the major focus of the course is on methods, as teachers are most interested in how best to present the language to the learner. Since that learner is now the young child, the teacher wants to know as much as possible about both first and second language acquisition. From Krashen's theories on second language acquisition the FLES teacher learns the importance of natural, meaningful language in the classroom. The now well-known Input Hypothesis emphasizes the necessity of providing the child with a vast amount of comprehensible language at the child's next linguistic stage. Most teachers ask how they can know what language is at the child's next level. According to Krashen and Terrell, however, "In practice, providing optimal input may be surprisingly easy" (Krashen & Terrell, 1983: 33). The authors refer to speech containing one structure at a time as "finely tuned input" and to speech that is understandable but uses some structures beyond the child's current linguistic stage as "roughly tuned input," and refer to this phenomenon as "casting a net" over the listener (1983: 33). The "net" idea allows the teacher freedom to communicate in the classroom without having to worry about linguistic overload for the listener. Our program stresses that allowing speech to emerge when the child is ready is a more natural way to acquire a language, as it gives the child time to internalize structures, syntax, pronunciation and intonation. In preparing their lessons, FLES teachers include activities that will promote good listening skills such as storytelling and Total Physical Response. The FLES teacher learns, too, that using the second language to integrate other content areas into the second language curriculum offers the advantage of placing the students' attention on meaning and concepts so that the second language becomes a tool for learning rather than an end in itself.

We feel that as methods instructors we can demonstrate good listening activities such as storytelling, Total Physical Response, describing and identifying pictures, etc. In this way teachers can learn that all these activities with understandable language and minimal student response prepare the child for later speech production. In addition, the demonstrations prove to the pre-service and in-service teachers enrolled in the course that their instructor is one of them, a colleague, involved in and interested in perfecting his or her teaching skills just as they are. Our demonstrations also provide the teachers with good examples of activities to use in their lessons for the practicum and for assignments for the course. These activities must integrate the curriculum of the elementary grades and the culture of the language as well as listening and speaking skills. As the teachers plan and teach the second language curriculum together, they become very familiar with the concepts that the young child is learning in his first language in math, language arts, science, social studies, fine arts, and healthful living. Some of the activities which the teachers use to integrate the second language with the elementary curriculum include sequencing story events, role playing, patterning, fantasy experiences, and culturally authentic songs, games, and counting rhymes. In planning and carrying out good lessons, the teachers must also ensure that they address the cognitive abilities and interests of the language learners by basing their teaching activities on concepts that relate to the children's developmental stages and to their world of thinking and living.

As methods teachers we share ideas from teachers whose classes we have observed. We also encourage experienced teachers in the class to bring in materials they have made and explain how they use them. A natural way that this exchange happens is through planning together for the practicum which is a part of the methods course. Some teachers who have never worked with the elementary child are unaccustomed to the constant search for materials that is a part of every elementary teacher's way of life. Our experience is that most successful FLES teachers learn to become scavengers, frequenting yard sales, dime stores, flea markets, and second-hand book stores as well as keeping a watchful eye for free and inexpensive items. Finally, we collect their suggestions for materials, add other resources that have come to our attention, and compile a list of available materials and addresses for the entire class. Participants will have seen how many of the materials can be used as they observe fellow teachers in the practicum.

PRACTICUM

The practicum which takes place in conjunction with the methods class is an important component of our FLES methods course. Young children between the ages of 6 and 10 who have had little or no prior experience in a second language come to the campus, where they hear only French or Spanish in the classes taught by the teachers in the methods course. We have found that the language classes provide a link between the community and the university and establish the rapport and involvement that are needed for successful second language programs.

During the sessions that precede the first day of the practicum, we work with the teachers of each language group to help them plan the curriculum and set goals and objectives for their teaching and their students. The second language specialists co-teach each class to allow all participants several opportunities to work with the children. Each session involves two consecutive lessons for each teacher. This is done in order to maintain some continuity with the children. The practicum gives the participants in the FLES methods course the opportunity to employ strategies that are appropriate to use with children in the elementary grades. When the participants are not involved in teaching, they are able to observe the other teams. Each session with the children is followed by a time for critiquing the lesson in order to point out successful activities and discuss ways of improving those activities that were less effective.

Our FLES methods course and the practicum have proved to be extremely successful and beneficial to both the second language specialists and the children. The second language specialists use their knowledge of the language, the culture, and the young child and how he or she can best learn a second language to provide optimal experiences for the children. The teachers have the opportunity to share ideas and to support each other in the teaching process. These two aspects of the course have been found to be of primary concern to all second language specialists. The involvement and support of the children's parents have also served to create positive attitudes toward second language learning that have helped promote FLES programs in the schools.

EVALUATION

The evaluation instrument we have developed has helped us determine the success of the course. At the end of the FLES methods course, we ask our students to rate us as well as the components of the course—the practicum, videos, texts, class discussions, activities which integrate the second language curriculum with the elementary curriculum—according to a scale of average, very good, or excellent. We also ask them to provide their personal comments concerning the aspects of the course they found most beneficial, what they would have liked to have been included that was not, and what they felt they contributed to the class. This evaluation tool has been valuable to us each time we have taught the course because it enables us to see how the course has been received and to determine how to improve the course the next time it is offered. For example, we have discovered that the second language specialists particularly like our demonstrations of teaching techniques and ideas, guest speakers who offer ways to enhance the second language program

(creative movement, drama, art, use of the computer), and some time devoted to sharing ideas about handmade and commercial teaching materials. The second language specialists seem to really enjoy the time that they have during the course to share their teaching experiences and to exchange ideas. We use our teachers' suggestions given on the course evaluation to improve our teaching and to enhance the content of the FLES methods course. As a result, we now include a segment on making materials and devote more time to critiquing the practicum. Their ideas provide us with an understanding of their needs as teachers and how we can best help them in our course.

The objectives of the FLES methods course continue to evolve as the FLES programs in the state expand to their full implementation in 1993. When we began our courses, the school systems were in the initial planning stages and FLES programs had not yet been started in the schools. At that time, students in the methods course were primarily secondary teachers who hoped to move to the elementary grades as the programs were implemented. These teachers had little or no teaching experience in the elementary school and therefore were not very knowledgeable about many aspects of a FLES program, the elementary curriculum, administrative involvement, teaching materials and resources, teaching techniques appropriate to use with young children, daily class load, and the high energy level demanded of the teacher. Now that the second language programs in the schools have had some time to become established and K-12 teacher certification programs in second languages have replaced the secondary level programs at the colleges and universities, the focus of the FLES methods course will continue to change to meet the needs of the undergraduate students who have no teaching experience, as well as the teachers who move from secondary to elementary school programs. The FLES methods course will also continue to address the increasing level of teaching competencies which is required as the program expands in the upper elementary grades and is articulated with the middle grades program.

DISCUSSION QUESTIONS

1. In a recent unpublished survey at the University of New Mexico involving 410 faculty members and 956 students, the single most important element of good teaching was judged to be "knowledge of the subject matter." If this is so across the board, and there is good reason to suppose that it is, should there be a proficiency requirement in the target language for foreign language teachers?

2. A common complaint about FLES programs in the past was "inadequate articulation"; i.e., the children who obtained substantial proficiency in a foreign language might find themselves in classes for rank beginners at the secondary level. What kinds of planning could be done to improve the articulation between elementary, middle school, and secondary school programs?

3. What are some of the ways teachers can benefit from observing other teachers and children in demonstration classes or other planned observations?

4. How can the knowledge of parents and others in the community who are speakers of the target language be brought into play in the foreign language classroom?

CHAPTER 12

Methods in Elementary School Foreign Language Teaching

Helena Curtain

EDITOR'S INTRODUCTION

The emphasis on meaning and comprehension, as Curtain describes the new look of FLES in the U.S., is as refreshing as a cool breeze on a hot summer day. Getting meaning and function across through scaffolding of meaning, as Curtain illustrates, is enormously more helpful than talking in English about the foreign language surface forms, grammatical rules, and the occasional cultural curiosity. By first understanding heavily scaffolded target language forms, by responding to commands, by understanding simple stories or dramas supported by gesture, pantomime, and lots of action, children work up gradually through yes-no questions, single word answers, and easy language into a comfortable speaking repertoire. The emphasis is on using the language naturally as a medium for real communication. Curtain wisely urges teachers to "use their acting abilities" and a number of distinct methods. In the background, I can see John Rassias saying "Yesssssss!" as he takes two running steps, bunches his head and hands into a thunderball, bends his knees, and slides clear across a Dartmouth classroom to where he imagines Helena Curtain is standing. He then leaps up, and on behalf of all the language teachers of America, kisses her on both cheeks.

INTRODUCTION

Methodology in elementary school foreign language programs has benefited greatly from today's emphasis on communication. This emphasis has shifted the focus of instruction from language *analysis* with a focus on form, to language *use* with a focus on function. Students are engaged in meaningful natural communication in situations which relate to their everyday communication needs. Methodologies of the past tended to isolate language into various parts, and as a result, elementary school foreign language programs were characterized by an emphasis on memorized patterns, lists, and labels. Concrete activities, songs, games, poems, and rhymes were often used, but frequently were not specifically related to the lesson of the day. When reading and writing activities were included, they were often carried out mechanically and without any meaningful context. The use of English often permeated the classroom for such activities as giving directions, checking comprehension, and teaching culture (Curtain & Pesola, 1988).

Methodology in today's elementary school foreign language programs emphasizes communication; classes are conducted in the target language, and elements of instruction are more integrated. Students no longer respond in a rote and mechanistic manner to long lists of isolated vocabulary words cued by a series of flashcards. Instead, as elementary school foreign language programs place greater value on the ability to communicate, even at the beginning levels of language learning, students are engaged in activities in which vocabulary is used in meaningful contexts. For example, they may use the names of foods in order to plan a nutritious lunch based on the four food groups, or use the names of animals to talk about animal habitats or animal body coverings. They may use classroom vocabulary to estimate and measure various sizes of common objects in the school, and color words to make a graph of colors of clothing worn by the students in the room. They may use the names of animals and colors in a pattern study which the class creates itself, perhaps based on a model such as *Brown Bear Brown Bear What Do You See?* by Bill Martin, Jr. (1983).

INSIGHTS FROM SECOND LANGUAGE ACQUISITION

While there are many variations in methodology and each program will be different depending on the program model and the goals of the individual school, there are some elements in common. One of the key elements in successful methodology for elementary school foreign language classrooms is that recent insights into second language acquisition are included. Research in second language acquisition suggests the need for early language experiences that provide many opportunities for listening comprehension especially at the early stages (Dulay, Burt, & Krashen, 1982). When listening comprehension rather than speaking is emphasized, students associate the new language with meanings before they make a conscious attempt to produce sounds and expressions. This is an important factor related to communicative methodology since early methodology placed a heavy emphasis on imitation and speaking.

Elementary school foreign language programs should be designed to take into account the natural stages of second language acquisition (Krashen & Terrell, 1983). An initial listening period should be planned for in which students are not expected to respond in the target language. Immersion programs provide a good model for this initial listening period. In immersion programs, students hear only the foreign language from the first day of school. All classroom instructions and directions are in the foreign language so that students acquire the foreign language in play and work situations that are related to meaningful communication. Even though the teacher is constantly using the foreign language, the students may use English among themselves and also in speaking to the teacher. This reduces anxiety and frustration and allows the children a period of time in which they can build up comprehension skills. Within one to two years in the program, the children move rather automatically into speech production.

Similarly, in other types of elementary school foreign language programs, the teacher should not feel obligated to restrict classroom language to that which the students can understand fully and attempt to produce themselves. When these teachers follow the immersion model, they enrich the language environment and surround the activity of the classroom with speech. Instead of calling for immediate imitation of words and patterns, they allow for an initial period when students are not expected to respond in the target language, thus encouraging the children to listen for meaning rather than listen for speech production (Curtain & Pesola, 1988).

Activities that encourage listening skills, especially in the early stages, include such strategies as active physical involvement, during which the students must respond to verbal commands by performing certain actions. Other activities that encourage listening skills are teacher demonstrations (with the teacher making use of props, pictures, and pantomime to aid comprehension), descriptions, and telling or reading a story. To use descriptions for listening practice, the teacher describes an object or picture, constantly using gestures and specific elements of the object or picture to make the meaning clear. The teacher can then check listening comprehension through yes-no, short answer, or either-or questions, or by pointing or having students otherwise identify information from the picture.

Communication as the Main Goal

Another key element in methodology for elementary school foreign language programs is that communication is the main goal. In content-based classroom settings such as immersion, the context within which communication takes place is well established and is relatively easy to identify. The context is the regular school curriculum and everything else that is part of a regular elementary school class. The language becomes a tool of instruction, and information exchange is assured. In non-immersion classes, the elementary school foreign language teacher must create within the classroom the settings that will give the learner the opportunity to use the target language in a natural communicative way. Tasks such as grammar or pronunciation drills don't provide students with the chance for exchanging authentic messages.

A basic element in promoting communication as the main goal is that the target language is used as the primary means of interaction so that children are immersed in an environment where the language is used naturally as a real means of communication. The teacher helps the student understand the target language through use of gestures, visuals, and concrete examples, and through the routines and rituals of the lesson and the school day. Especially with entry-level students, it is important that teachers use their acting abilities, as well as concrete objects, to illustrate meaning. In most language classes, students are surrounded by language that is made meaningful because of the context and because of the way the teachers speak to them. This language of the classroom environment is assimilated by students and later drawn upon when they are ready to express messages of their own in the target language.

Other Elements of Methodology

Written forms of familiar language can also be used, even in early stages of language acquisition, with children who are literate in their first language. Games, pair work activities, pen pals, and classroom exchanges all help motivate students to communicate and will provide situations in which communication is natural and meaningful.

Because most programs are dealing with children at concrete stages of cognitive development, successful approaches to elementary school foreign language classes emphasize concrete experiences and good use of visuals and physical activity. Teaching strategies that incorporate concrete experiences, especially in early stages, are extremely

successful. Other successful strategies are integrated experience-based approaches to reading and writing, planned experience-based culture activities, and incorporation of crafts activities and experiences with food.

Effective methodology in elementary school foreign language programs incorporates the student's interest in drama and play. Role play, games, action songs, and songs that tell a story can provide such opportunities. Children's literature and folk and fairy tales from the new culture enable students to participate in storytelling and re-telling, puppetry, and drama.

In contrast with the artificial separation of the skills which was common in the past, listening, speaking, reading, and writing are now integrated holistically into communicative experiences. While in beginning stages of instruction there is more emphasis on listening, reading and writing activities are not excluded, and flow out of listening and speaking activities. The amount of time devoted to reading and writing activities varies according to the age and grade level of the students.

In all areas of the elementary school foreign language curriculum it is important that teachers integrate the foreign language curriculum into the regular curriculum. This integrated approach looks first at the foreign language curriculum and then looks for ways to integrate the foreign language into other subject areas.

Holistic, integrated, thematic instruction is an important emphasis in today's elementary schools, and this emphasis must be carried into elementary school foreign language programs. Thematic teaching provides a focus for learning experiences. In thematic teaching the curriculum is organized around themes which can originate from the classroom, school, or environment, and activities are planned so that they relate to each other and fit within the framework of a lesson or a thematic unit.

Such integrated holistic approaches are based on the premise that when students are engaged in meaningful activities they acquire language, including writing, as naturally as they learn to walk and talk. In first language teaching, this kind of an integrated, thematic approach is often labeled "whole language" (Goodman, 1986). The hallmarks of such an approach in the first language are the following: it takes into account total language needs, focuses on meaning, revolves around learning activities with specific content, and follows natural developmental stages of literacy development. In second language teaching, the same hallmarks apply, except that literacy development may not be as important since many students in early language learning programs are already literate in their first language.

STRATEGIES AND ACTIVITIES

Strategies and activities used in elementary school foreign language methodology are extremely diverse, as is the methodology used for teaching any curriculum area at this level. There is really no single approach or method that is most effective with all children. Below are some methods, strategies, and approaches currently in use that contribute to effective elementary school foreign language teaching.

Total Physical Response (TPR)

In this approach, developed by James Asher (1988), students respond with physical activity to increasingly complex teacher commands. Students are not expected to respond orally until they feel ready. Early oral responses often involve role-reversal in which the student takes on the role of the teacher and gives commands to others in the class. An important aspect of the strategy is the creation of novel commands, to encourage creative and careful listening, and the combination of commands, to encourage performances of sequential actions.

The Natural Approach

In this approach (Krashen & Terrell, 1983) students learn new vocabulary through experiences and associations with the words in a meaningful context. Extended listening experiences include TPR, use of vivid pictures to illustrate concepts, and active involvement of the students through physical contact with the pictures and objects being discussed—by means of choice-making, yes-no questions, and game situations. The Natural Approach outlines a useful sequencing of teacher questions which moves students from a listening mode to a speaking mode; the first level (except for the use of "yes" and "no") gives a demonstration of listening comprehension only, while the last three levels move the student into speaking (Curtain & Pesola, 1988).

Descriptions and Demonstrations

The teacher describes an object or a picture, preferably brightly colored, that has high interest and vivid action and/or cultural value, constantly using gestures and elements from the object or the picture to make the meaning clear. Listening comprehension is checked through yes-no, short answer, or either-or questions, or by means of pointing or otherwise identifying information from the picture. In a demonstration the teacher gives instructions on how to complete a task (such as folding a piece of paper), making heavy use of props, pictures, pantomimes, and other visual aids to comprehension. There should be frequent rephrasing during the presentation—just as might occur in real conversation—and regular comprehension checks throughout (Curtain & Pesola, 1988: 130).

Telling or Reading a Story

Storytelling is an important method for providing natural language experiences even during very early stages of language acquisition. Stories should be highly predictable or familiar to the children from their native culture, and include a large proportion of previously learned vocabulary. They should be repetitive, making regular use of formulas and patterns. In the best story choices, these elements of repetition will provide language that children can later use for their own expressive purposes. The story line should lend itself to dramatization and pantomime and to the use of visuals and props to help clarify its content.

Shared oral reading with "big books" gives students oral language input and the opportunity to participate in shared reading. A big book is an enlarged piece of commercial—or student made—literature. It has a predictable story line with a strong rhythm, rhyme, repeated patterns, logical sequence, and supportive illustrations. Students follow each word in the big book as it is read. Students in literacy development programs begin to "read" by reciting and memorizing, recognizing sight words, and decoding. Students in foreign language programs can begin to match their oral language with the written word.

Games, Songs, Rhymes, and Finger Plays

Games are a familiar method by which elementary school teachers create a setting for second language acquisition. In addition to context, games also provide motivation and a sense of play that can enhance both learning and memory. Teachers can choose or invent games for introducing and practicing the language that students need for communication.

Many songs, rhymes, and finger plays for young children incorporate actions, which help to make the new language more meaningful. Finger plays are rhymes built entirely around the use of the hand and the fingers to enter into the performance of a rhyme. Culturally authentic songs, rhymes, and finger plays can be found in the target language to bring concepts and common expressions to life for children and to add a cultural dimension to the lesson.

Props and Concrete Materials

Another important factor in creating context for communication is the use of props and concrete materials. Children throughout the elementary school years continue to learn best from concrete situations; the more frequently the manipulation of actual objects can accompany language use, especially objects representing the cultures being taught, the greater the impact of the language itself.

Pair and Small-Group Work/Dialogs/Role Play/Simulations

Pair and small group work incorporate the benefits of cooperative learning, and are excellent vehicles to help students communicate in the second language. When students work cooperatively in pairs or small groups, their opportunities for language use are multiplied many times over. Often while engaged in pair work, meaningful communication stems from "information gap" activities in which one partner or member of the group has information that the other partner does not have. Cooperative learning (see Johnson & Johnson, 1987; Kagan, 1990) offers an approach to small group work and student-student interaction that has natural applications for a foreign language program in which communication plays a key role. Goals of social development can be reinforced through cooperative group work in the foreign language class, as students are placed in a position where they have need and motivation to communicate with one another.

Another cluster of strategies for creating context to motivate communication is the development of simulations, dialogs, and role plays. Dialogs can provide a structure for communication and develop a situation that will later be part of a story or a fairy tale in the curriculum or a simulation or role play the students will act out.

Role play moves a step beyond the dialog and places students in a situation in which they are called on to cope with the unexpected or with a new setting, using the material they have learned through other classroom activities.

Content-Based Instruction

Content-based instruction has arisen from the need in foreign language immersion programs to teach the standard curriculum while focusing on instruction in a second language. In content-based instruction, the goals of the language curriculum are broadened to include reinforcement of goals of the regular elementary school curriculum. In a content-based foreign language lesson, the foreign language teacher carefully selects concepts from the regular curriculum that are clearly defined and do not require an excessive vocabulary load. The teacher takes into consideration the language skills, content skills, and cognitive skills required by the students in order to achieve success with the lesson. Content-based instruction is gaining more and more attention, because it allows schools to combine the goals of the second-language curriculum with some of the goals of the regular curriculum. Content-based instruction enables the second/foreign language teacher to focus on academic needs and critical thinking skills, while, at the same time focusing on second language needs. It provides many more contexts for communication than would be possible if the language were taught in isolation from the rest of the school program.

Integration of language and content goals also correlates closely with the move toward communicative language teaching and more holistic instruction. In order for communication to take place, there must be some knowledge or information to be shared. In content-based teaching situations, this information is the school curriculum, and students develop communicative ability as they exchange information about measurement, animal properties, distances, and so forth.

Culture and Global Awareness

Students will learn about culture most effectively through meaningful experiences with cultural practices rather than through discussion, slides, reports, and readings. Methodology used to provide cultural and global awareness must relate to concrete experiences. Because the language itself is the single most important evidence of the culture available to the children, it provides both an important starting point and the obvious vehicle for culture learning. Letter, tape, and picture exchanges with children from the target culture can bring new meaning and importance to the experience of learning a language. Most important, real information from the culture must be a daily part of the activities of the classroom. Sometimes cultural information can be the object of instruction in the same way that mathematics or social studies curriculum content might provide the focus. Cultural practices like bowing or handshaking can be employed as a part of daily routines and classroom activities.

READING AND WRITING STRATEGIES

The following are meaningful, integrated strategies focused on reading and writing.

The Language Experience Approach

The Language Experience Approach uses language produced by the students to record experiences in writing. The stories are used for reading activities and later as springboards for writing activities. Students are able to read the stories since the only vocabulary used is that which came from their own oral language. The sequence to a language experience lesson is the following (Hansen-Krening, 1982):

1. Teacher plans a shared experience for the class.
2. Students become directly involved in the experience.
3. A student responds orally to experience.
4. A student responds by writing (or the teacher writes what a student dictates).
5. A student reads the written response.

The language experience approach is used successfully with both first- and second-language learners. In second/foreign language classes the experiences are often planned by the teacher since there is a need to maintain control over the vocabulary load. In first language classes this is not the case, and many of the experiences for language experience stories come from outside of school. While the steps in the process are similar for both groups, the second/foreign language teacher spends much more time creating the experience and less time with the dictation process. The actual language dictated by the children is usually modified and sometimes translated by the teacher at this step.

The language experience approach must be adapted somewhat for second language classrooms to allow for firmer direction from the teacher, but the central concept remains the same—use of the students' own vocabulary, language patterns, and background experiences to create the reading text.

Process Approach to Writing

The "writing process" encourages collaboration among writers and provides numerous opportunities to create and use meaningful discourse in writing (Enright & McCloskey, 1988). The six steps, which can be used in full group and small group settings, are

1. Pre-writing
2. Drafting
3. Sharing and responding to writing
4. Revising
5. Editing
6. Publishing

This process can be used successfully in foreign language classes as long as students have the oral language necessary to participate fully in the process. The publishing stage provides a natural vehicle for error correction within a meaningful context.

Dialog Journals

A dialog journal is a written conversation in which a student and teacher communicate regularly (Peyton, 1987). Dialog journals provide a communicative context for language and writing development. Students write on topics of their choice, and the teacher responds with advice, comments, and observations, thus serving as a participant, not an evaluator, in a written conversation. Dialog journals can be used very early in the second/foreign language learning process. Students can begin by writing a few words and combining them with pictures.

CONCLUSION

Children who participate in a foreign language program using appropriate methodology can be enriched in many ways. They experience the joy of communicating in a new language. They develop a sensitivity to other cultures that will shape their understanding of the world. The methods used by elementary school foreign language teachers are the key to this crucial experience.

DISCUSSION QUESTIONS

1. Curtain recommends "role play, games, action songs, and songs that tell a story" to help students to become acquainted with the culture(s) of the target language. What planned cultural experiences, such as field trips, can be related to and integrated with these?

2. How are the target language forms scaffolded to make the meaning optimally accessible to students in each of the methods recommended by Curtain?

3. If the integration of skills and modalities of expression is as valuable as the integration of meaning (content) with form (the foreign language), how can the classroom activities recommended in Chapter 12 be incorporated in the target language into meaningful forms that are heard, spoken, read, and written by students?

PART 3

CONTENT-BASED LANGUAGE PROGRAMS FOR ADULTS

At least since Lambert, Just, and Segalowitz (1970), but certainly after Lambert and Tucker (1972) appeared, foreign language teachers of adults have grown increasingly interested in the idea of immersion-type or content-based programs for language teaching which were developed originally with children. More recently, as the rush of demographic change has begun to be felt more intensely in higher education, Swain and Lapkin (1989) have asked explicitly: "What's the connection [between] Canadian immersion and adult second language teaching?" In fact, a spate of excellent books and articles have appeared in recent years about "comprehension-based" and "discipline-based" second language teaching (e.g., Brinton, Snow, & Wesche, 1989; Short, 1991; Swaffar, Arens, & Byrnes, 1991; Courchêne, Glidden, St. John, & Thérien, 1992; Richard-Amato & Snow, 1992).

In Chapter 13, Ann Masters Salomone shows specifically how the methods of Canadian immersion experiments in elementary education are relevant to adult second (or foreign) language teaching. Whereas Swain and Lapkin (1982, 1989) had reviewed the results of Canadian-style immersion programs, showing that the methods of those programs are relevant to language and content teaching across the board, Salomone looks to the methods themselves rather than results common to immersion-type classrooms. Her review contains some interesting, if modest, surprises.

For instance, contrary to some of the claims that have been made on behalf of immersion approaches, it appears that immersion teachers do give some attention, at least, to surface grammar. They even correct errors. In this connection, Helen Johnson's article on "defossilizing" (Chapter 25) is relevant. Perhaps the best answer to criticisms such as that of Hammerly (1987), who insists that immersion produces inferior competence in the target language, is to point to the results that can be achieved in context-rich (heavily scaffolded) settings where apparently even "fossilized" errors can be adjusted so that progress is made (see also Arevart & Nation, Chapter 27). At any rate, it comes out in Salomone's essay that grammar is not just taken for granted even in immersion programs. The implication is that perhaps it also ought not to be taken for granted in content-based instruction at higher levels as well. Clearly, this is a theme that has recurred from the early chapters of this book (see especially Chapter 5, about the Rassias methods).

However, neither Salomone nor any of the other professionals in Part 3 are recommending that lone-minority children ought to be scattered here and there ("submersed") throughout a school system, in what are sometimes bewildering and unfriendly environments. Professional language teachers and bilingual educators do not recommend "submersion" or any other form of "subtractive bilingualism." They reject the simple equation of "immersion" programs by Baker and de Kanter (1983) with the failure-prone "submersion" approach which is still used in too many U.S. communities. The problem is that an unsupportive and uncomprehending environment—where attempts of the minority child to communicate are apt to be met with a blank, monoglottotic stare (even from well-meaning teachers; see Simon, 1980)—is a sure-fire recipe for the abortion of further attempts at communication (see Watzlawick, Beavin, & Jackson 1967; Vigil & Oller, 1976). As attempts at communication are extinguished, the possibility for language acquisition drops to such a low ebb as to become effectively nonexistent. Is it any wonder, therefore, that "submersion" approaches generally fail?

Brinton, Snow, and Wesche (Chapter 14) expand on the idea of extending immersion approaches to higher education and recommend content-based language instruction. They review the results of immersion-type programs and show how those same kinds of results can be achieved in foreign or second language classrooms. Teaching non-primary languages in content-based approaches should not surprise anyone, because, after all, understanding the abstract aspects of any subject matter depends on comprehending representations in some language or other. In fact, it can be shown rigorously that the publicizing of abstract ideas (and all social organization depends ultimately on such abstractions) can only take place through the kinds of symbolic systems dependent on natural languages and derivative systems—e.g., beliefs, myths, customs, literature, music, math, law, medicine, art, architecture, etc. The proof of this fact is developed extensively in the writings of C. S. Peirce (in the Harvard series edited by Hartshorne & Weiss, 1931-1935, and by Burks, 1958; and in the Indiana University series now in progress: Fisch et al., 1982; Moore et al., 1984; Kloesel et al., 1986) and is summed up in Oller (1989). Therefore, content-based language instruction makes sense both for conveying content and for language instruction.

The trick is to jump-start the process so that the target language can be made comprehensible. One of the ways of doing this is through "sheltered" classes—these are out-of-the-mainstream classes where students with less than native-like skills in the target language nonetheless pursue content study in that language. In these cases, the common knowledge of the content, plus a lot of meaningful scaffolding, enables students to acquire language skills while also advancing in content knowledge. In Chapter 15, Krashen reviews the evidence and theory on such approaches and shows them to be a particularly advantageous variety of immersion or bilingual programming. In the sheltered class, the focus is mainly on subject matter, but with students for whom the language of instruction is not their primary language.

Finally, in Chapter 16, we reach the historical and logical limit of what has traditionally been an almost content-less kind of instruction, and, as a result, a colossal educational failure—the U.S. foreign language curriculum. Allen, Anderson, and Narvaéz show that foreign language acquisition can be enriched by content-based approaches. Sternfeld (Chapter 18 in Part 4) will offer additional evidence along the same lines even in the case of rank beginners. The great advantage afforded by content-based teaching is that the linguistic forms through which the content is expressed achieve sufficient determinacy to become comprehensible. This sort of determinacy is missing from content-less utterances dropped out of the blue sky on hapless foreign language students in traditional foreign language curricula.

CHAPTER 13

Immersion Teachers:
What Can We Learn from Them?

Ann Masters Salomone

EDITOR'S INTRODUCTION

According to Swain and Lapkin (1989), in their thorough review of Canadian immersion experiments, the integration of content and language is essential, and the "principles should generalize to any second language instructional setting." Salomone, in this chapter, takes this generalization seriously. This will come as no surprise to well-informed language teachers, but they may take heart from seeing that what immersion teachers often do intuitively is apt to involve the very methods that are known to be generally applicable in language teaching. Another outcome of the Canadian research, one that Salomone does not stress but which will also be heartening to many foreign language teachers who work with subjects beyond the early grades—a fact noted by Swain and Lapkin (1989)—is the finding that adults quite generally have the advantage over children in acquiring a new language. Older children and adults simply have more cognitive muscle to apply to the task and generally excel except with respect to the mastery of subtle aspects of surface form such as the phonology and morphology of the new language. Literacy skills and related knowledge bases afford older students a marked advantage over younger children. Owing to what is known of the interrelatedness of language skills and semiotic capacities in general (Cummins, 1981, 1983, 1984; Oller, 1979; Oller et al., 1991), it ought not to be surprising that more-mature learners are relatively better off with respect to transferable elements of their skills and knowledge than less-mature ones are. Another possible surprise from the Canadian research, and one noted here by Salomone, is that immersion teachers do emphasize surface grammar. According to Swain and Lapkin (1989), they overtly correct about 20% of student errors and also use some explicit teaching of "grammar," as Salomone also shows (in addition see Johnson, Chapter 25). Most importantly, however, Ann Masters Salomone details, perhaps for the first time, that methods that work elsewhere in literacy and language teaching are precisely the ones that immersion teachers typically employ.

Immersion can then be viewed not only as content-based language learning, but as a key example of the integration of content and language teaching, the principles of which should generalize to any second language instructional setting (Swain & Lapkin, 1989).

For over 20 years, French immersion research has concentrated on the achievement of immersion students. In Canada, where French immersion has flourished since 1965, some researchers have found that students attain near-native levels in second language receptive skills while maintaining their English-language abilities and performing as well as their English-language educated peers in subject matter areas. (See Swain & Lapkin, 1982, for a thorough review of the research.) Conversely, other researchers argue that immersion students err consistently in their French-language utterances and speak a pidginized dialect rather than accurate French (see Hammerly, 1987; Lyster, 1987; Pellerin & Hammerly, 1986; Spilka, 1976).

The central point here is that these traditional directions of immersion research have concentrated on student performance while giving little attention to teacher behavior. The intention of this article is to focus on the behaviors and thoughts of immersion teachers. As principal players in the immersion scenario, these teachers have not received enough attention, in spite of their pivotal role as the "native French-speaking model" in the classroom (Swain, 1982). Certainly, descriptions of immersion teachers' activities are interesting to future immersion teachers and to teacher trainers. But, according to Swain and Lapkin (1989), many elements of immersion teacher practices could be useful to any second language classroom teacher. In essence, immersion teachers base their classroom behaviors on pedagogical principles that other second language teachers might consider.

In order to examine the implications of this statement, we must first know what immersion teachers are currently doing. Several scholars have expressed the need for descriptive research in immersion classrooms. Carey (1984) states that there are few studies that actually document what immersion teachers do in immersion programs. Tardif and Weber (1987) suggest more qualitative studies; Klinck (1985) asserts that the expertise of the classroom teacher must be coupled with research; Willets (1986) contends that both researchers and teachers need to know what is actually happening in the classroom; and Genesee (1987) calls for a program of research to investigate how immersion teachers integrate academic and language instruction.

Descriptive research of this type is best handled by a qualitative approach, which is a relatively new direction in educational research. Qualitative research is characterized by data collection in a natural setting (usually in the schools); acknowledgement of the researcher as an influence

on the study; emergent research design (the research design can be modified as data collection progresses); inductive data analysis; negotiated outcomes (analyses are discussed with respondents); and a case study reporting mode (see Lincoln & Guba, 1985).

As part of a larger study sponsored by a United States Department of Education grant,[1] extensive observations and interviews of six elementary French immersion teachers were conducted during the first three months of the 1988-89 school year at "Glenwood" School, an elementary alternative school in a large midwestern city. Five of the teachers were native French speakers; one was English-speaking but also proficient in Italian. This "early total immersion" program provides all instruction in French in kindergarten and grade one. One hour of English language arts is introduced in grade two and progressively increased until grade five, when about half of the day is in French, half in English.

Qualitative research yields an enormous amount of data, which often proves unwieldy. However, by selectively focusing on certain immersion teacher behaviors, we can consider not only these immersion classroom activities, but also the relevant underlying principles that can generalize to any second language instructional setting (Swain & Lapkin, 1989).

Often, the typical pattern in a second language class is that textbook exercises are conducted in the target language, while all other classroom communications are conducted in English. However, the meaningful communication inherent in daily "housekeeping" tasks of all second language teachers can become a significant enhancement of the second language learning process.

At Glenwood School, elementary immersion teachers' daily tasks include circle time, presentation of the daily routine, and lining-up activities. The kindergarten teacher, Pierre, begins circle time with a song: "Bonjour, mes amis, bonjour" ("Hello, my friends, hello"), which he repeats with several individual students' names, thereby enhancing student self-images while providing motivation for repeating the song.

Denise, a first-grade teacher, discusses the daily routine with her students and models the second language while involving students in the planning: "Voilá ce qu'on va faire aujourd'hui" ("Here is what we're going to do today"), and eventually she writes:

1. *ours brun* (brown bear)
2. *une dinde multicolore* (a multicolored turkey)

jaune	*orange*	(yellow)	(orange)
rouge	*brun*	(red)	(brown)
vert		(green)	

3. *math*
4. *journal*

Before she writes, however, she discusses in French each activity with the children, thereby encouraging their second language production. *"On va faire le livre poisson rouge?"* ("We're going to do the goldfish book?") They respond negatively and tell her that the book is *"ours brun"* ("brown bear"), which she then lists as number one. As part of the presentation of the *programme,* it is interesting to note that teachers at Glenwood School often suggest an incorrect response to induce a correct one. This technique serves as a means to elicit student speech while providing an analogous second language model.

"On va commencer l'action de graces. Qu'est-ce que c'est?" ("We're beginning Thanksgiving. What is this?") Denise shows a ditto of a turkey with color names marked on its feathers and answers her own question: *"C'est une dinde. Cette dinde va avoir beaucoup, beaucoup de couleurs. Regarde comment je l'appelle."* ("It's a turkey. This turkey will have many, many colors. Look at what I call her.") She writes *"une dinde multicolore"* on the easel, has the class repeat, and then asks them to read with her as she points to the words. To illustrate number 3, Denise shows the class the math ditto they will complete; number 4 is their daily journal.

At the more advanced third-grade level, Patrice uses restroom lining-up activities to expand upon and reinforce the second language. First, she calls *"les filles qui portent un pantalon"* ("girls wearing pants"), *"les filles qui portent une robe"* ("girls wearing dresses"), and *"les filles qui portent une jupe"* ("girls wearing skirts"). Then she calls the boys: *"les garçons avec les yeux bleus"* ("boys with blue eyes"), *"les garçons qui portent des chaussures blanches"* ("boys wearing white shoes"), and *"les garçons qui portent des pantalons bleus"* ("boys wearing blue pants").

Any second language teacher can expand language instruction during daily "necessary" activities; textbook exercises should not be the only vehicle for language practice. Although high school/college classrooms have no circle time, daily warm-ups can be conducted in the L2. Presenting the *programme* is also possible in a traditional second language classroom: The teacher can list the day's activities while discussing them in the L2 with the students. Even "lining up" activities occasionally occur in secondary classrooms (for fire drills and special assemblies). Other tasks that can be conducted in the L2 include calling roll, assigning homework, announcing future academic events, and directing classroom activities. Not using the language for these daily tasks implies to students that the second language is reserved for textbook exercises. Conducting these activities in the L2 signifies to students that the language is a *tool* for meaningful and useful communication.

Researchers assert that between 65% and 90% of all communication is nonverbal, with some estimates exceeding 90% (Burgoon, Burgoon, & Woodall, 1989; Mehrabian & Ferris, 1967). While attempting to communicate in a language that is unfamiliar to their students, teachers nearly automatically resort to some form of *nonverbal communication.* Because Glenwood immersion teachers often spend six hours per day communicating in a non-familiar language, they use concrete materials and body movements extensively.

The need for concrete materials to reinforce and clarify early language learning is widely accepted: "Language environments rich in concrete referents appear to be a necessary environmental characteristic for beginning second language learners" (Dulay, Burt, & Krashen, 1982). At Glenwood School, for example, Pierre holds up a giant blue crayon to ensure students' comprehension of the sky's color; Denise uses large posterboard cutouts to illustrate various colored animals during reading lessons; Nadine, a second-grade teacher, uses students' leaf collections as a basis for science and math lessons; and Estelle, a fifth-grade teacher, gives a body-parts quiz that demands that students draw their answers: *"Il faut dessiner un menton. Il faut faire une image. N'écris pas le mot."* ("You must draw a chin. You must make a picture. Do not write the word.")

Using concrete materials can enhance second language learning at any level and appeal to students' varying learning styles. Some high school (and even college) students may still be in the "concrete-operational" stage (see Inhelder & Piaget, 1958), and need the support of "concrete-empirical props." All second language teachers could benefit from the words of Estelle: "I'll do anything that will get them involved using their hands."

Body movements also aid language retention, according to Pierre, who has his kindergartners sing *"Frère Jacques"* while performing appropriate body movements. They repeat the song several times, once singing softly, then humming to help memorize the song while performing the body movements, a technique Pierre calls *"intériorisation"* ("internalization"). Based on theories of Piaget and Vygotsky, this association of language and movement has been expanded successfully in Asher's Total Physical Response approach to second language teaching (Asher, 1982).

Patrice often uses body-movement comprehension checks with her students because of their limited language ability; *"Debout si c'est chaud"* ("Stand up if [you think] it is hot"), for example. During her physical education class, students associate familiar and unfamiliar vocabulary with their body movements: *"Mains sur la tête, les épaules, en haut, sur les hanches. . . On se tient bien droit."* ("Hands on your heads, on your shoulders, up high, on your hips. . . . Sit up very straight.") The exercises are performed slowly, with yoga-like control.

Using concrete materials and body movements enhances second language communication in any setting. Consciously capitalizing on this non-linguistic support in the classroom is a wise practice.

The use of *related vocabulary* (or "notions") is a central component in the functional-notional approach to second language teaching (see, for example, Finocchiaro and Brumfit, 1983). This practice is also apparent in any "situational" activity in traditional grammatical-structure oriented classrooms. "At-the-post-office" or "in-a-restaurant" activities depend upon thematic vocabulary for their success.

At Glenwood French immersion school, thematic vocabulary is used extensively and varies with the seasons or special topics. Teachers reinforce vocabulary in different subject-matter lessons over a period of two or three weeks. To the tune of "Who's Afraid of the Big Bad Wolf?" Pierre's kindergartners sing a song that he created using Halloween vocabulary:

> *Qui a peur du petit fantôme?*
> *Ce n'est pas nous, ce n'est pas nous!*
> *Qui a peur du petit fantôme?*
> *Ce n'est pas nous du tout!*
> *Qui a peur de la sorcière? (etc.)*
> *Qui a peur du grand squelette? (etc.)*
> *Qui a peur du gros chat noir? (etc.)*

("Who's afraid of the little ghost? Not us, not us! Who's afraid of the little ghost? Not us at all! Who's afraid of the witch? [etc.] Who's afraid of the tall skeleton? [etc.] Who's afraid of the fat black cat? [etc.]")

Expanding on the song and integrating language studies and math, Pierre asks a student to show him *la sorciere*. Camille points to the witches hanging from the ceiling, and the class counts to ten in French. Pierre then asks for the *"gros chat noir"* ("fat black cat"), the *"petit fantôme"* ("little ghost"), and the *"grand squelette"* ("tall skeleton"), which the children identify.

In high school/college second language classes, and perhaps more often in the language-for-special-purposes setting, thematic vocabulary can lend coherence to grammar-based lessons. According to Ausubel, Novak, and Hanesian (1978), retention is promoted by learning vocabulary items as a meaningful and active cognitive process that relates to the student's cognitive structure. By grouping related vocabulary items together and using them in varying contexts, teachers provide the necessary concept-relatedness required for meaningful learning.

In *Language and Content* Mohan (1986) asserts that second language learners can be *peer teachers.* All six Glenwood immersion teachers capitalize on this concept. Marie has students teach one another the hallway routine: She states, *"On regarde. . ."* Some children answer *"Devant."* Marie: *"On a les bras. . ."* Children: *"En bas."* *"On a la bouche. . ."* *"Fermee."* *"On ne marche pas. . ."* *"Comme les canards, comme les pingouins, comme un cheval"* ("We look. . ." "Ahead." "We have our arms. . ." "Down." "We have our mouths. . ." "Closed." "We don't walk. . ." "Like ducks, like penguins, like a horse.") In this case, by reiterating the hallway rules, students socialize one another in proper Glenwood School behavior. Classroom regulations and subject-matter content are often transmitted from child to child, and all six Glenwood teachers encourage students' sharing of information, in either the first language or the second.

Individual peer teaching, in which one student addresses the class, is also common at Glenwood: Nadine has students take turns leading the class in song while they point to the words on the blackboard. Estelle names one student as leader for math activities: This student is responsible for reading the mathematical statements presented by three other students, two of whom hold posterboard numbers and one of whom decides which direction to face his greater-than/less-than symbol.

Such involvement is also possible with older students: Peer teaching is sometimes more effective than teacher-centered instruction. According to Pica and Doughty (1985a), more L2 utterances occur in a small-group situation than in a teacher-fronted classroom; and results of a study by Porter (1986) show that grammatical errors are no more common in student-to-student activities than in those conducted by the teacher. Not only can older students lead traditional classroom activities, but they can also teach one another in pair or small-group situations.

Various *organizational structures* enhance students' awareness of the daily lesson. According to Wong-Fillmore (1985), consistency in organization is a structural characteristic of successful L2 classes. Carefully articulating a daily routine, specifying sub-activities, and using boundary markers give the students an idea of what to expect, both linguistically and instructionally.

Glenwood teachers agree: Denise believes that without a familiar routine, her students would question her constantly about what to do next. Marie specifies the sub-activities of her *"ours brun"* lesson by writing the following on the board:

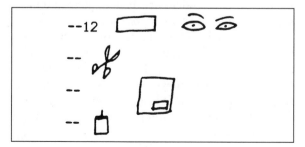

And she then explains the order of activities: *"Numéro un, je regarde; numéro deux, je decoupe; numéro trois, je les place; numéro quatre, je les colle."* ("Number one, I look; number two, I cut; number three, I position them; number four, I glue them.") Wong-Fillmore (1985) noted that teachers use lesson scripts that they have adopted for each subject. Once they learn the sequence of sub-activities for each subject, students can follow the lesson without having to figure out afresh what is happening each day.

Pierre often uses boundary markers between activities to provide familiar clues and "frame" the event for the students: To mark the end of circle time, Pierre and the class recite and perform the rhythmic finger play:

Frappe, frappe, frappe, les doigts croisés;
Frappe, frappe, frappe, les bras croisés;
Frappe, frappe, frappe, les mains fermées;
Frappe, frappe, frappe, les pouces levés.

("Clap, clap, clap, fingers crossed; clap, clap, clap, arms folded; clap, clap, clap, hands closed [into a fist]; clap, clap, clap, thumbs raised.")

At a more advanced level, teachers may state simply, as did Patrice, *"Les mathématiques maintenant. Quelle multiplication?"* ("Mathematics now. What multiplication?") to mark the end of one activity and the beginning of another. Or a simple "Take out your pencil and paper," spoken in the L2 can indicate to secondary school/college students that a writing activity will soon begin.

By providing as much structure as possible and depending on visuals and formulaic clues, language teachers can eliminate confusion and make it possible to use the L2 more in their classrooms. Recognizing that classroom directions are sometimes the most meaning-based communications of their day, second language teachers should exploit these inherently meaningful situations by structurally clarifying their L2 use as much as possible.

Immersion teachers often integrate *different subject-matter areas*. Pierre moves easily from language studies (singing a Halloween song) to math (counting Halloween characters). Patrice integrates reading and math: After lunch, she begins a story, *"Casquettes à vendre"* ("Caps for sale"), and asks comprehension questions while showing the illustrations. In answer to how many hats of each color there are, Patrice tells the students, *"Comptez par quatre—quatre, huit, douze, seize, et un égalent dix-sept"* ("Count by four—four, eight, twelve, sixteen, and one equals seventeen").

Estelle integrates math, science, language, and francophone culture in a three-step process for converting Fahrenheit temperature to Celsius:

1. Fahrenheit temperature (e.g., 77) - 30 = 47
2. 47 ÷ 2 = ~ 24
3. 24 + 10% (2.4) = 26.4 or 27 degrees Celsius.

At the secondary/college level, teachers often present different content: history, culture (lifestyle studies, art, music), math (flashcards to learn numbers, bingo games), and science (metric system, weather). When possible, these various subject-matter areas can be integrated. For example, when discussing weather, teachers can incorporate vacation activities, distances between cities, and attitudes toward travel in the target culture. Interdisciplinary possibilities in second language classes arise frequently, and these opportunities should not be squandered.

Confusing students' intellectual functioning levels with their language abilities, language teachers often limit their classroom discussions of reading passages to lower-order questions. At Glenwood School, in spite of the students' limited linguistic prowess, reading comprehension questions on higher levels of cognitive functioning are used (see Barrett, 1972; Bloom, 1956). Patrice, especially, asks *higher-order questions*. While reading *"Cosquettes à vendre"* ("Caps for sale"), she asks the children to guess what happened to the hats when the vendor in the story falls asleep with them on his head and all but one disappear. This inferential-level question easily becomes a creative exercise. The children answer imaginatively: *"Ils allaient dans le vent"* ("They went in the wind"), *"Une personne vient vendre les casquettes"* ("A person comes to sell hats"), and *"Comment dit-on 'dreaming'?"* ("How do you say 'dreaming'?").

Even Pierre, at the Kindergarten level, asks "Why?" questions, thereby encouraging the children to think analytically; *"Pourquoi est-ce que la citrouille est triste?"* ("Why is the pumpkin sad?"), for example. In this case, students answer in English, and Pierre translates their responses.

At the secondary/college level, asking "thought" questions is even more necessary, given the students' intellectual maturity. Language teachers at these levels should be careful not to restrict questioning because of students' limited linguistic ability. Using nonverbals, offering two possible answers for students to choose from, and prompting with an incorrect answer are techniques used at Glenwood School that can easily be adapted to secondary/college classrooms to facilitate students' L2 responses. In spite of their restricted second language abilities, mature students can be encouraged to respond creatively to intellectually challenging questions.

CONCLUSION

All of the practices and underlying principles described above have one common theme: Language is integrated into the teaching of content. Snow, Met, and Genesee (1989) list several rationales for the effectiveness of integrating content and language teaching, notably that content provides a cognitive basis for language learning in that it provides real meaning that is an inherent feature of naturalistic language learning. Further, they suggest ways that their "conceptual framework" can accommodate different types of elementary school second language learning situations. However, in second language classes at any level, teaching concepts should be the top priority. These concepts can be linguistic, as is the French notion that grammar rules can be modified to promote fluent pronunciation (e.g., *"Vas-y! Mon amie. . . Parle-t-elle?"*) or sociological, such as the French sense of privacy (e.g., walls around French houses, reluctance to discuss personal matters). It is important to address basic concepts in order to avoid superficiality and rote memorization of language. Not addressing underlying concepts can lead students to believe that language learning is a mere spelling exercise.

The six Glenwood immersion teachers who participated in this study are dedicated to teaching concepts integrated with the teaching of a foreign language. Because they nearly always communicate in a language that is unfamiliar to their students, they have refined many techniques that are transferable to all levels of language teaching.

Conducting housekeeping tasks in the L2, using nonverbals extensively, involving students as peer teachers, structuring classroom routines, integrating various subject matter areas, and asking higher-order questions can improve any second language classroom.

NOTES

1 This research was supported by United States Department of Education grant #R168F80060.

DISCUSSION QUESTIONS

1. In addition to the fact that adults generally know more than children, what other factors differentiate the experience of children versus adults in acquiring a new language? For instance, suppose an adult says something that other adults do not understand. How will they respond? But, suppose the speaker is a child and the hearers are also children. How will the children respond? Also consider the difference between the way adults react to children versus children to adults. How might these differences impact the acquisition of the subtleties of surface forms (e.g., a native-sounding accent, perfect surface morphology and syntax, etc.)?

2. What results should be expected if the opportunities for language students to produce comprehensible output were to be increased? Or suppose students have lots of opportunities to understand input but little or no opportunity to produce output. If comprehended input always must involve an active production of an interpretation by the person doing the comprehending, in what sense, exactly (from the student's point of view), is comprehended input less difficult than comprehensible output?

3. What sorts of social factors contribute to the stabilization or destabilization of the sort of system characterized by Hammerly (1987) as a "terminal classroom pidgin"?

4. In what ways are immersion classroom activities scaffolded to aid comprehension?

CHAPTER 14

Content-Based Second Language Instruction

Donna M. Brinton, Marguerite Ann Snow,
and Marjorie Bingham Wesche

EDITOR'S INTRODUCTION

Following the lead of immersion experiments, Brinton, Snow, and Wesche define content-based instruction as "the integration of particular content with language-teaching aims," and they assert unequivocally that "language is most effectively learned in context." However, they reject the notion that odd bits and pieces of linguistic discourse can be parachuted into some context in such a manner as to create an authentic text. Better, they suggest, to rely on the sorts of discourse that naturally occur in real contexts. This is the same as insisting on connected discourse of the true narrative type (see Chapter 37 for a definition) as the foundation for language instruction. Very sensibly, Brinton, Snow, and Wesche maintain that the content (or facts) should "dictate the selection and sequence of language items [representations] to be taught rather than vice versa." Both teacher and students, then, are engaged in an activity of negotiating the forms and arrangements of target language forms (the representations) in such a manner as to put them in appropriate correspondence to the content (i.e., to the facts at hand). They stress, correctly in my view, that this will result in "truly contextualizing" the target language.

The claim that language is most effectively learned in context is hardly a new or revolutionary one. Regardless of the specific methodology used, language teachers have generally found it desirable to present new items through meaningful content; in fact, "contextualizing" lesson presentations has become a widely accepted rule of good language teaching. Yet much of the controversy about second and foreign language teaching which has surfaced in the past several decades has centered precisely around the question of what role content should play in language teaching. What, for example, is the importance of meaningful content in the language acquisition process? Is it essential that content be understood in order for acquisition to proceed? If so, to what extent is this a sufficient condition for acquiring different aspects of language? Are texts which have certain grammatical and discourse features more appropriate than others for particular language-teaching purposes? What are the implications of using varied subject matter as opposed to developing the same theme in depth? How can we know which topics will be of interest to our students? How can a given content best be integrated with language-teaching purposes in the language classroom?

These and other related questions have led methodologists to carefully examine the role of content in language teaching. This investigation has led to a widely shared belief that simply "contextualizing" language lessons which are organized around structures or functions is not enough. Rather, theorists and practitioners have suggested as a starting point the use of *authentic texts* which are relevant to the learners' second language needs —i.e., written or oral texts which were created for a purpose other than language teaching. These provide in concrete form the structures, functions, and discourse features to be taught. One view is that these features, once identified, can then be taught at least partially in isolation, with lessons focused on particular language forms, functions, and patterns. A second view is that the emphasis on the informational content itself provides an effective means for incidental acquisition of the language features it presents. Content-based language-teaching approaches, in fact, often combine focus on form with experiential techniques.

In this volume, we define content-based instruction as the integration of particular content with language-teaching aims. More specifically, since we are dealing primarily with postsecondary education, it refers to the concurrent teaching of academic subject matter and second language skills. The language curriculum is based directly on the academic needs of the students and generally follows the sequence determined by a particular subject matter in dealing with the language problems which students encounter. The focus for students is on acquiring information via the second language and, in the process, developing their academic language skills. Ultimately, the goal is to enable students to transfer these skills to other academic courses given in their second language. Thus, both in its overall purpose and in its implementation, content-based instruction aims at eliminating the artificial separation between language instruction and subject matter classes which exists in most educational settings.

In a content-based approach, the activities of the language class are specific to the subject matter being taught, and are geared to stimulate students to think and learn through the use of the target language. Such an approach lends itself quite naturally to the integrated teaching of the four traditional language skills. For example, it employs authentic reading materials which require students not only to understand information but to interpret and evaluate it as well. It provides a format in which students can respond orally to reading and lecture materials. It recognizes that academic writing follows from listening and reading, and thus requires students to synthesize facts and ideas from multiple sources as preparation for writing. In this approach, students are exposed to study skills and learn a variety of language skills which

prepare them for the range of academic tasks they will encounter. This type of approach has important implications for course design. The course design must indicate the means by which the content is to be integrated with language objectives. Accordingly, the curriculum and materials must reflect this overall design.

A content-based instructional approach has a number of implications for language teachers as well. First, language instructors are asked to let the content dictate the selection and sequence of language items to be taught rather than vice versa. They are asked to view their teaching in a new way, from the perspective of *truly* contextualizing their lessons by using content as the point of departure. They are almost certainly committing themselves to materials adaptation and development. Finally, with the investment of time and energy to create a content-based language course comes even greater responsibility for the learner, since learner needs become the hub around which the second language curriculum and materials, and therefore teaching practices, revolve.

A RATIONALE FOR CONTENT-BASED LANGUAGE TEACHING

At least five different rationales for integrating the teaching of language and content are implicit in content-based approaches. First, proponents of English for Specific Purposes (ESP) note that for successful language learning to occur, the language syllabus must take into account the eventual uses the learner will make of the target language. Thus, focus is on the language forms and functions which will best serve the learner, based on systematic description. Second, even though learner language needs and interest may not always coincide, the use of informational content which is perceived as relevant by the learner is assumed by many to increase motivation in the language course and thus to promote more-effective learning. Third, content-based approaches apply the pedagogical principle that any teaching should build on the previous experience of the learner, as they take into account the learners' existing knowledge of the subject matter and of the academic environment as well as their second language knowledge. A fourth rationale is that language should be taught through a focus on contextualized *use* rather than on fragmented examples of correct sentence-level *usage*, the former a critical feature of a content-based approach. In this way, the learner will become aware of the larger discourse level features and the social interaction patterns which are essential to effective language use, as well as of the correct grammatical conventions.

Finally, the fifth and probably the strongest argument for content-based courses comes from research in second language acquisition. Much recent research suggests that a necessary condition for successful language acquisition is that the "input" in the target language must be understood by the learner (Krashen, 1985a; 1985b). Since input which will serve for language acquisition must also contain new elements to be acquired, comprehension is accomplished with the help of cues from the situational and verbal contexts. These interact with the learner's imperfect knowledge of the language and with his or her world knowledge and expectations. The associations of form and meaning which are required for successful comprehension feed into a developing stock of formal, functional, and semantic relationships as the learner acquires new elements in the language. While there is some controversy about whether novel, comprehended input in the target language is a sufficient condition for acquiring productive skills in the second language, there is strong evidence that it is a necessary condition, and that it is sufficient for the acquisition of a high level of proficiency in listening and reading. This process requires that the learner be focused on meaning rather than on form. The role of output has also been discussed in the literature and may be a necessary condition to enable learners to move from semantic to syntactic processing (Swain, 1985). The learning of significant, relevant content through a second language, the shared principle of all content-based approaches, can satisfy both these conditions.

LANGUAGE LEARNING THROUGH LANGUAGE USE: SOME HISTORICAL ANTECEDENTS

While the movement toward content-based language instruction is a contemporary one, its roots can be traced back many centuries. As early as 389 A.D., St. Augustine stressed the need for a focus on meaningful content in language learning:

Once things are known knowledge of words follows . . . we cannot hope to learn words we do not know unless we have grasped their meaning. This is not achieved by listening to the words, but by getting to know the things signified.[1]

There is, in fact, ample historical evidence of the human ability to learn a second language through meaningful exposure to its use. For centuries, upper-class European families have recognized the utility of direct contact and communication needs in effective language learning by sending their children to live and study in regions where the language of interest is spoken, or importing governesses and tutors who would use the language with the children. Likewise, soldiers, traders, immigrants, inhabitants of border areas, prisoners of war, footloose students, and even tourists have throughout history proven able to acquire the second language skills they need through contacts with speakers of the language, provided the contact is extensive enough and their motivation sufficient.

Notwithstanding the above, educators have often viewed both the goals and the appropriate methodology of school second language learning somewhat differently. Language study in school was long considered to be training in mental discipline, as well as a key to foreign literatures and cultures for the educated classes. Such attitudes still persist in many foreign language-learning situations in schools and universities, although approaches which advocate language learning for communicative purposes through meaningful language use have become influential in situations where the language to be learned is a second language with clear functional utility for the learner. The situation in which learners need to improve their second language skills for purposes of university study unites formal second language instruction with real and present functional needs. Here again, communicative language teaching and needs-related, content-based instruction merge in their respective objectives.

THE 1960S-1980S: THE ROOTS OF CONTENT-BASED LANGUAGE TEACHING

Current interest in language-teaching approaches which emphasize the mastery of particular informational content as an integral element of second language instruction represents a coming together of practical experience and theory. In light of the assumption that language can be effectively taught through the medium of subject matter, these approaches view the target language largely as the vehicle through which subject matter content is learned rather than as the immediate object of study. At the same time they recognize that important gains in language proficiency occur "incidentally" (albeit purposefully in a methodological sense), as language is used in the understanding and expression of meaning. Thus, the traditional focus of both native and second language classes on awareness of linguistic form is largely subordinated to a focus on acquiring information *through* the second language. Such an approach has been increasingly espoused by teachers and researchers involved in the teaching of native language skills across the curriculum, and it is also the cornerstone of such innovations in second and foreign language teaching as immersion language programs. In the following section, we will present some examples of how content-based language instruction is currently being implemented in native, foreign, and second language settings.[2]

Language Across the Curriculum

The language across the curriculum movement as a means of first language development received a major impetus in 1975 from the report of a committee commissioned by the British government to consider "all aspects of teaching the use of English, including reading, writing, and "speech" (cf. Bullock Report, 1975). A major finding of the committee was that first language instruction in the schools should cross over all subject matter domains. Accordingly, there followed a recommendation for a policy of teaching language as a part of instruction in other curricular areas in British schools. The committee's report and the experimentation which followed it have been very influential in North American schools as well.

The principles of language across the curriculum for native speakers of English have been further specified in instructional programs at the postsecondary level (Griffin, 1985; Thaiss, 1987). In programs for reading and writing across the curriculum, the perspective taken is that of a reciprocal relationship between language and content

learning. Students are not only given opportunities to learn to write and learn to read but are also encouraged to *write to learn* and *read to learn* in order to fully participate in the educational process. These objectives, by definition, necessitate cooperation between language teachers and subject matter teachers, with the language teachers emphasizing instruction focused on language problems in reading and writing English and the content teachers complementing this with activities requiring reading and writing in the learning of subject matter. As a consequence of this cross-curricular focus, the language across the curriculum movement has resulted in new developments in teacher training and materials development. For example, several publications describing strategies for cross-curricular teaching at the secondary and postsecondary levels deal with such issues as designing effective writing assignments and essay questions, improving the writing process, and evaluating student work (Anderson, Eisenberg, Holland, Wiener, & Rivers-Kron, 1983; Simmons, 1983).

In short, the language across the curriculum movement is an attempt by both British and North American educators to offer native English speakers access to the full range of educational activities in which language and content are inextricably woven together. It provides students who have highly developed functional skills in their own language with an opportunity to further refine the language skills required for advanced schooling—those needed in understanding and expressing complex content using the more-decontextualized skills required in academic reading and writing. This movement has influenced second language instructional theory and practice. It is particularly relevant to the development of content-based second language instructional programs of the type treated in this book, in that it provides a methodology for students with varying degrees of proficiency—those who need to develop their skills in precisely those areas required for successful learning of academic content.

Language for Specific Purposes

Language for specific purposes (LSP) is perhaps the best known and most documented of the content-based language models. LSP courses generally involve pragmatic, experience-based instruction and are aimed at preparing learners for real-world demands. This type of language program has been most notably developed in Britain for the teaching of ESP. Most common at the university level and in occupational settings, LSP courses are particularly suitable for adult clients with identifiable second language objectives, and are a response of academic as well as commercial language-teaching programs to the specialized requirements of postsecondary students and those engaged in business or other occupations. In LSP courses, the primary emphasis has traditionally been on the "what" of language instruction—language content which reflects the second language needs of learners "for whom the learning of English is auxiliary to some other professional or academic purpose" (Widdowson, 1983). Materials are usually created in relation to a systematic analysis of the learner's second language needs. These may take the form of a taxonomy of microskills and functions such as that proposed by Munby (1978), they may take the more flexible approach of the Council of Europe (Richterich & Chancerel, 1977), or they may be defined in terms of a particular set of texts to be mastered by the learner.

LSP courses, obviously, are possible only when the characteristics, needs, and purposes of a group of students are relatively homogeneous. They generally serve specific occupations, fields, or levels of study. Thus, an ESP course for Canadian police officers may be different in almost every way from one for Saudi Arabian oil company employees, international air traffic controllers, Chinese teachers of English, or international students entering an American university to study economics. The unifying feature is that the objectives and language content of each course are defined according to learners' functional needs in the second language. English for Academic Purposes (EAP), which prepares students for study in English speaking countries, accounts for a major subset of LSP courses.

A common body of second language needs does not in itself lead to the teaching of language via subject matter presentation, since the language elements identified can be isolated and reorganized for instructional purposes. Nonetheless, LSP courses, through the frequent use of authentic materials and attention to the real-life purposes of the learners, often follow a methodology similar to that of other content-based models in which a major component is experiential language learning in context.

Immersion Education

A third major example of experimentation with content-based language teaching can be found in second and foreign language instruction in Canada and the United States. The St. Lambert, Quebec, French immersion project, begun in 1965, was designed in accordance with the theory of the day on how second or foreign languages are best acquired (Lambert & Tucker, 1972). Intensive exposure to the target language through natural communication with a native speaker was considered essential, as was starting at a young age. The experiment began with a classroom full of English-speaking kindergartners receiving the regular half-day curriculum entirely through the medium of French from a French-speaking teacher. As year-by-year research results demonstrated the success of immersion for the mastery of both functional French and school subject matter, programs were begun by other school boards. Two decades later, "immersion" has become a mass educational movement in Canada, where over 240,000 Canadian children in all provinces and territories receive much or all of their school instruction through a second language. This instruction takes place in a variety of immersion formats for different age groups, and while it primarily involves French, it also is used for instruction in heritage languages such as Hebrew, Ukrainian, and Canadian Indian.

Since 1971, with the establishment of a Spanish Immersion Program in Culver City, California, immersion education has also spread in the United States as an alternative to traditional Foreign Language in the Elementary School (FLES) programs. While the student enrollment in immersion programs is still far smaller in the United States than in Canada, the American immersion programs reflect both geographical and language diversity. There are approximately 25 immersion programs around the country offering foreign language instruction in Cantonese, Spanish, German, Japanese, and French (Rhodes, 1987).

The immersion model is a carefully researched example of content-based second language instruction at the elementary and early secondary levels. It illustrates the effectiveness for kindergartners to adolescents of instruction which focuses on teaching subject matter through the medium of the second language. While the language itself is largely learned incidentally, there is also, as in first language instruction in the schools, some explicit focus on language rules and forms. Since the successes of the immersion model have been achieved almost exclusively with language majority children—those whose home language is that of the larger community and is thus not at risk—its main application is to foreign language teaching. For such children, constant out-of-school exposure to the first language, as well as first language instruction in school, ensures its continued development throughout their school years.

Immersion-type education through the second language has been notably unsuccessful with language minority children where there is inadequate input and support for continued mother tongue development, such as in some programs in English for native Americans and Canadians on reservations. It is also unlikely to be an appropriate alternative for young immigrant children learning the dominant language of their new country in school if it is not accompanied by first language instruction.

For language majority children who wish to add a second language in school, 20 plus years of immersion studies in both Canada and the United States have yielded remarkably consistent findings (Genesee, 1987). After several years of intensive exposure to the second language, immersion students achieve a high level of functional ability in the second language, with near-native proficiency in receptive skills by the time they graduate from an elementary school immersion program or a late immersion high school program. While their speaking and writing skills fall short of native speaker performance, such students normally achieve functional skills at a level far beyond what other second language instructional approaches have been able to produce in the schools. Immersion is thus highly successful in developing advanced second language speakers who can subsequently perfect their skills through real-life interactions with native speakers of the language. As for first language and subject matter learning, primary immersion students catch up to their monolingual peers in scholastic achievement, and they rapidly catch up in native language skills after first

language instruction is introduced. The immersion approach is used successfully with complex subject matter in bilingual secondary school programs as well, yielding impressive proficiency gains together with mastery of the content. In Canada, for example, these programs generally follow an early or late immersion sequence, with students taking 40 to 50 percent of their courses through the medium of French. Some forms of content-based instruction at the postsecondary level are in fact an extension of these secondary school programs to the university setting.

CONCLUSION

The above discussion suggests that content-based instruction can be a very effective way to teach both first and second language skills in school contexts. Practical experience with language teaching, systematic thought about language teaching and learning, and empirical research on classroom language learning all suggest that content learning through the medium of the target language can serve well as a major component of instructional programs for all age groups. It further suggests that such instruction is particularly appropriate where learners have specific functional needs in the second language.

How, then, does it work? Classroom experience and second language acquisition theory both tell us that rich second language input in relevant contexts is the key, where the attention of the learner is focused mostly on the meaning rather than on the language. This experiential component appears to be a vital element in the development of functional second language skills, with contextualized analytical activities which focus explicitly on language forms, functions, and patterns playing a complementary role in the development of accuracy and precision in language use (Allen, Carroll, Burtis, & Gaudino, 1987; Stern, 1978, 1992).

NOTES

1 St. Augustine 60: XI, as cited in Kelly (1969: 36).
2 We have selected these three examples of content-based instruction in different settings in part because of our own personal experiences and in part out of the clarity of the three models and their well-documented implementation with fairly homogeneous populations.

DISCUSSION QUESTIONS

1. If Brinton, Snow, and Wesche are correct in their argument for content-based instruction, why is the content teacher in a somewhat better position with respect to teaching a non-primary language (all else being equal) than the foreign language teacher is?

2. Supposing content (relatively well-determined facts) to be the fulcrum of successful language instruction, what becomes of the time-honored analytic approach to the separation of skills? If we can listen to discussions of the facts, talk about the facts, read about them, write about them, dramatize them, illustrate them, diagram them, mathematicize them, put them to music, interpret them aesthetically in art and dance, etc., what advantage is to be gained by separating listening and speaking activities into relatively content-less courses supposedly aimed at teaching just composition, or just conversation, or just listening skill? (Imagine, for instance, the relative effectiveness of a Dr. Pepper ad that appeals only to one single modality of sense—i.e., instead of seeing a lot of action accompanied by snappy dialog, music, sound effects, dance, visual setting, a brief episodic plot, etc., suppose we just heard against a blank background the message "Drink Dr. Pepper." Which is apt to be more effective, the advertiser's approach or the analytic language curriculum?)

3. How does the "language across the curriculum movement" reflect the natural ways in which "language and content are inextricably woven together," as Brinton, Snow, and Wesche put it?

CHAPTER 15

Sheltered Subject-Matter Teaching

Stephen D. Krashen

EDITOR'S INTRODUCTION

Krashen says that "subject matter teaching in a second language, when it is comprehensible, is language teaching, because it provides comprehensible input." Sheltered teaching can occur when all the students are more or less at the same level of development and when the focus is on the subject matter. Krashen distinguishes two kinds of research showing the effectiveness of some form of sheltering: research that focuses on the acquisition (1) of the subject matter and (2) of the target language. Both sources show that sheltered language teaching works. Another alternative is the "adjunct (or pull-out) model," in which non-native speakers of the primary language system are put in regular classes (along with natives) for subject matter but have one or more additional classes to help them master the language of each particular subject area. In addition, Krashen recommends supplementary activities such as role playing and board games to enrich opportunities for negotiating and increasing the amount of comprehensible input in the target language.

Inspired by the success of Canadian immersion programs (see e.g., Lambert & Tucker, 1972), sheltered subject matter-teaching (SSMT) derives from one important concept: Subject-matter teaching in a second language, when it is comprehensible, is language teaching, because it provides comprehensible input.[1] A history class, given to second language acquirers, if it is comprehensible, is a language class.

There are several crucial characteristics of SSMT:

1. In SSMT, only second language acquirers are allowed in the class. When all students are second language acquirers, when all students are in the same linguistic boat, it is easier for the teacher to make the input comprehensible .

2. In Sheltered Subject Matter classes, the focus of the class is on subject matter, not language. This encourages a focus on meaning, not form, and results in more comprehensible input,

and thus more language acquisition. Sheltered subject-matter classes are thus not "ESL Math" or "ESL History" but are "math" and "history."

If possible, the tests and projects also focus on subject matter and not language. When the test is on subject matter, students will listen to lectures, participate in discussions, read the required and recommended texts, and obtain a great deal of comprehensible input. When the tests are on language, students will be tempted to conjugate verbs and memorize nouns, and little language acquisition will take place. Similarly, when projects and papers deal with subject matter, students will read extensively in the second language and will obtain comprehensible input.

3. In SSMT, teachers attempt to make input comprehensible. This is done in several ways, including frequent comprehension checking, which indicates to teachers when they need to adjust the input they are providing, and the use of extra-lin-

guistic information (pictures, charts, realia, and occasional readings in the students' first language).

SSMT may be part of the solution to the "transition problem." There are several beginning language teaching methods that have been shown to be highly effective. Students in these comprehensible-input-based methods typically outperform traditionally taught first year foreign language students on tests involving communication and do as well or better on discrete-point grammar tests (Asher, 1988; Bushman & Madsen, 1976; Hammond, 1989; Nicola, 1990).

These methods, however, are limited in that they provide only "conversational" language. Second language students need more. It has been shown that conversational language does not make a large contribution to academic success among language minority students (Cummins, 1981; Saville-Troike, 1984). Conversational language is also not enough to allow the foreign language student to read the classics, engage in the serious study of literature, use the language for international business, or do advanced scholarship. Students need, in other words, the advanced vocabulary, grammar, and discourse structures necessary for truly sophisticated language use. SSMT is intended to help provide this competence.[2]

RESEARCH ON SSMT

Research on SSMT has shown that students in these classes acquire considerable amounts of the second language, typically doing at least as well as students in regular language classes, and they also learn impressive amounts of subject matter. Thus, SSMT is very time-efficient; students get both language and subject matter knowledge at the same time.

We can divide the research into two categories:

1. *Second Language Medium Studies:* Here, second language acquirers are tested on, and given course credit for, subject matter-learning.

2. *Content-Based Second Language Studies:* Here, subject matter is focused on, but students are not tested on subject matter. They get credit only for language. Some content-based classes have a grammar component, but when grammar is included, it is considered to be peripheral.

SECOND LANGUAGE MEDIUM STUDIES

The best known of the second language medium studies are the many reports of Canadian-style immersion (summarized in Lambert & Tucker, 1972; Swain & Lapkin, 1982). It has been shown repeatedly that children in these programs acquire impressive amounts of the second language, and learn a great deal of subject matter. In addition to the immersion studies, a number of research projects confirm that SSMT works for older students as well.

The Ottawa studies (Edwards, Wesche, Krashen, Clement, & Kruidenier, 1984; and Hauptman, Wesche, & Ready, 1988) showed that university students could learn both subject matter (psychology) and make progress in a second language at the same time. Participants, who were volunteers, had already studied one semester of college psychology in their first language (English or French), and had at least low intermediate knowledge of the second language (French or English). The sheltered course was second semester psychology (in Hauptman et al. one experimental group did sheltered psychology for two semesters), and was supplemented by a half-hour weekly session with a language teacher, who did no direct grammar teaching, but focused on comprehension of content and "developing strategies for effective reading and class interventions" (Hauptman et al., 1988: 445).

In general, subjects made progress in second language acquisition equivalent to students in regular second language classes, and acquired subject matter just as well as students who took the same course in their first language.

Ho (1982a) (see also Ho, 1982b) reported that tenth graders in Hong Kong who had had second language medium instruction for three of their eight years of EFL were far more proficient in English than comparison students with eight years of traditional EFL. (The English medium students may have had more total exposure to English as well, however.) Ho also reported that second language medium students learned as much physics through English over a three-month period as comparison students did in their first language.

In Ho (1985), eighth graders in Hong Kong who took courses in English learned as much subject matter as comparison students who took courses in their first language in four out of five courses. Second language medium instruction did not appear to result in additional second language acquisition. Both experimental and comparison students in this study, however, did all subject matter reading in English, which reduced the treatment differences. (Swain, 1988, in discussing this study, also suggests that the fact that nonnative speakers taught the Second Language Medium class may have been a factor, as well as the methodology used.)

Buch and de Bagheera (1978) found that ESL teachers who were not native speakers of English made significant gains on the Michigan Test and non-significant gains on a cloze test and writing test after taking eight applied linguistics courses in English. No comparison groups were used in this study for either language acquisition or content-knowledge learning.

Two studies (Saegert, Scott, Perkins, & Tucker, 1974; Gradman & Hanania, 1991) found a significant relationship between years of subject matter instruction through a second language and second language proficiency among students of English as a foreign language. In both studies, years of subject-matter instruction through English was a better predictor of English proficiency than was years of formal instruction in English.[3]

CONTENT-BASED SECOND LANGUAGE TEACHING

Schleppegrell (1984) reported that EFL students made significant gains on an essay test and test of listening comprehension after a five week content-based economics course. No comparison groups were used. (These subjects outperformed a comparison group that did a sheltered economics course in which the emphasis was on output rather than input. Comparison subjects took the essay test only.)

Lafayette and Buscaglia (1985) reported that fourth-semester university level students of French as a foreign language who studied French civilization and culture did just as well as a traditional fourth-semester class on several measures of French proficiency (listening and reading), and made better gains on a speaking test. On a writing test, however, the comparison class was slightly better, gaining about 5 points (pre = 169.3; post = 174.54) as compared to the experimental class's 3-point gain (pre = 165.29; post = 168.47). Lafayette and Buscaglia noted that the writing test was really a grammar test, with more than 20% of the items on the subjunctive. The comparison group focused on grammar, with two units on the subjunctive, while the sheltered classes relied exclusively on acquisition. Since it is quite likely that the French subjunctive is late-acquired (for evidence from Spanish, see Stokes, 1988; Stokes & Krashen, 1990), it is no surprise that the sheltered class did not do quite as well on this test.

A very impressive finding is that more of the sheltered students intended to enroll in additional French courses, and more students in this class reported that their interest in studying French had increased as a result of taking the course.

Peck (1987) found that students of Spanish as a foreign language (second-semester college level) made significant gains on an oral test and a listening comprehension test after taking a seven-week course on social work, which included some direct grammar instruction. There was no comparison group.

Sternfeld (Chapter 18) is unique because it involved beginning foreign language students. First-year college Spanish students who studied Latin-American history, geography, and culture did as well as traditionally taught students on tests of reading comprehension and listening comprehension. Comparison students did better on a writing sample, however. Sternfeld noted that this may have been due to the fact that the topic of the writing test was familiar to the comparison students, but was not included in the sheltered class.

Milk 1990 provided content-based second language teaching as part of a teacher training program to 17 bilingual and ESL teachers at the University of Texas at San Antonio. Students participated in one of two summer sessions, held for two hours per day for five weeks (42 contact hours). Students read and heard mini-lectures on second language acquisition theory, designed classroom activities in groups, and kept dialogue journals in Spanish. Participants varied considerably in initial Spanish competence, but significant group gains were found on a variety of language tests. No comparison group was used.

THE ADJUNCT MODEL

SSMT is not the only possible way of teaching language using content. The only alternative that has, to my knowledge, been empirically tested is the "adjunct model," in which students enroll in regular classes with native speakers, but also participate in an additional language class "linked" to the regular class.

In the Hauptman, Wesche, and Ready (1988) study cited in the text, one group of ESL students (1984-85 cohort) did not do sheltered psychology but were enrolled in the adjunct model, taking regular psychology with native speakers of English and also a supplementary class for one and a half hours per week. The adjunct class included "supplementary assignments, including readings related to the course topics, written summaries and critiques of the readings, and oral presentations . . ." (p. 446). Adjunct model students did well, making gains in English that were greater (p < .09) than gains made by comparison students enrolled in ESL classes. (Recall that sheltered students in the Ottawa studies also had a supplementary class, but only for a half-hour per week. Adjunct students received a separate grade for the extra class, but sheltered students did not.)

Snow and Brinton (1988) reported on twelve university ESL students who attended adjunct classes for 12 to 14 hours per week that were linked to one of several regular classes (psychology, political science, history, geography, computer science) which they attended for eight hours per week. The adjunct classes focused on "essential modes of academic writing, academic reading, study skills development, and the treatment of persistent structural errors" (p. 557). In addition, students had tutorial and counseling services. The program lasted for seven weeks (summer session). Adjunct students did as well as comparison students enrolled in regular ESL classes in the fall on a simulated academic task (answering objective questions and writing an essay after hearing a brief lecture and reading a short text). Since the comparison group had higher scores on a test of English language proficiency, Snow and Brinton concluded that the adjunct class had had a beneficial effect.

Thus, both studies of the adjunct model yielded positive results. From these studies alone, how-ever, it cannot be determined which factors of the adjunct model were helpful, especially since the adjunct classes in the two studies were somewhat different.

OBJECTIONS TO SSMT

Swain (1988) maintains that "not all content teaching is necessarily good language teaching" (p. 68). In content teaching in a second language, according to Swain: 1) students do not produce enough output, and do not produce enough complex output. More demands for output, according to Swain, will "help learners focus their attention on particular form-function relationships" (p. 73); 2) there is little correction; 3) the input is "functionally restricted," that is, "certain uses of language may simply not naturally occur, or may occur fairly infrequently in the classroom setting" (p. 71).

I have argued (Krashen, 1991) that points (1) and (2) are not a problem, since language acquisition does not require output or error correction. In fact, Swain's findings showing that sixth-grade immersion students get little correction and produce only modest amounts of language are excellent arguments that output and correction are not necessary, since these children have clearly made excellent progress despite having so little output and correction. (This is not, of course, to say that output is bad for language acquisition. I have argued in several places, e.g., Krashen, 1982, 1985a, that output helps indirectly, by inviting comprehensible input, as well as affectively.)

There are two possible solutions for the third problem Swain mentions, restricted input. One possibility is to "contrive contexts," deliberately introduce contexts that ensure the use of certain forms. This is difficult to do, since it requires knowing what rules students are ready to acquire ("i + 1").

A second possibility is simply to expand activities and the range of topics and subjects covered, which will naturally include more functions and forms (Swain, 1988: 77). This solution is easier and is more interesting for teachers and students. I will have some specific suggestions below.

NEW DIRECTIONS IN SSMT

SSMT has been successfully applied to much of the elementary school curriculum (Swain & Lapkin, 1982), and, as we have seen, to subject matter at the university level. Students have learned psychology (Edwards et al., 1985; Hauptman et al., 1988), culture and civilization (Sternfeld, Chapter 18; Lafayette & Buscaglia, 1985), economics (Schleppegrell, 1984), social work (Peck, 1987) and applied linguistics (Buch & de Bagheera, 1978; Milk, 1990) in SSMT.

I have discussed some other possibilities for sheltered courses for foreign and second language students elsewhere (Krashen, 1982, 1985a). These courses would probably provide much of the variety of input that Swain maintains is currently lacking from many content-based courses.

Two of the most promising areas for sheltered classes that would be usable for all levels are courses in popular literature and games. Popular literature and games promise to provide a wide variety of input, using activities that students find not merely interesting but often compelling.

POPULAR LITERATURE

Including a sheltered popular literature class may be a good way to combine pleasure reading and sheltered subject-matter instruction, two very effective means of moving beyond conversational language.

There is very strong evidence that pleasure reading is a major source of our advanced linguistic competence (see e.g. Krashen, 1985b, 1989a). In fact, there is evidence suggesting that merely making some popular literature available has a positive effect on literacy development (Rucker, 1982).

The goal of a popular literature class is to introduce students to many kinds of popular literature so that eventually students will read on their own. This includes comic books (for a review of the research, see Krashen, 1989b), magazines, newspapers, and popular novels.

Such a class will also give students a considerable amount of information about the everyday culture of the speakers of the target language, as well as linguistic competence.

GAMES

Several kinds of games might be very effective at the intermediate level. Straightforward board games promote interaction, and have the potential of supplying some subject matter knowledge: Britannia (Avalon Hill Game Co.), for example, takes place in Britain in the first century. While playing, participants inevitably learn a great deal of history.

The fullest potential of games is reached in what are termed "role-playing games," extremely complex games which require demanding solitary reading for character creation, and extensive group interaction in playing the actual game. The best known of the role-playing games is Dungeons and Dragons, but many variants exist, including some that set their adventures in actual historical locations, such as the China and Vikings modules from the GURP (Generic Universal Role Playing) system. Playing these games should result in significant subject-matter learning as well as language acquisition.

While there has been no evaluation of the value of role-playing games in language acquisition, it is a safe bet that they will be effective. Role-playing games provide input through reading, as well as input through interaction, and research suggests that interaction is extremely helpful in making input comprehensible (e.g., Pica, Young, & Doughty, 1987). In addition, Rhoda McGraw and Sian Howells have been offering role-playing games as part of advanced English as a Foreign Language at the École Nationale des Pont et Chassées in Paris, with great apparent success.

An obvious problem with games, as with all interaction activities, is that students hear primarily the speech of other students, or "interlanguage talk" (Krashen, 1981). I have argued that interlanguage talk probably does more good than harm, but if students hear only interlanguage talk, there is some chance they may acquire the errors they hear, leading to fossilization (Krashen, 1985a). The cure for this is to include native speakers in the games. Including native speakers as game participants violates one of the principles of sheltered subject matter teaching, but is consistent with a deeper principle: comprehensible input. When native speakers are in the game, their input can be highly comprehensible and useful; because of the constraints of the game, the students will have background knowledge to help them understand what the native speakers are saying.

For second language acquisition, finding participants is not a problem, since enthusiastic gamers are present in all school and university campuses. For foreign language situations, native speakers are harder to find, but when they are available, their task in the classroom will be obvious—simply to participate in the game.

IMPLEMENTATION

Implementation of SSMT requires some planning and effort, but it is not as hard to do as some exotic language teaching methods. One possibility is to move toward SSMT gradually, beginning with short modules as part of traditional intermediate classes. As these modules are developed and introduced into the curriculum, the language courses will take on the character of content-based second language classes and second language medium classes.

NOTES

1 I am assuming some familiarity with the Input Hypothesis, the hypothesis that we acquire language in only one way, by understanding messages. See, e.g., Krashen (1982, 1985a).

2 SSMT is not the only way of helping students move beyond conversational language. Other techniques include encouraging free voluntary reading and the proper use of the student's first language (bilingual education). (For supporting arguments, as well as ways in which SSMT can be combined with bilingual education, see Krashen, 1985a, 1985b.)

3 Increasingly Saegert, et al. (1974) also found that instruction using French as a language of instruction was also a significant predictor of English proficiency. French/Spanish as a language of instruction was not a significant predictor in Gradman and Hanania's study, however. The strongest predictor of English proficiency in Gradman and Hanania was "extracurricular reading."

DISCUSSION QUESTIONS

1. Consider the "input hypothesis." Try to imagine a way of progressing in target language acquisition without access to and comprehension of its surface forms. Why is mere exposure to such surface forms inadequate? For instance, why would merely listening to Chinese on the radio not be an inadequate method of acquiring Chinese?

2. In what ways specifically does sheltered subject-matter teaching encourage students to go beyond the limits of input with which they are already comfortable? How, for instance, does negotiating meanings in a new subject area affect vocabulary growth? Syntactic advances? Phonological development? And so forth.

3. If a group of non-native speakers are playing, say, Monopoly, with a native, in what ways do the facts of the game and the realia on the board constrain the negotiations? Suppose someone wants to buy a hotel for Pennsylvania Avenue: what sorts of facts constrain the price of the hotel, its location, its size, color, owner-to-be, etc.?

CHAPTER 16

Foreign Languages Across the Curriculum

Wendy Allen, Keith Anderson, and León Narvaéz

EDITOR'S INTRODUCTION

It has been known for a rather long time (Carroll, 1967) that for the great majority of students, foreign language education in the United States generally falls short of the goal of getting students to the point where they can communicate effectively in the target language. More likely, they will learn a few words and get some limited and oversimplified ideas about the "grammar" of the language, and beyond that they will remain almost as monolingual as most of them were when they started out. One of the reasons for this often lamented fact is, as Allen, Anderson, and Narvaéz note, that the connection between the target language and the kinds of subject matter that the foreign language student both needs and often wants to study is rarely made. Content-based instruction is a logical way to make the connection between the foreign language and its meaningful uses. Instead of teaching verb paradigms, a minimal vocabulary, and a few sentence patterns with little or no connection to experience, Allen, Anderson, and Narvaéz suggest that foreign language students at a fairly advanced level of development in the target language ought to be given a variety of opportunities to study subject matter in the language. Faculty response, student enrollments, and informal reports indicate a positive reception of such programs at St. Olaf College in Minnesota.

CURRICULAR ISOLATION OF FOREIGN LANGUAGE LEARNING

Despite three decades of programs designed to promote widespread language learning in the United States, only a small fraction of students achieve functional language competence. Even in postsecondary institutions having a one- or two-year foreign language requirement, foreign language study still is often focused primarily on the formal aspects of the target language, and the practical proficiency developed is usually limited to that required for the most basic social needs. Students acquire an initial vocabulary which they then work to expand; they study the verb tense system of the language; they begin to put the various elements of the language together, first in sentences and then in paragraphs. But, by the time they are becoming ready to focus more on the use of a foreign language to acquire and process content knowledge, i.e., to employ the tool which they have so arduously mastered, the requirement is completed and they move on to other areas of the curriculum. Consequently, students experience a sense of intellectual fragmentation with respect to their foreign language learning experiences.

Our foreign language requirements rest on the premise that as students acquire foreign language competence they also acquire a broad awareness of foreign cultures and a deeper understanding of language as a human phenomenon. Yet, because of the typical discontinuity between language programs and the rest of the curriculum, students often tend to view the foreign language requirement as just one more obstacle they must surmount on the path to graduation. The study of languages is seen solely as the acquisition of language skills divorced from any meaningful connection to the study of other disciplines, such as history, philosophy, political science, sociology, and art history. Students generally remain unaware of how the knowledge of a second language can enhance understanding of subject matter in practically all fields of study.

Furthermore, if language *study* is divorced from the heart of the undergraduate enterprise, language *use* is even more isolated. On many campuses, foreign language is studied and used only in the foreign language building or at special foreign language department events. Students have little or no opportunity to observe faculty in the humanities, the sciences, and the fine arts using a language other than English to communicate with colleagues for purposes of research or casual exchange. By the same token, due to narrowly drawn divisional and departmental lines, these same students are prevented by the curriculum itself as well as by major and other requirements from bringing together their language study and their study of other disciplines.

CONTENT-BASED INSTRUCTION

One approach to increasing integration between language learning and disciplinary content which has rapidly gained attention nationally, particularly in the field of ESL (see Cantoni-Harvey, 1987; and Crandall, 1987), is content-based instruction (CBI). Leaver and Stryker (1989) identify four features that characterize CBI: (1) the fundamental organization of the curriculum is derived from subject matter, rather than from forms, functions, or situations; (2) the core materials are selected primarily from those produced for native speakers of the language; (3) students use the foreign language to learn new information and to evaluate that information based on their emerging cross-

cultural understanding; and (4) instruction is tailored to the cognitive and affective needs of students and to their proficiency level.

Brinton, Snow, and Wesche (1989 and Chapter 14) provide what is to date the most comprehensive attempt to define CBI: "the traditional focus . . . on awareness of linguistic form is largely subordinated to a focus on acquiring information *through* the second language" (p. 137 this volume). They view interest in CBI as a coming together of the theory of second language acquisition specialists such as Krashen (1985b-c), on the one hand, and practical experience on the other. As these authors express it,

> Classroom experience and second language acquisition theory both tell us that rich second language input in relevant contexts is the key, where the attention of the learner is focused mostly on the meaning rather than on the language. This experiential component appears to be a vital element in the development of functional second language skills, with contextualized analytical activities which focus explicitly on language forms, functions, and patterns playing a complementary role in the development of accuracy and precision in language use (p. 139).

According to Brinton et al. (Chapter 14), CBI normally involves the concurrent teaching/learning of subject matter and of language:

> The language curriculum is based directly on the academic needs of the students and generally follows the sequence determined by a particular subject matter in dealing with the language problems which students encounter. The focus for students is on acquiring information via the second language and, in the process, developing their academic language skills. Ultimately, the goal is to enable students to transfer these skills to other academic courses given in their second language (p. 135).

CBI encompasses a wide range of curricular options, including the teaching of native language skills across the curriculum (e.g., language or writing across the curriculum programs), immersion programs (first begun in St. Lambert, Canada, in 1965 and currently experiencing a revival in U.S. elementary and middle schools), and language courses designed to prepare learners for specific, real-world demands. Although examples can be found as early as the 1920s, CBI did not play a significant role in college curricula until the 1980s. The primary model was the "special purposes" elective course in areas such as business, health care, and technology. Another model described by Jurasek (1988) was the "integrative" approach taken by Earlham College in an NEH-sponsored project which identified and prepared texts written in languages other than English for use in courses across the curriculum. To suggest that CBI is a unified "movement" is problematic; it is more accurately described as a bifurcated movement, with one branch focusing on language and the other on content.

Brinton et al. (1989 and Chapter 14) in their *Content-Based Second Language Instruction* describe three models for CBI at the post-secondary level. In theme based courses, often used in an ESL context, the language class is organized in terms of content "modules," and the language teacher teaches both the subject matter and language. (One of several Monterey Institute of International Studies CBI programs is based on this model.) In sheltered instruction, such as that offered at the University of Ottawa, a subject matter course is taught to a segregated class of second language learners by a content specialist, sometimes accompanied by supplementary language instruction and sometimes not. Finally, in adjunct instruction, as in the UCLA Freshman Summer Program, students are enrolled concurrently in a language course and a content course that are "paired." While all three models seek to promote teaching language through content, they differ in the relative emphasis given to language and to content learning, in overall structure, and in the levels and situations for which they are appropriate. They represent points along a continuum:

LANGUAGE   Theme-based Sheltered Adjunct   MAINSTREAM

CLASS ◄――――――――――――――――――► CLASS

(Brinton et al., 1989: 23)

The two projects described below, while having some of the features associated with the adjunct model cited above, nevertheless differ to some extent from it and from CBI in general, in that their goal is not content-*based foreign language* instruction, but foreign language-*enriched*

content instruction. Here we emphasize the concept of enrichment because, while our projects are multidisciplinary in origin and development, and while, clearly, they foster students' foreign language proficiency, their primary purpose is not so much to enhance foreign language acquisition as to enrich disciplinary study.

THE ST. OLAF PROJECTS

St. Olaf College, a private, church-related liberal arts college located in Northfield, Minnesota, is attempting to address the problem of language/content integration via a two-year project funded by the National Endowment for the Humanities (NEH) and a three-year project supported by the Fund for the Improvement of Postsecondary Education (FIPSE). The St. Olaf programs have all four of the characteristics cited by Leaver and Stryker. They share features with the Earlham project, but go beyond it in terms of level and range of second language use.

The St. Olaf projects have three objectives. The first objective is to identify a core group of faculty across the curriculum who have advanced foreign language proficiency and who are willing to incorporate foreign language texts into their courses. The second objective is to create appropriate foreign language materials for use in a group of specially adapted courses. The third objective, and perhaps our principal concern, is to encourage students to continue second language study and use beyond the three semester requirement by offering them the opportunity to combine advanced language work with disciplinary study, typically carried out in the context of institution-wide general education and distribution requirements, and/or requirements for a major.

The participating faculty members have all had significant international experience. Language faculty have demonstrated their commitment to language teaching and have been involved in teaching and doing research about the culture and history of their areas; non-foreign language discipline specialists have studied and conducted research in their language(s) of competence and have interest and expertise in cross-cultural analysis and interdisciplinary work. Both groups are committed to integrating language study and disciplinary work in order to broaden and deepen students' understanding of particular disciplines.

Critical to the success of our projects is the involvement and support of non-foreign language faculty, for it is obvious that student attitudes and behavior will not change unless faculty members demonstrate their commitment to changing the status quo. In a curricular context, this means faculty working to overcome the perceived low status of second language study and the typical absence of connection between disciplinary study and second language study. In a student context, faculty must encourage student advisees and other students with whom they have contact to do more than simply "get through" the second language requirement as quickly as possible. Also, students need to see non-foreign language faculty in their major departments as positive role models with respect to second language proficiency and use. Thus a major thrust of both projects is faculty development, for which grant funds provide released time, overload stipends, and summer salaries for course preparation and improvement of second language skills.

Students, too, in order to participate in an applied language program must first attain sufficient mastery of the language through formal language instruction or as a result of extended residence or study in a non-English-speaking environment, whether in the U.S. or abroad. Successful completion of the fourth-semester language course—one beyond the current requirement—or demonstration of equivalent proficiency is therefore required for participation in the program. (Based on surveys of student enrollments in fourth- and fifth-semester language courses, it was decided to focus the initial stage of these programs on French, German, and Spanish, each of which had a potential student participant pool of approximately 100 to 175.)

Simply offering the opportunity to develop and apply advanced language skills, however, is not enough to ensure student participation. Students also want academic recognition for their work. Consequently, in order to encourage students to enroll in applied foreign language courses, St. Olaf has created two special certifications:

a. The "Applied Foreign Language Component (AFLC)," parallel to the already-existing "Advanced Writing Component," is indicated on student transcripts. In order to receive this certification, students must complete the prerequisite courses in a particular foreign language (or demonstrate equivalent proficiency) as well as apply and extend their foreign language competence in two AFLC courses.

b. Students who wish to combine the study of a foreign language with the study of the history and culture of the respective language community in a program carried out in that language may receive (in addition to the AFLC) a "Foreign Area Concentration," which also is indicated on the transcript. These concentrations require five semesters' study of the same language plus successful completion of four courses which address the history and culture of the particular area. At least two of these courses must offer the AFLC.

Although the two projects have certain elements in common, they nevertheless differ in significant ways. They are, therefore, described individually below.

THE NEH PROJECT: "FOREIGN LANGUAGES IN THE DISCIPLINES"

Purpose

The NEH project seeks, first, to bring together a core group of faculty, representing the range of the humanities to study and discuss, in a structured seminar setting, the central role of language in the humanities and its implications for the undergraduate liberal arts curriculum. A second goal is the integration into courses taught by these faculty of significant foreign-language texts in order to promote among students a greater understanding of the relationship between language and the humanities, a broader and deeper understanding of foreign cultures, and a greater mastery of foreign languages.

"Foreign Languages in the Disciplines" is designed to demonstrate to students that the achievement of foreign language competence is an integral part of a liberal arts education and that their understanding of the humanities will deepen as their mastery of the language increases. Extending the use of foreign language materials to courses beyond those offered by foreign language departments gives students access to important texts not normally studied in language classrooms and often unavailable in English.

More importantly, students learn how, in diverse disciplines, language itself influences the shape as well as the content of the discipline. In a German history course, for example, students who read in the original language some of Wilhelm von Humboldt's writings on education learn that *Kultur und Bildung* carries implications much deeper than the English translation of "culture and education" would suggest. Reading these texts in the original leads students to explore the meaning of culture and its emergence in Europe in the eighteenth and nineteenth centuries as an autonomous category with ethical connotations. The class then examines the enormous importance in German society of the *Bildungsbürgertum*—another term whose meaning is partly lost when translated into English as the "educated middle class."

The students who elect to apply their foreign language proficiency in a particular humanities course are not the only beneficiaries of this decision. The entire class gains from the deeper level of discussion and the increased attention to meaning made possible by allowing at least part of the class to work directly with non-English texts in their untranslated original form. Gradually, the conventional wisdom of students is changing. Students who read particular texts in their original language are seen by their teachers as well as their peers to have attained far greater depth than those who have had to rely on English translations or instructor summaries. In time, it will become part of the "student culture" that it is both advantageous and interesting to do more than simply "satisfy" the foreign language requirement. Students will come to recognize the compromises, judgment calls, distortions, and sheer blunders involved in translation, and this recognition will make their reading of even the daily newspaper more sophisticated and thoughtful.

Student language competencies also are enhanced as students read, analyze, interpret, and discuss foreign language materials pertinent to a particular discipline. Students who have limited their language study to the requirement are encouraged to continue further by the opportunity to apply their foreign language proficiency to the subjects of interest to them, albeit subjects rarely included within the curriculum of most foreign language departments.

Project Design

The NEH project is a two-year effort (June 1989-June 1991) centered on faculty development, course adaptation, student recruitment, library acquisition, and program evaluation. The core group of fourteen faculty members (seven pairs, each pair composed of a foreign language specialist and a humanities specialist) modify seven already-existing humanities courses to include foreign language texts. In these courses, which are designated as having an "Applied Foreign Language Component" (AFLC), students who enroll in the AFLC "track" of the course may elect to complete approximately half of the course readings and other assignments in a particular foreign language. The AFLC students, in addition to the regular class meetings, meet in weekly discussion sessions conducted in the foreign language, which are led by a faculty pair consisting of the foreign language teacher and the course instructor.

Faculty Development and Course Adoption

The core group of faculty participates in an ongoing program of faculty development. First, these faculty meet in a week-long introductory seminar in which they explore the relationship between foreign language study and the study of other humanities disciplines, and the curriculum and pedagogical implications of integrating foreign language texts into traditional humanities courses. After the seminar, faculty pairs devote four weeks to modifying courses in history, literature, philosophy, and religion, so as to include an Applied Foreign Language Component (AFLC). Three courses were modified the first year of the project, and four additional ones the second year. These courses, together with the language of their AFLC, are as follows:

Backgrounds to British and American Literature (Spanish)
Modern Germany (German)
The Christian Tradition in History (French)
Essentials of Christian Theology (German)

Liberation Theology (Spanish; taught in
Mexico during the January 1991 term)
Modern France (French)
Progress and Poverty in Modern Latin
America (Spanish)

During the four-week period of summer work, faculty pairs discuss and shape the teaching methodology of the course in light of the introductory seminar discussions; identify, in collaboration with library resource consultants, materials for library purchase; select appropriate foreign language tats for course use; and, finally, prepare study guides, glossaries, and other course materials for students choosing the AFLC option.

Student Recruitment

The student aspect of the project begins with student recruitment, which is undertaken twice a year (in April and November) by the project director and faculty teaching AFLC courses the following semester. Computerized records of students who have completed the fourth-semester course in French, German or Spanish—those eligible to enroll in AFLC courses—are maintained by the project director and updated each semester. In early November or April, all eligible students are sent a letter by the project director. The letter explains the AFLC program, provides information concerning the courses to be offered the following semester, and explains specific registration procedures. Interested students are encouraged to contact the project director and/or appropriate faculty for additional information. In addition to this formal mailing, faculty pairs visit third-semester and fourth-semester language classes to describe the course they will offer and respond to student questions. While student recruitment is labor-intensive and time consuming for both project director and faculty, we believe that "the personal touch" is largely responsible for the success we have had in recruitment.

The AFLC Course

Student participation in the program begins with enrollment in one of the humanities courses featuring the Applied Foreign Language Component. All of the students enrolled in one of these courses complete a basic set of (English-language) readings. But those who elect the AFLC will do at least fifty percent of the total course reading and related research in the foreign language. (Those who do not elect the AFLC will complete this additional reading and research in English.) Written work for AFLC students may be submitted in English or in the foreign language, depending on the writing proficiency of the student. In addition to the three hours per week of class required of all students enrolled in the discipline course, those who elect the AFLC discuss their reading and research in weekly one-hour sessions conducted in the foreign language and led by the faculty member from the language department together with the course instructor. Students who elect to enroll in the AFLC section of these specially designated humanities courses receive an additional one-quarter course credit for their participation in the required weekly foreign language discussion sessions.

Library Resources

Another important component of the project is a coordinated program of library acquisition. A professional librarian with expertise in the humanities and in foreign languages works in close collaboration with the project director and faculty. These individuals determine the strengths and weaknesses of the college's current collections of books, journals, newspapers, government documents, maps, and video and film resources in various disciplines, written or produced in languages other than English, and identify additional foreign language resources appropriate for student use in the specially adapted humanities courses offering an AFLC.

THE FIPSE PROJECT: "FOREIGN LANGUAGES IN THE NATURAL BEHAVIORAL SCIENCES"

This is a three-year project (September 1989-August 1992) which extends the possibility for applied foreign language study to the natural and behavioral sciences, and to mathematics.

Project Design

The FIPSE project contains many of the same features as the NEH program, but also offers several additional options for students to complete the AFLC. Students can earn Applied Foreign Language Component credit in a variety of ways:

1. Partial foreign language immersion (the NEH model).
2. Directed readings. Individuals or small groups of students work with disciplinary faculty members who have foreign language competence to complete directed study projects in a foreign language.
3. A total immersion January term course. During St. Olaf's January term, courses which normally are taught in English are taught in a foreign language by two faculty members, one from the sciences and the other from foreign languages. Courses may be taught on campus or abroad.
4. A science course taken in a foreign language abroad Certain of St. Olaf's study-abroad programs allow students to enroll in science or mathematics courses taught in the language of the host country.
5. An internship in a foreign language community abroad This includes individually arranged internships as well as group experiences in which a St. Olaf faculty member accompanies a group of students who complete a one-month internship abroad during the January term.
6. Partial immersion semester. During certain semesters, two-course or three course interdisciplinary seminars are offered in a given foreign language. The thematically integrated program of study constitutes half or three quarters of the students' academic load for the semester.

FIPSE offerings to date include, in addition to five directed readings courses, the following team-taught disciplinary courses:

American Foreign Policy (Spanish)
Ethical Management: Germany and America (German)
Marriage and the Family (Spanish)

Library Resources

Holdings of foreign language editions of books in the natural and behavioral sciences are quite limit-ed in the typical undergraduate library. Thus, to support the AFLC courses, a coordinated program of library acquisitions is being carried out. The work is directed by a professional librarian with expertise in the sciences and in foreign languages, working in close collaboration with the faculty participants.

PROJECTED OUTCOMES

These projects will determine whether or not, at a four-year undergraduate liberal arts college, significant numbers of students who are non-foreign language majors will elect to continue foreign language study beyond the graduation requirement when given the possibility of attending use of their foreign language to general education requirements and/or their major fields of study. The several options for content learning in a foreign language will be evaluated and compared with respect to their contributions to subject matter mastery and to enhancement of students' foreign language abilities.

The projects also seek to build a cadre of disciplinary faculty members who will become mentors and role models for students who wish to apply their foreign language study to their non-language majors. This is accomplished both through support of existing faculty who are reactivating and enhancing foreign language competencies, as well as by making command of a second language a factor in the recruitment of new faculty.

The identification, acquisition and development of appropriate learning resource materials for content learning in foreign languages is a further goal of the project. This includes primarily library materials, but also other media such as films and videotapes.

The long-term "global" outcome which both projects hope to achieve is a gradual erosion of the traditional separation between foreign language study and the study of other disciplines in the minds of both faculty and students. The projects do not propose to make chemists into German teachers or French teachers into historians. Rather, the two projects seek to open a dialogue and develop the basis for interdisciplinary cooperation, a process which will yield enhanced relevance for foreign language study and add a new and exciting dimension to many students' work in a range of disciplines.

Project Evaluation

It is too early in these two projects to assess with any degree of certainty their ultimate impact on faculty and student attitudes toward foreign languages and toward proficiency in them, or to project their impact on curricular structures. The extent to which they will help break down the traditional curricular isolation of foreign languages is impossible to predict, as is the success they will have in encouraging students to continue their study and use of a second language after completion of the requirement. Nevertheless, certain aspects of the grant initiatives are now complete. As of this writing, two initial workshops have been held, and nine team-taught courses with an AFLC, plus five directed readings courses, have been offered. Based on analysis of the results to date, we offer certain preliminary conclusions.

First, the June 1989 and June 1990 faculty workshops offered a structured setting in which colleagues from across the curriculum had the opportunity to discuss an issue which is at the heart of our work as teachers and scholars in a liberal arts institution, namely, the role of language in the liberal arts and sciences. The one week seminars revealed that non-foreign language specialists are inclined to underestimate the amount of text preparation and accompanying activities necessary for students to engage fully a given text. Language faculty experienced the challenge confronting their disciplinary counterparts of structuring and adapting courses covering large quantities of material, virtually all of which is normally viewed as essential. The seminars provided opportunities for participants to discuss pedagogical concerns such as the merits of lecture, full-class discussion, and small-group work, as well as possible balances among the three. The opportunity to discuss pedagogical issues—and to do so in a multidisciplinary context—was highly valued by seminar participants.

In evaluations completed by faculty at the end of the seminar, there was unanimous assent for the value of forums such as these. Faculty reported that their participation in the seminar—in particular the opportunity to share ideas about the integration of methodology, topics and texts, and to discover

additional sources of information—would influence not simply their AFLC course, but all of their teaching. This suggests that the ultimate impact of the two projects will go well beyond the creation of materials to be used in a relatively limited number of courses in the humanities and sciences.

In terms of the faculty as a whole, the AFLC program has generated more discussion about foreign language competence and use than has occurred on the campus for many years. The fact that many faculty—and not simply language faculty—are talking about languages and the degree to which they are currently used on campus by both faculty and students is a positive development. In the fall of 1990, over a dozen non-foreign language faculty were enrolled in language courses, with the intent of using their language in a variety of contexts including, in some cases, the AFLC program. These developments constitute progress toward one of the major goals of the applied foreign language projects, namely, attending foreign language study and use across the campus.

As for student response, the goal of averaging seven to ten students per AFLC course has been met. All indications are that this enrollment pattern will continue. For example, nineteen students are enrolled for a three-course interdisciplinary immersion seminar offered in the fall of 1991 under the auspices of the FIPSE grant.

Student evaluations confirm students' recognition of the value of the program. They particularly appreciated the opportunity to discuss ideas and issues of substance made possible by the weekly AFLC discussion session. As one student wrote, "I had an additional hour per week to concentrate on thinking and speaking about the material." This opportunity enabled a number of students to contribute in a substantive way to full class discussions involving both AFLC students and students enrolled in the English-language track. AFLC students were able to contribute insights they might not have had in the absence of the weekly foreign language discussion sessions.

Students reported they had been able to maintain their language skills and to apply them to new material. As one observed, "I enjoyed being able to apply my language to another discipline, and it was good to be able to read firsthand many primary documents." Many students cited their expanded and improved second language vocabulary and a perceived strengthening in their reading comprehension. Most recognized that participation in the AFLC track of the course helped them focus on what was critical to the course and, in general, aided their preparation for and participation in the regular class sessions. As students stated, "Often in the AFLC we discussed more elaborately topics that were pertinent to the [regular disciplinary] course" and "I gained more insight into the readings."

The majority of students conveyed either verbally or in writing appreciation for the ability to work directly with materials written in a second language. The responses of students enrolled in the German AFLC section of a history course on Modern Germany were typical: "Some things, some words, are not easily translated and by reading [the text] in German, I could better understand what was being conveyed," and "Reading about the average German's life in German gave it a meaning that would have been lost in translation." Certainly the student support for this experiment has been more than sufficient to justify its institutionalization.

St. Olaf's Applied Foreign Language Component program and similar programs at other colleges and universities in the U.S. and Canada have received considerable attention within the foreign-language teaching profession and beyond (Moline, 1990; Straight, 1990; Watkins, 1990). These programs provide multiple ways of encouraging second-language use across the curriculum and thereby help to overcome the curricular isolation of second languages to which we referred earlier. We envision a future in which the academic use of languages is seen as an integral part of the undergraduate curriculum of most colleges and universities—and we and others are beginning to make that vision a reality.

DISCUSSION QUESTIONS

1. If one of the objectives of foreign language education is for students to "acquire a broad awareness of foreign cultures and a deeper understanding of language as a human phenomenon," can such a goal be achieved at all in the absence of a substantial degree of competence in the foreign language? If learning a few words in Spanish and a brief exposure to a few structures in that language will not produce the kind of knowledge and multicultural understanding that foreign language instruction aims to instill, what more will be required?

2. It is argued that substantial competence in a foreign language can enhance comprehension of the broad spectrum of subject matter. How is this possible?

3. Content-based instruction is "bifurcated with one branch focusing on language and the other on content," according to these authors, who also say that it is the connection (or "integration") of target language with content that is crucial. Discuss the bifurcation and integration relative to the theory of pragmatic mapping (see Chapter 37).

4. If the goal of content-based instruction is to "enrich disciplinary studies," how can it be demonstrated that this has occurred? What sorts of evidences could be marshaled (for instance, course enrollments, faculty participation in the program, student reactions, scores on standardized tests in the disciplines, etc.)?

PART 4

LITERACY IN ALL ITS GUISES

Becoming literate means much more than just becoming able to read and write. It involves the acquisition of the skills needed to relate written representations in the language of literacy to relevant aspects of experience in general. The literacy connection does not merely relate to this momentary here and now, though that connection is everyone's starting point, but to the whole world around us with its past, present, and future, together with all of their diversities and complexities. Becoming literate in this broader sense means being empowered in such a manner as to become a participant in the larger world community—a community of many languages, cultures, political entities, and of increasingly complex multinational organizations of all sorts. In the twenty-first century, being literate means having the intellectual tools and skills that give access to all sorts of meanings and possibilities that would otherwise remain out of reach. Practical literacy means knowing how to negotiate physical space more efficiently, as in using public transportation systems. It means being able to consider and select from a wider range of alternative courses of action than would be possible in a preliterate state. It means greater freedom, responsibility, and the power to participate in social, economic, educational, political, and other activities of the larger world communities. In a sentence, literacy is the essence of a practical education for modern living.

Therefore, Part 4 is about literacy in this broad sense of the term. It is new in this edition of *Methods That Work* and is predicated on the growing realization among educators everywhere that acquiring a language and learning to read are part and parcel of the same fundamental problem of actively comprehending representations. For readers familiar with the writings of Krashen (1981, 1982, 1985b, 1989a, 1991) and those of Frank Smith (1978, 1982, 1988), the close analogy between acquiring another language and learning to read will not come as a surprise. But regardless of whether the relation between these educational objectives seems familiar or surprising, the insight is well-grounded. Acquiring a language and becoming literate are fundamentally similar problems. This can be proved through sound theory, empirical research, and methods that work in both literacy and language instruction.

The first chapter of Part 4, Chapter 17, is aimed at elementary teachers and others who work mostly with children at the early stages of becoming literate. The principles explained there, among them the scaffolding of discourse to enhance its comprehensibility and to establish its social purposes and motivations, are thoroughly grounded in pragmatic theory. In addition, the methods advocated in Chapter 17 have been tested with populations of subjects where the failure rate in previous decades had approached the limit of 100%. Hardly any of the children in those contexts were accorded any hope of learning to read and write prior to the family of programs described in Chapter 17. With the changes recommended in classroom contexts by Walker and his collaborators, the picture has been completely reversed, from near 100% failure to near 100% success. Essentially all of the children who attend school regularly, even in very difficult third-world contexts, become enthusiastic readers and writers. These results are the more impressive when the demographic characteristics of the communities where they have been achieved are taken into consideration. Educators and others who have tried to explain away high failure rates on the basis of difficult demographic contexts (low socioeconomic status, a history of illiteracy, etc.) will be hard-pressed to account for the fact that the turnaround from almost total failure to near complete literacy has occurred in some of the world's most difficult demographic contexts.

The argument that essentially all children can become literate, even in a language other than their first, is carried forward to the case of adults in foreign language studies by Sternfeld in Chapter 18. Following the immersion model of the Canadians (see Parts 2 and 3), Sternfeld presents evidence showing that even first-year foreign language students in a university setting can progress in understanding of the target language and in literacy and knowledge of the target culture, all at the same time. However, Sternfeld insists, following Krashen (1982), that expectations concerning early output in the foreign language need to be "adjusted downwards" and that "compensatory strategies" focusing on comprehension in "sheltered" contexts should be employed. Students in the immersion/multiliteracy program report heightened interest in the foreign cultures and in broadening their educational experience. Presently, projects are under way at the University of Utah in Spanish, French, German, Chinese, and Japanese.

In addition to showing the connection between the acquisition of literacy and language acquisition (in Chapters 17 and 18), another purpose of Part 4 is to explore in greater depth the processes that underlie literacy in the broadest sense of the term. It is argued more fully in Chapter 37 that the episodic structure of ordinary experience underlies all true narrative representations. In addition, it can be shown that all fictional representations achieve their comprehensibility (to the extent that they are comprehensible) by virtue of their resemblance to those of the true narrative type. The comprehensibility of descriptive, reportative, expository, exhortatory, and all other kinds of texts and discourses depends ultimately, as is shown in Chapter 37, on representations of the true narrative kind, which are the only kind determinately grounded in experience—a fact which is logically proved there. For all of these reasons, scaffolding of the type exemplified in Chapter 17 is dependent in the final analysis on the *actual* experience of the persons benefiting from it. One of the principal elements of such scaffolding—one that is singled out for attention in the research reported in Chapters 17–22 of Part 4—is the temporal or sequential arrangement that typifies the episodic organization of experience in general. Because the spatio-temporal (episodic) aspect of experience is known only through representations of the narrative type, it follows that narrative representations must play a crucial role in all aspects of literacy. Moreover, as researchers look more closely into the nature of the episodic side of narrative-type representations (fiction included), it is clear that there is strong empirical evidence sustaining the theoretical (logical) necessity of the episodic organization of experience itself.

Chapter 19 deals with what Patricia L. Carrell calls a "formal schema" for stories. She, and others, have argued that such a formal schema (which transcends any particular exemplar of a story) is probably universal across languages and cultures. In Chapter 37, we will see logical proof that the formal schema underlying narratives, in fact, *must* be universal. Further evidence supporting the universality of a formal schema for narratives is seen in Chapters 20–22. In Chapter 20 a series of seven different studies, involving narratives, expository texts, and descriptive prose, shows that literate native speakers of English, as well as non-native users of English from a variety of language backgrounds, are able to understand and reconstruct portions of texts more easily when those texts appear in their original schemata-constrained arrangements. As will be argued in Chapter 37, that order is grounded ultimately in the formal schema associated with the episodic structure of experience itself. Empirically, there is confirming evidence that the logical basis underlying narratives is universal across language and cultural backgrounds. By contrast, however, comprehension of the particular content of texts (what Carrell in Chapter 19 has called "content schemata") appears to be dependent on particular experience and familiarity with certain kinds of subject matter as is shown in Chapter 20. As a result, knowledge of content schemata appears to be language and culture specific to a much greater extent than formal schemata are, and this is exactly what the theory (Chapter 37) predicts.

Chapter 21, by Yukie Horiba, goes some distance toward helping us to see just what a narrative schema might be like. It turns out that an analysis of native and non-native protocols in think-aloud readings of a story in Japanese reveals a linear propositional structure with multiple inferential links between its overt and covert propositional structures. By investigating such complexities, Horiba offers insight into the character of narrative schemata. It appears that such schemata are grounded in nothing other than inferential logic coupled with particular facts of ordinary experience. Horiba's data show that native speakers of Japanese are, as we would expect (and as the research of Chapter 20 also shows), more capable than non-native speakers in sorting out and expressing the relations between the propositions underlying the comprehension of a story in that language. Non-natives, however, are able to compensate for their lack of skill in Japanese by appealing to their knowledge of the world and the scaffolding that it provides in helping them to understand the story (also see Taira, Chapter 28). Horiba's work helps to put a particular shape to the otherwise nebulous concept of a formal schema.

The last chapter in Part 4, by Tudor and Tuffs, extends schema theory to the processing of video materials. The authors show that both formal and content schemata are important to the processing of an eight-minute expository video. The subjects of their research were students of business administration at a university in Belgium. The video in English (a second language for the subjects) concerned the pros and cons of a private road system in Britain. The results show that advance knowledge of the formal schema underlying the video, as well as specific facts contained in the video (the content schema), are helpful in improving both comprehension and recall of the material. It appears that scaffolding, just as pragmatic theory predicts (see Chapter 37), is helpful in video comprehension as in other forms of literacy.

CHAPTER 17

Literacy in the Third World for All the Children

Richard F. Walker, Saowalak Rattanavich, and John W. Oller, Jr.

EDITOR'S INTRODUCTION

Building literacy is a challenge. Even for children from relatively privileged backgrounds, traditional approaches widely produce unacceptably high failure rates. When literacy must be provided to children who do not yet know the language in which they need to become literate, failure is the norm more often than not. In this chapter, we offer an alternative pioneered by Richard F. Walker of Australia, Saowalak Rattanavich of Thailand, and colleagues from Australia, Thailand, and elsewhere. Results with Aboriginal children at Traeger Park School in central Australia (at Alice Springs in the Northern Territory) led Walker and colleagues to believe that what came to be known as the CLE (Concentrated Language Encounters) approach could work in almost any difficult context. For his efforts to bring literacy to third-world countries Walker was made a Member of the Order of Australia on June 8, 1992. The fundamental thesis of his work, and that of his colleagues (see Hart, Walker, & Gray, 1977), has been that we ought to consider what children can do in actual discourse contexts rather than to pre-judge what they might not be able to do on the basis of some preconception or other. It turns out that all normal children can do more than many of the theoreticians have supposed. They can even acquire a language while becoming literate in it. The proof is found in thousands of cases where children in difficult third-world contexts have achieved literacy in a non-primary language. It is generally assumed that six or more years of formal education will be sufficient to produce persons who can read and write, but this is not always true. Even in developed countries that have had compulsory public education for several generations, substantial numbers of illiterates can be found, and all over the world, many children leave school each year with inadequate literacy skills. Actual failure rates vary, but figures above 50% are not uncommon. While the skills required vary across situations, is it unrealistic to expect the great majority of students to complete their school years with essentially all the literacy skills they will need for adult life? This chapter addresses that question and concludes that it is possible to teach virtually all children to read and write, regardless of their language background or prior experience.

HOW CHILDREN LEARN TO READ

Children from actively literate families seem to acquire naturally a basic understanding of what reading and writing are about.[1] A surprising number of them begin to read before they ever set foot in a classroom (Smith & Johnson, 1976: 28). Success in reading is essentially a problem of connecting written language with experience. But to do so, as in solving any other representational problem, the child must have some notion about the feasibility and benefits of doing so. On this account, learning to read is fundamentally the same as the general problem of comprehension (see Chapter 37). As a result, children who begin school with little or no prior experience with written language are faced with an unfamiliar code of unknown benefits. They still have in front of them the full task of puzzling out its nature, its various forms and conventions, and its uses and usefulness. When compared against children who come from highly literate contexts with books, newspapers, and evidences of reading all around them, it is easy to see why those from relatively non-literate backgrounds will have a more difficult time learning to read. Wells (1981) showed that children from low-to-nil literacy backgrounds are, therefore, most likely to fail at school. High failure rates are also observed among minority language populations and socioeconomically depressed groups. In these latter cases linguistic, sociocultural, and other socioeconomic or political conditions are often cited as causal factors. Children for whom the language of instruction is a second language or dialect are seen as having the doubly difficult task of learning to participate in the spoken as well as the written discourse of the classroom. Multiple difficulties of all these kinds exist among minority populations in developing countries and among language minorities in urban contexts throughout the modern world.

Some have argued that children who do not learn to read are simply not yet capable of such a demanding "intellectual activity" and that we should therefore "postpone . . . reading activities and move children more slowly through the developmental reading process" (Smith & Johnson, 1976: 38). The remedy of postponing reading until some threshold of "readiness" is achieved is a little like not letting children get in the water until they learn to swim. It sounds protective and wise until we realize that the children can never learn to swim unless they get in the water. Without denying the relevance of socioeconomic and political conditions, we believe it is unacceptable for educators to appeal to such factors in order to explain away the high failure rate of literacy programs worldwide. Rather, the known likelihood of failure in difficult sociopolitical contexts should enliv-

en our interest in seeking out methods that work, even with oppressed populations.

We are convinced that success or failure in enabling children to learn to read has more to do with what goes on in classrooms than with what the children bring by way of background. As teachers, we prefer to look to cases where success occurs despite the odds, and to see how methods that work can be created for the full range of students who come to school—not just for those whose family background happens to fit a preconceived profile for success. The evidence shows, at any rate, that privileged children of high socioeconomic status are likely to learn to read even before they come to school and that most of those who do not do so beforehand will go on to become literate pretty much in spite of what the schools do or don't do. Therefore, it is apparently just as inappropriate for the schools to take full credit for observed successes in the case of the privileged and well-to-do children as it is to blame high failure rates of the less successful groups on socioeconomic factors. The sad fact is that in a large percentage of cases the schools are less helpful than we might hope in enabling children to become literate. On the other hand, if we turn to methods that work, the hopeful news is that we stand to learn a great deal. We can learn from the children who read before going to school and from those few programs where even highly oppressed minorities experience nearly 100% literacy achievement at school. There is good reason to suppose that we can indeed teach *all* the children to read. The Concentrated Language Encounter (CLE) techniques described here have been proved in practice to suit a much wider range of children than traditional literacy programs. In fact, we will argue that the evidence shows that such procedures can work with virtually all the children at school, even in difficult third-world contexts.

Before proceeding, a few words on the phrase *concentrated language encounter* (CLE) are in order. The name for the CLE approach comes from Cazden (1977). She argued that children acquire language mainly through occasions where they are intensely involved in understanding and being understood. We agree with this idea and see the fundamental task of educators as figuring out ways to increase the density of such intense communicative successes in the experience of school-children. Our job is to make high motivation communicative successes occur as regularly as possible in classrooms. In this chapter we describe a philosophy of language and literacy teaching which accomplishes this fundamental objective. We begin by discussing some actual samples of discourse in the hope that we will be able to show (rather than just tell) our readers how CLE approaches really work in practice. Then, we go on to discuss the overall organization of CLE programs, especially in Thailand, where successes in teaching children to read and write in Thai, even when their first language is not Thai, encourage us to believe that it is possible to teach all normal children to read regardless of their socioeconomic profile or their experiential background before coming to school.

LANGUAGE RESEARCH EVIDENCE: MARY

The fundamental principles of CLE language and literacy teaching were worked out in searching for a solution to the gross failure among Aboriginal students at Traeger Park School, in the Northern Territory of Australia (Gray, 1983). Mary was a beginning student at that school. The transcripts that appear in this section reveal what her language use was like in teacher-child interactions (Transcript A) and while playing (Transcript B) and working with other children (Transcript C). Our point is to show how child-teacher and student-student interactions can be enriched through CLE teaching (Transcript D). The transcripts were made in a language research project soon after Mary started going to school (Walker, 1981).

As we find her early in the school year, Mary speaks a dialect of English in addition to her Aboriginal first language. In English, she can understand what is said to her and make herself understood, but, according to traditional wisdom, she is almost certain to fail in school. Her teachers will attribute her failure mainly to limited English proficiency perpetuated by unfavorable socioeconomic factors. The first sample of discourse, Transcript A, involves Mary and her classroom teacher. Another child named Jane, a friend of Mary's, is seated side-by-side with her on the classroom floor, where they have been making

things out of colored rods and fittings that connect them (what Americans call "tinker toys"), in a free activity period at the beginning of the school day.

Transcript A

Teacher: What are you making, Mary? (Mary does not respond.) What are you making? (No response.) Very nice. (The teacher examines Mary's construction.) What's this part? Is that pink? (Mary shakes her head, indicating that it is not pink.) No? What is it? (No response from Mary.) Blue?

Mary: Yeah.

Teacher: Mm. It's blue. What's this one here?

Mary: Blue.

Teacher: Good. That's blue. What's this one? Yellow? (Mary nods her head.) Can you see another yellow one? (Mary points to another yellow one.) Very good. . . . (The same procedure is repeated for other colors.) What are you doing now, Mary? (No response.) What are you doing, Love? (No response.) Are you putting it together? Building something? (No response. Mary goes on working.)

Mary: (As she works, Mary says:) Making chair.

Teacher: Making a chair? Oh? Who's the chair for?

Mary: Sitting down.

Teacher: For sitting down? Oh. Who's going to sit on it? (No response.) Is Jane going to sit on the chair or you? (No response.) Who's going to sit on it?

Mary: Jane.

In this conversation, the teacher works hard to establish communication with Mary. She tries to teach the names for objects and colors, on the basis of Mary's own activity. Simultaneously she seems to be trying to see whether Mary already has those concepts and the English labels for them. The teacher's first try only requires that Mary name the object she has been making, but Mary does not respond even to a second trial of that probe. The teacher tries to establish a better relationship by admiring the chair that Mary has built.

She then tries to make her next question a more specific one by referring to the color of a part of the chair. The demand on Mary is made as light as possible by naming the color and asking only for affirmation or negation. Mary replies with a shake of her head, and on that basis, the teacher tries, more ambitiously, to get Mary to supply the name of the color. That fails, and the teacher goes back to requiring only affirmation or negation. She now makes some progress because Mary speaks up for the first time. She says, "Yeah." She even says the word *blue* after the teacher has used it. The teacher then goes back to requiring affirmation only and pointing out other pieces of the same color.

Apparently encouraged by this cooperative turn-taking by Mary, the teacher then goes back to her original gambit of asking what Mary is doing, but that fails entirely—even when the question is reframed to require only affirmation or negation. The teacher seems to think that Mary may not understand the verb. She goes on to use "making," "doing," "putting together," and "building," all for the same process, as she attempts to elicit a response. Mary understood the first try, as far as words were concerned, because a little later she volunteers "making chair." The teacher tries appealing to Mary's imagination by asking who the toy chair is for. She suggests that it might be for Mary or for Jane. We may note in passing that the difficulty of such a fiction is greater than that associated with any actual fact. Such fictionalizing requires Mary to conjure up a contrary-to-fact state of affairs that cannot actually occur. The chair will be too small for either Mary or Jane to sit in. All in all, the attempt to establish a basis for communication falls short of eliciting any intensity of interest, effort, or success, though the transcript is typical of many actually occurring interactions between teachers and children like Mary in traditional classroom contexts.

What we see in Transcript A is a teacher working hard to establish, as best she knows how, a basis for communication with Mary. However, the teacher moves to a lower and lower level until she settles on exchanges appropriate for a child with virtually no English. Mary seems (to the teacher) to be either unable or unwilling to communicate at a complexity beyond the simplest concepts and labels. But Transcript B, which is a

record of a playground interaction *on the same day,* reveals that Mary can operate at a level far above what the teacher was able to elicit. Mary is sharing a double push-pull swing with Sue. The two girls are sitting on the same seat, one behind the other, with Mary in front and in control of the push-pull bars. Two other girls are sharing a similar swing nearby, and a fifth is dancing around the swing, awaiting a turn. We notice that here Mary is relating to actual material events in which she and the other children are presently involved.

Transcript B

Mary: On again. On here again. Me push. (She says to Sue:) Look, you push me. You push. (To the other pair of girls, Mary says:) We'll go really fast like you. (To Sue:) Like this, eh? Hey, Marilyn! Fall down and . . . (Mary tells the fifth girl, who's dancing around, to repeat the trick she's just done). (Then to Sue:) Move back, Sue! (Mary is slipping off the front of the seat.) No. You! No! Hey, Sue! (Mary is annoyed because Sue has slipped along the seat.) I'll take you really fast. Sue! You thing! (She's annoyed that Sue is wriggling around.) (Now, both girls get off the swing.) Me turn. Jane and me and Jane now. Me and Jane now. (To Jane:) You and me. (To the other girls:) You and Sue at the back. Jane, other side, other side.

In this playground episode, Mary is garrulous and dominant to the extent that no one else has a turn to speak. More significantly, her dominance of the others is achieved and maintained through using English. Clearly, she can use English confidently and powerfully in this context. At the end of the day, in free classroom time before leaving for home, Mary is playing with large colored beads on the floor, and we get some additional insights into her ability to use English.

Transcript C

Mary: The colors, the colors, colors. (Bill, a classmate, moves over to Mary and begins to annoy her. She threatens him quietly:) I'll tell on you.

Vera: (Mary's classmate Vera says:) Bill Brown! Leave her alone!

Mary: (Calling softly for the teacher:) Mrs. Peters? (Then to Bill:) I'll tell on you, Bill. You're making troubles. You're making troubles. Not me. (Bill retires, and Mary continues playing. Looking at the colored beads, she says:) All the colors, all the colors.

From Transcript C we learn that Mary understands classroom dynamics well enough to mount an appeal to the teacher's authority. She also knows how to attribute blame for a breach of expected behavior. Finally, after Bill's aggression is quashed, Mary's returns to her almost poetic use of English as she expresses her appreciation for the colors of the beads.

On several other occasions, different ones of Mary's teachers try to draw her into an instructional dialogue. In each case, a stereotypical dialogue of the adult-to-infant kind develops (such as in Transcript A)—where the adult ends up providing answers sought from Mary. By this method, the teachers obtain almost no idea of what she can do in English as evidenced in Transcripts B and C. In all the transcripts (many not shown here), it is clear that Mary's teachers are unaware that she can use English at a much higher level. They act as if Mary were a bare beginner in English. For her part, Mary is content to play the game as the teachers have unwittingly defined it. Why take any new risks? Better to play the safe bet of waiting for the adult teachers to supply whatever responses are required. This leaves them with the self-perpetuating impression that Mary is a nonparticipant. But what would happen if the classroom game were substantially changed? Transcript D was recorded on the next morning in a "concentrated language encounter." This was one of the first CLEs at Traeger Park School specifically designed to enable Aboriginal children to participate fully in classroom learning. This session, which had been performed twice on previous days, involved making toast in a corner of the classroom.

Transcript D

Bill: Can I put some butter?

Teacher: We have to wait first until the toaster is ready to pop up. What color do you think the bread will be when it pops up? What color?

Bill: Brown.

Mary: Brown.

Teacher: Brown. That's right.

Mary: It pop up.

Sally: I can smell it now.

Teacher: (To the other children:) Can you smell it?

Mary: (Enjoying the smell of the toast.) Hey!

Teacher: Does it make you feel hungry, Mary?

Mary: (Nods her head.) My mother got peanut butter.

Teacher: Your mother's got peanut butter, has she?

Bill: We got some peanut butter home.

Teacher: You've got peanut butter at home too?

Bill: Yeah, and one of these.

Teacher: And a toaster?

Mary: And one of these.

Teacher: (To Mary:) What's that called? (She's interrupted by the toaster popping.) Oh! It's popped up!

Mary: Black now. It's black.

Teacher: D'you think it's burnt?

Mary: Yeah.

Teacher: I think it's probably all right.

Mary: (Excited:) It's black! Black! It's black!

Teacher: Dinner time. Yeah. It's dinner time.

Mary: Dinner time. Dinner time.

Teacher: Take the toast out of the toaster now, Bill. (Bill does so.) What are we going to do now, Mary?

Mary: Clean it.

Teacher: (Surprised:) We're going to clean it?

Mary: (Demonstrates:) This way.

Sally: Scrape it. Scrape it.

Teacher: Why do we have to scrape it?

Mary: It's yucky!

Sally: With the knife.

Teacher: No, that's all right. (She thinks the toast doesn't need scraping.) Then what do you have to do? What are we going to put on it now?

Mary: Peanut butter.

Teacher: What are we going to put on it before the peanut butter?

Mary: Butter.

Teacher: Good girl! Come on, then, you spread this. A nice piece of toast. Bill's going to put some butter on the other slice of toast.

Mary: This one?

Teacher: Yes! Good girl! Do you help your mother to butter the toast at home, Mary?

Mary: (She nods.)

Teacher: What's happening to the butter?

Lynette: It'll melt.

Teacher: It's melting. That's right, because the toast is hot. This (the butter container) feels nice and cold.

Lynette: I take it. I take it. (She picks up the butter container to feel it.)

Teacher: The toast melts the butter.

Mary: It's melting. Look there. It's melting. Look.

Lynette: Mine melting too. (Looking at Mary's toast.)

Note how different Mary's participation is here than in Transcript A in spite of the fact that *the same teacher* and *the same children* (still with the same socioeconomic backgrounds) are involved. It is also worth mentioning that Transcripts A and D were recorded on consecutive days. Not only does Mary now respond confidently to the teacher's questions, but she also initiates interactions with the teacher and with other students. All this happens in the presence of the teacher, without prompting. More importantly, Mary is now confident and involved enough to adopt and argue a point of view, even with the teacher, about whether or not the toast should be "scraped." Not only does Mary understand the facts pertaining to the physical actions being performed and the objects in question, but she has a deeper understanding of the facts of the social context and her role in it. She does not feel threatened (as she probably did previously when things were less clear to her, in the setting of Transcript A). She understands what she can and cannot do freely within the context in her role as active participant. As a result of changes between Transcript A and Transcript D, which takes place on the very next day, Mary and the teacher (and the other children as well) all have a better basis for negotiating meanings than they did under the traditional approach (see Transcript A). They know much better what the facts of the context (both physical and social) really are. For instance, even where fiction comes into the toast-making discourse (e.g., that it's dinner time), the activity underway provides plenty of scaffolding so that the fiction works. The participants know what is going on and what is expected of them. The fiction is fully comprehensible. It closely relates to the facts at hand, which are known in lots of ways other than just through deciphering spoken English. The objects can be seen and touched, and the toast is about to be spread with butter and peanut butter and is about to be eaten. The supportive social relationships between children and each other and the teacher are coded in facial expressions and gestures that are readily observable and comprehensible in the context. The social facts are out in the open, so to speak. The case is very unlike trying to imagine someone, for whom a tinker-toy chair might have been made, possibly sitting in it, or why the teacher would be concerned about such a possibility, exclusively on the basis of talk about those hypothetical (unreal and immaterial) possibilities—especially when the talk is supplied only in a non-primary language, English. There are huge differences, as a result, between Transcripts A and D.

The reasons for the differences between Transcript A and D become clear to participants in the CLE process. The teacher realizes that because Mary (and the other children) have shared in toast making on several occasions, they have become familiar with it. They know the names of things, what is to be done with them, and the sequence in which those events will occur. As a result, Mary knows what the role of toast maker requires, because she's seen others take turns in that role. Finally, Mary has realized that all the language demands to be made on her as toast-maker will be based on procedures with which she is already familiar and comfortable. In other words, she can articulately relate all that is said in this context to objects, persons, and events so as to comprehend essentially everything that goes on. She relates the surface forms of the language used, even unfamiliar ones, to what she sees happening, and to what she knows is expected of her in the context. She participates in bringing about the on-going transformation of the immediate context of experience from one phase of the toast making to the next until the activity is completed.

In the terms of the theory of Chapter 37, she has a rich basis of pragmatic scaffolding from which to advance easily, seemingly without effort, to previously inaccessible levels of linguistic performance. For example, notice the dialectal switch she makes during the session shown as Transcript D. Early in the session, when the toast pops up she volunteers, "It pop up." We note here that she does not use any surface marking on the verb. No copula appears as in "It's popping up," nor does the third person singular (non-past) morpheme {-s} on the verb *pop* appear, as in "It pops up." However, as the discourse progresses Mary consistently switches to forms that overtly show the copula as in "It's black," "It's yucky," and "It's melting." The other transcripts do not show any such elaborated surface forms. Why? Apparently, Mary is naturally sensitive (subconsciously, just as Krashen claims, 1985b, 1989a-b, 1990, 1991, 1992, and in Parts 2 and 3 of this volume) to dialect changes. As a result, without any special effort she switches to "It's black" after the teacher says "It's popped up," and then she continues in the teacher's more elaborate dialect. She does not need to be explicitly "taught" such standard structures, and all indications are that such explicit teaching would fail to produce the desired results in any case. However, in a rich CLE-type context, once a variant has been modeled for meaning and function, Mary can use it for similar purposes quite naturally.

In the carefully planned context of a CLE, the natural use of the teacher's primary language or dialect works, precisely because the modelling has full contextual support. There is plenty of scaffolding to make the meaning transparent from the point of view of the participants in the toast-making activity. Also, because of the cooperative aspect of the learning experience, there is a predisposition on the part of the children to unconsciously assimilate the elaborate language of the teacher. There is no threat and, therefore, no reason not to accept and use that language.

Remove the scaffolding of the CLE, however, and the classroom scene will revert back to the sort of discourse seen in Transcript A, where the most at-risk children are almost certain to remain confused. As Gray (1980: 3) put it, they just don't know "what is required from them in the learning task." This in turn leads to "low self-esteem as learners" (just as Gray observed) and an ever-renewed cycle of failure after failure. The children are not incapable in any general way, but relative to the specific classroom alternatives that they are presented with, they just aren't apt to understand what is going on or why. They have little chance of understanding what the teacher is getting at or why. Social relationships and motives are unclear. The child is apt to feel threatened or at-risk because of such uncertainties. Therefore, we *must change the classroom context.*

There are children like Mary in schools everywhere. They are have sufficient intelligence—no matter what sociopolitical contingencies may have been dealt to them by circumstances beyond their control. The "Mary's" of the world's classrooms are not all Australian Aborigines, and they are not necessarily from any particular language or ethnic minority, but there are many of them out there. We have only to visit the schools, and this is especially true in developing countries, to realize that exclusion from classroom learning occurs on a gigantic scale. With children like Mary, whose first language is not the language of instruction, a particularly effective recipe for wholesale failure is to allow only teacher-directed interaction in the classroom, and to "cover" just those concepts, words, and structures that are set down in some textbook to be drilled. In all too many cases, across large regions of the world, and even in developed nations in many places, literacy teaching begins with the alphabet and progresses through phonic drills to individual words, later to sentences (mostly chosen to illustrate particular phonological and syntactic patterns), and often bogs down in a morass of decoding confusion before the children can become readers.[2] In such cases, real reading and writing (for useful purposes) are postponed indefinitely—even permanently for many children. As a result, whole generations of students have found themselves engaged month after month in puzzling, laborious, analytical, boring activities that have no apparent purpose. Before long, they give up trying.

Such direct, analytical approaches to the teaching of language also discourage students from any real learning outside the formal lessons on which they are taught to rely. Moreover, the confusion is self-perpetuating as the new crop of teachers in each generation of educators slogs through the same old ineffective methodologies and is taught to believe that they are the best ones available. In the United States of the 1990s, for instance, in spite of an embarrassing reading failure rate even in relatively privileged middle class contexts (Crandall & Imel, 1991), not to mention the more severe cases of oppressed ghetto and minority language contexts (Kerka, 1989; Kirsch & Jungeblut, 1986; Savage, 1984), advertisements still promote the relatively ineffective "phonics" (sound-it-out) method as if it were a sure-fire solution for children and adults who keep on growing older without becoming literate. To respond to such needs, approaches to literacy that would eventually become known as CLE were conceived.

ORIGINS OF CLE

The first CLE program applied to highly at-risk children, whose primary language was other than the language of instruction, took place in Australia. It involved, among other children, Mary, the child featured in Transcripts A–D above. She was in one of the first groups of Aboriginal children to benefit from CLE techniques. Gray and his colleagues at Traeger Park School figured out how to create classroom contexts that would involve all of the children in understanding and participating in whatever was going on. They developed activities from which students would be able to comprehend, talk, read, and write in English, while also progressing in other skills and knowledge. They included only the sorts of activities that would have worthwhile applications in real life. Over a period of about five years, roughly from 1979–1984, Gray and his colleagues developed a program for the early grades of the Traeger Park School in which virtually all the students who regularly attended would become enthusiastic readers and writers. During the same period there was a noticeable improvement in school attendance as well. All of this is the more remarkable when it is taken into consideration that most of the children were not only becoming literate but were doing so in a second language.

Meanwhile, CLE techniques were introduced into Thailand in 1984 owing to efforts at the Brisbane College of Advanced Education (Rattanavich & Walker, 1990). In the following section, we will describe in greater detail how the CLE approach works in practice, but first it may be useful to summarize the order of events in which the Thai-language program was developed, piloted, and subsequently implemented on a trial basis with substantial numbers of some of the most at-risk minorities in that country, which would lead in 1991 to its being adopted for the entire nation (approximately six million primary school children) by the Ministry of Education as part of its National Plan for 1992–1996. The program is presently being implemented throughout the nation. In the meantime, pilot projects for new CLE programs are simultaneously underway near Hugli in India and in several schools near Dhaka, Bangladesh. It is interesting that what began as a kind of ESL and literacy program for Aborigines of Australia went on to develop into various similar programs in third-world nations, and at last has come full circle to an ESL program in addition to the Thai-literacy program in Thailand.

The Thai-literacy piloting projects began first in the drought-stricken provinces of northeastern Thailand, where 97% of the children speak Khmer, Lao, or some other minority language. Only 3% have Thai as their primary language. Then the pilot programs (called "lighthouse" projects) were begun in the southern border provinces, where Malaysian is the predominant mother tongue. Later the CLE concept would be carried to the extreme northern provinces, where a variety of hill-tribe languages and dialects are spoken. During 1991, CLE demonstration schools were set up in the remaining parts of the nation in preparation for implementation of the 1992–1996 National Plan. By the summer of 1992, CLE methods were already being used in more than 16,000 Thai schools.

WHAT IS THE CLE FAMILY OF APPROACHES?

As he worked with Aboriginal students at Traeger Park School, Gray noted that the most successful teaching sessions were those in which students were involved in contexts where they were doing interesting and useful things, but where they had to face up to challenging language tasks to get things done.[3] This same principle underlies all CLE programs and activities. Connected to the action principle is the matter of "scaffolding." The more that what is said relates to and is supported by the context—by what is perceivable, by what is happening, by the actions students are performing, by the accompanying gestures and tone of voice, and by the previous experience of the participants—the easier it will be for students to comprehend, participate successfully in what is going on, and thus to acquire language and literacy skills from that context. Scaffolding is important to all forms of discourse. Just understanding what is going on can be a tremendous help in figuring out what is being said and how to participate in it. In addition, knowing the facts pertaining to any activity or context of meaning is crucial to breaking the code of written discourse pertaining to those facts. The facts, of course, include not only the objects and material setting but also the social relations between participants, their goals, demeanors, and manners of communicating with each other. The already established connection between utterances and the facts of experience is crucial in enabling the preliterate child to begin to become literate.

In keeping with these observations, CLE programs can be divided into three major "stages" which in turn can be broken down into several "phases." The latter, in turn, can be further reduced to units or activities in the classroom. We realize that any such parsing of time segments is arbitrary, but in fact, schooling is inevitably parsed up into distinct time segments. In CLE programming, Stage 1 roughly embraces the first two to three years of schooling and typically begins with children in kindergarten or first grade. However, it is applicable in many preschool settings. The objective of this first stage is to produce enthusiastic readers and writers of the language used for instruction. Stage 2 aims to broaden the students' repertoire of text genres so as to encompass the full range of texts they will be apt to encounter throughout their schooling and in later life. This stage usually occupies the middle portion (about two years) of the primary grades. Stage 3, then, completes the primary schooling and may extend into the secondary school program. The main objective of this last stage is to teach students to organize their knowledge in terms of the full range of text genres they will need in later life. In this stage, they will learn to create such texts, to learn from the process of creating them, and, in general, to understand the vast and varied connections between texts and literate discourses of all types and the contexts of experience to which they relate. Here we concentrate primarily on Stage 1 of CLE programs. Readers who want to know more about Stages 2 and 3 are encouraged to read Rattanavich (1992).

Stage 1

The overall objective of Stage 1 in any CLE program is for students to become readers and writers. At the end of Stage 1, they should be able to read various types of simple texts and to recall and discuss what those texts are about. They should be able to write brief texts of several kinds, observing spelling and other conventions of writing. In progressing through this stage, they will learn the written forms of hundreds of words, many more phrases, and how to bring effective strategies to bear in recognizing and writing words they have not previously encountered in a written form.

Stage 1 of a CLE program usually covers two or three years, depending on whether or not it is used in preschool or kindergarten classes. The program for each school year is organized into units, each of which extends over a number of weeks. The actual number of units that are covered in a year varies from class to class, but most Stage 1 classes in Thailand will do ten to fifteen units in a year. Within each Stage 1 unit, the teacher and students progress through five "phases." There are two kinds of Stage 1 program units, both of which are illustrated in Figure 17.1. Based on Chapter 37 and, in fact, all of the chapters of Part 3 concerning content-based approaches, we should predict just the two avenues that have materialized in CLE approaches.

On the one hand, Figure 17.1 shows "activity-based" approaches, grounded in the experience side of Figure 37.1 in Chapter 37, and on the other, there are "text-based" approaches which are grounded in the representational side of Figure 37.1. Text-based approaches begin with written material. Language teachers, and especially linguists, might expect that activity-based approaches would be best when working with children whose first language is not the language of the classroom. However, experience teaches that either activity-

FIGURE 17.1

(I) The Activity-Based Route

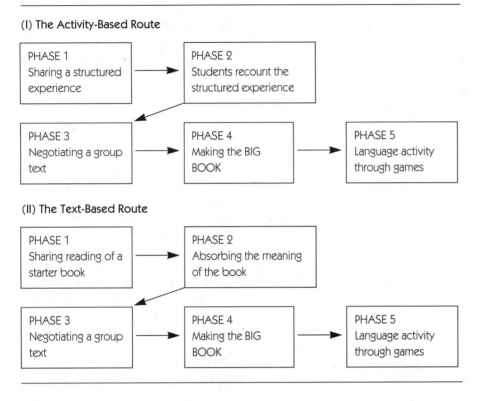

(II) The Text-Based Route

based or text-based approaches can be used with children regardless of whether or not they are already comfortable with the spoken language of the classroom. As is often the case, the expectation from the theoretical side is not borne out by experience. We have found that text-based approaches, perhaps owing to their more readily fixed routines of talk and presentation, work best with all students. Stories like "The Little Red Hen" and "The Three Little Pigs," with their repetitive structures, work well. The "executive" (classroom management) language is similar from class to class within the "text-based" approach, and this probably accounts for the ease with which children typically acquire the spoken language quite incidentally (also see evidences suggesting this outcome in Parts 2 and 3 above, but especially in Part 2, which is about immersion programs).

Figure 17.1 highlights the differences and common elements of the activity-based and text-based routes to literacy. In Transcript D given above, Mary and her friends were engaged in an activity-based CLE unit—in that case, making

toast. Additional activities that have been used in the CLE programs of Thailand include making a paper hat, learning to preserve beans, breeding fish, planting a garden, and many others.[4] Text-based units, by contrast, start with shared reading of a Starter Book, usually based on an interesting narrative. A favorite narrative with the children of Thailand is a story about a monkey and a tiger that are friends when they are little but get separated and later meet in the jungle as adults. Since the two are natural enemies, as rural Thai children can readily appreciate, the question is whether the tiger will eat the monkey. In the climax of the story, which has an American ending, the two old friends recognize each other and all is well.

With programs using published CLE materials (thanks to the generous help of Rotary volunteers), a "How To" Starter Book is provided. Some of these may be used as reference items for certain activity-based units, but more often than not, the activity-based route will begin with a practical demonstration by a visiting teacher, trained in

CLE procedures.[5] As can be seen from Figure 17.1, Phases 3, 4, and 5 are similar for both kinds of program units. However, in the "text-based" option, Phases 1 and 2 depend on a story and make it necessary to determine what the facts are via dramatization, pictures, etc. By contrast, the "activity-based" approach begins with an experience and then converts it into a discoursal representation in Phase 3. In both cases the discourse forms are pragmatically supported by a rich scaffolding of action and dramatization.[6] If the scaffolding is well developed, there is little danger that children will fail to understand what the facts of the story or activity are. Then, regardless which route was chosen in Phases 1 and 2, by the time Phases 3, 4, and 5 roll around, children become directly involved in the business of creating written discourse. These last three phases involve negotiation of a group text (a text created by consensus), the making of a Big Book (a clean copy of the previously agreed-to group text), and follow-up games. This process virtually guarantees total acquisition of the material, skills, and social strategies connected with all of the negotiations of meaning that will have taken place.

Here we come to what is no doubt a critical difference between the CLE approaches and more traditional methods—namely, that in CLE programs we never give a text or activity a glancing exposure and then pass on to something new and unfamiliar. Owing to the kinds of games, cooperative learning (also see Kagan, 1992), and related activities that always accompany the development of a Big Book, every negotiated text is brought to a level of comprehension that saturates the entire context and fully connects it to the experience of each and every participant. This never occurs (and logically cannot occur) in the sort of exchange that we saw above in Transcript A, but it does inevitably occur with the sorts of repeated cycling exemplified in the toast-making activity of Transcript D. In fact, in a CLE context properly developed, saturation of the entire context with readily accessible meanings can hardly be prevented from occurring naturally.

It remains to be seen in more detail what is involved in each of the several phases for the two CLE routes just described for Stage 1. We work first through the activity-based route and then look at the text-based approaches.

Phase 1 of an Activity-Based Unit

In Phase 1 of an activity-based unit, the teacher demonstrates an activity such as making toast. The demonstration usually involves several steps: (a) talking about what will be happening; (b) showing students the materials and equipment that are needed; (c) showing how the task is carried out; and (d) having students share in the activity with the teacher by performing it for themselves. From the beginning, the teacher and students talk about what they are doing as they do it. This talk is structured, not in accordance with anything laid down in a program text, but in accordance with what is going on. We follow the principle recommended by good writers of showing rather than just telling (Peck, 1980; Swain, 1980). Neither the talk nor the sequence of actions, however, is randomly arranged, but proceeds according to the requirements of the activity itself.

For instance, in making toast, we don't just go willy-nilly through any series of steps, but we work through a fairly determinate sequence of steps owing to the very nature of the activity itself. In consequence, as with any purposeful process, we end up going through a highly predictable (redundant) series of steps that must occur in a fairly fixed order. As a result, the talk that occurs relative to the actions being carried out by those who are cooperating in completing the task will similarly be structured around and thus richly scaffolded by an awareness of the steps being taken. In every case, the children and teacher talk about each step in the process, e.g., taking the bread out of the bag, putting it in the toaster, etc. They talk about what is happening while it is going on. They talk about what is needed for each step along the way. They are apt to do this before it happens, while it is happening, and after it has happened. They talk about who will do, is doing, and has done what, when, and where. They also talk about how they feel about what is happening all along the way. The overall result is lots of comprehended input and lots of negotiated output in a highly redundant, context-rich, affectively positive setting.

Phase 2 of an Activity-Based Unit

Phase 2 in the activity-based route involves absorption of the facts. In this phase we make certain that the students understand the various steps of the activity and what is involved in it. Processing and recall are required. Here the students note the equipment and materials that are required for the activity and tell how to do the activity, step by step. Just like Phase 1, this one too is constrained by the actual requirements and limitations of the activity itself as well as by the collective memory of the group and its individuals of what took place on previous executions of the activity. For instance, who really made the toast? What materials were used? Did they put butter on it before they applied the peanut butter? Who was involved? Who was responsible for what? That is, to say, there are actual facts (about things, actions, persons, social relations, goals, etc.) that constrain how a true representation of what happened might be developed.[7] The facts are largely remembered from the activity that has already taken place, or, as the occasion requires, they may be reconstructed by re-enacting the activity itself, e.g., having someone else be the toast-maker this time around. As students recount the shared activities on repeated cycles, the talk is naturally enriched. The students do not merely travel a circle repeatedly, but they move in cycles that increase in scope in the manner of a growing spiral. The children have already accumulated a good deal of common knowledge and new linguistic skills, and their skills and knowledge continue to grow as the cycles expand, as shown in Figure 17.2.

FIGURE 17.2 The Growth Spiral Over Time

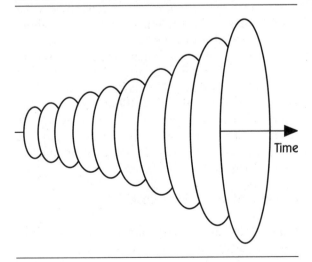

Time

Growth is assured as the teacher, or students themselves, direct their attention to different aspects of what is going on or as they bring into the developing discourse elements of their own experience, e.g., that Mary's mom puts peanut butter on toast at her house, and that, when the toast gets too dark, they just scrape off the blackened surface with a knife, and so on. As a result, there is an inevitable and natural progression from what is going on in the here and now to the richer world of experience beyond the classroom.

As soon as the students are confident in talking about an activity, they will be able to comfortably make the transition to written forms. However, since Phases 3, 4, and 5 are common to both activity-based and text-based routes, we next consider Phases 1 and 2 of the text-based approaches.

Phase 1 of a Text-Based Unit

When the sequence begins with shared reading, the Phase 1 objective is to get the children to understand the Starter Text thoroughly. This means from the overall structure down to the specific facts such as what happened, who did what, and the detailed characteristics of people, objects, and events. The reading should be a leisurely, informal process supported by dramatization, pictures, gestures, and realia wherever possible, in order to scaffold the language comprehension in every available way. In some cases, where the native language of the children differs from the language of the text and where the teacher knows that primary language, it may be necessary to describe some elements of the story in the stronger language of the children to make certain that the facts of the story are fully understood.

However, the reading of the text must not devolve merely into a translation. The goal is to get the children to understand the story in the language of the text itself. If we want the children to become able to read in Thai, translating stories to them in Malaysian will not get us to our goal. If the children cannot get the gist of the story in Thai (or whatever the primary language may be), then we should not be using a text-based unit yet. Children who lack sufficient language skills at least to comprehend the gist of the text will probably benefit most from an activity-based approach until they are somewhat farther along in their language skills.

However, even in cases where the children have some significant comprehension of the language of the text, the substance of classroom talk, and to a large extent the language needed for that talk, still needs to be supplied to the children. It must, therefore, be modeled in such a way (chiefly through dramatization) so that at least some of the students begin to understand and are able to help the others to do so. In addition to reading the story, acting it out, and repeated cycling with new props and additional scaffolding, songs and dances on the same theme can also help the children to understand and remember the story. Such activities also increase their enjoyment of the whole process and provide the essential changes of pace and activity that are so important for young children.[8] Songs and dances that are drawn out of the story context can also help the children to understand and remember the facts of the story. These activities can provide a rich form of scaffolding for comprehension.

Teachers should be patient with the less-confident students, giving them praise for non-linguistic involvements and waiting for their confidence to build up to the point where they can join in the talk. But first, the children must get the gist of the story in Thai (or whatever language is being used). At first, this might even be accomplished in their primary language, but they must be brought to a point where the language of the story itself is also understood. At any rate, once they become involved as participants, the children will have permanently left their most serious difficulties behind them.

Phase 2 of a Text-Based Unit

Assuming that students are already fairly competent in the language of the text, Phase 2 can come almost immediately on the heels of Phase 1, the shared reading of the text. The objective of Phase 2 is to have the students recall what they have heard during the Phase 1 reading. We must make sure they understand what was read and dramatized, etc. This phase usually begins with a warm-up period of questions about what happened, who was involved, what song was learned during Phase 1, and the like. The teacher elicits at this point a

retelling of the story. (Obviously, this step would be too difficult in most cases for students who do not yet have substantial facility in the language the story was told in. In those cases, as noted above, the activity-based approach is preferred.)

After the story has been retold once or twice, role play is recommended as a means of involving all of the students in recalling the story and in using the language in which it has been told. The utility of role play will vary as will the point at which it should be introduced. The biggest factor, of course, is whether the language of the story is the primary language of the children. If it is not, role play will probably need to be delayed or simplified. When it can be introduced, role play will give many opportunities for different children to become increasingly familiar with elements of the text. Repeated role plays are excellent devices for instilling language skills in an interesting, familiar, and nonthreatening context. At any rate, by the time Phase 2 is completed, whether the students began with an activity basis or a text basis, they will be ready to proceed to Phases 3, 4, and 5.

Phase 3: Negotiating a Group Text

By the end of Phase 2, both activity-based and text-based students will be able to draw on shared language and experience to talk about what they have learned. The former group is ready to tell how the activity in question is performed (e.g., what do you do to make toast?), and the latter is prepared to tell what happened in the story (e.g., did the tiger eat the monkey?). The foundation that has been laid down for Phase 3, therefore, is a whole language experience or text, not some isolated bits and pieces of a possible text or experience. Therefore, in Phase 3 we do not attend to single isolated words, phonic relations, verb forms, or any other analytic aspect of literacy. Phase 3, like the ones before it, looks to the whole experience of what you do when you make toast, or what happened when the monkey and the tiger met after they had grown up. The teacher asks the students to tell the story or recount the experience so that the group can write a book for themselves. As in Phase 2, the emphasis is on episodic development: "What happened first?" "Then what happened?" and so on. The difference is that in Phase 3, she now writes each sentence on a large sheet of paper, transforming the students' spoken forms into written ones before their eyes. This little bit of magic has long since lost its glory for most literate adults, but children in the early stages of literacy can still sense the significance of this remarkable transformation.

Each time the teacher writes a sentence, as suggested by a given child, she asks the other students if they want to say it a different way. If another form is preferred by the group, in a diplomatic and supportive manner, the teacher may change the sentence in order to make it fit the facts more adequately. Thus, the students negotiate an entire written text, sentence by sentence. They are cooperating all the while to make the text fit the facts correctly as they understand them. In this process of negotiation, they get lots of practice in talking about the facts, listening to comprehensible input about the facts, and inventing new ways of representing the facts, and they also read and reread their developing text many times as they proceed through the entire exercise. They experience literacy from the ground up, thus removing much of the mystery, but none of the magic, that has formerly been associated with writing. Along the way they read the text many times, often in chorus. The teacher will often say, "Let's see what we have up to here," and then will read the text from the beginning or ask the students to do so.

It is preferable to work with groups that are small enough so that all the students can make contributions to the text. This will enable them also to agree on its wording. The teacher does not dictate what is written, but modifies sentences as needed to observe grammatical conventions of the target language. The teacher functions less like a person giving dictation than like a helpful stenographer who reads back the text to the children who are creating it. In this way, the teacher models the corrected version many times along the way.

For the first few units of the Stage 1 program, the teacher must do all the writing. As each word is written down, it is read aloud. The teacher points to words and syllables even as children echo in chorus. Later, students will take pleasure in "being the teacher" and doing some of the writing themselves. For example, they will be able to insert punctuation and Thai tone marks, early on.

The pages used for writing group texts should be large enough for students to see individual symbols clearly, to chorus read from the developing text, and to check the accuracy of reading by other students. Spaces may be left at appropriate places for art work to be added later. To decide where those spaces should be, and how large they will need to be, students need to understand the content and decide how to illustrate it. Since the negotiation of a group text is almost never finished in one session, certainly not in the early developmental stages, it is left in place between sessions, which allows students to discuss it at leisure. Before beginning another session as a group, everyone reads the text in chorus up to the point where they left off previously. Here, a student can be asked to play the part of the teacher, pointing to the words of the text as the others read it.

As soon as the text is completed, students and teacher read it aloud, considering whether there is any part that might be improved. If the teacher has proceeded patiently and carefully in negotiating the text with the students, most of them will be able to read the whole text and to identify any word by "reading up to it." That is, the cognitive momentum of knowing how things begin and what comes after each event or description along the way enables the students to benefit from the expectancies that episodic organization engenders. They will be able to "recognize" words in their larger context (in the developing text) before they reach the point that they can recognize them in any other (and less-familiar) context. Words, phrases, and other elements presented out of context will need to be related back to the familiar group text at first in order for them to be easily recognized.

Phase 4: Making the Big Book

Once Phase 3 is completed, then a "fair copy" (or "clean" one, as Americans would say) is made of the negotiated text. This is the Big Book. Now that students have learned to work in small groups, there can be as many Big Books as there are activity groups. Additional books will be made, normally in Phase 5. A book that is to be used with the whole class needs to be as large as a full-sized poster or chart. Books for use with smaller groups may be only one-fourth that size.

In some parts of Thailand, the "Big Book" was just a few large sheets of paper stapled together. At Traeger Park School, by contrast, elaborate hard-covered Big Books of intriguing shapes were made. What is done will vary according to local conditions. The procedures used in making books will also change as students become more experienced and become able to work with less supervision. In any case, the first task is to decide on page layout and illustrations. This process involves reading the text and discussing what should be in the illustrations and where they should be placed on the pages.

As students work in small groups to print the book for themselves, the more-able students are called on to help those who are struggling to read the text[9] so that all can share in the decision making. The teacher will have prepared for this, while the students were still working as a single group, by modeling helping behavior and then having prospective leaders "be the teacher" from time to time. Watching students at work in small groups making their Big Books reveals much about their ability to read and write. It is particularly important to monitor how the groups go about editing their book so that they develop habits of systematic and effective proofreading and self-evaluation.

Phase 5: Games and Other Group Activities

By the time a group of learners have produced their own book, they will be able to chorus read it with ease. Most will be able to read it individually, with minimal prompting. As a group exercise, they will be able to identify any word within its context by chorus reading up to it. They will also be able to do this individually. Some will already be able to identify some of the words in isolation. Most importantly, all will have a firm grasp of the meaning of the text, from its overall structure down to sentences and individual words. The book now becomes a resource for language activities in which students can focus on the smaller elements of the written language, such as sentences, words, letters, and even the time-honored phonic correspondences (sound-letter relations). Even spelling and parsing exercises such as sentence diagramming may be undertaken on the basis of the Big Book.

What makes all of this vastly more meaningful than it would be in a traditional analytically oriented classroom is that in the background of all these analytic activities is the whole textual basis for the Big Book, which has been, by now, thoroughly grasped by the students. The rule for CLE programs is that until such understanding has been established to a high degree of saturation, analytic activities pertaining to such things as phonics (sounding-out-words) and the like should not be undertaken at all. Language games offer many ways to practice language skills and to draw attention to particular items and features without inducing boredom. As a new activity or game is introduced, the students are first trained to take part in the activity and then to manage it by themselves, in small groups.

In determining when to move on to Phase 5 activities, teachers generally take a number of factors into account. Enjoyment and responsiveness of students to the activity are important indicators. Students get more from tasks they like to do. Also, the activities must cover the full range of objectives for each given unit of study. Table 17.1 gives some ideas of the range of games and activities Thai teachers employ in Phase 5 of Stage 1 CLE programs.

CONCLUSION

Of course, determining just when the transition should be made from Stage 1 to Stage 2, where a greater variety of texts will be encountered, or determining when to go from there to Stage 3, where students will learn to produce essentially any kind of text and to learn from the process of doing so, is a judgment call. However, program experience suggests that two to three years will be needed, as a rule, for each stage. We do not describe those other stages here, as they are dealt with in detail elsewhere (see Walker, Rattanavich, & Oller, 1992). Instead we will conclude by summing up our central message.

There is no need for so many children to fail to learn to read either in industrialized nations or in third-world countries. It is simply not true that "ILLITERACY MAY BE INHERITED" as an article in *The Australian* (a national newspaper) has suggested (June 29–30, 1991). The article

TABLE 17.1 Sample Activities for Stage 1, Phase 5

1. Recognizing words that occur in the group-negotiated Big Book by matching a word or word sequence on a card with one in the Big Book. (For this activity the students and teacher can collaborate in preparing cards for all the different words and important phrases of the Big Book.)

2. Reading sentences that contain a certain word or word sequence from the Big Book or filling in missing words in sentences from the Big Book.

3. Writing the words or phrases from the Big Book by playing hangman or taking dictation.

4. Making up oral sentences that contain certain words or phrases from the Big Book to go with a given picture. Provided there are plenty of pictures, this can be done competitively by giving out pictures for sentences.

5. Reading and writing sentences that include words from the Big Book. This may include reading competitions, dictations, and pair work.

6. Making up sentences orally with new words. This can be done competitively by having different teams come up with new words that they can use in appropriate sentences related to the Big Book and challenging other teams to try to do so. Whichever team can come up with the largest number of most appropriate sentences with the new words provided by the other team wins.

7. Reading and writing new sentences can be done in jigsaw fashion by cutting up elements from the Big Book and asking the teams to see who can be first in reassembling them in the right order.

8. Reading competitions may also involve new texts from prose, songs, or poetry, in which the task is to guess certain words or figure out what a given sentence says.

9. Teams may be challenged to recount some text from everyday life or to role play an interview with a well-known TV personality.

10. Students or groups may compete for jobs as storytellers, TV or radio newscasters, or masters of ceremonies for game shows.

11. Charades and Twenty Questions (Is it a person, place, or thing?) are ever popular with children.

12. Games or competitions may involve composing a special card for someone's birthday or some other occasion, finishing a fictional story, or writing a poem.

---

continued by stating that a high proportion of children who are non-readers have at least one parent who also cannot read. Therefore, the article claimed the following:

> There is strong evidence that illiteracy is an inherited trait, and some educationists believe it is a contagious disorder best cured by treating the whole family.

The article noted that in one study,

> 30 per cent of the families admitted or were strongly suspected of at least two generations of illiteracy.

It barely stopped short of suggesting that any possible cure for illiteracy would have to extend back beyond the living.

People reasoning in such a manner would have had to recommend special "treatment" of Mary for hereditary illiteracy. But the evidence shows that Mary and all of her Aboriginal classmates became enthusiastic and capable readers. CLE approaches have by now succeeded in enabling many thousands of low socioeconomic status (at-risk) children to become fully literate. The fact that this has been done in contexts where there has been a long history of gross failure (where only a tiny percentage of the children became literate) suggests that it can be done with any children in almost any socioeconomic context.

The case of the little Aboriginal girl named Mary is not an isolated one. She was able to become literate in a non-primary language. When capable, normal children such as Mary fail, it is not their failure, but rather that of school language and literacy programs. The key to teaching virtually all children to read and write in whatever the language of instruction may be is to present language and literacy tasks in heavily scaffolded contexts where the children can see how the language in whatever form it may appear fits with whatever else is going on. If they are provided with such rich contexts of experience, the children will not only see the connections between linguistic forms and the facts of experience, but they will also readily be able to determine how texts and discourses of all types fit into the larger power structures of social organization. The children who can read and write in the languages that are used to shape and control social structures will themselves be enriched and empowered. As this occurs, they will to a great extent be released from their "disenfranchised" condition.

NOTES

1 The authors gratefully acknowledge funding of approximately $700,000 from the Rotary Foundation of Rotary International and approximately $100,000 from Rotary clubs in Australia for the projects in Thailand that are mentioned in this article. We are also grateful to the Srinakharinwirot University, the Thai Ministry of Education, and a number of volunteers from other countries who helped to make CLE literacy programs a reality for children in Thailand and elsewhere in Asia. It has indeed been an inspiration to see people with vision from education, from government, and from Rotary, cooperating in an all-out sustained effort that has changed the lives of literally millions of students and many thousands of teachers. Even before the conclusion of the five-year Rotary-funded project in Thailand, these workers had successfully introduced the CLE approach to teaching literacy into more than 16,000 schools scattered throughout most of the 71 provinces of that kingdom. We cannot name all those courageous and dedicated people, but we can say, sincerely, that our hearts go out to the wonderfully diverse people of Thailand, "The Land of Smiles," who joined in the quest to teach all the children of Thailand to read. (Also, Rattanavich and Oller congratulate their senior colleague and coauthor, Dick Walker, on his being made a Member of the Order of Australia as well as being awarded an honorary doctorate in curriculum and instruction from Srinakharinwirot University for his work on third-world literacy projects.)

2 In fact, as was noted in Chapter 16 by Allen, Anderson, and Narvaéz, the same sort of analytical teaching also occurs in many language classrooms with the same depressing results. Building language up from meaningless bits and pieces just doesn't work as a curriculum. It doesn't work for getting children to read, and it doesn't work for getting people to acquire non-primary languages.

3 We are reminded here of Krashen's "input hypothesis" (1985b, 1991, 1992), which says that advances occur when acquirers are pressed just beyond the limits of the language with which they are already comfortable—to what Vygotsky (1934) called their "proximal zone of development" or what Krashen calls "$i + 1$" (the stage just beyond the ith level which they have already achieved).

4 It should be pointed out that some of the pilot programs in the drought-stricken areas had to be placed in schools where the children were suffering from insufficient and unsanitary drinking water. This problem, therefore, had to be solved before any real progress toward literacy could be made. With volunteer help and funding from Rotary International, it was determined that a reservoir could be dug to a sufficient depth and size to fill the water supply needs. The tank would fill during the monsoon season, and absorption and evaporation were determined carefully by qualified engineers so that there would be sufficient water to carry through the drought season in subsequent years. Drinking water was separated into a distinct reservoir while the main tank was also stocked with fish. It was further determined that a poultry farm could economically be positioned over the fish farm with the poultry droppings feeding the fish. (It may not sound too appetizing, but it is ecologically efficient.) The children and teachers at the school would manage the fish and poultry farms, thus gaining valuable skills while also meeting the need for an adequate supply of water and sufficient protein in the diet of the children and much of the larger community. In addition, it was possible to cultivate vegetable gardens by using water from the newly created reservoir. So far, over 100 such projects have been completed, and about 1,000 are planned. In communities where this work has been done, the water problem has been solved so that children and teachers are able to devote sufficient attention to their educational objectives. In these communities, a great many literacy activities are built around the management of the fish and poultry farms

(which provide income to the schools) and to the management and care of the small vegetable gardens.

5 In fact, most of the training is accomplished by enabling teachers to see how the CLE procedures work in practice. The principal means of disseminating those procedures has been through regional week-long seminars with key administrators and selected teachers, followed up by weekend (three-day) sessions with grass-roots teachers. The method involves training a few teachers for the pilot ("literacy lighthouse") programs, thus enabling them to prepare themselves to teach others. From the outset, the CLE projects have been disseminated mostly by local personnel rather than by outside experts. However, it would be a mistake to underestimate the catalytic role played by key outsiders that have been brought to Thailand periodically, mainly through the help of the Rotary Foundation. The objective from the beginning, nonetheless, has been to create a self-sustaining approach with all of the built-in mechanisms for constant improvement developing from the inside. In this last respect, evaluation plays a critical role along with ongoing research efforts.

6 All of Part 1, which discusses ways of creating scaffolding, is relevant here.

7 Incidentally, as shown in Chapter 37, these activities and all others like them can only be reported accurately through representations of the true narrative type.

8 Song and dance are both activities that many Thai teachers are ready to supply at the drop of a hat. They are not only willing to invent catchy tunes and clever choreography, but they are very capable of doing so. Though some teachers would no doubt be daunted by the suggestion that they should compose a simple song or create a dance to go with it, the response of children to such activities seems to be universally positive, and there is little doubt that all elementary classrooms can be enriched by task-related, richly redundant activities of this sort. It may also be worth noting that even adult second language learners seem to be highly responsive to songs, games, and related activities in the target language (see Part 6).

9 On peer teaching, see Assinder's chapter in Part 5.

DISCUSSION QUESTIONS

1. What evidence shows that success in school is more apt to be a function of what happens in classrooms than it is of the demographic traits of school populations? Relate the discussion to the general tendency of educators to appeal to "deficits," "disorders," "disabilities," and the like to explain high failure rates in schools.

2. Compare the relative degrees and kinds of scaffolding available to Mary in the contexts of Transcripts A, B, C, and D. What sorts of contextual cues and social motivations are present in B, C, and D that are missing in A? Where is the dependence on linguistic forms greatest among the four transcripts?

3. Suppose Mary doesn't yet know the word *who* as used in the question "Who's the chair for"? How can she figure it out, based on the context of Transcript A? By contrast, suppose she encounters the same problem in the context of Transcript D? What sorts of cues will make the problem solvable? Or consider other question words such as *what, where, how,* and *why*. Or take a content word such as *melting*. It is likely that some of the Aboriginal children would not know it in advance of the toast-making activity. How and why is it a solvable linguistic problem in that context?

4. Does it surprise you that the activity route is not the easier one for children whose primary language is different from the language of the classroom?

CHAPTER 18

Immersion in First-Year Foreign Language Instruction for Adults

Steven Sternfeld

EDITOR'S INTRODUCTION

The previous chapter showed that children of low socioeconomic status (i.e., in situations with a traditional failure rate of nearly 100%) can in fact acquire literacy in a second language provided they are given sufficient scaffolding for the oral and written discourses of the classroom. In this chapter, Sternfeld reports on an approach to first-year foreign language instruction for adults at the University of Utah. He recommends an immersion-type experience which puts the students directly in touch with literature of the target language and culture. Although other authors, notably Brinton, Snow, and Wesche (Chapter 14), Leaver and Stryker (1989), and Allen, Anderson, and Narvaéz (Chapter 16), had advocated immersion-type or content-based approaches with adults (following the models employed so successfully with children by the Canadians), extensions of such concepts into the teaching of foreign languages to adults were usually limited to applications with students at the advanced intermediate stage or beyond. However, Sternfeld shows that foreign language students in their first year of foreign language study can also benefit from immersion-type exposure. As in the case of children in difficult socioeconomic settings, the evidence shows that students are often capable of more than the traditional theories suggest.

INTRODUCTION

Much has been written over the past sixty years about the place of modern foreign language (FL) study in the humanities and about the contribution that FL study makes to a liberal education.[1] A recurring theme in the post-WWII literature is that modern FL departments can strengthen their position in the humanities and enhance their contribution to liberal education by creating area studies programs. Kelly (1969) traces this interest in area studies to attempts made in Army Special Training Programs (ASTP) during World War II to "prevent American soldiers from offending the sensibilities of those whose language they were learning" (p.

379). On the heels of these ASTP courses, universities began to develop "language and area programs," a form of interdisciplinary study drawing on the fields of foreign language, history, and geography.[2] Kelly hastens to add that while ASTP courses were the catalyst for the creation of interdisciplinary programs in the modern languages, the model for these "new" programs came from the classics:

> The traditional classics course includes a thorough treatment of both the history and geography of the Roman Empire and an account of daily life in classical times, in other words, a full area program subordinated to the literary and linguistic content (p. 379).

Thus, the movement towards extending the area studies model to modern FL study is not new, and the University of Utah's Immersion/Multiliteracy (IM/ML) Program is but one of many outgrowths of this movement. Where the IM/ML Program has sought to innovate is in the creation of a first-year language program which espouses the area studies model. The designation Immersion/Multiliteracy is intended to capture both the methodology and aim of the program. The methodology of the IM/ML Program is based on the Canadian Immersion Model (see below). The program's aim is to promote multiliteracy,[3] i.e., the pursuit of intellectually challenging and culturally broadening activities in more than one language. Just as genuine first-language literacy requires not just the ability to read but also a fund of cultural knowledge, so multiliteracy requires both proficiency in a second language and basic background knowledge of the culture(s) associated with that language.[4]

THE IMMERSION APPROACH AND COLLEGE FL INSTRUCTION

As developed in Canada, the immersion approach to second-language teaching differs from conventional skills-based (SB) instruction in that immersion students use the target language primarily as a vehicle for studying other subjects in the school curriculum. Genesee (1983) describes immersion as

> a type of bilingual education in which a second language (or second languages) is used along with a child's native language for curriculum instruction during some part of the student's elementary or secondary education (p. 3).

First implemented twenty-eight years ago in the Montreal suburb of St. Lambert, by 1983 the Canadian Immersion Program was providing over 100,000 Anglophone students with some part of their regular daily curriculum instruction in French. Extensive evaluation of the program has shown that immersion students match their English-language schooled Anglophone counterparts with respect to both English language development and academic achievement. Moreover, they develop significantly higher levels of French

proficiency than do students in conventional SB French language programs. Not only do immersion students outperform students in traditional SB Programs, but they equal native French speakers in their receptive skills. While communicatively competent in speaking and writing, they do not generally reach native-like levels of grammatical accuracy. Finally, immersion students show positive attitudes towards learning French and an interest in continuing to study French; this is in contrast to students in conventional SB courses, who express relatively negative attitudes towards their French programs and towards learning French in general.[5]

The impressive results of the Canadian Immersion Program have already led to the creation of similar programs in half a dozen school districts across the United States.[6] College FL instruction, however, has yet to embrace the immersion model. There has, of course, been increased interest in incorporating content into SB programs in the form of authentic materials. However, the rationale for "content-mediated" (Patrikis, 1987) instruction is that authentic materials facilitate the development of language skills by providing learners with more highly contextualized and motivating input.[7] Thus, while content-mediated instruction and immersion programs have in common the use of authentic materials, their goals tend to differ: content-mediated instruction uses subject matter as a vehicle for teaching a second language while immersion programs use a second language as a vehicle for teaching subject matter.

Sternfeld (1988) identifies two notions which may account for the fact that the immersion approach itself has failed to make its way into college FL programs: 1) the notion that immersion is most effective, or indeed only effective, with very young learners, and 2) the notion that immersion works only when learners have multiple hours of daily contact over a period of many years. According to Sternfeld, current research does not support the "too little, too late" argument. Comparisons of proficiency levels attained by early vs. late immersion students have shown that in many cases children who begin immersion in Grade 7 are able to catch up with children who begin in kindergarten (Genesee, 1985, 1987; Swain, 1978; Lapkin et al., 1983). Moreover, the research on the effectiveness of short-term (e.g., one-semester), non-intensive subject-matter teaching has shown that students in subject-matter courses make linguistic gains equal to those of students in SB courses and also learn their subject matter (Edwards et al., 1984, Lafayette and Buscaglia, 1985). Sternfeld concludes that subject-matter learning could conceivably be "pushed down" (Krashen, 1982: 173) to the beginning level of college FL instruction provided that two conditions are met: 1) that expectations concerning initial production and comprehension are adjusted downwards, and 2) that compensatory pedagogical strategies are employed. Such strategies include focusing initially on comprehension, not forcing production, and modifying the format of written assignments and tests.

THE UNIVERSITY OF UTAH'S PILOT IM/ML PROGRAM

The goal of the pilot IM/ML Program at the University of Utah was for Anglophone students to use Spanish in an exploration of some facet(s) of Latin American studies. In these "sheltered" classrooms,[8] Spanish was the language of instruction while Latin American history, geography and current events constituted the content of instruction. Rather than learning to survive in a Spanish-speaking *country,* IM/ML students had to learn to survive in a Spanish-speaking *classroom.*

In 1985–86 two first-year IM/ML courses in Spanish were piloted by a professor in the Department of Languages and Literature. One of these courses met one hour a day, five days a week for three quarters; the other was offered as a summer intensive which met three and one-half hours a day for seven and one-half weeks. Eighteen students completed the year-long course; 25 completed the summer intensive course. To avoid self-selection and thereby enhance the generalizability of the results of this pilot program, neither pilot course was previously advertised as being part of the IM/ML Program. No students chose to withdraw upon being informed of the nature of the course, and attrition for the first-year IM/ML and SB programs was comparable.

A questionnaire was administered to all students completing the IM/ML Program and the con-

ventional SB program at the end of the first year. Students were asked to describe previous language instruction (school, year, and length of instruction) and informal contact (both in the United States and abroad) for *all* languages to which they had been exposed. These data indicate that absolute beginners were actually in the minority in both the IM/ML and SB Programs. In the case of false beginners, the fact that these students' initial exposure to Spanish had usually been brief (one or two years) and had not immediately preceded their enrollment in college Spanish would explain their presence in these first-year courses. Many students also indicated some informal contact with Spanish through friends, relatives, work, and/or travel. Over half the students had had some exposure to another foreign language besides Spanish.

DESIGN OF INSTRUCTION

In keeping with the principles of the Canadian immersion approach, none of the four language skills was explicitly taught initially. Thus, there was no underlying linguistic syllabus (grammatical, notional/functional, or situational), nor were there any vocabulary, structure, or pronunciation exercises. Following Krashen (1982, 1985b), it was assumed that the "comprehensible input" which would result from students interacting with the spoken and written language would lead to their acquiring Spanish.

Four activities were designed to promote student interaction with oral and written discourse: 1) daily reading assignments, 2) pre-reading lectures, 3) classroom discussions, and 4) subject-matter quizzes.

1 Daily Reading Assignments

Extensive daily reading assignments constituted the core of the IM/ML Program. These assignments were "purposely longer. . . than students can study crypto-analytically" in order to encourage rapid sketchy reading (Newmark, 1971: 16). For the study of history and geography, we adopted Spanish-language texts typically used in upper-division introductory civilization courses.[9]

For current events, students received five issues a week of *La Opinión,* a Spanish-language daily newspaper published in Los Angeles. *La Opinión* articles averaged about 300 to 500 words in length. Students in the year-long course were normally assigned four articles a night, students in the summer intensive course, eight. The use of the Spanish-language newspaper in the context of a beginning-level FL course deserves some special commentary. What might strike one as a difficult medium for beginning language students—because it is written for native speakers—is for several reasons an excellent medium for both subject-matter teaching and developing reading skills. First, students are already familiar with "genre schemas" (Fillmore, 1981) for newspapers, e.g., the use of the inverted pyramid format and the difference between news and commentary. Second, the newspaper frequently provides extralinguistic cues to meaning, such as photographs and other graphic devices. Third, by following news stories that continue over a period of weeks or even months, students are able to engage in the narrow reading (Krashen, 1985b) that greatly facilitates the acquisition of vocabulary and background knowledge. Fourth, since *La Opinión* is an American newspaper, it provides coverage of much the same news reported in the U.S. English-language media. This allows for an initial period of concentration on articles which report on U.S. and U.S.-related news. Focusing on these articles maximizes the amount of background knowledge students can draw on and provides a simple means for students to remedy insufficient background knowledge (they need only read the first section of the local daily newspaper). Finally, the variety of issues addressed in the newspaper allows for a progression from more concrete, action-oriented news to more abstract, issue-oriented topics.

2 Pre-reading Lectures

Students were prepared for each nightly reading assignment through a pre-reading lecture in Spanish. Initially, these lectures were a fairly extensive retelling of the text, involving elaborate non-verbal communication.[10] The retellings served as powerful "advanced organizers" (Ausubel, 1985) so that even absolute beginners were able to achieve a minimum level of comprehension with-

out recourse to a dictionary. As students' linguistic competence and background knowledge increased, the need for such comprehensive pre-reading activities was considerably reduced. By the end of the course, pre-reading lectures were presented only when the subject of the reading assignment was new to the students.

3 Discussions of Reading Assignments

In order to compensate for students' minimal comprehension skills in the early stages of the program, most of the class period was given over to pre-reading lectures; relatively little time was left for discussion of the reading assignments. Moreover, in order not to place too great a demand on student production, early discussions took the form of a question/answer period in which students could ask the instructor for clarification of words and phrases in the previous night's reading assignment. Students were able to learn quickly the simple formulaic language necessary for this type of interaction.

As the need for comprehensive preparation for the reading assignments diminished, more time could be devoted to discussion. Furthermore, as students' linguistic competence and subject-matter knowledge increased, and as more abstract, issue-oriented readings were assigned, discussions moved beyond teacher-centered textual clarification to highly interactive group discussions involving commentary and analysis.

4 Subject-Matter Quizzes

Students were quizzed daily on the reading assignments. The purpose of these quizzes was to encourage students to keep up with the extensive daily reading and to provide a means for teacher and students to monitor progress in reading comprehension and subject-matter knowledge.

Three types of quizzes were used in the course of the one-year program. Initially, students were asked to write an interpretation in English of the contents of several paragraphs selected from the previous night's reading, 60–90 seconds being allotted for each paragraph. Dictionaries were not allowed, and the only grading criteria were coherence and plausibility.

These four instructional strategies—the designation of the quiz as an "interpretation," the imposition of a rather severe time limit, the exclusion of dictionaries, and the rather lenient grading criteria—were intended to encourage students to assign quickly a global meaning to the text, even if that personally assigned meaning was at variance with the actual meaning of the text. Of course, early interpretations were very impressionistic, as students relied almost exclusively on readily identifiable cognates, context, and whatever background knowledge they brought with them to the course.

After about 75 contact hours, students' linguistic competence and background knowledge had developed sufficiently to allow greater emphasis to be placed on accuracy and completeness. It was at this point that the interpretations were reclassified as translations. It should be kept in mind that the ability to produce accurate Spanish-to-English translations was not an explicit goal of the IM/ML Program. As previously mentioned, the purpose of the interpretation quizzes was to encourage students to keep up with the reading assignments and to monitor the development of students' reading comprehension skills and background knowledge. In order to maintain this same focus with the translation quizzes, it was essential that students not be allowed to use dictionaries.

About two-thirds of the way through the course a short-answer quiz format was introduced. These open-book quizzes required students to write short responses in Spanish to simple questions on the material in the newspaper and the civilization textbooks. At first these questions were written on the board; later they were dictated to the students.

PROGRAM EVALUATION

Two questions were of primary concern in our evaluation of the pilot IM/ML Program:

- What was the program's impact on students' Spanish-language skill development?
- What was the program's contribution to students' liberal education?

Spanish Language Skill Development

Students' Spanish language skills were assessed for the purposes of ongoing evaluation of the IM/ML Program and articulation with the SB Program.[11] Thus, the same battery of tests was administered to all first-year students, i.e., those in the two sections of the pilot IM/ML Program and those in the four sections of the conventional SB program taught by graduate students under the supervision of a Spanish faculty member.

The considerable differences in the goals, curriculum, instructional strategies, and internal evaluation procedures of the IM/ML and SB Programs posed particular problems for test development. Given the problems inherent in "program-fair evaluation" (Beretta, 1986) and constrained as we were by practical considerations in the development, administration, and scoring of language tests, we initially limited ourselves to developing tests to measure just three skills: reading comprehension, listening comprehension, and extemporaneous writing. We adopted a combination of strategies to minimize test bias, including the use of pragmatic tests (Oller, 1979), the careful manipulation of test format and/or content both within and across tests, and the development of a dual scoring system.

Two reading tests were devised to measure extensive and intensive reading skills. The Reading Summary (RS) required students to summarize in English an essay written in Spanish, while the Reading Translation (RT) involved the translation of a short prose passage from Spanish into English.[12] In an analogous fashion, two tests of listening comprehension were developed. The Lecture Summary (LS) required students to summarize in English the contents of a videotaped lecture given by a professor of Spanish on the history of Spain during the reign of Philip II; the Dictation (DT) was based on a passage taken from the videotaped lecture. Writing was assessed with a single measure, a Writing Sample (WS). Students were given a prompt in Spanish on eating habits in Latin America and then asked to write, in Spanish and without the aid of any reference materials, about their own eating habits.

SCORING

For each of the five tests, two scores were awarded: a fluency score and a holistic content score. The fluency score was based on the number of words in a response. The content score was based on the degree to which a given response was factually correct, linguistically accurate, logical, and comprehensible. To increase the reliability of the content score of the Dictation, Reading Summary, and Writing Sample, each of these tests was rated by three Spanish-language instructors who participated in a 6-hour training program modeled on that used for training raters to evaluate University of Utah Freshman Writing placement essays. A consensus system was used whereby a final content score was awarded when at least two of the three raters assigned the same score and the third rater's score was no more than one point away. In this case the final score awarded was that of the majority. When there was more than a one point difference among raters, the test was re-rated until a consensus was reached. Raters did not see students' names, nor did they know to which group a given student belonged.

RESULTS AND ANALYSIS

Since not all students took all five tests, a total of 14 cases were deleted from the analyses (seven from the IM/ML Program and seven from the SB program). This left a total of 36 subjects in the IM/ML group and 46 in the SB group. Test scores for these subjects are reported in Table 18.1. For the purposes of statistical analyses, all raw scores were converted into z-scores. The content scores and the fluency scores were subjected to separate multivariate analyses of variance (MANOVA). Table 18.2 reports the results of the two MANOVAs.

No significant difference was found between the two groups with respect to fluency scores. The content scores were found to differ significantly ($p < .05$). The five pairs of content scores were therefore subjected to univariate F-Tests, the results of which are reported in Table 18.3. The only significant difference ($p < .05$) found was on the Writing Sample, where SB students outperformed IM/ML students.

DISCUSSION

The statistical analyses indicate that IM/ML students developed listening, reading, and writing skills which, for the most part, equaled those of SB students. While the MANOVA showed the content scores to differ significantly between the two groups, subsequent univariate F-tests indicated that the SB students outperformed the IM/ML students on only one of the five tests, the Writing Sample.

The question remains, then, whether this last result reflects actual differences in the development of writing skills or whether it is an artifact of test design. Indeed, the design of the writing test was rather problematic, given the very different roles which writing plays in the two programs. Since the primary function of writing in the SB program is to provide students with controlled practice in the use of the vocabulary and structures presented in their text, writing for SB students tends to invoke heavy monitor use (see Krashen, 1982, 1985b, for a discussion of monitor use). In contrast, given the focus on subject matter and the lack of formal language instruction in the IM/ML Program, IM/ML students were essentially incapable of monitoring their writing for grammatical accuracy.

The decision to test extemporaneous writing skills was made in an attempt to minimize monitor use, thereby ensuring a more equitable basis for comparison of the two groups. Yet this decision placed SB students at a disadvantage, since they lacked experience with unmonitored writing. To compensate, a guided composition format was chosen using a topic discussed in some detail in the SB students' textbook (eating habits). In the end, this may have placed IM/ML students at an even greater disadvantage. Since the subject of personal eating habits was not part of the content of the IM/ML course, many IM/ML students had not had prior experience in handling this subject in Spanish. As a result, IM/ML students were less likely to have the appropriate lexical items in their active vocabulary. Finally, the overall greater accuracy of SB students may reflect the fact that SB students, unlike IM/ML students, could rely in part on memorized routines, the accuracy of which generally surpassed that of their developing interlanguage.

TABLE 18.1 Summary of Mean Scores

Score	Group		Test				
			RT	RS	DT	LS	WS
Fluency	SB	(n = 46)	−.16	−.23	−.17	−.10	−.14
	IM/ML	(n = 36)	−.03	.33	.19	.16	.12
Content	SB	(n = 46)	−.02	.08	−.05	.12	.23
	IM/ML	(n = 36)	.11	.01	.06	−.16	−.33

TABLE 18.2 Multivariate Test

Score	Wilks-*Lambda*	Rao's *R* (Form 2)	*df*	*P*
Content	.8366264	2.968205	5,76	.0167*
Fluency	.8895743	1.886825	5,76	.1057

*$p < .05$

TABLE 18.3 Univariate Tests of Content Scores

Test	*F*-Ratio	*df*	*P*
Reading Translation	.3343	1,80	.5717
Reading Summary	.0930	1,80	.7551
Dictation	.2418	1,80	.6299
Lecture Summary	1.5886	1,80	.2086
Writing	6.5588	1,80	.0119*

*$p < .05$

THE IM/ML PROGRAM AND LIBERAL EDUCATION

Since the aim of the pilot IM/ML Program was to enhance the contribution of introductory FL study to liberal education, we were particularly interested in assessing the extent to which students had been intellectually stimulated and culturally broadened by their study of Latin America. An open-ended essay format was chosen as most appropriate for our purposes. Open-ended questions are a data gathering tool frequently used in qualitative evaluation (Patton, 1980).

Since students' views on the meaning of a liberal education differ considerably, we did not attempt to query students directly on their perceptions of the contribution which the IM/ML Program had made to their general education.[13] Rather, we chose to ask students to describe what they felt they had learned in the course; from this data we hoped to draw our own conclusions concerning the program's contribution to students' liberal education.

The essays were written in English during the last week of the program. Students were asked 1) to trace the development of their understanding of and attitudes towards Latin America over the course of the pilot IM/ML Program, and 2) to evaluate each component of the course (newspaper, civilization texts, lectures, discussions) in terms of its contribution to these changes. This second evaluation was included to provide program developers with feedback on the perceived utility of the various instructional activities.

RESULTS AND ANALYSIS

An initial analysis of the data has yielded five major categories into which the majority of reported learning outcomes fall. All students listed at least one of these major learning outcomes; many students mentioned several of these outcomes; others mentioned outcomes which had only a tenuous relationship to the aims of liberal education.[14]

The five outcomes are listed below, each followed by an excerpt from a student essay which is representative of the responses grouped under that learning outcome.

Learning Outcome 1: Students acquired basic (background) information useful for understanding more complex issues which they were already familiar with or became familiar with during the course of the program:

> The books provided me with much needed dates and places. My schema for geography included Guatemala and Argentina in the same sentence and dates for the independence of Latin American countries were often placed a couple of centuries earlier. Later when I read the newspapers it was very helpful to know general geography and dates because I was better able to understand the economic, political and social development of the country and how that fit with the problems they face today.

Learning Outcome 2: Students became aware of current issues in the United States and Latin America:

> The newspaper also made me aware of some of the issues that I had not even been aware of. I was not aware some people were trying to have English made the official U.S. language. The newspapers provided a feel for contemporary Latin American issues that would have been difficult to find elsewhere.

Learning Outcome 3: Students gained access to an additional and often differing point of view:

> The almost daily updates in *La Opinión* about aid to the Contras and Ortega's pleas to the U.S. for a negotiated settlement helped me grasp a much better understanding through seeing the issue from the point of view of Nicaraguans, both Sandinista and Contra, rather than from the point of view of American commentators.

Learning Outcome 4: Students developed greater awareness of the complexity of issues with which they were already familiar:

> I had thought that I understood the problem of illegal immigration in this country, but reading the articles on the "paramilitaries" from Alabama and the citizens' arrest made in Arizona really altered my view. I started to look at illegal immigration not as the problem, but as a result of the problem, which is poverty.

Learning Outcome 5: Students expressed an interest in further developing their understanding of Hispanic culture:

> The great thing about this class is that I can now *ask* a lot of questions. I have a subscription to *La Opinión* and I will continue to look for these answers because I am now *very* interested in what is going on in Latin America. I will also be searching the city and talking to Latins here in Salt Lake to see their viewpoint and how they fit into the picture.

DISCUSSION

Recall that it had been our intent to enhance the contribution that introductory FL study makes to our students' liberal education by promoting multiliteracy, which we defined as the pursuit of intellectually challenging and culturally broadening activities in more than one language. Assuming that these self-reports are not totally unfounded, it appears that the IM/ML Program has indeed made an important contribution to undergraduate education.

A definitive response to this question is, of course, not possible on at least two grounds. First, in the absence of pre- and post-tests, we are unable to confirm whether more objective measurements of learning outcomes would substantiate students' perceptions. Second, the above-mentioned outcomes may be criticized as failing to fulfill the role which traditional SB foreign language study has played in the undergraduate curriculum, namely that of a principled examination of the structure of language. Nevertheless, those who support an area studies approach to FL instruction will consider these outcomes central to the aims of liberal education.

CONCLUSION

The initial results of the Immersion/ Multiliteracy Program indicate that subject-matter teaching can indeed be "pushed down" to first-year language courses. A comparison of the reading, listening, and writing skills of IM/ML and SB students shows that IM/ML students are, for the most part, keeping up with their counterparts in the SB program. Moreover, data gathered from IM/ML students' English-language essays can be interpreted as lending support to the claim that an area studies approach can enhance the contribution that beginning FL study makes to liberal education.

These preliminary results encouraged us to proceed with the development of the IM/ML Program. In 1987 we received a grant from the Department of Education to improve the design, implementation, and evaluation of the IM/ML Program. We now have IM/ML Programs in Spanish, German, French and Chinese and will be beginning a course in Japanese this fall. Subject matter varies from course to course, for the most part the result of the availability and/or accessibility of reading material. The Spanish course, in addition to *La Opinión,* now uses the *Pequeño Larousse Ilustrado* (1976) instead of the civilization textbooks to present background information on Latin America. The French course has adopted *Journal Historique de la France* (Billard, et al., 1986), a history of France written in journalistic format. The German course has been built around a 3-volume world history text, *Unsere Geschichte* (Hug, 1985), which is used in secondary schools in Germany. For the Chinese course, special materials have been developed under the OED grant, including an outline of Chinese history, an overview of lifestyle in modern China, and stories based on classic Chinese proverbs.

Additional university funding was received in 1988 to aid in the development of a master curriculum for the languages taught in the IM/ML Program. Scholars from the fields of history, fine arts, political science, sociology, etc. will be asked to draw up a program of study that will 1) provide the Department of Languages and Literature with guidelines for the training of teaching assistants in our MAT (Master of Arts in Teaching) Program who serve as IM/ML instructors, and 2) provide IM/ML instructors in turn with a framework for designing new curricula for IM/ML courses. Considerable work lies ahead; nonetheless, we are convinced that an area studies approach to first-year college FL instruction holds promise for enhancing the contribution that FL study makes to liberal education.

NOTES

1 An initial search has produced nearly 100 articles written over the past sixty years on this topic. The vast majority of these articles have appeared in *The Modern Language Journal,* the *ADFL Bulletin,* and the *French Review.* A review of this literature is in progress.

2 There is considerable hesitation as to the appropriate label for such programs, the three most common ones being "area studies," "interdisciplinary studies," and "multidisciplinary studies." Although not widely used, the term *nondisciplinary* is perhaps the most appropriate. Coined by classics professor Harald Reiche, it was intended to describe tests which "predated—and even called into question—the very intellectual division represented by our [modern day] disciplines" (Elbow, 1986: 5). Such variations notwithstanding, these programs may be intradepartmental or interdepartmental (cross-curricular) in conception. A number of perspectives serve as a focal point of area studies programs: ethno-linguistic (e.g., Slavic Studies, Germanic Studies), socio-cultural (Women's Studies, Afro-American Studies), geographic (e.g., Latin American Studies, Asian Studies), historica (e.g., Renaissance Studies, Medieval Studies), and sociopolitical (e.g., International Studies, Multicultural Studies). For a general discussion of area studies programs and departments of language and literature, see Champagne (1978), Dease (1982), Giamatti (1979), Jorden (1982), Jurasek (1988), Lee (1983), Nelson (1972), and Tonkin (1985). For a discussion of foreign languages and International Studies, see Burnett and Robinson (1985), Dirks (1976), Haenicke (1979, 1976), and Knoll (1976).

3 The term *multiliteracy* is borrowed from Hirsch (1987), who contrasts it with multilingualism. As Hirsch points out, one can be multilingual without being multiliterate.

4 In this sense, multiliteracy is closely tied to multiculturalism, although the latter does not necessarily imply a background of shared *literate* knowledge. In the field of ESL, EAP (English for Academic purposes) Programs have as their aim multiliteracy, since their

goal is to provide international students with both the linguistic skills and the "cultural competence" they must have in order to study in English-speaking educational institutions.

5 For more detail on these results, see Genesee (1983, 1985), Hornby (1980), Lambert (1974), Lambert & Tucker (1972), Lapkin (1984), and Pawley (1981). For a review of criticisms of the Canadian Immersion Program, see Hammerly (1987).

6 Immersion programs have been implemented in Cincinnati, Milwaukee, Montgomery County (MD), Culver City (CA), Alpine School District (UT), and San Diego. See Campbell (1984) and Genesee (1985) for program descriptions.

7 For a more detailed discussion of content-mediated or content-based instruction, see Gamel (1984), Graman (1987), Meyer and Tetrault (1988), Rogers and Medley (1988), Stevick (1980), Suozzo (1981), Swaffar (1985), and VanPatten (1987).

8 A "sheltered" classroom (Krashen, 1985b) is reserved exclusively for non-native speakers. The exclusion of native speakers ensures that the instructor will make the necessary modifications to compensate for the linguistic deficiencies of the second language learners. As in the immersion program, the subject of instruction is not the second language, but some other subject in the curriculum (math, science, history, etc.).

9 See Incera (1980) and Marbán (1983, 1974). In order to compensate for the fact that students in the year-long course received more than three times as many issues of *La Opinión* as did students in the summer intensive course, the year-long section used only one history/geography text while the summer intensive course used three.

10 The fact that more than one student likened the instructor's early pre-reading lectures to a game of "charades" conveys a sense of the role played by nonverbal communication.

11 Indeed, the long-term viability of the IM/ML Program depended in part on IM/ML students developing skill levels comparable to those of students in first-year SB courses. Since it was not clear how the two groups would co-articulate at the beginning of the second year, one section of second-year Spanish was set aside for continuing IM/ML students. This two-quarter sequence was taught by a professor familiar with the goals and methodology of the IM/ML Program.

12 The essay *El Conflicto entre los sexos* was taken from *Perspectivas* (Kiddle & Wegman, 1988). The short prose passage was taken from the opening paragraph of *Macario* by Bruno Traven (1971).

13 Nevertheless, as Morello (1988) points out in a recent article, we should not overlook the importance of the relationship between students' perceptions of their progress and their attitudes toward foreign language study. See also Rivers (1985), who admonishes FL teachers to "look with our students' eyes at the way our curriculum appears to them" (p. 42).

14 For example, one student, whose husband was an English/Spanish bilingual who only used English at home, noted that she was finally able to speak to her mother-in-law on the telephone.

DISCUSSION QUESTIONS

1. Early in his article, Sternfeld rejects the "too little, too late" argument against teaching foreign languages to adults. How does that argument compare with the claim that children before a certain age or threshold will not be able to become readers?

2. What are some of the advantages of working with news stories? What kinds of representations are they? (See Chapter 37.) What scaffolding do they provide? What other sources of information will help the student to understand the newspaper? What will help students relate the news to their own experience?

3. Discuss the advantage of skills-based (SB) students in Sternfeld's study over the immersion/multiliteracy (IM/ML) students in writing and the lack of any contrast on the other tests. What other sorts of testing procedures might be conceived to make an optimal comparison between two such diverse groups of foreign language students?

4. How can intensive study of a foreign language and its cultural bases contribute to a liberal education? What ways are evidenced in comments received from the students in Sternfeld's study?

CHAPTER 19

Evidence of a Formal Schema in Second Language Comprehension

Patricia L. Carrell

EDITOR'S INTRODUCTION

*E*xpectations concerning what a given text or discourse may represent are apparently of two kinds. The first relates to particular facts and can be directly associated with what we would call "content" (the left side of Figure 37.1), and the second kind pertains to representations themselves and what we call "form" (the right side of Figure 37.1). Both kinds of expectations are called by many names, including schema (by Piaget, 1947; and Carrell, for instance), models (Johnson-Laird, 1983), episodic structure (Glenn, 1978), scripts (Schank, 1975, 1980; Schank & Abelson, 1977), plans (Miller, Galanter, & Pribram, 1960), expectancies (Oller, 1974, 1983b), and so forth. Depending partly on the vantage point we assume, we may prefer the term plan (from the producer's side) or expectancy (from the receiver's). Regardless, at their basis, the kinds of structures and processes involved seem to be very similar if not the same. Therefore, perhaps an abstract term (which is biased neither toward producer or receiver, nor toward content or form) such as schema ought to be preferred. Carrell chooses such an approach. However, as she shows in this chapter, it is useful to distinguish between content-oriented ("content") schemata and form-oriented ("formal") schemata. For reasons given in Chapter 37, the most basic "formal" schema is of the narrative type and happens to be the kind Carrell looks at in this chapter. The essence of a narrative schema (a kind of grammar of expectancy and planning) is some person experiencing events unfolding in time and space. An example in this chapter of such a temporal unfolding is one of the unlucky twins losing her dollar bill and suffering the consequences, or it is some other character struggling through some other connected series of events. The key (Dewey, 1916) is development over time. Here, Carrell shows that the formal schema for narratives is just as important to non-native speakers of English as it is to native speakers. Subsequent chapters of Part 4 continue to bear out this finding.*

Research on discourse or text comprehension has shown that comprehension is determined not only by the local effects of sentences or paragraphs, but also by the overall suprasentential or rhetorical organization of a text.[1] Each type of text—e.g., stories, fables, expository and scientific texts—has its own conventional structure; knowl-edge of these conventions aids readers[2] in comprehending the text as well as in recalling it later (Kintsch & van Dijk, 1975, 1978; Meyer, 1975; Thorndyke, 1977). Following Bartlett (1932), this knowledge has been called a *schema,* or more specifically, following Carrell (1983a), a *formal schema.*

The most extensively studied text schemata are the ones for stories. Bartlett, as long ago as 1932, explored the involvement of schemata in story comprehension. More recently, the study of story comprehension has again become an active research topic among cognitive psychologists, and in much of this research the concept of a story schema plays a crucial explanatory role (Bower, 1978; Kintsch & van Dijk, 1975; Kintsch, 1974, 1977; Mandler, 1978a; Mandler & Johnson, 1977; Johnson & Mandler, 1980; Rumelhart, 1975; Thorndyke, 1977). This recent empirical research has shown that stories have schematic structure and that readers are sensitive to such structure and use it to guide both comprehension and recall. For example, Thorndyke (1977) and Kintsch, Mandel, and Kozminsky (1977) have shown that stories presented in scrambled order are recalled less well than those presented in normal order. Mandler (1978a; Mandler & Johnson, 1977; Johnson & Mandler, 1980) has shown the powerful effects of story schemata in first language comprehension for both adults and children. Mandler's data show that not only do adults use their knowledge of story structure to guide comprehension and recall, but that children as young as first grade have acquired story schemata and use them to organize their comprehension and recall (cf. also the research of Adams & Collins, 1979; Adams & Bruce, 1980; Glenn, 1978; Stein & Glenn, 1979). Yet little comparable research has been done to empirically investigate the role of rhetorical schemata in second language comprehension.

This paper reports an empirical study of the effects of story structure or narrative rhetorical organization on reading recall in English as a second language. The research described in this paper is adapted from a paradigm used by Mandler (1978a) to investigate the effects of story schemata on first language comprehension during both encoding and retrieval of simple stories. Because of some important differences between the two studies, however, this is not a replication of the Mandler study.

This study of the effects of a particular story schema on ESL reading comprehension represents but one aspect of the general investigation of cross-cultural and culture-specific effects of both *formal* and *content* schemata on second language comprehension. Within the context of the study of formal schemata[3] (background knowledge of the rhetorical structures of different types of texts; Carrell, 1983a), narrative, story schemata are not the only rhetorical schemata of interest and relevance to ESL reading comprehension. The effects of different types of expository rhetorical organization, in the sense of Meyer (1975, 1977, 1979; Meyer, Brandt, & Bluth, 1980; Meyer & Rice, 1982; Meyer & Freedle, 1984), are another important area of investigation. A number of studies are beginning to emerge to demonstrate the relevance to ESL reading and writing of the investigation of formal, rhetorical schemata—for example, the research of Connor and McCagg (1983a, 1983b), comparing the performance of Japanese and Spanish readers of ESL on an expository text with a given rhetorical pattern; the research of Hinds (1979, 1983a, 1983b), comparing Japanese and English readers, reading in their respective native languages, on texts with a typical Japanese rhetorical structure; the research of Burtoff (1983), comparing the different rhetorical patterns of English expository prose produced by native speakers of Japanese, Arabic, and English; and the research of Carrell (1983c), comparing the written recalls from different types of expository prose by different native language/cultural groups of ESL readers. All of these studies illustrate the importance of investigating formal, rhetorical schemata in ESL reading comprehension.

Because narrative schemata have been claimed to be developmentally prior (Freedle & Hale, 1979; Glenn, 1978; Stein & Glenn, 1979) to expository schemata, and have also been claimed to be more cross-culturally universal and less culture-specific than expository schemata (Mandler, Scribner, Cole & DeForest, 1980)—although this latter claim is not without debate (Kintsch & Greene, 1978)—it would seem important to test for the effects of simple narrative schemata in comprehension in English as a foreign or second language. To my knowledge, no previous research of this type has been conducted in ESL.

STORY SCHEMATA DURING ENCODING

A story schema may be thought of as the rhetorical structure or the grammar of a story. It has even

FIGURE 19.1. Underlying Structural Schema for Stories Used in This Study

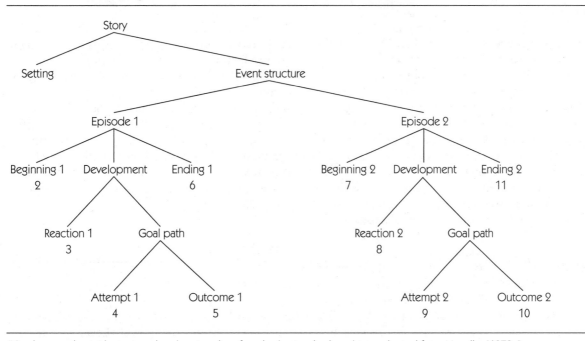

(Numbers under each story node = input order of nodes in standard versions; adapted from Mandler [1978a] and used with permission.)

been characterized as a grammar which generates a tree structure consisting of labeled nodes, the constituents of a story (see Figure 19.1).

As can be seen in Figure 19.1, each story consists of a common Setting plus an Event Structure, which consists of a series of causally or temporally connected Episodes. (The stories used in this research consisted of two temporally connected episodes, Episode 1 and Episode 2, as illustrated in Figure 19.1.) Each Episode consists of a Beginning, a Development, and an Ending. The Development consists of a Reaction and a Goal Path, the latter consisting of an Attempt and an Outcome. Mandler (1978a: 16) defines these simple story components or nodes as follows: A Setting usually consists of stative information about one or more of the characters, usually their location in time and place; the Beginning is usually some action or event that begins the story; the Reaction is an internal reaction of a character caused by the beginning event—the reacting character becomes the protagonist of the episode; in the Goal Path, the protagonist formulates a plan to deal with the problem created by the beginning; the Attempt comprises

the efforts and actions of the protagonist to try to reach that goal; the Outcome tells us whether the attempt was successful or not; the Ending usually consists of some further consequences or emphatic resolution to a series of events, or may also include a reaction on the part of another character. Only the terminal nodes in the diagram are actually realized overtly as segments of the text. The other, nonterminal nodes, as in a sentence diagram, represent the hierarchical organization of the story.

The story schema may also be thought of as a set of expectations about stories, about the units of which they are composed, the way those units fit together and are sequenced.

This cognitive schema guides both the encoding of a story during input (i.e., as it's being read) and during retrieval (i.e., as it's being recalled). During encoding, the schema provides a framework within which the incoming material may be structured; it helps the reader know which aspects of the material are more or less important or relevant, and it also lets the reader know when some part of the story is complete and can be stored, or that some proposition is still incomplete and must be kept in working memory because related material is yet to come.

Although some kind of very general text or discourse schema is activated at the time the encoding is begun, if the material is to be comprehended at all, details of the input guide the selection of the more specific details of the story schema. *Once upon a time* or some other type of setting statement alerts the readers to expect a subsequent sequence of statements far different from those they might hear if they were reading a research report, a recipe, or the transcript of a political speech. The process of comprehending a text is an interactive one between the text and certain key elements in it, on the one hand, and the appropriate background schema being activated by the reader, on the other hand.

Mandler and Johnson (1977) describe an explicit set of rules governing the structure of episodes in various kinds of stories, and they claim that knowledge of such a general set of rules is what enables a reader to organize incoming propositions while reading a story. A reader may go wrong at any number of places, even in a well-structured story. If any story nodes are omitted or are displaced from the ideal order, the chances of confusion or of encoding an unstable, novel structure increase.

STORY SCHEMATA DURING RETRIEVAL

At retrieval time, the story schema also plays a crucial role. First, it tells the subject what general sort of information is to be retrieved—i.e., it points to a general area of memory. Next, it provides a temporal sequence within which to find specific content—it tells the subject which address in memory to move to next. Finally, if the exact content of a category cannot be retrieved, the schema allows the subject to generate an approximation, based on the structure of the schema itself, before moving to the next address. Thus, a story schema may account for certain kinds of distortions and additions which are produced when the exact content of a story node is not retrievable. Similarly, since the schema directs temporal sequencing, if a story has been presented in irregular fashion, the output should be affected by the ideal order (the schema-dictated order) rather than the order actually read.

HYPOTHESIS

The main question in this study was whether ESL subjects are influenced by a simple story schema in comprehending stories read in their second language, English. The question was addressed by comparing recalls of two types of stories—one well-structured and the other deliberately violating the sequence of events prescribed by the story schema. It was hypothesized that if ESL subjects are influenced by a story schema, then when stories are read which violate the expected story schema, quantity of recall and temporal sequencing of recall will be affected.

METHOD

Subjects

Forty ESL subjects participated in the experiment. They were intermediate-level (Level 3) ESL students enrolled in the Center for English as a Second Language (CESL), an intensive program for prematriculated foreign students at Southern Illinois University at Carbondale. Their overall English proficiency was in the range of 50 to 60 on the Michigan Test of English. Their native language backgrounds included Arabic ($n = 12$), Spanish ($n = 8$), Malaysian/Indonesian ($n = 8$), and Japanese ($n = 5$), as well as others (African, Greek, Turkish, Chinese, and Korean).

Materials

Three simple two-episode stories were constructed according to the story grammar outlined in Mandler and Johnson (1977). In fact, one of the stories was one of four used by Mandler (1978a) in her first language research with both adults and children. Figure 19.1 illustrates the analysis of each story. Each story has a common Setting, followed by two temporally connected episodes. This structure is a loose one, in which the protagonist and events of the second episode bear only a temporal relation to the first. However, in all the stories the events made a sensible whole, and the two protagonists—one per episode—were closely related and were united by the common Setting in which they were both introduced.

TABLE 19.1 An Example of a Standard and Interleaved Story

STANDARD VERSION

	Setting:	Once there were twins, Tom and Jennifer, who had so much trouble their parents called them the unlucky twins.
	Beginning 1:	One day, Jennifer's parents gave her a dollar bill to buy the turtle she wanted, but on the way to the pet store she lost it.
EPISODE 1	Reaction 1:	Jennifer was worried that her parents would be angry with her so she decided to search every bit of the sidewalk where she had walked.
	Attempt 1:	She looked in all the cracks and in the grass along the way.
	Outcome 1:	She finally found the dollar bill in the grass.
	Ending 1:	But when Jennifer got to the store, the pet store man told her that someone else had just bought the last turtle, and he didn't have any more.
	Beginning 2:	The same day, Tom fell off a swing and broke his leg.
EPISODE 2	Reaction 2:	He wanted to run and play with the other kids.
	Attempt 2:	So he got the kids to pull him around in his wagon.
	Outcome 2:	While they were playing, Tom fell out of the wagon and broke his arm.
	Ending 2:	Tom's parents said he was even unluckier than Jennifer and made him stay in bed until he got well.

INTERLEAVED VERSION

Setting: Once there were twins, Tom and Jennifer, who had so much trouble their parents called them the unlucky twins.

Beginning 1: One day, Jennifer's parents gave her a dollar bill to buy the turtle she wanted, but on the way to the pet store she lost it.

Beginning 2: The same day, Tom fell off a swing and broke his leg.

Reaction 1: Jennifer was worried that her parents would be angry with her, so she decided to search every bit of the sidewalk where she had walked.

Reaction 2: Tom wanted to run and play with the other kids.

Attempt 1: Jennifer looked in all the cracks and in the grass along the way.

Attempt 2: Tom got the kids to pull him around in his wagon.

Outcome 1: Jennifer finally found the dollar bill in the grass.

Outcome 2: While the kids were playing, Tom fell out of the wagon and broke his arm.

Ending 1: But when Jennifer got to the store, the pet store man told her that someone had just bought the last turtle, and he didn't have any more.

Ending 2: Tom's parents said he was even unluckier than Jennifer and made him stay in bed until he got well.

(from Mandler [1978a], used with permission)

Each standard story was then rearranged to create an interleaved version. In these versions, following the Setting, the five basic nodes of each episode were presented in interleaved fashion: two Beginnings (Beginning 1, followed by Beginning 2), two Reactions, two Attempts, two Outcomes, and two Endings. In these sets of paired nodes, the node from Episode 1 was always presented first. An example of a standard and an interleaved story and its division into the basic nodes is shown in Table 19.1. Appendix 19.1 contains the complete text of all three stories, in both their standard and interleaved versions. The propositions and sentences in both versions are identical except for occasional substitution of proper nouns in the interleaved versions for pronouns in the standard versions to provide clear, unambiguous referents.

Procedures

Subjects were tested in their ESL classrooms. Half the subjects read the three standard versions, and the other half read the three interleaved versions. The stories were each typed on separate sheets of paper as a single super-paragraph, indented only at the beginning of the story. Order of presentation of the three stories was counterbalanced across subjects and was accomplished by stapling the three stories together in the six possible orders. Story booklets consisting of either three standard or three interleaved stories in each of these six counterbalanced presentation orders were randomly distributed to the subjects in their classroom groups.

Subjects were told that we were interested in how ESL students understand and remember stories. They were told to read the stories they were given, in the order in which they were stapled together, taking as much time as they needed to understand and remember the stories. They were told that they would be asked to write what they could remember of the stories sometime later, so they should read carefully and try to understand each story. They were not told when recall would be asked for, and they were not allowed to make any written notes. The story booklets were collected from them individually, as they finished reading. Although reading time was individually controlled by each subject, as a group they took approximately 15 to 20 minutes to read all three stories. After the stories were all collected, regular classroom activities were resumed and the stories were not discussed or even mentioned again.

In order to provide one measure of compatibility with Mandler's native speaker subjects, recall was elicited 24 hours later. In eliciting their recall, subjects were given recall booklets consisting of three stapled sheets of paper. At the top of each page was a story's title, intended as a recall cue; otherwise, the sheet was a blank piece of lined paper. To ensure that order of recall was the same as order of presentation, the order of the

titled pages corresponded to the order of the original stories for each subject. Subjects were asked to write their recall of each story, writing as much as they could remember of each story, as exactly as they could remember having read it, in the same order in which they read the stories. They were told to write as well as they could, but not to be overly concerned with their writing. They were told that not only would they not be given a grade on their writing, but that, in fact, their writing teachers wouldn't even see what they wrote. We emphasized that we were interested in how much and how well they could write it down. As with reading time, writing time was subject-controlled. However, as a group, they spent approximately 35 to 50 minutes writing their recalls of all three stories.

Scoring Procedure

A loose criterion[4] of recall was used. Two raters had to agree that the essential meaning of a story node had been reproduced, allowing possible slight distortions or additions in meaning. Interrater reliability exceeded .90. Disagreements were settled by a third rater. Distortions included the following: (1) recall of only a subsidiary part of a node, possibly even leaving out the main event being described; (2) repetitions of previously recalled nodes, in which other nodes were produced before the repetition; (3) character and event confusions, consisting of importations from one episode into another, or from one node into another within the same episode. The most typical character confusions were a single character being used as the protagonist for both episodes or a character from one episode appearing in the other. Additions were of the following types: (1) redundancies, i.e., saying the same thing twice, often in a slightly different way; (2) reasonable presuppositions in which obviously inferable material was added to the original node—for example, in the Unlucky Twins story (see Table 19.1), Attempt 1 might include something like "She retraced her steps" before continuing with the original node; (3) exaggerations, in which a statement was intensified in some way; (4) irrelevant or wrong information added to an otherwise correctly recalled node. This last kind of information was in contrast to reasonable presuppositions and exaggerations.

TABLE 19.2 Quantity of Recall

Story type	Intermediate ESL $N = 40$		L1 adults and children $N = 96$ (Mandler, 1978a)	
	Standard $n = 20$	Interleaved $n = 20$	Standard $n = 48$	Interleaved $n = 48$
Stories recalled	90% (54/60)	87% (52/60)	89%	89%
		n.s.		n.s.
Episodes recalled	90% (97/108)	83% (86/104)	86%	96%
		n.s.		**
Nodes Recalled	75% (402/539)	68% (330/482)	72%	67%
		**		**

$**p < .05$

Although these were frequently related to the story line, they could not logically be assumed to be the case. For example, in the Unlucky Twins story the subject might have written for Outcome 2 "Tom broke his arm and had to go to the hospital." The only type of additions which were not included were those in which irrelevant or wrong material was *substituted* for the essential meaning of an entire node. For example, in the Unlucky Twins story it might have been recalled that the girl found her dollar, and not being able to retrieve the Ending, the subject might have written "She felt glad and went home." Thus, if there was virtually any recognizable piece of the meaning of the node present in the recall, the node was scored as being present. Otherwise, it was scored as missing.

RESULTS

Quantity of Recall

The results indicating the quantity of recall are given in Table 19.2.

In addition to reporting the results for the ESL subjects of this study, I will also indicate how they compare to the first language results obtained by Mandler (1978a). However, I will make no statistical comparisons outside the ESL group. Furthermore, it should be noted that Mandler's first language subjects operated in the oral medium (listening to and retelling the stories); these ESL subjects operated in the written medium (reading and writing the stories). It was noted earlier that Mandler's subjects also had a 24-hour recall interval.

The same number of stories was recalled in both the standard and the interleaved story conditions. A story was counted as having been recalled if any part of it was recalled. The ESL subjects in this study recalled 54 out of 60 (or 90%) of the standard and 52 out of 60 (or 87%) of the interleaved stories. (N.s. in Table 19.2 indicates that the pair-wise comparisons are not statistically significant according to the test of significant differences in proportions from independent samples. If the difference is statistically significant at the level $p < .05$, a double asterisk is shown.) Thus, there were no differences between the standard and the interleaved conditions in the number of stories recalled in whole or in part.

When the story was recalled, in whole or in any part, there were also no significant differences in the number of episodes recalled in whole or in part: 90% (97 out of a potential 108) standard versus 83% (86 out of a potential 104) interleaved. In Mandler's results (1978a), more entire episodes were omitted in the standard versions (14%) than in the interleaved versions (4%). Mandler explains this by suggesting that the loose, temporal *then*-connection between the two episodes may lead to the belief that in the standard version the story is "complete" when one episode has been retrieved. In an interleaved story, the material from both episodes is continuously interwoven during input, and this fact, according to Mandler, may be sufficient to increase the likelihood that something from both episodes would be recalled. No such difference in the number of episodes recalled was found for the ESL subjects in this study.

The next level of analysis was for the proportion of total story nodes recalled when an episode was recalled in whole or in part. This analysis includes the Setting nodes, which, since they occurred only once per story, were scored on the basis of the number of stories recalled, rather than the number of episodes. Given that anything of an episode was recalled, the ESL subjects in the standard story condition recalled 75% (402 out of a potential 539) of the nodes in comparison to 68% (330 out of a potential 482) in the interleaved story condition. (Test of significant differences in proportions from independent samples $z = 2.48$, $p < .05$.) This finding is similar to Mandler's results (1978a).

The main analysis carried out on quantity of recall was on the mean number of nodes recalled per episode, given that an episode was recalled at all. Since the Setting is not part of any episode, Setting is excluded from this analysis (see Table 19.3).

In this analysis, episodes are treated as independent units. When an episode was retrieved at all, the number of nodes recalled in it (ranging from 1 to 5) was tallied. These were then summed and averaged over the number of episodes.

There was a significant difference between the number of nodes per episode recalled in the standard story condition and in the interleaved story

TABLE 19.3 Mean Number of Modes Recalled per Episode

Standard	Interleaved	t-Test independent samples
M = 3.62	M = 3.21	$t = 2.06$
SD = 1.211	SD = 1.493	$df = 182$
Range = 1, 5	Range = 1, 5	$p < .05$
N = 97 episodes	N = 86 episodes	

condition. After a 24-hour recall interval, a greater number of nodes were retrieved for the standard stories (M = 3.62) than for the interleaved stories (M = 3.21). Mandler (1978a) reports a similar significant difference for her native English speaking adults and children taken as a single group; in her results, more nodes per episode were recalled from standard stories (M = 3.5) than from interleaved ones (M = 3.2). However, her native English speaking children behaved quite differently from her adults. Her second-graders recalled relatively little of either type of story (M ≅ 3.0 for both versions); adults showed equally good recall of both types (M ≅ 3.8 for both versions); and her fourth- and sixth-graders were both quite good at recalling standard stories (M ≅ 3.6) but had more trouble recalling interleaved stories (M ≅ 3.1). On this measure, the ESL subjects in this study are most like Mandler's fourth- and sixth-graders.

The final analysis carried out on quality of recall was on the types of nodes recalled. Figure 19.2 shows that some types of nodes were recalled much better than others. The abscissa represents the ideal, schematic order. In the case of the standard stories, this also represents the input order; in the case of the interleaved stories, this does not represent the input order. More will be said about the temporal sequence of recall in the next section.

It is obvious in Figure 19.2 that Reactions—defined as the protagonist's internal reaction to the Beginning (a thought or emotional response, etc.)—were the least well recalled; action nodes were far better recalled. As Figure 19.2 illustrates, this finding also corresponds to Mandler's finding

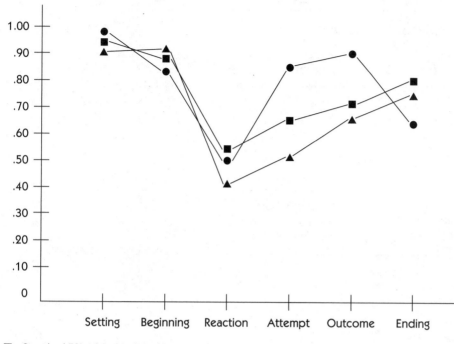

FIGURE 19.2 Types of Nodes Recalled

■ Standard ESL (.94, .90, .54, .66, .73, .79)
▲ Interleaved ESL (.92, .91, .38, .53, .69, .76)
● Standard & Interleaved L1 Adults (.98, .85, .51, .85, .90, .64)
(Mandler, 1978b) approximate proportions

(1978a, 1978b) for native English speakers. In fact, Figure 19.2 illustrates a remarkable degree of consistency in the pattern of type of nodes recalled between Mandler's native English subjects and ESL subjects in this study. The only difference in the patterns between the ESL subjects and Mandler's native subjects was in the Ending nodes. The native English subjects tended to recall the Endings less well than all other nodes with the exception of Reactions; the ESL subjects tended to recall these somewhat better than Outcomes and even Attempts.

Temporal Sequence of Recall

Of central interest is the order in which the story nodes were recalled. As Mandler (1978a) found for native English speakers, the ESL subjects' recall of the well-structured stories followed input order, almost without exception. Although there were nodes missing from episodes, there was no inter-leaving of the episodes; nodes from each episode were recalled contiguously. Further, Episode 1 was routinely recalled before Episode 2; from all 20 ESL subjects recalling stories, with a total of 54 stories recalled, there were no recalls in which Episode 2 was recalled before Episode 1. Within an episode, if the nodes were recalled at all, they were recalled in the standard order, with rare exceptions. The only exceptions were that four times an Attempt preceded a Reaction and two times a Reaction preceded a Beginning.

Of particular interest is the extent to which subjects in the interleaved condition followed the input order or the ideal, schematic order in sequencing their output. If a story schema affects second language retrieval, then the evidence of that effect is the extent to which the interleaved versions were recalled according to the ideal order rather than to the input order.

One measure of this evidence was calculated by taking those recalls in which at least one node

TABLE 19.4 Interleaved Stories/Probability that Structurally Adjacent Nodes and Input Adjacent Nodes Were Recalled Sequentially

	STRUCTURALLY ADJACENT NODES				
	B1, R1 + B2, R2	R1, A1 + R2, A2	A1, O1 + A2, O2	O1, E1 + O2, E2	
Intermediate ESL n = 20	.73	.58	.66	.78	
Mandler (1978a), all L1 subjects N = 48	.69	.66	.76	.64	

	INPUT ADJACENT NODES				
	B1, B2 + B2, R1	R1, R2 + R2, A1	A1, A2 + A2, O1	O1, O2 + O2, E1	E1, E2
Intermediate ESL n = 20	.42	.18	.21	.10	.42
Mandler (1978a), all L1 subjects N = 48	.46	.24	.12	.15	.41

B = Beginning; R = Reaction; A = Attempt; O = Outcome; E = Ending
1 = Episode 1; 2 = Episode 2

was recalled from one episode and two or more nodes were recalled from the other episode and determining the extent to which the episodes were recalled intact or whether there was interleaving of the nodes from the two episodes. Of such interleaved stories, 38% (14 of 37) were recalled with each episode intact, with no intervening nodes from the other episode. In fact, six different ESL subjects in the interleaved condition produced ten almost complete stories with a virtually complete Episode 1 followed by a virtually complete Episode 2. These subjects reconstituted the entire story according the ideal, schematic order. Some of these are illustrated in Appendix 19.2. Thus, the tendency was for the story schema to operate during retrieval, to produce stories closer to the ideal than to their interleaved input order.

This tendency to retrieve the interleaved stories according to their ideal story-schematic order rather than their input order was also apparent when pairs of adjacent nodes in output were

examined. To determine whether certain pairs of adjacent nodes in output were more likely to occur than others, two measures were computed (see Table 19.4). The first measure was the frequency of two structurally or ideally adjacent nodes from the same episode (e.g., Reaction 1 and Attempt 1, or Outcome 2 and Ending 2) recalled together in correct sequential order, given that both were recalled. (This is the top part of Table 19.4, labeled "Structurally Adjacent Nodes.") The second measure was the frequency of two nodes adjacent in input recalled together in correct input order, again given that both were recalled. (This is the bottom part of Table 19.4, labeled "Input Adjacent Nodes.")

Much higher percentages of structurally adjacent nodes than of input adjacent nodes were obtained. The recall frequencies for the structurally adjacent nodes are all 58% or higher. The frequencies for the input adjacent nodes are all considerably less than 50%. Mandler (1978a) reports similar findings for her native speakers. Thus, when the unstable, interleaved input order is stored in memory for a relatively long period of time (24 hours), it tends to be converted to the ideal, story-schematic order and tends to be recalled according to that schema.

DISCUSSION

The differences found in quantity of and temporal sequence of recall between the standard and interleaved stories in this study demonstrate the effects of a simple story schema on the comprehension of simple English stories by ESL readers. Quantity of recall was enhanced when the story was structured with a rhetorical organization that conformed to the reader's schema for simple stories—i.e., one well-structured episode followed by another—when the story was structured with a rhetorical organization that did not conform to the reader's schema. Further, the recalls produced by the readers of those stories which violated the story schema showed a strong schema effect in the tendency of temporal sequencing to reflect the story schematic order rather than the input order. In both of these findings regarding quantity of and temporal sequencing of recall, the ESL readers behaved similarly to native English speakers, especially to fourth- and sixth-grade children.

The finding that the ESL subjects in this study are most comparable to Mandler's fourth- and sixth-grade native English-speaking children and not to younger children or adult native speakers may reflect their developing linguistic systems as well as the effects of the story schema. The greater difficulty of retrieving story information from interleaved stories may reflect less flexibility on the part of ESL learners' retrieval processes when compared to Mandler's native-speaking adults. In general, the ESL learners had relatively more difficulty in retrieving information from the interleaved stories. This may also be due to confusions occurring at the time of encoding material presented in an unfamiliar format. Native-speaking adults don't have to devote as much effort to linguistic encoding and can therefore devote more effort to encoding the incoming interleaved stories in their ideal schematic form as two separate episodes, tagged with an interleaving algorithm.

Non-native readers who must devote more effort to linguistic encoding are less able to devote attention to sorting interleaved input into an ideal schematic form.

The fact that Ending nodes were better recalled by the ESL readers in this study than by the native speakers in Mandler's research (1978a) is an interesting anomaly which must await future explanation. I have no satisfactory explanation for the fact that these non-native readers apparently found material at both the beginning and the end of episodes particularly salient and memorable. The reasons for the particular salience of Endings over Outcomes for the ESL readers, compared to the reverse for native speakers, will require further investigation.

In addition to the further investigation of story schemata of the kind represented in this study, research into the effects on ESL reading comprehension of other kinds of rhetorical organization is needed. In particular, as mentioned at the beginning of this article, more research is needed on the effects on ESL reading comprehension of different types of expository rhetorical organization, in the sense of Meyer (1975, 1977, 1979; Meyer, Brandt, & Bluth, 1980; Meyer & Rice, 1982; Meyer & Freedle, 1984). The research of Connor and McCagg (1983a, 1983b), of Hinds (1979, 1983a, 1983b), of Burtoff (1983), and of Carrell (1983c), previously discussed in this article, all demonstrate the relevance to ESL reading and writing of the investigation of a wide variety of formal, rhetorical schemata. Pursuing the investigation of such formal schemata cross-linguistically and cross-culturally—in the spirit of contrastive rhetoric (Kaplan, 1966, 1972; Kaplan & Ostler, 1982; Houghton, 1980; Houghton & Hoey, 1983)—will enable us to determine which rhetorical patterns appear to be cross-cultural, or even universal, and might therefore require minimal emphasis in ESL reading and writing pedagogy (e.g., the simple story schema of this study), and which rhetorical patterns tend to be culture-specific and therefore require greater teaching emphasis for different groups of learners (cf. Carrell, 1983c).

In addition to investigating the interaction of texts of different types of rhetorical structures and the formal schemata of different groups of ESL readers, research in schema theory has shown the effects on ESL reading comprehension of content schemata (background knowledge of the content area of a text). One group of studies demonstrates the general effect on ESL comprehension of familiarity or prior experience with content (Hudson, 1982; Johnson, 1982; Alderson & Urquhart, 1983). Another group of studies shows the effects of culture-specific content knowledge on ESL reading comprehension (Steffensen, Joag-dev, & Anderson, 1979; Carrell, 1981; Johnson, 1981).

From the perspective of schema theory, reading comprehension is a function of the reader's possessing and activating the appropriate formal and content schemata in interaction with a text (or more specifically with the linguistic cues the author of the text has put there). Comprehension failures may be due partly to the reader's lacking the appropriate schemata required by the text. Second language comprehension failure may be due to mismatches between the schemata presumed by the text and those possessed by the reader. To the extent that the formal and content schemata presumed by the text are possessed by the second language reader—e.g., the simple story schema illustrated in this study—accessing the appropriate schema in second language comprehension may be a relatively simple and straightforward process. To the extent that other formal or content schemata may be presumed by a text and may not be possessed by the second language reader, second language reading may be impeded. As the research shows, second language comprehension failure may be due in part to schema failure, over and above language proficiency factors (Hudson, 1982). Second language acquisition can be viewed, in part, as the process of acquiring appropriate new formal and content schemata and of learning to instantiate or activate the appropriate schema during comprehension.

NOTES

1 I wish to thank my two research assistants, Kazuko Matsumoto and Jiang Zi-Xin, who helped with the project; my husband, Craig, who drew the figures; and my son, Michael, who assisted with the calculations. I would also like to thank colleagues in CESL who cooperated in this study by allowing access to the subjects who participated in this study. This research was partially supported by an internal grant from SIU-C's Office of Research Development and Administration.

2 The research reported in this study will be limited to the written medium; therefore, the focus will be on the reader. However, much of this research is generalizable to the oral medium, and would be applicable to listeners as well as to readers. Mandler's research has frequently employed the oral medium (Mandler, 1978a; Mandler & Johnson, 1977).

3 For the effects on ESL reading of content schemata (background knowledge of the content area of a text, Carrell, 1983a), see, for example, the research of Steffensen, Joag-dev, and Anderson (1979), Johnson (1981, 1982), Hudson (1982), Alderson and Urquhart (1983), Carrell (1981, 1983b), Carrell and Wallace (1983), and Carrell and Eisterhold (1983). These studies are reviewed briefly in the discussion section at the end of the article, where formal and content schemata are joined in a unified schema-theoretical view of ESL reading.

4 Although Mandler (1978a) scored her recall data using both a loose and a strict criterion, disallowing slight distortions and additions, only the loose criterion seemed appropriate for scoring the recall protocols of these intermediate-level ESL readers. Due to their inexpert control of the vocabulary and grammar of English, it would have been virtually impossible to tell whether what appeared as slight distortions or as reasonable additions were really such and hence due to schema effects, or whether they were due to inexpert control of English grammar and vocabulary. For example, in one recall of "The Studious Roommates," a subject wrote, ". . . When the examination started, suddenly he felt sleep. He didn't finish and did properly so he didn't improve anything." Is the word properly a distortion of the original text or a problem of vocabulary control in which the student intended the word poorly? It was decided to give these ESL readers the benefit of any doubt and not to penalize them for vocabulary and grammatical shortcomings. Therefore, only the loose criterion was used in scoring their recall protocols, and no arbitrary decision had to be made as to whether the information recalled was distorted or added to or not. If the information met the loose criteria, it was counted as having been recalled, period. Therefore, distortions and additions are not separable from recall of the essential idea; distortions and additions are not available for separate quantitative analysis by standard versus interleaved conditions as they were in Mandler's study (1978a).

Three Standard and Three Interleaved Stories

THE UNLUCKY TWINS
(standard version)

Once there were twins, Tom and Jennifer, who had so much trouble that their parents called them the unlucky twins. One day, Jennifer's parents gave her a dollar bill to buy the turtle she wanted, but on the way to the pet store she lost it. Jennifer was worried that her parents would be angry with her, so she decided to search every bit of the sidewalk where she had walked. She looked in all the cracks and in the grass along the way. She finally found the dollar bill in the grass. But when Jennifer got to the store, the pet store man told her that someone else had just bought the last turtle, and he didn't have any more. The same day, Tom fell off his bicycle and broke his leg. He wanted to run and play with the other children, so he got the children to pull him around in his wagon. While they were playing, Tom fell out of the wagon and broke his arm. Tom's parents said he was even unluckier than Jennifer and made him stay in bed until he got well.

THE UNLUCKY TWINS
(interleaved version)

Once there were twins, Tom and Jennifer, who had so much trouble that their parents called them the unlucky twins. One day, Jennifer's parents gave her a dollar bill to buy the turtle she wanted, but on the way to the pet store she lost it. The same day, Tom fell off his bicycle and broke his leg. Jennifer was worried that her parents would be angry with her, so she decided to search every bit of the sidewalk where she had walked. Tom wanted to run and play with the other children. Jennifer looked in all the cracks and in the grass along the way. Tom got the children to pull him around in his wagon. Jennifer finally found the dollar bill in the grass. While the children were playing, Tom fell out of the wagon and broke his arm. But when Jennifer got to the store, the pet man told her that someone else had just bought the last turtle, and he didn't have any more. Tom's

parents said he was even unluckier than Jennifer and made him stay in bed until he got well.

THE PLAYFUL PETS
(standard version)

Once there were two playful pets, a dog and a cat, who lived together with their master in a big city apartment. One day the master gave the cat a new toy mouse to play with, but as soon as her master left for work, the cat chewed big holes in the toy. The cat didn't want her master to take away her toy, so she looked for a place to hide it. She looked under all the furniture and in all the closets for a hiding place. She finally found a good hiding place in the kitchen. When her master came home and found the chewed up toy, he scolded the cat and threw her toy away. The same day, the dog ran away from the apartment. He wanted to run and play outside with other dogs. So he ran around the neighborhood barking and barking with other dogs. While the dogs were running loose, the dog-catcher came and took them all away to the dog-shelter. The master was so angry when he had to go get his dog and pay a fine that he kept the dog tied up after that.

THE PLAYFUL PETS
(interleaved version)

Once there were two playful pets, a dog and a cat, who lived together with their master in a big city apartment. One day, the master gave the cat a new toy mouse to play with, but as soon as her master left for work, the cat chewed big holes in the toy. The same day, the dog ran away from the apartment. The cat didn't want her master to take away her toy, so she looked for a place to hide it. The dog wanted to run and play outside with the other dogs. The cat looked under all the furniture and in all the closets for a hiding place. The dog ran around the neighborhood barking and barking with the other dogs. The cat finally found a good hiding place in the kitchen. While the dogs were running loose, the dog-catcher came and took them all away to the dog-shelter. When the master came home and found the chewed up toy, he scolded the cat and threw her toy away. The master was so angry when he had to go get his dog and pay a fine that he kept the dog tied up after that.

THE STUDIOUS ROOMMATES
(standard version)

Last year at SIU there were two students, John and Paul, who were roommates at Wilson Hall. One day, John's physics professor told John he could re-take the test he had gotten a bad grade on the week before. John was very glad to have this chance to get a better grade, so he decided to study hard for the new test. He studied physics all that day and late into the night. He went to take the test the next morning. But when he started to take the test, he was so tired that he fell asleep during the test and didn't get a better grade. The same day, Paul received a letter from his girlfriend in Chicago saying she was going to come and visit him. Paul was happy that his girlfriend was coming, so he decided to do all his studying ahead of time to be free for the weekend. He studied very hard all week long. On Friday, he went to meet his girlfriend at the train station. But Paul's girlfriend wasn't on the train; she had gotten sick and had to stay home. Paul had studied hard for nothing.

THE STUDIOUS ROOMMATES
(interleaved version)

Last year at SIU there were two students, John and Paul, who were roommates at Wilson Hall. One day, John's physics professor told John he could re-take the test he had gotten a bad grade on the week before. The same day, Paul received a letter from his girlfriend in Chicago saying she was going to come and visit him. John was very glad to have this chance to get a better grade, so he decided to study hard for the new test. Paul was happy that his girlfriend was coming, so he decided to do all his studying ahead of time to be free for the weekend. John studied physics all that day and late into the night. Paul studied very hard all week long. John went to take the test the next morning. On Friday, Paul went to meet his girlfriend at the train station. But when John started to take the test, he was so tired that he fell asleep during the test and didn't get a better grade. But Paul's girlfriend wasn't on the train; she had gotten sick and had to stay home. Paul had studied hard for nothing.

Sample Recall Protocols; Interleaved Version Read, Standard Order Recalled

THE UNLUCKY TWINS
(recall produced by an Arabic speaker)

There was two twins John and his sister Marry. His sister asked her father to give her a dollar to by a turtul from the pets store and he gave her a dollar bill. She went to the turtle store, but she found that she lost the bill. So she was afraid from his father. Then she decided to look for it when she was back she found it on the grass. Later she picked it up and went to the pets store to buy the small turtul. But for sorry he told her that he doesn't have any he just sold the last one. This was what happened with her.

Now we'll now what happened with her brother. While he was driving his bicycle he fall down and he broke his leg. Then he was playing with his friend and broke his arms. So for sure it was a bad day for the two twins.

THE PLAYFUL PETS
(recall produced by a Malaysian speaker)

One day a master bought a mouse toy and gave it to his cat. The played and chewed a big hole at a toy. So it tried to hide this toy from its master. Lastly he found in the kitchen. When the master came back he found the toy was chewed with big hole. He scolded the cat and threw away the toy.

Then the master left home, the dog also wanted to run away and played with the other dogs. It barking at the neighbor house, calling it's friend. On the same time the dog catcher came and carried him to the shelter. The master was very angry and had to pay for the dog. So he tied up the dog.

THE STUDIOUS ROOMMATES
(recall produced by a Spanish speaker)

Once time there were 2 students living in the same room. One of them was very bad in his class and he need pass the course this semester. So, he studied too hard for about 3 days, in the morning, in the afternoon, and in the night. But when he went to the school he was very tired. Then he can't pass the text.

The other student received a letter from his girlfriend, sayind him tha her will come the next week. So, he studied all yours next class to can leave all time with her. But when he want to the train station she don't come in it.

DISCUSSION QUESTIONS

1. If there were no such thing as a "story schema," what effects on recall could be expected to be caused by scrambling the sentences of a story? Or coming at the question from the other direction, assuming that there is a formal story schema, what kinds of effects would scrambling the sentences of a narrative be expected to produce?

2. Why should narrative schemata be "developmentally prior" and "cross-culturally universal"? (Also see Chapters 20, 28, and 37.)

3. Discuss the formulaic openings of stories that begin "Once upon a time . . . " (see Chapter 33) and conclude " . . . and they all lived happily ever after." What other cues are typically used in the surface forms of text or discourse to inform us what sort of schema (factual, fictional, narrative, expository, hortatory, etc.) ought to be employed?

4. What evidence does Carrell offer to show that non-native speakers as well as native speakers seem to rely on the same underlying type of formal schema? Also, what explanations can be given in this connection for the lack of contrast in some cases between the sequential and interleaved episode structures that Carrell used?

CHAPTER 20

The Impact of Discourse Constraints on Processing and Learning

John W. Oller, Jr., Tetsuro Chihara, Mary Anne Chávez-Oller, Grover K.H. Yü, Liza Greenberg, and Romelia Hurtado de Vivas

EDITOR'S INTRODUCTION

This chapter draws together results from a series of experimental studies. The idea that a discourse is more easily understood when it appears in a meaningful sequence, i.e., one that fits common expectations grounded in textual form, is certainly not new (see Foote ca. 1854, in Cooke, 1902: 221–222). However, attempts to measure the impact of formal constraints and/or formal schemata (adopting the term of Carrell, Chapter 19) date from Bartlett (1932). Almost four decades would pass before any of the authors of this chapter would try to tackle the question (Oller & Obrecht, 1969), and it would require a number of projects over another quarter of a century (Oller, 1975a; Chihara, Oller, Weaver, & Chavez-Oller, 1977; Oller & Yü, 1986; Chavez-Oller, Chihara, Weaver, & Oller, 1985; Oller, Yü, Greenberg, & Hurtado de Vivas, in press; and Oller & Jonz, in press) before we could claim any real breakthroughs on the experimental side. Now, however, it appears that we have some empirical evidence for the universality of the formal schema for narratives. Also, we can show a dramatic learning benefit attributable to formal constraints—though the underlying schema is presumably only one aspect of the full range of constraints that are at work and the schema itself remains nebulous. Apparently, formal schemata are nothing other than structures built up from logical inferences. We get some more ideas about how they are built, from Chapter 21 by Horiba. In this chapter, however, we have evidence showing why children and adults in all kinds of classroom contexts profit so much more from episodically organized verbal materials (Schank & Abelson, 1977; Schank, 1980; Oller, 1983b; and especially Taira, Chapter 28, this volume) than from isolated bits of discourse dropped out of the blue. The best understood exemplar of episodic organization is the kind we see in a chronologically told narrative that relates to actual experience. The results, summed up here, tell why activity-based and text-based approaches of the sort recommended in Chapter 17 work as well as they do. The primary method in the research reported is known as "cloze procedure" (also see Oller & Jonz, in press).

Everywhere in the world, people know more about their own experience than about anything else. Moreover, everywhere in the world, experience is arranged more or less in the form of a narrative text. It is chronologically arranged like a story unfolding across time. The events of the experience-story, it turns out, however, are highly constrained. They don't just occur in any old order. Actual experience, after all, is not altogether fictional. It is constrained by physics—by what *can* and *cannot* happen in the material world. It is also constrained by physiology—by what we can perceive of what happens in the world. This doesn't always keep people from making mistakes or having illusions, but it does enable us, in many cases, to correctly distinguish actual experience from fantasies and fictions of many sorts.

As a result, materials to be studied in classrooms will be easier to understand at the start, easier to recall, and easier to learn from, if they conform to the kinds of experience that people are built to understand. If the material is arranged in a meaningful sequence, that is, if it is episodically organized in the manner of ordinary experience, students will naturally have a better chance of understanding it. In fact, this is partly because the students know more about episodically organized materials in advance. They have an *a priori* familiarity about them. We know what kinds of things are likely to happen and in what ways they are normally constrained in experience. If young Margie's recently acquired balloon at the fair blows away and strikes a tree and bursts, we understand her crying (see Rumelhart's discussion, 1975). She is disappointed about the loss of the balloon. In the past she was happy to get it, and now in the present she is sad about losing it.

The fact is that we know a great deal about any episodically organized materials before we even get around to studying them. All of this is pretty obvious to anyone who thinks about it, but it is also often disputed by theoreticians and/or ignored in practice. Instead of studying meaningful, episodically organized materials at school, children learning to read are often exposed to relatively unorganized and unmotivated materials such as the *Dick and Jane* readers, or exercises just like them that make no more sense than the kinds of things Dick and Jane did and said. ("Jump! Jump! Run, Spot, run! See Spot. See Spot run. Look! Look! Jump, Dick! Jump! Run! Run! Run!" Etc. It never, apparently, occurred to the writers of the *Dick and Jane* type readers to ask where Spot was going or why he was running or what Jane and Dick were jumping about.)

In language classes, isolated phonemes, words, and sentences are not commonly studied anymore, but conversations (textual and video-type social vignettes) typically parachuted from the blue sky are probably the most common denominator of most current foreign and second language programs. It may or may not occur to students to ask why Ms. Jones is asking permission to leave work early, or why Mr. Smith refuses to let her go, but in many cases, the vignette, having been dropped from the blue sky, actually has no past and no future. It is exceedingly unlike *ordinary* experience in this way because ordinary experience absolutely cannot exist without a past and a future. The brain-damaged patient on a recent PBS program who thought he was just waking up or becoming conscious for the first time every two or three minutes was a decidedly abnormal (tragic) case and could not be said to have any normal experience at all. He could not, for instance, recognize his wife from one two-minute segment of his life to the next. He had the illusion that he was meeting her anew during each new segment of time. In this respect, his experience closely resembled that of the fictional characters in many basal readers and language programs—characters who just suddenly come into existence, without any known past in one lesson and disappear forever before the next lesson, where students find a whole new cast that has recently come into existence, and so on and on it goes through an unending series of unconnected vignettes.

In Chapter 28, Taira shows that such a disjointed series of vignettes that appear, more or less randomly, in many language programs are less conducive to successful comprehension and language acquisition than exactly similar materials arranged in the form of a sequentially developing story line. But, to mention that, we are getting ahead of our own story. Here we are concerned with a series of experiments that lay the groundwork for Taira's important breakthrough. In this chapter, we want to show only that sequentially arranged text is easier to understand and to learn from than the same text that has been disrupted by a scrambling procedure. The technical details of our story are contained in Oller and Jonz (in press), so here we will try to stick just to the main outlines of the research projects so that teachers and other users of the second edition of *Methods That Work* will be able to appreciate the powerful empirical evidence that has been amassed supporting the central thesis of this whole book (especially as spelled out in detail in Chapter 37)—namely, that heavily scaffolded, multi-modality, episodically organized experience in the classroom will give better results in literacy and language teaching than isolated bits and pieces of language or even vignettes of sociocultural interaction. The method used here, in the seven studies reported, is cloze procedure. Therefore, a few words of explanation and a bit of history about that technique may be useful before we sum up our seven experiments.

WHAT CLOZE PROCEDURE IS

The term *cloze* was invented by Wilson Taylor (1953) for a very general kind of reading exercise or test that can be applied to just about any kind of text or discourse. The term comes from Gestalt psychology. It stems from the idea that a great deal of our perceptual understanding of sensory information as well as our ability to conceptualize our experience are dependent on the filling in of missing data. We never see all of a scene, but what we do see suggests a great deal more than it immediately represents to us; it may be linked via other perceptual modalities (such as hearing) with aspects of a scene that we do not perceive directly at all but fill in via what the Gestaltists called "closure." For instance, sitting in his study (at this very moment about 12:20 p.m. on December 3, 1992), Oller can hear the rumbling of a distant aircraft. The plane is not visible, but is surely out there approaching (or possibly leaving) the Albuquerque International Airport. In fact, such ideas and their connections—the idea that the plane is out there making the noise that is heard, that it is coming from or leaving the airport in Albuquerque, that the airport lies to the south of the city, that the city is west of the house where this study is located, etc.—all of them are known via the sort of mechanism that makes a more complete whole pattern (Gestalt) out of what would otherwise be a disjointed, unconnected series of sensory impressions.

The great insight of Gestalt psychology was the realization that all perception and, indeed, all conceptualization of any sort, require the building up of patterns (Gestalts) out of representations that are always partial, truncated, or abbreviated in some way. Wilson Taylor applied that insight to texts and came up with a new name—"cloze procedure"—for the old method of replacing words or phrases in a text with blanks and asking readers to guess the missing elements (see Harris, 1985;

Ebbinghaus, 1897). Taylor (1953, 1954, 1956, 1957) also improved the procedure by providing it with a much richer research basis than it ever enjoyed prior to his work.

Nowadays, researchers distinguish between cloze tests (or exercises) that involve deleting every nth word (where n is usually a number between 5 and 9) and ones where the researcher carefully selects the words or other elements to be deleted (see Bachman, 1985, 1990). The first type of cloze exercises are called "fixed-ratio" tests. The latter are called "rational-deletion" exercises and fall into the broad class of "variable-ratio" approaches. In this present chapter, all of the cloze tests employed were of a kind of hybrid "fixed-ratio" and "rational-deletion" type. In general, in creating the cloze exercises in the research reported here (see Appendices 20.1 and 20.2), every nth word was deleted, but in a few instances, if deleting the word at the nth position would have resulted in an impossibly difficult item (say, it was a date or name used only once in the text), that item might be skipped in favor of the word just after it or just before it.

There are many well-known applications of cloze research to educational tasks, but especially to aspects of literacy. For instance, cloze exercises may be used to determine, roughly, whether a given text is suitable in terms of its difficulty level for a given group of students. Table 20.1, from Oller and Jonz (in press), gives some rough guidelines for interpreting cloze scores over a given text relative to the reading abilities of a typical group of subjects.

TABLE 20.1 Rough Estimates of Readability Based on Cloze Scores Between 1/5 and 1/7 Deletion Ratios

Roughly Defined Levels of Readability	Exact-Word Scores	Contextual-Appropriatness Scores
Independent (Easy)	53% and up	85% and up
Instructional (Moderate)	44% to 52%	66% to 84%
Frustrational (Difficult)	43% and below	65% and below

The term *independent readability*—including exact-word scores (roughly) of 53% or above and contextual-appropriateness scores of 85% or better—has been used to refer to that level at which a written discourse can be understood without special study helps (such as a dictionary or tutor); *instructional readability*—applied (roughly) to exact scores between 44% and 52% or contextual scores between 66% and 84%—has been used to indicate the level at which learners generally understand enough of a discourse to benefit from it in a classroom or other study setting; and *frustrational readability*—applied (roughly) to exact scores of 43% or lower or contextual scores at or below 66%—means the text is too difficult to be of much benefit. (Again, it must be stressed that these guidelines are rough. A good deal of elaboration is given, however, in Oller & Jonz, in press.)

THE IMPACT OF FORMAL CONSTRAINTS

In this chapter, we are interested in more than just the readability of any given text or the literacy of any given group of subjects. Here we are concerned with the impact of formal constraints (including the special case of formal schemata) on the relative redundancy of any given text as measured by cloze items inserted in that text. More specifically, we want to test the hypothesis that a sequentially arranged text will be easier to understand and to learn from than one that is disrupted by some degree or other of randomization (scrambling). Since it is true that grammar-based expectancies ranging beyond five to ten words on either side of a cloze blank can help subjects to guess missing words, then cloze procedure is sensitive to formal constraints. In fact, this is now well established both on theoretical and empirical grounds (see Bachman, 1990; also the concluding chapter of Oller & Jonz, in press). In addition, it is now known that the point of diminishing returns for the effect of discourse constraints ranges across sentence boundaries and much larger segments of text than was previously supposed by some researchers such as MacGinitie (1961), Carroll (1972), Alderson (1979a, 1979b, 1980), Porter (1978, 1983), Shanahan, Kamil, and Tobin (1982), and Shanahan and Kamil (1983).

In addition, the point of diminishing returns, if it exists, is not a limitation on formal constraints *per se,* but on the capacities of human producers and interpreters to use them. While a constraint on human ability *is,* in a way, a constraint on the representations we are capable of producing and/or understanding, this does not reduce the logically independent theoretical status of the constraints themselves. A text in its material existence is as different from an act of using it as a baseball is from an act of being thrown or caught. Though it remains true that the size, weight, shape, etc. of the ball depend greatly on the size, shape, and strength of a human hand, the shape of the human hand does not make it logically impossible for a baseball to be constructed so as to be either too large or too small for any pitcher to ever throw it. In the same way, the characteristics of texts are limited by the capabilities of our minds, but nonetheless have a separate, real existence that is independent of ourselves. In any case, the results discussed in the following experiments show conclusively, we believe, that contexts beyond the five-to-ten word level are generally helpful in enabling subjects to infer intended meanings and in enabling them to supply missing material in cloze items. This is true for texts of the narrative kind as well as at least some texts of a descriptive or expository sort, as we will see. More importantly, we know now that a great deal more is learned from working through cloze exercises over texts where the underlying formal constraints are undisturbed than in the same exercises over the same texts where the formal arrangement has been deliberately disrupted (by some degree or other of scrambling).

In what follows, we sum up the results of seven studies in which one or more of us participated. The first two deal with the degree to which formal constraints impact scores on cloze exercises over descriptive, narrative, and expository texts by native and non-native subjects while the last four experiments concern the relative amount of learning (or information gain) that occurs when natives or non-natives work through narrative texts arranged according to a typical formal schema of the narrative type versus the same texts where the sequence has been disrupted by a scrambling procedure. As we progress, we will discuss only as much background and analysis as we think is essential to understanding the study in question. Readers who want to see the statistical and design details for each of the studies in question are referred to Chapters 7, 8, and 17 in Oller and Jonz (in press).

STUDY 1: NATIVES AND FORMAL CONSTRAINTS

Background of Study 1

To test and actually refute the claim that cloze items are sensitive only to about five to ten words of context on either side of any given blank, an experiment was conceived using 5 distinct segments of prose of a little more than 100 words each. Following the intention of Miller and Selfridge (1950) to create different degrees of approximation to English prose, Oller (1975a) started with normal prose and worked backward toward lesser and lesser approximations rather than following the Miller and Selfridge method of trying to work up toward normal prose, through one-word, two-word, three-word, and so forth approximations. In a nutshell, the trouble with their method, as shown by Coleman (1963), was that they tried to get different native speakers to invent meaningful text by adding a word to an already existing one-, two-, three-, or *n*-word sequence. This method was fundamentally flawed. In creating any one of the Miller and Selfridge "orders of approximation" to English prose, one subject would provide a one-word ("first order") approximation which a different person would add to in order to get a two-word ("second order") approximation. A still different person would add another word to get a three-word ("third order") approximation, and so forth. The trouble was that their method only drew closer to normal prose up to about the 7th word and after that became increasingly nonsensical. To avoid the difficulty Miller and Selfridge fell into, Oller (1975a) used 5 normal texts of a little more than 100 words each to begin with and then proceeded to cut and scramble those 5 initial texts into 50-word, 25-word, 10-word, and 5-word segments. (See Appendix 20.1 for these texts and the details of their segmentation.)

These pieces of text were then rearranged into 5 distinct cloze tests of 100 items each (20 items per each of the 5 texts). Each of the five 100-item cloze tests was structured so that a text of 100+ words of normal prose appeared first and the remaining 4 texts, divided into scrambled segments of 50, 25, 10, and 5 words, appeared next in a random order. These segments of varying lengths, which formed varying degrees of less than sensible prose, were printed on the page immediately following the 100+ words of text as if they all formed a single paragraph. On each of the 5 cloze tests, therefore, all 5 of the texts were represented but each one in a different order of approximation owing to the cut-and-scramble procedure applied. Each cloze test also represented all 5 orders of approximation, and each text appeared in each order of approximation on exactly one of the 5 cloze tests. The design was systematically counterbalanced to distribute variations in passage difficulties equally over the 5 orders of approximation to English prose. Also, the skills of subjects were assured to vary only randomly by the way the 5 cloze tests were handed out to each participating group of subjects. The tests were stacked from number 1 to number 5 and handed out so that nothing but the luck of the draw, and where any individual was seated, could determine what subgroup of subjects might work on Test 1, 2, 3, 4, or 5.

The intent of the experiment was to show that the 100+ segments, arranged in the order constructed by their original authors, would be easier to process (as shown by higher cloze scores) than the same texts cut into 50-word segments presented in a random order. Similarly, the 50-word segments presented in random arrangements would be easier to process (again, shown by higher cloze scores) than the randomly arranged 25-word segments, and so forth. The 5-word segments would be the most difficult to process.

Materials and Tests of Study 1

Four of the 5 passages used for Study 1 were excerpted from selections in a reader edited by Gorrell, Laird, and Freeman (1970) intended for college readers of English. The fifth was a passage taken from a novel by Victoria Holt (1973). The texts ranged from (I) a *description* of a carry-out restaurant of the 1950s, to three *expositions* covering such diverse topics as (II) how to get an education, (III) how to construct a paragraph, (IV) what a sentence is, and (V) a fictional narrative about the death of Sir Edward Travers. Each passage was at least 100 words in length plus a lead-in sentence and a lead-out sequence of at least 5 words beyond the 100th word.

By deleting the 3rd word of the 2nd sentence of each passage and every 5th word thereafter until exactly 20 cloze items were attained, 5 cloze tests of 20 items each were constructed over each of the 5 passages. These cloze tests yielded 5 tests at the 100th+ approximation to the actual texts these segments were each taken from. Each 100-word segment contained exactly 20 cloze items, each of which, except for the first and last, was separated from other items before and after it by exactly 4 words. To achieve the 50th order of approximation, each of these initial texts of 100+ words was duplicated and cropped at the ends so that it was exactly 100 words long. Then it was divided in the middle to produce two 50-word segments. To get the 25th, 10th, and 5th orders of approximation, the 50-word segments were duplicated 3 more times and cut 3 more times into 25-word, 10-word, and 5-word segments. This yielded a pool of 100 cloze items, each item appearing in all 5 orders of approximation to normal prose (100th+, 50th, 25th, 10th, and 5th).

For example, following the lead-in sentence in passage I, in the 100th+ condition, there were 20 cloze items of the form:

For those who hang out there, the Carry-out offers a wide array of sounds, sights, smells, tastes, and tactile experience which titillate and sometimes assault the five senses. The air (1) warmed by smells from (2) coffee urns and grill (3) thickened with fat from (4) deep-fry basket. The jukebox (5) up a wide variety (6) frenetic and lazy rhythms. (7) . . .

The 5th order approximations consisted of the same items, but in 5 word segments, such as

fat from (4) deep-fry basket. wide variety (6) frenetic and The air (1) warmed by . . .

and so forth. The 10th order approximations consisted of the same items but arranged in randomized 10-word segments as in

The jukebox (5) up a wide variety (6) frenetic and The air (1) warmed by smells from (2) coffee urns . . .

Therefore, 100 distinct items times the 5 conditions of arrangement (i.e., the 5 orders of approximation to normal prose) gave a grand total of 500 items from which to construct 5 distinct 100-item cloze tests. Each of these tests would contain one of the 5 passages in the 100th+ condition, another in the 50th word condition, another in the 25th, another in the 10th, and the remaining one in the 5th. All passages would appear in all 5 tests, and each passage would appear exactly once in each of the 5 orders of approximation to English prose. It is crucial to note that every single item appeared exactly once in each of the five orders of approximation. The items in each approximation were identical except for the scrambling procedure applied in each case.

Subjects of Study 1

Ninety-three adult native speakers of English each completed one of the 5 cloze tests. Subjects were drawn from introductory linguistics and English classes at the University of New Mexico and from a group of participants at the Sixth Annual Michigan Conference on Applied Linguistics in February 1975. Subjects ranged in age from the late teens to over 50. There was a nearly equal balance of males and females.

Results of Study 1

Tests were scored by two methods. First, the exact-word scoring method was used, and, second, words other than the exact word which fit the total context of the original passage were counted correct. The latter method is referred to here as the "contextually acceptable" (A) criterion and is contrasted with the "exact-word" (E) criterion. If formal discourse-level constraints make a difference, and assuming cloze is sensitive to such constraints, scores should be highest on the 100th+ order of approximation to normal prose and should be ordered in descending rank from 50th, to 25th, to 10th, to 5th. Figure 20.1 shows that this prediction was sustained for all conditions and for both the exact-word and contextual scoring methods averaged over the five texts. The means on which Figure 20.1 is based are the column means of Table 20.2. An appropriate analysis-of-variance (see Oller & Jonz, in press) showed that the

TABLE 20.2 Means by Orders of Approximation and Passage

Passage	Score	100th+	50th	25th	10th	5th	Row Means
I	A	17.5	15.3	12.4	9.7	5.8	12.1
	E	8.3	6.5	5.5	4.3	3.0	5.5
II	A	15.5	12.3	11.5	8.2	4.2	10.3
	E	5.3	4.2	4.3	3.6	1.3	3.7
III	A	16.3	13.6	9.6	6.8	6.0	10.5
	E	8.5	7.4	6.0	4.9	4.3	6.2
IV	A	16.6	12.5	11.1	5.8	5.3	10.3
	E	12.7	9.0	8.1	4.2	3.9	7.6
V	A	19.2	14.4	12.6	10.5	6.3	12.6
	E	11.3	8.3	8.4	6.3	4.6	7.8
Column Means	A	17.0	13.6	11.4	8.2	5.5	11.6
	E	9.2	7.1	6.5	4.7	3.4	6.2

predicted contrasts were significant. In fact, the predicted contrasts actually observed in every case could be expected to occur by chance less than one time in 1,000 tries ($p < .001$). Equally important, as intended by the experimental design, the contrasts across the five distinct groups of subjects created by the random assignment of the five distinct cloze exercises to the various subjects was nil. That is, the groups of subjects (as intended in the design of the experiment) were not significantly different from one another, but the effects owed to disrupting discourse constraints were highly significant as predicted.

As can be seen from Figure 20.1 and from Table 20.2, the 93 native speakers tested found sequential prose a lot easier to understand than the same material in any of its less sequentially arranged forms. Moreover, as the disruption became more and more severe (from the 50-word segments down to the 5-word segments), the effect became more pronounced. The fact that subjects attained higher scores on cloze items embedded in higher order contexts than on the same items embedded in lower order contexts is merely another special demonstration of a very general fact—namely, that long-range context (beyond five to ten words on either side of a blank) is important to the processing of verbal material. Or, looked at from a more abstract point of view, we see evi-

FIGURE 20.1 Contrasts Over All Passages in Five Orders of Approximation to English Prose

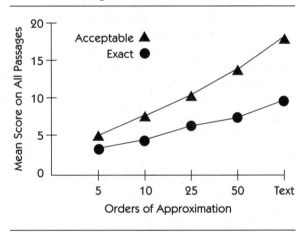

dence that formal constraints on textual material really do make a difference to its comprehensibility. The only surprise here, based on a reasonable theory (see Chapter 37), is that such an outcome should be a surprise to anyone (and we must suppose that it *is* surprising to people who have argued that cloze procedure cannot be sensitive to discourse constraints beyond the five-to-ten word level). The cloze procedure is sensitive to discourse constraints, and the possible point of diminishing returns for that sensitivity must be well beyond 50 words of context, not at 5 or 6 words, as previously argued by Miller and Selfridge (1950). Neither are cloze items generally limited in sensitivity to material within the immediate sentence context, as argued by MacGinitie (1961), Carroll (1972), Alderson (1979a, 1979b, 1980), Porter (1978, 1983), and Shanahan, Kamil, and Tobin (1982; also Shanahan & Kamil, 1983).

STUDY 2: NORMAL NATIVES AND NON-NATIVES

Background of Study 2

Ramanauskas (1972) had shown that cloze items embedded in whole sentences presented in a random order were more difficult than the same items embedded in the same sentences presented in their original order as part of a narrative. The result, however, was achieved with educable mentally retarded subjects. Therefore, the experiment by Chihara et al. (1977), which is summarized here as Study 2, set out to see if the Ramanauskas result could be achieved with normal natives and non-natives. Another purpose of the Chihara et al. study was to rule out the possibility that the procedure used in Study 1 above (Oller, 1975a) might have biased results against a negative outcome by cutting and scrambling segments of prose irrespective of sentence boundaries.

Although Study 1 demonstrated that greater amounts of meaningful surrounding context (other things being equal) increased the ease with which native subjects supplied missing words in a variety of cloze exercises (narrative, expository, and descriptive; see Appendix 20.1), it had not been shown explicitly for normal natives and non-natives that cloze procedure would be sensitive to constraints ranging across sentence boundaries. Nor had the degree to which such constraints were available to language users at different levels of proficiency been investigated. Our first hypothesis for Study 2, then, was that cloze items would be sensitive to constraints ranging beyond sentence boundaries, and our second hypothesis was that increasingly proficient language users would be better able to capitalize on this fact. In other words, the abstract formal schema and other dis-

course-level constraints underlying narrative texts would be more accessible to more proficient English speakers than to less proficient ones. Our first hypothesis had already been supported in part by Carroll et al. (1959), Ramanauskas (1972), and by Study 1, but our second hypothesis had not been tested prior to our own Study 2.

Materials and Tests of Study 2

Two passages of prose were selected from texts written for non-native speakers of English. Text A was a narrative from Praninskas (1959: 217) about Joe going off to college and all the things his mother made him do before he could leave. Text B, from Wright, Barrett, and Van Syoc (1968: 327–328), was a similar narrative about a Greek boy named Nicholas going off to Athens to work for his uncle in a mechanic's shop. Two cloze tests were constructed over each text. Roughly every 7th word was deleted from A and every 6th word from B to get two sequential cloze tests (sequential A and sequential B). No lead-in or lead-out (unmutilated text at the beginning or end) was allowed for either test. Then the tests were divided roughly into thirds. Divisions were always at sentence boundaries. In this way each sentence that appeared in the sequential version would also appear in the very same form, but not in the same order, in the scrambled version. The last sentence of the last third of A in the sequential form became the first sentence of the scrambled version of A. The last sentence of the second third of A in the sequential form became the second sentence of A in the scrambled version, and so on, until all sentences were exhausted. Then the same procedure was applied to passage B. There were 56 cloze items in A in each of its forms (sequential and scrambled) and 48 items in B in each of its forms. The four tests appear in Appendix 20.2.

Subjects of Study 2

Adult students of English as a foreign language at the Osaka YMCA, 201 in all, and 41 native speakers of English at the University of New Mexico served as subjects. The non-natives, all native speakers of Japanese, were enrolled in basic, intermediate, or advanced EFL classes at the Osaka YMCA in Japan. Four groups were distinguished by level of proficiency in English. First, there were 71 subjects at the basic level (group 1); second, there were 66 intermediates (group 2); third, there were 64 advanced EFL learners (group 3); and, finally, there were the 41 native speakers of English from UNM (group 4). Approximately equal numbers of subjects in each group were males and females. All were adults above 18 years of age. Group 4 was composed of native speakers of English enrolled in an undergraduate introduction to linguistics at the University of New Mexico. Again, there were about equal numbers of males and females, and all were above 18 years of age.

METHOD AND DESIGN OF STUDY 2

The native speakers of English were all tested during a single class meeting, and the non-natives were tested in groups of 15 to 35 depending on class size. Every subject took a test over one of the texts in the sequential condition and a different test over the other text in the scrambled condition. Assignment of a particular condition (sequential or scrambled), text (A or B), and order (which arrangement of condition and text came first and which came second) was randomized. Each subject took two tests—either A sequential and B scrambled, or B sequential and A scrambled. However, unlike the Ramanauskas design, no one took both the sequential and scrambled versions of the two tests over the same text. The reason was that we didn't want subject performance in our design to be influenced in any way by prior learning that would occur from working through the same text twice. The design here was also counterbalanced (as was done by Ramanauskas) to control for a possible effect of the order in which subjects encountered either text A or B and the order in which they encountered either a sequential or scrambled version of A or B.

There were four random blocks of subjects made up of four combinations of condition, text, and order of presentation: (i) sequential A, scrambled B; (ii) scrambled B, sequential A; (iii) scrambled A, sequential B; and (iv) sequential B, scrambled A. These arrangements were crossed with the four proficiency levels. That is, about equal numbers of subjects within each proficiency level were assigned to each of the blocks. This was accomplished by random assignment of tests to subjects in each test setting. First the tests were stacked alternating between the four combinations. Later, when they were passed out in each classroom context, they were handed out in that same arrangement. This resulted in random selection of the four blocks of subjects (i–iv, defined above) with approximately equal numbers in each block. Moreover, the four blocks were about equally distributed over the four different levels of proficiency defined earlier. All of this is important because our results depend not on the equivalence of the randomly created blocks of subjects but on the difference between the four proficiency levels (beginning, intermediate, advanced, and native).

The design, speaking somewhat technically only for a moment, therefore, involved two completely crossed between-subjects variables (groups 1–4 and blocks 1–4), and three within-subjects variables each nested within the other two: order (first or second) was nested within text (A and B), which in turn was nested in the main variable of interest, condition (sequential or scrambled). In other words, approximately half of the subjects did A in the sequential version and B in the scrambled ($n = 120$), while the remainder did B in the sequential version and A in the scrambled ($n = 122$). Of the half that did A in the sequential version, approximately half did it first while the remainder did it second, and so forth.

Results of Study 2

Table 20.3 gives mean scores and mean differences (mean sequential scores minus mean scrambled scores) across conditions (averaging over texts and orders) for each of the four groups.[1] From Table 20.3, it is apparent that the scrambled texts were, as predicted in our first hypothesis, more difficult on the whole than the sequential texts. Further, we see from Table 20.3 that the relative effect of long-range constraints as shown in the contrast between sequential and scrambled texts (see the columns labeled "Difference") increases as the proficiency of subjects increases. This finding conforms to the prediction of hypothesis two. In addition, taking a tip from Cziko (1978, and also personal communication from him), we followed up in our recent re-analysis of these data with the appropriate sort of statistical "trend analysis" and were able to show

TABLE 20.3 Mean Percentages of Exact-Word Scores Between Groups by Condition

Group	n	Sequential (Q) Mean	SD	Scrambled (R) Mean	SD	Difference Mean	SD
1 Beginners	71	17.93	6.88	16.92	7.85	1.01	9.82
2 Intermediates	66	31.79	7.69	26.36	8.56	5.43	11.94
3 Advanced	64	41.13	8.82	33.19	8.89	7.94	13.29
4 Natives	41	71.57	8.75	60.29	9.69	11.27	8.87
Marginals	242	36.93	19.61	31.15	16.90	5.79	11.84

that the tendency for more proficient subjects to become increasingly sensitive to discourse constraints—as shown in the increasing difference scores from beginning to intermediate to advanced to native subjects in our data—is a linear trend. The growth pattern is completely consistent with the original prediction. Further, it is clear that both native speakers of English and non-native speakers (Japanese-speaking EFL learners, in this case) are sensitive to discourse constraints. Exactly as semiotic theory predicts (see Chapter 37 and Oller et al., 1991), non-natives become increasingly more sensitive to the impact of discourse constraints as they improve in English proficiency. Beginners are hardly able to benefit from discourse constraints at all, intermediates are benefited somewhat more, advanced subjects more than intermediates, and native speakers even more than advanced EFL students.

Appropriate analyses of variance showed that, as intended by the experimental design, there was no difference among the randomly assigned blocks of subjects but that there was a highly significant contrast ($p < .001$) across the various levels of proficiency. Moreover, separate analyses of variance for each contrast (see the "Difference" scores in Table 20.3) across groups—beginners with intermediates, intermediates with advanced, and advanced subjects with native speakers—showed that each of them was also significant. Indeed, the contrasts became more and more dramatic with each successive comparison.

Another interesting result, one that was not predicted, but that is investigated in detail by Chihara et al. in the updated version of the 1977 project in Oller & Jonz (Chapter 8, in press) was

that the non-native subjects (speakers of Japanese) apparently had more difficulty understanding the text about Joe going off to college than the one about Nicholas going to Greece, while native speakers of English found the Joe text (A) a little easier than the one about Nicholas (B). Further, this difference appeared to be somewhat independent of the level of English proficiency of the subjects. It seems that this contrast has to do with culturally engendered expectations—the sort of schemata that Carrell (Chapter 19) distinguishes as "content schemata." The text about Nicholas traveling to Athens is apparently more consistent with the experience of the Japanese adults studying EFL than the one about Joe's mother sending him here and there on various errands before he gets to go off to college. The latter experience is apparently unfamiliar and unexpected by Japanese subjects.[2] Beginning, intermediate, and advanced EFL students (all native speakers of Japanese) consistently found text B about going to Athens easier. This result has also been replicated relatively recently (in a study with an entirely different focus) with a different group of Japanese students at Osaka Jogakuin Junior College by Chihara, Sakurai, and Oller (1989). However, owing to the way texts and conditions were counterbalanced, the contrasts between the two texts could not unduly influence the contrast over conditions. The latter sort of contrast has to do with the "formal schema" (see Carrell, Chapter 19) underlying the two narratives that is quite independent of their specific content. The contrast in subject performance on the sequential versus the scrambled variant of each narrative stands independent of the difference in performance on the two narratives.

The contrast between conditions and its interaction with groups was quite different in its patterning from the contrast between texts, as is shown in Figure 20.2. As subjects increase in proficiency, they become increasingly able to benefit from the kinds of discourse constraints (in accord with our second hypothesis) that range across sentence boundaries and enable the whole story in each case to make sense. The pattern is shown clearly in Figure 20.2, which graphs differences between sequential and scrambled texts against groups as contrasted with differences between texts across groups. The patterns are clearly distinct. We conclude, therefore, that as learners become more proficient in a language, they do, as expected, become more sensitive to discourse constraints and better able to profit from higher-order formal constraints. In view of all the evidence, therefore, we conclude that sensitivity to discourse constraints (including formal schemata as measured by cloze procedure in this study) has a facilitating effect and, as predicted, one that becomes relatively greater as subjects become more proficient in the language. Furthermore, conforming to the theory expressed by Carrell (Chapter 19), we can clearly distinguish effects owed to the formal narrative schema (refer to the line graph in the top part of Figure 20.2) from those owed to content schemata (refer to the line in the lower part of Figure 20.2).

STUDY 3: EFL TEACHERS IN THAILAND

Background of Studies 3–6

Our next series of studies, in addition to further testing the results of Study 2, went on to examine the learning effect (or information gain) owed to working through the items of a cloze exercise with sentences arranged in a sequential order as opposed to the same exercise but with the sentences in a randomized order. Naturally, we predicted that high-order formal constraints underlying the normal arrangement of sentences in a narrative text would enhance not only its immediate processing but also the amount of information gained from that experience. Our hypothesis, based on the findings of Oller and Yü (1986)[3], was that more information would be gained from

working through cloze items over a text arranged in a normal order than in a disrupted order. The new element in our experimental design, therefore, had to involve a method to measure information gain (the learning effect).

Previous studies, showing the sensitivity of cloze items to discourse constraints, had often employed a design with two or more texts (e.g., see Ramanauskas, 1972; Oller, 1975a, Study 1; Chihara et al., 1977, Study 2; and Cziko, 1978) explicitly to exclude or control any learning effect. Researchers involved in those studies assumed that working through a single text more than once *would* produce a learning effect. Taylor (1956) and Ramanauskas (1972) had also already demonstrated that working through a passage in its normal order would impact performance on a subsequent cloze test over that same passage (provided only that subjects were able to understand the text).

To avoid the possibility of such a learning effect, which would have contaminated (and sometimes did contaminate!) the very differences of interest in many previous studies (e.g., Porter, 1978), two options have generally been employed. One possibility, preferred by Marshall (1970) and by some other researchers (Alderson, 1979a, 1979b, 1980; Porter, 1983; and Shanahan et al., 1982), was to test different groups of subjects over the various conditions that a given text might be put into (e.g., a sequential order versus some degree of scrambling or other distortion). This option, a between-subjects design, however, has the undesirable effect of mixing whatever differences there may be between the groups with any differences owed to arrangements of the text *per se*. So that design option has generally not been approved.

Another option, used independently by Ramanauskas (1972) and by Oller, Bowen, Dien, and Mason (1972), is, technically speaking, a "within-subjects, randomized-block design" where group differences are distributed over more than one text to avoid a learning effect. In the case of the two-text option (in the design of Oller, Bowen, Dien, & Mason, 1972; and also Study 2 above), half of the subject pool takes a certain version of one text first and a different version of a different text next. By this procedure, recommended to us by J. Donald Bowen, it is possible to average

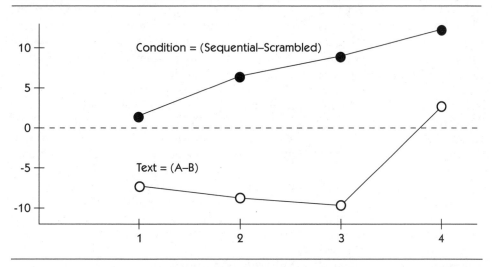

across texts and across conditions so as to distribute group differences in a manner that effectively eliminates them. (This was explicitly demonstrated for Studies 1 and 2 above, in each case by the lack of contrast across randomly created blocks of subjects. It was also demonstrated independently for Studies 3–7 below; see Oller & Jonz, in press, for details.) This latter option is preferable to using different intact groups of subjects, because in general the differences across individuals (and groups) are large relative to any effects owed to contextual constraints in experimental treatments. The reason is easy to understand: differences in levels of proficiency across individual subjects and/or groups are acquired over months and years of experience whereas differences produced in an experimental context are usually (but see Taira, Chapter 28, this volume, for an exception) due to experience that takes only a matter of minutes or an hour or two at the most.

In previous studies (especially, Studies 1 and 2 above; also in Cziko, 1978) one of the main goals was to see whether cloze items were sensitive to different levels of constraints within texts. It was desirable in those studies to avoid any learning effect, because it might have obscured the contrasts owed to different degrees of disruption of coherence experimentally imposed on the texts. Here, however, in addition to replicating the contrasts owed to sequential versus scrambled arrangements of texts, we needed to measure *the*

learning effect itself. We wanted to know just how strong that effect might be and whether we would find it in advanced non-native users of English as a second language as well as native speakers of English and whether such groups would differ in their degree of sensitivity to coherence (as was observed in Study 2).

We predicted that the learning effect (or information gain) owed to the experience of having worked through a passage in its normal order would be greater than any learning attributable to working through the same cloze items in a text whose sentences had been scrambled. The reason for this prediction is straightforward: scrambled text will (usually) contain less information and be less coherent than the unscrambled sequential basis from which the scrambled version was derived. The reason is that some of the formal and content constraints (e.g., the formal schema and the content schemata underlying the text) will be violated by the scrambling procedure.

It is important to note early on, however, that the hypothesis that information gain will be greater from episodically organized material does not derive from cloze procedure *per se* nor from any empirical research with cloze or any other testing method. In fact, it derives from the semiotic theory spelled out in Chapter 37 of this volume (also in Oller, 1990; Oller et al., 1991; and Oller & Damico, 1991). More specifically, the result predicted here derives from what is called (see

Chapter 37) the "connectedness perfection" of narrative texts—i.e., the fact that one event in a narrative leads to another and that every scene has a past and a future to which it is related by logical inferences. This "connectedness perfection" (which Chapter 37 proves to be unique to true narratives, i.e., genuine experience), is posited, therefore, as a universal factor underlying all narrative-type discourse processing.

In Studies 3–6, we report four replications of what is known technically as a "Latin-Squares design" (see Maxwell & Delaney, 1990: 483). We treat each study separately, and then in the final section of our report, Study 7, we examine the contrast between natives and non-natives by combining groups. Our expectation is that native speakers will be more sensitive to discourse constraints (i.e., to the contrast between sequential and scrambled versions of texts) than advanced non-natives. More-proficient subjects, in other words, will experience a relatively greater learning effect from working through sequential material (as contrasted with a scrambled variant) than less-proficient subjects.

Method of Study 3

The experiment described here replicated one that was conducted in Kyoto, Japan, in 1984 (see note 3 above), though in this case the subjects were Thai-speaking secondary and post-secondary English teachers in Thailand. The cloze tests used in the Kyoto study and in this replication were the same ones used in Study 2 (see Appendix 20.2). Based on the results of Study 2, as well as those of Oller and Yü (1986), it was expected that these texts would neither be too easy nor too difficult for teachers of English as a foreign language in Thailand (see the Subjects of Study 3 section below). According to the results of Study 2, the texts in question (see Appendix 20.2) fell at the lower edge of the "instructional" range (compare Tables 20.1 and 20.2) for advanced EFL students at the YMCA in Osaka and were easily within the "independent" range for native speakers (again compare Tables 20.1 and 20.2). The results of the Oller and Yü study in Japan showed that college teachers of EFL in Japan scored about 19 percentage points higher on the average than the most advanced students at the Osaka YMCA and only about 10 points below the native speakers of Study 2. Therefore, high school and college EFL teachers in Thailand should not find the tests too difficult or too easy.

Subjects of Study 3

Participants were teachers of English as a foreign language (total $N = 90$) who attended three regional seminars for English language teachers sponsored by the United States Information Agency in collaboration with the Thai Ministry of Education and the Teachers Colleges at Khon Kaen ($n = 30$), Chiang Mai ($n = 31$), and Songkla ($n = 29$). About two thirds of the subjects were females and ranged from their early twenties to age 63. All were native speakers of Thai and, at the time of testing, were practicing teachers of English as a foreign language at a college or secondary school in Thailand.

Design of Study 3

Each subject completed all four cloze tests in two consecutive 50-minute testing sessions with an

TABLE 20.4 Random Assignment to Blocks

Subject	Block	Occasion One		Occasion Two	
1	i	A Sequential	B Scrambled	B Sequential	A Scrambled
2	ii	B Scrambled	A Sequential	A Scrambled	B Sequential
3	iii	A Scrambled	B Sequential	A Sequential	B Scrambled
4	iv	B Sequential	A Scrambled	B Scrambled	A Sequential
5	i	(same as Subject 1)			
...	...	(continue cycling)			
n				...	

intervening break of about 20 minutes. In the first period of testing, subjects were given a pair of tests consisting of either text A or B in the sequential condition and the remaining one in the scrambled condition. The pattern of test distribution (a randomized block design) is displayed in Table 20.4. During the second testing period, depending on which pair of tests had been completed by the subject in the previous period, subjects were allowed an additional 50 minutes to complete the complementary pair of tests consisting of either B or A in the scrambled condition and the other text in the sequential condition.

The design allowed us to measure directly the learning effect of working through a story versus working through the same sentences that made up that story but in a random order. There were a rather large number of hypotheses to be tested, but the one of greatest interest here was that subjects would make substantial gains owed to working through the sequential material and essentially no gain at all from working through the same material in a scrambled arrangement.

Results of Study 3

Table 20.5 shows the mean scores of interest, and Figure 20.3 graphs the results. To test the hypothesis of greatest interest here, we must compare the mean scores on occasions one and two on the two sequential cloze exercises with the mean scores across the two occasions on the two scrambled texts. The reason that these mean scores are the right ones to compare can be understood by a little bit of reflection. First, we suppose that the expected mean score on either of the sequential texts (had there been no prior experience with either of those texts) would be exactly the mean across both texts that was actually obtained on the first occasion. This assumption is sound because subjects did, in fact, obtain that mean and they did do so without any prior experience with either of the two cloze tests. Second, we make the same assumption for the mean on the corresponding pair of scrambled tests. Again, the assumption is sound. The mean attained on occasion one by the subjects under study was attained without any prior study of either of the two texts. Therefore, we assume that the expected mean for these same subjects on the second occasion when they

TABLE 20.5 Mean Percentage Scores on Cloze Tests by Occasion and Condition for Thai EFL Teachers (N = 90)

Occasion	Condition	Mean	SD
One	Sequential	56.03	11.58
	Scrambled	50.37	9.78
Two	Sequential	55.86	10.52
	Scrambled	58.13	11.10

encounter the corresponding pair of sequential texts will be the one they obtained on the first occasion. Any difference observed would be owed to learning from the prior experience with the scrambled variants. The same holds for the scrambled texts encountered on the second occasion. Any difference between the mean attained on that occasion and the mean for the scrambled texts on occasion one must be owed directly to a learning effect. The reason that these assumptions are logically valid is because, in fact, no experience intervened between occasion one and two that might produce any observed difference.

So what do we see? The results are shown most clearly in Figure 20.3. Compare the mean over the two sequential texts on occasion one,

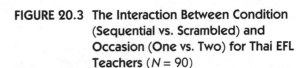

FIGURE 20.3 The Interaction Between Condition (Sequential vs. Scrambled) and Occasion (One vs. Two) for Thai EFL Teachers (N = 90)

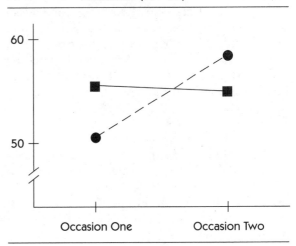

56.03 percentage points, against the mean over the two sequential texts on occasion two, 55.86 percentage points. In fact, the contrast is not significant statistically, but subjects fell on the average .17 of a percentage point owing to having experienced the scrambled variant of one of the two cloze exercises on the prior occasion. But what about the impact of working through the sequential exercise on the first occasion? Compare the mean of the two scrambled texts on the first occasion, 50.37, against the mean of the two scrambled texts on the second occasion, 58.13. Here we see a difference of 7.76 percentage points, which proves to be significant by the appropriate sort of analysis of variance (see Oller & Jonz, in press, for the details) at a probability of less than .0001. That is, such a large contrast could be expected to occur by chance only once in 10,000 similar experimental designs. The moral of our story, therefore (looking ahead to the punch line), is that language teachers really ought to do whatever is necessary to find materials that are episodically organized in the manner of a narrative rather than the isolated bits and pieces of texts that commonly populate the pages of too many textbooks. (In fact, we will see in Chapter 28 that even unconnected sociocultural conversational vignettes ought not to be used.)

STUDY 4: NORTH CAROLINA

Essentially the same texts and procedures were used here as in the previous study. Study 4, however, was conducted as part of a joint meeting of Carolina TESOL (Teachers of English to Speakers of Other Languages) and a workshop for English and foreign language teachers in the Carolinas and neighboring states held in Greensboro, North Carolina, in the spring of 1991 (co-sponsored by the North Carolina Department of Public Instruction and Carolina TESOL).[4]

Subjects of Study 4

There were 63 participants who were either teachers of English as a second language or foreign language teachers. Many of them were also members of the Carolina TESOL organization. The women in the study, as in the previous one, outnumbered the men about two to one.

TABLE 20.6 Mean Percentage Scores on Cloze Tests by Occasion and Condition for Carolina Teachers (n = 63)

Occasion	Condition	Mean	SD
One	Sequential	73.28	7.44
	Scrambled	62.35	8.99
Two	Sequential	74.44	6.91
	Scrambled	73.75	7.37

Design of Study 4

Each subject completed all four cloze tests in two consecutive 40-minute testing sessions with an intervening break of about 10 minutes, as shown above in Table 20.4. Otherwise, except for allowing less time for these native speakers, the design and test administration was as in the preceding study in Thailand.

Results of Study 4

Table 20.6 shows essentially the same pattern as with the Thai data, except that the contrasts with native-speakers as subjects are more pronounced. As before, the contrasts of interest can be seen in a graph (Figure 20.4). The mean over the sequential

FIGURE 20.4 The Interaction Between Condition (Sequential vs. Scrambled) and Occasion (One vs. Two) for Carolina EFL Teachers (n = 63)

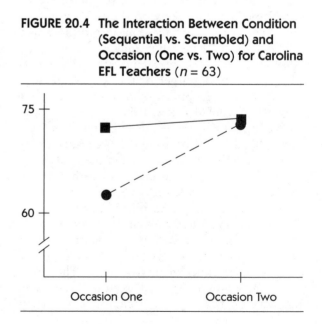

texts on the first occasion was 73.28 percentage points, as compared against the mean of 74.44 for the sequential texts on the second occasion. On the average, the native speakers gained 1.16 percentage points from the first to the second occasion, owing to the experience of working through one of the scrambled texts on occasion one. However, as in the Thai study (Study 3), this contrast was not statistically significant. Again, subjects benefited very little, if at all, from the experience of working through one of the two texts first in its scrambled form before encountering it in its normal narrative sequence. On the other hand, the contrast between the mean over the scrambled texts on the first occasion, 62.35, and the mean attained on the second occasion, 73.75, shows a substantial gain of 11.40 percentage points that can be reliably attributed to the information gained from having worked through the sequential variant of the corresponding cloze exercise on occasion one. Again, a difference this large would be expected to occur less than one time in 10,000 tries.

STUDY 5: FLORIDA NATIVE SPEAKERS OF ENGLISH

Our next study was conducted as part of a series of Florida in-service training seminars for teachers in the Broward County Schools in the summer of 1991.[5]

Subjects of Study 5

In this study, the 89 participants were either teachers of English as a second language, content area specialists (math, English, social studies, etc.) working with children identified as of limited English proficiency, or teachers in bilingual programs in Florida. All 89 were native speakers of English. In this case there were, again, about twice as many women as men (again, see Oller & Jonz, in press, for details).

Design of Study 5

Each subject completed all four cloze tests in two consecutive 40-minute testing sessions with an intervening break of about 10 minutes. The design was similar to that of Studies 3 and 4.

TABLE 20.7 Mean Percentage Scores on Cloze Tests by Occasion and Condition for Broward County Teachers ($n = 89$)

Occasion	Condition	Mean	SD
One	Sequential	69.34	9.88
	Scrambled	61.67	9.11
Two	Sequential	69.73	8.75
	Scrambled	69.42	9.45

Results of Study 5

Table 20.7 gives the relevant means. In fact, as predicted, the contrast between performance on the sequential texts on occasion one (with a mean of 69.34) versus the sequential texts on occasion two (69.73)—a difference of .39 percentage points favoring the second occasion—was not significant, but the contrast between the mean for the scrambled texts on the first occasion (61.67) versus the second occasion (69.42)—a difference of 7.75 percentage points—was highly significant. Again, such a large contrast would rarely be expected to occur by chance ($p < .001$). (Because the results are so similar to those of the two preceding studies, we will not present a graph.)

STUDY 6: FLORIDA NON-NATIVE SPEAKERS OF ENGLISH

The same texts and procedures were followed here as in Study 5. This replication was also conducted as part of the series of Florida in-service training seminars conducted in the summer of 1991 for teachers in Broward County Schools.

Subjects of Study 6

In this case, there were 38 participants who were either teachers of English as a second language, content area specialists (math, English, social studies, etc.) working with children identified as limited in English proficiency, or teachers in bilingual programs in Florida. All indicated some language other than English as their primary language. The majority were of Haitian background (about

TABLE 20.8 Mean Percentage Scores on Cloze Tests by Occasion and Condition for Broward County Non-Native Speakers of English ($n = 38$)

Occasion	Condition	Mean	SD
One	Sequential	63.58	10.20
	Scrambled	53.57	9.94
Two	Sequential	62.65	11.79
	Scrambled	62.93	9.76

50%), or Hispanic (about 25%), mainly from Cuba or Puerto Rico, plus a miscellany of other backgrounds (the remaining 25%).

Design of Study 6

Each subject completed all four cloze tests in two consecutive 50-minute testing sessions with an intervening break of about 10 minutes. The design was the same as in the previous study except that the time limits were extended.

Results of Study 6

Table 20.8 shows the relevant means. As with the Thai subjects, this group did slightly better on the sequential texts on the first occasion (63.58) than on the second (62.65), but the contrast, as predicted, was not significant. However, on the scrambled texts, there was a contrast of 9.36 percentage points, indicating a substantial gain owed to the experience of working through the corresponding sequential text on the first occasion.

STUDY 7: NATIVES AND NON-NATIVES COMBINED

Background of Study 7

From all of the foregoing, it is apparent that textual coherence as determined by connections ranging across sentences is a factor in cloze scores both for native speakers of English and for advanced non-natives as well. A remaining question suggested by the contrast across different proficiency levels

(groups 1–4) in Study 2 is whether a higher degree of proficiency will result in a greater sensitivity to discourse constraints for subjects from Studies 3–6, as was observed in Study 2. Based on the second hypothesis of Study 2, we predicted that a greater degree of proficiency would in fact correspond to a greater sensitivity to discourse constraints for the native speakers of Studies 4 and 5 as contrasted with the non-natives of Studies 3 and 6. To test this hypothesis, the data from the four preceding studies were combined.

Subjects of Study 7

The subjects for Study 7 were merely the combined non-natives and natives of Studies 3–6. The non-native group included the 90 Thai EFL teachers and the 38 Broward County teachers who were non-native speakers of English ($N = 128$, advanced non-natives) to be compared against the 63 Carolina teachers and the 89 Broward County teachers who were all native speakers of English ($N = 152$, native speakers of English). In all, therefore, the two groups combined resulted in a total $N = 280$.

Design of Study 7

The test scores employed in the analyses were those described in Studies 3–6.

Results of Study 7

Table 20.9 gives the relevant means of groups. As expected, owing to the second hypothesis of Study 2, the natives outperformed non-native speakers of English and were also significantly more sensitive to the formal schema underlying the narratives presented in their sequential form as contrasted with the same materials arranged in a scrambled form. In both cases—that is, for the natives and for the non-natives—the contrast between the mean sequential scores on occasions one and two was nil (i.e., not statistically significant), but the contrast between the two corresponding performances on the scrambled texts was highly significant for both groups. Moreover, the contrast for the non-natives was significantly less (a difference of 8.26 percentage points) than for the natives (9.55). Again, both of these last differences were

TABLE 20.9 Mean Percentage Scores on Cloze Tests by Occasion and Condition for Natives ($N = 152$) and Non-Natives ($N = 128$)

Group	Occasion	Condition	Mean	SD
Natives	One	Sequential	70.97	9.17
		Scrambled	61.95	9.07
	Two	Sequential	71.40	8.45
		Scrambled	71.50	8.85
Non-Natives	One	Sequential	58.27	11.35
		Scrambled	51.29	9.95
	Two	Sequential	57.91	12.89
		Scrambled	59.55	11.38

significant at $p < .0001$, and the contrast between the pair of differences was also significant at $p < .001$. It does appear that native speakers on the whole are indeed more sensitive to discourse constraints than even advanced non-natives. The mean difference between the scrambled text on occasion one versus the sequential text on the same occasion for native speakers was 9.02, as against a mean difference of 6.98 for advanced non-natives. Natives benefit more than non-natives on the first occasion from the sequential text. This is proved by the fact that the natives had higher scores on both types of tests and yet, nevertheless, had a greater spread between the sequential and the scrambled text on the first occasion than the non-natives did.

However, it should be noted that the advanced non-natives in the data pool for Study 7 benefited proportionately more than the native speakers did on occasion two from the prior experience of working through a text in its sequential form. This can be seen by noting that the contrast between the sequential versus the scrambled performance for natives on occasion one was already 9.02%, as against the corresponding 6.98% for non-natives. However, the non-natives gained proportionately more (from 6.98% to 8.26%) from working through the sequential exercises than the natives did (from 9.02% to 9.55%). This, we believe, is further evidence in favor of the universality of episodic organization as a factor underlying the interpretation of narratives.

The fact that non-natives gained almost as much (in total percentage points, 8.86%) across the two occasions as the natives did (9.55%) from prior acquaintance with the respective story line contrasts markedly with the noteworthy differences between their observed levels of overall proficiency. For instance, averaging across the various cloze scores in Table 20.8, we get a mean of 68.96 for the 152 natives and 56.76 for the 128 non-natives—an average difference of 12.21%. In view of this difference, the non-natives gained more from the narrative schema than they would be expected to do solely on the basis of their proficiency in English. Just as Horiba (see Chapter 21) argues, proficiency in the target language is clearly not all that is at work here. It seems that a formal schema, just as Carrell supposed (Chapter 19), really is at work.

CONCLUSIONS

This series of studies confirms previous findings and extends them. First, it confirms that cloze tests *are* highly sensitive to discourse constraints in at least *some* fairly typical narrative, descriptive, and expository texts. Second, it shows that the amount of learning owed to working through a narrative text in a sequential form is substantial whereas the learning owed to working through the same text in a scrambled version is next to nothing. For classroom applications this finding is far-reaching. It suggests that we ought never to use isolated bits and pieces of language dropped out of the blue (also see Taira, Chapter 28). Third, the degree of benefit gained from discourse constraints ranging beyond sentence boundaries does indeed appear to be linked to the degree of proficiency of subjects (as hypothesized by Chihara et al., 1977)—more-proficient subjects gain somewhat more benefit from discourse constraints than do less-proficient subjects.

It was also interesting that while text A was generally easier than B for some groups, for three different samples of Japanese subjects, B was consistently easier than A (Oller & Yü, 1986; Chihara et al., 1977; and Chihara, Sakurai, & Oller, 1989). In spite of this contrast across linguistic and cultural groups, the effect of discourse constraints and the higher degree of learning produced by coherent text (a formal schema for narratives) have remained quite consistent across languages and culture groups suggesting its universality (see Chapter 37). Also, the greater sensitivity of more-proficient subjects to discourse constraints has held up regardless of primary language or cultural background. This suggests that the contrasts observed across the two texts used in Studies 2–7 may be due to experiential and cultural factors (an overlay of what Carrell has called specific "content schemata") while contrasts in the impact of narrative discourse constraints (a "formal schema" posited by Carrell and others) are probably owed to semiotic universals. The formal schema of experience-based narratives, it would seem at any rate, can be expected to play a central role in the workings of intelligence in general, as well as in the processing and language acquisition related to narratives. These, it is argued in Chapter 37, form the foundation for the discourse processing that results in normal language acquisition and literacy.

APPENDIX 20.1

Passage I[6]

For those who hang out there, the Carry-out offers a wide array of sounds, sights, smells, tastes, and tactile experiences which titillate and sometimes assault the five senses. || The air (1) IS warmed by | smells from (2) THE coffee urns | and grill (3) AND thickened with | fat from (4) THE deep-fry basket. | The jukebox (5) OFFERS up a | wide variety (6) OF frenetic and | lazy rhythms. (7) THE pinball machine | is a (8) STANDING challenge to | one's manipulative (9) SKILL or ability | to will (10) THE ball into | one or (11) ANOTHER hole. Flashing | lights, bells (12) AND buzzers report | progress or (13) ANNOUNCE failure. Colorful | signs exhort (14) CUSTOMERS to drink | Royal Crown Cola and (15) EAT Bond Bread. On | the wall, (16) ABOVE the telephone, | a long-legged (17) BLOND in shorts | and halter (18) SMILES a fixed | wet-lipped smile (19) OF unutterable delight | at her Chesterfield (20) CIGARETTE , her visage || unmarred by a mustache or scribbled obscenities. In the background, a sleek ocean liner rides a flat blue sea to an unknown destination (Gorrell, Laird, & Freemen, 1970: 29).

Passage II

It is possible to get an education at a university. || It has (1) BEEN done; not | often, but (2) THE fact that | a proportion, (3) HOWEVER small, of | college students (4) DO get a | start in (5) INTERESTED, methodical study, | proves my (6) THESIS, and the | two personal (7) EXPERIENCES I have | to offer (8) ILLUSTRATE it and | show how (9) TO circumvent the | faculty, the (10) OTHER students, and | the whole (11) COLLEGE system of | mind-fixing. My (12) METHOD might lose | a boy (13) HIS degree, but | a degree (14) IS not worth | so much (15) AS the capacity | and the (16) DRIVE to learn, | and the (17) UNDERGRADUATE desire for | an empty (18) BACCALAUREATE is one | of the (19) HOLDS the educational | system has (20) ON students. Wise || students some day will refuse to take degrees, as the best men (in England, for instance) give, but do not themselves accept, titles (Gorrell, Laird, & Freemen, 1970: 33–34).

Passage III

The statement of the main idea, discussed in the preceding chapter, helps the writer organize the subdivisions of his paper. ‖ As he (1) WRITES, he also | recognizes and (2) UNIFIES material within | the subdivisions, (3) USING the paragraph | as his (4) UNIT of composition. | Paragraphs can (5) BE written in | many ways, (6) BUT one basic | type is (7) SO useful for | expository writing (8) THAT we are | calling it (9) THE standard paragraph. | It includes (10) THE following: (1) topical | material to (11) INTRODUCE the subject; | (2) development to (12) ILLUSTRATE or support | or extend (13) THE subject, material | that may (14) BREAK into divisions | or even (15) SUBDIVISIONS; and (3) sometimes | a conclusion. (16) USING this pattern, | the most (17) OBVIOUS and most | useful way (18) TO construct a | paragraph is (19) TO write a | topic sentence (20) AND add specification ‖ to support it (Gorrell, Laird, & Freemen, 1970: 26).

Passage IV

On some occasions, a single word—"Fire!" or "Murder!" for example—is a complete message; context and tone of voice supply the unspoken information. ‖ Usually, however, (1) COMMUNICATION requires more, | that we (2) NOT only name | a topic (3) BUT say something | about it— "(4) THE fire is | spreading" or " (5) THE fire was | caused by (6) FAULTY wiring." A | simple sentence, (7) THE horse is | eating, gets (8) UTTERED not because | we think (9) OF the topic | horse and (10) THEN search for | something to (11) SAY about it | but because (12) WE want to | report on (13) WHAT we have | observed, want (14) TO say something | about the (15) HORSE. If we | have a (16) GREAT deal more | to say (17) ABOUT a horse, | the result (18) MAY be, not | a simple (19) SENTENCE but an | article or (20) A book. Writing ‖ a simple sentence or a longer composition includes at least a topic and a comment about it, although the line between the two may not be precise (Gorrell, Laird, & Freemen, 1970: 1).

Passage V

When Sir Edward Travers died suddenly and mysteriously there was consternation and speculation, not only in our neighborhood but throughout the country. ‖ One newspaper (1) HEADLINE ran: SIR | EDWARD TRAVERS VICTIM (2) OF CURSE? Another | reported: SUDDEN (3) DEATH OF EMINENT | ARCHAEOLOGIST BRINGS (4) ABRUPT END TO | EXPEDITION. A (5) PARAGRAPH in our | local paper (6) STATED, "The death | of Sir Edward Travers, (7) WHO recently left | this country (8) TO carry out | excavations among (9) THE tombs of | the pharaohs, (10) HAS caused us | to wonder (11) IF there is | any truth (12) IN the ancient | belief that (13) HE who meddles | with the (14) RESTING place of | the dead (15) INVITES their enmity." | Sir Ralph Bodrean (16) AT Keverall Court, our | local squire (17) AND Sir Edward's | closest friend, (18) HAD given financial | aid to (19) THE expedition, and | when, a (20) FEW days after ‖ the announcement of Sir Edward's death, Sir Ralph had a stroke, it was hinted that his misfortune was the result of the same curse (Holt, 1973: 325).

APPENDIX 20.2

Form A Sequential

Joe is a freshman and he (1) IS[7] having all the problems that most (2) FRESHMEN have. As a matter of fact, his (3) PROBLEMS started before he even left home. (4) HE had to do a lot of (5) THINGS that he didn't like to do (6) JUST because he was going to go (7) AWAY to college. He had his eyes (8) EXAMINED and he had his cavities filled, (9) ALTHOUGH he hates to go to a (10) DENTIST, and he got his watch fixed (11) BY a neighborhood jeweler. Then, at his (12) MOTHER'S suggestion, he had his father's tailor (13) MEASURE him for a suit. He didn't (14) HAVE a suit made, though, because his (15) FATHER wouldn't let him order one. "You're (16) STILL growing, son," he said. "You're growing (17) SO fast that you'd outgrow a suit (18) IN no time. Buy yourself a pair (19) OF slacks and a sport jacket. Klein's (20) HAS such a large selection that I'm (21) SURE you will find something you like (22) THERE." Joe's father always suggested Klein's for (23) CLOTHES. Joe went to Klein's in order (24) TO please his father but he didn't (25) FIND anything that he liked there so (26) HE went to another store to buy (27) THE slacks. He took them out of (28) THE box as soon as he got (29) HOME so that his father wouldn't notice (30) WHERE they came from. When Joe was (31) ALL ready to leave for school, his (32) MOTHER suggested that he visit all his (33) RELATIVES. "What do you want me to (34) DO that for?" he asked, and she (35) ANSWERED, "To say good-bye." She made him (36) GO to see his cousins in Bellevue (37) AND his Uncle Ned in Plaintown and (38) HIS Great-Aunt Lizzie who lives in (39) THE southern part of the state. He (40) DIDN'T want to visit all those people (41) BUT he did it anyway because of (42) HIS mother's insistence. On the day that (43) HE left for college his sister helped (44) HIM pack his clothes. She let him (45) BORROW her suitcase because he didn't have (46) ONE of his own. When everything was (47) ALL ready, he got his father to (48) DRIVE him to the station and the (49) WHOLE family went along. Of course his (50) MOTHER insisted on kissing him good-bye in (51) SPITE of his embarrassment. As soon as (52) THE train pulled into the station Joe (53) JUMPED on and hurriedly found his seat. (54) BY the time it pulled out he (55) WAS already contemplating his new life away (56) FROM home.

Form A Scrambled

1. BY the time it pulled out he <u>WAS</u> already contemplating his new life away <u>FROM</u> home.
2. "What do you want me to <u>DO</u> that for?" he asked, and she <u>ANSWERED</u>, "To say good-bye."
3. "You're <u>STILL</u> growing, son," he said.
4. As soon as <u>THE</u> train pulled into the station Joe <u>JUMPED</u> on and hurriedly found his seat.
5. When Joe was <u>ALL</u> ready to leave for school, his <u>MOTHER</u> suggested that he visit all his <u>RELATIVES</u>.
6. He didn't <u>HAVE</u> a suit made, though, because his <u>FATHER</u> wouldn't let him order one.
7. Of course his <u>MOTHER</u> insisted on kissing him good-bye in <u>SPITE</u> of his embarrassment.
8. He took them out of <u>THE</u> box as soon as he got <u>HOME</u> so that his father wouldn't notice <u>WHERE</u> they came from.
9. Then, at his <u>MOTHER'S</u> suggestion, he had his father's tailor <u>MEASURE</u> him for a suit.
10. When everything was <u>ALL</u> ready, he got his father to <u>DRIVE</u> him to the station and the <u>WHOLE</u> family went along.
11. Joe went to Klein's in order <u>TO</u> please his father but he didn't <u>FIND</u> anything that he liked there so <u>HE</u> went to another store to buy <u>THE</u> slacks.
12. He had his eyes <u>EXAMINED</u> and he had his cavities filled, <u>ALTHOUGH</u> he hates to go to a <u>DENTIST</u>, and he got his watch fixed <u>BY</u> a neighborhood jeweler.
13. She let him <u>BORROW</u> her suitcase because he didn't have <u>ONE</u> of his own.
14. Joe's father always suggested Klein's for <u>CLOTHES</u>.
15. HE had to do a lot of <u>THINGS</u> that he didn't like to do <u>JUST</u> because he was going to go <u>AWAY</u> to college.
16. On the day that <u>HE</u> left for college his sister helped <u>HIM</u> pack his clothes.
17. Klein's <u>HAS</u> such a large selection that I'm <u>SURE</u> you will find something you like <u>THERE</u>.
18. As a matter of fact, his <u>PROBLEMS</u> started before he even left home.
19. He <u>DIDN'T</u> want to visit all those people <u>BUT</u> he did it anyway because of <u>HIS</u> mother's insistence.
20. Buy yourself a pair <u>OF</u> slacks and a sport jacket.
21. Joe is a freshman and he <u>IS</u> having all the problems that most <u>FRESHMEN</u> have.

22. She made him <u>GO</u> to see his cousins in Bellevue <u>AND</u> his Uncle Ned in Plaintown and <u>HIS</u> Great-Aunt Lizzie who lives in <u>THE</u> southern part of the state.
23. You're growing <u>SO</u> fast that you'd outgrow a suit <u>IN</u> no time.

Form B Sequential

Nicholas Rizos was not a tourist; <u>(1) HE</u> was in Athens to <u>(2) WORK</u>. He had arrived from America <u>(3) THE</u> day before on a Greek cargo <u>(4) SHIP</u>. During his last year in <u>(5) HIGH</u> school, his uncle had invited <u>(6) HIM</u> to spend a year in <u>(7) GREECE</u> and to help him in <u>(8) HIS</u> garage. Nicholas accepted the invitation <u>(9) BECAUSE</u> he wanted to become a <u>(10) MECHANIC</u>; he thought that the <u>(11) WORK</u> would be good experience for <u>(12) HIM</u>. He would also have an <u>(13) OPPORTUNITY</u> to learn more about the <u>(14) COUNTRY</u> where his parents were born. <u>(15) FOR</u> several months he had studied <u>(16) THE</u> Greek language at night school <u>(17) IN</u> his home town. He wanted <u>(18) TO</u> speak it as well as <u>(19) POSSIBLE</u> and to be able to <u>(20) READ</u> signs, at least, when he <u>(21) ARRIVED</u>; but now he wished he <u>(22) COULD</u> have practiced it more with the <u>(23) SAILORS</u> on the ship. That first <u>(24) MORNING</u>, Nicholas woke up and looked <u>(25) AROUND</u> at the unfamiliar room. Everything <u>(26) WAS</u> strange to him. From his <u>(27) WINDOW</u>, he could see the Acropolis <u>(28) AGAINST</u> the bright blue sky. Then <u>(29) HE</u> remembered; he was in Athens! <u>(30) HOW</u> happy he was to be <u>(31) THERE</u>. He got dressed quickly and <u>(32) JOINED</u> his aunt and uncle in <u>(33) THE</u> kitchen. They seemed pleased when <u>(34) HE</u> said "Good morning" in their <u>(35) OWN</u> language, but it was difficult <u>(36) FOR</u> him to continue. They knew <u>(37) VERY</u> little English, and at first <u>(38) HE</u> was afraid to try his <u>(39) GREEK</u>. Before long, however, they were <u>(40) ALL</u> talking and laughing together. After <u>(41) BREAKFAST</u>, Nicholas and his uncle left <u>(42) TO</u> go to work. They walked <u>(43) RATHER</u> fast because his uncle was <u>(44) IN</u> a hurry; in fact, he <u>(45) WAS</u> later than usual that morning. <u>(46) NICHOLAS</u> would have liked to walk <u>(47) MORE</u> slowly in order to enjoy <u>(48) THE</u> unfamiliar sights along the way.

Form B Scrambled

1. <u>NICHOLAS</u> would have liked to walk <u>MORE</u> slowly in order to enjoy <u>THE</u> unfamiliar sights along the way.
2. <u>HOW</u> happy he was to be <u>THERE</u>.
3. <u>FOR</u> several months he had studied <u>THE</u> Greek language at night school <u>IN</u> his home town.
4. They walked <u>RATHER</u> fast because his uncle was <u>IN</u> a hurry; in fact, he <u>WAS</u> later than usual that morning.
5. Then <u>HE</u> remembered; he was in Athens!
6. He would also have an <u>OPPORTUNITY</u> to learn more about the <u>COUNTRY</u> where his parents were born.
7. After <u>BREAKFAST</u>, Nicholas and his uncle left <u>TO</u> go to work.
8. From his <u>WINDOW</u>, he could see the Acropolis <u>AGAINST</u> the bright blue sky.
9. Nicholas accepted the invitation <u>BECAUSE</u> he wanted to become a <u>MECHANIC</u>; he thought the <u>WORK</u> would be good experience for <u>HIM</u>.
10. Before long, however, they were <u>ALL</u> talking and laughing together.
11. Everything <u>WAS</u> strange to him.
12. During his last year in <u>HIGH</u> school, his uncle had invited <u>HIM</u> to spend a year in <u>GREECE</u> and to help him in <u>HIS</u> garage.
13. They knew <u>VERY</u> little English, and at first <u>HE</u> was afraid to try his <u>GREEK</u>.
14. That first <u>MORNING</u>, Nicholas woke up and looked <u>AROUND</u> at the unfamiliar room.
15. He had arrived from America <u>THE</u> day before on a Greek cargo <u>SHIP</u>.
16. They seemed pleased when <u>HE</u> said "Good morning" in their <u>OWN</u> language, but it was difficult <u>FOR</u> him to continue.

17. He wanted <u>TO</u> speak it as well as <u>POSSIBLE</u> and to be able to <u>READ</u> signs, at least, when he <u>ARRIVED</u>; but now he wished he <u>COULD</u> have practiced it more with the <u>SAILORS</u> on the ship.
18. Nicholas Rizos was not a tourist; <u>HE</u> was in Athens to <u>WORK</u>.
19. He got dressed quickly and <u>JOINED</u> his aunt and uncle in <u>THE</u> kitchen.

NOTES

1 In 1991, these data were completely re-analyzed on the University of New Mexico IBM 9121 using the MANOVA program, version 4.0 of *SPSS*[X]. Contrasts were cross-checked following procedures laid down in Maxwell and Delaney (1990: 516–539) using Lotus 1-2-3 on an IBM PC.

2 We will see below that Thais show exactly the reverse response to the distinct content schemata of texts A and B.

3 We thank not only the subjects who participated in a July 22–29, 1984 seminar on English teaching in Kyoto, Japan, but also the organizers of the Eighteenth Japan Association of College English Teachers (JACET) Summer Seminar, who sponsored Oller's travel to Kyoto, Nagoya, and Yokohama. We especially thank Professor Minoru Tada of Ohtani University in Kyoto and his co-workers in JACET. Also, we note that the report of Oller and Yü (1986) appeared in Wangsotorn et al. (1986: 54–71). The replication of that original research in Japan, now in Thailand, was made possible by the sponsorship of the United States Information Agency in collaboration with Thai TESOL and the Chulalongkorn University Language Institute in Bangkok for Oller to travel to Thailand. The authors especially thank Professors Kanchana Prapphal and Achara Wangsotorn as well as Messrs. Bill Royer, Ron Smith, and Steve Madeira for their help in arranging seminars in Khon Kaen, Chiang Mai, and Songkla. We are indebted equally to the teachers who participated in those seminars.

4 We are especially grateful to Mr. L. Gerard Toussaint, Director of Curriculum and Instruction for the Department of Public Instruction in North Carolina, for setting up the joint workshop and seminar. Mr. "Bill" Simmons H. Isler IV was also helpful in arranging Oller's participation in the Carolina TESOL meeting that ran concurrently and at which some of the results of the several studies reported here were discussed (*after* the experimental data from some of the participants, incidentally, had already been collected). We also thank Ms. Jacqui L. Asbury of the South Carolina State Department of Education as well as Professor Jane Tucker Mitchell of the Department of Pedagogical Studies and Supervision at the University of North Carolina at Greensboro and Professor Alice Ann Goodwin of the Byrnes International Center at the University of South Carolina. It has been the consistent friendship and encouragement of people like these, especially Gerard Toussaint, that have brought the research reported here to fruition.

5 Special thanks are due to Mary Obfenda and Mayra Menéndez of the Broward County Multicultural Education Department for their part in organizing the sessions, preparing exercise materials, and initiating sponsorship for Oller to travel to Fort Lauderdale, Florida. Most of all, of course, the participants in the several seminar sessions are to be thanked.

6 In this Appendix, double bars mark the beginnings and ends of the 100-word segments while single bars mark the boundaries between 5-word segments. There were six cases where proper nouns were counted as one word. For instance, in Passage I, *Royal Crown Cola* was counted as one word as was *Bond Bread*. In Passage III, parenthesized numbers were not counted as words. In Passage V, *Edward Travers* was counted as one word on its first appearance, and *Sir Edward Travers* was counted as one word on the next appearance. *Ralph Bodrean* and *Keverall Court* were each counted as one word. Otherwise, blanks were spaced with exactly four words between them in each case. Hyphenated forms were, as is customary in cloze applications, counted as one word.

7 While the blanks shown in this Appendix (and the preceding one) conform to the size of the word, in the actual tests, blanks were all of a standard length, and, of course, the answers which are printed here in capital letters did not appear.

DISCUSSION QUESTIONS

1. For the texts discussed in this chapter (see Appendix 20.1), what high-level constraints or formal schemata can be discerned? Why is there no point of diminishing returns between 50 and 100 words of text, as many theoreticians predicted?

2. Work through one of the cloze tests in Appendix 20.2 in the scrambled version and the other in the sequential arrangement. Then do the alternate versions over each text. Reflect on the kinds of discourse constraints that are violated in the scrambled variant. What happens between the sequential text and the scrambled variant of that same text? Did you remember the story? What about between the scrambled variant of the other text and its sequential version?

3. Consider the finding that more-proficient English speakers are better able to make use of formal schemata and discourse constraints in general. Why must this be so? Why are beginners relatively unable to use such high level constraints?

4. For Japanese EFL students, the text about Joe was more difficult than the one about Nicholas (see Appendix 20.2), while for Americans, Thais, and non-native speakers of English tested in Florida, the reverse appeared to be true. The Joe text was easier. What sorts of factors might account for this outcome? By contrast, why would the benefit gained from formal discourse factors (especially from episodic organization) be, as it apparently is, consistent in its effects across all the groups examined?

CHAPTER 21

Narrative Comprehension Processes: A Study of Native and Non-Native Readers of Japanese

Yukie Horiba

EDITOR'S INTRODUCTION

We come now to a research project that tries to get a closer look at the inferential processes that sustain both the content and form of the knowledge that constitutes the basis for textual coherence. Horiba asserts here that persons who are not able to access pertinent content and formal structures relevant to any given discourse or text will be hard-pressed to understand it, regardless how well they might know the language of the material. The research paradigms of the previous chapter show that when content and formal schemata are deliberately disrupted, being an advanced non-native or even a native speaker does not necessarily make the disrupted text comprehensible. Horiba's think-out-loud protocols help to add to our understanding of the kinds of propositional connections that underlie the narrative basis of discourse. The fact that the protocols were elicited from native speakers and L2 learners of a non-Indo-European language may also be of some interest. The propositional analysis of the narrative structure posited for the simple story about Yoshiko and the bus reveals at once the deceptive simplicity of the linear causal sequence and the inferences that link various points (propositions) on the line into a complex network of relations.

We now conceive that reading comprehension involves both "top-down" and "bottom-up" processing and that both operate simultaneously rather than sequentially.[1] Researchers in second language (L2) reading have increasingly paid attention to the reader as an active processor who receives information from a text (bottom-up processing) by applying his or her background knowledge in order to make sense (top-down processing). However, few empirical data are available about the interaction of top-down with bottom-up processing while the reader is trying to construct a coherent representation of the text.

The study reported in this paper attempts to explore this issue.

BACKGROUND

Defining Reading Comprehension

L2 reading research has increasingly provided evidence that, as in L1 reading, what is understood depends as much on the reader as it does on the text (Bernhardt, 1984). Schema research has demonstrated that to comprehend a text, a reader's background knowledge or schemata must interact with the text itself. The more links the reader makes between new and previously acquired knowledge, the greater the depth of processing is, and the easier the retrieval of information from memory (Anderson & Pearson, 1984). In other words, *the more familiar a text is, the more likely it will be remembered.* As in the case of L1 research, it has been demonstrated that L2 students will better comprehend and recall when they have access to background knowledge or schema relevant to the content and/or the formal structure of a text. Those who do not have such access will have difficulty in comprehension and recall, regardless of their understanding of the language.[2]

Some researchers have reported the effects of schemata or top-down processing on the comprehension of specific linguistic items. Adams (1982) demonstrated that activated "script" knowledge of the topic of a text aided recognition of unfamiliar vocabulary which appeared in it, both in English as L1 and French as L2. Lee (1987) found that students who had never been instructed in the Spanish subjunctive mood were able to comprehend the meaning of sentences which contained this verb form, implying that the readers give meaning to the text through interaction between their knowledge and the content of the passage.

Although L2 reading research has favored schema-theory based studies during the last decade, most of these studies are vague in the sense that the comprehension process is inferred from what is reproduced after reading has been completed. Most of the studies investigate the effects of schemata by utilizing free recall and/or comprehension questions as a measure of comprehension; none of them examines the ongoing comprehension process. [Editor's note: Cloze procedure research is, of course, an exception.] Furthermore, many studies treat ESL readers as a group whose linguistic and cultural backgrounds are diverse. This heterogeneity in readers' variables seems to increase variability in the way information is encoded in memory and later retrieved. Therefore, it is difficult to infer what takes place in these individual readers' heads. Our understanding of the effects of schematic knowledge on L2 reading comprehension will be enhanced if the processes are investigated *on line* as well as *off line,* with the readers' cultural and linguistic backgrounds held constant.

Language Competence and Reading Comprehension

Some theories have suggested that L2 readers' inadequate command of vocabulary and grammar may interfere with conceptualizing the text content and can inhibit reading comprehension. With the limited processing capacity of the human mind, unfamiliar language and schemata necessitate "controlled processing" in which component processes are evoked by stimuli only with conscious efforts (Shiffrin & Schneider, 1977). The LaBerge & Samuels model (LaBerge & Samuels, 1974; Samuels, 1977) shows that both decoding and comprehension require attention. One can infer that in L1 skilled reading, the relatively low-level processes such as feature and word recognition and the language-specific processes such as parsing and segmentation are most likely to be automatic, while unfamiliar features, such as words and grammar in L2, need to be allocated to the reader's cognitive attention, resulting in insufficient opportunity for conceptualizing and resultant comprehension to take place.

A number of studies on the processes of L2 reading comprehension conclude that a reader's limited command of language increases reliance on graphic information and inhibits use of effective reading strategies. McLeod and McLaughlin (1986) investigated strategies used by ESL readers and native readers who were taking oral cloze and oral reading tests. They found that, although advanced ESL readers scored better in both tests, their error patterns on the oral reading test were the same as those of beginning ESL readers. The proportion of the meaningful errors committed by advanced ESL readers was significantly lower than in the case of native speakers. McLeod and McLaughlin speculated that the advanced students were aiming at decoding rather than comprehension. The reader is cautioned to recognize that oral reading may impede the L2 reader's comprehension because the extra task of pronouncing words results in insufficient attention paid to conceptualization (Bernhardt, 1983b).

Comparing eye movements of L1 and L2 German readers, Bernhardt (1983a) found that inexperienced L2 readers spent more time overall and spent longer sampling information from the text than experienced L2 readers and L1 readers.

She also noted that the readers seem to pay more attention to function words as proficiency improves. Thus, inexperienced L2 readers seem to attend to individual letters and words and employ inappropriate "English-like" behaviors. As a result, their short-term memory may have been overloaded and could not allocate sufficient attention to conceptual and schematic information.

Few data are available about the relationship between language competence and the processes of comprehension. Does a limited command of the language make the reader rely more on the linguistic information given in the text or on his/her general knowledge? How does the L2 reader process linguistic and nonlinguistic information in the attempt to conceptualize a text?

Text Comprehension as a Problem-Solving Process

Recent research in English as L1 has increasingly paid attention to the importance of causal reasoning in narrative text comprehension (Black & Bower, 1980; Graesser & Robertson, 1988; Schank, 1975; Trabasso, Secco, & van den Broek, 1984). Theories resulting from that research view narrative comprehension as a problem-solving process in which the reader understands each of the events portrayed in the text by discovering the causes (events producing them) and effects (events resulting from them) by utilizing information provided in the text and his/her own knowledge of the world. By discovering the causes and tracing the consequences of the events, the reader generates a sequence of causal links that connect a text's opening to its outcome. In this approach to the study of text comprehension and recall, a text's causal structure is seen as the primary determinant of recall. This structure is derived by parsing a text into individual states then using the criterion "necessity in the circumstances" (Mackie, 1973; Trabasso & Sperry, 1985) to determine the causal connections between these states. Thus, X is said to cause Y if it is the case that Y would not have occurred in the circumstances described by the text had X not occurred. By this criterion, enablement, motivation, and psychological and physical causation are all considered "causal" relations. Several studies provide evidence that the information,

which is on the causal chain in the causal structure of the text and the information which has more causal links to other information is more memorable and easier to recall (Fletcher & Bloom, 1988; O'Brien & Myers, 1987; Trabasso & van den Broek, 1985; Trabasso, van den Broek, & Suh, 1989). These studies suggest that people tend to construct a causally coherent representation of text in comprehension and use it for retrieval.

Applying this theory and evidence to L2 comprehension research, we can assume that L2 readers also try to build a causally coherent representation of a story as long as their processing capacity is not used up for decoding, but is available for higher-level processes (i.e., integration of meaning). In other words, when readers operate causal reasoning on the basis of their naive "causal theory" of the world, they might bring missing information into the text and accommodate it to insufficient understanding of vocabulary and grammar (top-down processing). As a result, they might be able to elaborate appropriately or they might inappropriately distort what is intended by the author. On the other hand, when too much processing capacity is used for linguistic information in the text (bottom-up processing), readers are most likely unable to perceive appropriate connections between statements in the text, resulting in the construction of a less causally coherent representation of it.

The present study examines the comprehension processes that occur as a person reads a text and what a reader remembers and recalls after the text has been read. The study utilizes Trabasso and van den Broek's causal network model (Trabasso & van den Broek, 1985; Trabasso, Secco, & van den Broek, 1984) as an analytical tool (both the original and that reproduced by the subjects). Off-line data (recall) are obtained as a retrieved mental representation of the text and analyzed in terms of the size and causal structure of the representation. As an on-line measure, the think-out-loud method (TOL) (also called the think-aloud method or concurrent introspection) is used to tap the content of the reader's immediate awareness or short-term working memory during reading. The TOL data are taken not as direct reflections of thought processes, but as correlated with underlying thought processes.[3]

STUDY

Research Questions

The research questions this study addresses are: 1) Will L2 readers pay more conscious attention to different aspects of their mental states (categories of TOL productions) during reading than L1 readers? 2) Will recall protocols provided by L2 readers differ from those provided by L1 readers in terms of how much information of the text is recalled and what kind of information is recalled? 3) Will repeated reading affect TOL productions and recall provided by L2 readers?

Subjects

Nine native and eleven non-native advanced adult speakers of Japanese participated in this study. L1 subjects were all female, aged twenty-three to thirty-five plus. The L2 group consisted of American students taking the third-year Japanese language course (advanced level) or equivalent-level Japanese courses, seven males and three females, all native speakers of English, aged twenty to twenty-two (plus one forty-one years old). Most of the L2 subjects had never been to Japan. They were all students at a metropolitan university in the Midwest at the time the study was conducted (June 1988).

Materials

The test text was a simple story in Japanese titled *Yoshiko and the Bus* (Appendix 21.1). The title and each of the ten sentences were typewritten on separate index cards. A stack of cards was created for the text, with a blank card placed between every two cards to prompt the subject's production of TOL protocols (Appendix 21.2). The title of the story was placed as the first stimulus so as to activate the readers' familiar schema for the story.

Design

Within each language group, half of the subjects were randomly assigned to read the text with the TOL method (TOL subgroup), the other half without it (Control subgroup).[4] This procedure was followed to check possible effects of the TOL

method, because the readers who did the TOL procedure might process information differently from those who did not do it. After reading, each subject was asked to recall the text. The L2 group was also asked to repeat the same procedure twice: that is, read a text, write a recall, read the text again, and write another recall. This allowed the researcher to examine learning effects among L2 readers.

Procedures

The procedures were the same for all the subjects except for two details. Half of the subjects read with the TOL method; the other half read without it. The L2 group repeated read-recall; the L1 group did not. The TOL method was used following the recommendations in Ericsson and Simon (1980) and in Olson, Duffy, and Mack (1984). Each subject in the TOL group practiced the TOL method with a warm-up story, a simple story presented in a stack of index cards. Subjects were told to read each sentence silently, flip the card, and report what was in their mind. Since simply instructing subjects to "think out loud" was deemed inadequate, the kinds of things which might be talked about were listed and presented to the subjects prior to the task. Subjects were told not to try to explain to the investigator why they were doing a particular activity. They were also told to read for the meaning of the text because they would be asked later to recall it in their native language. Each TOL protocol was audiotaped. Subjects practiced until they felt familiar and comfortable with the method. While a subject was engaged in the task, the investigator was seated away from him/her and kept silent unless some mechanical trouble occurred which required intervention. When the subject finished recording and called the investigator, he/she was given a sheet of paper on which he/she was asked to write everything remembered of the text in his/her native language. Subjects were also asked to write their recalls in complete sentences, using exact words from the story when possible.

Analysis of the Data

The story (Appendix 21.1) was analyzed in two ways. First, it was propositionally analyzed using procedures recommended by Bovair and Kieras (1985). A proposition is a semantic unit consisting of a predicate and one or more arguments. For example, the sentence *She checked her purse and realized that she didn't have any change* can be analyzed into five propositions: P1 (*check Yoshiko purse*), P2 (*possess Yoshiko purse*), P3 (*realize Yoshiko P4*), P4 (*neg P5*), P5 (*possess Yoshiko change*). P1 is a simple verb frame consisting of the predicate *check* and two arguments: the logical subject, the word concept *Yoshiko* referred to by *she*, and the logical object, the word concept *purse*. P2 represents that *her* in *her purse* is not a simple modifier like *red* in *red purse*, but it is the logical subject *Yoshiko* who *possesses* the logical object *purse*. The verb *realized* takes a proposition as an argument expressed by a *that*-clause, so that P3 contains P4 as an argument. Propositions are negated by means of the *negate* predicate. *Negate* has one argument which is always a proposition; in this way P4 and P5 are obtained. Using this method, a list of propositions was obtained for the original text (Appendix 21.3). The list was used in scoring the amount of information contained in subjects' recall protocols. A strict scoring criterion was adopted such that a subject was credited with recalling a proposition only if it or a close paraphrase of it was explicitly present in the protocol. Some consideration was made, however, for scoring linguistic differences such as explicit existence of pronouns in English versus their ellipsis in Japanese (Hinds, 1982; Kuno, 1978). For example, when a proposition in a Japanese subject's recall did not explicitly contain a pronoun which should be included in the English counterpart, it was given a credit only if the referent meaning was clearly understood, judging from the discoursal context of the recalled text.

Second, the text was analyzed in terms of the causal structure, using procedures recommended by Trabasso, Secco, and van den Broek (1984). The text's causal structure was derived by parsing it into individual states (or clauses), then determining the causal relations between those states by using the "necessity in the circumstances" criterion and mapping the states and connections into a network representation (Appendix 21.4).[5] For example, the first sentence of the story (*It was raining when Yoshiko finished work and came out, so she decided to ride the bus home instead of walking.*)

can be analyzed into five causal units: 1) *It was raining;* 2) *Yoshiko finished work;* 3) *Yoshiko came out;* 4) *Yoshiko decided to ride the bus home;* 5) *Yoshiko decided not to walk.* That Yoshiko was finished working enabled her to come outside, which in turn enabled her to perceive it was raining. If she had not finished work, she would not have come out and would not have perceived it raining. Yoshiko's decision to take a bus home was motivated by her perception of the rain. If it had not been raining, she might not have decided to take a bus home. Her perception of the rain also psychologically motivated her to decide not to walk home, and so on. The obtained causal network of the story is shown in Figure 21.1. Since English-as-L1 research has shown the effects of the links and chain of a causal network on comprehension and recall of narrative text, the causal analysis of this text was also used in scoring the subjects' recalls. More specifically, the subjects' recalls were analyzed in terms of the number of causal states, connecting the text's opening to its outcome, and in terms of links between the causal states.

For the TOL data, each subject's recorded TOL productions were transcribed. Relative frequencies of types of talking in the TOL data were calculated for eight categories: 1) predictions; 2) questions; 3) comments on structure; 4) comments on own behavior; 5) confirmation of predictions; 6) references to antecedent information; 7) inferences; and 8) general knowledge and associations. Table 21.1 shows the categories and some examples from the TOL productions. Each TOL production was analyzed by using a clause as a unit. One subject's TOL protocols produced during reading the story are shown as an example in Appendix 21.5.

Inter-rater reliability for scoring recall data for the idea units (propositions and causal states and links) and for scoring TOL productions for the categories was ninety-two to ninety-nine percent. All discrepancies were solved through discussion. Group means were obtained for the proportions of categories for TOL productions and for the number of propositions, causal states, and causal links for recall protocols. These means were statistically compared between groups (*t*-test; repeated measure for the first reading—second reading comparison within the L2 group). The TOL productions were also qualitatively analyzed.

FIGURE 21.1 Causal Network of *Yoshiko and the Bus*

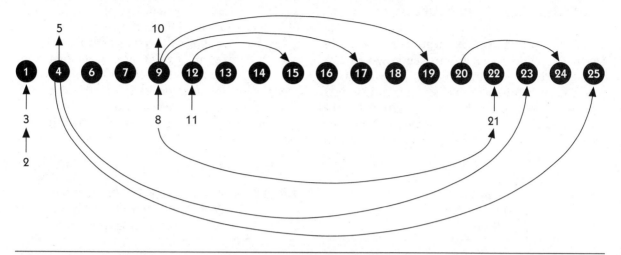

(The numbers represent the *n* causal states in the story. Lines represent causal links between states, with the arrow representing the direction of the link. The numbers circled represent causal states on the causal chain.)

TABLE 21.1 Examples of Categories of TOL Protocols

Predictions	"Maybe she is gonna miss the bus." (A2) "She'll miss the bus." (J1)
Questions	"Someone wasn't there? Or there was no one there?" (A3) "What kind of vending machine was there?" (J1)
Comments on structure	"That was the end, I guess." (A3) "Since the title is 'Yoshiko and the Bus,' maybe . . ." (J3)
Comments on own behavior	"Trying to get change, that's all I know." (A5) "I am imagining relieved expressions on her face." (J5)
Confirmation of predictions	"Oh, I was right." (A2) "Oh, I was wrong." (J2)
References to antecedent information	"She saw it and she got the change by putting a dollar in." (A1) "When she went to the bus stop, there were other people waiting there. So she asked them." (J4)
Inferences	"And maybe she can get some pop there." (A4) "Yoshiko is in trouble." (J3)
General knowledge and associations	"Very, very interesting." (A5) "Sometimes you find a change machine but it's broken." (J5)

RESULTS AND DISCUSSION

TOL Productions: Quantitative Data

The total raw frequency of categories for each subject had a wide range: from twenty-two to 115 within the L1 group, thirty-nine to fifty-eight within the L2 group for the first reading, and twenty-one to eighty-eight within the L2 group for the second reading. Table 21.2 shows the total raw frequency for each category per group. The raw frequencies were transformed into relative frequencies for each subject and then for each group. Table 21.3 shows the summary of the proportion of each category in TOL productions.

Table 21.4 shows the results of statistical comparison between the two groups. In the first reading, the differences between the L1 and the L2 groups were found to be statistically significant in three categories: comments on own behavior ($p <$ .03), inferences ($p <$ .006), general knowledge and associations ($p <$ .02). No significant differences

TABLE 21.2   Total Raw Frequency for Each Category in TOL Production for Each Group

Category/Group	L1	L2(1st)	L2(2nd)
Predictions	32	37	7
Questions	16	12	6
Comments on structure	6	10	8
Comments on own behavior	3	28	40
Confirmation of predictions	5	6	0
References to antecedent information	75	99	95
Inferences	73	46	31
General knowledge and associations	46	1	18
Total	256	239	204

TABLE 21.3   Proportion of TOL Productions in Each Category for Each Group (Means and Standard Deviations)

Category/Group	L1	L2 (1st)	L2 (2nd)
Predictions	.15 (.07)	.15 (.15)	.04 (.08)
Questions	.06 (.05)	.05 (.03)	.01 (.03)
Comments on structure	.01 (.02)	.04 (.04)	.01 (.03)
Comments on own behavior	.01 (.01)	.11 (.08)	.23 (.36)
Confirmation	.03 (.03)	.02 (.03)	.00 (.00)
References to antecedent information	.27 (.11)	.43 (.13)	.50 (.37)
Inferences	.30 (.09)	.19 (.09)	.13 (.09)
General knowledge and associations	.18 (.09)	.00 (.01)	.06 (.09)

TABLE 21.4   Results of Tests on Proportion of TOL Productions for Each Group (Two-Tailed)

Comparison	L1 vs. L2 (1st)		L2 (1st) vs. L2 (2nd)		L1 vs. L2 (2nd)	
	t	p	t	p	t	p
Predictions	.169	.8739	2.535	.0643	4.673	.0095*
Questions	.423	.6938	5.031	.0073*	1.745	.1559
Comments on structure	.202	.1135	.668	.5405	1.043	.356
Comments on own behavior	3.489	.0251*	.762	.4887	1.389	.2371
Confirmation of predictions	.288	.7878	2.067	.1076	2.162	.0967
References to antecedent information	1.923	.1268	.557	.6071	1.143	.317
Inferences	5.511	.0053*	1.125	.3236	3.29	.0302*
General knowledge and associations	4.222	.0135*	1.632	.1781	1.734	.1579

* $p < .05$

appeared in any other category. The proportion of comments on behavior was significantly higher in the L2 group than in the L1, whereas the proportions of inferences and general knowledge and associations were significantly higher in the L1 group than in the L2 group. With a repeated measures comparison between the first and second reading by the L2 group there was a significant difference only for questions: a higher proportion in the first reading than in the second ($p \leq .008$). When comparing the second reading by the L2 group and the first reading by the L1 group, significant differences were found in predictions ($p \leq .01$) and inferences ($p \leq .04$). Both of these categories were proportionally larger in the L1 group than in the L2 group's second reading. From the first to second reading by the L2 group, confirmation of predictions decreased in proportion as well as predictions, but they did not lead to any significant statistical differences.

In the first reading, the L1 readers reported inferences and elaborations and used general knowledge and associations proportionally more frequently than the L2 readers. The L2 readers, on the other hand, stated proportionally more comments on their own behaviors than the L1 readers. This result seems to indicate that the L1 readers attended more than the L2 readers to filling gaps between pieces of information given in the text for reconstructing cognitive schema. L1 readers seemed more aware of making connections between the information newly coming from the text and their already acquired general knowledge based on life experiences. On the other hand, the L2 readers seem to have attended to what they were doing in the reading comprehension task.

In the second reading, the L2 readers had proportionally fewer questions than in their first reading and proportionally fewer predictions than the L1 readers. This result is hardly surprising. As clearly seen in their recall data later, these readers understood and comprehended the story through the first reading; therefore, few questions remained when they read the story for the second time. The fact that the L2 readers in the second reading did not produce proportionally as many inferences as the L1 readers might be due to the task requirement of recalling the text as closely to the original as possible, as well as their high level of comprehension of the story from the first reading

TOL Productions: Qualitative Data

The quantitative data tell something about the TOL productions provided by these readers, but the data cannot relate much about their characteristics. Generally speaking, the characteristics of the TOL productions differed between the L1 and L2 groups (depending on category). Both groups made similar predictions at similar points in the course of the story (see Appendix 21.1). Both groups predicted at the third sentence that the protagonist would miss the bus; at the fourth sentence, they wondered whether the people at the bus stop would be able to help Yoshiko with change; at the sixth sentence, they supposed that Yoshiko would go to the place where she could get change; at the ninth sentence, they saw Yoshiko would barely catch the bus. These predictions are specific and directly related to the causal structure of the story. Some differences were observed at the first and seventh sentences. At the first sentence, three L2 readers stated a vague prediction that something was going to happen to Yoshiko; at the seventh sentence, three L1 readers made predictions about the condition of the building ("being locked") and the vending machine ("being broken," "being a vending machine but not a change machine"). At these positions, no one from the other group made such predictions.

Content questions, such as how she would get change, what she would do next, and whether or not she was wet, were observed in both L1 and L2 groups, but content questions were made far more often in the L1 group. However, questions related to meaning of specific vocabulary and sentences were found only in the L2 group.

Comments on their own behaviors made by the L2 readers seem to reflect the heavy attention paid to language mechanics; these comments were almost exclusively about the degree of understanding vocabulary—*kozeni* (change), *ryoogaeki* (change machine), *jidoohanbaiki* (vending machine), *toochaku* (arrival), *ryookinbako* (farebox)—and phrases—*nurezu-ni* (without getting wet). The data seem to indicate that the L2 readers consciously monitored their recognition and understanding of vocabulary and sentences, although they were mostly successful in deducing the meaning of them. On the other hand, very few comments on their own behaviors were produced by the L1 readers. None of their comments were on language mechanics, suggesting that they automatically processed the linguistic information in the text.

As for inferences, the L1 and L2 groups stated many similar inferences. At the first sentence which introduced the initiative event (it is raining) and the protagonist's goal (taking a bus home), both groups mentioned the protagonist's usual behavior: that Yoshiko would normally walk home. At the point in which a problem is introduced, both groups made psychological inferences concerning the protagonist: at the second sentence and at the fifth, common inferences were that Yoshiko is in trouble. At the same places, some readers in each group inferred the outcome that Yoshiko could not get on the bus without change. Both groups also made inferences about physical distance between objects: the building and the bus stop, Yoshiko's house and her place of work.

Although some inferences about the protagonist's actions and the scene were similar between the L1 and L2 groups, there were some differences in the degree of elaboration. At the sixth and seventh sentences, both groups inferred that Yoshiko would go to the building. However, at the ninth sentence, two L2 readers stated: "The bus was waiting there." "She starts to walk. She sees the bus just stopping at the bus stop"; at this same point, three L1 readers stated inferences: "She waved her hand to the bus driver and has him stop the bus and wait for her." "She has one dollar's worth of change in her hand." "She has to run hard. Now, she starts running!" These inferences made by the L1 readers are very descriptive, though not crucial, concerning what the protagonist might be doing and how she might look in the scene.

Use of general knowledge and associations were virtually not observed in the L2 readers'

TOL productions, while in those by the L1 readers this category was rather rich. Many of them were about the readers' evaluation of the protagonist's attempts and their outcomes. At the fourth sentence, two L1 readers stated a judgment (good) about the protagonist's request for change. At the point where a possible solution to the problem is introduced, two other L1 readers judged the protagonist as being "in luck." Where a goal is achieved at the eighth sentence (getting change) and at the tenth sentence (riding the bus home), four L1 readers stated "lucky" and "good." Other statements in this category produced by the L1 readers indicate use of their world knowledge about the bus system and change machines: "Bus schedules are irregular." "It seems that American buses are a 'one-man' (without conductor) system like Japanese buses." "Sometimes you have a change machine, but it is broken." Responses indicate reactions from personal experience ("I'm sorry for her." "I hope she has an umbrella." "I hope the office building is close.") and a saying or moral ("Bad things will happen, one after another." "You should have some change ready all the time [when riding a bus]").

In sum, some quantitative and qualitative differences were found between the TOL productions given by the L2 readers and those given by the L1 readers. Comparisons of each category in TOL protocols indicate that the L2 readers more frequently made comments on their own behaviors than L1 readers, and that these comments were about their self-monitoring of vocabulary and sentence comprehension. The L1 readers more frequently made inferences and elaborated from their general knowledge. Together with use of general knowledge and associations, some of the predictions and inferences made by the L1 readers seemed to reflect more detailed schematization and

TABLE 21.5 **Number of Propositions Recalled for Each Group**

Group	L1		L2 (1st)		L2 (2nd)	
Means (SD)	38.3 (8.6)		35.4 (7.4)		46.6 (9.1)	

Subgroup	L1 TOL	Control	L2 (1st) TOL	Control	L2 (2nd) TOL	Control
Means (SD)	36.4 (9.3)	40.8 (8.2)	35.6 (5.6)	35.2 (9.6)	42.4 (9.3)	50.8 (7.4)

attention to conceptualization of the story than in the case of their L2 counterparts.

Recall: Propositional Analyses

Table 21.5 shows the number of propositions recalled by each group. Table 21.6 displays the results of comparisons between groups. In the first reading, no significant differences were found in amount of propositions recalled between the L1 group and the L2 group. No differences were found between the TOL and Control (sub)groups within each language. In the second reading, the L2 group produced significantly better recall, not only than their first reading ($p \leq .003$), but also than the first reading of the L1 group ($p \leq .007$). In the second reading, those L2 readers in the Control (sub)group did significantly better in recall than the TOL (sub)group ($p \leq .006$).

Recall: Causal Structure Analyses

In order to examine the nature of information recalled from the story, the number of causal states, causal links, and states on the causal chain recalled were compared between subject groups. Table 21.7 shows the summary data of the number of causal units recalled by each. Table 21.8 shows the results of statistical comparisons between groups. No significant differences were found between the L1 and L2 groups for the first reading. A similar pattern of differences was found within group comparisons. From the first to the second reading, the L2 group significantly improved their recall of causal states ($p < .003$); however, they did not outperform the first reading of the L1 group.

Tables 21.9 and 21.10 show the summary data of the number of causal states on the causal chain in recalls. The results of the statistical comparisons were very similar to those for the number of causal units recalled. No significant differences were found between the L1 and L2 groups for the first reading; the L2 group significantly improved in recall for the second reading ($p < .02$) but did not outperform the L1 group.

Finally, the subjects' recalls were analyzed in terms of the number of causal links between statements. Tables 21.11 and 21.12 show the summary data of the number of causal links recalled by each group. The results of the comparisons between groups indicate that in the first reading, significant differences existed between the L1 group and the L2 group: the L1 group recalled a significantly greater number of causal links than the L2 group ($p < .04$). The rest of the results were very similar to those for the number of causal states.

Thus, these recall data indicate that when reading the story for the first time, the L2 readers comprehended and recalled as many idea units (propositions and causal states) as the L1 readers. Considering the TOL production data discussed above, it seems that although these L2 readers

TABLE 21.6 Results of t-Tests on Number of Propositions Recalled for Each Group (Two-Tailed)

Comparison	t	p
L1 vs. L2 (1st)	.442	.6705
L1 vs. L2 (2nd)	-3.685	.0062*
L2 (1st) vs. L2 (2nd)	-4.311	.002*
L1 within: TOL vs. Control	-1.269	.2941
L2 (1st) within: TOL vs. Control	.164	.8778
L2 (2nd) within: TOL vs. Control	-5.468	.0054

* $p < .05$

TABLE 21.7 Number of Causal Units Recalled for Each Group

Group	L1		L2 (1st)		L2 (2nd)	
Means (SD)	19.1 (2.5)		15.8 (3.1)		20.9 (3.2)	

Subgroup	L1 TOL	Control	L2 (1st) TOL	Control	L2 (2nd) TOL	Control
Means (SD)	18.8 (3.1)	19.5 (1.7)	16.2 (2.6)	15.4 (3.8)	19.2 (3.4)	22.6 (2.1)

TABLE 21.8 Results of *t*-Tests on Number of Causal Units Recalled for Each Group (Two-Tailed)

Comparison	*t*	*p*
L1 vs. L2 (1st)	2.011	.0791
L1 vs. L2 (2nd)	-2.021	.0779
L2 (1st) vs. L2 (2nd)	-4.135	.0025*
L1 within: TOL vs. Control	-.552	.6376
L2 (1st) within: TOL vs. Control	1.372	.242
L2 (2nd) within: TOL vs. Control	-4.185	.0139

* $p < .05$

TABLE 21.10 Results of *t*-Tests on Number of Causal States on the Causal Chain Recalled for Each Group (Two-Tailed)

Comparison	*t*	*p*
L1 vs. L2 (1st)	1.796	.1102
L1 vs. L2 (2nd)	-.725	.4888
L2 (1st) vs. L2 (2nd)	-2.862	.0187*
L1 within: TOL vs. Control	-.48	.6638
L2 (1st) within: TOL vs. Control	.667	.5415
L2 (2nd) within: TOL vs. Control	-3.586	.0231

* $p < .05$

TABLE 21.9 Number of Causal States on the Causal Chain Recalled for Each Group

Group	L1		L2 (1st)		L2 (2nd)	
Means (SD)	14.6 (1.7)		12.4 (2.4)		15.1 (2.4)	

Subgroup	L1 TOL	Control	L2 (1st) TOL	Control	L2 (2nd) TOL	Control
Means (SD)	14.4 (2.2)	14.8 (1.0)	12.8 (1.9)	12.0 (2.9)	13.6 (2.4)	16.6 (1.3)

TABLE 21.11 Number of Causal Links Recalled for Each Group

Group	L1		L2 (1st)		L2 (2nd)	
Means (SD)	22.4 (3.6)		17.3 (4.0)		24.7 (5.1)	

Subgroup	L1 TOL	Control	L2 (1st) TOL	Control	L2 (2nd) TOL	Control
Means (SD)	21.6 (4.0)	23.5 (3.3)	18.2 (3.1)	16.4 (4.9)	22.4 (5.7)	27.0 (3.7)

paid more conscious attention to the lower-level processes and were limited in the degree of elaborative schematization during reading compared with the L1 readers, the L2 readers successfully constructed a mental representation by encoding as much information from the original text as that constructed by the L1 readers. We cannot predict how much information from the text they would recall based on what they reported during reading and vice versa. However, the comparison of the number of causal links recalled suggests that the L2 readers' mental representation of the text was dif-ferent from that held by the L1 readers in terms of the structure: the L2 readers' representation of the text contained fewer causal links between events and states than that of the L1 readers. In other words, the L1 readers' representation might be more causally coherent than that of the L2 readers, possibly due to their facile use of linguistic information in the text and general background knowledge during mapping antecedent-consequence relations between statements for schematization.

From the first reading to the second, the L2 readers significantly improved their recall of the idea units. The L2 readers in the second reading outperformed the L1 readers in terms of recall of propositions, but not in terms of recall of causal states. This result seems to indicate that the L2 readers who read the second time learned and recalled more pieces of information, both detailed and causally important, than when they read for the first time, but that learning effects were stronger for detailed information not crucial to the causal structure of the story's content.

The data on the TOL-Control group comparisons indicate that the TOL task neither distracted nor impeded either L1 or L2 readers' comprehension during the first reading. However, during the second reading by the L2 readers, the Control group improved their recall more than the TOL group. The data seem to imply at least some alteration of the comprehension processes in the TOL readers. When reading the same story for the second time, the L2 readers who did not report their thoughts during reading might have been attending to the reading task more effectively for the purpose of recall than the L2 readers who reported. On the other hand, though statistically not significant, the initial advantage of the L2 readers who read with the TOL method over the L2 readers who did not might suggest that those who were verbalizing their thoughts were comprehending the text differently, possibly more actively engaged in the whole "problem solving" processes, from those who were just silently reading.[6]

CONCLUSIONS

Because the present study explores the processes of L2 story comprehension, its results should be treated as preliminary in nature. Some possibly important variables, such as the subjects' native language verbal skills, intelligence, and (cultural) personality factors, were beyond the control of the investigation. Despite these limitations, the data obtained here provide unique and valuable information about the narrative comprehension processes of these L1 and L2 readers and for L2 text comprehension research in the future.

First, the present data on the content of the readers' short-term working memory during reading (obtained by the TOL method) seem to support the previous research finding that L2 readers

TABLE 21.12 Results of *t*-Tests on Number of Causal Links Recalled for Each Group (Two-Tailed)

Comparison	t	p
L1 vs. L2 (1st)	2.552	.0341*
L1 vs. L2 (2nd)	-1.724	.123
L2 (1st) vs. L2 (2nd)	-4.686	.0011*
L1 within: TOL vs. Control	-.598	.3994
L2 (1st) within: TOL vs. Control	1.45	.2205
L2 (2nd) within: TOL vs. Control	-2.875	.0452

* $p < .05$

whose command of the language is limited pay more attention to vocabulary and grammar than do L1 readers, whose behavior is automatic in such lower-level processes. They attend more to the meaning of the text (Bernhardt, 1983a; McLeod & McLaughlin, 1986).

However, in most cases these L2 readers were successfully figuring out the meaning of unfamiliar vocabulary and sentences by utilizing available contextual information. Data seem to indicate that these L2 readers apparently utilized a familiar schema (getting on a bus) and activated relevant information (e.g., what might happen, what might be involved) in the schema, and that, while carefully self-monitoring understanding of linguistic information from the text, they were sensitive to the constraints on the initial representation of the story. As a result, most of the L2 readers were successful in the process of deducing vocabulary. This finding supports the representation of meaning rather than linguistic units in memory, and seems to account for the effects of an activated script or schema on vocabulary and syntax recognition (Adams, 1982; Lee, 1987).

The brevity of the text and the way it was presented possibly influenced the readers' behaviors in some way. Presenting such a short text sentence by sentence possibly encouraged the readers to attend to the conceptualization and schematization of the content of the text. Further research is needed to examine the relationship between the readers' allocation of conscious attention during reading and their language competence with more natural reading settings and to explore the relationship between a text's comprehensibility and how readers process it, by closely examining the effects of the text's topic, structural organization, cohesive devices, vocabulary, and syntactic complexity.

Second, the study shows that use of both on-line and off-line measures helps enhance our understanding of the nature of comprehension processes. The TOL and recall data are not equivalent, but complementary, in providing information on how readers process information during encoding into a mental representation and then retrieving it from memory. However, from the comparison between those who read with the TOL method and those who read without it, we can speculate that there are possible effects of using the method (impeding and/or aiding comprehension). Future research should not only examine the effects of concurrent introspection on comprehension by utilizing data from a group who read without this secondary task as baseline, but also conduct other on-line measures such as eye movement and reading rate to gather convergent evidence for concurrent introspection.

Third, an analysis of recall and its interpretation requires caution and theoretical motivation. The present study, applying both propositional and causal analysis (Trabasso & van den Broek, 1985; Trabasso, Secco, & van den Broek, 1984), demonstrates that an individual's comprehension is dependent on the way the recall of text is scored. The data suggest that we must examine not only how much information is remembered, but also how much of what kind of information is remembered and what kind of information is further created from the repeated reading. As for the generalizability of the causal model to the L2 comprehension, more research with a variety of texts and populations is needed. The model might serve as a tool for a closer analysis of comprehension and recall, especially for the examination of the interaction between linguistic and causal-world knowledge. It would be interesting to examine the readers' recall, not only mapping it onto the original text, but also as it is. A causal analysis of the subjects' recall might be able to better illustrate their memory representation of text which contains both information from the original text and information which reflects elaborations and distortions.

Fourth, the present findings help us describe in part the processes of L2 narrative comprehension, but we cannot extrapolate to comprehension of expository texts except for lower-level processes such as decoding. Some evidence exists from English-as-L1 research that readers employ different strategies between narrative and expository texts. The reader of a story adopts a *prospective* orientation, looking ahead, trying to anticipate where the story is going. In contrast, the reader of an essay is *retrospective,* trying to relate each new element in the essay to earlier elements with general expectation about the overall structure of the argument (Olson, Duffy, & Mack, 1984). L2 reading literature has no data on this issue. With lack of well-developed models of representation of expository texts, research is necessary to investigate how L2 readers process expository texts, by carefully considering factors such as readers' knowledge of the content area and the relationship between logical and semantic relations in the L2 text and the way the readers reason in their native language.

Although the study reported in this paper is not instructional, some implications for classroom application can be derived from it. First, the data suggest that the reader's involvement in the reading task, especially at the acquisition stage, is crucial for the construction of text representations in memory and later recall. Learners should be encouraged to conceptualize the content of the text and to monitor their own comprehension processes. It is important to select texts which are interesting for the learners and to provide time and tasks which provide maximal opportunity for the learners to become cognitively active in conceptualizing the content of the text. Useful activities include reading a text for later recall in their native language and practicing specific strategies for vocabulary and syntax recognition and inference-making.

Second, the selection of reading materials should consider the learners' background knowledge, both linguistic and nonlinguistic. The study suggests that if the content of the text is familiar, readers have a better chance to figure out unfamiliar vocabulary and syntax in the text. Familiarity with content will provide opportunity for the students to learn vocabulary and syntax in the text itself. For example, texts describing events and situations which are commonly experienced in the students' own culture can be useful reading material.

Third, teachers may find it useful to assess student comprehension with such tools as the TOL and free recall methods. Each student's verbal report might tell the teacher how the individual approaches the reading comprehension task and what aspects of the particular text seem to cause comprehension difficulties. Similarly, each student's recall protocol might indicate common linguistic and conceptual difficulties experienced through the reading or those which are specific to the individual. Thus, teachers can gain insights into the nature of their students' comprehension and therefore can meet their students' needs more effectively.

NOTES

1 This research was supported in part by the Center for Research on Learning, Perception, and Cognition at the University of Minnesota. I am grateful to professors Dale L. Lange, Paul W. van den Broek, and Charles R. Fletcher of the University of Minnesota for their insightful comments on an earlier version of the manuscript. I wish to express thanks to the anonymous reviewers for the valuable suggestions. Parts of this work were presented at the 1989 MIFLC annual meeting, Clemson, South Carolina.

2 See, for example, Steffensen, Joag-Dev, and Anderson (1977); Johnson (1982); and Carrell (1987) for the effects of knowledge of culture-specific content on comprehension and recall. See, for example, Walters and Wolf (1986) and Carrell (1987) for the effects of story grammar.

3 For a collection of theoretical and empirical discussions on use of introspection in second language research, see Faerch and Kasper (1987).

4 Although it seems to be a "must" among English-as-L1 researchers to obtain the baseline data from a control group who read texts without the TOL task, most studies which have attempted to examine L2 learners' comprehension and learning strategies have not done so. Considering the limited processing capacity of the human mind, I felt that L2 research should also empirically look into the effects of the TOL task which competes against the primary task for short-term working memory resources during comprehension.

5 Van den Broek personally communicated that the causal model can be used to analyze a variety of texts, from a short story to a novel, and possibly other kinds of things which are narrative in nature (e.g., television stories, real-life events). Units of analysis can vary depending upon the researcher's interests (e.g., propositions, clauses, chapters, real-life events).

6 There is some evidence in comprehension research in English-as-L1 that moderate effort in initial processing information (e.g., making connections between statements) at the acquisition stage benefits the retention and later recall of the information (e.g., Myers, Shinjo & Duffy, 1987).

APPENDIX 21.1 The Test Text: *Yoshiko and the Bus* (English Translation)

T.   *Yoshiko and the Bus*
S1. It was raining when Yoshiko finished work and came out, so she decided to ride the bus home instead of walking.
S2. On the way to the bus stop she checked her purse and realized that she didn't have any change.
S3. The bus wasn't due to come for ten minutes so she thought she'd have a chance to get change for a dollar and still catch the bus.
S4. There were a few other people waiting for the bus so she asked them for change.
S5. They all looked in their pockets and purses but no one had change.
S6. One of the women at the bus stop told Yoshiko that there was a change machine in the office building on the corner that she could use.
S7. Yoshiko went into the building and saw the vending machine area right inside the lobby.
S8. She put a dollar in and got change from the machine.
S9. The bus was pulling up just as she walked out of the building.
S10. Yoshiko got on the bus and dropped two quarters and a dime into the fare-box and rode home dry.

APPENDIX 21.2 The Way in Which the Sentences of the Story Were Presented to Each Subject

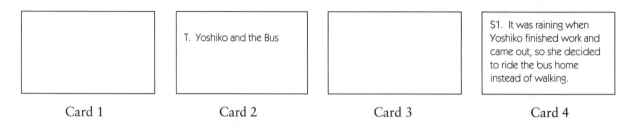

	T. Yoshiko and the Bus		S1. It was raining when Yoshiko finished work and came out, so she decided to ride the bus home instead of walking.
Card 1	Card 2	Card 3	Card 4

APPENDIX 21.3 Propositional Analysis of the Text (English Translation)

P1 (Is Raining)
P2 (Time P1 P4)
P3 (Leave Yoshiko Work)
P4 (Cause P2 P6)
PS (Decide Yoshiko P7)
P6 (Ride-home Yoshiko Bus)
P7 (Instead-of P6 P8)
P8 (Walk Yoshiko)
P9 (During P10 P11)
P10 (Go-to Yoshiko Bus-stop)
P11 (Check Yoshiko Purse)
P12 (Possess Yoshiko Change)
P13 (Realize Yoshiko P14)
P14 (NEG P15)
P15 (Possess Yoshiko Change)
P16 (NEG P17)
P17 (Due Bus)
P18 (Duration P16 Minutes)
P19 (Quantity Minutes Ten)
P20 (Cause P18 P21)
P21 (Think Yoshiko P22)
P22 (Possess Yoshiko P23)
P23 (Chance-to Yoshiko P26)
P24 (Get Yoshiko Change)
P25 (For Change Dollar)
P26 (Set-members P24 P27)
P27 (Still P28)
P28 (Catch Yoshiko Bus)
P29 (Exist People)
P30 (Quantity People Few)
P31 (MOD People Other)
P32 (Wait-for People Bus)
P33 (Cause P32 P34)
P34 (Ask-for Yoshiko People Change)

P35 (Quantity People Change)
P36 (Look-in People P37)
P37 (Set-members Pockets Purses)
P38 (But P36 P39)
P39 (NEG P40)
P40 (Possess People Change)
P41 (Quantity Woman One)
P42 (LOC Woman At-bus-stop)
P43 (Tell Woman Yoshiko P44)
P44 (Exist Change-machine Building)
P45 (LOC Change-machine Building)
P46 (MOD Building Office)
P47 (LOC Building On-corner)
P48 (Able Yoshiko P49)
P49 (Use Yoshiko Change-machine)
P50 (Enter Yoshiko Building)
P51 (See Yoshiko Area)
P52 (MOD Area Vending-machine)
P53 (LOC Area Inside-lobby)
P54 (Put-in Yoshiko Dollar)
P55 (Get Yoshiko Change)
P56 (From P55 Machine)
P57 (Pull-up Bus)
P58 (Time P57 P59)
P59 (Leave Yoshiko Building)
P60 (Get-on Yoshiko Bus)
P61 (Drop Yoshiko P63)
P62 (Quantity Quarter One)
P63 (Set-Members Quarter Dime)
P64 (Quantity Dime One)
P65 (Into P61 Fare-box)
P66 (Ride Yoshiko Home)
P67 (MOD P66 Dry)

APPENDIX 21.4 Causal Analysis of the Text (English Translation)

1. It was raining.
2. Yoshiko finished work.
3. Yoshiko came out.
4. Yoshiko decided to ride the bus home.
5. Yoshiko decided not to walk.
6. On the way to the bus stop Yoshiko checked her purse.
7. Yoshiko realized that she didn't have any change.
8. The bus wasn't due to come for ten minutes.
9. Yoshiko thought she'd have a chance to get change for a dollar.
10. Yoshiko thought she could still catch the bus.
11. There were a few other people waiting for the bus.
12. Yoshiko asked them for change.
13. People all looked in their pockets and purses.
14. No one had change.
15. One of the women at the bus stop told Yoshiko something.
16. There was a change machine in the office building on the corner that she could use.
17. Yoshiko went into the building.
18. Yoshiko saw the vending machine area right inside the lobby.
19. Yoshiko put a dollar in.
20. Yoshiko got change from the machine.
21. The bus was pulling up.
22. Yoshiko walked out of the building.
23. Yoshiko got on the bus.
24. Yoshiko dropped two quarters and a dime into the fare-box.
25. Yoshiko rode home dry.

APPENDIX 21.5 An Example of TOL Production by an L2 Reader

T. This is going to be a story about Yoshiko and a bus.

S1. So the story is starting out with her taking . . . her taking the bus because it was raining when she left her job. And I'm not sure exactly what's going to happen on the bus, but I'm sure it's gonna be some interesting sort of . . . predicament, maybe.

S2. I'm not ex . . . on the way to the bus . . . I think she realized that she didn't have it, any change. But I'm not sure about that, but we'll see.

S3. Since there's gonna be a few more minutes to the bus, she went to get a dollar changed, I think. And I . . . at this time I'm kind of thinking that maybe she is gonna miss the bus. I'm not sure, though.

S4. She asked everybody else, who was waiting at the bus stop. There was quite a few people. And . . . my feelings are that they proba-

bly won't be able to help her, but we'll see.

S5. I was right. She . . . nobody had any change. So, now she's gonna have to look elsewhere.

S6. One of the girls at the bus stop suggested that Yoshiko go, I think, to some building, office building, and they had maybe a change machine or something. I'm not sure which . . . there.

S7. She went into the building in the lobby, entrance, maybe. Um . . . there was some . . . maybe a parking machine or something like that sitting there.

S8. She saw it and she got the change by putting a dollar in.

S9. Just as she was coming out of the building, the bus had come. And I still wonder if she's going to make it. And if she does, it will be just barely.

S10. So she got home, just fine. And that's it.

DISCUSSION QUESTIONS

1. Why should we expect advanced L2 learners to devote more attention to the "bottom-up" aspects of processing texts in the L2 than L1 users might? Why would it be more difficult for L2 learners than for L1 speakers to access appropriate "top-down" formal schemata or knowledge structures? What evidence from Horiba's study, in fact, supports both these expectations? Also, why would L1 users be more apt to evaluate, moralize, or express empathy for Yoshiko?

2. It is observed that L2 subjects tended to make more predictions and ask more questions on the first think-aloud protocol than on the second. How can this contrast be explained?

3. The English translation of the story says that "Yoshiko decided to ride the bus home instead of walking," yet both L1 and L2 readers inferred that she usually walks home. How do they know this? In other words, how is this inference grounded in the story?

4. How do we account for the fact that the non-natives were able to recall essentially all of the salient propositional elements of the story in spite of the fact that they were also more apt to comment on vocabulary and grammar than the natives? Also, it is noted that the think-aloud L2 users seemed to have a slight edge in making sense of the story in Japanese. What reasons are given, and how do they relate to the suggestions for teaching that Horiba offers at the end?

CHAPTER 22

Formal and Content Schemata Activation in L2 Viewing Comprehension

Ian Tudor and Richard Tuffs

EDITOR'S INTRODUCTION

With the increasing availability of video materials for both language and content teaching, the research in this chapter by Tudor and Tuffs will undoubtedly be welcomed by many teachers. The authors provide solid evidence that instruction can help L2 consumers of video (accompanied by aural discourse in the L2) to prepare both for the content and the formal structure of the video presentation. Their work will help us to better understand such integrative video-literacy tasks. The video used in the research reported here was of an expository, documentary type concerning the possibility of developing a system of private roads in Britain alongside the present government-controlled national network. The consumers for this material were Belgian students at the university level studying business administration. Three groups of subjects were distinguished. One group received preparation aimed at helping them to build up an appropriate formal schema for the problem-solving type of discussion they would encounter, on the merits and drawbacks of a privatized road system. A second group was given a specific content schema informing them in advance about facts they would encounter in the video, e.g., names of people, places, and institutions. A third group, designated as a control group, received no special preparation at all prior to viewing the video. Comprehension was measured by questions immediately after viewing the video and a week later. Also, subjects in all three groups were asked to write a summary after viewing. Interestingly, the formal schema group benefited most from the preparation, but the content schema group also enjoyed a significant advantage over the control group. In brief, it appears that preview-scaffolding activities of both types help but that the special kind of formal schema provided by the researchers in this study worked better than merely forewarning subjects about certain facts that would appear in the video. The upshot is that "appropriate previewing activities" can help learners "gain access to authentic video materials." In this respect, visual literacy is a great deal like textual literacy. Moreover, there is little doubt that these distinct kinds of literacy can support each other in classroom contexts of all sorts.

Schema theory (Rumelhart, 1980) posits that the manner in which language users process textual material is dependent not only on the information present in the target material but also on the relevant mental structures or schemata which they bring with them to the processing of this material. Adams and Collins (1979: 3), writing within the context of first language (L1) reading comprehension, describe the objectives of schema theory in the following terms:

> The goal of schema theory is to specify the interface between the reader and the text—to specify how the reader's knowledge interacts with and shapes the information on the page and to specify how that knowledge must be organized to support the interaction.

This approach to the study of language comprehension has, over the last decade, provided a powerful stimulus to the analysis of the process of comprehension in second language (L2) learners, in terms of both reading (Barnitz, 1986; Carrell, 1983a; Carrell & Eisterhold, 1983) and listening (Kasper, 1984; Markham & Latham, 1987) comprehension. Very little work, however, has been conducted in the area of viewing comprehension, namely the comprehension of film or video material involving the combination of visual and verbal input. Given the increasing role played by video materials, both in the L2 classroom and in the wider domain of education and training (instructional video cassettes, interactive video, satellite broadcasting), not to mention the potentially significant role of recreational films and television as a means of cultural assimilation and a source of "comprehensible input" (Krashen, 1982) for learners of English as a Second Language (ESL) in North America and the United Kingdom, this is clearly an omission.

In the light of these considerations, at least two main lines of research emerge. The first, and in logical terms the more basic, relates to the process of viewing comprehension in an L2. Under this heading research is clearly called for to determine the extent to which viewing comprehension may be seen as a skill in its own right, separate from listening comprehension—in other words, the way in which the visual element in television or film material interacts with information provided by the verbal element (cf. Boeckmann, Nessmann,

& Petermandl, 1988 and Pezdek, 1986 for instances of L1 studies in this area). In addition, it is also of interest to examine the cultural aspect of viewing comprehension, in terms of the role of familiarity with culture-specific knowledge or beliefs (cf. Tuffs & Tudor 1990) or with specific genres such as news, game shows, and soap operas and discourse formats such as those present in current affairs broadcasts and documentaries. In other words, there is ample scope for the replication, within the domain of viewing comprehension, of studies such as those of Carrell (Chapter 19; 1985), Johnson (1981), and Steffensen (1986) conducted in the field of L2 reading comprehension. The second line of research, and that in which the present article is situated, relates to the possibility of enhancing L2 learners' viewing comprehension by means of appropriate priming techniques, this having strong links with the growing body of research into pre-reading and reader priming in L2 reading instruction.

A number of studies have indicated that L2 learners' prior knowledge of the content (Alderson & Urquhart, 1983; Aron, 1986; Johnson, 1981; Markham & Latham, 1987; Nunan, 1985; Steffensen, 1986) or rhetorical structure (Carrell, Chapter 19; 1984) of textual material in the L2 can have a significant effect on their ability to comprehend and assimilate this material. These findings have, not surprisingly, generated research into strategies for building or activating learners' text-relevant background knowledge as a preparation for text processing. For instance, the explicit pre-teaching of cultural background knowledge (Floyd & Carrell, 1987; Johnson, 1982) or of elements of the rhetorical organization of texts (Carrell, 1985) has been shown to enhance the text comprehension of L2 learners. In a similar vein, studies into the effect of pre-reading activities on text comprehension (Hudson, 1982; Taglieber, Johnson, & Yarbrough, 1988; Tudor, 1990) have illustrated that such activities, if geared appropriately to both learner and text characteristics, may play a valuable role in enhancing L2 learners' comprehension of written material. The present study describes an attempt to apply a similar approach to the enhancement of L2 viewing comprehension. Two forms of pre-viewing were experimented with (cf. Carrell, 1987), one geared to the activation of formal schemata relevant to the rhetorical structure of the target video sequence, and the other geared to the activation of content schemata relevant to the conceptual content of the sequence.

METHOD

Subjects

The subjects (age 21 to 23; N = 108) were ESL learners following English courses as part of a five-year degree program in business administration at the Université Libre de Bruxelles, Belgium. They were in the fourth (n = 55) and fifth (n = 53) years of their program, and had followed English courses for three and four years respectively at the Université Libre (no English courses being given during their first year of study), in addition to an average of four years of English at secondary level. The English courses were an integral part of the subjects' study program, and levels of motivation and attainment were high. Both groups of subjects may safely be considered as advanced learners. Testing was conducted with three class groups in each year, these groups being constituted to be homogeneous in terms of linguistic proficiency on the basis of subjects' end-of-course examination results from their previous year of study.

Video Sequence

The video sequence on which the experimentation was based was an off-air recording (length 8 minutes and 2 seconds; number of words 1,217) from a British weekly television program concentrating on economic and business matters and aimed at an intelligent and well-informed audience. The target sequence deals with possible plans of the British government to set up a network of privately financed roads alongside the existing national network, which in Britain is government controlled. The sequence outline in Figure 22.1 provides a breakdown of the main stages in the development of the topic. It should be noted, however, that the main topic development divisions highlighted in Figure 22.1 were not explicitly signaled in the video sequence itself other than by television production techniques such as scene change, topic shift, or intonation, with subjects having to abstract these thematic divisions from the visual and verbal input themselves. A variety of presentation formats were used in the video sequence, the most frequent being commentary by the reporter on screen; voice-over commentary by the reporter accompanying a topic-relevant scene; interviews with key participants (e.g., representatives of the government and of construction firms). The sequence thus represented a dense and relatively complex body of both verbal and visual information involving frequent changes of scene, speaker, and perspective on the target topic.

Video material from the same source and of a similar level of complexity was frequently used in the classroom with the subjects concerned. Furthermore, the experimental video sequence had been used as an end-of-course viewing comprehension examination with a population of 48 final year students at the end of the first semester of the academic year 1988–89 (the experimentation was conducted in the second semester of the same year), mean scores obtained on a summary writing task (cf. elicitation procedures, below) being 10.6 out of 21 (SD = 2.7). The sequence was thus judged to be of a challenging but acceptable level of difficulty in both linguistic and conceptual terms for the present experimentation.

EXPERIMENTAL TREATMENT

Rationale

The aim of the present experimentation, as mentioned previously, was to study the effects of two types of schemata activation, one formally oriented and the other content-oriented, on the viewing comprehension of a population of ESL learners. The rationale underlying both approaches is the same, namely that activating learners' existing knowledge by providing them with a number of key concepts pertinent to the target text will aid the learners to process the text more meaningfully, and thereby facilitate assimilation and recall of the target material. The difference, of course, lies in the nature of the schemata activated and the way in which these relate to the processing of the target text. *Formal schemata* are knowledge structures relating to the way in which textual information is organized and presented, and help language users

FIGURE 22.1 Topic Development and Presentational Formats of Video Sequence

TOPIC DEVELOPMENT	SPEAKER AND FORMAT	VISUAL ACCOMPANIMENT
Topic statement: Is the creation of a private road network a good idea? Is it feasible?	Commentator: voiceover	Scene of traffic congestion

1. SITUATION

Worsening traffic situation in the U.K. is source of economic problems	Commentator voiceover/conversation between participants in vignette	Vignette: delivery truck arrives late; goods unloaded

2. PROBLEM

Late and slow deliveries cost the economy five billion pounds a year	Commentator: voiceover	Scene of traffic jams
Situation worsening with increase in the number of cars	Businessman: interview	Businessman in his office

3. SOLUTION

Create a private road network to supplement the existing national network	Minister of Transport speaking at a Conservative Party conference	Minister making his speech/audience
Private funding already employed in a few projects	Commentator: voiceover	Scene of Minister at the inauguration of a new motorway bridge
Private sector has been successful in other parts of the economy: why not in privatization of roads	Junior Transport Minister: interview	Minister in studio

4. EVALUATION

Construction companies not enthusiastic about government's plans	Commentator: on screen	Commentator in front of road being constructed
Uncertainty about political will to overcome the practical difficulties	Construction company representative A: on screen	Representative interviewed on motorway being constructed

Problem 1 Size of the Road Building Program

Expanding private investment could reduce state investments, resulting in no overall gain in projects	Commentator: voice over	Scene of road surveyors at work
As last point	Construction company representative A: on screen	Background of motorway construction scene

Problem 2 Competitive Tendering

In a tender system a firm proposing a project could lose the contract to a competitor.	Commentator: voiceover	Scene of engineer preparing plans for a motorway tunnel
This could result in heavy losses for the firm making the original proposal.	Construction company representative B: on screen	Background of bridge construction work

Problem 3 Planning Permission

Local opposition can seriously delay road construction.	Commentator: voiceover/vignette of conversation between local protesters	Scenes of countryside and historic house
Delays in obtaining planning permission could deter private investors.	Commentator: voiceover	Scenes of countryside
Difficulty of giving powers of compulsory acquisition to private firms	Construction company representative C: on screen	Representative in his office

Problem 4 Return on Investment

How to provide a payback to private investors on their investment	Commentator: on screen	Background scene at an historic toll bridge, motorists paying tolls to an official
Political problems of charging tolls on road	Construction company representative B: on screen	Background of bridge construction work
Charging only for new roads will discourage motorists from using them if existing roads remain free.	Commentator reading the text of a statement from the Minister of Transport	Picture of the Minister of Transport plus the text written on screen
Is the government willing to put a charge on existing roads?	Commentator: voiceover	Scene of toll booths outside a motorway tunnel
The government does not intend to charge for use of existing roads: new, privately funded roads will provide greater choice for the motorist.	Junior Transport Minister: interview	Minister in studio

to predict the development of a text, locate topic-relevant information, and interact with a text as a piece of structured discourse. *Content schemata* relate to the subject matter or topic of a text, and help language users to disambiguate and to perceive links between textual information and what they already know about the topic in question. Formally oriented schemata activation, then, makes learners aware of the structural and organizational properties of the target text, while content-oriented schemata activation focuses their attention on the subject matter or topic of the text. In the present study, the formal pre-viewing treatment was built around Hoey's (1979) problem-solution model, the content treatment providing background information of a referential nature and then focusing on the key concept of the sequence, privatization.

Formal Treatment

Hoey's problem-solution model offers an analytical framework able to accommodate the presentation and discussion of a variety of problem situations, either productively (as in the preparation of a written report) or receptively (as in the present context). This model was chosen for use in the current experimentation in view of its relevance to the topic development of the target video sequence (cf. Figure 22.1), which moves from the identification of a problem (road congestion) through the proposed solution (privatization of a part of the road network) to an evaluation of the difficulties arising from this proposed solution. The model thus provides a global analytical framework within which the details of the target sequence may be meaningfully accommodated and interpreted. Naturally, the problem-solution model represents just one formal framework, chosen for its relevance to the target sequence, and other sequences, with a different conceptual organization, would call for differently oriented formal priming activities.

The experimental treatment lasted 20 minutes and was subdivided into three stages. In the introductory stage (ca. 2 minutes) the experimenter (Tuffs) informed subjects they were going to watch a video about the future of the road network in the United Kingdom and that, prior to viewing the video, they would receive some preparatory materials introducing them to a model for analyzing problem situations of the type encountered in the video. In the second stage (ca. 5 minutes) subjects received the first problem-solution handout (cf. Appendix 22.1) outlining the problem-solution model. The experimenter talked through this sheet, clarifying the goals and operation of the model. In the third stage (ca. 13 minutes) subjects received the second handout, the problem-solution task sheet, and worked on the task in groups of four or five. The results of the group work were briefly pooled and discussed. Subsequently, the video was viewed. Both examples used in the problem-solution materials were selected to be familiar to the subjects.

Content Treatment

The content-oriented treatment had two goals. The first was to fill in the gaps in the subjects' knowledge of culture-specific entities referred to in the target sequence, and the second was to activate their existing knowledge relevant to the general topic of the sequence. The source program from which the target sequence was drawn was aimed primarily at an educated British audience, and thus incorporated assumptions of shared background knowledge relating to entities and events referred to in the sequence, a number of which were unlikely to be familiar to the subjects. Part of the experimental treatment was thus devoted to filling in some of these referential gaps in the subjects' general background knowledge of the target situation. While gaps existed on this culture-specific level of reference, the subjects could, given the business orientation of their studies, be safely assumed to have a fair level of knowledge of privatization in general and also of those privatizations undertaken by the British government in the last few years. On this wider conceptual level, then, the content treatment sought to activate subjects' existing knowledge of privatization so that they could approach the target sequence within the appropriate ideational framework. The content treatment thus operated in terms of both providing information and activating knowledge—in other words, both input and activation.

The administration of the content treatment paralleled that of the formal treatment. In the introductory stage (ca. 2 minutes) the experimenter (Tudor) informed subjects that they were going to watch a video about the future of the road network in the U.K. and that, prior to viewing the video, they would be given some background information about the target situation and asked to think about the topic of the video, privatization. In the second stage (ca. 5 minutes) subjects were given the first content handout (cf.

Appendix 22.1) listing key people, institutions, and places featured in the video. The experimenter talked through this sheet and drew a map on the blackboard illustrating the location of certain places and projects mentioned in the handout. In the third stage (ca. 13 minutes), subjects were given the content task sheet and worked on this in groups. The results of the group work were, as in the formal treatment, pooled and briefly discussed.

The two treatments thus had a parallel structure in terms of input and activities performed. Stage 1 involved an introduction to the topic of the video and an overview of the type of preparation subjects were to receive. Stage 2 involved the provision of background information, either on the goals and operation of the problem-solution model (in the formal mode), or on elements of culture-specific knowledge (in the content mode). Stage 3 involved a learner-centered task-based activity, subjects attempting to apply the problem-solution model to a familiar situation, or reflecting on the advantages and disadvantages of privatization. Both experimental treatments lasted 20 minutes. As preparation for a video sequence of 8 minutes shown only once, this treatment-text ratio might appear somewhat top-heavy, but it was felt to be justified in view of the specific nature of viewing comprehension. Video material calls for the rapid processing of significant amounts of both verbal and visual information (cf. Figure 22.1), and the meaningful processing of such input seems likely to call for the possession of relatively stronger interpretative schemata than is the case in written material, where the reader can easily skim forward or reread to build up or confirm predictions. While this hypothesis clearly merits further investigation, it seemed sufficiently plausible to justify the treatment-text ratio adopted.

Administration

The testing was conducted simultaneously with three class groups of fourth year subjects and then, a month later, with three class groups of fifth year subjects. In each case, one group received the formal treatment prior to viewing the video and undertaking the tests (cf. below), another group receiving the content treatment, and a third control group viewing the video and completing the tests without any preparatory treatment. The class groups at each level were homogeneous in terms of linguistic and academic attainment, and were allocated randomly to a given experimental condition. The formal treatment was administered at both levels by Tuffs and the content treatment by Tudor, both working from prepared notes. All testing was conducted during subjects' normal class hours. Due to random absences, subject numbers in the content condition were slightly higher on both testing sessions (4th and 5th years) than in the two other conditions (Formal $n = 33$; Content $n = 41$; Control $n = 34$). Subject numbers on the recall test (cf. below) were slightly lower on all conditions, again due to random absences (Formal $n = 29$; Content $n = 37$; Control $n = 30$).

Elicitation Procedures and Statistical Analysis

Two elicitation procedures were employed, a summary and a set of open-ended comprehension questions. Prior to viewing, subjects were informed that they would be required to write a summary in English of the video sequence, which they would see only once, and then answer a set of comprehension questions. Subjects were allowed to make notes while the video was being shown and use these notes to help them write their summary, fifty minutes being allowed for summary writing. At the end of this time subjects' notes and the completed summaries were collected and the comprehension questions distributed, fifteen minutes being allotted for this task. Summaries were evaluated on the basis of idea units: the experimenters had analyzed the video sequence into 21 idea units, and subjects received a point for each of these idea units judged present in their summary (the maximum possible score on the summary thus being 21). The comprehension questions (14 in number) contained both factually and inferentially oriented items, each item being scored either correct or incorrect. One week after the initial experimentation subjects were given the same set of comprehension questions again in order to monitor their level or recall.

The three sets of data (summary and both immediate and recall comprehension questions) were each analyzed by means of a univariate analysis of variance to determine treatment effect, and subsequently a comparison for differences in mean scores was carried out on the same data.

Results and Discussion

The results presented in Figures 22.2 and 22.3 and in Tables 22.1 and 22.2 show that both formal and content treatments produced significant levels of comprehension facilitation, this being evidenced on all three elicitation procedures employed. In general terms, then, the results would seem to indicate that pre-viewing instruction has a potential for facilitating the viewing comprehension of L2 learners. With respect to the relative effectiveness of the two pre-viewing treatments, the formal treatment emerges as having exerted the more powerful effect on subjects' comprehension, this difference being the most marked on the immediate measures of comprehension (summary and comprehension questions). Here, levels of significance for the formal group attain .001, whereas for the content group significance is reached at only .05 (cf. Table 22.2). While the same trend persists on the recall, the relative difference between the effect of the two treatments is less marked, the results of the content group here reaching significance at .01 against, again, .001 for the formal group.

These observations would seem to indicate that, although both previewing treatments provided subjects with substantial assistance in their processing and comprehension of the target video sequence, the formal treatment offered subjects a more powerful aid to or framework for comprehension than the content treatment. The difference in the relative effectiveness of the two treatments seems, however, to be more marked in the short-term, which may indicate that treatment type may not be a major determinant of the longer-term retention of message content providing the treatment is sufficiently learner-sensitive and focuses subjects' attention on crucial aspects of the target sequence in a meaningful manner.

The results taken as a whole indicate that the activation of text-relevant schemata (either formal or content) prior to the viewing of a video sequence can produce significant gains in both comprehension and recall of message content. They thus provide support, within the relatively under-explored area of viewing comprehension,

FIGURE 22.2 Mean Scores per Condition: Summary

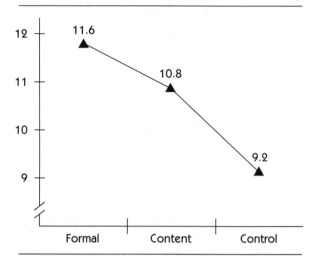

FIGURE 22.3 Mean Scores per Condition: Comprehension Questions (Immediate and Recall)

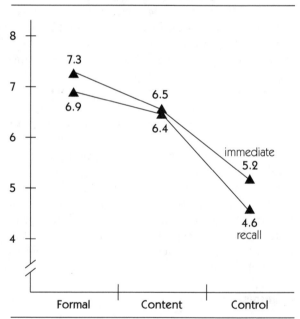

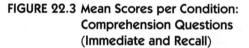

for the results of other schema-based studies of L2 comprehension, and in particular studies involving the explicit building of learners' background knowledge and the use of pre-reading techniques, such as those of Floyd and Carrell (1987) and Hudson (1982) referred to earlier. Naturally, it would be unwise to draw sweeping generalizations

TABLE 22.1 ANOVA per Elicitation Procedure

Elicitiation procedure	Source	df	SS	MS	F
Summary	between groups	2	95.65	47.82	6.63*
	within groups	105	757.20	7.21	
Comprehension questions (immediate)	between groups	2	77.86	38.93	7.53*
	within groups	105	534.05	5.17	
Comprehension questions (recall)	between groups	2	90.02	45.01	9.06*
	within groups	95	461.98	4.97	

*$p < .01$

TABLE 22.2 Comparisons for Differences Among Means per Elicitation Procedure

Elicitation procedure	Treatments	t
Summary	Control vs. Formal	3.57***
	Control vs. Content	2.48*
	Formal vs. Content	1.27
Comprehension questions (immediate)	Control vs. Formal	3.82***
	Control vs. Content	2.54*
	Formal vs. Content	1.48
Comprehension questions (recall)	Control vs. Formal	4.02***
	Control vs. Content	3.30**
	Formal vs. Content	0.95

*$p < .05$ **$p < .01$ ***$p < .001$

from the present study, given that a relatively specific learner population was involved and that only one video sequence was used. Nor should it be overlooked that the experimental subjects were advanced-level ESL learners for whom the target sequence, while not without difficulty in purely linguistic terms, was at least reasonably accessible. There is thus no guarantee that lower-level learners, for whom the processing of the target sequence would represent a substantially greater linguistic challenge, would have been able to avail themselves of the facilitative potential of the experimental treatments either to the same extent or in the same manner as the present subject population.

Both experimental treatments were informed by extensive contact, if not with the individual experimental subjects, at least with numerous other members of the same learner population—an element which would seem crucial for the effective development and use of any priming techniques. The problem-solution model had been used pedagogically with several class groups to guide both productive (report writing in the main) and receptive (study of both written and video texts) language practice activities. The authors were thus able to feel reasonably confident that the experimental population would be able to respond to and make use of this type of formal schema. The same may not be true of other learner populations with different learning styles or study habits (cf. Snow & Lohman, 1984). Similarly, the content treatment was developed on the basis of the experimenters' familiarity with the learner population's background knowledge of political and economic events in the U.K. and also their general level of knowledge of economic policy. It is worth pointing out that there is a high degree of cultural proximity between Belgium (the subjects' home culture) and the U.K. (the source culture of the target video sequence): the two countries share relatively similar political systems and face the same sort of economic and social problems. There is also a generally positive attitude among Belgians to British culture. The authors were thus able to assume the presence of a relatively well-developed set of general content schemata among subjects and develop the experimental treatment accordingly. In the case of subjects from a more distant culture, with a less developed knowledge of recent political and socioeconomic events in the U.K., the content treatment might have needed to assume a markedly different form.

In a similar vein, British television is easily accessible in Belgium and was watched regularly by a sizable proportion of the subject population. This means that the experimental population was, by and large, familiar not only with the general format of the television report but (albeit, implicitly) with the specific techniques employed, such as the juxtaposition of a verbal message with supporting/reinforcing visuals (e.g., outlining of the problem of traffic congestion against a visual background of traffic jams, mention of the difficulties of obtaining planning permission for the construction of new roads against a background of "unspoilt" countryside—cf. Figure 22.1). In other words, the subjects were familiar with the discourse and presentational conventions of the target medium, even if gaps did exist in their familiarity with a number of culturally specific referential elements (cf. content treatment, above) and there were evident difficulties in terms of language comprehension. A similar level of medium familiarity might not exist with learners from a culture in which television may play a less important social and communicative role, or where the relevant medium conventions are different. To what extent such mismatches might affect L2 learners' ability to process and comprehend television or video material, or how far they would affect the potential effectiveness of pre-viewing

activities is unclear, and would therefore seem an area that merits further research.

These considerations relating to the study style, content preparedness, and medium familiarity of the subjects do not undermine the results of the present experimentation as they stand. At the same time, such considerations should be borne in mind in assessing the possible generalizability of the present results to other learner populations. While further research in this area clearly needs to pay careful attention to text-specific factors such as format, structuring, presentational conventions, and assumptions of shared background knowledge, it equally well needs to view these factors in the light of considerations of the preferred learning style, content preparedness, cultural proximity, and medium familiarity of the target learner population.

CONCLUSIONS

The results of the present study indicate that the prior activation of text-relevant schemata can serve to meaningfully enhance the comprehension and retention of the message content of authentic video materials by L2 learners. In this way the results fit in well with and lend support to the schema-theoretic approach to the study of L2 comprehension, illustrating the applicability of this approach to a medium which has so far been relatively little explored—most schema-theory-based research to date focusing on the written medium. On the level of classroom practice, the results clearly provide support to the use of pre-viewing activities, indicating that if such activities are appropriately structured and sufficiently learner-sensitive, they can play a significant role in aiding learners to gain access to authentic video materials.

Naturally, given the limited nature of the experimentation, the results of the present study need to be viewed with a degree of caution until further research has been conducted into the domain of viewing comprehension in an L2. Such research could, on the one hand, focus on whether pre-viewing can exert a similarly facilitative effect on a wider range of video materials, including culturally oriented genres such as situation comedies and soap operas (genres which offer the possibility of focused study of the concerns, attitudes, and value systems of the target community). Also and potentially more importantly, research could address the question of whether repeated exposure to previewing treatments (possibly along the lines of those used in the present experimentation) could have a carry-over effect to learners' private viewing, in other words whether they could serve to help L2 learners to develop an independent viewing strategy.

APPENDIX 22.1 The Problem-Solution Model

The problem-solution model is a useful model which is designed to structure reports.

The model has four parts:

1. SITUATION   at the beginning of the report the writer/speaker outlines the situation
2. PROBLEM   then the writer/speaker outlines the problem or what is wrong with this situation
3. SOLUTION   the writer/speaker proposes a solution to the problem
4. EVALUATION   this solution is evaluated to see if it works

We can look at this model again with a concrete example.

Example

One of the main goals of the English courses at the Institut de Phonetique is to help students to be able to speak English fluently. However, with classes of up to 24 students it is not easy to develop fluency in speaking.

SITUATION   students need to speak more
PROBLEM   large classes mean that students do not speak enough
SOLUTION   use group work in the class so that more students have the opportunity of speaking
EVALUATION   students may speak in French, but the teacher will not be able to correct all the students

The above example illustrates that the problem-solution model is not just a four-step model leading to a perfect solution. In fact, in any situation people may disagree as to what the problem or problems are. The solution may lead to a situation that also has a problem as in the above example, and so the model could be recycled.

This flexibility makes the model a very useful tool when we want to write or understand a wide range of business reports.

TASK

Try and apply the problem-solution model to a situation which is familiar to you—the linguistic problem in Belgium.

Working in groups, make an analysis of the situation and offer ONE solution which should then be evaluated. What problems might your solution lead to?

SITUATION

PROBLEM

SOLUTION

EVALUATION

BACKGROUND INFORMATION

The following people, institutions, and places appear or are mentioned in the video which you are going to watch.

1. Governmental representatives

Paul Ghannon, Secretary of State of Transport

> The member of the government who is responsible for transport planning in Britain.

Michael Portillo, Minister of State for Transport

> A junior government minister who is on the staff of Mr. Ghannon.

2. Institutions

Department of Transport

> The government ministry responsible for all matters relating to Transport in the United Kingdom.

Whitehall

> A street in London where many government ministries are located. The term "Whitehall" is often used to refer to the British government.

The Treasury

> The government ministry which deals with the country's finances.

White Paper

> An official report which gives the policy of the government on a particular issue.

Construction companies

> Tarmac
> Mowlem

3. Places

Thames Estuary

> The river Thames flows through London and then widens into an estuary which meets the North Sea east of London.

Dartford Tunnel

> A road tunnel underneath the Thames at Dartford, east of London, which is now part of the M 25.

M 25

> A motorway (auto route) which encircles the outskirts of London.

M 40

A partly constructed and planned motorway linking London, Oxford, and Birmingham. The motorway has encountered fairly strong local opposition.

Swinford Toll Bridge

An old bridge where users have had to pay to cross for 200 years.

TASK

1. One of the best-known aspects of Mrs. Thatcher's government is the extensive privatization of previously state-owned companies and parts of the economy. Make a list of the privatizations carried out by the Thatcher government.

2. Make a list of what you consider to be the advantages and the disadvantages of privatization .

DISCUSSION QUESTIONS

1. What are the salient differences between formal and content schemata, as described in this chapter?

2. Why, do you suppose, building a formal schema might be a more powerful previewing activity than instilling prior knowledge of specific facts to be encountered in a given video viewing?

3. If contrasts as great as those observed here could be produced in a matter of 20 minutes or so, what should we expect for treatments extended over a much longer period of time, say, several years, as in the literacy programs described in Chapter 17?

4. What carry-over effects might be expected for previewing, viewing, reviewing, reading about, talking about, and writing about the kind of video materials explored in this chapter? What sorts of implications follow for educational curricula in general?

PART 5

SOMETHING OLD, SOMETHING NEW . . .

It is commonly said by researchers that they "stand on the shoulders of giants" (Edgerton, 1988: 7). This presumably makes them taller and gives them a better vantage point from which to see things of interest. However, Seldin (1990: 5) and Edgerton note that, as teachers, we generally "stand on the ground." In fact, just as Piaget (1926, 1947, 1981) has shown with children, adults, too, often have to rediscover what they had already known at some earlier time. Never mind the cases where we find out for ourselves things that others had found out long before. New insights, it seems, often involve something temporarily forgotten that has to be rediscovered in some new context. Teaching, like communication in general (cf. Watzlawick, Beavin, & Jackson, 1967), tends to begin anew on each occasion almost at the year zero. But this is not altogether bad since each new school year, each course of study, and even each class meeting begins with something like a clean sheet to write on. Along with whatever ideas and plans we bring to our teaching, new faces appear and new opportunities and challenges are sure to arise. At any rate, insights about teaching are always, without exception, some mixture of something old and something new.

As was noted above in Part 2, elementary teachers have long been scavengers, always on the lookout for new materials that might be used in the classroom. For teachers of adult foreign language students, a common resource that is readily available via satellite communication just about everywhere and in many different languages is the daily news. In Chapter 23, Maureen Weissenrieder shows how this resource can be tapped for building up listening skills in Spanish. Her contribution connects with Part 4 by showing what a formal schema for newscasts might be like. In this she follows Van Dijk (1983), who argues that the typical news story consists of two or three main parts: a summary or introduction followed by a main episode and possibly commentary after that. Thus Chapter 23 carries forward an important theme from Part 4 of this book and leads smoothly into the theme developed in Chapter 24 by Wendy Assinder, who also used video recordings of newscasts in teaching English as a second language in Australia.

However, Assinder's main focus is not on the newscasts *per se,* nor even the video recordings of them, but on ways they can be developed into peer teaching and cooperative learning experiences in the classroom. In fact, Assinder aims to extend the full range of the linguistic and social capabilities of her students from listening comprehension to reading, writing, and speaking. A wonderful old idea, seen here in a bright new light through the intelligent and sensitive eyes of Wendy Assinder, is that students can also be teachers. In fact, all teachers will agree that believing in their students' abilities is crucial to empowering them as learners. Only through believing that students can do what they need to do will it be possible for teachers to hand over to them a greater measure of responsibility for teaching and learning, as Assinder, Spencer Kagan (1985–1992), Nunan (1988, 1989), Prapphal (Chapter 34, in Part 6, this volume), and others are advocating. Students can teach and learn much more, as experience with cooperative learning clearly shows, than they have generally been given credit for in traditional classrooms. Besides, Assinder also reminds us simply but persuasively through the advances her students see in themselves that teachers [*the peer teachers*] *are also learners.* Or as Gerald Dykstra and Shiho S. Nunes put it back in 1970 (reprinted in Oller & Richards, 1973: 287–288) in reference to a peer teaching program with children in Hawaii,

> a great deal has been learned about . . . peer teaching in recent years. When a child participates actively in communicating to another something that he [or she] has learned, a sense of responsibility, purpose, and self-fulfillment are important outcomes, but at least equally important from a skills-learning standpoint is the gain that accrues to the child who teaches. Helping another learn constitutes a review, but it is review in a situation that appropriates real-life activity with an adult-type purpose [genuine responsibility] to enhance it. It is also a delayed test of the tutor's own learning. . . . Evidence already accumulated . . . shows far superior gains for children who teach than for comparable children who do not teach. There is, further, for the "tutored" child, convincing evidence to indicate that children *learn* effectively from their peers. . . .

Not only does peer teaching work for the students who teach and for those who are taught, but it frees the teacher up, as Dykstra and Nunes noted more than two decades ago, to perform higher professional tasks than record keeping, test giving, and low-level classroom management. As Assinder shows, the teacher can give feedback and guidance and perform a higher and more effective professional role as overall orchestrator and facilitator.

Lately, D. F. Clarke (1989) has underlined the fact that language teachers ought not to bear the whole burden of materials selection and preparation for adult language classes. Nor should they do all the teaching that goes on in the classroom. The greatest resource available to the teacher is not material that can be obtained from outside the classroom, as important as that material may be, but the students who are in the class. Since 1985, Spencer Kagan has been advocating cooperative approaches to learning that involve the students in more responsible roles. There are many advantages to such cooperative learning approaches. Among them is the fact that once the student escapes the role of passive-recipient of information—for which the teacher has traditionally been exclusively responsible—the students themselves become active investigators preparing materials and taking on the role of presenters and teachers themselves. It is an old but true adage that teaching something ensures more profound learning than learning by itself ever could.

Another benefit is that having students do more for themselves frees the teacher to do the things for students that they cannot do for themselves nearly so efficiently. The teacher can concentrate, for example, on such things as individualized help and specific feedback to students. In particular, the teacher will be able to provide feedback on such things as form, content, and presentation. These kinds of feedback can help students refine their skills and knowledge. In this process, surface forms of language are not ignored. The idea of nudging grammatical development along is followed up in Chapter 25 by Helen Johnson, where she discusses "defossilizing." In the meantime, peer teachers, as they actively engage in preparing to teach and discuss video materials and accompanying exercises, also advance in their understanding of current events, politics, geography, science, and nature. Because they are focusing attention mainly on subject matter (the content basis; see Part 3), they advance in language skills quite naturally, and as a bonus they also gain a lot of subject matter knowledge. However, I for one (like Swain, 1985) have never been quite convinced by the argument that accuracy in production will *necessarily* follow from mere listening comprehension.

On the contrary, I subscribe to the theory (cf. Vigil & Oller, 1976) that relatively stable grammatical systems—which are sometimes referred to a little misleadingly as "fossilized" systems (following Selinker, 1972)—can only be destabilized and caused to advance when the learner, for whatever reason, raises his or her own personal standard of communicative demands. For instance, suppose a person had a job as a laborer where all needs in the target language up till then had been about hands-on tasks which could readily be met via gesture and demonstration. But now imagine that same person wants to become a real estate broker or a certified school teacher, or wants to be promoted to a managerial role. There will need to be some adjustments in the worker's own standard of what success in communication is. While a heavily accented, pidginized variant of the target language might work for the role of a laborer, if the person in question intends to advance to a position with greater communicative demands, the standard of communicative success will have to be advanced. Many actual cases in ordinary experience support the hypothesis that we advance in our communicative abilities (within vague limits) according to the perceived demands of the ordinary contexts of communication that we commonly encounter. Grammar and the details of surface form, it turns out (as Helen Johnson shows in Chapter 25), are not forgotten after all. They are merely treated in a manner that makes them properly subservient to the demands of communication.

While Weissenrieder (Chapter 23) and Assinder (Chapter 24) exploit the existing resource of newscasts through their peculiar episodic schema, and while both Assinder (Chapter 24) and Johnson (Chapter 25) stress the benefits of peer teaching and cooperative learning, Ben Christensen in Chapter 26 adds another resource to the ones already discussed in this book. He recommends teenage adventure novels. They have the virtue of plenty of episodic organization, a high degree of redundancy and predictability in plotting, and lots of action. Among the advantages of narrative material with rich episodic organization is the relative ease with which they enable readers to add new vocabulary. In fact, Krashen (1985a–c, 1989a–b, 1990, 1992) has argued, and I am persuaded by the evidence he offers, that we acquire writing skills, including vocabulary and spelling, mainly through reading.

Here is a story told by Jim Shooter (as cited by Krashen, 1989b) that illustrates what is at stake:

> On a November day in 1957 I found myself standing in front of Miss Grosier's first grade class in Hillcrest Elementary School . . . trying to think of a really good word. She had us playing this game in which each kid had to offer up a word to the class, and for every classmate who couldn't spell your word, you got a point—provided, of

course, that you could spell the word. Whoever got the most points received the coveted gold star.

"Bouillabaisse," said I, finally.

"You don't even know what that is," Miss Grosier scolded.

"It's fish soup."

"You can't spell that!"

"Can too."

"Come here. Write it," she demanded.

I wrote it. She looked it up, and admitted that it was, indeed, correct.

Easiest gold star I ever won. And right here, right now, I'd like to thank, albeit somewhat belatedly, whoever wrote that Donald Duck comic book in which I found the word "bouillabaisse." Also, I'd like to thank my mother who read me that comic book and so many others when I was four and five. . . . I learned to read from those sessions long before I started school. While most of my classmates were struggling with "See Spot run," I was reading Superman. I knew what "indestructible" meant, could spell it, and would have cold-bloodedly used it to win another gold star if I hadn't been banned from competition after "bouillabaisse." . . .

I repeat this story because it shows two fundamental points about scaffolding in language and literacy acquisition: First, we need narrative-like context—episodic organization together with pictures, dramatization, etc.—to help us work out the meanings of unfamiliar surface forms and to enable us to correctly solve the content side of the comprehension problem. Second, we need to experience the surface forms of language in their natural episodic contexts where they are sensibly used in order for those surface forms themselves—how they sound, how they are spelled, how they feel rolling off the tongue, etc.—to get hung on the proper mental hooks. A word or surface form that has no place in my experience is a word I don't know how to use and one that I am likely to misuse, misspell, mispronounce, or just neglect altogether.

But what evidence is there that practicing the production of surface forms actually provides some advantage to language users? Swain (1985; also Swain & Lapkin, 1989) sticks with the contention that perfection of the surface forms of speech and writing is invariably linked not only with comprehension *per se* but ultimately with speech production and practice in writing. In fact, it can be shown on the grounds of pure logic (especially by the methods of Chapter 37) that comprehension itself is never altogether passive but that it must involve the active production of an interpretation that corresponds to perceived forms of language. But, setting that argument to one side, is there any compelling empirical evidence that grammatical accuracy or just plain fluency can be improved by merely practicing speech production? Chapter 27, by Arevart and Nation, addresses just that question and comes up with positive evidence. When students in a second language context at the University of Wellington in New Zealand merely told the same story a second and a third time (to different listeners), they improved significantly (on the average) both in grammatical accuracy and in fluency. Apparently practice in producing meaningful output really does make a difference. It's an old idea that "practice makes perfect," but Arevart and Nation provide some new evidence on the subject.

There are many new technologies to be considered by language specialists these days, and in Chapter 28, by Tatsuo Taira, we address the matter of interactive computer programs. The key point in Taira's research is to show that episodic organization of materials (see especially Part 4, this volume), even on the computer, results in noteworthy advantages to language learners. Of course, there is already some excellent material on how to select videotexts, perhaps the lowest common denominator of the most widely used classroom technologies in the 1990s (cf. Joiner, 1990; as well as Altman, 1989, and Smith, 1989). For example, Pesola (1991) points out the need to reach beyond the surface forms of culture (those that can be displayed to our senses) to the deeper meanings of videotexts, stories, and other cultural manifestations. Her point is to help students acquire a deeper and richer understanding of other cultures, as foreign language education has long sought to do. Another exciting possibility for accomplishing this is "telecommunication," discussed by Juan Carlos Gallegos (1992)—where students separated by half a world can see and talk to each other via satellite. But Taira's chapter concerns the more immediate issue of enabling students to make optimal use of an interactive computer program for learning English in Japan. His results, I believe, will be extensively applied in the coming century to further the development of computer-assisted language learning and teaching. Taira argues for episodic organization in all kinds of texts and videotexts used in computer-assisted language teaching. The reasons for exploiting the cognitive advantages of meaningful sequence together with opportunities for dramatization, video illustration, and the like are myriad and have been explored in Parts 1 and 4 of this book. What is new, however, in Taira's chapter, is the employment of computing technologies to demonstrate the power of what I understand as the strongest form of the episode hypothesis. Taira shows that episodic organization doesn't just contribute to comprehension—which we already knew—but that it does indeed also contribute to language acquisition in general. Moreover, Taira shows that this is so at high levels of episodic organization extended over multiple episodes and an entire semester of study.

Finally, Part 5 concludes with Chapter 29 from Jack S. Damico and Sandra K. Damico. This study shows that what works with "normal" populations also works with "special" cases of "impaired" populations. Many practicing speech-language pathologists, clinicians, and teachers of special education have long known that additional context in a range of sensory modalities (scaffolding) is especially helpful to children or adults with organically based limitations or difficulties. However, in Chapter 29, Damico and Damico tie the important practice and research in the vast fields of special education and speech-language therapies to what is known about methods that work in language teaching and literacy training in general.

CHAPTER 23

Listening to the News in Spanish

Maureen Weissenrieder

EDITOR'S INTRODUCTION

The following chapter by Weissenrieder appeared in a longer form in The Modern Language Journal *in 1987. News stories are useful, as Weissenrieder contends, partly because they are (in most cases) grounded in actual facts of experience. When a newspaper or TV story reports that Donna Reed, star of the film* From Here to Eternity, *died at age 64 at her home in Beverly Hills, we suppose that the event really occurred about when and where it is reported to have occurred. To the extent that news stories are grounded in facts, they enjoy all the benefits of episodically organized narrative reports of any actual experience whatever. These benefits make them relatively more comprehensible than pure fictions are apt to be. Certainly, news stories are easier to understand on many counts than surface forms of any language dropped out of the blue sky. For instance, as is shown in Chapter 37, news stories (and all narratives that are true) benefit from (1) relatively greater determinacy of meaning (we know fairly accurately which Donna Reed died in 1989 and where Beverly Hills is located), from (2) connectedness between facts in experience (e.g., that Beverly Hills is in California, not far from Hollywood, a favorite nesting place for actors, commonly featured in films, etc.), and from (3) generalizability (e.g., that Donna Reed and all of us, apparently, are just about exactly as mortal as Socrates was). Furthermore, news stories captured in print, on video, or more likely both ways, are susceptible to multiple passes in which the student (as reader, viewer, and comprehender) improves the degree of comprehension of the news story on each pass. Weissenrieder shows how.*

The goal of this study is to suggest a pedagogical direction to facilitate the comprehension of Spanish-language newscasts for second language learners. It assumes that listening skills are best facilitated if comprehension strategies and how they interact with the target register are adequately understood. Essential to the understanding of this interaction are the following issues: 1) a discussion of the role that listening comprehension plays in language skill formation and, in particular, the need to teach comprehension of the news; 2) a description of the relevant linguistic properties of the broadcast register in Spanish; 3) a discussion of the listening task in general and how it pertains to the news in particular. Although I do not give suggestions for specific classroom strategies, I do outline a framework, based on that of Oller and Oller (Chapter 6, this volume) within which classroom techniques can be elaborated. My conclusions are based on the Spanish language alone, although parallels to other languages are easily drawn.

LISTENING IN LANGUAGE SKILL FORMATION

A quick perusal of the literature on language teaching will reveal the ever-increasing interest of pedagogues in listening skills.[1] Much of this interest is based on sound theoretical principles which stress the primary role of aural comprehension in first language acquisition. Psycholinguists insist axiomatically that no child learns to speak his/her native tongue prior to exposure to great quantities of comprehensible input. Much experimental work in L2 acquisition, such as that of Krashen (1982), suggests that listening comprehension is not only necessary to production skills, but may in and of itself be sufficient for production to take place spontaneously.

Whether or not one accepts the strong form of this theory, which states that aural comprehension spawns automatic production, and thus should precede it methodologically, is no of concern here. After all, few would suggest that students learn to comprehend specialized registers, such as news broadcasting, in order to produce them. Rather, we present the more moderate hypothesis that listening should be taught for listening's sake alone. In other words, to the extent that the acquisition of other skills will not automatically lead to aural comprehension, listening must be singled out pedagogically. Obviously, oral signals differ from visual ones, and, as Weaver (1972) points out (p. 12), reading abilities do not necessarily correlate with listening skills. It follows that students who read well, particularly in more academic registers such as literature, will not necessarily be able to comprehend aural registers such as newscasts. Moreover, we cannot assume that production skills will correlate positively with successful comprehension. Perceptive foreign language professionals, such as Belasco (1971, 1981), have noted how students who are relatively fluent in terms of production are often lost when they find themselves on the other side of the communicative act. This inability to comprehend is exacerbated in specialized, passive registers such as newscasting since the language to be comprehended is significantly different from that to which the typical student has been exposed. These register differences compound the listening task and, therefore, need to be addressed pedagogically.

THE LANGUAGE OF NEWS BROADCASTING

Economy of language is evident at the discourse level, where news briefs may last no longer than twenty seconds. Much more interesting than time span or the reduced number of sentences which make up the majority of news pieces, however, is the way in which news ideas are concentrated into the discourse. Discourse analysts, such as Van Dijk (1983), have shown that distinct registers of language can be characterized, not only by specific sentence-level structures and vocabulary, but by the way in which basic ideas or "propositions" are organized into a recognizable whole. Thus, at the most general level, discourse has a superstructure. Business letters are framed by a salutation, body, and closing while fairy tales and other stories are often recognizable by their introduction, complication, resolution, evaluation, and moral. More importantly, as indicated by Larsen (1983), the organization of discourse structures plays an important role in the way information is listened to and processed.

Although detailed analysis and testing have yet to be done, Van Dijk (1983) proposes a hypothetical superstructure for written news registers which is of interest here. According to Van Dijk, prototypical news articles may be characterized by a theoretical discourse superstructure or schema which is reproduced below in reduced form.

NEWS STORY
1. Summary/introduction
   1.1 Headlines
   1.2 Lead
2. Episode
   2.1 Events
      2.1.1 Previous information
      2.1.2 Antecedents
      2.1.3 Actual events
      2.1.4 Explanation
   2.2 Consequences/reactions
3. Comments

Each category in the above schema is a macro-proposition into which many different ideas or propositions may fit. Thus, a newspaper headline and lead statement(s) (category one above) serve to summarize news stories. Episode (category two) details main events within context and may describe consequences or reactions to the details. Finally, comments (category three) may add the point of view of the reporter or news journal. Naturally, macropropositions may be absent in any given newspiece or moved from the order in which they are given in the hierarchy.

THE LISTENING TASK

For the instructor of language, the reliance on previous world knowledge provides an ancillary tool to student comprehension. Once isolated words and phrases are perceived, they can be used as a springboard to unraveling the main gist of the news story, provided that the instructor takes advantage of the students' knowledge of the world and encourages them to guess at possible associations and to anticipate related themes. Armed with an understanding of the organizational relationships within news discourse, the instructor can add direction to the anticipatory and reconstructive processes. Where students perceive detail, appropriate instructor prompting will help them backtrack to the lead concept. Conversely, if students grasp the lead, the instructors will be able to direct them to comprehension of detail.

Pedagogically, the need to listen for restricted amounts and types of information leads, as Oller has suggested, to cyclical treatment of the material. Students are asked to focus on one or two simple perception or comprehension tasks in each of several listenings. With the aid of instructor guidance, each cycle builds on the knowledge accumulated in the previous cycle until ultimate comprehension goals have been reached.

The exact form of the instructor's guidance within these comprehension spirals will be based on various factors such as the language level or interests of individual students and the linguistic idiosyncrasies of the news piece. Given these diverse factors, it is difficult to prescribe an exact recipe for the creation of any given spiral. The following example, however, demonstrates how a spiral might be presented. Consider the news brief given below, which in its written form would present little difficulty for the intermediate student. Presented orally, on the other hand, it requires considerable elaboration:

La secretaria de transporte de los Estados Unidos, E. D., ordenó una intensa inspección de las compañías de aviación con vuelos de alquiler especialmente esas empresas que rentan sus aviones para vuelos militares. Esta es la cuarta inspección ordenada después del accidente de AeroAir en que murieron doscientos cuarenta y ocho soldados.

The lead in this piece involves an official order to inspect aircraft. The inspection is, in turn, a result of a recent airline disaster. Students are likely to hear cognates such as *inspección* on a first listening but still not comprehend what is being inspected or why. The first cycle in the spiral, represented below, involves a vocabulary search where, through instructor prompting, the students are directed to focus on a few topically important language fragments. As indicated by the parentheses in the student responses below, less-experienced students will supply smaller pieces of information than more-prepared classmates.[2]

CYCLE ONE

Instructor: This news brief deals with flying. As you listen, write down the words you hear that you would associate with flying.

Students: planes, (rented) flights, (military) flights, aviation

In the second cycle, the instructor relies on the students' understanding of the world and their interest in current events.

CYCLE TWO

Instructor: When are airplanes generally mentioned in the news?

Students: When there is an accident.

Instructor: Think of a recent airline disaster. As you listen, see if you can hear it described in the news brief.

Students: (Two hundred and forty-eight) soldiers died (in an AeroAir accident).

Now that the episodic detail has been supplied, the instructor can direct student attention to the lead.

Instructor: We react to aviation disasters in several ways—enacting new laws, checking equipment, and investigating causes. Listen again for the reaction described in this case and write down the words that you associate with it.

Students: (The Secretary of Transportation ordered) a thorough inspection; (this is) the fourth inspection (since the accident).

Depending upon student level and comprehension goals, cycles can be added or deleted. Of interest for an advanced-level class are the lesser known vocabulary items *empresa* and *alquiler*. Although the information they contain is in the background and is thus of lesser importance to the overall understanding of the piece, they afford the instructor the opportunity to increase student vocabulary. Owing to the condensed nature of the news, these items are repeated in the cognates *compañia* and *rentan*. Instructors can elicit this vocabulary either through the comprehension of content or a perception drill.

CYCLE FOUR

Instructor: AeroAir is a privately owned airline. Listen to see if you can hear why there were so many military personnel on the flight.

Students: Companies rent their planes for military flights.

Instructor: Who has heard an alternate way to say *compañías*?

Students: *empresas*.

Guiding a student's attention through a comprehension spiral like the one given above provides an external, pedagogical analogue to the "chunking" process. Language pieces which are given primary focus in earlier cycles are backgrounded to form the building blocks of wider-scoped comprehension in later cycles. Processing information is thus progressively amplified so that more information is attained with each listening without further taxing the student's limited linguistic skills. Comprehension goals are sufficiently focused within each cycle so that overloads are avoided.

Multiple listenings by themselves, of course, are unlikely to advance the student through the spiral. As seen in the example given above, the instructor plays a crucial interactive role. As arbiter between the material and the student, not only does the instructor set focused goals and thus pinpoints attention, but he/she must supply clues to meaning. In this way, the direction the instructor supplies in leading the student search through the cycles serves as a crutch to the novice listener's inability to reconstruct linguistically. Providing clues to meaning itself, this instructor guidance encourages students to guess constructively so that they may perceive concepts even when transmitted in unfamiliar linguistic constructions. Further, this leads to the bonding of concept to new vocabulary and structures, thus allowing for new language forms to be discovered rather than given. As many of these forms reappear in different news pieces, their status as characterizing routines and patterns can be established.

CONCLUSION

Imparting listening comprehension skills to L2 students has not always been an obvious or universally accepted goal within our profession. Yet, to the extent that students who can successfully manipulate other skills lag behind in aural comprehension, listening needs to be taught. This need is particularly acute for the newscasting register, whose role in an information-oriented world underscores its importance, but whose unique nature makes it a particular challenge for the novice listener.

We have described the peculiarities of newscasting in Spanish, not in an attempt to give a thorough linguistic characterization, but rather to reveal what we believe to be a major source of comprehension difficulties. We have seen that in performance, organization, and structures, the language of newscasting is motivated economically. Its condensed, telescoped form concentrates a higher information load in a reduced linguistic space. The resulting need on the part of the listener for greater processing efficiency explains what every sensitive teacher of foreign language already knows—student attempts at comprehending the news can be frustrating, and very often, unsuccessful endeavors.

Obviously, any pedagogical approach that purports to teach comprehension of the news must address the demands created by the register. The approach suggested above responds to these demands by teaching comprehension within the framework of a graduated spiral. In recursive sweeps through each cycle, comprehension goals are focused narrowly to meet the linguistic level of the student. For some, this may be no more than the recognition of isolated lexical items; for others, it involves interpretation and analysis of detail. In this system, teacher intervention serves as a catalyst between what students perceive and what needs to be perceived. The instructor gives direction, focuses attention, encourages guessing, and, when needed, reveals partial information. In this patchwork fashion, the patterns which make up the news can be discovered and then established as familiar, clue-giving regularities.

The above discussion reveals clearly that the language of newscasting differs significantly from that of daily use. As such, it is unlikely that students will learn to master it through unguided exposure. Moreover, we cannot expect students to pick up the news synergetically, for the ability to understand other registers does not in and of itself guarantee success in understanding the news. To the contrary, listening to the news must be specifically taught. Pedagogical techniques, such as comprehension spirals, that enable the instructor to uncover register-specific language patterns while reducing the increased processing load offer us a hopeful direction for the future.

NOTES

1 See Byrnes (1984, 1985), Dunkel (1986), Higgs (1985), Long, Pino, and Valdés (1985), Ostyn and Godin (1985), and Rivers (1981, 1986).

2 These procedures were used in a class in listening given at Ohio University in 1986. Students enrolled in the class were intermediate and advanced students who had studied one academic quarter in Mexico. All interaction was conducted in the target language but is represented here in English for reader ease.

DISCUSSION QUESTIONS

1. When Weissenrieder says "we cannot assume that production skills will *correlate* [my emphasis] positively with successful comprehension" (p. 266) she apparently means that language users may sometimes be able to comprehend a discourse without being able to produce it. Thus, the term *correlate*, as she uses it (also see Weaver, 1972; and Belasco, 1981), is taken in the restricted sense of "correspond quite perfectly." On the other hand, there is ample evidence that language skills in comprehension and production generally are "correlated" in the less restricted statistical sense (cf. Carroll, 1983; Bachman, 1990; Oller, 1979; Oller et al., 1991). Discuss the special sense, nonetheless (of Weissenrieder), in which our productive skills may require special work in order for them to come close to our capacity to comprehend. But can production ever catch up fully with comprehension? Can we reasonably expect, for instance, to produce as well as we can understand the plays of Shakespeare (cf. Spolsky, 1973), or the plot of the 1943 film *Casablanca*? Recall that this film was re-released in 1992, which invited some viewers to see it again. Discuss, therefore, the susceptibility of film to multiple passes by comprehenders.

2. Consider the kinds of information that a student who does not know Spanish might be expected to extract from the news item on p. 267 even on the first pass. How might that comprehension be improved through a video element? What are the theoretical limits of comprehension that might be achieved by further cycles through the story? Review the cycles suggested by Weissenrieder and discuss them.

3. In addition to listening comprehension for newscasts, what other genres of discourse might also need special attention in the foreign language classroom? Why do you think these particular cases ought to be singled out for attention? What special advantages do these genres afford to comprehension, and what special problems do they present?

Peer Teaching, Peer Learning: One Model

Wendy Assinder

EDITOR'S INTRODUCTION

In Chapter 24, Wendy Assinder, presently Director of Education at the Australian College of English, tells what happened when she had her students start doing for themselves some of the things she had been doing for them. It occurred to her that she could have her students preview video segments of the news and prepare vocabulary keys, study questions, cloze exercises, and oral presentations of the material. As Assinder notes, the peer teaching approach puts students at the center of classroom activities. It also enables the teacher to step back to a higher remove and to serve as a counselor (a facilitator and expert language consultant) in the family of language teaching methods known under the guise of "counseling learning" (Curran, 1961, 1976, 1983). Probably the single most important advantage of Assinder's approach was the enhanced motivation and the corresponding effort by her students. Because they were thoroughly involved in activities and research for which they took responsibility, the students were willing to put out more effort over longer periods of time and consequently enjoyed greater success.

BACKGROUND

The Course and Class

Last year I spent two mornings (six hours total) per week teaching a class of twelve students on a full-time "English for Further Studies" course.[1] The students were from Korea, Japan, Indonesia, Thailand, China, and New Caledonia. Their levels ranged from lower- to upper-intermediate, and their academic backgrounds were diverse, but most were intending to continue, ultimately, with some kind of higher education in Australia. The objectives of the course were to prepare the students, in terms of the skills and language they would need, for their further education courses, and to equip the students with the level of general knowledge, of Australia and the world, that might be expected of an average Australian high-school graduate. The two mornings that I taught were devoted to current affairs. The remainder of the week was allocated to topic-based input (history, economics, and science), study skills, grammar, and seminars.

The Current Affairs Materials

For the first few weeks I used authentic materials, taken from the radio, TV, and newspapers, with tasks and activities aimed at developing vocabulary and listening, reading, note taking, and speaking skills. Students commented that they liked the materials. In particular, a weekly current affairs program, *Behind the News,* broadcast weekly in Australia as part of the ABC's TV for high schools and primary schools, was very popular. The program typically includes two or three main items, each 5–10 minutes long, taken from the week's news. The items are informative and of general interest, often with an Australian or Asian bias. A typical lesson based on *Behind the News* would include some vocabulary input, skills work (listening comprehension, note taking, etc.), a focus on language, and some discussion.

The Idea

One day, as I was pre-viewing a video item for potentially new vocabulary and compiling some comprehension questions, it occurred to me that perhaps the students could do this for themselves. I felt that this would increase their responsibility for their own learning, vital if these students were to continue to further education courses as well as providing more opportunities for learning and developing a greater range of skills. Further, if students were to produce their own worksheets and then present the video item to another group, this would not only provide a clear goal to the task, but would consolidate, or even test, what they had learned. It would also give useful practice in presentation skills. Most importantly, the students would be forced to take total responsibility throughout. With the idea conceived, I went into class.

SETTING THINGS UP

I asked the students if they would like, as an experiment, to prepare some video materials to "teach each other" the following day. The response was positive, and a discussion ensued on how "best" to teach. There seemed to be a consensus that a "good" lesson, based on a short video item, would consist of some vocabulary input; some listening practice, with comprehension questions; some accuracy work, probably based on a cloze exercise, which could be used to develop grammar, vocabulary, and/or intensive listening; and a discussion. This exercise in itself was productive in that it increased students' awareness of why certain classroom activities are useful.

We also talked about the nature of questions, in particular the difference between the "closed" questions (e.g., true/false, short answer, yes/no, or multiple choice) often used to check comprehension, and the more "open" nature of questions intended to stimulate discussion (e.g., "Why . . .?" "Should there . . .?" "What do you think about . . .?" etc.).

The students divided into two groups of six, and each group was given a different video item (taken from recent *Behind the News* program) on which to work. Each group went into a separate classroom with a video recorder. Asked how long they thought it would take to prepare their lesson, which was to include a typed worksheet, to be presented to the other group the following day, they estimated (accurately) that they would need the rest of the morning (just over two hours). They set to work. I made myself available as a consultant/monitor, but otherwise kept a very low profile.

WHAT DID THE STUDENTS DO?

Video Preparation

First, the groups watched the video items for gist. The students then talked about what they had seen and heard and how they would approach the task, and organized who would do what. One group delegated a video operator, a note taker, a "dictionary consultant," a "questions committee," someone to take down dictation, and a typist.

The students tried to isolate new vocabulary and to check its spelling and meaning: they consulted each other; they used dictionaries. They talked about the topic and had lengthy discussions about their perceptions of the situation, negotiating meaning until they were satisfied that they all had a good general understanding. They watched and listened, they talked, they listened again. They summarized, re-phrased, circumlocuted, took notes, took dictation, and took responsibility for themselves and for the group.

The groups argued about which items of vocabulary would be most useful for the other group to learn; which segment would be most representative of the whole program to transcribe for the cloze exercise, and which words should be gapped. Individuals argued about the appropriateness of different questions for comprehension and/or discussion; they fought over what they had "heard," meaning, pronunciation, and points of grammar. In most cases a consensus was reached. As a last resort, in cases of unresolvable conflict, I was called upon to act as a consultant or mediator.

By the end of the morning each group had drawn up a worksheet, to be typed out later by one member of the group, and had discussed how they, as a group, would present their video lesson the following day to the other group.

A sample worksheet, produced entirely by the students, is given in Figure 24.1.

The Presentations: Learners Teaching Learners

The following day, the two groups took an hour each to teach the other group. What took place was actually remarkably similar in form to what might have taken place had I prepared and taught the lesson myself, except that the students were in control. The six "experts" on each topic had taken on roles such as introducer of vocabulary, video operator, checker of answers, chairperson of the discussion, and so on.

In the initial presentation, it was interesting to see many of my own techniques being used by the "teachers": brainstorming the topic at the start of the lesson, marking the stress and drilling the pronunciation of new vocabulary, getting the "learners" to predict the answers to the comprehension questions, to guess the part of speech of the gapped words in the cloze exercise, or to check answers in pairs. Other techniques were clearly their own preferences: I was in the habit of putting students in small groups for open discussion; the students seemed to prefer whole-class discussion.

The first hour was a resounding success. The "teachers" clearly revelled in their new roles as "experts"; the "learners" were respectful of the work that had gone, and was going, into the lesson and found the topic interesting and the worksheet challenging. A lengthy discussion on the topic was generated.

The students then exchanged roles and the "learners" became "teachers." This lesson was an equal success.

After a break, the final hour of the morning began with a class discussion on the usefulness of the previous two days' work. The response was overwhelmingly positive, and the students asked for more of the same. We agreed to repeat the exercise the following week.

THE REST OF THE COURSE

The following week, I took into the class a list of the recently videoed *Behind the News* items available in the school archives, with a brief description of each, and allowed the groups to choose which item to prepare, thus giving the students even greater choice and responsibility. One group previewed several times and then came to a consensus on what would be most useful and interesting for the other group to learn about the following day. The experiment was equally successful the second time around, and once again the students asked if they could continue with the approach. Figure 24.2 outlines "my" two mornings per week during the remaining seven weeks of the ten-week course.

The last hour each week was devoted to a whole-class feedback session, in which the groups evaluated each other's performance (not just their linguistic performance, but also their self-confidence, presentation skills, etc.), or watched videoed segments of their own teaching and then self-evaluated. This would be followed with my own comments and some error analysis and/or remedial pronunciation work, based on the two days' oral samples. Homework, such as an essay or remedial grammar exercises, was then set.

Students also attended individual tutorials/counseling sessions, during which they discussed their strengths and weaknesses, plans and progress, and were assigned individualized homework. Towards the end of the course, we also experimented with the two groups; instead of teaching *each other,* they taught groups of students from *other* intermediate (general EFL) classes. This too was considered by both parties to be useful and successful.

The Teacher's Role

The total student-centeredness of this approach, where students were preparing and presenting their own materials, presented me with a unique opportunity to watch carefully my students in action, and I learned a great deal about them: their personalities, their linguistic strengths and

FIGURE 24.1 A Worksheet Produced Entirely By the Students

BEHIND THE NEWS: CHINA
(Donna, Toshi, Iwan, Tae-Jung, Wirot)

VOCABULARY

- tragedy: a terrible, unhappy, unfortunate event
- modernize: to make (something) suitable for modern use
- interfere: block the action of another
- conservative: not liking change, especially sudden change
- crack down: to become more severe

COMPREHENSION QUESTIONS

1. How long has the Communist Party controlled the People's Republic of China?
2. What kind of system did the Communist Party use?
3. How did the Chinese people get the overseas news?
4. What was the only way to modernize China?
5. When did the first students' demonstration happen in China?

GAP-FILL EXERCISE

The Communist Party has controlled the People's Republic of China for nearly 40 years and for the first 30 of those years it made sure China was kept isolated from the rest of the world. Under the communist system of government everyone worked for the state, whether on farms, producing food, in factories producing _____ or weapons, or in government _____, like schools or health centres. The reason China was able to _____ isolated from other countries was that it worked in a closed system. Chinese farmers provided food for the people _____ factories provided tools and other _____ goods and government workers provided services like education for everyone. Under this closed system the Communist Party also controlled the media and the only way Chinese people knew about what happened in other parts of the country or overseas was through official and _____ newspapers, radio, and more recently, television. After 30 years of China's closed system, the most powerful members of the Communist Party, led by Deng Xiaoping, became concerned that their China was falling behind the rest of the world. China's weapons were out of date and no _____ for those of other countries and the same _____ for other areas of technology, like medicine and agriculture. Deng Xiaoping decided that the only way China could modernize _____ _____ start communicating with other countries.

DISCUSSION QUESTIONS

1. What do you think about the closed system in China?
2. What are your opinions on the future of China?

FIGURE 24.2 A Weekly Plan

Day 1		
9:00–9:30	Whole class together: checking homework, arranging groups, deciding on topic	
9:30–11:00	GROUP A Prepares video and worksheet	GROUP B Prepares video and worksheet
11:30–12:30	Talks about how to present it	Talks about how to present it

Day 2	(Whole class together)
9:00–10:00	Group A teaches Group B (or a group from another class)
10:00–11:00	Group B teaches Group A (or a group from another class)
11:30–12:30	Peer evaluation of each group's performance; feedback from teacher; error analysis/pronunciation work; home-work assigned (e.g. essay or remedial grammar exercises).

(outside class hours)

15-minute slot per student per fortnight	Individual tutorial/counseling session

weaknesses, strategies for learning, other skills and attributes that they possessed (organizational skills, leadership, people management, technical know-how, etc.), and their knowledge (or, in some cases, lack of knowledge) and views on world affairs.

I made myself available as a "resource" for language queries, an "on-the-spot checker," and a "sounding-board" for ideas, opinions, and inter-pretations of political scenarios. Mostly, however, I was an "observer," gathering data on the students and their interlanguage for use in follow-up feedback sessions, accuracy work, and remedial language work. This role put me in an excellent position to diagnose the problem areas of each individual. On a card for each student, I noted

oral errors that each learner was making, general comments on their performance, and my percep-tions of their needs. I also made video and audio recordings of some lessons, to be used in subse-quent feedback sessions.

Initially, I was concerned that my own role, somewhat in the background, might be perceived as not giving "value for money." It has sometimes been my experience that group work is not popu-lar with students: they may feel that it lacks pur-pose, that the teacher is being lazy, that they learn each other's errors, or that they do not have suffi-cient correction or feedback. When I tentatively voiced these doubts, however, they were immedi-ately dispelled by the students, who were positively glowing with their own responsibility. The students were aware that I was observing them intently, diagnosing their problem areas, and prescribing and preparing remedial work for use in the class feedback session or the individual tutorials.

Because my own preparation time had been drastically reduced, I was in a position to devote time outside class hours to these individual tutorials/counseling sessions, in which I used the cards as prompts and prescribed appropriate remedial tasks for individual students. Thus, I maintained my own *raison d'être,* as well as giving each student more individual attention.

PEER TEACHING, PEER LEARNING

Evaluation by Students

In addition to the weekly oral feedback session, the students were asked to complete a questionnaire at the end of the course. The following questions were asked:

1. Did you enjoy this kind of lesson? Why/Why not?
2. What did you learn?
3. What did you practice?
4. What was your role in the lesson?
5. What was the teacher's role?

A selection of the students' comments is listed below:[2]

Question: Did you enjoy this kind of lesson? Why/Why not?

Answers: (without exception)
Yes! It was very valuable.
I really enjoyed these lessons.
I think this is a good way to learn English.

Because: It made us think.
We not only got the news, but improved our English.
I enjoyed the variety of topics and all the information about the world that I got while studying English.
I'm interested in world topics.
Studying *difficult* topics (e.g., political

situations) forced us to *think* in English.
The subjects were very interesting, and we practised listening, writing, speaking, and understanding at the same time.
We practised so many things in one lesson.
We learnt English by enjoying it.
We learnt a lot about English.

Question: What did you learn?

Answers: A lot!
Vocabulary
Many things about the world
A lot of information
All about Tasmania, Iran, NATO, Panama . . .
How to understand news programmes better
How to listen better
Other students' opinions and ideas
Knowledge about science, current affairs, and nature

Question: What did you practise?

Answers: Listening
Writing
Spelling
Grammar
Composition
Typing
Dictation
Pronunciation
Using new vocabulary
Making questions
Finding and checking meanings in dictionaries
Getting the main ideas
Summarizing

Question: What was *your* role in the lessons?

Answers: Helping to choose what we did
Asking questions
Organizing who did what
Controlling what we did
I was a sort of "director"

I wrote the main ideas on the board
I took notes

Question: What was the *teacher's* role?

Answers: Preparing the equipment
Providing the videos
Advising students
Assisting with the dictation and giving
suggestions
Helping when we had a problem
Checking the grammar, pronunciation
and spelling: without her, it would
have been much more difficult
Collecting and correcting mistakes

My Own Observations/Reflections

The students' comments, all of which were resoundingly positive, speak for themselves. I should, however, like to add a few of my own observations and reflections:

Increased Motivation

Without exception, all students appeared more motivated, and this motivation was sustained over the entire course. Students seemed to be enjoying themselves more, be much more willing to contribute, have increased concentration spans, and engage in many more spontaneous conversations than previously.

Increased Participation

Even students who had previously been fairly passive in the class became more involved. All the talk was initiated by the students, and, as well as vastly increased student talking time, the nature of the discourse changed to include far more questions, more checking, more clarifying, and more negotiation than in previous lessons. Students also appeared to listen to each other more carefully.

Increased "Real" Communication

Discussions were lengthier and more meaningful. I was struck by the richness and variety of exchanges that took place—analyses of information and political situations; discussion about learning and the value and aims of different components of the task; negotiation of group organiza-

tion; and discussion of the relative merits of different dictionaries.

Increased In-depth Understanding

Group negotiation seemed to result in deeper understanding for all concerned. There was some mixture of ability among the students; stronger students often had their linguistic resources stretched to the limit when called upon to explain something, be it content or grammar, to a weaker student, who, in turn, had his or her own threshold raised to a new level. I was impressed by the persistence of the groups to ensure that each member of the group had achieved a thorough understanding of whatever was being discussed.

Increased Responsibility for Their Own Learning and Commitment to the Course

As well as being responsible to his or her own group (in terms of sharing the work) and responsible to the other group (in terms of teaching), each individual assumed complete responsibility for what, and how much, was learned. Vocabulary development, for example, was very individualized, with each student isolating a number of new items each day. The students themselves chose what, and how much, to learn.

Increased Confidence and Respect for Each Other

Each student was able to excel at something (not necessarily linguistic). Being able to bring their own adult knowledge and skills to bear, increased both their self-confidence and their respect for each other. Each student was, at some stage, materials writer, problem solver, learner, teacher, expert, evaluator, technician, manager, or even typist. This multiplicity of roles further increased self-confidence and respect for peers.

Increased Number of Skills and Strategies Practiced and Developed

I was struck, in lesson after lesson, by the richness of any one session in terms of the number of skills and strategies which were practiced, and the amount of learning which seemed to take place.

Increased Accuracy

The students took immense pride in producing accurately written worksheets for the other group.

Consequently, there were often lengthy debates on points of grammar; the negotiated end product was always of a level of accuracy far greater than that of the written work of any individual group member.

RATIONALE

It is not my aim here to discuss the underlying principles of task-based learning, student autonomy, learner involvement, negotiated syllabuses, and individualization. These themes have been widely documented elsewhere. What I have intended to do in this article is to show how some of these themes have been realized in the classroom. I should, however, like to comment upon six factors which I believe were of key importance in the success of this practical experiment:

Six Factors

1 Subject Matter

The input, *Behind the News,* was perceived as interesting and relevant. Students were able to bring their own life experience and knowledge of politics, geography, and world events to bear; but students who did not know the background to any particular topic were not disadvantaged as each program item was delivered as a "whole" unit, with adequate background information to the topic, rather than assuming previous knowledge .

2 The Task

Producing a worksheet and presenting the program to the other group provided a clear goal. Students were using language to get things done and to acquire and impart information and knowledge; thus all communications were genuine. The task stimulated the learners to mobilize all their linguistic resources, to try persistently to extend their linguistic limits. As in real life, a variety of skills were integrated in the task; students were able to practice and develop those skills in a meaningful framework.

3 Learner-Centeredness

The giving over of control to the learners meant that they were able to share in the planning and development of the course, and to exercise their own choices in the subject matter, how the task was attacked, what was learned, and how much personal effort was invested. This not only increased motivation, sense of purpose, responsibility, and commitment, but allowed for different abilities and learning styles.

4 Group Work

The power of group work was evident. My own observations certainly support arguments in favor of group work (e.g. Nunan, 1988). In particular, the increased opportunities for negotiation of meaning within the groups seemed to me to be an important factor regarding the amount of learning taking place. It has been suggested (Long & Porter, 1985) that learners need the opportunity to "negotiate the new input, thereby ensuring that the language which is heard is modified to exactly the comprehensibility they can manage." They also claim that small-group work provides the optimum environment in the classroom for this to take place, as well as giving opportunities for production. Long and Porter cite second-language acquisition research where language has, in the course of negotiating meaning, been modified by learners, thereby increasing the amount of comprehensible input to which the learners are exposed. This, it is hypothesized, increases the rate at which they learn (Long & Porter, 1985).

The fact that my own class had quite a range of ability also seemed to increase the amount of negotiation, and consequent learning from each other, taking place—particularly as responsibility to one's group to give a good presentation meant that each individual needed a full understanding. This fostered a very supportive group atmosphere. The group feeling was compounded by the pride taken in the presentations.

5 Error Correction, Feedback, and Counseling

The weekly class feedback sessions and the individual tutorials seemed to be important factors in giving the course validity. The students were reassured that although, for the main part, they were concentrating on the task, they would have an opportunity to focus on the language and be offered some remedial help with their weaknesses. Thus, the students felt able to take full advantage of the opportunities presented by the task for fluency work and experimentation. The fact that follow-up language work stemmed from the students' own errors provided a personalized approach and made the language work itself more motivating.

6 The Presentations—Peer Teaching

I believe that the goal of "teaching each other" was a factor of paramount importance. Being asked to present something to another group gave a clear reason for the work, called for greater responsibility to one's own group, and led to increased motivation and greatly improved accuracy. The success of each group's presentation was measured by the response and feedback of the other group; thus there was a measure of built-in evaluation and a test of how much had been learned. Being an "expert" on a topic noticeably increased self-esteem, and getting more confident week by week, gave a feeling of genuine progress. The presentations were also seen as useful practice for university seminars and tutorials.

In addition, thinking about teaching seemed to bring about a greater awareness of learning. "Peer teaching" really seemed to be resulting in "peer learning."

NOTES

1 I am indebted to the following students for providing me with stimulation and support, and for allowing me to use their comments: Hiroyuki, "Steven," "Donna," Tae-Jung, Caroline, Wirot, "Bill," Supaporn, Kim, Cholatip, Toshi, Iwan, and Shanti.

2 A full list of student reactions is available from the author or the Australian College of English, P.O. Box 82, Bondi Junction, NSW 2022, Australia.

DISCUSSION QUESTIONS

1. What kinds of scaffolding are offered by video segments of the sort described? How do news segments contrast with fictional videos or with texts conjured up by language specialists?

2. Why should we expect increased participation from students in a peer teaching and cooperative learning context?

3. While EFL and foreign language teachers in traditional classrooms often lament the diversity of abilities with which they must contend, in a class where students work together through peer teaching and cooperative learning, diversity seems to afford some special advantages. What are they?

CHAPTER 25

Defossilizing

Helen Johnson

EDITOR'S INTRODUCTION

*A*ll language teachers know students who suffer from what Helen Johnson calls "chronic intermediate-itis." Their target language development seems stalled on a permanent learning plateau well short of nativeness. In my experience, one student I remember well was one I'll just call "Rada" (her nickname actually). Among other things, there were a few little phonological problems we singled out for attention in a tutorial setting. At UCLA, in those days, there was a course for TESL teachers to learn how to teach pronunciation and another for foreign students (some of whom also wanted to be English teachers) to improve their English pronunciation. Having just read Dykstra and Nunes (1970), I got the idea of putting these two groups together into a peer teaching experience (all 70 of them: about 35 in each category, tutors and "tutees" as one of the tutors called them). Because I wanted to be closely involved with the whole experience (since it was in California), I took on a non-native speaker too. Enter Rada. Yes, she was willing to sound more American, but she allowed as how she really sounded that way already. She didn't, according to her, produce any retroflex t's, d's, n's, or r's. None. Never mind the rest of the "foreign accent" that the diagnostic readings turned up. It was like beating my head against the Rock of Gibraltar, transformed into an East Indian accent. The course ended and a summer intervened. Then one day at Sunset Recreation Center, I heard someone yelling from across the parking lot: "Hey, John! Listen to my d's! No more retroflex alveolars!" And she was right. The alveolars and surrounding vowels were all perfectly American sounding. Rada had been transformed, alas, into a Valley Person. My point is that if students can become aware of subtle problems in pronunciation and syntax, and if they want to adjust toward a more native-sounding norm, it's possible. The key is resetting the internal calibration of the student's own perceptions of what is required. But, the body builder's caveat applies: no pain, no gain. In this chapter, the term deep end strategy may suggest a person learning to swim. The "deep end" of the pool, of course, is where you have to swim or drown. Now, neither Johnson nor I recommend the "deep end strategy," but here's her story.

The aim of this article is to consider what can be done for intermediate students of the sort we might entitle "fluent-but-fossilized," in other words, people whose communicative ability is rather high but whose accuracy is poor and showing no signs of improving. The assumed relationship within communicative language teaching between communicating and learning is explored, and methodological modifications are proposed for attempting to ensure that the communicative phase of a lesson counteracts rather than reinforces fossilization.

THE "FLUENT-BUT-FOSSILIZED" INTERMEDIATE STUDENT

We have all come across them at one time or another. Easily recognizable by their inability to move in any direction except sideways and by the glazing of their eyes when you mention the present perfect tense, I am, of course, referring to students suffering from chronic "intermediate-itis," students whose fluent and extensive output consists almost entirely of communication strategies and very little grammar—the "fluent-but-fossilized." Encouraged to follow the communicative path, these students have become hapless victims of their own success at achieving the goals we set up for them. Every method has its Frankenstein's monsters, grotesque parodies of whatever it is the teaching has emphasized, and these tediously inaccurate chatterers are the unfortunate creations of the communicative approach. In despair, at the end of another seemingly pointless lesson where much was said and all of it wrong, we may even question the whole wisdom of *allowing* communication in the classroom if we are to get such students to improve.

Action Research in the Classroom

How can such good communicators be such poor learners? This was the central question which sparked off the thinking behind this article. It led to the undertaking of a small-scale piece of action research, conducted with a class of "fluent-but-fossilized" students, where the relationship between communicating and learning was investigated. The main conclusions to which this led, as we shall see below, were that communicative interaction does hold great potential as an aid to learning, but that standard methodological procedures adopt a rather naïve, hope-for-the-best view of the communicating/learning relationship and may need re-thinking, if we are really to put pressure on students to move on.

The process of action research (Kemmis & McTaggart, 1982) involves identifying a problem, reflecting on the reasons why it exists, formulating an "action plan" to deal with the problem, and implementing it. We have identified our problem—the "fluent-but-fossilized" phenomenon. The rest of the article reports on the outcomes of the

other stages in the process. With reference to our particular field of enquiry, this means that we shall first of all explore the role of communicative interaction in communicative language teaching and attempt to identify aspects of standard procedures which may be leading to fossilization. We shall then formulate a set of principles for combating these tendencies and give some practical examples of how these might work.

COMMUNICATIVE INTERACTION IN COMMUNICATIVE LANGUAGE TEACHING

One might argue that there are two basic views of communicative interaction within communicative language teaching. In what we might term "conventional procedure," it comes at the conclusion of a sequence which begins with presentation and controlled practice. Naturalistic communicative interaction is seen as the necessary last step in a steady build-up to new learning. Another view stands this procedure on its head and starts the sequence with communicative interaction, with presentation and practice arising, in a relevant and motivating way, it is claimed, out of learners' mistakes in the first phase. We shall now look at these in more detail to try to see why it is that, for some students, neither of these works as a spur to learning.

"CONVENTIONAL" PROCEDURE

With students in the "fluent-but-fossilized" category, the conventional pedagogic process of presentation, controlled practice, and free practice may long since have ceased to be effective. If you are lucky, they will sit politely through your presentation and even join in when required, but interest is not engaged. When you reach the free-practice spot, the structure or function of the day will be conspicuous by its total absence from all classroom discourse.

If these were true beginners, one might say they were simply not ready yet; the internal syllabus had not caught up with the day's teaching. What we are describing here, however, are people whose internal syllabuses last made a move in 1986, then settled down comfortably and pulled up the drawbridge. Instead, therefore, it seems feasible to suppose that, for students such as these, there may be an essentially unmotivating aspect to this procedure. We noted above that when the communication phase is reached, it is as if the teaching had never happened, so totally have the students failed to engage with it. Perhaps this is because the content of the teaching phase is determined by the teacher and imposed on the students before they are made to feel any particular need for it. It could be that for fluent, blasé students to realize a relationship between learning and communicating, the relevance of any teaching needs to be highlighted with much more force than this procedural organization can manage. If this is the problem, then the next procedure should be more effective.

THE "DEEP END STRATEGY"

The "deep end strategy," a term coined by K. Johnson (1982) to describe a technique also discussed by Brumfit (1979), turns conventional procedure on its head, proposing instead the following (cyclical) outline (cf. Brumfit, 1979):

1. Students communicate with available resources.
2. Teacher presents items shown to be necessary.
3. Drill if necessary.

A central purpose behind this procedure is that it "should help to develop in the student a type of confidence essential to learning a foreign language: the confidence to attempt to say something which he knows that he does not really know how to say" (K. Johnson, 1982). Its main claim, then, is that the communicative interaction will move students on communicatively rather than linguistically. A second claim is, however, made. In the "deep end strategy," formal teaching, stage 2, occurs after a need has supposedly been established for it (stage 1). Students are expected to have difficulty in expressing themselves at stage 1 and therefore to be open to stage 2 teaching which is aimed specifically at these difficulties. The teaching should come, as Brumfit (1979) says, at a time when the students "clearly perceived themselves to need to improve." This suggests that starting from communicative interaction will provide a framework for teaching which is more student-centered, more relevant, and more motivating

than a conventional lesson where the teaching precedes the practice. It should, therefore, be good for the "fluent-but-fossilized."

There is, in addition, another theoretical perspective which might be imposed on the "deep end strategy"—that which derives from studies into communication strategies. According to Faerch and Kasper (1983), positive use of communication strategies creates learning opportunities. By trying at all costs to get one's message across, by conveying what it is one is attempting to say, one creates the possibility of learning, through the feedback one receives, how to convey it more correctly. The "deep end strategy" starts by requiring students to communicate "using available resources" and then goes on to supply the appropriate new linguistic resources. It should thus enable the sort of student being discussed here, good users of so-called "achievement strategies," to use their strategic competence for the enhancement of their linguistic competence.

Claims can thus be made for the learning potential which arises out of communicative interaction, particularly for the "fluent-but-fossilized," it would seem, if it comes first procedurally. Starting from the students' attempt to say something offers the possibility for very personally meaningful teaching, which is more likely to break down the immunity of these students than blanket doses of arbitrarily directed instruction. In addition, starting from the students should allow us to take advantage of what they are good at—using communication strategies—since, as we have seen, these can promote learning.

PROBLEMS WITH THE "DEEP END STRATEGY"

Experience shows that for students in the "fluent-but-fossilized" category, the procedure, as it stands, is not, after all, very useful. The stage 2 teaching and practice still do not seem to engender any great enthusiasm: in fact, it is all downhill from the peak of effort and interest at stage 1. Why should this be?

Success Through Strategic Competence

The first reason for failure lies in the fact that the initial goal of the "deep end strategy"—

"Communicate"—is achievable by these students through the application of their highly developed strategic competence. This means that "success" is achieved too early in the game, since, although it will take some effort, students *will* probably manage to cope at stage 1, communication of sorts *will* occur—perhaps even accompanied by the highly rewarding feeling of having amused one's classmates with creative use of language and gesture. The procedure operates by imposing a pressure to communicate, and, when this is achieved, albeit haphazardly, there is no subsequent pressure to improve: if you are told that the main aim of swimming is merely to stay afloat, you are unlikely to bother to learn the butterfly stroke. Instead of revealing a need for teaching, therefore, the "deep end strategy" merely serves to show the already fluent student that by normal standards he or she is managing perfectly well. Only a language teacher would judge otherwise.

The Teacher as Arbiter of Success

It is, of course, unfashionable to suggest that it is an absolute requirement for progress that the teacher should be the arbiter of success, but this is, in fact, a key observation and one for which we can find support from a variety of sources. Vigil and Oller (1976), for example, point out that it is the nature of the feedback which people receive during their attempts to communicate which is the determining factor in whether their grammatical systems move on or not: "any forms that elicit favorable feedback ["I understand"] will tend to fossilize." Since the "deep end strategy" has as its primary aim the transmission of a message to a peer audience, the feedback the communicative student receives in the course of stage 1 is, in Vigil and Oller's terms, favorable—and risks being too favorable, in fact, for progress to occur. To counteract this over-positive tendency, Vigil and Oller argue forcefully for the necessity of corrective teacher feedback.

Intrinsic and Extrinsic Feedback

The crucial role of the teacher as a provider of expert feedback is also stressed in the literature on skills acquisitions (discussed in Johnson, 1988). This distinguishes between two types of feedback

which a learner can receive when learning a skill: "intrinsic" feedback—the student's own experience of "whether the rudiments of survival have been met" (Johnson, 1988)—and "extrinsic" feedback—information on "whether externally imposed norms have been adhered to." Intrinsic feedback is a very blunt instrument: it will tell you only what *works*—and what works may be far from what is *correct*. As Johnson points out, "the rudiments of survival can be met by a form of pidgin." If the only feedback available is whether or not something works—the sort of feedback students give each other in a communicative task—it is likely that these pidgin forms will become established. Because the "norms" of language—refinements such as irregular past tense forms or adverbial endings—are to such a great extent arbitrary and, strictly speaking, unnecessary for survival, they will develop only if extrinsic feedback is available—that is, information as to whether or not something is correct, and the only reliable provider of such extrinsic feedback in the classroom is the teacher.

All this is recognized by the "deep end strategy," and indeed it does not rely solely on peer feedback: stage 2 is specifically designed for the giving of extrinsic feedback by the teacher. It is not, however, enough for it to be there; to be effective it has to come at the right time. If it comes after students have received an abundance of overwhelmingly positive intrinsic feedback, negative extrinsic feedback has little chance of making any impression: the swimming teacher's comments on the finer points of arm position will fall rather flat if you have already won the race with your own version of the stroke! Since the extrinsic feedback in the "deep end strategy" is given *after* the communication phase, which students will have survived using their present pidgin, there is a risk that they will feel no motivation to acquire the niceties they managed without, such as the third person -*s* or the past tense, even if these are corrected and practiced at stages 2 and 3.

Wasted Potential

In terms of communication strategy theory, we can see that there is a lot of wasted potential here. The students' achievement strategies do not lead to new learning, largely because no new learning is felt by the student to be needed for "deep end" survival: the strategies work perfectly well as substitutes. In addition, the structure of the "deep end strategy" is such that, even if a student makes an appeal to the teacher *during* stage 1 for a new piece of language which he or she feels *is* needed, the risk is that it will be forgotten as soon as it has served its communicative purpose. A possible reason for this lies in what we know about the concept of attention, the relevant fact being that attention is limited: we have only a certain amount available at any one moment, and, if there are too many demands on it, something will be ignored. In stage 1 of the "deep end" procedure, with all attention on communicating under the difficult circumstances of insufficient linguistic knowledge, there is very little attention to spare for learning. However, if the new language comes at stage 2, when attention is, in theory, available, it is too late, since success will already have been achieved without it, as we have seen above. Thus, the danger is that when the language is desired, it cannot be learned, and when it could be learned, it is no longer desired.

To summarize, then, in terms of the needs of the "fluent-but-fossilized," the "deep end strategy" allows the main goal of the task to be achieved too early and relies too much on students' own limited criteria for success. The teaching which takes place is mistimed, failing to observe what we have identified as the two learning requirements of perceived need and attention. It thus reinforces "coping mechanisms," encouraging students to flail about in pidgin rather than swim in English. As Vigil and Oller (1976) say, "unless learners receive appropriate sorts of cognitive feedback concerning errors, those errors can be expected to fossilize." In the light of the above discussion, we can begin to interpret this word *appropriate* as having to do with factors such as teacher involvement and, even more crucially, with the timing and interrelationship of the learning and communicating phases.

TOWARDS A MODIFIED PROCEDURE

For students with long experiences of communicative methodology, the same processes will be at work even when "conventional procedure" is used. They will soon learn that they can manage communicative pairwork without the demanding and fiddly linguistic refinements introduced in the first part of the lesson. Subsequent lessons will confirm this, increasingly reducing the attention students will devote to the teaching phases. In addition, there is the further disadvantage already identified that here the content is teacher-led and imposed on the students before they know precisely what it is for, so there is no attempt to create a specific motivation to learn either. What we can now identify as its advantage over the "deep end strategy"—that the teaching comes before the communicative aim is achieved—is cancelled out by the fact that there is no personal investment in the teaching phase on the part of the students.

All this might lead us to conclude that communicative interaction is not useful for the "fluent-but-fossilized"; perhaps it is better at showing unconfident students that they can cope communicatively than at showing the over-confident that they cannot cope very well linguistically. However, quite apart from the fact that we could not stop fluent, sociable students from communicating with each other, we have seen that this sort of interaction does have theoretical potential as an aid to learning. In examining reasons why it typically does not achieve its potential, what we have established is not necessarily that there is no relationship between communicating and learning, but perhaps that it is not a simplistic linear one. We might, then, begin to look for better ways of ensuring a relationship, ways which would capitalize on the best aspects of the procedures described above and deal with their faults.

The challenge we would face might then be formulated in the following terms: to find a way of starting from the students' desire and ability to communicate, which, unlike the "deep end strategy," would postpone the experience of communicative success until after new learning had had a chance to occur.

THE "TENNIS CLINIC STRATEGY"

We are already drowning, as it were, in metaphors, but, to find an appropriate name for our modified procedure, we shall leave the essentially solitary sport of swimming and turn to the game of tennis. Like language use, this is a two-way interaction; you can practice in advance and perfect your best shots, but each game is an essentially unpredictable encounter.

A "tennis clinic" is where people come along to receive advice on their game from an expert: "My serve isn't long enough—what can I do?"; "Am I holding the racquet correctly?"; and so on. The coach watches the player in action, advises, and sends the player off to impress the next match partner with newly learned skills.

Translating this into classroom tennis, we shall imagine the teacher as the coach and the students as players seeking advice on their "shots."

THE PROCEDURE IN PRACTICE

As an illustration of the proposed procedure, I shall describe a task which falls into the well-worn "survival games" category. Here are the students' instructions:

> You and your friends are going to go on a "Survival Expedition" to a desert island for a month. Each group of four is allowed to take ten items. There is water on the island and a natural supply of food (fruit, fish, etc.).
>
> 1. Work alone. Make a list of the ten items *you* would like to take. (If you don't know how to say any of these in English, write them down in your own language.) Plan, too, what you will say to persuade your friends to choose your items.
> 2. Check your list with the teacher. Try to get her to give you the English words you need.
> 3. Work with a partner. Explain your lists to each other and agree on *one* list of ten items.
> 4. Work with another pair and do the same again.

The language focus here is primarily on vocabulary, but the "persuading" aspect will occasion certain key structures and functions.

Phases of the Procedure

If we analyze what is going on in the task, we can see the following stages:

1. *Communicative goal* is set;
2. Students *plan* what they will want to say, including things they need to learn;
3. Students *learn* (through communicating individually with the teacher);
4. Students *communicate*.

Stage 1 of this procedure ensures the same overall focus as the "deep end strategy," that is, the desire to communicate. Note, however, that fulfillment of this aim is postponed until stage 4. This is to allow time for learning to occur—at stages 2 and 3—before communicative success has been achieved.

Stage 2 is new, and, whereas the "deep end strategy" merely reveals—to the teacher—a need for learning, this is an attempt to arouse a desire for learning, a desire for some new "shots," within the student. The fact that students are allowed to write in their own language should create the possibility for them to stretch their linguistic resources, rather than just stick to what they know already. Predicting language needs is, of course, usually regarded as the teacher's responsibility; handing it over to the students is not cheating: it is a way of increasing their active involvement in their learning.

Stage 3 is the actual "coaching" stage and has slightly different purposes for teacher and student. While the teacher is actually using the overall communicative aim of the procedure (stage 1) to motivate the student to learn, the student is encouraged to view this learning phase as a tool towards communication. It is predicted that learning has at least a chance of occurring here because it comes at a stage when there is still a student-initiated communicative need for it and, as it is clearly differentiated from the communication phase itself, because the students have time to give it their attention.

Given this timely sub-aim of learning and given that the interaction is with the teacher, it is now more likely that the students' communication strategies, which they will inevitably use in explaining their notes to the teacher, will lead to the uptake of new linguistic resources. The learning is thus *for* communication—which is what these students enjoy—and is achieved *by* communication—which is also what they are good at.

For the student, stage 4 is the culmination of the procedure, a real tennis match; for the teacher, it is a test of the effectiveness of the teaching and learning at stage 3.

APPLYING THE "TENNIS CLINIC STRATEGY" TO A TASK

As the no doubt familiar example above shows, with a bit of modification, this procedure can be applied to existing tasks. What is required is that the basic task should call for peer interaction with a communicative aim, which might, for instance, take the form of a discussion, a role play, or a simulation. As an example, many of the activities in Penny Ur's excellent *Discussions That Work* (1981) could be handled in this way. The only stipulation might be that the actual communication phase should be quite substantial, in order not to be *entirely* predictable in advance, which would render it unnatural and boring, and in order not to be outweighed by the preparation stage.

Normally, as we have seen, any teaching associated with such tasks takes place either before, where students' language needs are anticipated by the teacher, or after, where the teacher builds on students' mistakes. Modifying the task to incorporate the "tennis clinic strategy" will mean requiring the students to determine their own language needs for the task and to elicit instructional input from the teacher before they embark on it.

There are two categories of task language which students can be asked to plan: the interactional language which the task will require and the task data itself.

PLANNING FOR THE INTERACTION

We may decide that what we want to do is to take a task as it stands and ask students to predict some of the interactional language it will require ("Plan what you will say to your partner to describe/persuade/explain/find out . . . ," etc.). In the example task above, students are asked to do this. Such a process will require them to think functionally, structurally, and lexically.

Having thought about it and made some notes, in their own language if necessary, students then go through their ideas individually with the teacher, as we have seen above. This allows stu-

dents to receive instruction, correction, and reassurance, all of which they have asked for, at a useful point in the lesson.

PLANNING THE TASK DATA

Another way of modifying a task in order to introduce the element of student initiation is to examine whether some of the existing task data could be deleted and created instead by the students during the planning and learning phases. The usual version of the survival task type above presents students with complete task data in the form of a list of objects from which they have to choose, say, ten items. The modified version requires students to create the task data themselves in the form of individual lists. Not all tasks are amenable to this treatment, since some depend on the provision of well thought-out data, but many are.

The question we need to ask if we are looking to modify a task in this way is whether there is anything random about the task data. The materials designer may have produced an interesting set of data full of useful language, but if the content is random—that is, if an alternative set of data would allow the task to be done just as well—then the opportunity exists for this to be produced by the students. They may learn something different from what was envisaged by the writer, but at least they might learn *something*.

Once again, the teaching input will come as elicited feedback on the students' plans, before they take their data to the peer interaction. As a further example of this type of modification, we might take a similar task to the survival task, again involving a list, which comes from Penny Ur (1981: 173). This involves giving students a sample list of attributes for such people as a teacher, husband, soldier, which students then put in order of importance (e.g., intelligent, attractive, fair, has sense of humor, etc.). Once again, students could instead produce individual lists of attributes, with words checked with and learned from the teacher, which they would then negotiate with each other as above.

Another category of tasks which may be modified in this way is that which Penny Ur terms "choosing candidates" (1981: 73–80). Here students receive biographical data about various people and have to choose the best one for a particular purpose. Ur herself says that in a "sophisticated" version of such tasks, students can make up the candidates' data themselves. I would argue that this is indeed more sophisticated, not in the sense of being more difficult, but of being more motivating and more likely to lead to new learning, if this phase is regarded as a chance for student-initiated instruction-based interaction with the teacher.

SOME COMMENTS ON THE "TENNIS CLINIC STRATEGY"

The first obvious point to make about this modified procedure is that it cannot work as it stands as a large class activity; the teacher would simply not get around to everyone. With smallish classes it is fine, since when the teacher is with an individual, other members of the class will be refining their notes, double checking with the dictionary or grammar book, and generally preparing themselves in the time it takes for the teacher to spend some minutes with everyone.

To adapt it for large numbers might mean dividing the class and using this as an activity for a particular group, while the rest do something else, perhaps a reading or writing activity. Alternatively, one could compromise on the individualized aspect of the procedure and put students in pairs or groups for the initial planning stage, before being paired with someone from another group for the actual task. This would retain the spirit of the procedure in that each individual student would have had some input into the plan.

Another aspect of the procedure which may strike some as questionable is the fact that the final communication activity is rendered less spontaneous by the preparation stage. (Given the sort of students we have been discussing, this is entirely

intentional!) This could perhaps be objected to on the grounds that one is interfering with the students' freedom in some way, or on linguistic grounds. To the first objection I would say that, while there *is* an attempt to manipulate language use through teaching, *what* is taught is entirely left to the students. From the linguistic point of view, there is still, in fact, a high degree of unpredictability in the task, since no student has any idea what their partner will propose. The newly learned language will be a useful tool in the negotiation, but the negotiation interaction itself is unrehearsed and will still demand spontaneous communicative skills. Indeed, communication strategies will still need to be used, not as a substitute, but as a support, in that a partner will not necessarily understand the new word the student has just learned from the teacher and will need to have it explained. This in turn gives the partner the chance to learn the word as well. Paradoxically, therefore, through bringing forward the role of the teacher, the students have a greater possibility of learning from each other.

CONCLUSION

I hope that what the above discussion has shown first of all is that communicative interaction can be considered as a valid, learning-enhancing activity. What we do need to turn our attention to, however, is better and more subtle ways of capitalizing on it methodologically, with a specific focus on the relationship between communicating and learning. The "tennis clinic strategy" may not in itself be an immense discovery of vast importance, but I hope it serves as a practical example of how such thinking might help to create a "forward-moving" ethos in the communicative classroom. There may be no instant cure for "intermediate-itis," but we can at least try to give our students the will to recover.

DISCUSSION QUESTIONS

1. Why do we insist that if there is to be any improvement, the student must perceive the need for it? Why is it that someone with a fairly noticeable accent may not be able to hear it (even when listening repeatedly to a self-recording over a course that lasts about ten weeks)? Is the capability to monitor one's own speech patterns, especially the "fossilized" elements, prerequisite to changing them?

2. If mere communicative success, intrinsically motivated, in a particular context were all that mattered, why would a fossilized student bother with a few retroflex consonants and distorted vowels? But suppose that such a person really wanted to sound like a Californian (who knows why!). How would that person get the needed feedback in "ordinary" contexts? As Johnson sees it, "when the language is desired, it cannot be learned and when it could be learned, it is no longer desired" (p. 283).

3. Johnson urges that determining the language needs for the "Survival Game" is better done by the students than by the teacher. In fact, she says it isn't "cheating" but rather a way of "increasing their active involvement in their learning." Compare what she says with the cooperative learning and peer teaching ideas of Weissenrieder (Chapter 23) and Assinder (Chapter 24). Why are students more apt to comprehend and internalize language they need for a task that they will repeat many times over? (Also see Chapter 27 by Arevart & Nation.)

CHAPTER 26

Teenage Novels of Adventure as a Source of Authentic Material

Ben Christensen

EDITOR'S INTRODUCTION

In addition to their natural episodic organization, teenage novels of adventure, as Christensen suggests in this chapter, also contain peer-level characters that secondary and college students may identify with in the target language. Their "suspense, intrigue, fast action, opposing forces of tension, and cliff-hanging chapter endings have sustained the reading interest of millions of American youth during this century" (from Christensen's abstract, 1990: 531). He goes on to say that "editions of such novels with culture notes, glossaries, and classroom activities have much to offer the foreign language classroom." In addition to reference to The Hardy Boys *by Franklin W. Dixon and* The Nancy Drew Series *by Carolyn Keene, Christensen recommends* Las Aventuras de Héctor *by Pedro Casals for Spanish classes. Readers of Chapter 24 by Assinder will, no doubt, see plenty of potential for involving the students themselves in the preparation of the critical editions that Christensen has in mind for such adventure novels. The students, for example, are in an ideal position to advise the teacher on which vocabulary items belong in a glossary. They might even be able to point out the cultural elements that seem to merit explanation. They will readily be able to imagine ways to dramatize dialogues or act out scenes of particular interest in a given story.*

The category identified as "Authentic Materials" covers a wide range. Some people have defined *authentic materials* as those items that are "produced by members of the culture for members of the culture." Included are such sub-categories as physical objects, artistic renditions, advertisements of various sorts, and other writings, such as postcards and telephone messages or printed material, including such disparate items as dry cleaning tickets and literary pieces, which in turn may be further sub-categorized into various genres.

Currently, the foreign language teaching profession is interested in exploring how teachers might best use authentic materials for helping students acquire the target language as used in the "real world." For instance, on first glance at a magazine ad, one might not notice material that could be used profitably for instructional purposes in a classroom. Yet, teachers are finding interesting ways of using such material for gathering cultural information. For example, a typical Hispanic newspaper ad might contain one or two telephone numbers. A tight focus on these could help beginning students practice numbers as they are used in the real world, and demonstrate how telephone numbers are usually grouped in pairs, such as 9–23–46–21, rather than recited separately.

As we consider authentic material for possible use in the classroom, let us not overlook possible new uses of more traditional, "authentic" material. The authentic material suggested here is imaginative literature, specifically, the genre of the teenage detective novel.

Many will recall with fond memories how the Hardy Boys series (Dixon, 1959) in English captured their interest. Each novel in the series was an adventure-packed story with abundant intrigue and action. The Hardy Boys series and the Nancy Drew series (Keene, 1939), which have entertained countless young readers throughout the years, reflect the popularity of detective novels among the American adult reading public of earlier decades. The language of the "hard-boiled" brand of detective novel (Billman, 1986: 80), as exemplified in the works of Erle Stanley Gardner, Dashiel Hammet, and Raymond Chandler, was toned down in the Hardy Boys series, while the intrigue was maintained at a high level. Sons of a famous American detective, the Hardy Boys helped solve many thrilling cases after school hours and during vacations, as they followed up the clues they unearthed in their quest to bring criminals to justice. The level of language, of course, was carefully constructed to allow the reader to follow the plot without getting bogged down in cumbersome verbiage. One of the primary purposes of the Hardy Boys series was to help stimulate curiosity in young readers and, thereby, instill a desire to continue reading.

Franklin W. Dixon's first Hardy Boys title, *The Tower Treasure,* appeared in 1927. In 1984, Mr. Dixon published volume 80 of the Hardy Boys series, *The Roaring River Mystery.* The three-year period from 1983 to 1986 saw sales of over two and one-half million copies, demonstrating that this genre continues to have wide appeal and lasting value, even in the age of "hard-core" television watching. The Nancy Drew series has been featured in many book-length studies of the series book phenomenon. Articles about Drew's creator, Carolyn Keene, have appeared in scholarly journals, and prominent essayists, such as Ellen Goodman and Frances Fitzgerald, have written about the teen detective's literary significance (Billman, 1986: 100).

Many of the teenage adventure novels of the U.S. between 1900 and the end of World War II were developed around fixed formulas and themes of war, science, school, and sports. Over time the literary conventions of the basic adventure tale crystallized and were reduced to easily recognizable and repeatable formulas, which never seemed to fail in arousing curiosity. The repetitive, predictable structure of these works helped to pace the young reader's efforts.

Works of detective fiction are different from pure crime stories; the former "must be mainly or largely occupied with detection and should contain a proper detective, whether amateur or professional" (Stewart, 1980: 14). Of all the many teenage detective series, the Hardy Boys and Nancy Drew series have been the most popular. These two series exemplify the juvenile mystery genre in stark and formulaic relief, with the fast action of chases, attempts at code breaking, stereotypical villains, detectable clues, and a crime-infested environment where justice finally prevails and the "good guys" are enthusiastically commended by one and all.

The reader's interest is maintained through intrigue, mystery, and fast-paced action. While some may call detective fiction "sensational," it is, in fact, the opposite. Winks states that although the action may be sensational, "the process is to illuminate a special perspective on rationality. Rather than depend on the sensations alone . . . , detective fiction insists that there must be some explanation" (Winks, 1980: 5). In this connection, detective work arouses curiosity. The rational and objective process of detection is a part of science, which uses clues to uncover facts. Much of western civilization is based on the development of scientific fact and evidence. As Barzun states (1961: 15), "The detective tale arouses a double curiosity—what can the solution be? and how was the solution arrived at?" With insatiable curiosity, young readers often developed, consciously or unconsciously, a love for reading and, consequently, improved command of the language. These skills may not have been a direct result of these readings, but were likely partially due to them.

For many young readers, the act of opening a book invites the release of imagination and simulates the experience of peeking into a treasure box full of the unknown. As readers move through the book, they constantly look both backward and forward (a process language teachers pray for!), taking knowledge they have gained and using it to make guesses about what is still a mystery. They then revise these guesses as they read further and come upon more narrative evidence about the true direction and final outcome of the story. The mystery series, with its recognized clues as to the crime's solution and its cliff-hanging chapter endings, offers extraordinary stimulation for apprentice readers just beginning to experience comfort in the act of reading a novel.

If novels of this genre exist in the countries of the foreign languages we teach, and if such novels contain similar factors as those that have rendered the Hardy Boys and Nancy Drew series so successful, then a case can be made that such novels will be of interest to young readers in foreign language classes. Some of the more apparent factors involved in the success of the Hardy Boys series are action, suspense, and intrigue; dynamic opposing forces that set up tension, unusual characters; intelligent peer heroes; and the novelistic device of allowing the reader to have access to the characters' secret thoughts. In short, many of these factors are used to facilitate the release of the reader's imagination. Imagination is a key element in stimulating the student's interest in pursuing more actively the acquisition of the language and the target culture. In this connection, Peter Schofer (1990) makes a convincing argument about the use of literary elements as "authentic" material with which students might develop their reading skills and acquire language and a knowledge of the target culture.

The length of the novel is important; it should be relatively short so as to facilitate closure and a sense of finality and success. Editing of such novels is needed: the addition of glossary, footnotes, and some instructional activities. With this accomplished, teachers have "authentic" material for different levels of language proficiency in secondary schools and colleges.

ENTER PEDRO CASALS

A new series of teenage detective novels has recently been written in Spanish. The series is called *Las aventuras de Héctor* (Casals, 1989)[1] and contains a marvelous combination of the familiar world of adolescence and adventure-filled daydreams converted into a literary reality. So far, six short novels have been written. The author, Pedro Casals Aldama, a gifted storyteller, lives and works in Barcelona, Spain. His works have had a prestigious position on Spain's top ten best seller list for more than three years. He is the author of three different types of novels: l) a series of detective novels for mature readers in which the main protagonist is a "post-industrialist type" attorney with an MBA from Harvard, who possesses detective instincts, and whose clients are very wealthy and powerful chiefs of multinational corporations or other large enterprises; 2) the Héctor series, which is, itself, a detective genre for teenagers and young adults; and 3) historical novels. Casals approaches the work of writing novels from a Stendhalian perspective: the novel is a social chronicle steeped in the contemporary culture of the period that frames it.

Stylistically, Casals, like Hammet, Chandler, Gardner and other greats of the detective genre, utilizes the techniques of the *novela negra* ("dark novel") to probe those obscure zones that pulsate below the appearance of social norms. Casals has written several novels for adult readers, and some of these works have been translated into several languages, including Russian, German, and Portuguese. However, without abandoning the undemanding tone of his style, Casals has created characters in the Héctor series who act out diverse dramas of detective work and mystery with freshness and vigor. A number of critical works dealing with detective fiction suggest that the genre has now achieved respectability (Hart, 1987). Pérez (1988) indicates that the value of the *novela negra* is receiving increasing recognition in Spain as a reflection of the culture and a vehicle for analyzing the socioeconomic complexion of Spanish society. According to Pérez, contemporary scholars of the Spanish scene should be aware of the genre's potential.

THE HÉCTOR SERIES

The main characters of the Héctor series are a well-intentioned group of six teenagers, four boys (Héctor, Toni, Benjamín, and Luis) and two girls (Susana and Isabel, Luis' *novieta*).[2] These six youngsters form a gang that Casals calls the *tropa* and are caught up in a thousand and one adventures, some of which are typical pranks of mischievous minds. Another character in these novels is a police inspector who plays off the youngsters for his own purposes. The inspector puts their trust-worthiness to the test: he will forgive them for their pranks if they will help him gather information about criminals operating in the vicinity. The inspector represents one of the opposing forces, and this helps to establish the necessary tension to keep the reader involved. Each of the teenage characters reflects a different set of strengths and attributes which, presumably, are to be understood or admired by young members of the Spanish society. However, it is not surprising to find that the traits attributed to the main characters are rather universal and therefore understandable to young readers in U.S. Spanish classes. Incidentally, the group's inclination toward good-natured pranks is at once both humorous and culturally set, reminding one of the practical jokes the Bowery Boys set in motion many years ago in American movies. Although the members of the "tropa" seem not to be endowed with sleuth instincts to the same high degree as the Hardy Boys or Nancy Drew, the series is imbued with mystery, action, and adventure, with the tropa always gaining the upper hand over sinister characters. One salient feature of the Héctor series is the chain of assaults made upon the members of the tropa and the victorious results which fall in the members' favor.

According to Casals[3], the amount of reading in which Spanish youth are engaged is in decline. In the interest of making a humanistic attempt to encourage Spanish youth to read more, the author has added an unusual element in his Héctor novels: frequent reference to various literary classics. The police inspector is an avid reader of the classics. When the band of teenagers gets into a tight, suspenseful situation, the inspector is able to call upon a reasonable solution he has read about in the classics. As an example, Héctor and his friends are trapped underground due to a cave-in, and they believe they will suffocate. Through means of a walkie-talkie the inspector has entrusted to them, they are told to light a match. If the flame bends in one direction, that means there is a draft of air, perhaps too imperceptible to detect without the aid of the delicate flame. This solution came to the inspector after having read *King Solomon's Mines*. Other classics referred to in the novels of this series are *Tom Sawyer*, *The Count of Monte Cristo*, *Treasure Island*, *The Three Musketeers*,

and *Robinson Crusoe*. According to the author, the sixth novel in this series alludes to Joseph Conrad and features a boy with Down's Syndrome, whom the members of the *tropa* befriend. In the end, the boy is celebrated as everybody's hero. Since Casals' Héctor series is currently experiencing great success in Spain, perhaps the author has combined the right ingredients for meeting his humanistic aims while providing intrigue and mystery.

AUTHENTIC CULTURE

By almost every measure, the primary element of this kind of fiction is its action-based plot. The intrigue, as well as the interaction—sometimes humorous, sometimes serious—among the six teenagers moves the story forward at a fast pace. The plot, being fictional, is extraordinary and represents only certain facets of reality that the author provides to add a touch of verisimilitude. Furthermore, the author's style of writing is an important part of the overall value of each story. Casals allows the young reader to enter into a fictitious world of adventure that is filled with universally affective elements with which most young readers can identify: beliefs, emotions, personal values, or fantasies. Nevertheless, the author is a product of his cultural environment and society. That environment leaves its mark on the author and on his work. Here and there, throughout each story, we discover traces of cultural elements worthy of comment for the benefit of our students' understanding of Hispanic culture.

For example, in book 2 of the Héctor series, one can find the following topics to which the teacher may draw students' attention for broadening their cultural awareness:

- the extended family
- making friends
- tiles as common building materials
- soccer and football for youngsters
- adults' need to protect youngsters
- adults' need to preach to youngsters
- a Latino bar vs. a North American bar
- equal sharing of food among friends
- many idiomatic expressions that reflect cultural values

- *compadrismo*
- trust in close friends
- portable clothes closet
- flamenco music
- slang forms of speech
- door-to-door beggars
- good luck charms
- various gestures

These topics, among many others, can be useful in directing students' attention to specific details underlying the target culture. In-class discussions may lead students to an understanding of the differences and similarities that relate to the attributes of members of both cultures. In one novel, for example (novel #2, p. 18), one finds the followings description: *". . . penetraron agachados en el pasadizo descendente debajo techo que olía a iglesia vieja . . ."* (". . . they crept along the descending passageway under a roof that smelled like an old church . . ."). The reference to the smell of an old church is loaded with cultural information: A visit to any one of Spain's old gothic-style churches provides an unmistakable olfactory experience due to the musty ambience of centuries of mildew and dust accumulation. Pictures of the interiors of some old Spanish churches help students understand the relationship between musty odors and antiquities and to the author's allusion.

On another occasion, Susana, one of the gang members, enters the group's hide-out and begins to dance and *"dar palmadas . . ."* A bit of culture may be "teased out" of this scene by focusing on the Spaniards' penchant for engaging in a special type of clapping that usually accompanies flamenco music. American students could be treated to samples of both the music and the accompanying clapping. One popular Spanish group, the Gypsy Kings, has recently toured the U.S. and has an album in which one can hear the typical *palmadas*. When two or more Spaniards engage in this clapping activity, a unique sound is created. The cadence comes from the coordinated descant-type of clapping created when one person's hands move away from each other after the clap and another person's hands, at that precise moment, come together. This rapidly repetitive counterpoint action creates a wonderful percussion sensation, which has been developed to perfection in Spain.

An interesting look at one specific cultural behavior of Spaniards is related to this clapping activity. Spanish youth often walk along the streets at night in groups, enjoying this flamenco-type clapping as a form of togetherness and companionship. Excerpts from Carlos Saura's film *Carmen* would allow students to experience flamenco music and dance as a fascinating element of Spain's culture. As a follow-up activity, the teacher might ask students to think of comparable ways American youngsters engage in "friendship" activities.

As another example of a specific element of culture, Héctor, the leader of the group, congratulates Luis, one of the gang members, for his ingenuity in tricking a thief. Héctor says: *"Eres un genio! Te lo has toreado!"* (You're a genius! You have really bullfought [i.e., tricked] him). Reference to the activity of bullfighting in this context conjures up the art of the toreador, who taunts the beast again and again with feints and dodges, until the bull becomes tired or bewildered and seems to give up the fight. In the context of bullfighting, all the *toreando* comes before the so-called moment of truth, which is secondary to the skill the toreador must display to guard his own life in the bullring. In the Héctor novel, the allusion to the trickery of the bullfighter is well placed in the context of the adventure the gang members have had with the thief. Again, in this connection, Barzun makes a cogent statement, "Only in the detective tale is the hero demonstrably as bright as the author says he is" (1961: 17).

AUTHENTIC MATERIAL AND COOPERATIVE LEARNING: THE JIGSAW

In recent years, several studies (Pica & Doughty, 1985b; Webb & Kenderski, 1984; Long & Porter, 1985) have focused on the effectiveness of small-group interaction in second language acquisition. The results of Ballman (1988) suggest that class time is best used in meaningful, communicative tasks. Rivers (1987) states that communication derives from interaction, i.e, sharing something of interest with someone else, and that interactive language teaching is, by nature, student-centered. In order to teach for communication, teachers must develop a store of interactive teaching techniques that can be adapted to specific instructional environments, resources, and learner characteristics.

Among some of the more contemporary and successful interactive classroom activities suitable for foreign language practice are cooperative learning activities, whose fostering of mutual cooperation can help to enrich the ambience in which students work to meet curricular objectives. Generally, teachers want students to be interested in what they are learning. Apart from the content of the material, another factor that causes young minds to focus on any particular objective is peer allegiance. Of interest to the foreign language teacher is how to harness this in guiding to focus on class objectives.

In discussion or analysis of literature, particularly narrative or prose literature, the "Jigsaw" activity of cooperative learning is particularly appropriate. In this activity teams of four students are formed ("best friends" grouping should be avoided if there appears to be a social rather than an academic agenda).

Once teams have been formed, each team member receives a number from 1 to 4. Prior to class, the teacher has identified four topics for discussion, chosen from the pages the students were previously assigned to read as homework. For example, the following topics, originally given in Spanish, were developed for one of the Héctor novels (novel #2, pp. 5–30) and were used in an intermediate conversation class at the college level.

1. Inspector Mora: Who is he? What is he like?
2. H Bomb (Susana): Who is she? What is she like?
3. Héctor: Who is he? What is he like?
4. The meeting between Héctor, Susana, and Mora: What happened?

Later on in the course, another set of topics is used (pp. 87–101).

1. All the things Mora did before arriving at the building.
2. All the things Héctor did before Mora arrived at the building.
3. All the things Mora did after arriving at the building.
4. All the things Héctor did after Mora arrived at the building.

Each of the four topics is assigned to the correspondingly numbered team members. Students are given about ten minutes to scan the pages they had read as homework in order to gather information for support of the topic each student has been assigned.

All students with number one are then directed to move to one corner of the classroom to exchange (in the target language) information they were able to uncover about their topic through the scanning activity. They become the so-called "experts" on their particular topic. Likewise, groups 2, 3, and 4 are directed to congregate in other corners of the room to exchange ideas and information about their topics.

This exchange of information takes approximately ten minutes. Students are encouraged to take notes based on their discussion. After this phase of the "Jigsaw," students are asked to return to their original teams, so that each team is composed of 4 experts on 4 different topics.

In their original teams, each student informs the other three team members about the topic he or she discussed in the "expert" group. Team members may be given about two minutes each to convey as much pertinent information as possible. When all four team members have presented their "expert" information, the whole class is given a short quiz over pertinent information based on the content of the assigned homework pages. The design of the quiz questions should not necessarily focus on discrete content items (i.e., specific dates, names, etc.) but rather on questions they may answer from inference, based on their "expert" group discussions and subsequent presentations to their team members. The quiz is needed as a stimulus to spur students on toward meeting the objectives of communicating to exchange information.

The "Jigsaw" process provides ample opportunity for students to listen to and speak about concrete ideas found in the pages they were assigned for previous reading. What is challenging in the "Jigsaw" is the freshness of the four discussion topics the teacher plans beforehand and gives to the four members of all teams on the day of group conversation. Classmates are challenged to read carefully during their homework activity and, later, to scan carefully about the topics they have been assigned. Moreover, students feel compelled to listen carefully and to contribute to the overall body of information pertinent to the topic of the "expert" group and to relate that information concisely to their original team members. Thus, in this type of activity, students read, listen, speak, and write notes at their own level of proficiency. As is often the case in this type of cooperative activity, students want to say more. Their level of proficiency is stretched, because they have chosen to stretch it.

Students who have used the "Jigsaw" activity to discuss Casals' Héctor novels have found the experience rewarding and enriching. More in-depth communication seems to be achieved through this activity than through other types of small group tasks. However, as for any lesson preparation, the teacher must carefully decide on the topics that the small groups will use for their discussions.

To read several novels of a series, one after another, is to come to know the idiosyncrasies of the characters. Héctor, the natural leader of the *tropa,* reveals himself by allowing the reader to know his thoughts. Héctor is a responsible and reflective individual whose leadership qualities are admirable. Benjamín, on the other hand, is a feisty yet humorous youngster whose qualities include a fascination for the intricacies of chemistry. He is the specialist in the use of cherry bombs. Again and again, the author of the series instills in each of the individual characters special traits and strengths with which American youth may come to identify. For years, young American readers have identified with similar traits and strengths in the many teenage novels on the American scene. These personal traits taken collectively, over time, provide a framework for accessing the culture of their origin. In this respect there can be no doubt that the teenage novel of detective adventures is a bona fide source of authentic material for the foreign language classroom. And, like Nancy Drew and the Hardy Boys, the Héctor series holds great promise for displaying enduring power and for stimulating access to the language and the culture.

NOTES

1 The publisher of the Hector series is Planeta, one of the largest publishing houses in Spain. The author plans to write more of these novels on a regular schedule during the next several years. The print size on each page is rather large, and the length of each novel is approximately one hundred and twenty pages. The dimensions of the printed page are three and a half by six inches. Thus, the total amount of reading matter in one of these novels is quite manageable during a normal term of instruction. Classroom editions are forthcoming from Heinle & Heinle Publishers, Boston, MA.

2 The term *novieta* may just be the felicitous term Spanish teachers have been seeking for so many years to refer to the English equivalent of *girlfriend.* As is known, the term *novio* or *novia* refers to *fiancé* or *fiancée,* respectively, and not to the popular relationship of *boyfriend* or *girlfriend.*

3 Personal communication with Pedro Casals.

DISCUSSION QUESTIONS

1. Consider the ways that fictional scenarios in any adventure novel resemble real-life experiences.

2. Some might complain that the Hardy boys, Nancy Drew, and even Héctor are too tame for today's foreign language crowd. That they need something racier, a little more contemporary. In response to that complaint, compare any one of the novels discussed by Christensen with the typical materials that are produced by authors of foreign language textbooks. Or, for that matter, take most any anthology of great literature down from the shelf and compare. Which story is easier to visualize? Which is more apt to generate suspense? Which one contains the greater degree of contextual constraints to help students figure out its meanings? And, finally, the clincher: which one has sold millions of copies to eager readers?

3. In the "Jigsaw" cooperative learning activity, Christensen says that students often want to say more than their present level of proficiency will allow. As a result, "their level of proficiency is stretched, because they have chosen to stretch it" (p. 294). Why is this stretching apt to be more effective than any the teacher might try to impose?

CHAPTER 27

Adjusting Fluency and Grammar Through Repetition

Supot Arevart and Paul Nation

EDITOR'S INTRODUCTION

This entry is actually a combination by the editor (with the permission of the authors in question) of two earlier research reports that appeared in the RELC Journal *in 1989 and 1991. The report (by Arevart & Nation, 1991) given in this chapter (with a few changes) as Study 1 dealt with fluency improvement owed to repetition of a discourse task. Arevart (1989), included here with some changes as Study 2, singled out a particular individual's performance and examined it for improvements in surface form. On both accounts, the mere repetition of the task (under increasingly severe time constraints—in four minutes, three minutes, and two minutes) was apparently effective in producing improved fluency and grammatical accuracy. The idea that repetition will help a student work out a more fluent presentation is not too surprising, but that it also results in improved grammatical accuracy may have some surprise value for certain theories. In yet another study, Nation (1989) found that repetition also enabled subjects to increase the complexity of the constructions they used in speaking. At any rate, the method of asking students to repeat a discourse or segment thereof in a target language is not a new one, but it is seen here, I think, in a new light. Moreover, however simple it may be, repetition works.*

Fluency in language learning includes the ability to make the most effective use of what is already known. Fillmore (1979) describes four kinds of fluency, the first of which is "the ability to fill time with talk." This requires learners to be able to draw quickly on their language resources in order to put their message across. A lack of fluency is characterized by a slow and hesitant delivery and in some cases by grammatical errors owed partly to inefficient planning of speech. It was hypothesized that the repetition of a talk would result in improvement in both the fluency and accuracy of the language used. Study 1 examines improvements in fluency owed to repetition, and Study 2 looks closely at gains in grammatical accuracy for just one subject.

THE FOUR, THREE, TWO (4/3/2) TECHNIQUE

In an attempt to provide practice in speaking for learners of English as a second language, Maurice (1983) devised the 4/3/2 technique. In this technique, learners deliver a 4-minute talk on a familiar topic to a partner. Then they change partners and deliver the same talk to a different partner but with a 3-minute time limit. Finally, they change partners again and deliver the same talk in 2 minutes to their new partner. Thus, each speaker has to deliver the same talk three times to three different people, with a decrease in the time available for each delivery. Each of these three features—a changing audience, repetition, and decreasing time—makes an important contribution to improved fluency.

The changing audience, the first feature, makes sure that the speaker's focus continues to remain on the message, because although the message is repeated, it is delivered each time to someone who has not heard it before. This also reduces the speaker's need to add new information to the talk. If it were delivered to the same listener more than once, the speaker might feel the need to keep the listener interested by changing the content. The second feature, the repetition of the talk, has a major effect on fluency because it increases the speaker's familiarity with both the form and content of the material and thus increases the speed with which a speaker can access wanted forms. The third feature, the decrease in time from 4 to 3 to 2 minutes, has several effects. First, it puts pressure on the speaker to increase the rate of speaking. Second, it greatly limits the opportunity for the speaker to add new material in the 3- and 2-minute deliveries of the talk. This is important because the addition of new material would reduce the proportion of repeated material between the talks. Repeating the same material from one talk to the next allows the speaker to reach a level of fluency and accuracy higher than his or her usual performance.

In Study 1, the performance on the 4-minute delivery is assumed to be the speaker's usual level. The 3-minute and 2-minute deliveries are compared with the 4-minute delivery to see if there is improvement. It is hypothesized that fluency will improve from the first to the third repetitions. In Study 2, the same sort of assumption is made except that we concentrate on grammatical contexts (complexes of structures and content) which occurred in at least two deliveries of the talk. It is hypothesized that errors committed are apt to be corrected on successive repetitions so that the second will be more accurate than the first and the third more accurate than the second.

STUDY 1: FLUENCY

Research on speaking fluency has shown that repetition has positive effects. Goldman-Eisler (1968) asked subjects to describe and interpret cartoons. With unlimited time allowed, the speakers were asked to repeat the task six times. Goldman-Eisler found that the duration of pauses gradually decreased from the first to the sixth repetition.

Heike (1981b) studied a procedure he called Audio-Lectal Practice (ALP). In Heike's procedure, graded texts of increasing length and complexity in vocabulary and sentence structure are recorded at normal native speed. First, learners listen to the text while silently reading it. Second, while listening and looking at the text, they simultaneously speak onto the tape in an imitative fashion. Third, they listen to their own versions, comparing them with the model and jotting down phonological errors and all other deviant features. Finally, the learners repeat the second step, but at this stage they must reduce their errors. Repetition continues until their version matches the model as much as possible. In Heike (1981b), tests were given before and after 12 sessions of training to 29 intermediate to low-advanced students studying English as a foreign language. The format of each test was identical. In the first part of each test, the subjects were asked to listen to a 5-minute short story once. They were not allowed to take notes. Then they had to paraphrase the story in three minutes. In the second part of each test, the subjects told a story based on a series of cartoons. The recordings were transcribed and analyzed. Fluency was measured by calculating the number of syllables uttered divided by total speech time. Hesitation phenomena were also counted. The comparison between the results of the pre- and post-tests of both kinds showed that the speaking rate increased and the number of hesitations decreased. Further, Heike found that *uh*-phenomena decreased more than did repeats and false starts.

A study involving the effects of repetition on the control of content was carried out by Brown, Anderson, Shillcock, and Yule (1984). Their subjects were asked to work on two types of tasks, namely a static task and a dynamic task. In the static task, the speaker had to provide the hearer with sufficient instructions on how to reproduce a diagram, rearrange a particular model, or put parts of an object together. In the dynamic task, the speaker had to describe pictures so that the hearer could either choose the correct picture according to the order or identify persons or things appearing in the pictures. Two studies were conducted, each of which consisted of two sessions one week apart. In the first study, the subjects were given practice in speaking on the tasks. In the second type, the subjects acted as hearers immediately prior to performing the tasks as the speakers. The talks were analyzed for the amount of detail they contained.

Brown et al. found that the amount of required information increased in the second occasion of each study. Further, it significantly increased if the subjects had been in the hearer's role before they performed as the speaker. Brown et al. concluded that speakers improve as a result of prior experience in speaking on the tasks, and even more so if they also act as hearers immediately before speaking.

In a study involving only six speakers, Nation (1989) found that while doing the 4/3/2 technique, learners significantly increased their speed of speaking, reduced the number of hesitations, reduced certain types of grammatical errors, and used two or three more complex constructions to convey the same information. The present study is an attempt to replicate the previous study with a larger group of people and to look at the relationship between speed of speaking and hesitation. It investigates the following questions: Does repetition of a talk result in increased fluency as measured by words per minute and hesitations per 100 words? Are both of these measures necessary to assess fluency?

Subjects and Procedure for Study 1

The 20 subjects in the experiment were 10 males and 10 females, with ages ranging from 19 to 50 years. They came from 16 different countries, including Switzerland, China, and Tonga. They were all members of an English proficiency course at Victoria University of Wellington, New Zealand, and had obtained total scores on dictation, vocabulary, and cloze tests that placed them within an intermediate range of proficiency. The study was conducted after the subjects had been following the course for eight weeks.

The speakers talked to classmates who shared the same daily experience, and the relationships among the learners were established through the experience of the preceding eight weeks. As the transcripts show, the learners had no difficulty in addressing one another and talking at length. To avoid the effect that shared L1 backgrounds might have on the speaking tasks, the subjects were split into five groups. Each group participating in the

experiment consisted of students with four different first languages. Initially, the subjects were told to talk about their own experiences, but topics of common interest were also permitted since they made the subjects feel at ease. It was decided to have the subjects select the topic according to personal interest because such a topic might encourage a better performance, owing to motivation and confidence.

TABLE 27.1 The Arrangement of the Subjects

Sequence	Speakers	Listener 1	Listener 2	Listener 3
1	Subject A	Subject B	Subject C	Subject D
2	Subject B	Subject C	Subject D	Subject A
3	Subject C	Subject D	Subject A	Subject B
4	Subject D	Subject A	Subject B	Subject C

Table 27.1 summarizes the way speakers and listeners were arranged. For example, when Subject A was speaker, B, C, and D in turn played the role of listener. As soon as A finished the task, A became the third listener for subject B as speaker, and so forth as shown. The talks were tape-recorded and later transcribed. Where necessary, the transcriptions were checked by the speakers. Hesitations, repetitions, long pauses, and errors were all included in the transcripts. The 9 minutes of talk from each subject (4 + 3 + 2 = 9) took about an hour and a half to transcribe. Appendix 27.1 contains one full transcript of the Swiss subjects' three deliveries. That transcript was selected as typical.

Analysis and Results of Study 1

Fluency was measured in words per minute and hesitations per 100 words. In determining words per minute, contracted forms were counted as separate words, e.g., *I'm* was counted as two words. Hesitations included *uh*-phenomena (*uh, er, um*), repairs (*you had hadn't you had never met*), sentence incompletion (*before they said that the it mean that it is 1975*), repetition (*if anyone don't go to work they they accuse that . . .*), markers of correction (*about five years or sorry about five or seven year*), and intrusions such as throat clearing or sighs. Each hesitation unit was counted as one item. So one repair containing four words was

TABLE 27.2   Changes in Speed of Speaking for 20 Subjects Over Three Deliveries of the Same Talk

Subjects	WPM in the 1st delivery	WPM in the 2nd delivery	WPM in the 3rd delivery	Percentage increase
1	106.75	91.33	118.50	11.0%
2	97.00	110.33	127.00	23.6%
3	56.75	62.33	57.50	1.3%
4	122.75	120.00	121.00	-1.4%
5	78.75	84.66	88.00	11.7%
6	84.00	87.00	105.00	25.0%
7	88.25	95.00	104.00	17.8%
8	94.00	105.66	111.00	18.1%
9	64.25	70.33	82.50	28.4%
10	85.50	101.00	111.00	29.8%
11	66.25	76.33	82.00	23.8%
12	130.00	139.00	151.50	16.5%
13	89.00	88.66	101.00	13.5%
14	66.75	85.33	108.19	62.1%
15	58.75	65.33	82.50	40.4%
16	101.00	120.00	114.50	13.4%
17	110.50	117.66	112.50	1.8%
18	49.50	71.00	77.00	55.6%
19	79.00	96.33	120.00	51.9%
20	60.00	65.66	77.00	28.3%
Average	84.44	92.65	102.59	21.5%

counted as one hesitation. Each repetition was counted as a hesitation. So *to to to go to different schools* included two hesitations, the second and third utterances of *to*. Research by Lennon (1990) supports the use of speech rate (words per minute) and filled pauses (hesitations) as indicators of fluency improvement.

As seen in Table 27.2, there was an average increase of just over 18 words per minute (an overall improvement of 21.5%) from the first to the third delivery. If the first delivery is taken as the subjects' normal average rate, we can see that by the third, they are performing well above normal. Only three subjects showed little change, and two of these were speaking fluently on their first delivery. PROC GLM in SAS was used to analyze the data, with subject as a random effect crossed with occasion (1st, 2nd, or 3rd delivery). Using the occasion-subject interaction as an error term for the test of an effect due to occasion produced a highly significant effect across occasions, $F_{2, 38} = 33.41$, $p < .0001$. Subjects increased their rate of speaking significantly across the three deliveries.

(See also Figure 27.1.) Corresponding to an increase in words per minute, we would expect the number of hesitations to decrease. Table 27.3 shows that this happens. On the average, speakers decreased by 3.88 hesitations per 100 words from the first to the third presentation, with 17.52 hesitations in their first delivery and 13.64 in their third (a decrease of 22.1%). The decrease was significant, $F_{2, 38} = 8.65$, $p < .0008$, as expected.

Although five of the subjects (Table 27.3) increased their number of hesitations per 100 words from the first to the third delivery, three of them simultaneously increased their rate in words per minute, supporting Lennon's (1990) finding that learners may improve on different variables. The two measures on the whole, however, as seen in Figure 27.1, both show that repeating a talk results in greater fluency. The figure also shows the strong correlation between hesitations per 100 words and words per minute. In fact, these variables are so strongly correlated that combining them explains 95% of the variance in the covariance matrix. With both hesitations and words per

TABLE 27.3 Changes in Rate of Hesitations for 20 Subjects Over Three Deliveries of the Same Talk

Subjects	Hesitations per 100 words in the 1st delivery	Hesitations per 100 words in the 2nd delivery	Hesitations per 100 words in the 3rd delivery	Percentage decrease
1	5.39	4.02	1.27	76.4%
2	22.42	16.92	15.35	31.5%
3	15.86	12.30	13.91	12.3%
4	10.00	15.56	18.18	+ 81.8%
5	22.86	16.93	18.75	18.0%
6	7.44	8.81	10.48	40.9%
7	13.88	11.23	6.25	55.0%
8	22.87	15.77	17.57	23.2%
9	21.01	21.80	13.94	33.7%
10	19.30	16.83	18.02	6.6%
11	17.74	13.54	11.59	34.7%
12	2.70	2.16	1.98	26.7%
13	10.39	9.77	5.94	42.8%
14	33.71	23.05	24.38	27.7%
15	25.53	26.02	26.06	+ 2.1%
16	6.43	5.83	6.55	+ 1.9%
17	12.67	9.63	13.78	+ 8.8%
18	36.36	22.54	20.13	44.6%
19	9.81	6.57	7.75	21.0%
20	34.00	26.40	21.00	38.2%
Average	17.52	14.28	13.64	22.1%

minute in a multivariate analysis of variance, F 2, 38 = 33.49, $p < .0001$, which is only slightly larger than the F-ratio for words per minute alone. This shows that words per minute alone would be a good index of improvement in fluency.

Discussion of Study 2

The significant improvement over the three deliveries shows the value of repetition with a focus on the message. Even when the subjects know the words or form, they may still have difficulty accessing them when their attention is focused on conveying a message. Given repeated opportunities, however, as in the 4/3/2 technique, learners are often able to come up with the lexical material and structures that they need. With practice, through repetition, they may improve their fluency to a level well beyond where they started out in the first session.

Moreover, the 4/3/2 technique can be used with small and large classes. We have used it in large lecture halls with the people at the ends of rows moving and those inside staying seated. Maurice (1983) has suggested that the learners in a pair might stay together until both persons have taken a turn at delivering their talk before they move on to new partners. In Study 2, however, we had speakers repeat their talks immediately to maximize their tendency to repeat material they used in prior deliveries. Allowing students to pre-plan their talks ought to produce some advantage in fluency, but we have not yet tested this idea experimentally.

Our study shows that fluency can be improved through a repetition task that involves fairly long turns (4, 3, and 2 minutes). It is expected that improved fluency owed to repetition of the sort described here will carry over to other speaking tasks, but that demonstration awaits further study. In the meantime, in Study 2, we look at the impact of the 4/3/2 procedure on the grammatical accuracy of a single individual.

FIGURE 27.1 Change in Number of Hesitations and Words per Minute Over the 4/3/2 Procedure

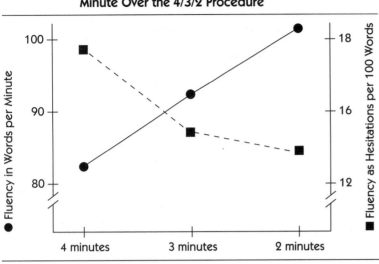

STUDY 2: GRAMMATICAL ACCURACY

There is no question that hesitation phenomena are linked with the sort of planning that determines the surface structures that are actually produced in spontaneous speech. Goldman-Eisler (1968: 31) observed that speaking is "a highly fragmented and discontinuous activity" because the speaker does not always have everything planned out before beginning to produce the message. Planning what to say, what to omit, what to include, or how to convey the message usually begins at the time the speaker is about to speak and continues while the speech is being produced. As a result, the speaker is apt to hesitate, revise, replan, repeat, and sometimes backtrack. This study focuses on how such planning and reworking (while speaking is in progress) may be affected by repetition, specifically the 4/3/2 procedure.

While the significance of hesitation phenomena is not perfectly understood (Leeson, 1975), they have been known for some time to be associated with a variety of cognitive activities (Henderson, Goldman-Eisler, & Skarbek, 1966; Goldman-Eisler, 1967) that are involved in speech production. For instance, hesitations are often associated with anxiety (Mahl, 1956; Mahl & Schulze, 1964). They are also known to be involved in planning and selection of novel constructions (Temple, 1985). They may be essential for the speaker in producing well-planned utterances

(Heike, 1981a). In some cases, they are probably owed to individual style of speaking (Deuz, 1982).

On the whole, hesitation phenomena can be divided into two main types: (1) silent or unfilled pauses and (2) lapses or filled pauses, each with its own features that may vary depending on the speaker (Maclay & Osgood, 1959) and task (Goldman-Eisler, 1968). Unfilled pauses occur most often at clause boundaries. *Lapses*, a term applied to filled spaces where something has gone awry, are commonly accompanied by kinesic phenomena (significant gestures or body movements—Ragsdale & Silvia, 1982; Butterworth & Beattie, 1978) and consist most frequently of *uh*-phenomena (Ragsdale & Sisterhen, 1984). Lapses may involve a single sound, a syllable, a word, or a string of words. They are quite generally related to lexical selection (Maclay & Osgood, 1959; Goldman-Eisler, 1961). Another common kind of lapse consists of repetition, repair, or stuttering (Ragsdale & Sisterhen, 1984; Ragsdale & Silvia, 1982) often associated with anxiety (Mahl, 1956; Mahl & Schulze, 1964; Ragsdale, 1976; Siegman & Pope, 1965). Of course, the functions or causes of hesitation phenomena may overlap such that those at the beginning of a string are related to those occurring later. Loban (1966: 8) points out that lapses, in particular, do not "constitute a communication unit and are not necessary" to it. When the lapses are removed, the grammatical acceptability of the communication is not reduced.

In any case, it seems that the hesitation phenomena that are common to spontaneous speech always signal some form of planning, editing, or searching for information. To explain the phenomena actually observed in the 4/3/2 tasks, a three-step model is proposed in Figure 27.2. In step 1, the speaker becomes aware of a problem in production. This awareness is apt to be revealed in one or more hesitation phenomena. In step 2, adjustment of some kind occurs in the surface form but usually not without one or more lapses or unfilled pauses. Finally, in step 3, the surface form appears without further adjustments and without accompanying hesitation phenomena.

FIGURE 27.2 A Model of Self-Correction

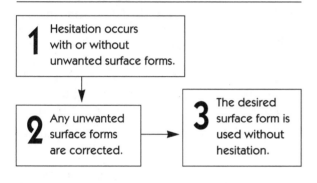

Procedure for Study 2

In fact, the Swiss subject from Study 1 served as the single case to be examined closely here (see the transcripts in Appendix 27.1). Each of the three talks was recorded in a soundproof room. During each session, while the speaker was delivering the talk to one of the listeners, the other two were seated in a separate room so that they could not hear what was being said. As soon as the speaker finished the 4-minute session, the first listener left the room and the next listener entered.

As with all of the transcripts for Study 1 above, wherever the recording was unintelligible the subject was asked to listen to the tape and interpret what was being said at that juncture. The subject for this case study (from here on referred to as B) was a 34-year-old female, native Swiss-German speaker who had begun studying English as a foreign language in Switzerland at the age of 27. At the time of the study she reported using English at home along with Swiss-German and

German. When the study began, she had been in New Zealand for about 4 months and prior to that time had never studied in a university.

Her three talks, all about the festival called *Fastnacht* (see Appendix 27.1), were given to three listeners from Japan, Taiwan, and Samoa, respectively. B spoke at a rate of 88, 92, and 104 words per minute in the first, second, and third deliveries. She had 14 lapses per 100 words in the 4-minute delivery, 13 in the 3-minute, and only 6 in the 2-minute turn. A number of hesitation phenomena were observed in her talks. They seemed to serve four distinct functions, which are discussed in order of descending frequency of occurrence with examples.

Editing

Editing may involve (1) substitution of one surface element for another to achieve greater semantic and syntactic accuracy, (2) making an element more explicit or specific, and/or (3) omission of unnecessary elements. Editing always yields a successful outcome: the target error is changed and a correct form is produced. For B, 90% of the observed hesitation phenomena are of the editing type. Most commonly, in the 17 cases seen in the data, B reaches a solution which satisfies her immediately following the lapse. Here are a few typical examples:

(1) . . . it's called eh /kə/ eh Fastnacht it's in English means carnival . . . [1]/[2][1] (1st delivery)

. . . it's called Fasching or carnival . . . [3] (3rd delivery)

In this example, two categories of hesitation phenomena occur: an *uh*-phenomenon and an omission. The first *eh* indicates that the speaker has a word in mind which she is about to say. The /kə/, together with what follows, shows the desired word to be *carnival*, which is only partly produced on the first try. The following part of the utterance shows what the speaker wanted to say. After her unsuccessful attempt she uses a mother-tongue word. Then, after the second *eh* she comes up with the intended English word. So the problem is solved in the first delivery and is not carried over into the second and third.

(2) . . . you can have eh hot sausage they make hot sausages and you can buy them and eat them . . . [1]/[3] (1st delivery)

In (2) what is said at first does not satisfy the speaker. The *eh* preceding *hot sausage* indicates the speaker is uncertain about how to express her intention. Then she repeats *they* and reconstructs. Again she solves the problem in the same delivery where it first occurs, and it does not appear again.

(3) . . . and then they walking during the day through the street . . . [1] (1st delivery)

. . . and they walking to the through the street . . . [2] (2nd delivery)

. . . and they are walking during the day through the street . . . [3] (3rd delivery)

Example (3) involves a more complex process of correction. During the first delivery, a piece of discourse is planned and presented, though the speaker obviously knows it contains some mistakes, such as the omission of *are* before *walking.* In the second delivery, the phrase *to the* is repaired and *during the day* is omitted. In the third delivery, the presentation is apparently refined as much as the speaker's level of English allows, and there are no hesitations. In example (3), by contrast with (1) and (2), there are changes across all three deliveries.

Searching

In searching, the speaker first repeats the utterance from the previous turn. Then unacceptable forms appearing in the presentation are picked out and corrected, though a successful outcome remains unattainable. Attempted corrections may involve (a) putting a new surface element in the place of a problematic one and (b) changing around the construction containing it. B committed 6 lapses of this type, and it seems that the trouble is grammatical—she uses the same pattern repeatedly and the same lexical items appear when the information in question is presented on subsequent occasions. In some cases a word or sequence is not repeated from the previous occasion because it does not easily fit into the pattern B produces next. Here we see many evidences of uncertainty on the part of the speaker.

(4) . . . then eh make this ball goes on till 2 o'clock in the morning . . . [1] (1st delivery)

. . . and it's it's going on till 2 o'clock in the morning . . . [2] (3rd delivery)

In (4) B apparently intends to communicate the same information on the first and third deliveries, but in the first the string *make this ball goes* appears after an *eh* indicating uncertainty about how to express what is meant. Perhaps because of this uncertainty the string in question is omitted in the second presentation altogether. The same problem manifests itself in the repetition of *it's* on delivery three.

(5) . . . (B laughs) oh it's it's very funny . . . [1] (1st delivery)

. . . it's a very funny eh event . . . [2] (2nd delivery)

Example (5) involves laughter, the interjection of *oh,* a repetition of *it's,* and an *eh.* Laughter and the interjection *oh,* no doubt, reflect the state of the speaker, who appears relaxed and enjoying herself. The repetition of *it's* is used to fill in while she searches for a descriptive word or phrase. She does not seem satisfied and on the second delivery comes up with the word *event* but only after an *eh,* which indicates that she is still searching for a better descriptive term even on the second occasion.

(6) . . . eh this eh festivity means they would like to throw away the winter . . . [1] (1st delivery)

. . . these events means the the spring or summer should come very soon because they don't like the winter . . . [2] (3rd delivery)

In (6), besides changing the grammatical pattern, the speaker refines the information presented earlier. It seems that what was said before did not precisely serve the speaker's intention. Two *eh*'s and a repetition of *the* may reveal an attempt to introduce a new idea and look back to something said before, all at the same time, and also make changes where necessary.

Abandonment

In spontaneous speech, with a limited amount of time for planning, organizing, and presenting the message, the speaker sometimes gives up in mid-utterance. Abandonment is a kind of content repair. Whatever preceded the decision to abandon is omitted in later deliveries. Here are several possible reasons for the abandonment phenomenon: (a) The global form that the intention requires (the syntax) is not known in the target language; (b) the structure already initiated may require a word, phrase, or idiom that the speaker is unable to access; (c) the content itself may elude the speaker, e.g., as in trying to think of an example to illustrate a generalization; (d) the idea that the speaker is trying to express may turn out not to fit the theme at hand, so further attempts to express it are no longer desirable; (e) the speaker may become so involved in processing that the intention is actually forgotten in midstream; and (f) the speaker may remember what was said on an earlier occasion but choose not to use that material.

A wide range of phrases signal abandonment, e.g., *what would I say, I don't know, that's all,* etc. Often some information is partially coded in surface forms which abruptly reach an impasse. The beginnings of the information may even appear in a complete sentence, but in most cases the speaker will explicitly indicate her difficulty in saying what she intends. For instance, in describing floats in the parade at *Fastnacht*, she says:

(7) . . . and they make also make some wagons carriage with eh eh events who happens during the year you know like political (3 seconds elapse) events or or I I don't know and then after then when you watch them . . . [1]/[2] (1st delivery)

In example (7) the speaker searches for a word or descriptor, and after saying *eh* twice she settles on *events* but is not satisfied with it. She pauses for three full seconds after the word *political* and comes back again to *events*. She indicates her dissatisfaction with this solution by saying *I don't know*. The entire context is absent from the second and third deliveries.

(8) . . . so after 12 o'clock they they mask their face so the pe the people know them with whem [*sic*, whom? them?] they enjoy the evening (2 seconds) um (3 seconds) it's very cold what would I say and it's it's going on till two o'clock . . . [1]/[2] (3rd delivery)

The flow seems to break down in (8), with the speaker running out of anything to say. Her difficulty is signaled by two long pauses and by *um*. She fills in by saying *what would I say,* and then repeating *it's,* she manages another idea about the festival.

Elaboration

In this kind of correction, the speaker has a certain bit of content in mind but seems to ramble since she is not yet satisfied with the way she has expressed it so far. In terms of Figure 27.2, the speaker seems stuck at the second stage of the model. She may pick out a particular element and reform it entirely. In doing so, she is apt to hesitate while selecting a lexical item or a syntactic structure. Sometimes she stops to plan or even retraces what has already been said in order to correct it or to check whether it is understandable. These elaborations will typically be omitted from later deliveries, but unlike cases of abandonment they do not result in immediate omission of the problematic element.

Two instances of elaboration occurred in the speech of B:

(9) . . . but it's very cold because it's winter time do you know the winter time in eh do you have winter in Japan winter winter it is very cold and snow so sometimes we have to go in a restaurants to warm up us to get warm you know . . . [1]/[2] (1st delivery)

The speaker seems to want to confer with the listener. Since the speaker does not know if there are cold winters in Japan, she seeks confirmation and attempts to elaborate the concept of *winter*. The elaboration is manifested partly in the false-start question *do you know the winter time in* followed by *eh* and then repeated with adjustment as *do you have winter in in Japan*. The uncertainty of the speaker is manifested in the repetition of *in* while apparently searching for and then finding the word *Japan* and then is shown again by repeating the word *winter* with an intonation indicating that it is a question. After the listener responds, the talk is continued but at a slower rate. Maybe this is because the speaker must reconstruct her own intentions. Or perhaps she intends to elaborate the consequence of the cold, that *we have to go in a restaurants to warm up us* which is repeated *to get warm* followed by the formulaic *you know*.

(10) . . . children are also involved in these events they dress up also sometimes the most of them are clow clowns you know nice faces and and they have pipes to make noise and (2 seconds) there are some people they watch them when they go through the street (2 seconds) um . . . [1]/[2] (2nd delivery)

In (10) attention is called to *the most of them are clow clowns,* which is done with falling intonation at a slow rate. This probably shows that B is unsure of the word *clowns* or thinks that the listener might not know the word. However, the intruding *you know,* which is stressed, indicates that the speaker intends to use *clowns* to describe the role of the children who *are involved in this event.* She elaborates by adding *nice faces and . . . make noise and,* after which she pauses for 2 seconds. Probably this is because she needs time to plan what will come next and possibly to allow the listener to decode what she has just said. Then, there is another burst of discourse followed by another 2-second pause and an *um.* B may realize that the listener does not follow what she is saying, or B may have run into encoding trouble again.

Discussion of Study 2

It seems clear from the research reviewed and from the data discussed above that hesitation phenomena are indicative of monitoring. On the one hand, hesitations (of the several kinds discussed) slow down the rate of speaking, but on the other, they seem to improve the chances of being understood. Krashen and Terrell (1983) point out that monitoring results in hesitations that impede fluency, but in practice we have seen that monitoring can also be beneficial: it may help to make a message comprehensible and thus enable the speaker to achieve communicative purposes efficiently. Both

Study 1 and Study 2 show that as familiarity with the content and its manner of expression increases through repetition, fluency and accuracy both improve. For a final example from Study 2—one that further demonstrates the increased efficiency owed to practice in speaking—consider the following from another subject's transcripts:

> (11)   . . . I realize that I have to go back to my country and hope that I will be able to finish the first year in the university . . . [1] (1st delivery)
>
> . . . so I realize that I'll have to go back to my country to continue my studies . . . [2] (2nd delivery)
>
>   . . . so I decided to go back to my country and finish my study . . . [3] (3rd delivery)

In (11) the repetition task results in two kinds of improvement: first, vocabulary items like *decide* and *study* describe the speaker's intention more accurately, and, second, the speaker is able to express the message more concisely. In the final analysis, the point that emerges is that through repetition of an output task, significant improvements occur.

NOTE

1 The numbers in square brackets indicate the number and order of the speaker's attempts to express some particular piece of information.

APPENDIX 27.1 TRANSCRIPT OF A 4/3/2 TALK

The Four-Minute Delivery

"Hallo Hiro I would like to tell you about eh events the traditional events who happened in Switzerland it's called eh/k/eh Fastnacht it's in English means carnival it happens eh in the month of the February and it's goes it happens one month the whole February and it is some people they dress up in fancy clothes long clothes coloured clothes and also they paint their face so you can't eh recognize them or sometimes they put on masks and then sometimes they wear big hats or without hats and then they walking during the day through the street and make noise with drums or they blow

et in in instruments and a lot of people watch them it ah all people are included or involved in this eh events also children they do the same and (2 secs) you can watch them and if you stand in the street and you hear the music you get very warm you know exciting because it's ah very ah exciting but it's very cold because it's winter time do you know the winter time in eh do you have winter in in Japan winter winter it is very cold and snow so sometimes we have to go in a restaurants to warm up us to get warm you know and they make also some wagons carriage with eh eh events who happen during the year you know like political (3 secs) events or or I I don't know and then after then when you watch them you can have eh hot sausage they they make hot sausages and you can buy them and eat them it's very funny and there in the evening there are are some balls you know for dancing the meet the people meet each other to dance by music also in these fancy clothes and you can't see the face before twelve o'clock after twelve o'clock they eh they they mask off their faces and then you can see who with who you enjoy the whole evening (laugh) oh it's it's very funny and shshsh then eh make this balls goes on till two o'clock in the morning then they go home you know also lots of alcoholic eh consumed consumed because eh it's ah ah happy things eh this eh festivity means they would like to throw away the winter thus the summer should come very soon so they like to have the time the warm time the the summer."

The Three-Minute Delivery

"Hello Sherry em I would like to tell you about a traditional events who occur in Switzerland and in the during the month of February it's eh nice events people they dress up ah in fancy clothes long clothes long long clothes coloured clothes in eh different kinds of of shape and also they paint their eh faces in many colours and sometime thick colour you know and also all mask them so you can't recognize them and they wear also big hat and they walking to the through the street um they sometimes they have instruments like drums or um to blow in blow in instrument children are also involved in these events they dress up also sometimes the most of them are clow clowns you know nice faces and they have some pipes to make noise and (2 secs) there are some people they watch them when they go through the street (2 secs) um (4 secs) after sometime it's very cold because it happens in the winter if you get cold you have to go inside to have eh some drink but if you stand outside if the people walk through the street and with this music you get very exciting you know

there is a lot of fun (3 secs) um after the af in the evening there are some balls you know people they go in these dresses for for dancing eh and also their faces eh with colour or masks and they dance the whole evening with somewhere maybe with different people and then after twelve o'clock they they mask and eh also put the eh paint away so the people can recog recognize with whom she they enjoy the evening it's a very funny eh events and it is a lot of fun I I was also sometimes clown eh dressed up and and you can make joke with people you you never done before (3 secs) and (2 secs) it it's eh go."

The Two-Minute Delivery

"So I talk you about the events who happens in Switzerland it's called "Fasching" or Carnival people they dress up in fancy clothes coloured clothes in different shapes also they colour their face or mask their face and wear hats they have also some musics instruments like drums or blow instruments and they are walking during the day through the street some people watch them also little children are children are involved in this a um events (2 secs) it is very cold at this time it's winter time and it happens during the whole February in the evening people meet each other in in for a ball for a dancing also in these fancy clothes in these fancy ah coloured face or mask and after twelve o'clock (3 secs) eh they make joke with people you know but they don't know them so after twelve o'clock they they mask their face so the pe the people know with whom they enjoy the evening (2 secs) um (3 secs) it's very cold what would I say and it's it's going on till two o'clock in the morning and it means because it's winter time they would like to come very soon the spring and summer these events means the the spring these events means the the spring or summer should come very soon because they don't like the winter."

DISCUSSION QUESTIONS

1. If speaking practice—target language output from the student—had no significant impact on the development of fluency, what would be the predicted outcomes in the several experiments described in this chapter? Consider the Goldman-Eisler (1968) description of cartoons, the Audio-Lectal Practice of Heike (1981b), the study by Brown et al. (1984), and the two studies by Arevart and Nation.

2. Heike's (1981b) study is particularly interesting because it suggests that practice in producing output in one kind of task generalizes to other tasks. Based on this result, what would be the predicted effect of the 4/3/2 procedure on other speaking tasks?

3. In Brown et al. (1984), practice in listening improved performance on speaking tasks. Why would listening to someone else perform a task just prior to doing it yourself be an advantage?

4. Consider item (3) of Study 2, where the speaker use the ungrammatical form *they walking* twice and then in her third talk on the same subject changes to the well-formed *they are walking*. How might practice in producing the output under time limits cause this sort of adjustment?

CHAPTER 28

Episodes on the Computer

Tatsuo Taira

EDITOR'S INTRODUCTION

In this chapter, Tatsuo Taira, rapidly emerging as one of the leading specialists in CALL (computer-assisted language learning; also known as CAI, computer-assisted instruction; CALI, computer-assisted language instruction; and other acronyms), applies his talents to a subtle question: Does episodic organization above the level of conversational vignettes make a difference? No one can seriously doubt that episodic organization does make a difference in many aspects of textual processing at lower levels (cf. Chapters 19–21 of Part 4), but what about organization across lessons? It was my Dad, John W. Oller, Sr., who introduced me to the idea of episodic organization (he just called it "meaningful sequence") when I was studying Spanish at Roosevelt High School in Fresno, California, back about 1959. His Spanish program of the 1960s exemplified that idea more completely than any other language program to date that I know of. At any rate, after all these years, Tatsuo Taira has used a CALL approach to finally put the question to the test. His results are as predicted. For over 25 years, I have sought ways to test the relevance of episodic organization to language teaching (cf. Chapter 20, this volume, and Oller & Jonz, in press), and here at last we are able to present, I believe, a study that tests the strong form of the episode hypothesis.

What teachers generally want to know about Computer Assisted Language Learning (CALL) is whether it can help their students acquire communicative competence.[1] A number of research studies have shown that study in pairs—that is, interaction among students while working on computers—does so (Chapelle & Jamieson, 1991; Ahmad, Corbett, Rogers, & Sussex, 1985; Higgins & Johns, 1984; Higgins, 1988; Underwood, 1984; Wyatt, 1983). Here it is taken for granted that the ultimate goal of CALL is to promote communicative competence (Murray, Morgenstern, & Furstenberg, 1989). If this is so, then an approach that emphasizes a rich context, including episodic organization, should be preferred. A number of recent studies (Kenning & Kenning, 1984; Underwood, 1984; Higgins &

Johns, 1984; Geoffrion & Geoffrion, 1983; Davies & Higgins, 1985) suggest that computers can be effectively applied to language acquisition because of their versatility, provision of immediate feedback, individually paced learning, appeal to intrinsic learner motivations, ease of materials modification, and ease of scoring and analysis of answers.

But the main purpose of this chapter is to explore the hypothesis (cf. Oller, 1983b, 1990; Oller & Damico, 1991) that episodically organized materials over the long haul (i.e., in a series of connected episodes over a full semester of study) will produce a significant advantage over less-organized materials. In this study, episodically organized materials are compared with nearly identical language materials decomposed into smaller but unconnected vignettes presented in a non-episodic arrangement.

Episodic organization, of course, is defined as having two aspects: First, texts that have it are structured so that each event or element, thanks to logical inferences, suggests others along the lines of Oller's expectancy hypothesis (cf. Oller, 1983b; Taira, 1991). Second, each episode involves some element of risk, surprise, or conflict (relative to the persons involved) which serves to motivate the discourse or text about the episode in the first place. The technique used in the research and teaching reported here was CALL of the cloze type. Cloze procedure is a technique for creating exercises or tests by deleting elements from a discourse by replacing them with a blank and having students fill in the blanks by guessing the missing part of the discourse. In the CALL procedures used here, the basic approach involved cloze procedure with an audio assist. Students heard an auditory version of the complete text. Therefore, the task was closer to what some have called "dicto-comp" (Brodkey, 1972) or partial dictation (Johansson, 1973), a dictation/cloze combination where the student hears the whole text along with the missing word that must be filled in.

But before describing the specifics of the method, it is important to clarify the hypothesis at stake in the present research. It is already well established by previous research (Oller & Obrecht, 1969; Stevick, 1976; and in this volume by Carrell in Chapter 19 and Oller et al. in Chapter 20) that episodic organization of texts tends to make them easier to understand and to recall. This is an idea that was first argued in relation to language teaching by Otto Jespersen (1904)[2] and was re-introduced to language teachers by way of the Spanish program of John W. Oller, Sr., in 1963 and 1965 (cf. Oller, Sr. 1963; Oller, Sr. & González, 1965). However, the research, till now, has focused on relatively narrow ranges of text under various terms—"informational sequence" (Oller & Obrecht, 1969), "formal and content schemata" (Rumelhart, 1975; Carrell, 1984 and Chapter 19, this volume), "scripts," "frames," and the like (Thorndyke, 1977; Schank, 1975; Kintsch & Van Dijk, 1978; de Beaugrande, 1980). The research has always been concerned with relatively narrow ranges of texts, e.g., a brief conversation, a really short story, or something similar. On the other hand, the episode hypothesis, as it was originally stated, said much more. It said that a series of connected episodes arranged like those of a novel or soap opera would be a more adequate basis for language acquisition than a disjointed series of unrelated episodes.

At the present stage of language teaching, nearly all professional practitioners—theoreticians, researchers, and teachers alike—have given up on the old-style "discrete-point" approaches that tried to teach, as Simon Belasco put it (1971: 4), "50,000 carefully selected structural features" in hopes that people would come out knowing the target language at the end.[3] They didn't, and as a result, those methods have for the most part been rejected. Instead, it is now common to teach larger chunks of conversational or textual discourse. Nowadays, most teaching works from discourse-styled vignettes—such as short conversations, bits of prose, news stories, etc.—that involve one or more persons and that are susceptible of various kinds of scaffolded representation along the lines of Chapters 2–8 in Part 1. Sometimes, for instance, the meaning may be portrayed by actors on a videocassette, videodisc, or through a comic strip, or by the teacher and students through mime, dramatization, role play, etc. However, it is uncommon, even these days, for the vignettes to have any connection between them. Rarely do the separate vignettes form a continuous story line as was recommended by Oller, Sr. (1963), Oller and Obrecht (1969), and Oller (1983b). However, there are exceptions such as Ferreira (1984). The main question addressed here is whether it makes any difference. In other words, will it help if the vignettes are connected in the manner of a series of episodes forming a larger story line as contrasted with the same (or very similar) vignettes presented in any which order? The episode hypothesis in its strongest form says that a series of episodes generated on the basis of a continuous story line will result in more efficient and sociolinguistically richer language acquisition over the long haul. In addition to this main hypothesis, which to my knowledge (and to Oller's) has not been tested experimentally until now, I also wanted to assess the effectiveness of a whole family of "cloze-based" approaches to CALL. In the present instance, a modified cloze-type approach was applied to the teaching of EFL in Okinawa, Japan, at the college level. The focus on a cloze-type approach may sound like it narrows down the generalizability, but Holmes (1984) quotes Hall as saying tongue in cheek that "the computer and the cloze test go together like *uña y mugre*" (p. 99). Presumably in this simile, the cloze procedure must be the dirt (*mugre*) while the computer is the fingernail (*uña*) that it gets under, but the point is made, and unlike the simile, it is a fact with positive as well as negative aspects.

CALL inevitably supplies all students with some context into which responses from those same students must eventually be inserted. Questions are asked and students must respond to them. "What," "who," "when," "where," and even "how" and "why" questions involve implicit blanks. Or in more overt cloze tasks, blanks are actually supplied on paper or on a CRT, and students fill them in. As a result, it is difficult to conceive of any CALL approach (cf. Alderson, 1990) or any other sort of language teaching method for that matter that is completely free of some essential cloze-type of activity. Besides, there is no need to apologize for using cloze-procedure in language instruction (cf. Oller & Jonz, in press). It works and can be shown to be similar in its functioning to the kinds of "wh-" questions that are characteristic of all languages. In all such questions, there is an implicit blank to be filled, as Chomskyan theory in recent years has greatly clarified (Chomsky, 1982, 1988; Cowper, 1992).

With the computer, cloze exercises can be generated, administered, scored, and analyzed (Hedges & Turner, 1983; Montgomery, 1984), and can also be applied to instructional purposes (Whitaker, Schwartz, & Vockell, 1989; Montgomery, 1984; Higgins & Johns, 1984; Bortnick & Lopardo, 1973). In using a cloze format, the learner is guided in a partially completed production but must discern shades of intention and the use of rhetorical devices, and must infer meanings within an existing context (Morrison, 1984). While such partial production is, of course, artificial in its surface form, it is, nonetheless, interactive and similar to real-life conversation in crucial ways.

Unfortunately, a great deal of CALL software lags behind the cutting edge of developing theory in language acquisition and teaching methods. Paradoxically, while language teachers are struggling to improve the communicative ability of their students, the instructional programs corresponding to the most recent technological advances in the classroom tend to be based on antiquated methods. CALL programs emphasize surface forms of language and often fail to relate to any meaningful situation whatever. In fact, in many cases, CALL still leans on "discrete-point" and "behavioristic" teaching with lots of drill (cf. Dalgish, 1987; Holmes, 1984; Robinson, 1989; Salisbury, 1990; Taira, 1986). The "discrete-point" philosophy, of course, was based on the idea that language is learned in tiny bite-sized pieces of surface forms that can only be connected with meanings long after they have become so familiar as to be automatized (from the habit theory of "behaviorism": Skinner, 1957). Underwood (1984: 46) points out how most CALL exercises are made:

> Creating these frames . . . means breaking the language itself down into bite-size chunks—discrete points of grammar or vocabulary, mostly out of context and devoid of any real meaning. The result: grammar fill-ins and vocabulary translation exercises, often called "flashcard programs."

We now know that the basis for discrete-point, surface-oriented language teaching put the emphasis in the wrong place. Not that we shouldn't deal with surface forms, but the whole approach failed to account for the synergistic, holistic, and pragmatic (rational) aspects of language acquisition which have been emphasized for many years now by people like Emma Marie Birkmaier (1960, 1963), Mary Finocchiaro (1964), the Ollers (1963, 1971, 1979; Oller et al., 1991; also see Taira, 1991), Krashen (1981, 1985c), Fraser (1983), Richard-Amato (1988), Stevick (1974, 1976, 1980, 1982, 1986), Savignon (1972, 1983), Halliday (1973), Halliday and Hasan (1985), Wells (1981, 1986), Leech (1983), Markkanen (1985), Kretschmer and Kretschmer (1989), and Hamayan and Damico (1991). But the present chapter is not merely concerned with the broad question of language in its holistic aspect; it is also concerned with the aspect of episodic organization (see Richard-Amato, 1988) that is somehow created through the inferential links that make narratives distinct from other kinds of discourse (cf. Chapter 37, this volume). I am concerned here, therefore, with the connectedness of episodic structures ranging across conversational segments that form a story line.

METHOD

My dissertation (Taira, 1993) deals with the details of the year-long project conducted in Okinawa, Japan. The work involved students of English as a foreign language at the University of Ryukyus.[4] The experimental instruction took place over a full academic semester (April-July, 1992). The hardware was standard NEC equipment, and the software was prepared by the author.

Subjects

Ninety-six students (19 males and 77 females) enrolled at the University of the Ryukyus in Okinawa in three different classes were randomly assigned to either an experimental group or a control group. The intent was to achieve groups that were as nearly matched as possible. The two groups contained 48 subjects each, with approximately equal numbers of males and females assigned to each group. The first one, designated as the experimental treatment group, was arbitrarily chosen to receive the episodically organized materials (described below), while the second one, the control group, would receive structurally similar conversational vignettes but arranged randomly (again, see below). A check (ANOVA of group by gender) showed the groups to be statistically equivalent for gender, but the control group was significantly older (F 1, 94 = 8.10, $p < .01$)[5] at 22.73 years versus 20.06 years for the experimental group, with an overall mean of 21.43. Also, it turned out that the control group was somewhat more proficient in English to start with, though this could only work against the episode hypothesis as stated above. All subjects were nearing completion of their second year, working for an associate degree in English. The two groups did not differ significantly with respect to years in school.

THE MATERIALS

I began, with the help of native-English speakers (which I am not, incidentally, as English for me is a foreign language), by constructing a series of episodes about a Japanese family traveling from Tokyo to New York. Actually, 18 episodically structured lessons were built from the following sequence of events in the lives of a fictional Japanese family. Here are the original episodes in brief: The Yamadas hear from Dad, who is in New York, and begin to plan to go there; they apply for visas at the American Consulate; they make reservations through a travel agency and buy their tickets; they get all packed up for the trip; go to the airport; get on the plane and fly to New York; go through customs; take a taxi to a hotel; speak with the clerk at the front desk and check in; eat out at a steak house; go to the subway station; visit the Statue of Liberty; go shopping; and call home. Corresponding to the 18 episodically arranged lessons, an exactly parallel set of unrelated vignettes (56 mini-episodes, with about 3 per episodic lesson) involving different characters was also prepared. Thus, the first set of materials consisted of an episodically organized series of 18 conversations progressing over sequentially arranged scenes in the manner of a play or novel. The second set, a similar set of 56 structurally identical conversational vignettes, was derived from the episodic lessons, but was arranged in a random order and with names of persons and places changed to remove any connection between vignettes. For each episode, two color pictures (26 in all) were drawn in the manner of early school experience (from the viewpoint of the Yamada children) to help illustrate the meanings conveyed within each episode or within the corresponding control group vignettes (see the examples below). The same pictures were used for both groups, except that names of persons and places were adjusted to fit the vignettes for the control group.

Each episode (for the experimental group) or series of vignettes (for the control group) consisted of a conversational exchange preceded by a description of the setting (actually given in Japanese as an advance organizer so that students would understand what was going on in each conversation). The description of the setting was structurally the same in both the episodically arranged sequence and in the randomly arranged series of vignettes, except that the names of characters and the sequence of conversations were changed.

Episodic Materials

To illustrate, here is the sort of material that students in the experimental (episodic) treatment group encountered (in Japanese) before working through the first English lesson:

Description of the Situation (Episodic Version)
The Yamada family in Tokyo—mother, Yoshie, age 38; five-year-old, Tsutomu (a boy); and twelve-year-old, Keiko (a girl)—receive a telephone call from Kazuo (the father of the children, 41), who has been working for an electronics company in New York for two years. Father wants them to come to New York City next month, in August, for a visit.

Next, here is the dialogue between Kazuo and Yoshie which took place in the imaginary situation and which served as the main material for the opening English lessons of the experimental group (the group that received episodically organized materials). The words that appear in square brackets, like [so], were blanked out in the material presented on-screen through the CALL procedure, which will be described in detail in the Procedures section:

Example of Experimental Materials
Episode One (Episodic Series of Lesson/Vignettes)

Kazuo: Hello. This is Kazuo [speaking].
Yoshie: Hello. Glad to [hear] from you. [How] have you been?
Kazuo: I'm fine. [How] are the kids?
Yoshie: They've really [grown].
Kazuo: I can imagine [how] they've grown. I [miss] them a lot.
Yoshie: They miss you, [too].

Kazuo: Will you [come] to New York [next] month, in August?
Yoshie: I'd love that. All [of] us?
Kazuo: Yes, I [sent] you a letter last week. Have you received it [yet]?
Yoshie: Not [yet], it'll [probably] come tomorrow. The kids'll be [excited].
Kazuo: I [hope] you can arrange to [come]. Call me [if] you have any problems.
Yoshie: Sure. Take [care] of yourself.

Non-Episodic Materials

For the control group (those who received non-episodically organized vignettes), an identically structured series of descriptions of setting were composed, but the connection from one vignette (or mini-episode) to the next was removed and the order of some elements was changed. For example, among the vignettes that were used with the control group are the following which correspond exactly (except for names) to the episode just given above. Note that the same words in the same sentential structures were blanked out. See the words in the control and experimental materials that are enclosed in square brackets. These would later be blanked out for the cloze exercises during instruction for the control group as well as for the experimental group:

Control Materials (Vignettes Derived from Episode One)
(A Non-Episodic Series of Lesson/Vignettes)

Lesson 1 (from Episode One)

Description of the Situation for Lesson 1 (Segment 1)
Charles wants Jane to come to Mexico next month, in April, for a visit [corresponds to

"Father wants them to come to New York City next month, in August, for a visit"].

Charles: Will you [come] to Mexico [next] month, in April.
Jane: I'd love that. All [of] us?
Charles: Yes, I [hope] you can arrange to [come]. Call me [if] you have any problems.
Jane: Sure. Take [care] of yourself.

Lesson 2
Mr. Suzuki: I [sent] you a letter last week. Have you received it [yet]?
Mrs. Suzuki: Not [yet]. It'll [probably] come tomorrow. The kids'll be [excited].

Lesson 3
The Harris family in Los Angeles—mother, Lucy, age 38; five-year-old, Jack (a boy); and twelve-year-old, Annie (a girl)—receive a telephone call from Clark (the father of the children, 41), who has been working for an electronics company in Taiwan for two years [corresponds to "The Yamada family in Tokyo—mother, Yoshie, age 38; five-year-old, Tsutomu (a boy); and twelve-year-old, Keiko (a girl)—receive a telephone call from Kazuo (the father of the children, 41), who has been working for an electronics company in New York for two years"].

Clark: Hello. This is Clark [speaking].
Lucy: Hello. Glad to [hear] from you. [How] have you been?
Clark: I'm fine.

Lesson 4
Grandma: [How] are the kids?
Daughter: They've really [grown].
Grandma: I can imagine [how] they've grown. I [miss] them a lot.
Daughter: They miss you, [too].

These examples are just to give an idea of the materials and how they differed across the two groups. I believe it must be agreed that the only structural differences between the two sets of materials pertain to episodic organization. The vocabulary and syntax of the two sets of materials, except for constraints ranging across vignettes, are the same. Of course, it must be kept in mind that

there were 18 episodic lessons used with the experimental group and that every one of those received a treatment similar to the first one, which we have just examined. Most importantly, as a result of the method in which the experimental and control group materials were prepared, all subjects in both groups would experience exactly the same cloze items in exactly the same kinds of contexts (lexical and syntactic), except for the richer episodic organization of the materials assigned to the experimental group.

Procedures

Teaching, testing, and questionnaires about student reactions to CALL procedures must all be described. Since three tests and one questionnaire were actually used before any CALL training took place at all, these will be described first. Then I will describe the CALL training and, finally, the post-testing and post-questionnaires reacting to the CALL procedures.

Pre-Testing and the Pre-Questionnaire

Three different pre-tests, one of which was divided into two parts, plus a questionnaire were given at the beginning of the semester. The pre-tests and the pre-questionnaire were used to assess the relative English proficiency and attitudes of the subjects before training and to establish benchmarks (or covariates) for the post-test comparisons of the experimental and control groups. In addition subject-participants were asked to fill out three questionnaires pertaining to their expectations and experience with CALL.

Pre-Tests

Three pre-tests were used. Since the CALL procedure would involve filling in blanks, the first pre-test was a written cloze test (omitting every fifth word) drawn from a general text (Pre-General Cloze). Second, the Standard English Placement Test (STEP), one that is normally taken by students throughout Japan ranging from junior high through the universities, was used as a pre-test (Pre-STEP). Third, another cloze pre-test was created in two parts by omitting approximately every fifth word from material that would appear in the episodic and non-episodic arrangements of the CALL exercises (Pre-Exercise Cloze). The first half of this third pre-test was drawn from the series of isolated vignettes (the non-episodically arranged conversations) while the second half was taken from the experimental (episodically arranged) materials. The purpose of all three pre-tests was to determine baseline proficiencies of both groups of subjects.

Pre-Questionnaire

A Pre-Questionnaire (15 questions) was to assess student expectations about CALL, prior experience with computers, and CALL as a method of EFL instruction. Like the pre-tests, the reason for including the Pre-Questionnaire was to provide data to assess any differential impact of CALL instruction on the two groups.

CALL Procedures

Between the pre- and post-testing (and the pre- and post-questionnaires) came the actual classroom experiences with CALL for the three classes selected for the experiment. There were actually thirteen 90-minute sessions during the whole semester. Both groups of subjects had exactly the same amount of time on task. In each class, students were paired off. They were asked to choose partners to work with among themselves, and after this was done, each pair was assigned to a computer. Each pair, for each class session, was given two 5.25" high-density floppy diskettes, each with 1.2 megabytes of memory. One of these was a system diskette containing the CALL EFL program designed by the author (Taira, 1987, 1989). The other diskette contained the EFL material. There were, in fact, two sets of EFL teaching diskettes (one for each group), 18 in each set. Pairs were allowed to work at their own pace during each 90-minute session and to determine along the way when they were ready to advance to the next lesson.

The computer hardware consisted of an NEC 286 AT machine operating at 12 MHZ (clock speed), with 640K of random access memory (RAM), 12K of text video RAM, 250K of graphics video RAM, and a color monitor of 640 x 400 dot resolution allowing 4,096 colors (from 16 underlying colors) with a 14" full color CRT screen. The hardware also included audio capabilities and a graphic interface enabling on-screen display of the appropriate picture while the EFL lesson was in progress.

At the beginning of each class session, here are the kinds of steps the students might follow during a lesson: First, they fill in their numbers and names to log onto the computer. Then, they are directed to read the description of the context for a conversational episode or vignette (the first or the next in the series they were working on). This description is given in English. After becoming familiar with the context, they hit a function key to advance the program. Each screen-sized bite of material includes the picture in the top half of the screen followed by a line of text with a word missing (see the illustrations above on p. 313). When the text appears on the screen, an audio version of the English utterance is also heard. This audio version is repeated as many times as the pair of students wants it to be. All they have to do to hear it again is hit the appropriate function key. Students are given two chances to fill in the blank before they are provided with the first letter of the word as a hint (or the second letter if the first letter is already correctly chosen). After the third try, the correct answer is given. At the end of each conversation (either an episode or vignette), the students are given some additional explanation (in Japanese) about difficult or important elements of the dialogue which they have just worked through (e.g., *"fallen* is the past participle of *fall"* would be given on the screen in Japanese). Only a handful of points are covered in each lesson in this way. Students are also provided with their scores. The computer automatically scores each item as the students work through the dialogue. They receive three points for a correct first entry, two points for a correct second entry, and one point for a correct answer with a hint. Also, the program automatically keeps a cumulative total of errors for each cloze item, which helps teachers identify problems with the exercises themselves or general problem areas of the students.

Thus, in keeping with John Carroll's observation (Carroll, 1965) that multiple modalities result in more rapid assimilation and longer retention of new language material (also in keeping with semiotic theory, cf. Oller et al., 1991; Taira, 1991, 1993), in the experiment students were exposed (1) to visual clues to meaning through the appropriate picture on the screen (see Figures 28.1 and 28.2); (2) to a brief explanation or description of the meaning or certain elements of the text in

Japanese; (3) to an auditory rendition of the appropriate English discourse, and, of course; (4) to the printed English forms on the screen. Finally, there was (5) the task requiring action (a motor response) on the part of the students. They had to decide what word they had heard, and then they were to write it in the blank on the screen. As they typed in their response, the letters would appear in blue. When they hit the RETURN key, if the answer was correct the letters of their response would turn green. If the answer was not correct, the letters they keyed in would turn red.

Although costly in terms of on-line memory, delayed speed of interaction, and disk space, it was possible to allow up to three correct answers in each blank. However, these had to be specified in advance, and it was necessary (owing to hardware limits, mainly) to keep alternative answers to the exact word deleted from the discourse plus the next two most common responses given by native speakers. (In fact, as the technology advances these limits will soon be overcome, and it should be mentioned that in quite a few cases only one or two words actually fit the context fully.) It is desirable, of course, in keeping with the recommendations of Oller (1972, 1979) and others for applications of cloze procedure *to instructional purposes* (also Stubbs & Tucker, 1974; Jonz, 1976) to allow any contextually appropriate response as correct. (Incidentally, the computer program [Taira, 1987, 1989, 1993] includes teacher authoring capabilities enabling any materials whatever to be included and developed into cloze-dictation exercises together with audio recordings and a limited number of full color pictures as well.)

In the event that a wrong answer was keyed in by the pair of students, after the letters turned red the students would see the same blank as before, in the same discourse context, but this time the first letter of the exact word would appear in green followed by exactly the number of letter spaces required for the rest of the word. Generally, as soon as a pair of students got the right answer for a given item, they would advance to the next item (i.e., the next turn in the conversation).

Each episode or sequence of vignettes in any given lesson format throughout the semester always involved three cloze-dictation exercises. That is, students in both groups always made three

passes through each segment of text. This idea is consistent with the general principle that multiple cycles through the material will tend to deepen and enhance comprehension on each successive pass (cf. Oller, Sr., 1963; Oller, Sr. & Oller, 1983; Weissenrieder, Chapter 23 this volume). As has already been shown by Arevart and Nation in Chapter 27, we also know that productive proficiency tends to be enhanced by such repeated cycles. However, in keeping with the idea of the learning spiral (cf. Vygotsky, 1934, 1978; Krashen, 1981, 1982, 1985b; Oller, 1983b; Richard-Amato, 1988), the task was made a little more difficult on each pass. The idea was to begin near the student's current level (what Krashen calls the "*i*th" stage) and to advance to the next level up ($i + 1$). On the first pass through a given episode or vignette, the cloze items were relatively easy words (as judged by the programmer; see Bachman, 1985 and 1990 for a justification of rational deletion). On the second pass, some new words would be deleted so that the task would become a little more difficult on the whole. On the third pass, a review session, students re-encountered deletions that they solved on the first and second passes. In the review session, no new deletions were introduced.

Post-Tests

The four post-tests involved three that were similar to the pre-tests but were based on different textual material. These three next 8 words post-tests, nearly parallel to the pre-tests, are accordingly designated in the Results and Discussion section below, as the Post-General Cloze, Post-STEP, and Post-Exercise Cloze (the latter, as in the corresponding pre-test, again divided into two parts, non-episodic and episodic). An important difference between the Pre-Exercise Cloze and the corresponding Post-Exercise Cloze was that the former used a fixed-ratio deletion procedure omitting every fifth word while the latter used a rational deletion procedure focused on more difficult items. The fourth post-test was a picture arrangement task (the Picture test). Since all subjects in both groups encountered the same pictures, though not in the same order, the Picture task required students to arrange eight of the pictures in the order in which they had been encountered during the CALL exercises. (Since the pre-tests occurred before any of the pictures had been encountered, there was no corresponding Picture pre-test.) The expectation was that those who experienced the episodic arrangement throughout the semester would be able to put the pictures in the right order, while those who studied the non-episodically organized vignettes would find difficulty in remembering the order in which they had encountered the pictures.

Post-Questionnaires

As their next-to-last responsibility for the course, students were asked to reflect on the CALL experience. Did they like it? Would they like to do it again? Did their level of anxiety about working on a computer increase or decrease? Did their English improve? Finally, the very last experience, a final review, involved working through both sets of exercises on the computer—those arranged in the form of a story and the randomly connected vignettes. After this review, they completed the final post-questionnaire, which asked which of the two approaches they preferred. Which did they find more interesting, and which set of materials was easier to learn EFL from?

RESULTS AND DISCUSSION

Table 28.1 gives means, standard deviations, and Cronbach α reliabilities for the pre-tests and post-tests for both the experimental and the control groups in text.

On the initial testing there was no significant contrast between the two groups on the Pre-STEP Test or the Pre-Exercise Cloze Tests, but the Pre-General Cloze showed a significant contrast favoring the control group ($F\ 1, 94 = 4.93, p < .03$). Since it was also observed that the control group obtained higher means on all pre-tests, it may be supposed that in this case, the luck of the draw worked *against* the experimental hypothesis—i.e., the control group had the advantage going into the experiment. At any rate, it was clear from the pre-test results that a multivariate analysis of variance treating the pre-tests as co-variates and both pre- and post-tests as repeated measures would be sensible.

The result of that MANOVA comparison between groups was $F\ 1, 93 = 16.14, p < .0001$, and across all three tests with the co-variates in the regression equation was $F\ 2, 187 = 39.00, p < .0001$, confirming the experimental hypothesis dramatically (for more details, see Oller & Taira, in press). Happily, there was no interaction between the group factor and the several tests. With respect to the pre- and post-tests, the most interesting contrasts, it would seem, were those between tests that were not directly involved in any way in the exercises performed during the CALL experience, namely the Post-STEP and the Post-General Cloze. The contrasts on these tests were significant in both cases with or without the respective pre-tests as co-variates at $p < .02$ (Taira, 1993). What these contrasts show is that episodic organization not only makes an impact on materials practiced and directly studied through CALL, but it also makes a significant difference to performance on materials that are independent of those actually studied. In other words, the gain owed to episodic organization generalizes to new tasks.

The last test comparison between the experimental and control groups was on the Picture test. It was expected that the experimental group, owing to its constant exposure to the developing meaning of the story all through the semester, would end up with better recall of the pictures and their order relative to the story line than would the control group, where the pictures were tied only to unrelated conversational vignettes. In fact, the prediction was confirmed. The contrast on the Picture test was significant ($F\ 1, 94 = 240.92, p < .0001$). This result shows that the experimental group easily recalled the relation of the episodically organized materials to the visual representations, whereas the visual dimension of the isolated conversational vignettes was hardly recalled at all by the control group. The experimental group apparently processed the discourse at a deeper level of comprehension.

None of this is really surprising, but it bears heavily on CALL theory and practice. A number of studies on memory had already shown that a great deal of information is normally stored in an episodic order (Layton, 1979; Rivers, 1983; Green, 1990; Umemoto, 1987). One element that distinguishes a story line—such as the kind the experimental group in this study experienced—is the recurrent appearance of surprise or conflict. A meaningful conflict can be any sort of a question

TABLE 28.1 Means (as Percentages), Standard Deviations, and α Reliabilities (Total *N* = 96) for Pre-Tests and Post-Tests for the Experimental Group (*n* = 48) and the Control Group (*n* = 48)

| Tests | Experimental Group | | Control Group | | Cronbach's α |
	$\overline{X}$	SD	$\overline{X}$	SD	(*N* = 96)
Pre-General Cloze	48.81	12.53	54.46	12.43	.68
Post-General Cloze	68.75	10.48	63.86	8.75	.31
Pre-STEP Test	48.69	11.75	48.54	12.63	.66
Post-STEP Test	73.57	10.49	68.15	10.54	.55
Pre-Exercise Cloze Test					
(Non-Episodic Items 1–25)	46.17	12.32	48.58	13.48	.61
Pre-Exercise Cloze Test					
(Episodic Items 26–50)	41.67	15.59	44.25	12.53	.60
Post-Exercise Cloze Test					
(Non-Episodic Items 1–25)	55.92	19.45	59.75	20.24	.83
Post-Exercise Cloze Test					
(Episodic Items 26–50)	61.75	17.81	50.75	20.06	.81
Picture Test	71.09	21.60	14.97	33.34	.83

occurring in the mind of the language user. When the student is brought into unfolding events with surprise value, effort is expended toward the resolution of the discomfort. That effort aims to find out what will happen and to connect the developing present with both a significant past and a future. As a result, textual interpretations are generated at a deep level as propositions are weighed, developed, compared, and so forth in the ongoing effort to resolve the conflict or eliminate the discomfort. When resolution is realized, the memory of the story is relatively well-established and the mapping process is terminated. The student is ready to go on to something new. This sort of conclusion, however, is not achieved either in the same way or to the same degree with non-episodically organized material. Both structure and motivation are deficient in the isolated vignettes that are so popular in language instruction.

At last we come to the pre- and post-questionnaires. I will not discuss them in detail because I have done that in my dissertation (Taira, 1993). However, it is worthwhile to note a number of trends. First, students on the whole became more positive about CALL regardless whether they were in the experimental or the control group. This result augurs well for CALL. For instance, on the

Pre-Questionnaire students were asked if they thought they would enjoy using CALL to study EFL. On the 6-point Likert-type scale (with 6 being defined as "very much" and 1 as "not at all") of the Pre-Questionnaire, the two groups did not differ significantly and had an overall mean of 4.74—indicating positive expectations about the course. It is interesting that their enthusiasm for CALL actually increased during the course. Though the two groups did not differ significantly on the corresponding questions of the Post-Questionnaire, the overall mean of the both groups had increased significantly above the Pre-Questionnaire level to 5.50.

There were remarkably few differences in reactions between the experimental and control groups to the very different procedures each had experienced. Foreign language students apparently do not seem to have any clear expectations about what kinds of materials are best for EFL study or CALL. However, at the very end of the course, after working through both sets of materials (something that took place *after* all the post-testing had already been completed), both groups agreed that the story line was easier to process. However, those who had worked through the episodic material (the experimental group) felt even stronger about it. The mean for the control group was 4.29, and for the experimental group it was 5.20 ($F_{1, 92} = 8.44$, $p < .005$).

Two conclusions are clear. First, the episode hypothesis is correct. Arranging discourse material from lesson to lesson in a story format makes a substantial difference over a semester. Second, in spite of the fact that CALL is still in an early stage of development, it is clear that students enjoy working together in a cooperative atmosphere interacting with a computer. CALL works, and the Japanese students examined here like it a lot.

NOTES

1 First, I must thank my colleagues and co-workers and my courageous, hardworking students at the University of the Ryukyus in Okinawa. Second, I want to acknowledge the help in planning the study and writing its results from Dr. John W. Oller, Jr. Also, Dr. Jack S. Damico helped in the planning stages. I never knew John Oller, Sr., but I am glad to have been able to demonstrate experimentally that the central thesis of his Spanish program was correct and can be generalized, apparently, to any language. My results, I believe, also confirm the findings of Chapter 20 and the other chapters in Part 4 of this book. Perhaps all of them together will contribute to moving CALL toward a better-developed and more meaningful theory of language acquisition and instruction. Of course, I take full responsibility for any errors that remain in this paper.

2 Joel Walz (1989: 161) says that Jespersen (1904: 11) cannot have been referring to language teaching relative to grammar in general when he said "there must be (and this as far as possible from the first day) a certain connection in the thoughts communicated in the new language. . . . Indeed not even disconnected sentences ought to be used." Walz says that Jespersen was talking about written texts and therefore not grammatical exercises, but it is hard to see how this could have been so since essentially all language teaching back at the turn of the last century *involved* written texts, just as it usually does today. Moreover, Jespersen was dealing with foreign language teaching in general. The fact is clear, in any case, that Jespersen was indeed recommending materials with episodic structure.

3 Belasco (1971), like many other theoreticians, more or less concluded that it wasn't really possible to teach a language in a classroom setting after all.

4 I am also grateful for the assistance received from Tomoaki Kamimura, a private consultant working for a software company.

5 The procedure used was MEANS from SPSS[X] 4.1 on the University of New Mexico IBM-9121. All the other procedures, including ANOVA and MANOVA discussed below, were done on the same hardware and with the same statistical package.

DISCUSSION QUESTIONS

1. Relate Taira's findings to Christensen's recommendations (Chapter 26) concerning the use of novels in foreign language instruction. What are some of the advantages of novels, and what reasonable expectations should teachers have concerning their use?

2. Taira's students seemed to appreciate very much the experience of working in pairs with a computer. Consider this result in the light of Assinder (Chapter 24) and Prapphal (Chapter 34). What role do you suppose peer work played?

3. Students were allowed in Taira's experiment to work at their own pace. Could this properly be called "autonomous" language learning? How so, or why not?

4. Why would students be relatively oblivious to the power of episodic organization until they were exposed to it? Why would they not naturally demand it of language programs? Why, for example, would adult non-readers gladly accept a program like "Hooked on Phonics," which hardly takes the normal episodic organization of experience into account at all? Or why would teachers of basal reading (teachers trying to get children to read for the first time) be willing for so long to accept the disjointed nonsense that is characteristic of such familiar programs as *Dick and Jane* or the more recent Science Research Associates, (an IBM subsidiary) *A Pig Can Jig*?

CHAPTER 29

Mapping a Course Over Different Roads: Language Teaching with Special Populations

Jack S. Damico and Sandra K. Damico

EDITOR'S INTRODUCTION

Long ago, J. J. Asher (1969b; also Humphrey, 1970, 1972) and more recently Andrade, Kretschmer, and Kretschmer (Chapter 10) have argued that even special education children can acquire a second language. Genesee (1992), Bruck (1982, 1985a-b, 1987), Bruck, Tucker, and Jakimik (1985), and Holobow, Genesee, Lambert, Gastright, and Met (1987) have also shown that most, though perhaps not all, limited or handicapped children are capable of acquiring a second language, though this point is not without controversy (Sparks, Ganschow, Javorsky, Pohlman, & Patton, 1992). The evidence suggests that many LD children, who have been seen as hopeless illiterates incapable of ever succeeding at demanding cognitive academic tasks such as becoming literate, really can join "the literacy club" (to borrow a phrase from Frank Smith, 1988). Regardless how the controversy over such cases will eventually be settled, the Damicos make it clear that the same methods that work with normal and even gifted populations are also largely applicable to children and adults with special kinds of neurological or other impairments. The key is to provide even richer scaffolding for children and adults with difficulties than would be necessary for unimpaired subjects. The Damicos also make the important connection between "whole language philosophy" and pragmatic theory. Instead of asking what impaired children cannot do, about which facile speculations have often been disproved, the Damicos urge us to apply the same principles that work with other populations—dramatization, role playing, story telling, appeal to episodic organization, use of multiple modalities and recursive cycles through materials and activities, lots of action-oriented peer teaching, cooperative learning, etc. In brief, they show that methods that work with normal students also work with special populations. If anything, ways of making comprehension easier are even more essential for special populations than for normal ones.

The laughter in the classroom faded away as the professor stopped reading the text. The point had been made. An excerpt from an ESL textbook revealed the absurdity of asking students to study uninteresting, unmotivated, and artificially organized text. "Now let's try something else," the professor suggested to his class. He reached down and picked up *The Pearl* by John Steinbeck. Within two minutes the class was mesmerized. We were soon transported into another world. Our bodies were sitting in the same chairs and our ears were listening to the same voice, but our selves had identified with the main character, Kino, and had been carried to that fictional world in which Kino lived, thanks to John Steinbeck. Just like Kino, we were afraid of the men who were searching for him with drawn pistols. Our hearts raced and we held our breath as the men approached his hiding place. We were transported to that hiding place ourselves. In a moment of insight, what the professor intended suddenly came through.

Steinbeck's text was motivated by conflict involving people who had become real to us in plausible situations that were relevant and loaded with conflict. We cared about Kino and were motivated to find out what would happen to him. How different it was from the ESL/EFL textbook that told an insipid and unremarkable tale. Oller's Chapter 1 in the previous edition of *Methods That Work* reminds us (we had to read it to recall) that the ESL/EFL story he used that day back in 1980 was about the Millers en route to Hong Kong. They were a bland "vanilla" couple (borrowing a term from Peck, 1980) in a world without any apparent conflicts. Their world was also strange because there was hardly any meaningful connection between the sequences of events that were portrayed. The Millers had recognized the flight attendant from a previous international flight to Hong Kong, so she promptly dragged out her photo album, and they all began to discuss whether her friend Fumiko was taller, thinner, older, etc. than she, Miss Yamada, was. Then, Mr. Miller became hungry and hoped it would soon be time to eat.

The pragmatically motivated text, in contrast with the more traditional dialogue (written as a language teaching lesson), had a significant effect on us as listeners. As teachers in training we began to realize what meaningfulness, comprehensibility and pragmatic mapping (see Oller, 1975b, 1983b and Chapter 37) were all about. There was a shift in our understanding of what language acquisition, language use, literacy, and all related educational activities really were. The point had been made. We began to see the relevance of episodic organization and all that it entails for educational uses of language. We began to appreciate why episodically organized materials would be easier to understand, to learn from, and to recall. We began

to get a glimmering of what native-speaker intuitions are made of.

This chapter focuses how such ideas about language teaching, especially the theory of pragmatic mapping discussed in that class in the early 1980s, can be applied to special populations in schools all over the world. More particularly, we believe we can show that the methods recommended throughout this book are about equally if not more applicable to special populations than they are with so-called normal subjects. We are referring especially to children or adults exhibiting language-based difficulties of a semiotic kind, whether they are grounded in neurological or other cognitive impairments. Even though the subject populations in question exhibit special types of problems, we believe that the principles discussed in *Methods That Work* (both the previous edition and the present one) are just as relevant, if not more so, to special populations as to those considered as normal or gifted. By organizing language teaching around meaningful, contextually embedded, and motivated activities, through texts and discourses that are comprehensible, we can maximize our effectiveness in remediating the language problems noted for special populations. In effect, we can apply the general concepts directed by pragmatic theory (and by the more general theory of semiotics laid out in Oller & Damico, 1991; and in Oller et al., 1991) to chart a course over different instructional roads—those traveled by language learners with special types of learning problems. By demonstrating the applicability of the theory to these populations, we believe we can lend additional support to the principles discussed throughout this volume.

SPECIAL POPULATIONS

Within any sizable population in any educational or medical context, there will be some individuals who exhibit special problems in acquiring and/or using language. Due to some known and some yet to be discovered etiological factors, some children never acquire the language proficiency needed to function within normal limits in social and/or academic situations. These children often end up in special education programs. They are apt to be referred to as "language disordered," "language-learning impaired," "language delayed," or "learning disabled." All of these categories are sometimes abbreviated to "LD." Within such special education programs, LD children are usually taught by speech-language pathologists or special educators trained to provide teaching especially designed for one or more of the LD subpopulations.

Similarly, in medical settings it is well known that many adults who previously exhibited normal language proficiency will eventually lose it to some neurological impairment or other. Depending on the etiology, individuals afflicted with neurologically induced language loss are identified as having impairment due to focal lesions resulting in "aphasia" (left hemisphere impairment) or "right hemisphere impairment" (with discourse difficulties)—or diffuse lesions such as "closed head injuries" or "dementia" and are also apt to end up being assisted by speech-language pathologists whose goal will be to help them recover lost language abilities.

Whether the learners are adults or children and whether their problems are the result of an acquired neurological deficit or some developmental factor (e.g., a genetic brain disorder), in addition to a host of medical and neurological questions, the speech-language pathologists or special education teachers who work with them must deal with the same questions regarding language teaching, restoration, and therapeutic intervention strategies that language teachers typically ask. In fact, speech-language pathologists and special education teachers must ask: How can we best teach a language? What strategies or techniques are apt to be most effective? How can we keep our students motivated? How can we ensure carryover from fictional to factual contexts? How can we ensure that the somewhat sheltered tasks of the therapeutic intervention (in the classroom or clinical context) will have the desired impact on performances in the actual material world of experience outside the teaching or therapy context? What kinds of language teaching materials will work best? How should our instruction or therapeutic intervention be organized? Or should we rely on huge amounts of merely "comprehensible input" without worrying much about organization at all?

For years, speech-language pathologists assumed that the answers to these questions would be different when dealing with "impaired," or so-

called "LD," individuals. Increasingly, however, we recognize that this is not the case (Brinton & Fujiki, 1989; Damico, 1988; Davis & Wilcox, 1985; Fey, 1986; Muma, 1978; Rhodes & Dudley-Marling, 1988). The best responses to questions about language acquisition actually must embrace the same general and natural principles of language learning and acquisition discussed by other language teachers (Atwell, 1987; Bruner, 1978; Goodman, 1986; Langer & Applebee, 1986; Nelson, 1985; Oller & Richard-Amato, 1983; Omaggio, 1986; Richard-Amato, 1988; Wells, 1986). While there appear to be some differences in the way that the principles are applied, and certainly in the diagnostic procedures required, the teaching process is much the same at its basis and is directed in both cases by the same kinds of theoretical considerations. We prefer to work within the theory of pragmatic mapping with its related idea of "scaffolding" (as laid out especially in this volume, Parts 1 and 4 and Chapter 37). This theory can also be conceptualized relative to what has come to be known in recent years as "whole language philosophy." We will discuss both frameworks in what follows.

MEANING-MAKING BY SPECIAL POPULATIONS

For language teaching and therapeutic intervention with special populations, the theory of pragmatic mapping, and especially the ideas about how to scaffold meanings in order to make them optimally accessible, are directly relevant. This is because effectiveness in language teaching and in related therapeutic interventions will be directly determined by our success in understanding and applying these concepts. Since Krashen's original statement of the input hypothesis was amplified relative to what were called the textuality hypothesis, the episode hypothesis, and the expectancy hypothesis (Oller, 1983b), a great deal of evidence has become available showing the essential empirical and theoretical validity of these general ideas. Also, the theory of pragmatic mapping has been amplified (Oller & Damico, 1991) and has been developed into a comprehensive view of semiotics (meaning systems in general) and of intelligence (cf. Oller et al., 1991).

Pragmatic mapping, in a sentence, is the process of creating meaningful representations of the world. More specifically, pragmatic mapping is defined as the systematic linking of external experience (its facts) to our internalized representations and thus to our understanding of those experiences (through texts, discourses, gestures, and other representations of various sorts). What we think of as intelligence is also the underlying basis of the comprehensibility of the material world. It is what enables us to make sense of that world and of all the fictions and other representations that we find in it. This intelligence, of course, must include our capacity to participate in all kinds of communication and to make sense of all sorts of sensory-motor and gestural representations as well. According to the theory of pragmatic mapping, all kinds of representations are thus manifestations of our ability to create effective pragmatic maps of factual states of affairs, which ultimately extend to include relationships, events, actual fictions, fantasies, imaginings, illusions, and hallucinations. Similarly, the process of acquiring and using any language (or languages) also depends on successful pragmatic mappings of the forms of that language (or those languages) onto the facts of experience (see Chapter 37).

Whether we see ourselves as language teachers or therapeutic interventionists, a comprehensive theory of how human intelligence works will be essential in determining how to best help our students or clients. According to the theory of pragmatic mapping, we need to help them create correct pragmatic maps of their experience. If we can determine how to best enhance this pragmatic mapping process, then children acquiring their first language, students learning an additional language, and special populations trying to overcome impairments are bound to be more successful than they would be otherwise.

Another way of conceptualizing the same general problem is through two critical strategies drawn from whole language philosophy. These strategies, which are consistent with pragmatic and semiotic theory (Oller & Damico, 1991; and Chapter 37, this volume), guarantee appeal to episodic organization and virtually ensure optimally comprehensible input. In fact, since pragmatic theory is elaborated in detail elsewhere, our main emphasis in this chapter will be on the two strate-gies related to what is known as whole language philosophy. We will also endeavor to show how that philosophy and those strategies are related to methods spelled out in this edition of *Methods That Work*.

WHOLE LANGUAGE PHILOSOPHY

Before considering the two strategies in particular, it is necessary to establish a few basic points concerning what whole language philosophy is all about. Of course, the idea is not new, nor is it unique to speech-language pathology. The general framework has been discussed and used in a number of teaching disciplines over several decades, especially in literacy and language arts, and more recently in relation to the teaching of ESL/EFL and foreign languages. By reviewing applications in these areas, several points come to light. First, the whole language framework is a *philosophy* of teaching. It is not any single curriculum or program (Edelsky, Altwerger, & Flores, 1990; Goodman, 1986; Norris & Damico, 1990). While we can discuss specific applications, an actual technique or a particular set of materials is not what is meant by the term *whole language philosophy*. This is because a whole language intervention model doesn't merely exist in the activities or materials themselves, but in the dynamic interaction between the activities, the interventionist, the materials, and the students (Damico, 1992). It is, in short, a philosophy of teaching.

Second, the whole language philosophy is built upon data obtained from *normal developmental research*. The research indicates that language acquisition (in all skill areas) is a *constructive* process that is best accomplished when the language and the intervention process are *meaningful, relevant, authentic,* and *contextually embedded*. Just as with children acquiring their native language in a home environment, all other forms of language and the intervention process itself must be natural and must focus on "making-meaning" (Wells, 1986). In this way, the whole language philosophy is entirely compatible with the suggestions contained in the rest of this volume.

Third, to maximally benefit from the constructive power of human language capacity and other semiotic abilities, it is essential to realize that meaning-making is the general purpose of all forms of language, discourse, and text. It is the central purpose of all representational skills. Therefore, it is important to provide the students with opportunities to work in all language skill areas and in related cognitive, affective, and sensory-motor domains. These conclusions, incidentally, are completely consistent with the hierarchical model of language proficiency, gestural, and sensory-motor capacities in relation to a general semiotic capacity (Oller & Damico, 1991). Abstract ideas are mainly expressed through language and language-related mechanisms (e.g., mathematical and other symbologies). Affect is expressed chiefly through gesture, facial expression, tone of voice, and other body-language or paralinguistic elements, and the interface between cognition and affect with the material world is effected mainly through sensory-motor mechanisms. Consequently, when working with special populations, teachers should engage the students in plenty of reading, writing, and listening activities as well as speaking tasks. Better yet, these four skills should be interwoven in all teaching activities, and all of them should always be developed, as Walker et al. (1992 and Chapter 17, this volume) have stressed, within the sort of context that is rich in all kinds of additional semiotic scaffolding so that meaning can be comprehended.

Finally, within a whole language framework—if language teaching activities include the three previous points—students will become *empowered* to be *active* and creative language users and meaning-makers (Beed, Hawkins, & Roller, 1991; Damico & Armstrong, 1990–1991). They will become increasingly independent and able to assist themselves as language users and as learners in general. They will acquire a dynamic array of ways to enhance their own pragmatic mapping capabilities. Or, looked at from a more traditional viewpoint, they will learn to learn. They will become able to build their own scaffolds and to develop their own agendas by seeking out whatever help they need and by doing on their own the kinds of meaning-making that are required.

But how, exactly, can all of the foregoing be accomplished within a whole language framework? We come now to the two strategies we said we would discuss: First, general changes must be made in the instructional environment, including the materials used. Second, the activities and the manner of use of materials must be modified. The aim of all these changes will be to achieve authentic language activities that are meaningful, relevant, contextually-embedded, and motivating. We will take the two strategies in turn.

CHANGING THE INSTRUCTIONAL ENVIRONMENT

The language teacher, speech-language pathologist, or special educator should strive to create an environment that will encourage active learning on the part of the students (Bashir, 1989; Edelsky, Draper, & Smith, 1983; Hoskins, 1990; Pardo & Raphel, 1991; Stabb, 1990). This can be accomplished by planning a general program that addresses the following elements:

1. Plan goals and objectives tailored to naturalistic principles and relevancy.
2. Give the students as many opportunities as possible to read, write, talk, and listen in various group structures.
3. Allow the students to think and discuss options, make decisions, and establish accountability for what they do when working with you.
4. Surround the students with print to build a literacy-rich environment.
5. Treat the students with respect and work to empower them as learners.
6. Use interesting and meaningful materials and activities.

There are numerous authentic language activities that may be used within the whole language context (Goodman & Goodman, 1983; Langer & Applebee, 1986; Oller & Richard-Amato, 1983; Paris, 1989; Westby, 1989; Willig & Ortiz, 1991). Damico (1992) discusses no less than 35 different activities that can be incorporated into this instructional framework. For example, Dialogue Journals (Staton, 1983) and Response Journals (Wollman-Bonilla, 1989), provided they are actually read and reacted to by the teacher, qualify as authentic because they are genuine interactive dialogues about real experience between a student and another interested individual. In these activities, the focus of the journals is on meaning and communicative function rather than on grammatical form *per se*. Consequently, the students are more willing to communicate and take risks with language forms than in classes where the emphasis is on surface form rather than meaning. Because the student journals result in the interlocutors getting to know one another as unique individuals, there is more motivation and interest on the part of both parties.

Another authentic language activity that can incorporate all forms of text in a meaningful and relevant manner is the establishment of a Writing Workshop in the classroom. As advocated by Atwell (1987), Calkins (1983, 1986), and Graves (1983), writing workshops fit easily into the whole language philosophy. Writing activities are meshed with discussions and reading assignments. The primary focus of the activities, however, is the writing process itself, and the student receives encouragement and instruction within this text manifestation. The focus on writing, therefore, is not on a skills-oriented approach but rather on well-motivated meaning transmission. In the writing workshop, the teacher/interventionist sets up a block of time during which the writing activities are the primary focus. It is during this time that the students have the opportunity to engage in writing as a meaningful and developmental activity that will eventually enable the students to use their writing skills across the entire curriculum.

Theme building (Norris & Damico, 1990; Stabb, 1991) is another possibility. It depends on repeatable context and experience. In theme building, recurring activities are designed around a particular theme that is chosen by the students themselves as an area of investigation. Multiple formats, various language functions, and numerous activities can be incorporated into a theme building unit. The language teacher, for instance, may develop activities surrounding a theme by incorporating relationships between people, objects, and events. For theme building activities, here are the steps that are usually followed: (1) Determine the theme (content) that will be the initial focus; (2) decide how to incorporate multiple modalities through the activities; (3) ask what language functions will be focused on during the

TABLE 29.1 A Theme Building Plan for a Group of Preschool Children

Theme: "Zoo Animals"

	Monday	Wednesday	Friday
Week One	Read aloud "A Zoo in Our House" and discuss it.	Reread book with pauses for predictions and discuss trips to the zoo.	Talk about zoo animals and draw favorites.
Week Two	Discuss how zoo animals act outside the zoo and pretend you are some animal. Use the book as a guide. Reread parts as appropriate.	Read a related story about a trip to the zoo. Learn the sounds of new animals.	Plan and organize a field trip to the zoo, using the two books as guides.
Week Three	Discuss what you may see at the zoo, using the two books as guides, and write notes on what to do.	Take a field trip to the zoo. Discuss the trip and dictate notes to an adult while there.	Discuss the field trip. Reflect on the two sets of notes. Dictate a story and illustrate it.

TABLE 29.2 A Theme Building Plan for a Group of High School Children

Theme: "Scientific Method"

	Monday	Wednesday	Friday
Week One	Read about the scientific method in the textbook. Create a flow chart description of it.	Read portions of Loren Eiseley's "The Man Who Saw through Time." Discuss why and how Bacon conceived the method. Students take notes. These are critiqued, and suggestions are given.	Discuss the advantages of the scientific method. Practice using it to solve a problem.
Week Two	Discuss the method's relevance to everyday occurrences. Give a demonstration. Review the components and assign observations of everyday events.	Discuss how the method can help in other classes. Practice strategies based on the method.	
Week Three	Comment and discuss how the students applied the scientific method in classes or in everyday situations.	Read excerpts from scientists reporting discoveries and applying the method. Write an essay on its significance in everyday life.	

activities; (4) choose the language texts, formats, and strategies that will be used; and (5) prepare the actual sequence and organization of activities that will be incorporated into the theme building instructional unit.

Tables 29.1 and 29.2 provide examples of theme building plans with two very different levels of students. In each case, the students engage in theme building activities for approximately 90 minutes three times a week. In both of these examples, many language-oriented activities and opportunities are available. In Table 29.1, the theme of "Zoo Animals" is employed for preschool children. In this three-week instructional plan, there is an initial attention-grabbing activity (in this case, an excellent piece of children's literature) that highlights the theme. Once the theme is established, the children are involved in activities using language in various manifestations. For example, there are opportunities to talk about zoo animals and zoos (cf. Brinton, Snow, & Wesche, Chapter 14; Walker et al., Chapter 17); there are reading activities, writing tasks, pretend play (cf. Stern, Chapter 8); dictation to adults; and even a field trip that is collaboratively planned and conducted by the students and the adults.

In Table 29.2, a theme building plan is illustrated for high school special students. In this plan, "The Scientific Method" was chosen as the theme because of its relevance to real classroom assignments. In this three-week plan, various techniques and activities build on the theme in interesting and relevant ways. The activities are motivating to the students because they fit typical academic experiences, and they are comprehensible because of scaffolding through experience, demonstrations, flow charts (Geva, 1983), and the like. It should be mentioned that the table offers only a bare, skeletal outline. Many more activities can be incorporated. These may include discussions, note taking, reading, writing, and field observations.

As the examples of theme building suggest (Tables 29.1 and 29.2), the focus on the same theme over time and across activities leads to recurring patterns of language use and of content that allow the students both the time and the opportunity to become familiar with the material and to gain the specific knowledge that they need in order to negotiate meanings relevant to the theme. The accumulating knowledge acts as a scaffold of known contextual information that assists the students in creating their pragmatic maps of subsequent activities within the theme building plan. It can be a kind of "sheltered" language experience for students in special education classes (Krashen, Chapter 15). Or for students in mainstream classes, peer teaching can be used to great advantage (Assinder, Chapter 24). High school students are also capable of doing a great deal of the planning for theme building, collection of materials, working out of activities and the like as suggested by D. F. Clarke (1989) and by Prapphal (Chapter 34). In working with young children, pantomime and mime are particularly effective, as recommended by Seaver (Chapter 32). Children are especially benefited by the kinds of dramatic play that can easily be incorporated and modeled by the teacher through creative story telling (Morgan & Rinvolucri, Chapter 33).

There are many other instructional techniques, activities, and strategies that can be effectively incorporated within the whole language context. For example, many speech-language pathologists working with aphasic adults and closed-head injured patients employ Mediation of Learning techniques (Damico, 1992; Nelson, 1990) such as the K-W-L Strategy (Ogle, 1986), Think Alouds (Davey, 1983; Wade, 1990), or Directed Reading-Thinking Activity (Stauffer, 1981). These are effective activities in preparing for daily living and occupational needs once these patients start recovering from their neurological difficulties. All of these strategies are compatible with the kinds of scaffolded language activities recommended by language specialists such as Asher et al. (Chapter 2; Kalivoda et al., Chapter 3; and Glisan, Chapter 4), as well as drama-based approaches of the sort practiced by Rassias (Chapter 5), and role plays of the type recommended by Rodrigues and White (Chapter 7) and discussed in some depth by Stern (Chapter 8). Persons who are limited in their capacity to handle material in one modality are also most apt to be benefited by discourse that is scaffolded in the ways recommended and illustrated by Oller, Sr. and Oller (Chapter 6). In fact, Wessels (Chapter 36) shows how improvisation relative to dramatic purpose captures the essence of the "whole language philosophy," and she also shows how "input" from various sources can be converted into fully comprehended "intake."

The reason that these tried and proven methods of language teaching work with LD populations is essentially the same as those given earlier in this book for the broad range of normal subjects: Multiple modalities of presentation increase the likelihood of comprehension of input. The procedure is more like a blanket or "net" approach (to use Krashen's term) than like a discrete-point, diagnosis-bound approach, but it works precisely because not all channels of the LD individual are closed off. Even if we do not know exactly which modalities are damaged or malfunctioning (and in many cases medical science is still uncertain of etiologies), by casting the net broadly with plenty of scaffolding, we increase the likelihood of success.

Here is a typical example. A California child at age 11-6, classed as "dyslexic" (and there are a wide variety of definitions and subcategories), may be able to suddenly begin reading on her own after years of failure. Becky was such a child and in the summer of 1992 became a reader. The key to unlocking her hidden abilities was to increase the scaffolding available to her through multiple cycles (as recommended, for instance, in foreign language teaching by Oller, Sr. & Oller, Chapter 6, and by Weissenrieder, Chapter 23) through a story with which she became increasingly familiar. Her mother read and reread the story without any apparent advance for several weeks. The child and her mother discussed the facts of the story until they were "over-learned" beyond anything that most school teachers would approve or attempt. Becky and her mom pointed to the appropriate pictures relevant to facts being read aloud. Mom asked questions, and the child, Becky, answered them.

Pig-simple methods (as Peck, 1980, would say), but they worked. After years of total failure and expensive but unhopeful diagnoses (largely uninterpretable to the child or the parents, and mostly grounded in speculative theory rather than in any empirically verifiable facts) by various physicians and speech-language pathologists, Becky suddenly cracked the reading problem. First she was able to read the over-learned story. It was almost as great a surprise to herself as it was to her mom. The proof of the pudding was when Mom asked Becky if she wanted to try one of the less-familiar stories in the same book. Becky was also able to read it, and the next, and the next. She had, for all intents and purposes, joined "the literacy club" (cf. Smith, 1988).

Within the school context, speech-language pathologists may use procedures like those of Becky and her mom, or they may prefer activities like Script Building (Creaghead, 1990), Storytelling (Peck, 1989; Morgan & Rinvolucri, Chapter 33), Communicative Reading Strategies (Norris, 1989; Walker et al., 1992, and Chapter 17 in this volume) and Literature Study Circles (Samway et al., 1991). The latter language activities are reflective of many required academic tasks in the classroom and hold much appeal for this reason.

ENSURING ACTIVE MEDIATION

The second strategy for working with special populations, already implicit in the first, is to ensure active mediation. This is necessary in order to make certain that students take on the active role in constructing pragmatic connections between the discourse or text they must solve for meaning (i.e., comprehend) and their own experience. Until this happens, no real acquisition of skills or language can occur. What makes the application of this strategy extra difficult with special populations is the nature of their special problems in effectively and/or efficiently creating pragmatic maps. Therefore, it is even more critical with these populations than with normal classes that the teacher help the student with the mapping process. For dyslexic Becky, for example, the help was repetitive cycling, reference to pictures, recounting the facts (*ad nauseam* almost), asking comprehension

questions to get Becky involved in the processing, and continuing with a variety of different modalities until the light came on (so to speak). While a number of competent diagnosticians had told Becky's parents that she would probably never be able to learn to read at all, the fact is that she *was* able to do so. Therefore, the need for active mediation can hardly be over-stressed.

This need for mediation is typically recognized in the special populations. It is not unusual for this awareness to be stated in the form of a question, which goes something like this: "Is there a difference between the language instruction conducted with special populations versus the language instruction with 'normal' language learners?" The answer is "yes," but with qualification. Although the basic principles derived from pragmatic mapping and the actual implications of the mapping process are the same for the normal and the special populations of language learners, there is one primary difference in providing language instruction to special populations: The teacher must make even greater effort to adapt the input to the special student so that this input meshes with the student's proficiency and capabilities. The closest analogue among "normal" populations would be the case of children from severely disenfranchised backgrounds (such as the Hill Tribes of Thailand; cf. Walker et al., Chapter 17) who are expected to learn to read a language that they do not yet know. However, the case of the special education (LD) child is a still more difficult problem in many instances. It may be compounded by socioeconomic factors beyond the control of the child or the schools. The key, nevertheless, is always to find and play to the student's strengths rather than weaknesses. To do this the teacher/therapist must act as an active *mediator* between the student and the language input or output. Also, the teacher or clinician must actively enlist all the capabilities of the child to ensure that whatever scaffolding is available is in fact being used to maximum benefit by the child.

The great advantage of the whole language philosophy is that it creates a meaningful, relevant, authentic, and empowering language environment within which meaning-making can occur. For the special population students, however, we must take additional steps in order to "pitch" the language to the student's level. As discussed by

Krashen, Oller, and others, we must ensure that during language instruction, the *input* becomes *intake*.

In order to ensure this objective during instruction, the teacher or speech-language pathologist has to function as an active mediator for the student. That is, the teacher places him/herself between the student and the environment and acts as a meaning-maker between the two (Canterfold, 1991; Wells, 1986). This process is typically accomplished by the mediator taking the incoming stimuli from the environment and modifying it so that it can be presented to the student within his or her zone of proximal development (Vygotsky, 1978) or at his or her level of comprehensible input (Krashen, 1983). Once the student acts upon this meaningful input, the mediator can help to adjust the student's output till it optimally fits the facts at hand in a manner appropriate and meaningful to the environment. This mediation is primarily achieved through conversational interaction or discourse between the teacher/interventionist and the student. The whole process is greatly aided over the long term through materials and activities that have strong episodic organization (Oller, 1983b and in this volume Part 4 and Chapters 28 and 37). In effect, through conversational interaction and the structuring of language learning activities, the language input from the environment to the student and the language output from the student to the environment are scaffolded to enhance the creation of well-equilibrated pragmatic maps (Boyle & Peregoy, 1990; Ninio & Bruner, 1978; Palincsar, 1986; Silliman & Wilkinson, 1991; and Oller et al., 1991).

From a practical perspective, interactional mediation can be implemented by following a three-stage process when interacting with the special students during instruction (adapted from Norris & Hoffman, 1990). Stage One involves providing the appropriate organization. At this stage, language learning activities are created and implemented that are appropriate to the developmental abilities or the language proficiency of the students. Establishing the appropriate organization can be achieved in three steps: (1) Observe and evaluate the special students and determine their appropriate levels of proficiency; (2) ensure that the activities and content provided during the language-learning activities are context-embedded and relevant to the experience of the students; and (3) maintain the theme or topic with logical episodic organization so that new activities logically extend and build upon previous activities (cf. Walker et al., Chapter 17, for illustrations concerning how this can be done).

Once Stage One is in place, Stage Two can be implemented: The instructor can engage in actual language teaching by providing an opportunity for successful pragmatic mapping to occur. At this stage, the teacher strives to place the special student in the role of the meaning-maker within the context of the activity. The teacher creates the opportunity for the student to map his or her language onto the experiential context, and the teacher then accepts the student's spontaneously occurring behavior as meaningful mapping, interprets it in a manner that is contextually appropriate, and becomes a collaborator with the student in reformulating the map as necessary to make it fit the context more effectively. (An example of how this can be done is given with respect to the Aboriginal child named Mary in Chapter 17 by Walker et al. We are referring specifically to the toast-making activity, shown in Transcript D, as contrasted with Transcript A, where sufficient scaffolding was notably absent.)

It is at this second stage of the mediational process that scaffolding is used as the primary method for providing the student appropriate opportunities to map and communicate effectively (Ninio & Bruner, 1978; Palincsar, 1986; Silliman & Wilkinson, 1991). This strategy serves to assist the student in formulating messages with greater complexity, specificity of meaning, accuracy, and clarity of expression.

Stage Three of the mediation process with special populations involves providing the student with natural consequences based on his or her behavior. Once the student does respond or interact to the opportunity provided at Stage Two, feedback should be given to the student that is natural, temporally constrained, and respects the logic of experience (Oller, 1979, 1983b; Vigil & Oller, 1976; Johnson, Chapter 25, this volume). That is to say, the feedback in order to be optimally successful must meet the "pragmatic naturalness constraints." It must be meaningful, and it must be provided in a timely manner so that it can be connected in the appropriate way with the ongoing experience of the student. This feedback should be directly related to the effectiveness of the student's mapping and to the student's effectiveness in influencing the listener or observer. If the student's response or output is effective and appropriate, then positive consequences such as acknowledgments and affirmations; restating and rewording; recounting events; semantically contingent remarks; sharing personal reactions, questions, and comments; and predictions and projections can be used to good advantage (Damico, 1992; Norris & Hoffman, 1990; Silliman & Wilkinson, 1991; Johnson, Chapter 25, this volume). These responses enhance the mapping process, respect the logical flow of natural interaction, and assist the student in fulfilling his or her expectancies about the ways that mapping and communication operate (Vigil & Oller, 1976).

If the student's mapping processes and interactions are not appropriate or effective, then the teacher responds with requests for repair that are also natural and contextual in nature. There are a number of repair strategies that can be used. For example, Brinton and Fujiki (1989) and Norris and Hoffman (1990) have offered at least nine relevant strategies: request for repetition, negation, modeling with revision, request for clarification, repetition with rising intonation, prompts to request information, phonetic changes, reinterpretations, and concept formation activities. Also see the suggestions in Walker et al. (1992, and in Chapter 17, this volume).

From a practical perspective, this three-stage process of mediation is typically very effective in the enhancement of pragmatic mapping in special populations. Regardless of what specific process is used, the important issue is that some way has to be found to achieve comprehensibility during the language teaching process. This is the central problem in all aspects of language instruction or other kinds of language-based teaching. The cru-

cial element is to enable students to achieve correct pragmatic maps relative to common experience (Krashen, 1983, 1985b; Oller, 1983b, 1990; Oller et al., 1991, and Chapter 37, this volume).

CONCLUSION

Regardless of whether a language teacher's instructional charges are facile language learners who could do well in spite of the teacher's worst efforts or whether the students are less-capable learners owing to neurological or other special impairments or just to societal factors beyond the child's control, the same fundamental principles apply. Students of any caliber must be motivated, interested, and given the opportunity to become meaning-makers for real and relevant purposes. Language teaching that provides less is simply not sufficient. By conceptualizing the process of language learning as a particular application of the theory of pragmatic mapping and by seeking out and creating logically consistent and pedagogically sound approaches based on that conceptualization (and related ones such as the whole language philosophy), our best hopes as language teachers can be fulfilled. The road to language acquisition and literacy may not always be smooth and level. Sometimes it twists and turns, crossing canyons filled with raging rivers. It is often strewn with rocks and obstacles that we cannot even make out for certain. But teachers, speech-language pathologists, and special educators can do a great deal to make the road smoother and more pleasant for children and adults with special difficulties. By serving as mediators and helpers, special educators can help many who have, till now, had little hope of attaining the reasonable goals of literacy and sufficient language proficiency to become fully empowered, functional members of the human community.

DISCUSSION QUESTIONS

1. Why does meaningful conflict (a character pursuing a desirable goal in the face of opposition) motivate interest? Consider examples from everyday experience, your own or those around you. What do people generally focus on in their talk? Why do they talk so much about conflicts, troubles, difficulties, surprises, and accidents? What are the underlying programs that cause people to attend to things out of whack while things going well are taken for granted?

2. Suppose a child is neurologically impaired in some unknown way. Suppose further that the child has some well-developed capabilities. For instance, take the case of Becky, who had well-developed oral language and social skills but had been diagnosed as "neurologically impaired" and had been loosely classified as "dyslexic." Or take another familiar case. What might be done for such a child to help him or her become a reader (or to acquire another language)? What strengths can we play to? How might these be used to scaffold the weak points of the child's development?

3. In a whole-language approach to teaching language or literacy (for instance, in the case of Becky), how does recycling through episodically organized material create a richly scaffolded basis for acquisition of the language or skill in question? What impact on learner confidence can be expected, for instance, from repeated readings and probing of understanding through comprehension questions about a story that becomes more and more familiar with each rereading? What effect will accrue from the rote recall of some lines in the story, through an oral cloze procedure (and then she said "_____"), where the student/client is able to supply the needed element from memory? What impact could be expected from having the child tell the story to someone else (e.g., to a younger sibling or to a friend)?

PART 6

SING 'N RAP: GAMES 'N GRAMMAR, DRILLS 'N DRAMA

Significant human behaviors include a much wider range of semiotic (meaning) devices than are commonly recognized in traditional language curricula, including foreign language curricula, those aimed at language arts, and even linguistics courses. For instance, when someone seems to be slipping over the edge of sane and acceptable behavior, it is not uncommon for a couple of intelligent and uninhibited observers (like the two of us are, of course) to confidentially turn to each other with knowing looks, and, like as not, one of us will raise his or her eyebrows and begin to hum in a sing-song cadence the theme of *The Twilight Zone*—na-na-NA-na, na-na-NA-na. Then we'll both chuckle, and our friend who was getting weird will probably blush and get real again.

In fact, human beings are apt to use almost any perceivable bit of experience as a sign to indicate or demonstrate some meaning to someone else. Such signs certainly include lyrics, tunes, rhythms (dum-ta-da-DUM-dum, dum-dum!), and in general anything that we could subsume under a heading like "Sing 'n Rap: Games 'n Grammar, Drills 'n Drama." In the previous edition of *Methods That Work* we included a similar section that we called "Fun and Games," but that designation might have suggested the items included there were not to be taken seriously—I mean, as bona-fide content-laden entries. But of course they were content items, though they were seen as desserts rather than main dishes. Well, this time around, the fun section still includes some creamy puddings and tangy tarts, but it ought to be kept in mind by all the patrons that a banana split includes most of your basic food groups. You've got your potassium in the banana, your calcium in the ice cream, your chocolate in the hot fudge, and so on. The main thing is that just about any combination of these items will make your meal both sweeter and more nourishing. Besides, if play for kids is their work, as some sage said, then work for adults ought to be play. Right? Right.

Subramaniyan Nambiar (Chapter 30) suggests songs as a resource, and commercial jingles, of course, could be added in. Don't you deserve a break today? Oh what a relief it is! Carolyn Graham (Chapter 31), with her M.C. Hammer-style jazz raps steamed up with some funky dancing, can do a lot even without even a TV commercial. Realia can also help. Whoa! Is that a great lookin' Pepsi can, or what! Or if you prefer pantomime instead of rhyme, you'll enjoy Seaver (Chapter 32), who argues that mime itself is a natural route in early cognitive and affective development of children and that it provides another means to help make the meaning clear in the foreign language classroom. He says that when teachers mime, "momentarily, students relate to that new, nonthreatening person rather than to the teacher as authority figure" (p. 342). They relax. And the miming, like a spoonful of sugar, helps the medicine go down. Target language forms are painlessly internalized, just as Krashen has long been saying that they ought to be.

Chapter 33, by Morgan and Rinvolucri, offers yet another source of authentic language material that can serve as comprehensible input in the classroom. Oddly, it is a source that has been greatly neglected by language teaching methodologists and has been scarcely tapped by literacy specialists either. Perhaps some educators have embraced the mistaken idea that telling a story is too close to going to the movies to count as any part of a school curriculum. But many creative teachers, like Morgan and Rinvolucri themselves, have realized that a well-told story is an especially rich source of input for language acquisition. Good stories are full of mental imagery that can easily be scaffolded by creative miming. Good stories are loaded with the kinds of conflict that students are apt to readily identify with. In fact, they may concentrate so completely on what is happening and how the characters are reacting that they are drawn into the experience until the target language becomes as transparent as their native language normally is. Perceptive teachers will see innumerable ties between this chapter, titled "Once Upon a Time," and all of the other methods that are recommended in this book.

Games, jigsaw readings, songs, and a host of potential cooperative learning experiences are explored in Chapter 34 by Prapphal, former President of Thai TESOL and renowned author of English materials for students in Thailand. Her classroom research with adults shows that even they, like younger students, are also receptive toward a wide range of "cooperative learning" and of "caring and sharing" experiences along the lines of authors like Spencer Kagan and Gertrude Moskowitz. The same theme is developed further, in a slightly more theoretical vein, by Jonathan de Berkeley-Wykes, in Chapter 35, where the fundamental virtues of connected text are extolled relative to "jigsaw reading." It is interesting that the cooperative learning aspect of such activities was fully anticipated by de Berkeley-Wykes, writing late in 1982, though his article predated the multitude of materials on cooperative learning which began to appear in the literature a couple of years later (esp. Kagan, 1985–1992).

Drawing it all together into a neat dramatic package, we come at last to Chapter 36, by Charlyn Wessels. If her classroom experiment in teaching English through drama will not naturally appeal to nearly every language specialist who should give it a moment's thought, then I know nothing of all those teachers and clinicians. I am not saying that the method itself, in any particular manifestation, is for all educational occasions, nor for all kinds and levels of students, nor for all sociocultural settings. Hardly. But I am saying that I really believe that what can be learned from Wessels' remarkable classroom research is bound to be universally applicable to the business of teaching and acquiring language skills. Wessels illustrates, elaborates, and demonstrates just about everything that this book has attempted to represent by way of language teaching methods. I cannot improve on the words of Damico and Damico, Chapter 29. They say that "Wessels shows how improvisation relative to dramatic purpose captures the essence of the 'whole language philosophy,' and she also shows how 'input' from various sources can be converted into fully comprehended 'intake'" (p. 324).

CHAPTER 30

Pop Songs in Language Teaching

Subramaniyan A. Nambiar

EDITOR'S INTRODUCTION

*N*ambiar addresses TESL teachers in this article, but the suggestions offered could easily be adapted to language and literacy programs of any kind. Whistling while you work or singing "I owe, I owe, so off to work I go" is a familiar theme for teachers everywhere (Richards, 1969; Finocchiaro, 1973: 174; Dubin, 1974). If the silk hat fits when you place it on your head, you too may begin to dance around. Music somehow helps to connect us with the past and the future. It has been suggested that the American cowboy could get his horse and dog back, not to mention the girl of his dreams, if he'd just sing his songs in reverse. Ballads, owing to their episodic organization, are especially adaptable to methods in Part 1 and for reasons given in Part 4 and Chapter 37. What makes ballads relatively easy to understand? They can be acted out and illustrated via their story line. But well-chosen pop songs, provided they are tastefully selected and not too out of touch with the host culture, are apt to find a ready response from students. So within reasonable limits, noise levels, and so on, why not! We'll sing along and even rock and roll. Dance and rap. Bungee jumping? Moshing? Raving? Uh . . . There must be some limits . . . But we're still cool and a little crazy, even after all these years. And if anyone asks, tell 'em, "Yep. We are having fun, yet" or still. Whatever.

At TESL conferences and in TESL journals, recommendations and suggestions are frequently given that teachers of English as a second language need to be more innovative, and creative and that they should use a wide variety of materials to enhance, foster, and motivate students to learn English. At times this seems to be an uphill task, especially in Malaysian schools where there are occasions when the entry of the English language teacher into the classroom is greeted with these words: *Datanglah guru bahasa haram!* Translated, this means, "Here comes the teacher of the infidel language!" Nevertheless, these English language teachers soldier on and try to use a variety of resources in English language teaching and learning.

One of the resources that can be utilized in the teaching and learning of English is the use of songs: pop, folk, rock, ballads, etc. According to Dubin (1974: 1) the use of songs in language learning and teaching is an "overlooked resource—at least one that has been overlooked by the 'establishment' in our profession." But see Richards (1969).

WHY USE SONGS?

Songs have a great tendency to attract the attention of people that other forms of the mass media may lack. Even the person who is totally tone deaf may at times consider himself a good singer, and a person who cannot understand the words of a song can still appreciate the song itself. Songs, especially current pop songs, exert a great influence over the younger generation from which our students come. The songs deal with the whole realm of human emotions and experiences—love (especially so) and hate, wealth and poverty, joy and misery, freedom and slavery, happiness and sadness, loneliness and companionship, life and death are all common human experiences, and songs that deal with these emotions appeal to the young and the old.

Secondly, students are often willing to learn to sing a song in a foreign language even if they do not fully understand or only partially understand the meaning of the words. Since one of the purposes of language learning and teaching is that students should learn to use the language instead of learning the usage of the language, the singing of the pop songs thus takes us one step towards achieving that ultimate goal, language use by the students.

The use of songs in the English language classroom allows the students to "hide behind the music" (McDonald, 1984: 35). According to him, the use of songs

> . . . avoids the heat of an early spotlight landing on a timid student. It also warps the students' preconceptions of how difficult it is to use the new language. The result is . . . a loss of certain inhibitions, a new respect for one's own voice and the learning of whatever vocabulary, grammar and punctuation the song has to offer.

By using songs in the language classroom, the teacher adds variety (which is badly needed in most language classrooms) to the teaching-learning process as the music, verse, and song constitute a total and dramatic departure from the normal pattern of language learning experience wherein the teacher drones for most of the time while the students use the language for only a brief moment of time, if they are allowed to use the language at all. By using songs, therefore, "language learning can be combined with recreation or aesthetic appreciation for a change of pace in the classroom to enhance motivation" (Finocchiaro, 1973: 174).

Songs introduce an atmosphere of gaiety, fun, and informality in the classroom which is a far more conducive environment for language learning than a strictly regimented atmosphere where students are pounced upon for the least bit of deviation from grammatical norms or for making any "unnecessary" noise.

Furthermore, songs permit maximum participation of students in that the whole class can sing simultaneously. Songs also aid language recall because it is easier to recall rhythm, rhymes, and verse than mere passages of prose.

BEFORE USING THE SONGS . . .

Before the songs can be used in the classroom, it is necessary for the English language teacher to undertake the following tasks:

a) The teacher has to shed whatever dislike he or she may have towards the current pop hits. Just because the teacher grew up listening to the songs of the sixties or the fifties, he or she should not expect the students to share such feelings for these "oldies." He or she has to realize and accept the fact that his or her students' interests in songs may be totally different. In fact, nothing would do better to dampen students' interest than the use of songs that students have no desire to hear at all.

b) It is necessary to have an adequate supply of recorded songs together with their lyrics.

c) There should be a tape recorder in working condition with an extension cord so that the machine can be moved around in the classroom with ease.

d) The teacher should be familiar with the linguistic features that predominate in each song. Certain songs have a lot of questions, others have idioms, similes, or metaphors, while still other songs have words that are culture bound and sociological in nature.

SOME SUGGESTED ACTIVITIES

The following is a list of suggested activities that could be carried out. This list is by no means exhaustive, and a creative and an innovative teacher could find new uses for songs in the language classroom.

a) Musical Dictation

Songs can be a very good substitute for prose passages in dictation exercises. The song can be played right through, with the students listening intently. Then the song is played a line at a time until the students are able to write out the lyrics of the song. Then the song is played again so that they can compare the words that they have written with the words that they actually hear from the tape recorder. Sometimes this may lead to amusing incidents as where a student after hearing the words "Oh, Carol, I'm but a fool," wrote "Oh, Carol, I'm a bloody fool." (A word of caution: It is imperative that the teacher have a correct copy of the lyrics of the song!)

b) Completion Exercises

The songs can also be used as a completion exercise. In this case copies of the song sheets are given to students with blanks in between. The students are required to listen to the song and complete the sheets by writing the words that have been left out. Here, a teacher may focus on a particular phoneme or sound. For example, in the song "The Traveller" the sound /r/ occurs frequently, and the students can be trained to listen to the words. Thus the verse may appear like this:

In. . . . the coast,   from

. . . . like the wind   riding

and . . . . the moon   racing

Shadows on the . . . .   road

dancing and a-weaving

like a . . . . fool   crazy

c) Cultural/Social Background

Songs frequently depict the social and cultural background of a particular society. Consequently, students can be asked to find out the meaning of certain cultural terms which may have a particular meaning in another society but a meaning that is totally different in the students' society. In the song "Uptown Girl," phrases such as "downtown guy," "whitebread world," "brown bread," and, of course, "uptown girl" occur. Students can be asked to find out the meaning of these phrases so that they will have a better idea of the song.

d) Similes and Metaphors.

Certain songs have a lot of similes or metaphors in them. As illustrated in the song above ("The Traveller"), similes such as "riding like the wind" and "like a crazy fool" occur. Students could be asked to explain the meaning of these similes and also to think of other similes or metaphors that have been used in other songs (e.g., "lips like cherries" from "The Green Green Grass of Home").

e) Grammatical Features

In some songs particular grammatical features occur with great frequency. In the song "Knock Three Times" there is an abundant use of prepositions and frequent use of the conditional clause beginning with *if*. In the song "Leaving on a Jet Plane" there are examples of the present continuous tense. In "Where Have All the Flowers Gone" the present perfect tense in the interrogative is used. Such songs can be used as a form of reinforcement for the particular structural item that had been taught in the previous lessons. (Alternatively, the songs could also be used as an introduction to the particular grammatical item.)

f) Vocabulary Learning

Active vocabulary learning is an activity that is seldom paid any attention in most language classrooms. It is here that songs can be of great help. Numerous words that deal with a particular theme or emotion abound in the songs. Students can be asked to identify these various words and then they can form a cluster of words. By using the song "Bridge over Troubled Waters," one can have the clusters shown in Figure 30.1.

FIGURE 30.1

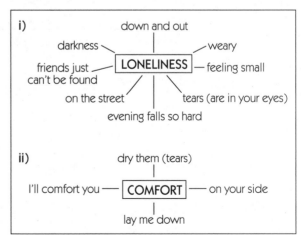

g) Phonological Features

There are also songs that focus on particular phonological features such as *wanna* for "want to" and *somethin'* for "something." Some of the songs by the Beatles are good examples ("I wanna hold your hand!").

h) Discussion Sessions

Where the students are able to speak fairly well, discussion sessions can be held in order to enable students to express their views or feelings about the song in general, and whether they agree or disagree with the views expressed in the song.

i) Singalong

The students can just sing along with the recording and learn to sing it themselves. It would be essential for them to have the words, and this is where the dictation exercise could be put to good use. Then the song can be learned verse by verse. It would be better for the students to learn to sing in groups so that they can hide behind the music and also because they can find security in numbers.

The availability of songs can be a problem. Some teachers may not have a selection of songs on tape, or they may not know how to use the songs during the English language lessons. The simple solution is to record the weekly BBC English by Radio program *Pedagogical Pop*. It is a program where the current pop hits are used as a resource for language learning and teaching. It is a 15-minute program and a bank of songs can be accumulated over the weeks. There are also commercially produced songs by book publishers which can be utilized as a resource material for language learning and teaching.

CONCLUSION

The need to make language learning more interesting is a pressing one, as this seems to be one of the ways of motivating students to want to learn a new language. Teachers should therefore throw away the archaic idea that a language can only be taught and learned through the use of a textbook. A language teaching and learning program that emphasizes the use of a variety of resources may hold a key to successful language learning in the classroom.

DISCUSSION QUESTIONS

1. What songs have worked for you? Why do you think they did?

2. In view of the recommendation of D. F. Clarke (1989) that teachers ought to enlist their students' help in finding and adapting materials (also see the suggestions in Chapter 24 by Assinder), why not have them pick the songs and invent supporting activities? What sorts of activities could you suggest for them to consider?

CHAPTER 31

An Excerpt from *Jazz Chants*

Carolyn Graham

EDITOR'S INTRODUCTION

"Jazz chants" are catchy repetitive drills that draw attention to rhythmic and kinesthetic properties of utterances. If they are linked to contexts of experience through imaginative dramatization, as is common with modern "rap music" (also see Part 1), and if they are linked to meaningful experience, they can be a powerful tool for enabling students to achieve a greater fluency and naturalness in uttering the forms of the target language. They may be used to help students over significant pronunciation stumbling blocks—as for instance, the little rhyme

> Erre con erre barril.
> Erre con erre carril.
> ¡Qué rápido corren las ruedas del ferrocarril!

has helped many Spanish students over the difficult hurdle of the trilled r. The danger of focusing attention too narrowly on surface form can be avoided by using the "jazz chant" technique sparingly and with sufficient dramatic props to make certain that whatever meaning exists in the chant is drawn into play. Of course, raps and chants can used not only to drill surface form, but also to produce a pragmatic effect.

Jazz chants are the rhythmic expression of Standard American English as it occurs in situational contexts. Just as the selection of a particular tempo and beat in jazz may convey powerful and varied emotions, the rhythm, stresses, and intonation patterns of the spoken language are essential elements for the expression of feelings and the intent of the speaker. Linking these two dynamic forms has produced an innovative and exciting new approach to language learning.

Although jazz chanting's primary purpose is the improvement of speaking and listening comprehension skills, it also works well in reinforcing specific structures used in a situational context. The natural rhythms and humor of the chants are highly motivating and may be used effectively for both classroom practice and individual home study.

The student of jazz chanting learns to express feelings through stress and intonation, while building a vocabulary appropriate to the familiar rituals of daily life. See the following example.

OUCH! THAT HURTS

Ouch!
    What's the matter?
I stubbed my toe.
    Oh, that hurts, that hurts.
    I know that hurts.
Ouch!
    What's the matter?

I bit my tongue.
> Oh, that hurts, that hurts.
> I know that hurts.
Ouch!
> What's the matter?
I got a cramp in my foot.
> Oh, that hurts, that hurts.
> I know that hurts.
Ouch! Ouch!
> What's the matter now?
I bumped into the table,
tripped on the stairs,
slipped on the carpet,
fell over the chairs.
> Gee! You're clumsy today!

The chants are written in two-part dialogue form. The dialogues include three basic forms of conversational exchange:

1. Question and response. This includes information questions, yes/no questions, and questions created by intonation pattern alone.
2. Command and response.
3. Response to a provocative statement.

The material in the chants includes the most frequently occurring structures of conversational American English and is intended to provide the student with patterns and vocabulary that he or she can comfortably use in the world outside the classroom.

In performing the chants, the students are actually learning to distinguish difficult vowel and consonant contrasts while they are actively engaged in a verbal exchange which can easily be related to their own experience.

The chants are particularly useful in developing listening comprehension skills. A comparison of the written text and the tape which accompanies it illustrates the striking difference between the written word and spoken American English. The students are being trained to comprehend the language of an educated native speaker in natural conversation.

THE PRESENTATION

The essential element in presenting a jazz chant is the clear, steady beat and rhythm. By setting the dialogue to a beat, we are not *distorting* the line but simply *heightening* the student's awareness of the natural rhythmic patterns present in spoken American English. A student practicing a specific rhythm and intonation pattern within the chant form should be able to use that same pattern in normal conversation and be readily understood by a native speaker.

The chants are based on a combination of *repetition* and *learned response*. Initially, the students should repeat the lines of the chant following the model provided by the teacher and/or the tape. This choral repetition allows the students to experiment with expressing strong feelings and, in some instances, raise their voices to an angry shout, without the natural shyness that would occur when speaking alone in class.

Once the students are familiar with the material, they progress from the simple choral repetition to giving a group response in answer to a question or statement. This introduces an important new element, as the class is now engaged in a dialogue with the teacher. This dialogue may then be transformed into a three- or four-part exchange.

It is extremely important that the students have a clear understanding of the meaning of the words they are saying and the appropriate situations in which they might occur.

Presenting a Jazz Chant, Step by Step

The following step-by-step plan for presenting a jazz chant is intended to suggest one of the many possible ways of using the material and to share some of the methods I use with my classes in jazz chanting at New York University. The teacher should feel free to experiment, improvise, and adapt the chants to the needs of the students. In short, if it works, use it.

1. The teacher explains the situational context of the chant. For example, in "Baby's Sleeping" we are learning the different ways in which you tell someone to be quiet. In this case, we are asking for silence because the baby is sleeping. The teacher should clearly explain any vocabulary items or expressions which might present difficulties, and may wish to discuss the cultural implications of the material.

SH! SH! BABY'S SLEEPING!

I said, Sh! Sh! Baby's sleeping!
I said, Sh! Sh!, Baby's sleeping!
    What did you say?
    What did you say?
I said, Hush! Hush! Baby's sleeping!
I said, Hush! Hush! Baby's sleeping!
    What did you say?
    What did you say?
I said, Please be quiet, Baby's sleeping!
I said, Please be quiet, Baby's sleeping.
    What did you say?
    What did you say?
I said, Shut up! Shut up! Baby's sleeping!
I said, Shut up! Shut up! Baby's sleeping!
    WAAAAAAAAAAAAAAAAAAA
Not anymore.

2. The teacher gives the first line of the chant at normal speed and intonation. The students repeat in unison. This simple choral repetition continues for each line of the chant. At this stage the teacher may stop at any point to correct pronunciation or intonation patterns. You may wish to repeat each line several times in chorus.

3. The teacher establishes a clear, strong beat by counting, clapping, using rhythm sticks, or snapping his or her fingers. The teacher continues to demonstrate the beat and repeats step 2.

4. The class is divided into two equal sections. There is no limit to the number of students in each section. A jazz chant can be conducted with two students or two hundred students. The teacher now establishes a clear, steady beat and gives the first line of the chant, using normal speed and intonation. The first section repeats the line. The teacher gives the second line of the chant. The second section repeats the line. This pattern is continued for each line of the chant, with the teacher's voice providing a model for the repetitions.

5. The chant is now conducted as a two-part dialogue between the teacher and the class. The teacher establishes a clear, strong beat and gives the first line of the chant. The class answers in unison with the second line of the chant. Until the students are thoroughly familiar with the material, they will probably wish to refer to their open text in class. This two-part dialogue between the teacher and the class is clearly illustrated in the accompanying tape. Notice that at this stage the class is no longer divided into two sections but is *responding* to the teacher as one choral voice, *without* the teacher's model.

DISCUSSION QUESTIONS

1. What precautions could be taken to select or create "chants" that are directly linked to meaningful contexts?

2. Based on the results of Arevart and Nation (Chapter 27), what effects can be expected to accrue over time from well-practiced "jazz chants" or rap-type language lessons?

3. Can you create a jazz chant from a socio-drama (or other role-play situation) to help students over some difficulty of surface syntax, morphology, or phonology? Can it be done with optimal meaningfulness and accessibility to the relevant context?

CHAPTER 32

Pantomime as an L2 Classroom Strategy

Paul W. Seaver, Jr.

EDITOR'S INTRODUCTION

A t least since Watzlawick, Beavin, and Jackson (1967) pointed out the distinction between content and relationship levels of communication, we have understood that the affective (emotional and personal) side of human relations is coded largely in nonverbal, gestural, and paralinguistic mechanisms such as tone of voice and facial expression, while the cognitive side tends to be coded mainly in words and other digital devices such as numbers. Raymond Birdwhistell (1970), who coined the term kinesics to cover all sorts of significant body movements, argued that nonverbal (analogue) modalities were even more important to communication in most situations than verbal (digital) ones. At any rate, no one doubts that nonverbal devices, such as how close we get to each other and whether or not and how we touch each other (proxemics), are loaded with nuclear-powered meaning. Nor is there any question (not since Watzlawick et al.) that if the affective side of communication goes sour, cognitive interaction tends to stop. Seaver's substantial chapter could as easily have been included above in Part 1. His essential point is that mime affords a kind of scaffolding for meaning distinct from all the others. It's a serious theoretical point, but most language teachers, I think, are still apt to see pantomime as belonging in the fun and games category, so I have put Seaver's chapter here in Part 6. Actually, acting of all kinds is probably closer to recreation than to any traditional idea of a language curriculum. So perhaps other parts of this book rightfully belong here with Seaver's chapter. Wherever it might appear, it is an important article (with a substantial list of scholarly references), and it fills a big gap in much current thinking about language and language teaching. If nothing more, surely Seaver will help us appreciate what Asher, Rassias, and others have been telling us all along: language acquisition always involves active comprehension, teaching is acting, and acting can be a lot of fun.

INTRODUCTION

In most communicative exchanges the impact of nonverbal modalities exceeds that of verbal channels.[1]

Communication is accomplished to a large degree through the paralinguistic features subsumed under the rubrics of proxemics and kinesics. "Proxemics" refers to the proximate distance between speakers. In cross-cultural situations miscommunication frequently results from a lack of understanding of the social implications of closeness to or relative distance from the interlocutor. Hammerly (1982) relates having seen numerous conversations between Latin Americans and North Americans in which the participants began speaking at one end of the room and gradually moved to the opposite end as "the North

American retreated to protect his 'bubble' of intimate space" (p. 521). In his seminal study of body motion and communication Birdwhistell (1970: 41) includes gesturing, touching, posture, eye, head and body movement, facial expression, and gait as belonging to the realm of kinesics. Other types of non-verbal communication involve whistling, laughing, pitch, intonation and timbre, mode of dress, and even the fragrances we wear. While most kinesic patterns are culturally learned and defined, individuals also have their own personal gestural systems.

In interpersonal communication the nonverbal domain is a powerful source of information that is often crucial to the proper understanding of the linguistic message. As Von Raffler-Engel (1980) observes, "man communicates both verbally and non-verbally and . . . the total message lies in the combination of the two modalities" (p. 227). Birdwhistell (1970) asserts that "probably no more than 30–35% of the social meaning of a conversation or an interaction is carried by the words" (pp. 157–158).[2] Berkowitz (1982: 311) estimates that communication consists of 63% body language and gesture, 30% eye contact and expression, and only 7% speech. Kinesic behavior, then, may reinforce, clarify, or "enrich" the message, or it may encode the real message in subtle ways.

As foreign language teachers we often do not appreciate the role the kinesic domain can play as a source of teaching strategies. In our classes we tend to focus on the surface linguistic features, perhaps reflecting a belief that communication is single- rather than multi-channeled.[3] Von Raffler-Engel (1980) asserts that to reduce communication "to the sole channel of verbalization is not communicating in full" (p. 229). This article will describe an approach utilizing the kinesic domain developed for Spanish students that has proven to be quite successful in the author's classes: pantomime. While this article draws on examples in Spanish, the principles are presumed to be applicable to any language.

BACKGROUND ON PANTOMIME

Pantomime or mime (used here as equivalent terms), according to Lawson (1957), is "an exercise of the imagination." Further, it is "the act of telling a story, expressing a mood or an emotion or describing an action without resorting to words. Instead, the artist uses movements and gestures made with every part of his body" (p. vii).[4]

Modern classical mime dates from 19th century France and employs specific, stylized techniques.[5] Theatrical mimes usually dress in black and wear white gloves and white make-up to emphasize their expressions, though they need not do so. Teachers themselves will rarely, if ever, want to adhere to the classical elements of mime; rather, they should emphasize their meaning with clear, dramatic gestures. As we shall see, the use of a few simple props helps to create the desired illusion of reality.

Mime affords the teacher a "natural" strategy for instruction since students, especially children, frequently imitate others. As Aristotle (1952) observed in *On Poetics,* "Imitation is natural to man from childhood, one of his advantages over the lower animals being this, that he is the most imitative creature in the world . . . it is also natural for all to delight in works of imitation" (p. 682). With respect to man's instinctual use of mime, Walker (1969) observes that "mime . . . is more natural than one's own native language, indeed, a child mimes before he speaks" (p. 11). Children use mime in several ways. They use it in play activities such as "cops and robbers" or in swordplay. They also take great pleasure in imitating people from the popular media or people in their immediate environment that they either admire or resent. Adults resort to mime and gesture to convey meaning when words are inadequate or when their command of the L2 is insufficient for their communicative needs. Travelers will often resort to mime when they possess little or no knowledge of the language of the country in which they are traveling.

Though gestures are often culturally defined, a certain amount of universal meaning can be conveyed by gesture. To some extent, teachers of elementary language have used simple mime for a long time, albeit not as an organized, conscious teaching approach, to teach directly in the target language (TL). Thus, if a student does not understand the verb *tomar,* the teacher may lift his or her outstretched thumb and little finger in imitation of drinking from a cup. Likewise, if a student cannot grasp the meaning of a noun, verb, adjective, or adverb, teachers often clarify meaning with an appropriate gesture. In fact, mimetic gesture may be required to help achieve the "comprehensible input" for which proponents of the Natural Approach strive. It is the purpose of this article to show how we can go beyond these simple gestural features to a more sophisticated, systematic approach to the use of mime in language instruction.

RESEARCH ON KINESICS IN CLASSROOM INSTRUCTION

A review of the published literature on kinesic approaches to classroom instruction reveals relatively meager attention to mime as a teaching device. Mention of the technique's application to the classroom environment is sporadic and generally unsystematic. One important exception is Carels (1981), who describes methods of using pantomime to act out fables, to retell part of a story in a literature class, or to describe new vocabulary in context. Otherwise, mime *per se* is mentioned only occasionally in articles and methodology texts.[6]

The predominant focus in the literature is on the use of gestures, and the importance of teaching gestures, to achieve more fully authentic communication.[7] Several researchers (Green, 1971, Brault, 1963; Kirch, 1979; Von Raffler-Engel, 1980; Wylie, 1977, and Nuessel, 1985) advocate systematic instruction in target culture (TC) non-verbal kinesic behavior (gestures, body movement, paralanguage, and proxemics) as an accompaniment to presentation of verbal language. These linguists maintain that to ignore TC gestures is to ignore an essential source of communication as it obtains in the natural environment. To that end, Kirch (1975) argues that "not only does nonverbal communication share various characteristics with language, but the two are complementary constituents of the whole process of interaction" (p. 423). Following this line of reasoning, Green (1971: 67) recommends that teachers gloss dialogues with high-frequency gestures indicating emotions and proxemic features. Similarly, Nuessel (1985: 1019) advocates enhancing the linguistic meaning of literary passages with common gestures designed to illustrate with a mental image what is going on in the visual domain of the work.

Hence, if a scene involved madness, recalling information, signaling an object or another person, or indicating a state of inebriation, the teacher would make a culturally appropriate gesture (pp. 1016–1018).

Other scholars outline the incorporation of personal gestures into classroom management procedures. Barnett (1983) advocates using gestures as signals in directing class performance and in modeling verbal concepts to reduce unnecessary explanation. Schachter (1981) proposes a hand signal system designed to provide feedback for error correction when students commit oral grammatical errors.

As an instructional adjunct, mime has been mentioned with respect to three modern methods: the Audio-Lingual, Total Physical Response (TPR), and the Audio-Motor Unit. As for the first, practitioners of the Audio-Lingual Method used mime in dialogue practice. Rivers et al. (1988: 32-33) suggest a group approach in which one group mimes the dialogue while the other supplies the lines. Kalivoda et al. (Chapter 3, this volume) describe the use of kinesic behavior including pantomime as part of the Audio-Motor Unit. This activity, designed to teach language and cross-cultural features, is a supplementary ten-minute lesson in which students act out 10–20 commands on a central theme given either orally or on tape. Activities utilizing this approach can involve how to set the table in another country or the French way to eat a piece of fruit. Students first watch the teacher to correlate sound and meaning. In groups or individually the students then perform commands (given in scrambled order to ensure internalization of meaning). Lacking appropriate realia, the teacher and students will have to mime their actions. In a similar manner, students taught by the Total Physical Response Method may act out the commands given them by their teacher in pantomime. This method, developed by James Asher, purports to imitate first language acquisition on the assumption that children acquire their first language through commands given by their parents, such as "Come here," "Don't touch the stove," and "Give me the ball." In the classroom, students observe the teacher carrying out a command which he or she gives either orally or on tape, and they then perform the same action. Grammatical instruction is avoided. More commands are added, previous ones reiterated, and finally commands are given in random order to ensure comprehension. In some instances, TPR can be enhanced by mimetic gestures while in others only a simple kinesic response is required; e.g., "jump," "write your name on the board," "stand up," "sit down," "turn around," or "put the red circle on top of the blue circle." Hence, pantomime of situationally appropriate communicative gestures as an adjunct to TPR is a useful strategy. It has been shown here, then, that pantomime can be done without TPR and vice versa. As will be suggested below, however, mime can play a much greater role in TPR than has been previously acknowledged.

JUSTIFICATION FOR THE USE OF MIME AS A CLASSROOM STRATEGY

Before examining more closely mime's potential as a classroom device, it is advisable to consider reasons for its systematic inclusion in the language curriculum. Recent research in learning styles and cognitive and personality differences clearly indicates that students' learning preferences vary considerably. Ely (1988) has studied how students' personality characteristics influence their attitude toward various learning activities in the language classroom. His findings indicate that "certain situation-specific personality factors significantly influence attitudes toward what occurs in the second-language learning environment." He concludes that "teachers need to consider carefully the affective makeup of their classes in designing language-learning activities" (p. 30). In another article, Ely (1989) links teaching language-learning strategies with personality and cognitive styles as a way to help students cope with tolerance of ambiguity. Thus, he reasons that it is not enough to make students aware of a strategy and to provide them with opportunities for its implementation. Teachers also need to "become aware of (and take into account) underlying personality and other affective variables which might tend to inhibit or promote the acquisition of new ways of approaching language learning tasks." As a consequence, teachers will want to "provide activities which might be able to alter the classroom-specific characteristics we have discovered . . ." (p. 443). Ehrman and Oxford (1989: 1), using the Myers-

Briggs Type Indicator (MBTI), also relate personality and cognitive style to language learning preferences. Their research found that there are clear differences in level and choice of learning strategies, given differences in sex and occupation in adult language learners.

One important conclusion to be drawn from this body of research is that the wide variation of learning types mandates a variety of teaching and learning strategies. What appeals to one student may not appeal to another. Some students enjoy working alone on cognitively based activities. Others prefer group work, role playing, games, handouts, or visual aids. Still others will show a preference for the dynamics of kinesically oriented approaches. Teachers need to recognize, then, that they must provide a variety of learning modalities to accommodate varying learner styles and personalities.

Foreign language teachers today are more cognizant of the important role of the affective domain in second language acquisition. Krashen's Affective Filter Hypothesis, for example, has had a great impact on the language teaching profession. According to Krashen (1982), learners acquire languages best when large amounts of "comprehensible" input at $i + 1$—that is, input just a bit above their present level of ability—is available in an environment of low stress and anxiety. When anxiety is low, acquisition is fostered. Conversely, high anxiety leads to a high Affective Filter, or barrier, that impedes acquisition.

Another important area in which pantomime can be a useful strategy is in the amelioration of student anxiety. The role of anxiety as an inhibiting factor in foreign language learning has concerned many researchers in recent decades. Horwitz et al. (1986) have observed that "the problems of anxiety represent serious impediments to the development of second language fluency as well as to performance" (p. 127). McCrashey (Foss & Reitzel, 1988) describes communication anxiety as an "abnormally high and debilitating level of fear associated with real or anticipated communication with one or more persons" (p. 438). Horwitz et al. (1986) see foreign language anxiety, however, as "a distinct complex of self-perceptions, beliefs, feelings and behaviors . . . arising from the uniqueness of the language learning process" (p. 128). Due to the complexity of the communicative task in the L2, students, when asked to perform, are apt to feel a challenge to their self-concept, leading to "reticence, self-consciousness, fear, or even panic" (p. 128). Psychophysiological responses to foreign language anxiety may encompass tension, trembling, palpitations, perspiring, and sleep difficulties. Anxious foreign language learners may put off language study until the last possible minute, miss classes, sit in the back of the room, be inadequately prepared, hesitate to volunteer or speak out and to experience poor performance (see Horwitz et al., 1986).

Attempts to alleviate foreign language anxiety range from counseling and using psychological techniques to specific methodological approaches. Several contemporary language teaching methods, among them Suggestopedia, Community Language Learning, the Natural Approach, and Total Physical Response, attempt to lessen the impact of anxiety by making the learning environment less stressful.[8] Foss and Reitzel (1988) report on the use of a relational model of communication, based on motivation, knowledge, skills, outcomes, and context, to alleviate anxiety, and McCoy (1979) has applied the tenets of the behavior modification model as a way to lower levels of anxiety.

THE ROLE OF PANTOMIME IN THE CLASSROOM

No claim is being made here that pantomime will totally eliminate foreign language anxiety. Nevertheless, it has proven to be a valuable strategy in creating a less stressful learning context with ancillary benefits in the affective domain. When teachers mime, and especially when they assume another identity, it is as if they were another person. Momentarily, students relate to that new, nonthreatening person rather than to the teacher as authority figure. Since teaching is a form of performing, mime permits teachers to tap their imagination and to do things that they would not normally do.[9] If the teacher looks relaxed, the students are more likely to relax. Further, experience has shown that mimed characters tend to take on realistic dimensions. Students remember audacious characters throughout the course and

speak about them as if they were real people. Some students even mention them as a memorable feature of the course in end-of-the-semester course evaluations.

In the classroom mime helps to foster class cohesion since students work as a group to decipher linguistically the actions they observe. Carels (1981: 407) correctly notes that when working together to interpret gestures, students lose their sense of individuality, hence, there is a momentary loss of self-consciousness. Reticence diminishes when they are encouraged to speak at any time in the L2 whether or not they have correctly interpreted or "worked out" the sequence. Inhibitions are lowered even more when they are invited to participate in the miming activities. If a variety of answers is permitted, given different, yet reasonable interpretations or use of structure, students learn that language is flexible and that more than one answer may be correct. My experience with mime further shows that weak students participate as enthusiastically as their more able classmates. With lowered inhibitions, the class begins to resemble a group of children who all want to speak at once. Greater student involvement helps to reduce anxiety about speaking in front of one's peers, an increase in *esprit de corps* ensues, and students come together as a group while a positive student/teacher relationship is promoted. Obviously, these benefits ought to prove attractive to teachers who are frustrated when their best efforts fail to elicit widespread verbalization or participation. Working as a group also encourages cooperative learning among students. Students who are easily intimidated and anxious can be "brought into the fold" through working in small groups and dyads. Enthusiasm for language class increases, as does motivation.

Mime, like many classroom techniques, is a useful approach to supplement rather than supplant the teacher's basic pedagogical orientation. It can be successfully adapted to classes employing a Cognitive Four Skill approach, the Natural Approach, Total Physical Response, the Proficiency Approach, as well as many other methods. At first, the teacher may feel self-conscious or students may experience uncertainty about their tasks, but these problems disappear with practice. If utilized every few weeks, the activity becomes quite natural. Indeed, if teachers "let go" of their self-image, students relax and participate eagerly and enthusiastically.

In order for mime to reach its potential, the context needs to be made clear before beginning the activity. The teacher can do this by writing an organizing theme on the blackboard; for example, *cosas que una persona generalmente (no) hace en una fiesta* or *quehaceres domésticos que está haciendo la nueva criada.* Actions mimed need to be clear and unambiguous since students have only the visual modality on which to rely for conceptual meaning. Exaggeration may be required for the sake of clarity. The miming of verbs like *trabajar* or *hacer* can prove to be difficult for elementary students to interpret rapidly. Verbs with kinesic properties like *bailar, cantar,* or *fumar* are most readily understood. If students do not understand, the teacher should repeat the action with greater clarity or express it with other gestures. The action should be terminated if students continue to have trouble. Obviously, if new or unknown vocabulary is to be used, it is best to review or gloss it on the board first. There should be something accessible and challenging to virtually all students. It will help, also, if the teacher works out in advance the sequence of gestures to be mimed and practices it. Visualizing the actions can give the teacher a mental picture of how best to proceed and how students will perceive their actions.

During mime the teacher should strive for flexibility. If students produce a response other than the desired one, but one that makes sense, it should be accepted and rewarded. The teacher can signal with his or her arms that students should try the same item again, if necessary. In this way they will be relaxed about testing the limits of their L2 competence. As Carels (1981: 409) suggests, if students have comprehended the actions but have given a slightly wrong response in terms of structure or syntax, the teacher should not continue but should "freeze" in place until the right answer is worked out.

Students' interest in mime can be sustained longer when they are involved in the activity. Initially, the teacher will do all the gesturing. Then, as the class members become more cohesive and comfortable with one another, they can take part either as a group, in dyads or individually. Selected students can be asked to mime to their classmates in order to avoid producing anxiety in the very shy, self-conscious, or linguistically limited students. Alternatively, students can work in small-group situations where more students can participate and the fear of "being on stage" is reduced. The success of mime can be further ensured when the person doing the mime assumes the role of an imaginary character. Common L2 names, like Raulito or Lupe, can be used.

WARM-UP ACTIVITIES EMPLOYING MIME

Mime can be employed at practically every stage of language learning. As a warm-up activity on the elementary level, students can be called on to engage in a rapid response oral drill of thematically related lexical items. Thus, beginning students can rapidly review new vocabulary that the teacher mimes in quick succession. In this vein, concrete examples such as sports vocabulary, the names of professions, expressions relating to health, and easily identified transitive verbs should be used. Alternatively, the teacher can give the new words and the students mime an appropriate action. Equally effective is a game format in which students, working in pairs, mime a short series of vocabulary to their partner from a sheet prepared by the teacher. The student's partner then has to correctly identify the word or expression. The class members should then be asked to go on to the more advanced function of creating original sentences using the new words and expressions. Yet another approach is for the teacher to mime 5–10 simple actions (for example, using the progressive mood on a single topic) while students write down an appropriate response to a question written on the chalkboard. Later, they can exchange papers and compare with a master list, or the teacher can call on individual students to identify the actions they have written on their papers. Whenever possible, teachers should strive to elicit more than one-word responses. To encourage sentence-length utterances, teachers can give a hand signal or point to items on the board which solicit additional information with words or expressions like *¿a qué hora?, ¿con quién?, ¿por qué?* or the prepositions *a, de, con, para,* and the like. Stringing together several questions or phrases will result in a more complex answer.

CULTURE AND MIME

In the cultural realm mime can be especially useful, for as we have already seen, gestures often are culture-bound. Many culture-specific gestures can and should be incorporated into normal classroom situations. If a student responds with a correct answer, the teacher of a Spanish class can lift an arm, form a circle with the thumb and index finger, and raise the other three fingers while saying *correcto*. Likewise, the Spanish teacher can advise a student to think further (*piensa*) by placing the index finger of the right hand on the forehead just above the nose. "Be careful" (*ojo*) is indicated in Spanish by touching the cheek below the right eye with the right index finger. Other gestures can be taught when introducing new structures. For instance, *tengo hambre* can be accompanied by rubbing the stomach with either the right or left hand in a clockwise circular motion. This motion can be followed by the gesture for *quiero comer*. To accomplish this gesture, one holds one hand with palm up and all fingers and thumb together in imitation of putting food into the mouth. Thus, when gestures are taught in a communicative context, it is easy to demonstrate that communication is not only a linguistic event but also, in large measure, depends on gesture and body language.

Refrains or proverbs can be easily mimed, as well. Some examples follow:

- *Aunque la mona se vista de seda, mona se queda* (an imaginary monkey jumps around, then puts on clothes and jumps around again)
- *Cada quien tiene su manera de matar pulgas* (kill imaginary fleas with varying methods—between the fingers, with a mallet, with bug spray)
- *Más vale pájaro en mano que cien volando* (hold an imaginary bird in one hand and flail about, trying to catch others).

In a game format, points are awarded to the first side to accurately identify a proverb that has been mimed.

MIME AS A METHOD OF INTRODUCING NEW VOCABULARY

Mime is an effective way of presenting new vocabulary. By means of a mimed action attention focuses on the concepts, and students learn the linguistic feature through induction. Similarly, the teacher is able to eliminate both teacher talk and interference from the L1. Carels (1981: 410) recommends an approach in which the teacher reads a short text that contains new vocabulary. In his example of the circus knife thrower, the teacher verbally emphasizes the target vocabulary (e.g., knife, sharp, long, pointed) while acting it out. Alternatively, the teacher can mime actions without any verbalization. Students may have either model sentences or a short text containing new vocabulary on a hand-out or on the board. As the activity progresses, the teacher can stress the new vocabulary by pointing to the words written on the board. Thus the teacher introduces new lexical items through a kind of "kinesic comprehensible input."

GRAMMAR AND MIME

Even advanced structures can be effectively taught through mimetic procedures. Frequently, teachers encounter difficulties explaining the *se le* form for unplanned occurrences. This author's experience has demonstrated, however, that by using mime, comprehension of the new structure is quicker than through explanations either in L1 or L2. Before beginning the class the teacher writes the model sentences he or she will need on the board. Then he or she places some items in the room to be utilized as needed. A few simple props will help—an empty milk carton, a plastic cup, a watch, and some chalk. The teacher mimes each action successively to the theme *Hoy todo me fue mal* and then successively points to the model sentences presented on the board as each action is performed. The following are offered as models:

- *Se me perdió el reloj.* (teacher looks at wrist, appears panicky, looks all over room until he or she "finds" the watch)
- *Se me acabó la leche.* (teacher shakes an empty milk carton into the plastic glass)
- *Se me cayó y se me rompió la tiza.* (teacher clumsily begins to write something on the board, "accidentally" dropping the chalk).

In each case students can be asked to follow each item with an explanation of the action's occurrence. Once the basic concept has been understood, the explanation of the use of the indirect object, as well as how to respond to questions with *¿A quién?*, is a relatively simple task.

Many students are clever mimes and enjoy miming for their classmates. In a completely student-student sequence, students can be called to the front of the room and given slips of paper with written instructions in the L2. Actions should be given out of normal order. The students then mime appropriate gestures that their friends have to identify in short, complete sentences. For example, a useful theme to practice reflexive verbs is *Cosas que hago todos los días.*

Sample Sequence:
Me levanto a las siete.
Me lavo los dientes con X.
Me baño por quince minutos.
Me pongo los zapatos.
Me visto rápido.

After students have correctly identified the actions, the teacher can call for additional information with questions like *¿por qué?* or with prepositions. Then the teacher can amplify further by personalizing with questions using the same verbs. This activity can also be accomplished in dyads or small groups, in which one student receives a list of actions to mime to his or her partner.

Commands given by the students to the teacher open up endless possibilities for using mime. One of my favorite sequences involves a naughty little boy named Raulito. A few props will add to the fun—a child's cap, an appropriate T-shirt, and a sucker. The teacher puts on the costume and plays the role of Raulito (or that of Lupita) and then mimes a series of actions in which the child misbehaves. Students imagine themselves as the teacher and give appropriate affirmative and negative informal commands. The activity begins with an introduction by the child: *Me llamo Raulito (Lupita) y tengo cinco años. No me gusta ir a la escuela. Prefiero jugar. Mi maestro dice que nunca me porto bien pero mi mamá dice que soy un angelito. ¿Qué creen Uds.?*

Sample Sequence
- *escribir en la pared* (act as if writing all over the walls)
- *dormir en el suelo* (curl up on the floor)

- *jugar en la basura* (appear to play with things in the wastebasket)
- *pegar a los compañeros* (lightly "hit" students)

The subjunctive can be practiced with mime in an activity in which the teacher plays the role of a maid. A bandana, an apron, and kitchen utensils are useful to create the appropriate setting. The teacher then asks mimetically if the students want her to do certain domestic chores. The students' task is to respond verbally to the inquiry using the verb *querer.* Thus, to the mimed question *¿Quiere Ud. que yo pase la aspiradora?*, the students would reply *Si/No quiero que Ud. pase la aspiradora.* Other possible exchanges can be based on the following questions:

> *¿quiere Ud. que yo planche la ropa?*
> *¿quiere Ud. que yo barre el suelo?*
> *¿quiere Ud. que yo vacie el cubo de basura?*
> *¿quiere Ud. que yo haga las camas?*
> *¿quiere Ud. que yo friegue los platos?*

TPR AND MIME

Since a large part of the effectiveness of Total Physical Response depends on kinesic activity, mime would seem to serve as a natural adjunct to TPR, although it is only mentioned occasionally and in passing in the literature on TPR (e.g., Glisan, Chapter 4, this volume). This is an optimal place, however, to incorporate mime. In the following interactive TPR sequence (presented in abbreviated form), students can either react with silent, dramatic actions or combine mimetic gestures with verbalization.

Sample Sequence
Context: Students reenact a scene in a doctor's office. Half the students play the doctor's role, the other half the patient's.
A los pacientes: entren en la sala de espera del médico
quítense el suéter/el sombrero
saluden a Carmen, la recepcionista
siéntense y lean una revista
ahora les toca/pasen al consultorio del médico/saluden al médico
A los médicos: saluden al paciente

preguntenle qué es lo que tiene (mime quizzi-
cal gesture)
*A los pacientes: señálenle (díganle) que están
congesionados*
señálenle (díganle) que les duele la cabeza
señálenle (díganle) que se sienten mareados
A los médicos:
*señálenle (díganle) al paciente que se
levante/señálenle (díganle) que respire profun-
damente*
señálenle (díganle) que tose

TESTING WITH MIME

Mime can also be used as a testing vehicle. In one
approach the teacher mimes a sequence of actions
relating to the question *¿qué estoy haciendo?*, to
which students write an appropriate response. An
alternative might consist of multiple choice
answers. The teacher can, as well, create a short
dialogue or narration with blanks left for the
actions he or she will mime. In this manner students have to invoke global knowledge of the text
to properly complete the missing items. Moreover,
they are required to use conjugated verb forms in a
contextual framework. Indeed, mime can be used
successfully as a testing format with several of the
activities previously described.

CAVEATS ON THE USE OF MIME IN THE CLASSROOM

The virtues of mime as a classroom technique
notwithstanding, it has, like any other pedagogical
approach, its weaknesses, which principally fall
into two areas. The first involves linguistic limitations. Carels (1981: 409) correctly observes that
mime best expresses feelings, emotions, and reactions to physical stimuli and actions. Abstractions,
complex concepts, thoughts and beliefs, communicative exchanges, verbs of being, human relationships, and words that are hard to convey with
one clear, unambiguous gesture are difficult to
mime. Student knowledge of lexical and structural
elements will also limit mime's potential. On the
affective side, as has been indicated earlier, some
students' learning preferences will not favor the
use of kinesic principles. At first some students

will think themselves too sophisticated or will be
too shy and insecure with their language skills to
participate. Others will be limited by their imagination and will initially only be able to carry out
basic gestures. Still others will feel constrained by
fear of peer judgment. However, with a little practice these inhibiting factors can be overcome.

CONCLUSION

A significant amount of interpersonal communication is almost always accompanied by nonverbal
forms. Nonetheless, in their classrooms, language
teachers frequently overlook the important role of
non-verbal communication, focusing almost exclusively on a verbal frame of reference. At the same
time, current research on learner cognitive styles
and learning preferences demonstrates the necessity for diversity of teaching strategies to accommodate different learning styles. Further, foreign
language anxiety is a well-documented phenomenon that language teachers are called on to com-
bat. The silent, dramatic, and mimetic elements of
pantomime, a universal human communicative
modality, have largely been overlooked as a teaching technique that has the potential to successfully
overcome these problems. Mime provides an alternative for multi-channel sensory input for language acquisition, reduces teacher talk, promotes
learning through induction and motor activity,
and provides a common conceptual frame of reference for the teacher and students. As an aid in the
amelioration of learner anxiety, it helps to lower
the student's affective filter. An effective pedagogical tool, mime can be used for a wide variety of
instructional purposes, as exemplified in the samples included in this essay. Teachers are invited to
incorporate their own mimetic routines into their
classes. All that is required is a little imagination.

NOTES

1 This article is a revised and expanded version of
an article published in the *PNCFL Newsletter* (XIII: 2,
1989) and is based on preliminary work presented at the
1987 Conference of the Hawaii Association of
Language Teachers and the 1988 Pacific Northwest
Council on Foreign Languages Conference.

2 Birdwhistell (1970: 85) refers to nonverbal methods of communication as a redundant feature of communication.

3 Brown (1980: 199) points out that verbal language uses only one of the five sensory modalities, that of hearing, which leaves three others basic to our communicative repertoire—the visual, olfactory and kinesic.

4 Readers interested in a concise review of the technique and history of mime should consult Lawson (1957).

5 With respect to the origin of the terms, the tragic players in Roman drama were referred to as pantomimi and buffoons as mimi (Walker, 1969: 48).

6 Rivers et al. (1988), for instance, describe the use of mime in games and other class activities.

7 Cultural gestures have received scant attention from textbook writers. Two do, however, present short inventories of gestures: *Modern Spanish* (Modern Language Association of America, 1960: 345–347) and *Communicating in Spanish, Level I* (Enrique E. Lamadrid, William E. Bull, and Laurel A. Briscoe, 1974), which presents 12 typical Spanish gestures interspersed throughout the text. Readers desiring longer gestural inventories in French and Spanish should consult Kany (1960), Green (1968), Brault (1963), and Wylie (1977).

8 For more information on these and other anxiety reducing methods, readers may consult Stevick (1980), Blair (1982), and Oller and Richard-Amato (1983).

9 Suggestopedia attempts to achieve a reduction in levels of anxiety in similar ways by assigning students a new persona. For more information on Suggestopedia, consult Stevick, 1980.

DISCUSSION QUESTIONS

1. As a research project, examine videos of authentic communication based in different languages and cultures. Which gestures and other kinesic elements appear to be universal, and which ones are distinctive or unique to a particular culture? Or observe a person who is thoroughly bilingual, speaking in similar contexts in both of his or her languages. Note the distinctive gestures, facial expressions, and the like that are used when the person changes languages. (A particularly dramatic case, typically, is a hearing child of deaf parents—a person who is fully bilingual in a spoken language such as English and a signed system such as ASL. Whereas in English the kinesic elements are essentially everything but speech, in ASL almost exactly the reverse is true. Speech, and gestures with the mouth, become part of the paralinguistic overlay in ASL.)

2. What kinds of personal risks does the teacher take in miming, or acting in general? What inhibitors prevent letting loose in this manner? What trust factors must be taken for granted if a normally dignified person is to allow herself or himself to step out of that guise and into another persona?

3. Suppose the teacher does "let go" of his or her own "self-image." What if the teacher wholeheartedly assumes distinct roles and personae, as Seaver recommends? What effect can this be expected to have on student inhibitions and their participation? What effect do such antics have on you, and why?

4. Discuss some of the ways that Seaver illustrates the incorporation of episodic organization into his classroom procedures.

CHAPTER 33

Once Upon a Time

John Morgan and Mario Rinvolucri

EDITOR'S INTRODUCTION

*T*he material in this chapter is from a book by Morgan and Rinvolucri (1983), titled Once Upon a Time: Using Stories in the Language Classroom. *Had their book appeared a year earlier, an excerpt from it might well have been featured in the previous edition of* Methods That Work. *Though their book itself is less than one hundred pages long, it contains a great deal more information than could possibly be included in this brief excerpt. Morgan and Rinvolucri offer a* vade mecum *of ideas about how to tell stories and in doing so how to enhance language acquisition. Perhaps the most important element of telling stories, the one that distinguishes it from other communicative acts, is the personal interaction between the storyteller and the person(s) to whom the story is told. But this interaction depends on the story's being understood. The story itself is distinguished by the fact that it has a plot, a certain meaningful connectedness and motivation. It develops over time somewhat in the manner of ordinary experience, though if the plot is fictional or fantastic, the story may be more or less constrained than actual experience. For instance, actual experience is apt to have many more characters than could ever be included in any consumable fiction, and a fantasy by definition always involves elements that do not and, in many cases, could not exist in the material world. The* sine qua non *of stories of all types, however, is some sort of episodic organization that is comprehensible, and good storytelling means finding a delicate balance between surprise value and coherence. It means involving the consumers of the story in such a way that they begin to consider alternative outcomes and to puzzle out what will happen. To some degree they live through the events of the story. To the extent that the storytelling succeeds, both the teller and the listener(s) are involved to such a degree that the experience of the character(s) in the story becomes their own. As a result, whatever language of the story is understood will also tend to be internalized along the way.*

TO THE TEACHER

Among both practicing language teachers and applied linguists there is an increasing awareness that successful second language learning is far more a matter of unconscious acquisition than of conscious systematic study. Stephen Krashen (1981) goes so far as to say that "the acquisition-rich environment is for everyone" (p. 38) and that

major function of the second language classroom is to provide "intake" for acquisition (pp. 46–50).

It is our view that the "intake" required to facilitate language acquisition will be very different from the materials currently provided in the classroom as part of systematic structural or notional courses. If unconscious processes are to be enlisted, then the whole person will need to be engaged.

"I Can't Tell Stories"

You could be right, but if so you're in a small minority. In our experience very few teachers of English can *read aloud* adequately, but almost all have a hidden talent as storytellers.

Listening Comprehension

The quality of listening that takes place when you tell your class a story (provided you tell rather than read aloud) is radically different from that during conventional listening comprehension from tape. The latter is always third-person listening, a kind of eavesdropping that is strangely uncompelling. To be told a story by a live storyteller, on the contrary, involves one in "I-thou" listening, where the listeners can directly influence the telling. Even if you are a non-native teacher of English (or whatever language), the communicative gain will outweigh the "un-Englishness" (or non-nativeness in whatever language) you may hear in your telling.

Following up a Story

"Comprehension questions" and paraphrase exercises are standard classroom follow-ups to listening work: after a story they at best dilute, at worst destroy, its effect on the listener. Alternatives are to allow the student to decide for himself or herself which questions (if any) he or she wants answered, and to hear the answers from a classmate. Role assignment can be used to explore feelings toward characters in a story. Drawing illustrations can enable students to put the story in a different form. All the exercises, at any rate, should encourage the recycling of the new language forms introduced through the story.

Retelling

Being required to retell a story to someone who has just heard it is a pleasure few of us would willingly repeat, yet this is often what teachers ask of their students. A better approach is to have students tell a familiar story to someone who hasn't heard it, or to have them tell something similar from their own experience.

Stories and Grammar

Many traditional stories abound in powerful repeated phrases. (E.g., "Who's been sleeping in my bed?") For elementary and intermediate students, such stories (suitably chosen) can be used as an almost subliminal grammar input.

From Listening to Oral Production

Teachers, of course, can collaborate with students in the production of the students' own stories (e.g., see Walker et al., Chapter 17; Damico & Damico, Chapter 29; and Wessels, Chapter 36). To include the entire class in the production, a Greek chorus technique can be used. The teacher can model vocabulary from within a group. Stories can be taped, illustrated, or dramatized for use in a language laboratory.

Oral Production

There are stories hidden inside everyone. Elementary students will bring them out in dramatic, excited half-sentences; advanced speakers will reach out for ever more vivid or exact expression. For all, adequate communication is an attainable miracle, if the teacher is prepared to allow it. Stories can be created and recalled from the experience of the students themselves by delving into either a real or an imagined past.

Picture Stories

We are all familiar with the "picture story" as a device for provoking narrative work. Unfortunately, anyone with normal eyesight produces much the same story, which robs the telling of any point. Symbolic pictures can be used to elicit a wide range of different stories. Once they have created their own story, students are keen to tell them and to find out what others have made of the doodlestrip:

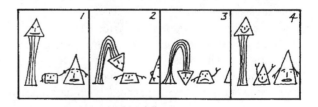

Story Pool

In our book, at the end, we give twenty story outlines like the ones included in this chapter. We have tried to make them as varied as possible, but recognize that we cannot span the range of tastes of all teachers, so we encourage them to add their own stories to the pool.

FAIRY STORIES

For very young learners and with adults, we recommend a variety of fairy stories. They are probably not a good bet in most classes of adolescents, where we suggest you concentrate on symbolic, literary, and problem stories. (For an example of this last type, see below.) There are, however, great advantages to working on fairy stories with older people. They are often familiar in outline (though seldom in detail) in the students' mother tongue; the language is simple, yet the meanings are evocative and many-layered; and the stories bring back, often in a flood of excitement, memories of one's own childhood and that of one's children.

TELLING, NOT READING

One can readily imagine the wide range of factors that might go into producing differences between telling and reading: the mood of the teller when he or she first encountered the story; his or her mood while telling; the background experiences that lead, for example, to one teller imagining a forest where another sees a desert; the number and seating of the audience; the teller's relationship to the audience; and so on and so on. And these differences are in turn reflected in the language: sometimes fluent, sometimes hesitant and uncertain, broken by irregular pauses, but always definitely spoken language, the language of personal communication that is so often absent from the foreign language classroom.

In some ways telling is easier than reading aloud: the reader may be forced to interpret speech patterns and rhythms very different from his or her own; he or she is forced to become aware of things normally taken for granted, such as breathing; and these technical problems may become a barrier between the reader and the author just as the book he or she is holding may become a physical barrier between the reader and his or her audience. In telling, on the other hand, one can shape the story to one's own needs, and while this may require the development of certain, perhaps buried, skills, the advantages are very great. In the first place, one can address one's audience directly: one can make eye contact or not as one chooses, use gesture and mime freely, expand or modify the form of one's telling as the occasion demands, and in general establish and maintain a community of attention between teller and listener.

Again, from the learner's point of view, it is of immense benefit to witness the process of framing ideas in the target language without, as in conversation, constantly having to engage in that process oneself: forcing students always to hear polished speech (or, words, the bland monotony of specially constructed oral texts) does them a great disservice.

Since first starting to work with stories, we have come to realize something of the extent to which narrative underlies our conversational encounters with others, and of the deep need that people have to tell and exchange stories. We have also learned something about the ways in which storytelling can take place in the foreign language classroom.

FINDING AND CHOOSING STORIES

Stories are everywhere: they include traditional fairy stories, folk tale collections, newspaper reports, literary short stories, films and plays, personal anecdotes, rumors, stories from our own childhood and from the childhood of our students, friends, and colleagues, and our own imagination. We have learned stories from our children and their friends, and from professional storytellers like Propp (1968) and Rodari (1973).

In selecting stories for the classroom, we have been guided by two main criteria: Is this a story that we would enjoy telling, and is this a story our students might find entertaining or thought provoking? We have seldom been influenced by purely linguistic considerations in our choice (though this sometimes plays a part), and we have never excluded a story because it originated in a language other than English.

MAKING SKELETONS

We found early on that a brief written outline (a skeleton) provided the best way for us to store material for storytelling. The skeleton should give, in minimal form, a plot outline, background information where necessary (e.g., cultural context if the plot is heavily dependent on this), and a certain amount of character detail. There is no need to produce a continuous text—indeed, this could be an obstacle to improvisation—or to observe the conventions of punctuation and "complete" sentences. The aim should be to record all those elements that are essential to the story, but only these.

The examples that follow are given in the form of skeletons. These are presented exactly as we would use them ourselves, and we have not attempted to present a "standardized" form. We think they will be at least adequate as they stand, and we are sure that teachers who wish to work from their own material, and thus produce their own story skeletons, will develop their own style and technique. It must be emphasized that the skeleton merely provides the bare frame of the story for the teller to work from, and must not be referred to *during* a telling.

A SKELETON

Here is an example of the kind of story skeletons that we use and recommend to teachers.

The River

Summer
They reached the river, had been at war three
  years
Lull in fighting
Three of them went bathing—three shots
HQ put river out of bounds

He crept through wood to river bank
Propped rifle against tree, undressed, swam
Water cool and clean
Caught branch in midstream
Saw head in water. Ours? Theirs?
Head went to other bank

He swam back to rifle, got there first
Aimed at other climbing out of water
Could not squeeze trigger
Let rifle fall
Saw birds rise as shot rang out
His face hit the ground

(after Antonis Samarakis, *Zitite Elpis*)

PREPARING TO TELL

In preparing to tell a story, we have worked directly from skeletons like the example just given. This has the effect both of distancing the teller from the rhythms and forms of the source (whether oral or written) and of focusing on what is essential to memorize—the plot and development. Except where formulaic expressions are essential to the story (e.g., in fairy stories such repetitions as "What big _____ you have, Grandmother"), we have consciously avoided all memorization or recording of *forms of words,* concentrating on plot line and pace, and on "getting the feel" of the story. A dress rehearsal, for example, in front of the mirror may at times be helpful, but it can easily lead to loss of involvement and, thus, in the classroom, failure to communicate; one rehearsal technique which gets around this is to replay the story in one's head while mumbling the rhythms of the story (but not the actual words of the telling) aloud. We have also found that a brief period of total relaxation before telling is of immense help.

OTHER EXAMPLES

Here is a skeleton of a story from a fairy tale genre (derived from "Kacuy" as it appeared in *South American Fairy Tales,* edited by John Meehan).

Kacuy

She lived with brother in cottage in forest
Did cooking, cleaning; he hunted
She was unhappy; cottage too small, isolated
One day he brought home animal:
She said: "Cook it yourself." He said nothing.

He knew she loved honey
Next day came home, told her about huge
    bees' nest up tree
Asked her to help him get honey—she refused
"If I go alone I'll spill the honey"
She agreed to help

He took hood and machete, they set off
Finally came to tall tree in clearing
She climbed ahead of him, wearing hood
Near top he whispered "Sh, stop or the bees'll
    hear"
He went down tree, lopped off branches above
    head
Left clearing, thought: "Now she will see she
    needs me"

Cold, night falling, she was terrified, wind
    rising
Began to grope her way down tree
Her foot slipped into space
Took off hood, looked down: no branches
Her arm itched, looked down: feathers
Felt back of head: something growing
Her feet on branch: claws
Gust of wind knocked her off tree
She was flying; called out brother's name,
    heard "Kacuy, Kacuy"
Ever since Kacuy bird has been searching for-
    est for brother

Here is another fairy tale, "The Billy Goats Gruff," with a repetitive theme related to birth order. We recommend an exercise of the birth-order type as found in Moskowitz (1978). After telling the story, ask which of the students are an *only* child, a first-born child, a last-born, or a middle child. Students can then be split up into birth-order groups and compare experiences about what it's like to be a first-born, last-born, etc.

The Billy Goats Gruff

Three goats in mountain valley
Bridge over river—under bridge troll—ate
    people
Goats wanted to eat grass other side—greener
    and sweeter

One day smallest goat onto bridge, trip-trap,
    trip-trap

Troll's ugly head appeared
"Who's that trip-trapping over my
    bridge?"
"Only me, the littlest Billy Goat Gruff."
"Then I'm going to eat you up"
"No, don't eat me, eat my brother—he's
    bigger and fatter than me"
"Mmmmmm, OK, off you go"
Littlest goat crossed bridge, began to eat
    grass

Next day middle-sized goat trip-trapped onto
    bridge
(same sequence as above, substituting "mid-
    dle-sized")
Biggest goat—long beard, sharp horns
TRAP TRAP TRAP onto bridge
"Who's that trap-trapping over my bridge?"
"It's me, the biggest Billy Goat Gruff"
"Then I'm going to eat you up"
"Oh no you're not"
Big goat lowered horns—ran at troll—tossed
    him into river

Since then bridge safe to cross

Finally, here is an example of the problem type.

The Two Doors

The king never condemned criminals to
    death—this is what he did:
The criminal was led into an arena with 2
    doors
Behind one a ravenous tiger
Behind the other a beautiful girl
The man did not know which door was
    which
Had to choose—be eaten or marry the girl
This was fair—man's fate in his own hands

King had daughter
She fell in love with poor soldier
King furious—young man arrested
In arena he looked up at king and daughter
Princess knew which door was which
What signal did she give her lover?

In our book, many other examples are given together with recommendations for exercises to follow.

STYLES OF STORYTELLING

There are many ways of telling a story. One can unroll one's mat under the nearest tree and call together a crowd; one can buttonhole a stranger in a railway carriage or bar; one can murmur in the ear of a sleepy child. These and many other traditional modes of telling can have their counterparts in the foreign language classroom. Standing, or sitting on a raised chair in front of rows of students, you can capture something of the one-person theater show, and aim to fire emotions or entertain by pure acting skill. In total contrast to this, sitting with the students, in a tight circle, can conjure up memories of childhood storytelling. By seeking and exchanging eye contact, one can draw the students into the story and give a sense of participation in the process of telling; withholding eye contact, on the other hand, can be used to increase the mood of fantasy and to encourage introspection. Body posture, voice level, and variation in the external environment (furniture, lighting, color) can also be made to heighten certain effects. Particular stories and groups of listeners will call for different styles of telling, and the teller should be aware of the range of possibility open to him or her. A certain amount of deliberate experimentation is very helpful to anyone trying to develop his or her own styles: see what happens, for example, if stories are told from behind the listeners, or with the whole group lying down.

DISCUSSION QUESTIONS

1. How does a good storyteller scaffold the meaning of the language used in telling a story?

2. The idea of there being a "troll" (a fantastic creature from Scandinavian mythology) under a bridge may be easier to get across to a child than, say, the idea of the sister in the "Kacuy" story turning into a bird. In general, fantasies of all sorts are more difficult to convey without words than are plausible fictions. Why is this so, and what implications does this have for the kinds of stories that ought to be used in the early stages of language acquisition?

CHAPTER 34

Cooperative Learning in a Humanistic English Class

Kanchana Prapphal

EDITOR'S INTRODUCTION

Spencer Kagan's ideas concerning cooperative learning are applied here with adult dentistry students in an English class at Chulalongkorn University Language Institute in Bangkok. Activities included a number of group projects which involved learners in selecting from and negotiating tasks, adapting materials in English, and participating in various songs, games, and other activities. Readers will note that this chapter has much in common with previous entries by Walker et al., Chapter 17, Assinder, Chapter 24, and Christensen, Chapter 26. It is included here in Part 6, however, because of its emphasis on games, songs, and activities in general that aim to make language acquisition more enjoyable.

This essay presents cooperative learning as an effective way to involve EFL students in using English and to make learning more enjoyable. This approach helps build rapport and, in the words of Moskowitz (1968), fosters a climate of "caring and sharing" in the classroom.

A study conducted in an English class at the Chulalongkorn University Language Institute illustrates how cooperative learning fosters commitment to tasks, encourages students to work cooperatively, to learn to be problem solvers, to become knowers rather than merely assimilators, and to act as evaluators and assessors. An informal evaluation of the study indicates that cooperative learning is a promising humanistic approach which increases student participation in EFL classes in the Thai context. It appears to facilitate the learning process both cognitively and affectively.

COOPERATIVE LEARNING

Kagan (1985) describes the cooperative learning system as consisting of team building, manage-

ment techniques, and rewards based on a complex system of points. He presents these five basic types of cooperative learning: 1) *peer tutoring,* where teammates teach each other to carry out given tasks; 2) *jigsaws,* in which each member of a group is given a piece of information and must share that information with the others in the group to complete a task; 3) *cooperative projects,* where the members of a group work together to complete a group project; 4) *cooperative, individualized projects,* where students work alone on a particular assignment or project, but evaluations of their individual progress contribute to a group grade; and 5) *cooperative interaction,* where each student is graded individually although completion of the task requires a cooperative effort. Richard-Amato (1988) views cooperative learning as a management technique. She suggests that "in cooperative learning, students help other students within groups of four to five persons in an effort to reach goals. Adaptations of cooperative learning can be effective at many age levels from the late elementary grades up through adult levels. It can be used in both second and foreign language teaching situations" (p. 193).

TEACHING MATERIALS

Cooperative learning utilizes materials which Rodgers (1988) categorizes as manufactured, modeled, modified, and mined. *Manufactured materials* are commercial texts. *Modeled materials* are those prepared by teachers based on, or supplementing, commercial materials. *Modified materials* are those taken from non-language learning sources and modified for language learning purposes, such as jigsaw materials—stories cut up into sections which are distributed among individual group members who then must share their information with the rest of the group in order to accomplish a specific task. Finally, *mined materials* are those that come from authentic sources.

Prabhu (1988) makes a distinction between course materials and source materials. The former refers to "the inputs to be presented to learners, in the order in which they are to be presented. They constitute both the teaching content and the teaching agenda, in the sense that their units are easily usable (and meant to be used) as lesson plans." However, source materials are "those which provide a range of possible inputs, without envisaging that all of them will be used in any classroom or that all classrooms will use the same inputs" (Prabhu, 1988: 11). The use of source materials requires the teacher to share classroom decisions with learners, an aspect of what Allwright (1981) calls learner training.

Clarke (1989) advocates learner involvement in determining what happens in the classroom. He proposes five principles underlying learner contribution in an external syllabus: 1) learner commitment; 2) learners as materials writers and collaborators; 3) learners as problem solvers; 4) learners as knowers; and 5) learners as evaluators and assessors.

Based on the belief that learners are active participants in the learning process, not passive recipients, and that teachers are facilitators, not drill leaders or mere presenters of materials, cooperative learning was tested in a Foundation English class at the Chulalongkorn University Language Institute.

THE STUDY

Subjects

Twenty-seven dentistry students who took the Foundation English Course in 1989 participated in this study. There were thirteen male students and fourteen female. In response to a questionnaire, eighteen students indicated positive attitudes towards learning English while nine students expressed a lack of interest.

Procedures

Since the Foundation English Course, which aims at providing communicative skills, is required for all first-year students, the same course materials are used by all teachers. However, since learners differ in abilities, attitudes, needs, learning styles, and strategies, source materials were introduced to encourage learner contributions to the course. Clarke's five principles were implemented as follows:

1. Learner Commitment

During the first hour the students were asked to indicate their preferences for cooperative projects by choosing from a list of possible projects given in a questionnaire prepared by the instructor. They were free to arrange their own groups or to let the teacher arrange the groups. Each group negotiated with the teacher concerning the nature of the tasks to be completed and the date of presentation. An informal contract was drawn up to encourage the learners to take responsibility.

2. Learners as Materials Writers and Collaborators

Once the project was approved, each group selected, adapted, or wrote the materials themselves outside of class. The materials had to correspond to the specified tasks. At this stage, the teacher acted as a consultant and facilitator. The learners could modify their projects, but they had to inform the teacher. Although Thai was allowed in the preparation stage, students were encouraged to use English as much as possible.

3. Learners as Problem Solvers

Each group was assigned the task of designing an activity in which their classmates could participate. This was very fruitful because each group was trained to present meaningful problems for their classmates to solve. They also learned how to work together and to share ideas. In addition, the task of designing the activities was in itself meaningful, creating situations which required the use of real and authentic language. During the presentations, the students of each team were responsible for classroom management. They divided their classmates into teams, and one member of the team read the directions while the others helped record scores and acted as facilitators. What follows are the activities they contributed.

Proverbs

(four group members)
1. Divide students into four teams.
2. Give a list of 10 Thai proverbs in English to each student.
3. Tell the stories which correspond to the proverbs, one at a time.
4. Ask teams to guess the right proverb in English and translate it into Thai.
5. The first team which answers correctly gets one point.
6. The team that gets the most points wins.

Directions

(three group members)
1. Divide students into five teams.
2. Ask students to listen to directions and find the right places on a map.
3. Read the directions twice.
4. The first team which answers correctly gets one point, and the team that gets the most points is the winner.

Songs 1

(three group members)
"Eternal Flame" and " Greatest Love of All"
1. Listen to the songs and fill in the missing words.
2. Answer questions about the songs. (Extra credit is given for difficult questions.)
3. The team which receives the most points is the winner.

Songs 2

(three group members)
"Wonderful Life" and "Different Seasons"
1. Divide students into five teams.
2. Listen to each song twice.
3. Fill in the blanks. Three points are given for the correct answer for the first listening, and two points are given for the correct answer for the second listening.
4. The team which receives the most points is the winner.

Comparisons

(three group members)
1. Write 15 names of rare animals on the board.
2. Read some information about the animals and let the other students guess the name of each animal. The student who guesses correctly gets one piece of candy.
3. Cite some special features (focusing on comparisons) and have the other students match the names of animals with the features described. Here the student who gets the correct answer gets two pieces of candy.
4. The winner is the one who has the most candy.

Descriptions

3 Mini-activities (three group members)
Mini-activity 1: Describe five students in the class and ask each team to match the names with the pictures.
Mini-Task 2: Give pictures of seven people to each student. Read the description of the thief twice and ask each team to find the thief.
Mini-Task 3: Guess the nickname of a student's boyfriend or girlfriend. Give clues by showing pictures. The first letter of the item in the picture is one of the letters in the student's name (e.g., a jar of coffee = the letter c). By recombining the letters, groups can guess the nickname of the student's boyfriend or girlfriend. The team which receives the most points is the winner.

Quizzes

(four group members)
1. Divide the students into four groups.
2. Ask general trivia questions. If a team member knows the answer, he or she writes the answer on a piece of paper. A correct answer to easy questions is worth one point. If the question is difficult, it is worth two points.
3. Let the two teams with the most points compete in the final round. Here, the questions will be more difficult than in the first round.

Vocabulary Revision

(four group members)
1. Select vocabulary from the previous lessons.
2. Play "anagrams" and ask the other students to write the correct words.
3. If nobody gets the correct answer, give the first letter. If nobody can get the right answer, give the meaning of that word.

4. Learners as Knowers

By designing these classroom activities, learners acted as knowers. They were not "assimilators" or "spoon feeders," using Allwright's terms. The tasks reinforced what the students had learned in their previous lessons as well as encouraged positive attitudes towards language learning.

5. Learners as Evaluators and Assessors

At the end of each group project, the students were asked to evaluate the performance of their peers on a 7-point Likert scale, ranging from 1 (disliked very much) to 7 (liked very much). The means of all the projects are as follows: Proverbs ($\overline{X}$ = 4.68); Directions ($\overline{X}$ = 4.79); Songs 1 ($\overline{X}$ = 4.91); Songs 2 ($\overline{X}$ = 4.85); Comparisons ($\overline{X}$ = 4.87); Descriptions ($\overline{X}$ = 4.94); Quizzes ($\overline{X}$ = 4.87); and Vocabulary Revision ($\overline{X}$ = 4.80). The results show that most students were satisfied with the performances of their peers. The group mean was the score the members of each group received and was counted as one part of their grade.

EVALUATION

In addition to the quantitative data, the students were asked to comment on the group projects.

Following are some of their opinions translated into English.

"I like group projects because they provide knowledge and a relaxing atmosphere. They also promote cooperation."

"I like group projects very much. I used to think that English was difficult, but now I think I can cope with it."

"Group projects make learning English more entertaining. Group projects should be continued."

"I like group projects very much. They make me feel relaxed. I think group projects don't have to strictly follow the lessons. They should focus on listening and games. Very good and very entertaining."

"I like group projects a lot because I was relaxed. They make us practice language skills such as listening. They provide world knowledge, new vocabulary and make the class enjoyable."

The only negative comment was that in designing the tasks some groups should have paid more attention to content. That is to say the tasks should not be too trivial.

CONCLUSION

Cooperative learning seems to be a promising humanistic approach which encourages student participation in English classes. It helps promote positive attitudes towards English and peer teaching, as well as teaching students to work together and developing their cognitive abilities. Moreover, it helps lower affective filters, which may hinder the process of language acquisition, by creating a relaxing and friendly atmosphere in the classroom. Cooperative learning helps develop a feeling of cohesiveness and caring that far exceeds what is already there and helps foster a climate of caring and sharing (Moskowitz, 1978). The extent to which this approach is examined and adopted depends on the caring, sharing, and daring of each language teacher.

DISCUSSION QUESTIONS

1. Consider some of the ways that "group projects" or "cooperative learning" can help "to lower affective filters" as well as create many new opportunities for negotiating target language forms. Better yet, observe a group project in progress and describe in detail the uses to which the target language is put. Ask what kinds of projects are apt to produce the highest rates of successful negotiations of the desired kinds.

2. Why do you suppose Prapphal suggests that "caring and sharing" (Moskowitz's phrase) requires "daring" on the part of the language teacher?

CHAPTER 35

Jigsaw Reading

Jonathan de Berkeley-Wykes

EDITOR'S INTRODUCTION

"Jigsaw reading" (JR) has been called by other names. For instance, a more colorful term which has been applied to much the same technique is "the strip tease." It is a kind of puzzle in which pieces of text are cut up and scrambled. The objective of the student, or group of students, to whom the jigsaw is assigned is to restore the pieces to their proper order—to make sense of the text. In writing this piece de Berkeley-Wykes was concerned not only with introducing the method as a practical classroom activity, but also with justifying it in terms of previous research on reading and related psycholinguistic processes. If used as a group activity where students communicate about the decisions of how to order the various pieces of the text, JR can elicit a great deal of communicative interaction. It also has a solid basis in reading research and in theories of discourse processing.

Research into the reading process has led to many theories and some models of reading, e.g., Gough (1972) and Rumelhart (1980). Interest in the processes underlying reading has not, however, been matched by a comparable interest in the production of classroom materials and applications of them for the teaching of reading to students of English as a second or foreign language.

Traditionally, reading series have been produced following prescriptions such as

(a) graded structural complexity,
(b) vocabulary frequency counts, and
(c) reading skills and strategies development (concentrating on sound-symbol correspondences and the like).

The assumption implicit in the derived reading courses is that identification of the language components and improvement of each of those components separately will eventually produce a cumulative improvement in student reading. Such atomistic approaches fail to recognize that reading, like language, is an integrated functional system. To quote a trite but true aphorism, "the whole is greater than the sum of the parts" (Watzlawick, Beavin, & Jackson, 1967).

Atomistic approaches to reading in a non-primary language also seem not to recognize that reading in a second language may depend on many of the same psycholinguistic processes, conceptions of discourse, and affective factors which enter into reading in the first language. However, these three aspects of reading can only interact to good effect if the materials selected naturally draw them into the process. Materials which are "episodically organized"—see Chapters 1 and 37 in this volume—will facilitate the necessary interaction. Jigsaw Reading (JR), an interesting and highly interactive classroom activity, can help to integrate the skills of communication and reading in a more holistic manner.

INTERRELATED PSYCHOLINGUISTIC PROCESSES

As Goodman (1975: 25) has argued,

> There is no possible sequencing of skills in reading instruction since all systems must be used interdependently in the reading process even in the first attempts at learning to read.

Therefore, sorting out the elements that go into the totality of the reading process may not only be unnecessary, but actually counterproductive.

To begin with, a JR is based on a full-fledged, relatively self-contained text (that is, it should not require access to other texts for its comprehension). The text is cut into segments, and the task of the students is to restore it to its proper order. A JR may include a title, or in the case of news articles, headlines. The value of titles has been shown by Bransford and Johnson (1972), and in Part 4 above, to establish a link in the reader's mind with his or her knowledge of the subject of a text. Activation of this knowledge sets up, in the reader, certain *predictions* of what he or she might expect to find in the text.

A similar orienting effect can be achieved by including pictures, cartoons, drawings, maps, charts, diagrams, or tables. Brown and Murphy (1975) show how the logical sequencing of pictures will cause a learner-reader to impose a *logical sequencing* on a narrative. Also, Paulson, Kintsch, Kintsch, and Premack (1979) show how a sequence of pictures can create a "story proposition" which subsequently facilitates reading.

In addition to *specific* predictions in text processing there are also *general* expectations. Readers always expect, for example, that a piece of writing will make sense (Bever, 1970) and will adhere to the cooperative principle (Grice, 1975) of being relevant, informative, more or less concise, and truthful. Presumably, these general expectations come either from previous experience with texts in the first language or from innate cognitive universals (or both). Peck (1980) argues that failure to take account of reader expectations explains why so many aspiring writers produce so much unpublishable fiction. On the other hand, recognizing the importance of such expectancies (Oller, 1983b) serves as a theoretical basis for the kind of text operations involved in JR.

Writers cater to detailed expectations about person(s) place, time, and setting by offering this information early on. The fact that readers can sometimes remember the first sentence of a paragraph verbatim while the remainder is only recalled in outline (Garrod & Trabasso, 1973) suggests (among other things) that reader expectations are particularly strong at the beginnings of passages. Expectations about how texts should begin may be due to a universal need in discourse processing to pragmatically tie down the context. Weaver (1980) has suggested that effective readers use context to confirm their unfolding tentative interpretations. A clear context will assist comprehension and set up further useful predictions concerning what is to follow later in the text (McCullough, 1976).

Olson (1974) has noted that a written text has to define the spatial and temporal terms of reference to enable the reader to accurately interpret it. Therefore, a useful constraint on JRs is that they should give the reader clear, contextual frames of reference. Through them, the learner-reader can make tentative comprehension decisions which will be confirmed, rejected, or refined (Goodman, 1975) as more pieces of the JR are put together.

The JR is cut into pieces at meaning boundaries. Johnson and Friedman (1971) showed how sentences which are meaningfully segmented are more easily comprehended and remembered. Also, Cohen and Freeman (1978) have shown how good readers naturally segment a text into phrase-like units. By presenting the JR in pieces, the learner-reader processes the passage in clausal units (Garrett, Bever & Fodor, 1966) since these segments act as psychological units (Carroll & Bever, 1976) in comprehension. Each piece of the JR, therefore, should be a natural *"chunk"* (Clark & Clark, 1977). Jarvella (1971), Caplan (1976), and Klieman (1975) have shown how comprehension processing tends to chunk material according to a semantic interpretation which is not necessarily related to surface syntax. Cutting the JR into pieces at meaning boundaries therefore encourages the student to use the normal psycholinguistic method of comprehension.

Psycholinguistic theories of the processes involved in reading are often characterized by "top-down" or "bottom-up" descriptions (e.g. by Kamil, 1978). Neurolinguistic research suggests that the two hemispheres of the brain process different types of information in different ways (Wittrock, 1977), but comprehension is the joint result of those differential processing systems. JR, therefore, engages both holistic "top-down" processes as well as sequential, analytic "bottom-up" methods which jointly contribute to meaningful reading.

At any point during its assembly, JR enjoins the reader to match the pieces he or she intends to add against the text already completed. This matching involves both holistic and sequential considerations. In order to fit correctly, each piece will have to be matched to a number of particular aspects of the text (Collins, Brown, & Larkin, 1980).

The addition of pieces, at a grammatical level, shows the student that agreements of gender and number can reveal constituent clauses of a sentence. Tense consistency within paragraphs can help with assignment of the pieces to the correct paragraph in longer passages. Similarly, punctuation may help. For example, pieces which end with a comma or a semicolon have to be followed by a continuation beginning with a small letter, whereas pieces ending with a full stop have to be followed by a capital letter. Using this awareness of grammar and punctuation can help the student arbitrate in cases of uncertainty.

Since the JR retains the natural redundant features of language, the learner-reader can use this redundancy to reduce the number of plausible contextual alternatives as the text progresses. As the student's ability to activate psycholinguistic processes improves, the number of plausible alternatives will presumably be reduced, thus enhancing comprehension (Smith, 1978). As the reader draws on different aspects of language redundancy, at the same time using different processing mechanisms, the "psycholinguistic guesses" (Goodman, 1976) become more accurately constrained. Thus, JR engenders a self-reliant approach, to use the known to aid in understanding the unknown. Self-directed handling of language aims to prepare the student to better cope with language outside the classroom.

CONCEPTIONS OF DISCOURSE

Not only can the student use psycholinguistic processes to aid in reading another language, but also he or she has experience and knowledge of discourse. Oller (1983b) proposed that language comprehension involves crossing the pragmatic bridge between individual experience and texts. Accomplishing this requires intricate and complex mental negotiations of the connections between structures of discourse and elements of experience. Rosenblatt (1978) has stressed the importance of the reader's personal store of knowledge in achieving this sort of comprehension. JRs are helpful in this respect because they encourage the reader to draw on prior knowledge and understandings of discourse in a surprisingly natural way.

Such interaction sets up an extra-linguistic link between the reader and a piece of text. When the text is in a foreign language, that interactive link can assist comprehension, for experience and knowledge of discourse are not necessarily bound to any one language. JRs capitalize upon a reader's non-language bound knowledge; therefore, JRs should relate to the interests and knowledge of the learner. With learners who are learning to read for a specific purpose, specialist texts can be used. Voss et al. (1980) have shown how subject knowledge, or specialized "expertise" (their term), is involved in comprehension. For learners with less specifiable purposes, passages on current affairs, topics in the news, and the history or geography of their country can be used. Such subjects bring the learners themselves more actively into the process of comprehension. This process, it is claimed, relies as much on the "information in the reader's mind as on the information in the written text" (Adams, 1980: 12).

Regardless of the kind of information contained in a piece of text, Morgan and Sellner (1980) have shown that effective readers naturally impose some kind of organizational structure. Rumelhart (1975) clarifies the nature of textual expectancies in terms of his "story schema." Together with foregoing arguments, this fact supports the "expectancy hypothesis"—the notion that cognitive momentum aids in the unraveling of a text (Oller, 1983b). JR encourages the reader to appeal to this expectancy momentum in assembling the pieces and thus restoring the text.

Completion of the JR relies on the coherence (Halliday & Hasan, 1976; or "conceptual connectivity," de Beaugrande, 1980) of a discourse being realized by means of the cohesion (Halliday &

Hasan, 1976; or "surface connectivity," de Beaugrande, 1980) of the language of the text. Anaphoric expressions are examples of cohesive language devices. They are intersentential elements which maximize comprehension (Huggins & Adams, 1980) by helping the reader update and refine hypotheses about the discourse (Webber, 1980).

In many texts written for language classes, however, natural anaphora is deleted. This attempt at preadaptation of passages is based on the mistaken belief that it makes the passages simpler and therefore easier for the non-native to understand. Though such a method may make passages seem simpler, it does the student harm in two ways: it "short-circuits" comprehension systems, since it upsets the surface connectivity of the passage, by removing much of its cohesion, and it encourages the development of false expectations about texts. These freakish expectations violate universal notions of conceptual connectivity and will, over the long run, be apt to hinder the comprehension of discourse.

AFFECTIVITY

A further effect of artificially pre-adapted reading materials is that they are less interesting than natural texts. D. V. Swain (1973) has suggested that prose momentum is essentially a linked series of units consisting of motivating stimulus and consequent reaction. These motivation-reaction units, D. V. Swain argues, are the basis for sustained involvement of the reader. Peck (1980) contends that interest is also naturally heightened as a character in a story encounters obstacles in the pursuit of a desirable goal. Similarly, linking the pieces of a JR may produce in the student sustaining interest due to the synergistic character of the text itself, and also the puzzle-solving esthetic of assembling the pieces. As each piece fits into the developing discourse momentum builds in the reader.

Clearly, the best classroom reading materials still depend to a great extent on reader interest. Piaget (1981: 8) has argued similarly that

> the technique by which a goal is attained requires coordinations, regulations, and always presupposes an energy whose origin appears to be essentially affective.

An additional aspect of affectivity which Piaget emphasizes is "valuation." How much value does the subject place on a particular goal? According to expert writers (e.g., D. V. Swain, Peck, and others), the valuation of a goal is best judged in terms of what the character will endure to obtain the goal. However, Piaget (1981) rejects any simple cost/benefit explanation which would attribute value strictly on the basis of potential reward. He argues that valuation of goals exceeds the limits of mere behavioristic "reinforcements." Corder (1978), following a similar line of thought, claimed that a learner will only move along the continuum towards more accurate language use when the improvement has merit in the learner's own eyes.

Partly because of the game-like character of JR, the value of the completed task is constantly reaffirmed as the student works through the puzzle. In keeping with the observation of Wilkins (1976) that using language as a tool is intrinsically rewarding, JR affirms the student's efforts through a satisfying solution of the puzzle. Also, in solving the puzzle, the student refines necessary skills in the target language. The intrinsic valuation of such performances helps to produce self-dependent learning and gives students a sense of personal achievement.

In an oft-quoted remark, Huey (1908) described reading as "the most remarkable specific performance that civilization has learned in all its history." JR is a modest step toward making this skill more accessible to language students. It depends for its effectiveness on the three-way interaction of psycholinguistic processes, prior experience and knowledge, and interest. It conscientiously avoids the prescriptive bases of artificially contrived reading materials. What is more, it works.

A Sample Jigsaw Reading

The text which follows has slashes inserted at cut points. The text would be typed on cardboard, cut up into segments, and then shuffled. The object of students is to restore the segments to their original order:

Sadat's Assassination
On 6th October, 1981/ there was a military parade/ in Al-Nasr stadium./ The President of Egypt, Anwar Sadat,/ the Vice-President,/ and their

guests/ were sitting in the President's box./ Some planes flew over the stadium,/ so everyone looked up at them./ While they were looking up,/ a lorry stopped in front of the box,/ and four young soldiers jumped out of it,/ and ran towards the box./ When Sadat saw them,/ he stood up,/ because he thought they were coming to greet him./ Suddenly, three of them began shooting at the President/ and the other people in the box./ Everyone got down on the floor,/ and some tried to hide/ on the floor under the chairs./ The fourth soldier ran round/ to the side of the box/ and shot at the people/ under the chairs./ When the shooting stopped,/ 11 people were dead/ and 18 were injured./ One of those was Sadat./ The Defense Minister radioed for a helicopter/ and it took Sadat to the hospital./ When he got there,/ the doctors tried to save him,/ but he died two hours later.

DISCUSSION QUESTIONS

1. Consider ways in which psycholinguistic processes, knowledge and experience, and affect might interact in solving a JR. For example, what specific and general expectations are used in solving the Sadat example?

2. Suppose the JR activity is done in small groups. What kinds of discussion might be expected to occur?

3. How might such JR activities be calibrated for maximal effectiveness at a particular level of instruction?

CHAPTER 36

From Improvisation to Publication Through Drama

Charlyn Wessels

EDITOR'S INTRODUCTION

In this chapter we return, as always it seems, to acting. The insight of John Rassias and others that acting provides an essential ingredient of all communication is affirmed and extended in this exciting chapter by Charlyn Wessels. She shows how improvisations created by students can be developed into materials for language teaching. In fact, the dramatic improvisations worked out here have been published by Macmillan as part of the "Bookshelf" series of readers. In Chapter 8, Stern offered evidence showing that students markedly preferred improvisation over acting out scenes from plays written by someone else. In this nourishing chapter by Wessels, we see some of the reasons why.

BACKGROUND: THE ENGLISH THROUGH DRAMA COURSE

Stevenson College in Edinburgh offers an EFL course for upper-intermediate and advanced students which is based entirely on drama techniques. The course includes classes on pronunciation, spoken communication skills, theater workshop activities, literature, and play production. Theater and cinema visits form an integral part of the course, which runs for ten hours a week for a total length of three months, and can be taken by both part-time and full-time students. A maximum of fourteen students can participate in the course each term.

The heart of the course is the improvisation of a full-length play (usually 20–25 pages in length) by the class, and this end product is usually performed at the end of term in front of an enthusiastic audience of fellow students, teachers, and guests. Past productions have included the following titles: *Soap Opera, Soap 2—The Sequel, That's*

What I Want! (about a bank robbery that goes wrong) and *City of Women* (about a world in which women control everything).

THE STAGES TOWARDS AN END PRODUCT

In the first week of the course, the class has to be transformed into a group of people willing to work together in a relaxed and friendly atmosphere. This is achieved through a range of group-dynamic activities, both verbal and nonverbal, such as warm-up and relaxation activities, name games, pair games, and group games. An example of a pair activity is "Mirrors," where one partner mirrors the actions of the other. And a popular group game is "Parties," where the entire group has a party in a variety of ways—as a group of philosophers, as punks, as babies, as animals, and so on.

Next, the group needs to be familiarized with learning through drama. This is done through a

FIGURE 36.1 Questionnaire for the Second Week of the Course

QUESTIONNAIRE

Choosing a play and a character

1. Read the brief description of the different types of genres, and then list, in order of preference, the type of play you would like the group to do. Use numbers to indicate your preferences, e.g., first choice ⬚**1**⬚, second choice ⬚**2**⬚, etc.

   a. Domestic plays—mainly concerned with relationships within a family, either comic or serious. ❑

   b. Crime and detection plays—murders, bank robberies, etc. ❑

   c. Death, grief, and social embarrassment plays—plays that highlight the more painful side of life either in a direct or surreal/absurdist manner. ❑

   d. Melodramas—sensational, often sentimental, plays with improbable plots dealing with exciting and sometimes shocking events. These tend to have standard stereotyped characters, e.g., villain, noble hero, suffering heroine. ❑

   e. Parable plays—plays which teach a moral lesson or general truth drawn from the events and characters in the play. ❑

   f. Historical plays—plays that cover dramatic episodes in the lives of well-known people in history. ❑

2. What type of role do YOU see yourself in?

   a. romantic hero(ine) ❑

   b. villain ❑

   c. detective ❑

   d. comic character ❑

   e. voice of wisdom and reason ❑

   f. strong, silent type ❑

   g. person of mystery (e.g., angel, god, deus-ex-machina) ❑

   h. nasty, vicious person ❑

   i. "angry young man/woman" ❑

   j. kind, gentle person ❑

3. Here are the plots of a number of one-act plays. If you would like us to practice extracts from some of these, state your preference.

   a. *Us and Them:* Two groups of people looking for a place to settle meet on the same piece of land. They divide the land, first with a line, then with a wall. From there on, the trouble begins. ❑

   b. *Look—Sea!:* Various characters, including holiday-makers, a marine biologist, the captain of an oil tanker, politicians, and a poet, react in different ways to the pollution of the oceans. ❑

   c. *The Patient:* Someone has tried to kill Jenny Wingfield. He or she will certainly try again—unless Dr. Ginsberg and Inspector Cray can prevent a murder. ❑

   d. *The Man Who Wouldn't Go to Heaven:* People arrive at the gates of Paradise. They are welcomed by the Angel Gabriel, although most of them don't understand why they were sent to Heaven. But one man refuses to enter Heaven—he thinks it is all a pack of lies. ❑

   e. *The Man in the Bowler Hat:* Madcap melodrama about John and Mary, whose humdrum lives are suddenly invaded by sensational characters in search of the Rajah's ruby. ❑

   f. *Pullman Car Hiawatha:* On an interstate train between New York and Chicago, the dreams, failures, and simple lives of the passengers become interwoven with commentary from a range of external characters who have contributed to the development of the railways (and thereby to the development of the country) and have caused the sudden death of one traveler. ❑

FIGURE 36.2 One Group's Relationship Tree for *Soap Opera*

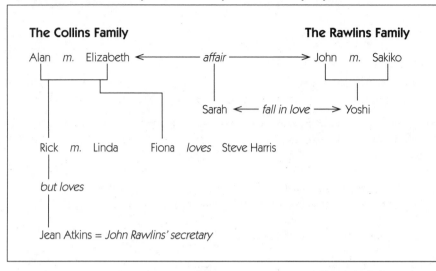

range of theater workshops, each of which focuses on a different aspect such as movement and mime, improvisation, scenework, and drama voice production. These sessions always begin with warm-up and relaxation activities, and end with a cool-down aimed at releasing tension and dissipating any negative energy which may have built up during the session. Carefully selected music plays a vital role during the warm-up and the cool-down phases. (The references at the end of this article are sources of group-dynamic and theater-workshop activities.)

The second week of the course starts with a questionnaire (see Figure 36.1) which is aimed at getting students to think about the type of play they would like to do, and the kind of character they would each like to portray. They answer the questions individually and then discuss their answers, first in pairs, then groups, then as a whole class plenary, thereby gradually reaching consensus on what they would like to do.

When they have finished discussing their responses to the questionnaire, the group decides on a plot and characters for their own play. This is done through brainstorming, and all the ideas are discussed until a consensus is reached. Gradually, a story line is developed, as well as the role of each character in the story. The teacher notes down this development on the chalkboard, and draws a rough "tree" to show the relationships between the characters. The relationship tree developed for

Soap Opera by a class of eleven students is shown in Figure 36.2.

Each student then writes, as a homework assignment, a detailed character profile of the character he or she is going to portray. It is quite important to let each student develop his or her own character first, before the final plot is agreed on, because the story will develop from the interrelationship between the characters.

Finally, an outline for the scenes is drawn up by the teacher and the class, and the actual work of improvising the scenes can begin. The draft outline for *Soap Opera* was as follows:

Scene 1—Sarah's birthday (to introduce the Collins family)
Scene 2—Narita airport, Tokyo (to introduce the Rawlins family)
Scene 3—The offices of Allied Enterprises (Alan and Rick meet John)
Scene 4—Home life (both families)
Scene 5—Sarah and Yoshi fall in love
Scene 6—Elizabeth and John meet again: the terrible secret is revealed
Scene 7—Alan sets fire to the office
Scene 8—A happy ending?

The draft outline simply serves as an initial guide, because the story line can still change depending on its improvised development and the strengths and weaknesses of individual characters.

The more "kitchen sink" the initial story line is, the easier it will be for students to identify with the situation, but more advanced students also enjoy fantasy and surrealism.

IMPROVISING THE SCENES AND CREATING A SCRIPT

Two days a week are set aside for improvising the play. These sessions begin with a discussion on the scene to be improvised, and a brief outline of the scene is noted down on the board. The scenes need not be improvised sequentially—it is perfectly permissible to jump from improvising scenes 1–3 to scene 8, as some scenes may prove more difficult to construct than others, and the solution to these scenes can often be found by first working out later ones.

As in normal theater workshop sessions, the group then warms up physically and vocally, and also does a number of group dynamic activities to relax bodies and sharpen concentration. The group then splits up into: (1) the characters required for the scene and (2) "scribes" (i.e., students who note down as much as possible of the dialogue produced by the characters).

But although the characters do all the acting, every member of the group assists in creating the dialogue and "blocking" (i.e., planning and practicing) the necessary movements. With numerous repetitions, a scene begins to emerge—usually within an hour.

Throughout the improvisation, the actors are reminded by the teacher to remain "in role" and to ask themselves constantly what their characters would do in a given situation and how this would affect their interaction with others. There follows a sample of an improvisation in progress, recorded during one session; the group was working on scene 6 of *Soap Opera*:

Elizabeth and John are meeting in secret for the first time in years.

ELIZABETH: You haven't changed.
JOHN Well, you have.
SCRIBE (interrupting): Just a minute! Surely John wouldn't be so nasty to his former lover? I thought he was a nice guy.

ACTOR PLAYING JOHN: Well, I think he's still very angry because she left him for Alan.
SCRIBE: But would he really be so cruel?
ACTOR PLAYING JOHN: Oh, yes!
TEACHER: How do you know?
ACTOR PLAYING JOHN: Look, I made him up, so I should know!
TEACHER: You're absolutely right. Continue.

The above exchange not only shows how students identify closely with the characters they create themselves, but also illustrates how much intensive language practice students can get through improvisation; with improvisation we have both learning and acquisition (see Krashen, 1982) at work. The students *learn* the correct language required for the end product and also *acquire* a good deal through the informal yet focused discussion which helps to create the scene, as they offer ideas, agree or disagree with each other, and describe possible actions. Because they are creating the play themselves, rather than responding to an existing text, there is usually no shortage of ideas, nor any unwillingness to contribute to the developing scenes. As with normal spoken communication skills classes, these sessions end with language feedback from the teacher, during which recurrent errors (from the actual improvisation as well as the discussions) are corrected.

At the end of the session, all the scribes' notes are gathered together and handed over to either one or two students, who write out the complete scene for homework. Each student in the group will have the chance either to write or to co-write a complete scene. The teacher edits the written scene, checking for errors in style, grammar, and vocabulary. The corrected version is then typed out and copies are given to the students, who are always delighted to see their own ideas in print.

This scene writing, together with the reviews the students write after they have seen a film or a play, ensures that the course has a writing component as well as an aural/oral one. A further writing assignment is the keeping of a "character diary," which records events that happen to individual characters as the play develops. The following is a diary entry made by one of the *Soap Opera* students:

NAME OF CHARACTER: Yoshi Rawlins
SCENE: One

Flew from Tokyo to London with Dad and Mom. Miserable to leave school pals and grandparents, but excited at thought of new life in Britain. Met at airport by Dad's new secretary, Jean. Boy, what a dish! My new school (which Dad also attended) is called St. Paul's.

Once all the scenes have been created in the manner described above, the more formal type of rehearsals with the complete script take place (see Wessels, 1987, Chapter 9 there). But here, too, we have managed to minimize the dominance of the teacher by allowing individual students to direct certain scenes. This is a very practical and enjoyable way of introducing the language and intonation of tact and diplomacy; for example,

"That was very good, but don't you think . . .?"
"With a little more emotion, you should be able to . . ."
"What do you think about/How do you feel about trying it out in this way?"
"If you put the emphasis on that word, the meaning would be clearer. . . ."
"Darling, you were wonderful! I'd just like the audience to see more of your lovely face, so how about looking up occasionally?"

And throughout the rehearsal phase, the script can still be changed and enlivened by different ideas from the group.

At this stage, we use the weekly pronunciation class to concentrate on correcting recurrent problems with the word stress, sentence stress, rhythm, and intonation of the newly created dialogue. Weaker students are also withdrawn from the group for individual assistance. Towards the end of the rehearsal phase (usually two to three weeks), photographs are taken, tape recordings are made of scenes, and a video recording is made of the whole play. Then the performance is held, bringing the course to an exciting and rewarding conclusion.

CREATING NEW TEACHING MATERIALS FROM AN IMPROVISED PLAY

From our improvised plays, we have been able to develop new teaching material for a range of levels (elementary to upper-intermediate), to cover all the skills:

Reading—using the complete script (with or without the audio or video recording) or, as in the case of *Soap Opera,* transforming it into a class reader (published in 1991);
Listening—to individual scenes from the tape recordings, or watching the video and answering comprehension questions;
Pronunciation—using the dialogue to teach or revise those aspects of speech mentioned above; with more advanced students, analyzing pronunciation errors made on the tape recording or video;
Speaking—matching photographs with correct extracts from the play, improvising different endings to scenes, discussing the characters;
Grammar—using the text to create cloze tests and exercises on prepositions, idioms, verb tenses, reported speech, and word order;
Writing—rearranging "jumbled" scenes, writing alternative scenes.

So the course is not only beneficial to the students, but also to the teachers, who can create banks of new material out of such "homemade" products, without worrying about copyright restrictions.

CONCLUSION

Student feedback at the end of each course has been very positive, and we now offer a second English Through Drama course for lower-intermediate and intermediate students. We also run a special drama option class once a week for anyone who wishes to attend. Here are some responses from students on the last upper-intermediate to advanced course:

"A significant experience I'll never forget"— Kumiko (Japanese, 50)
"Improving my English by creating was fantastic"—Gerardo (Italian, 37)
"I've improved my English, had fun, and I've got to know my friends much better—what more can I ask of a course?"—Sylvie (French, 20)
"In Drama we live the language"—Tereza (Spanish, 29).

And what effect does teaching through drama have on teachers? Well, those of us who use it as our main teaching technique freely admit that it is physically and mentally demanding, but it certainly helps to keep us young and staves off apathy!

DISCUSSION QUESTIONS

1. Wessels insists that each student should develop his or her own character (the one to be portrayed) "before the final plot is agreed on." Why do you suppose this point is stressed? Incidentally, how do "plots" normally develop in experience—before or after the characters of the persons involved are pretty well set? How do fiction writers handle character background in novels, for example?

2. Why should we expect any particular episode of experience (or a plot in a particular story) to have less effect (on the whole) in shaping a person's character than the history that precedes that particular episode? (In this connection, also note the willingness of a student improvising a part, see p. 367, to defend what the character says in a particular scene on the grounds of past but fictional experience. Why do you suppose the student is so sure of what "John" would be apt to say to "Elizabeth"?)

3. Why would "fantasy and surrealism" be apt to appeal to "more advanced students" rather than beginners? In this same connection, consider the language feedback from the teacher where recurrent errors are corrected (p. 368). Recall the discussion of "defossilizing" by Helen Johnson (Chapter 25) and discuss the connections in all of this.

4. Based on remarks from students who have had the course "English Through Drama" (see pp. 372–373), what are some of the ways that the "whole" person is involved in this whole-language experience?

CHAPTER 37

Reasons Why Some Methods Work

John W. Oller, Jr.

EDITOR'S INTRODUCTION

The purpose of the last chapter, included as an epilogue but not as an afterthought, is to provide a sound logical grounding for all of the practice, research, and theory which has preceded it in this volume. Frankly, at one point I had put all the material that appears here in Chapter 1. Then several colleagues (especially Dean Brodkey, the Damicos, Mari Wesche, and Sima Paribakht) reminded me that students and other users would have a better chance of understanding it after they had worked through a goodly portion of the preceding chapters. I believe that it will be useful to instructors of methods courses who use the book, for researchers who want to understand and apply its recommendations, and for all practitioners who really want to understand the whys and wherefores. Theoreticians and would-be critics, I believe, should not neglect it. The logical findings that are discussed here have been under development for about a quarter of a century—and much longer if traced back to the vein from which they were mined, the writings of C. S. Peirce who lived from 1839 to 1914. Some will, no doubt, find the abstractness daunting, but I urge them to take heart from the extremely practical and well-researched applications that such ideas, I believe, enable us to understand. If such a theory makes it possible, as I believe it does, to distinguish sharply between methods of instruction that nearly always work and ones that inevitably fail, it will be worthwhile for any teacher who takes the trouble to follow it out to its limits.

Theoretical advances are rarely made on the basis of the familiarity or immediate acceptance of arguments put forward. Rather, the question is whether the theory (and the hypotheses it suggests) can be fitted to the facts of common experience. I claim that the theory laid out here and the hypotheses it suggests fit the facts. I have included it here so that anyone who will take the trouble will see that the second edition of *Methods That Work* is a book with a theoretical basis.

The original groundwork was laid by C. S. Peirce in a systematic logic more consistently and comprehensively developed than any other even to this date (see Nagel, 1959; Eisele, 1979; Jakobson, 1980; Houser, 1986; and Sebeok, 1991). I will

endeavor to show some of the unique aspects of that comprehensiveness and consistency here, and I will try to point out how these ideas are applied and demonstrated to be correct in all the results attained by contributors to this book.

THE THEORY OF PRAGMATIC MAPPING

Content always has a dual aspect. On the one hand, there are the material facts that are, have been, or might be actually experienced. These are usually what is meant by subject matter. On the other hand, there are the abstract concepts and ideas that enable us to make sense of the facts.

FIGURE 37.1 Pragmatic Mapping of Representations Onto the Facts of Experience

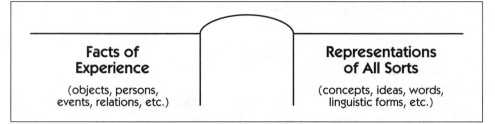

Facts of Experience		Representations of All Sorts
(objects, persons, events, relations, etc.)		(concepts, ideas, words, linguistic forms, etc.)

Between these two utterly different realms (Einstein, 1941)—(1) the actual things, events, states of affairs, etc. that we experience in the material world and (2) the abstract concepts that enable us to make sense of that world—there is a complex of representational systems usually including one or more languages. Concrete facts as well as abstract ideas are known to us exclusively through (often linguistic) representations. A simple (but correct) way of viewing the needed integration between content and language (as described by Swain & Lapkin, 1989, and by others throughout this book) is given in the pragmatic mapping diagram shown in Figure 37.1.

The problem is to link up the realm of abstract concepts (ideas) with the material world of experience (objects, events, and relations in space and time) through the interaction of various representational systems. The mediating process of pragmatic mapping usually involves a particular language, but sensations and movements (voluntary and involuntary), especially gestures (e.g., pointing, significant hand signs, head and trunk movements, etc.) and so-called paralinguistic devices (e.g., tone of voice, facial expression, etc.) are also commonly involved. Music, art, dance, mathematics, and other specialized sign systems may also enter the picture. There are really three distinct problems to be solved in working out any particular pragmatic mapping, though the three problems are not entirely separable and need not be worked out in any particular order. One aspect of the pragmatic mapping process is to determine the facts in some manner. This may be accomplished partly through sensory-motor representations. We see the cars collide and hear the crunch of metal. Another aspect of the pragmatic mapping process is to call into play the relevant concepts and ideas. This is the invisible part of the

process and is usually taken for granted or overlooked altogether. It is the means by which we conceptualize what is, has been, or might be. We classify the objects that are colliding as "cars" and the noise caused by the collision and the whole event as "a wreck." The categories (ultimately abstract forms) that we depend on must be indexed against actual experiences, and the experiences also, by the same means, must be linked to the categories. The experience suggests the categories to our minds, and each of the categories connects the particular experience in question with other experiences of the same type. Therefore, yet another aspect of the pragmatic mapping process is the connecting of the facts and the concepts via some medium of representation. In ordinary experience, sensory-motor representations are involved. We see, hear, touch, smell, and taste. We also have some volitional control over where we look, where we go, what we choose to do, etc. In order to share our thoughts and feelings with others, publicly observable sign systems (representations) such as gestures and language come into play. We point, frown, gape in disbelief, and comment "Oh! No! A wreck!" In normal human experience all three elements—facts (or actual states of things) representations, and concepts (abstract ideas)—are usually at work simultaneously.

THE GENERALITY OF THE THEORY

The theory of pragmatic mapping (which Peirce called "abduction"; see Oller, 1990) as a picture of all meaningful acts of representation holds true regardless whether we are thinking of the production, comprehension, or acquisition of sign systems. In this book we have generally been concerned with meaningful acts of language use, but not to the exclusion of other meaningful acts of representation such as sensation, significant volitional movement, gesturing, etc. To produce comprehensible output, the language user must utter, write, or otherwise produce a sequence of signs that is pragmatically linked with concepts on the one hand and with the world of experience on the other (in such a manner as might be understood by someone else). To comprehend material as input, a language user must similarly make the sorts of connections that the producer intends. To acquire a language, some level of comprehension is required as a minimal starting point and as a pre-requisite to the production of comprehensible output. Communication and thought are similarly dependent on such connections. Hence, the theory of pragmatic mapping covers all the cases of interest to language teachers, reading teachers, and in fact to teachers in general. Furthermore, it defines the methods that work (in language teaching and in teaching or communication in general). It describes what those methods must do and predicts which ones will succeed.

Owing to evidences currently available (many of them summed up in preceding parts of this book, but especially in Parts 2 and 3) and to theoretical advances, it is now possible to rigorously define certain logical properties of the pragmatic mapping process and to show both their central importance and comprehensive scope with respect to language processing and to the acquisition of language skills. Some of the advances (since the first edition of *Methods That Work*) fall into the realm of theoretical discoveries grounded in pure logic. To understand better the advantages of the particular brand of pragmatic theory summed up in Figure 37.1 (first broached somewhat tentatively in Oller & Richard-Amato, 1983: 5–6), it is essential to explore the unique logical properties of true narrative representations (i.e., correct pragmatic mappings of the sort shown in Figure 37.1), which, as we will see, are the only kind that can lead to actual understanding, to successful communication, and to teaching that really works. The logical properties in question are abstract and theoretical, but they have powerful empirical consequences that have already been demonstrated in many ways in previous chapters of this book and elsewhere in the vast and growing literature, as will be summed up below. Besides, there is no way

that the full force and comprehensiveness of the theory under consideration can be understood without examining the peculiar logical advantages of true narrative representations[1] of just the sort depicted in Figure 37.1.

THREE PERFECTIONS OF TRUE NARRATIVE REPRESENTATIONS

To begin with, a little reflection will show that the pragmatic mapping process of Figure 37.1 is that by which any true representation is truly related to its logical object—the state of affairs, the fact(s), of which it (the representation) is true. It turns out that such a true representation is exactly the sort found in a true story, or in any ordinary experience where neither illusion nor error plays a major role. That is, pragmatic mapping always and only results (if it succeeds at all and only to the extent that it succeeds) in a true narrative representation. The representation must be of the narrative type because it occupies a position in the temporal flow of actual, ongoing experience. I see the neighbor's cat leap through the open window into my pickup. A moment later I can no longer see it, but as I approach the vehicle, the cat jumps out again. In a narrative, states of affairs are conceived as being transformed so that what has been is changed into what is, and what is changes into what will be. That is, in every true narrative the events represented are transformed from ones that preceded them into ones that follow them in an unbroken, connected series. While I cannot see the cat inside the cab of my pickup, I know it is there, and my knowledge that it was in there, though the cat was momentarily out of sight, is confirmed when it leaps out of the truck again. All of this is merely a definition of what we normally understand true narrative representations to be. By this definition, true narrative representations have three real (actual) aspects of well-formedness (three logical perfections): (1) the logical object of the representation has a material, spatio-temporal aspect, i.e., the object (state of affairs, sequence of events, or whatever) referred to by the representation is real; (2) the representation itself is a particular logical object which also has a real aspect, e.g., it is noticeable in some way, takes up time, and occurs when the representor/interpreter is in some actual location at some time, etc.; and (3) the connection between the logical object and the noticeable form of the representation is actually made in real time by the producer/interpreter of the representation who relies on concepts and ideas correctly understood and applied to the representation and to the logical object in question.

The theoretical discovery of these three unique logical properties is important because they are associated only with true narrative representations and with no other kinds of representations. As a result, all true narrative representations can be proved logically to be relatively more complete (more perfect or well-formed in the rhetorical, grammatical, or logical sense of the term *perfect*) as compared against any and all other kinds of representations. Three proofs will be given, but before developing them it will be useful to state and briefly explain the character of the theorems to be proved.

First, true narrative representations can be shown to be the only kind that determinately relate (that is, that are connected in space and time) to actual, particular, concrete, material facts. We may call this the *determinacy* perfection.[2] Second, any true narrative representation relates truly to a plurality of other true representations which can be known by inference through presuppositions that pertain to facts that precede the one or ones in question, associations that are semantically linked to the one or ones in question, and implications that follow from the one or ones in question. We may call this the *connectedness* perfection. Third, only a true narrative representation of the sort depicted in Figure 37.1 can sufficiently determine any universal representation—the kind of proposition that purports to be true of all particular and even all possible facts of a certain type. An example is the proposition that human beings are mortal. This third property of true narrative statements may be called the *generalizability* perfection.

Proofs of the Three Pragmatic Perfections

For those readers who can see in advance that the foregoing theorems must be quite true, or for those who may have an aversion to logic (I've met a few humanists who report actually being allergic to axiomatic reasoning), I suggest that they might skip the section that follows. For conscientious readers willing to exercise some brain cells in order to thoroughly understand the argument, for theoreticians, and for all aspiring critics, the logical arguments that follow will need to be grasped entirely. Those arguments provide explanations and proofs of the three pragmatic perfections of true narrative representations along the lines of the logic of C. S. Peirce.

The Determinacy Perfection

(1) The proof that true narrative representations are the only kind that relate to particular, actual facts begins with the premise that at least they are one of the kinds of representations that do so. This is known from the definition of true narrative representations. What must be proved relative to the determinacy perfection, however, is that true narrative representations are the only kind of propositional forms that are related in a determinate way to particular facts. This can be proved by showing that the complement of true narrative representations—namely all other representations (false ones, fictional ones, true or false general representations, and non-factual ones of any type including fantasies, imaginings, etc.)—do not have the perfection in question.[3] Following Peirce, we may adopt the term *degeneracy* as the opposite of *perfection* (or Chomskyan *well-formedness*).[4]

Now, the very definition of fictional representations as well as false ones eliminates them as possible counterexamples to the thesis under consideration. They are all degenerate by definition because they are either false or fictional. More specifically, they fail to relate to their purported objects. For instance, the characters and events of a fictional story have no material aspect other than a fictional one except insofar as they may incorporate true narrative representations within them or insofar as the fictional events depicted may resemble real events and persons. Fictional representations, therefore, however interesting and engaging they may be, remain degenerate with respect to the material realities that they purport to represent but which are not real. With false representations, that which is represented to be actually is not. With fictional ones, that which is represented may exist in a fictional world but not in this material world. As a result, all false, and in fact, all non-factual representations are degenerate (relatively incomplete) with respect to what they purport to represent. Their logical objects lack the full material aspect that would be found if the fictional representations were factual ones. In terms of Figure 37.1, for false statements, the whole factual side of the diagram is not absent altogether, but is undetermined. We have no way of filling in what goes there unless we know how to make the false representation over into a true one. If the left-hand side were replaced with anything, it would be a fiction of a peculiar doubly degenerate form—one that is represented to have a material substance which in fact it does not have. Errors and mistaken representations would have this form. Lies, of course, are false representations, but with a peculiar additional degeneracy. To qualify as such, a lie must be known to be false by the person representing it for the truth. Therefore, lies are triply degenerate.

Returning to fictions, so long as they are plausible ones, they are degenerate only with respect to the material aspect of their objects. They pretend (though the pretense is not concealed) to represent things that are, yet those things only exist in imagination. If the fiction is implausible or difficult to imagine, even the imaginary purported facts may be difficult to conjure up, in which case the fiction becomes still more degenerate. In terms of Figure 37.1, fictions (including all hypotheticals and all contrary-to-fact conditionals and the like) involve a degeneracy in the material side. That is, the form may be perfect but without any complete material (concrete physical space-time) aspect.

Thus, we are left only with true general representations to consider as possible non-degenerate cases. A true general statement (e.g., that human beings are mortal) that is related to a particular fact or plurality of facts (e.g., that Socrates and the rest of us are mortal) is not merely general but, by definition, is itself determined by a plurality of true narrative representations. A general statement, however, that is not known to be determined by a multitude of true narrative representations is simply one that is not known (not determined) to be true at all. It would be the sort of general statement, which if it were true, could only be of uncertain meaning with respect to our experience. Therefore, our case is made for the first pragmatic perfection, the *determinacy* perfection: Only true narrative representations are determinately linked with particular facts of experience.

The Connectedness Perfection

(2) The second pragmatic perfection of true narrative statements—that they are logically connected to true presuppositions, associations, and implications (see Horiba, Chapter 21)—follows from the fact that any given fact in actual experience is part of a stream of related material facts. For instance, if I say truly that the cat disappeared through the open window of my pickup and if you believe me, you are also obliged to suppose that the cat was elsewhere before jumping into my pickup and that it continued to exist after disappearing into the truck. You could not be very surprised to hear that the cat jumped back out as I approached the truck. Nor could you reasonably doubt, granted the foregoing facts, that the cat would continue to enjoy some existence after jumping out of the truck. All of this illustrates the connectedness perfection, which, incidentally, is the basis of what were formerly called the "expectancy" and "episode" hypotheses (see Oller 1974; 1983b). In sum, every particular fact is connected with other facts. As a result, we cannot know any truly singular, particular fact all by itself. If we really know something of one fact, we know something of the ones to which that particular fact (and all others as well) are connected. If we assume only that the space-time universe consists of connected parts, or if we assume at least that the parts we know of are connected to each other, any fact that we can know about one part must be connected with facts concerning all of the other parts. Therefore, any true narrative statement that relates to any particular (actual) fact whatever is necessarily related to the entire material continuum. By the same line of reasoning, any true narrative representation is necessarily related (however indirectly) to the experience of the same material continuum by any experiencer whatever just to the extent (and only to the extent) that the true narrative statement is truly representative of some fact or facts. From the deductive proof that only true narrative representations have the determinacy perfection (see the proof above), it follows necessarily that only they (true narrative representations) can have the second pragmatic

perfection, the *connectedness* perfection, since the connections between facts in the material world, no matter how numerous they may be, are always particular ones.

The Generalizability Perfection

(3) The third pragmatic perfection concerns the determination of the meaning of universal propositions or concepts. A universally applicable concept (or a general concept) is one that can be applied to any conceivable exemplar. However, as noted by Immanuel Kant, C. S. Peirce, and Albert Einstein (see Oller, 1989), the vesting of any abstract concept with any particular content is entirely dependent on connecting it with some particular element in actual experience. This is the same as saying that only true narrative representations concerning particular facts can inform us in such a manner as to enable us to determine the content of abstract general representations which concern all facts of a particular type. The proof of the generalizability perfection is strictly deductive, but an empirical example will help to show in terms of experience (inductively) why the deduction holds and what it means. Imagine the sort of concept described by a certain word, though we don't know which word or in which language. Now a concept of that sort, it must be admitted, is about as indeterminate as a concept could be. It is indeterminate both with respect to the realm of pure ideas and also with respect to the realm of tangible things in the material world. But suppose I say that the word I am thinking of (actually, just thought of) is *shang* in the language Quang. Now you have only a little more to go on, but you still cannot determine the meaning of the word for two reasons. First, I just invented the word and the language a moment ago (both being pure fictions); second, I had not yet decided what a "shang" might be, until just now. It is a kind of mongrel dog like the one I used to call Chester. Now, if you had ever known my scruffy dog, Chester, you would be in a fair position to put some particular content to the abstract concept *shang*. In fact, if you have ever known any mongrel dog whatever, once having heard my description of Chester, you are in a fair position to imagine about the right sort of content to associate with the term *shang*. Remove all such experi-

ence from the picture, and the term *shang* or, in fact, any abstract concept whatever would remain altogether devoid of any determinate content. So much for the inductive aspect of the proof. It remains to give the more adequate deductive side of the case.

We begin (following Peirce) by finding the logical limit to the possible facts that might be known concerning the material world. By definition, a fact is such that it can be known only by being represented. An unrepresentable fact is one that is, to us, altogether unknowable. To us it could not therefore be any material fact at all. It would be fantastic beyond our imagination. Any fact that can be imagined is one that is not quite outside the limits of representation, so only those that are altogether unrepresentable are excluded. This leaves behind only representable facts. Therefore, only facts that are representable can be known. This is the limit on the material side. The next step is to determine the limit on the immaterial or abstract side. A representable fact is one that is (or can be) linked via pragmatic mapping to an abstract representation of some sort, i.e., to a conceptual form. The question is, can we define the extreme limit of the sorts of conceptual forms that can be known? It turns out that we can. For the reasons just given, conceptual forms, insofar as they can be known at all, must be representable. A conceptual form that could not be represented in any way would be the sort that could not be known at all. Its content, if it had any, could never be discovered and would be outside the reach of any representation whatever. Perhaps it ought to go without saying, as a prerequisite premise, that any act of representation whatever is a particular act because it occurs somehow in space and time. (Any act occurring anywhere in space and time, of course, must be a particular act.) This leads us to the door beyond which we find the inevitable conclusion of the deductive proof: any knowable abstract form (concept or proposition) or any knowable particular fact (material object or state of affairs) can only be known through some particular representational form that links the one with the other. Hence, only a particular true pragmatic mapping of the sort in Figure 37.1 can determine the meaning of absolutely any general or universal proposition. This holds for any general proposition whatever.

Thus we have established the generalizability perfection of true narrative representations.

The Upshot of the Theory: Summing Up and Looking Back

The three pragmatic perfections are summed up in the terms *determinacy* (only true narrative statements are determined relative to particular facts), *connectedness* (only true narrative representations are determinately connected to the material continuum of space and time), and *generalizability* (only true narrative representations provide a sufficient basis to determine the content of general propositions). Based on these perfections and on the empirical consequences that derive from them, it follows that the kind of representations we call experience are exclusively of the true narrative type. In those relatively uncommon instances where we are misled or deceived by what we take for actual experience, the representations that we mistake for perceptions prove out not to be of the true narrative kind. They are illusions, hallucinations, or errors of some other type.

For instance, hallucinations and illusions are special cases where we think things are really being perceived that turn out to be fictions created by our own representational systems. Saying this, in fact, is little more than affirming the common definitions of the terms *illusion* and *hallucination*. Though the border between illusion and hallucination may be fuzzy, illusions are usually construed as fictions that we mistake for valid perceptions in ordinary experience while hallucinations are usually drug-induced fictions or the result of organic malfunctions. Fantasies, imaginings, and other fictions (ones that we willfully indulge in), however, become hallucinations only if we should start believing them, i.e., regarding them in the same way as we do actual experience. Past and present experience, correct and incorrect expectations about future experience, memory, confabulation (the natural mixture of memory with fictional reconstructions), and every conceivable degree of hypothesis or hypothetical reasoning is therefore covered by the theory. In fact, every kind of representation whatever, according to the proofs given above, can only be determined (or defined) relative to true narrative representations. Therefore, each and every case of an illusion or hallucination or

any other form of fiction or fantasy, rather than drawing true cases into question, proves in fact that they must exist and that they are known. If this were not so, illusions and other fictional cases of representation could not be distinguished from true cases at all.

One of the results of all the foregoing is that a Peircean view of abduction (Oller 1989, 1990; Oller et al., 1991) or of *pragmatic mapping* (Oller 1975b, 1983b) describes both the necessary and sufficient conditions for language acquisition, for communication, for becoming literate, and for learning in general. It provides a logical foundation for an explanation of why some methods of language instruction are bound to work better than others. It shows why it is that only a small portion of what passes for language use in many foreign language classrooms, in many basal readers, and in much of what is called "language arts" makes any sense. The theory of pragmatic mapping shows explicitly why grammatical explanations unaccompanied by instantiations grounded in actual experience are next to useless. It tells us precisely why implausible fictions of all sorts are more difficult to process than more plausible ones and why scrambled or otherwise mutilated discourse is more difficult to process than discourse in a more normal arrangement (see Carrell, Chapter 19; Oller et al., Chapter 20; Horiba, Chapter 21; Tudor & Tuffs, Chapter 22; as well as Oller & Jonz, in press). Because of its relative comprehensiveness, the theory of pragmatic mapping provides a suitable basis from which to assess all sorts of hypotheses about language acquisition and language teaching.

No doubt some theoreticians will say that the foregoing argument is overstated. Those who hold to the skeptical view that no comprehensive theory can possibly ever be constructed are obligated by their own theory to say this. In fact, any such skepticism is fatally flawed. It professes to know enough to be able to absolutely prove that nothing whatever can be known for certain. In the meantime, it remains for critics to fault the present logical (purely deductive) argument. If the limits of cognition, one on the material side of experience and the other at the utmost reach of abstract reasoning, are validly defined, as I believe that they are (also see C. S. Peirce and Albert Einstein in Oller, 1989), then the rest follows apodeictically (i.e., with the full force of an axiomatic proof in mathematics). Besides, the theory of pragmatic mapping finds independent theoretical support. Giordano (1983: 34), for example, asserted that "the basis of semiotics [the Peircean science of all signs and representational forms] is pragmatics." On then next page he elaborates: "(1) semiotics should be based on pragmatics and on the study of sign-function; (2) the best key to understanding the sign function is through context and ground; (3) signs are highly complex functions which, far from being mutually exclusive, mix and conflate nature and culture" (p. 35). In addition, John Deely (1983) showed why all cognition (including the affective sociocultural aspect) must be viewed in terms of functional pragmatics. I have merely elaborated a portion of the groundwork for both sets of claims in the logical proofs developed above.

THE RELEVANCE AND NATURE OF EVERYDAY TRUTH

The pragmatic mapping process clarifies a particular version of the correspondence theory of truth—the one that lay persons everywhere more or less subscribe to—and it shows how that theory provides the basis for communication, language acquisition, literacy, and all kinds of social organization known as culture, society, law, education, and so forth. A true proposition is one that corresponds faithfully in its form to the form of the fact(s) that it represents. As such, therefore, in keeping with Peircean theory, truth is a property, strictly speaking, not of facts *per se* but of true representations of facts. This last result is not one that lay persons are apt to subscribe to because, for the most part, common sense is unaware that it knows facts only through representations. Lay persons are more apt to argue from common sense that facts are merely facts, and that things are just what they seem to be. Their position is a little bit naive, but only a little, inasmuch as errors, hallucinations, illusions, and the like require that we recognize the level of representations as distinct from the level of objects in the material world. But the association of truth only with representations and not with concrete objects or states of affairs is absolute. Since any interpretation of any representation is itself only another representation of a particular fact (or facts), truth is exclusively a property of representations and never of facts *per se* (things, objects, concrete situations).

TRUE NARRATIVE REPRESENTATIONS AND SOCIAL EXISTENCE

One of the far-reaching consequences of truth being connected only with representations is that the very possibility of cognition, communication, culture, society, and social existence of any known or knowable kind is entirely dependent on true cases in the sense elaborated earlier in this chapter. That is, if a sign is to have any determinate meaning whatever, it follows from the first pragmatic perfection (determinacy) in concert with the third (generalizability) that the determinate meaning in question can only be grounded in true narrative representations. At least, those representations must be relatively true. That is, they are true relative to what is truly known of some particular fact or constellation of facts. As a result, every cultural or communal manifestation of society, wherever it may be found, is entirely dependent on the narrative aspect of ordinary experience.

In fact, experience is a kind of true narrative representation, and it naturally forms the backbone (by virtue of the three pragmatic perfections given above) of all faithful representations of any sort—linguistic, gestural, paralinguistic, sensory-motor, visceral, musical, artistic, mathematical, or affective. Therefore, the shared meanings that constitute a community, culture, or society are completely dependent upon the sort of true narrative representations that undergird the meaningfulness of all experience. If a sign were just a sign and exactly no more, as Sebeok (1991) says in his title, *A Sign Is Just a Sign,* how is it possible for a reader to think of the tune, as I recently did, to the song from *Casablanca,* "As Time Goes By," before ever opening the cover of Sebeok's book? (His point, in part, was to parody the lyric "A sigh is just a sigh.") And, if a sign were only that and nothing more, how could the sign point any reader correctly to the song, the movie, prior viewings of the film, the love affair between Rick and Ilsa (in the story), the Second World War (the setting of the story), the persecution of the Jews by the

Nazis, the war itself and the parts played by the French, English, and Americans, the reader's own romantic experiences, and all the rest of the experiential facts to which the sign relates? Or how would the actual lyric of the song alluded to, "A sigh is just a sigh," come to mind with the very melody that I correctly applied by inference to Sebeok's enigmatic title? Or how would it be possible for Sebeok to make so much hay from just a few straws? A quotation from Rick to Ilsa in Sebeok's dedication of the book to his wife, Jean Umiker-Sebeok, a statement from Laszlo to Rick on the title page, and the title of the song which forms the opening phrase of Sebeok's Introduction, where he writes "As time goes by . . ." (p. 1).

The Something More: Material Reality

It soon comes out that Sebeok intends to use the relatively common knowledge of the fictional story of Rick and Ilsa as portrayed by Humphrey Bogart and Ingrid Bergman to give us a glimpse of his (Sebeok's) interpretation of Peircean semiotics (the theory of representations). But Peirce argued that "a sign is something, A, which demotes some fact or object, B, to some interpretant thought, C" (1903: 177). Now if only the sign existed, and nothing else, according to Peirce the sign itself would be disqualified as such. It wouldn't even be a sign. There must be something more than just the sign itself. That something more is the "fact or object" which is conceived of via the sign. Moreover, Peirce insisted that both the conceiving and its object were very real (1903b). He defined reality as whatever remains unchanged by however we may represent it to be.[5] For instance, if I say that *Casablanca* is a film about a story that supposedly takes place in the town by the same name in North Africa during World War II, my statement fits the facts. However, I might as easily say, something different, e.g., that Casablanca is a town in Latin America, or that it is the name of a new Korean-made luxury car, or that it is a word of unknown meaning probably from the language Quang. Regardless what I say, the real Casablanca is unaffected. Now, that reality which remains unaffected by however we might represent it to be (according to Peirce) forms the only satisfactory

basis for the existence of any common knowledge (or any conflict about that common knowledge) whatever. Remove that independent reality, and the very possibility of communication (along with any disagreement, confusion, ignorance, or illusion) will evaporate more quickly and more completely than a drop of water in the Sahara desert. It will absolutely not only disappear from view but will altogether cease to exist.

Concerning the possibility of finding a consistent skepticism about an external world of things and forms beyond mere representations of them, Peirce (1865a: 257) argued his case as follows. Concerning the existence of representations, first off, it is impossible to maintain any sort of consistent doubt because the doubt itself is a form of representation, and if a representation denies its own existence, it is a blatant self-contradiction. There cannot be any consistency in such a view. But the situation is different with respect to things (that is, material objects and their states of affairs in experience, e.g., a particular instance of a certain make of car such as the white 1991 Acura Integra parked in my garage). It is also different with respect to the abstract forms of those things (i.e., their underlying conceptual character, e.g., that which is common to all cars similar to the one parked in my garage). As we saw in proof (3) above, we only know universal abstract forms and particular concrete objects through representations. However, Peirce contends that it is not possible to introduce anything false into our understanding by supposing that both the car (that is, the physical thing with wheels, etc.) *and* its peculiar abstract attributes (its abstract form) *really* exist because both are known only relative to representations of them.

I cannot, for example, present the material white Acura to you here on this page. For one thing, it wouldn't fit. Yet, assuming that you are reading this book and know English, it's a good bet that you know very well what sort of object I am referring to and, supposing that you believe I have one in my garage, you would be correct in supposing that I own it or am paying off the bank that does. As Peirce concludes, "since all that we know of [things and forms] we know through representations, if our representations be consistent they have all the truth that the case admits of" (1865a: 257). In our thought, therefore, all representations answer ultimately only to other representations though things and forms answer exclusively to representations. In this much Peirce and Sebeok agree—a sign is only related to other signs. However, the representations of things and forms in the material world enjoy a special privileged status, for all the reasons outlined in the proofs given above. That is, some signs are signs of things and forms of experience whose existence we cannot reasonably doubt. Concerning the proofs related to this conclusion, I feel reasonably certain that Peirce would not have disagreed in any essential way.

NARRATIVE DISCOURSE AS THE BASIS

At any rate, this book has been developed on the basis of the theory explained in this chapter, especially the three proofs given above. On that basis, it is hypothesized that language acquisition in its normative, social, communal aspect as well as in its cognitive aspect can only prosper in contexts where the learner has access to the common experiences (the narrative sort of discourses) that constitute the target language community. Access to such experiences can be had in a variety of ways. Sensory-motor representations can be had directly by living in the target culture. These will be of two main kinds: (1) impressions of the linguistic forms of the target language as uttered, signed, or written down, and (2) impressions of the material contexts where the linguistic forms are observed. Similar kinds of representations can also be known through films and video and audio recordings. Even still pictures, artifacts, architecture, cuisine, dress, and the like offer a kind of vicarious and indirect access to the culture of a target language. Linguistic representations in a language known to the learner (other than the target language) may provide access to some of the narrative basis of the target language community.

For instance, we are apt to learn something of Spanish culture by reading a translation of *Don Quixote* by Cervantes. We could (with effort) even learn a great deal of the language by studying carefully the translation in English, say, alongside the original in Spanish. However, the *sine qua non* of language acquisition is the pragmatic mapping of surface forms of the target language (as they are

perceived and produced) onto the actual ongoing experience of the learner. This is as true for adults as it is for children. The difference is that adults have a richer representational repertoire of instantiated concepts and of ways of representing them and linking them to experience than children do. Because of the greater resources available to them, adults are in many respects superior learners (see Swain & Lapkin 1989; Genesee et al., 1989). Otherwise, the process of pragmatic mapping is similar for children and adults.

ON COMPREHENSIVENESS

In striving, by their lights, toward the unreachable goal of a comprehensive theory of language acquisition, some theoreticians (e.g., Spolsky, 1989) contend that we need to specify any and all of the motivational, social, political, and economic factors and all of their interactions as they impinge on the process of language acquisition. On this account Spolsky has come up with a list of about 74 factors which he thinks are, in some interactive fashion, responsible for second language acquisition. Of course, Spolsky does a service by showing that a rich constellation of factors impact language acquisition to some degree, but to call a list of hypothetical possibilities a comprehensive theory, or to suggest that it might someday be turned into one, is to fall into a deep confusion. Logical reflection shows that any taxonomy of tenuously related research objectives of the type Spolsky discusses is doomed by its very nature to remain forever uncomprehensive. Nor is such a tendentious list relevant to the implication that a comprehensive theory is necessarily out of reach. On the contrary, I believe that what is required is the sort of approach urged by C. S. Peirce: to begin with what we have no reasonable basis for doubting and to add nothing that we cannot show to be necessary (1865b: 340).

THE TEACHER AS CHIEF NEGOTIATOR

We teachers, all of us, know that we have a responsibility to find out what works and to seek out the best available information from theory, research, and practice in order to use it. We cannot abdicate that responsibility (as Kalivoda et al. made clear in Chapter 3). As Long (1985; also Long & Seliger, 1983), Richards (1974), and others have been pointing out for years (even Oller & Richards, 1973: vi), teachers in the classroom have access to a brand of empirical (research) evidence that has a high degree of validity independently of confirmation by any other evidence from any other source or any other observer. The teacher is in a *very* good position, generally a better position than anyone outside the classroom, to determine what works there in that kind of context. As a result, just as M. A. Clarke (1989, 1992) has persuasively argued, the teacher rightly maintains a high degree of autonomy and independent responsibility for whatever takes place in the classroom. And, of course, in arguing the case for teacher autonomy, Clarke is one of the first to note that students too must not be denied some of the same responsibility for initiative in determining what happens in the classroom. As Little and Sanders (1989) have pointed out, communication in the classroom presupposes a community that actually assumes responsibility for negotiating meanings. As a result, the teacher shares responsibility with the students, aides, the school administration, and the community at large, but the teacher remains the chief negotiator of meaning in the classroom. Teachers can share that burden with others, but carrying the brunt of the load is what makes us the teachers. It's also what we get paid for, even if we're underpaid. (And I, for one, admit that in a monetary way, at least, teachers surely are underpaid.) Fortunately, the negotiation of meanings in that wonderful process of communication (see Dewey, 1926: 265) has a value in itself that money can't buy. That's why many of us would rather be teachers than anything else. Teaching is more than a vocation, more than a profession, more than a passion—it's a calling.

THEORY AND PRACTICE

In the previous edition, Richard-Amato and I said that there is nothing more practical than a really good theory (except, of course, a better theory). The converse is also true. There is no theory that can improve much on the sort that is displayed in a method that works well (except for a method that works better). Really good practice is really good theory. Research is nothing more than finding a method to test a theory. And a theory that cannot be tested by translating it into a method is a useless theory in the first place. It ought to be called confusion, superstition, or supererogation—but not theory. Untestable hypothetical propositions strung together in endless profusion do not constitute a theory. Figuring out how to test a theory requires putting it into practice via some method that works, and, conversely, explaining how and why a given method works is the main job of theory construction. In fact, as Dewey argued long ago, the experimental connection between theory and practice—i.e., the method (an experiential or experimental application)—is "the only guarantee for the sanity of the theorist" (1916: 442).

In the meantime, no one really doubts that motivation, sociocultural context, political and economic factors, etc., are of great importance to the large picture. Even in individual cases such facts are likely to have some non-negligible impact. However, on the basis of the theory of pragmatic mapping (as argued above), it can be shown that all such factors are subordinate to the necessary and sufficient condition that the theory of pragmatic mapping defines. Suppose, for instance, a learner is put in a position where successful pragmatic mappings of the sort described throughout this chapter occur frequently and over an extended period of time in the target language. It will matter little whether that learner actually is highly motivated or relatively unmotivated, whether the learner has a high or low anxiety level, whether the motivation is integrative or instrumental, whether the language is one of a power group or an oppressed minority (see Walker et al., 1992 and Chapter 17, this volume), whether the learner comes from a low or high economic status, whether the learner knows more than one language or not, whether the target language is from the Indo-European stock or some other stock, whether the learner speaks English or Chinese, or is an adult or a child, well educated or not, literate or illiterate, etc. All such factors may influence the overall picture of language acquisition in all sorts of settings to some non-negligible degree, but they will amount to relatively little in comparison to sustained success in the process of pragmatic mapping, which is the *sine qua non*—a necessary and a sufficient condition—for comprehension, communication, language acquisition, and language teaching methods that work.

NOTES

1 Some might prefer for us to call the sort of representations depicted in Figure 37.1 "narrative-*type* representations" because, unlike true narratives, they may not tell the whole story. But the term *narrative representations* stands best without the adjustment because any true narrative whatever suffers from the same defect—if indeed it is a defect to leave out more than we actually code in words, or to always notice less than we actually experience. It remains true that every true representation humans are capable of producing is an abbreviation for a much richer conceptualization and that every story about spatio-temporal experience begins *in medias res*.

2 I must interrupt the argument at this juncture to point out that I am not saying that true narrative representations are perfectly determinate. That would be a false claim. What I am saying is that compared to all other kinds of representations, true narrative statements are *relatively* perfect. That is, they have a kind of completeness that is missing or defective in all other kinds of representations. This last claim is proved below. The point here is merely to remind the reader that none of the logical advantages of true narrative statements is claimed to be perfect (i.e., completely) in any absolute sense. Rather, they are relatively more perfect in these respects than absolutely any other kind of representations.

3 It must be noted here that exclamations, imperatives, and questions are generally judged to be neither true nor false. However, to the extent that such utterances have any appropriateness at all to the situations in which they are uttered, their appropriateness, it turns out, is precisely of the true narrative sort. For instance, an exclamation such as "Oh no!" in response to an accident suggests that something undesirable is happening. To the extent that the exclamation is appropriate to the occasion and actually reveals the sentiments of the utterer, it is of the true narrative type. An imperative can only have the force of an imperative to the extent that the utterer has the power and authority to issue such an imperative to the person(s) addressed. Further, every interpretable imperative can always be paraphrased into a declarative such as "I order you to do such and such" and to the extent that the deictic elements "I" and "you" are appropriately related to the first and second persons involved, they are related in the manner of true narrative representations to their objects. In fact, even the predication in the imperative form remains nothing but an abstract possibility until and unless the command is carried out by the appropriate act, in which case the predication corresponds to the act performed exactly in the manner of a true narrative representation of that act.

4 The reader is asked to keep in mind that only a "relative" perfection or degeneracy is at issue. Nowhere in the argument do we refer to absolute perfection—except perhaps by implication.

5 A definition, incidentally, which is altogether unaffected by the Heisenberg uncertainty principle (see Oller, 1990).

DISCUSSION QUESTIONS

1. What are some of the obvious differences between material objects and abstract ideas or representations of them?

2. If a true narrative representation (e.g., "Stephen went to school today while Mom was at work and Ruth Marie stayed home with Dad") can be used as a standard of relative "perfection," in what specific ways are fictions, falsehoods, and undetermined generalizations relatively "degenerate"?

3. In the final analysis, why is it a good idea all around to base foreign language instruction, the teaching of reading, and, in fact, education in general on true narrative discourse, or at least on discourse that resembles that of the true narrative type?

REFERENCES

Adams, J. J., & Bruce, B. (1980). *Background knowledge and reading comprehension*. Reading Education Report No. 13. Champaign, IL: Center for the Study of Reading, University of Illinois Press.

Adams, M. J. (1980). Failures to comprehend and levels of processing in reading. In Spiro, Bruce, & Brewer (1980: 12–32).

Adams, M. J., & Collins, A. (1979). A schema-theoretic view of reading. In Freedle (1979: 1–22).

Adams, S. (1982). Scripts and recognition of unfamiliar vocabulary: Enhancing second language reading skills. *Modern Language Journal, 66,* 155–159. Also in Oller & Richard-Amato (1983: 375–382).

Ahmad, K., Corbett, G., Rogers, M., & Sussex, R. (1985). *Computers, language learning, and language teaching*. New York: Cambridge University Press.

Alatis, J. E. (Ed.) (1978). *Georgetown University Round Table on Languages and Linguistics 1978: International dimensions of bilingual education*. Washington, DC: Georgetown University Press.

Alatis, J. E. (Ed.) (1989). *Georgetown University Round Table on Languages and Linguistics 1989*. Washington, DC: Georgetown University Press.

Alatis, J. E. (Ed.) (1990). *Georgetown University Round Table on Languages and Linguistics 1990: Linguistics, language teaching, and language acquisition: The interdependence of theory, practice, and research*. Washington, DC: Georgetown University Press.

Alatis, J. E. (Ed.) (1991). *Georgetown University Round Table on Languages and Linguistics 1991*. Washington, DC: Georgetown University Press.

Alderson, J. C. (1979a). The cloze procedure and proficiency in English as a second language. *TESOL Quarterly, 13,* 219–227. Reprinted in Oller (1983: 205–218).

Alderson, J. C. (1979b). The effect on the cloze test of changes in deletion frequency. *Journal of Research in Reading, 2,* 108–119.

Alderson, J. C. (1980). Native and non-native performance on cloze. *Language Learning, 30*(2), 159–176.

Alderson, J. C. (1990, April). Language testing in the 1990s: How far have we come? How much further have we to go? In S. Anivan (Ed.) (1991), *Current developments in language testing* (pp. 1–26). Singapore: SEAMEO Regional Language Center.

Alderson, J. C., & Urquhart, A. (1983). "This test is unfair. I'm not an economist." Paper presented at the 1983 TESOL Convention, Toronto, Canada. Also in P. Hauptman, R. Leblanc, & M. B. Wesche (Eds.), *Second language performance testing* (pp. 25–43). Ottawa, Ontario: University of Ottawa Press.

Allen, J. P. B., Carroll, S., Burtis, J., & Gaudino, V. (1987). The core French observation study. In J. P. B. Allen, J. Cummins, B. Harley, & M. Swain (Eds.), *The development of bilingual proficiency* (Vol. 2, pp. 56–189). Toronto: Modern Language Center, Ontario Institute for Studies in Education.

Allwright, R. L. (1978). Abdication and responsibility in language teaching. *Studies in Second Language Acquisition, 2*(1), 105–121.

Allwright, R. L. (1981). What do we want teaching materials for? *ELT Journal, 36*(1), 5–18.

Almanza, H., & Mosley, W. (1980). Curriculum adaptations and modifications for culturally diverse handicapped children. *Exceptional Children, 47,* 608–614.

Altman, H. (1989). *The video connection: Integrating video into language teaching*. Boston: Houghton Mifflin.

Altus, G. (1953). WISC patterns of a selective sample of bilingual school children. *Journal of Genetic Psychology, 83,* 241–248.

Andersen E., Dunlea, A., & Kekelis, L. (1984). Blind children's language: Resolving some differences. *Journal of Child Language, 11,* 645–664.

Anderson, J. R., Eisenberg, N., Holland, J., Wiener, H. S., & Rivers-Kron, C. (1983). *Integrated skills reinforcement: Reading, writing, speaking, and listening across the curriculum*. New York: Longman.

Anderson, R. C., & Pearson, D. C. (1984). A schema-theoretic view of basic processes in reading comprehension. In P. D. Pearson & M. L. Kamil (Eds.),

Handbook of reading research (pp. 255–290). New York: Longman.

Anthony, E. M. (1963). Approach, method, and technique. *English Language Teaching, 17,* 63–67.

Anthony, E. M., & Norris, W. E. (1969). *Method in language teaching.* ERIC focus report on teaching of foreign languages No. 8. New York: Modern Language Association of America. (ERIC Document Reproduction Service No. ED 031 984)

Arevart, S. (1989). Grammatical change through repetition. *RELC Journal, 20*(2), 42–60.

Arevart, S., & Nation, P. (1991). Fluency improvement in a second language. *RELC Journal, 22*(1), 84–94.

Aristotle. (1952). On poetics (I. Bywater, Trans.). In R. M. Hutchins (Ed.), *Great books of the western world. Vol. 9* (pp. 681–699). Chicago: Encyclopaedia Britannica.

Aron, H. (1986). The influence of background and knowledge on memory for reading passages by native and non-native readers. *TESOL Quarterly, 20*(1), 136–140.

Asher, J. J. (1964). Toward a neo-field theory of behavior. *Journal of Humanistic Psychology, 4,* 85–94.

Asher, J. J. (1965). The strategy of the total physical response: An application to learning Russian. *International Review of Applied Linguistics, 3,* 291–300.

Asher, J. J. (1966). The learning strategy of the total physical response: A review. *Modern Language Journal, 50,* 79–84.

Asher, J. J. (1969a). The total physical response approach to second language learning. *Modern Language Journal, 53,* 3–17.

Asher, J. J. (1969b). The total physical response technique of learning. *Journal of Special Education, 3,* 253–262.

Asher, J. J. (1972). Children's first language as a model for second language learning. *Modern Language Journal, 56,* 133–139.

Asher, J. J. (1979). *Learning another language through actions: The complete teacher's guidebook.* Los Gatos, CA: Sky Oaks Productions.

Asher, J. J. (1982–1988). *Learning another language through actions: The complete teacher's guidebook* (revised eds.). Los Gatos, CA: Sky Oaks Productions.

Asher, J. J. (1983). Motivating children and adults to acquire a second language. In Oller & Richard-Amato (1983: 329–336).

Asher, J. J. (in press). Brain-compatible instruction for stress-free learning of second languages, mathematics, and science. In R. J. Pellegrini & S. J. Meyers (Eds.), *Psychology for correctional education: Facilitating human development in prison and court school settings* (pp. 149–164). Springfield, IL: Charles C. Thomas.

Asher, J. J., & Garcia, R. (1969). The optimal age to learn a foreign language. *Modern Language Journal, 53,* 334–341.

Asher, J. J., Kusudo, J., & de la Torre, R. (1974). Learning a second language through commands. *Modern Language Journal, 58,* 24–32. (Reprinted in this volume as Chapter 2.)

Asher, J. J., & Price, B. S. (1967). The learning strategy of the total physical response: Some age differences. *Child Development, 38,* 1219–1227.

Atwell, N. (1987). *In the middle: Writing, reading, and learning with adolescents.* Portsmouth, NH: Heinemann.

Ausubel, D. P. (1968). *Educational psychology: A cognitive view.* New York: Grune and Stratton.

Ausubel, D. P., Novak, J. D., & Hanesian, H. (1978). *Educational psychology.* New York: Holt, Rinehart, & Winston.

Bachman, L. F. (1985). Performance on cloze tests with fixed ratio and rational deletions. *TESOL Quarterly, 19*(3), 535–555.

Bachman, L. F. (1990). *Fundamental considerations in language testing.* Oxford: Oxford University Press.

Bacon, R. M., & Schleipman, R. (1977). The thunder and lightning professor. *Yankee Magazine,* September, 108–113, 200–202, 205.

Baker, K., & de Kanter, A. (1983). *Federal policy and the effectiveness of bilingual education.* Lexington, MA: Lexington Books.

Ballman, T. L. (1988). Is group work better than individual work for learning Spanish? *Hispania, 71,* 180–185.

Baolin, M. (1987). Teaching language by using theater. *Beijing Review, 30*(29), I–III.

Barik, H., & Swain, M. (1978). *Evaluation of a bilingual education program in Canada: The Elgin study through grade six.* Paper presented at the Colloquium of the Swiss Interuniversity Commission for Applied Linguistics. (ERIC Document Reproduction Service No. ED 174 073)

Barik, H., Swain, M., & Nwanunobi, E. (1977). English-French bilingual education: The Elgin study through grade five. *Canadian Modern Language Review, 33,* 459–475.

Barnett, M. A. (1983). Replacing teacher talk with gestures: Nonverbal communication in the foreign language classroom. *Foreign Language Annals, 16,* 173–176.

Barnitz, J. C. (1986). Toward understanding the effects of cross-cultural schemata and discourse structure on second language reading comprehension. *Journal of Reading Behavior, 18*(2), 95–116.

Barona, A., & Barona, M. (1987). A model for the assessment of limited-English-proficient students referred for special education services. In S. Fradd & W. Tikunoff (Eds.), *Bilingual education and bilingual special education: A guide for administrators* (pp. 183–210). Boston: College-Hill Press.

Barrett. T. C. (1972). Taxonomy of reading comprehension. *Reading 360 Monograph.* Lexington, MA: Ginn.

Bartlett, F. C. (1932). *Remembering: A study in experimental and social psychology.* Cambridge: Cambridge University Press.

Barzun, J. (1961). *The delights of detection.* New York: Criterion.

Bashir, A. (1989). Language intervention and the curriculum. *Seminars in Speech and Language, 10,* 181–191.

Becker, W., & Gersten, R. (1982). A follow-up of follow through: The later effects of the direct instruction model on children in the fifth and sixth grades. *American Educational Research Journal, 19,* 7–92.

Beed, P., Hawkins, E., & Roller, C. (1991). Moving learners toward independence: The power of scaffold instruction. *The Reading Teacher, 44,* 648–655.

Belasco, S. (1971). The feasibility of learning a second language in an artificial unicultural situation. In Pimsleur & Quinn (1971: 1–10).

Belasco, S. (1981). "Aital cal aprene las lengas estrangieras." In Winitz (1981: 14–33).

Beretta, A. (1986). Program-fair language teaching evaluation. *TESOL Quarterly, 20,* 431–434.

Berkowitz, P. A. (1982). Foreign language: The university's sleeping giant. *Canadian Modern Language Review, 38,* 311–314.

Bernhardt, E. B. (1983a). *Text processing strategies of native, non-native experienced, and non-native inexperienced readers of German: Findings and implications for the instruction of German as a foreign language.* Unpublished doctoral dissertation, University of Minnesota.

Bernhardt, E. B. (1983b). Three approaches to reading comprehension in intermediate German. *Modern Language Journal, 67,* 111–115.

Bernhardt, E. B. (1984). Toward an informational processing perspective in foreign language reading. *Modern Language Journal, 68,* 322–331.

Beutler, S. (1976). *Practicing language arts skills using drama.* Report prepared at Bryant Community School, Ann Arbor, Michigan. (ERIC Document Reproduction Service No. ED 136 295)

Bever, T. G. (1970). The cognitive basis for linguistic structures. In J. R. Hayes (Ed.), *Cognition and the Development of Language* (pp. 288–331). New York: Wiley.

Bigelow, A. (1987). Early words in blind children. *Journal of Child Language 14,* 47–56.

Billard, Y., Dequeker-Fergon, J-M., Lepagnot, C., & Lepagnot, F. (1986). *Journal historique de la France.* Paris: Hatier.

Billman, C. (1986). *The secret of the Stratemeyer Syndicate.* New York: Ungar.

Birdwhistell, R. L. (1970). *Kinesics and context: Essays on body-motion communication.* Philadelphia: University of Pennsylvania Press.

Birkmaier, E. M. (1960). Modern languages. In C. W. Harris (Ed.), *Encyclopedia of educational research* (3rd ed., pp. 861–888). New York: Macmillan.

Birkmaier, E. M. (1963). Extending the audio-lingual approach: Some psychological aspects. *International Journal of American Linguistics, 32,* 122–138.

Black, J. B., & Bower, G. H. (1980). Story understanding as problem solving. *Poetics, 9,* 223–250.

Blackwell, P., & Fischgrund, J. (1985). Issues in the development of culturally responsive programs for Deaf students from non-English speaking homes. In G. Delgado (1985: 154–166).

Blair, R. W. (Ed.) (1982). *Innovative approaches to language teaching.* Rowley, MA: Newbury House.

Blatner, H. (1973). *Acting-in: Practical applications of psychodramatic methods.* New York: Springer.

Bloom, B. S. (1956). *Taxonomy of educational objectives, handbook I: Cognitive domain*. New York: David McKay.

Bobrow, D., & Collins, A. (Eds.) (1975). *Representation and understanding*. New York: Academic Press.

Boeckmann, K., Nessmann, K., & Petermandl, M. (1988). Effects of formal features in educational video programs on recall. *Journal of Educational Television, 14*(2), 107–122.

Bolen, D. (1981). Issues relating to language choice: Hearing-impaired infants from bilingual homes. *The Volta Review, 83,* 410–412.

Bortnick, R., & Lopardo, G. S. (1973). An instructional application of the cloze procedure. *Journal of Reading, 16*(4), 296–300.

Bovair, S., & Kieras, D. E. (1985). A guide to propositional analysis for research on technical prose. In B. K. Britton & J. B. Black (Eds.), *Understanding expository text* (pp. 315–362). Hillsdale, NJ: Lawrence Erlbaum.

Bower, G. H. (1978). Experiments on story comprehension and recall. *Discourse Processes, 1,* 211–231.

Boyle, O., & Peregoy, S. (1990). Literacy scaffolds: Strategies for first- and second-language readers and writers. *The Reading Teacher, 44,* 194–199.

Bransford, J., & Johnson, M. (1972). Contextual prerequisites for understanding: Some investigations of comprehension and recall. *Journal of Verbal Learning and Verbal Behavior, 11,* 717–726.

Brault, G. J. (1963). Kinesics and the classroom: Some typical French gestures. *French Review, 36,* 374–382.

Brinton, B., & Fujiki, M. (1989). *Conversational management with language-impaired children*. Rockville, MD: Aspen.

Brinton, D., Snow, M. A., & Wesche, M. (1989). *Content-based approaches to second language teaching*. New York: Newbury House.

Brodkey, D. (1972). Dictation as a measure of mutual intelligibility: A pilot study. *Language Learning, 22,* 203–220.

Brown, A. L., & Murphy, M. D. (1975). Reconstruction of arbitrary versus logical sequences by preschool children. *Journal of Experimental Child Psychology, 20,* 307–326.

Brown, G., Anderson, A., Shillcock, R., & Yule, G. (1984). *Teaching talk*. Cambridge: Cambridge University Press.

Brown, H. D. (1980). *Principles of language learning and teaching*. Englewood Cliffs, NJ: Prentice Hall.

Brown, R. A. (1973). *A first language*. Cambridge, MA: Harvard University Press.

Bruck, M. (1982). Language disabled children: Performance in an additive bilingual education program. *Applied Psycholinguistics, 3,* 39–61.

Bruck, M. (1985a). Consequences of transfer out of early immersion programs. *Applied Psycholinguistics, 6,* 101–120.

Bruck, M. (1985b). Feasibility of an additive bilingual program for the language impaired child. In Paradis & Lebrun (1985: 69–93).

Bruck, M. (1987). The suitability of early French immersion programs for the language disabled child. *Canadian Journal of Education, 3,* 51–72.

Bruck, M., Lambert, W., & Tucker, G. R. (1977). Cognitive consequences of bilingual schooling: The St. Lambert Project through grade six. *Psycholinguistics, 6,* 13–33.

Bruck, M., Tucker, G. R., & Jakimik, J. (1985). Are French immersion programs suitable for working-class children? *Word, 27,* 311–341.

Brumfit, C. J. (1979). "Communicative" language teaching: An educational perspective. In Brumfit & Johnson (1979: 183–191).

Brumfit, C. J., & Johnson, K. (Eds.) (1979). *The communicative approach to language teaching*. Oxford: Oxford University Press.

Bruner, J. (1978). The role of dialogue in language acquisition. In A. Sinclair, R. J. Jarvella, W. J. Levelt (Eds.), *The child's conception of language*. New York: Verlag, 1978.

Buch, G., & de Bagheera, I. (1978). An immersion program for the professional improvement of non-native teachers of ESL. In C. Blatchford & J. Schachter (Eds.), *On TESOL '78* (pp. 106–117). Washington, DC: TESOL.

Bugos, T. J. (1980). Defending the foreign language requirement in the liberal arts curriculum. *Foreign Language Annals, 13*(4), 301–306.

Bullock Report. (1975). *A language for life*. Report of the Committee of Inquiry appointed by the Secretary of State for Education and Science under the chairmanship of Sir Alan Bullock. London: HMSO.

Burgoon, J. K., Burgoon, D., & Woodall, W. G. (1989). *Nonverbal communication: The unspoken dialogue*. New York: Harper & Row.

Burks, A. W. (Ed.) (1958). *Collected writings of C. S. Peirce*, Volumes VII and VIII. Cambridge, MA: Harvard University Press.

Burnett, D. G., & Robinson, F. B. (1985). Foreign languages and international studies: A consortial approach to institutional development. *ADFL Bulletin, 17*, 9–13.

Burt, M., & Dulay, H. (Eds.) (1975). *New directions in second language learning, teaching, and bilingual education*. Washington, DC: TESOL.

Burt, M., Dulay, H., & Finocchiaro, M. (Eds.) (1977). *Viewpoints on English as a second language*. New York: Regents.

Burtoff, M. (1983). Organizational patterns of expository prose: A comparative study of native Arabic. Paper presented at the 1983 TESOL Convention, Toronto, Canada.

Bushman, R., & Madsen, H. (1976). A description and evaluation of Suggestopedia—a new teaching methodology. In J. Fanselow & R. Crymes (Eds.), *On TESOL '76* (pp. 29–38). Washington, DC: TESOL.

Butterfield, T., & Sieveking, A. (1989). *Drama through language through drama*. Banbury, England: Kemble Press.

Butterworth, B., & Beattie, G. W. (1978). Gesture and silence as indicators of planning of speech. In R. Campbell & P. Smith (Eds.), *Recent advances in the psychology of language: Abnormal and experimental approaches* (pp. 347–369). New York: Plenum.

Byrd, Charles W., Jr. (1980). Intensive language instruction at a small liberal arts college: The Dartmouth model at Emory and Henry. *Modern Language Journal, 64*, 297–302.

Byrnes, H. (1984). The role of listening comprehension: A theoretical base. *Foreign Language Annals, 17*, 317–348.

Byrnes, H. (1985). Teaching toward proficiency: The receptive skills. In A. C. Omaggio (Ed.), *Proficiency, curriculum, articulation: The ties that bind* (pp. 77–108). Middlebury, VT: Northeast Conference on Teaching Foreign Languages.

Cabello, F. (1983). *Total physical response in first year Spanish*. Los Gatos, CA: Sky Oaks Productions.

California State Department of Education (1984). *Studies on immersion education: A collection for United States educators*. Sacramento, CA: California Office of Bilingual/Bicultural Education.

California State Department of Education (1986). *Beyond language: Social and cultural factors in schooling language minority students*. Sacramento, CA: California State Department of Education. (ERIC Document Reproduction Service No. ED 1.31012 304 241)

Calkins, L. (1983). *Lessons from a child: On the teaching and learning of writing*. Exeter, NH: Heinemann.

Calkins, L. (1986). *The art of teaching writing*. Portsmouth, NH: Heinemann.

Campbell, R. N. (1984). The immersion education approach to foreign language teaching. *Studies on immersion education: A collection for U.S. educators*. Sacramento, CA: California State Department of Education.

Campbell, R. N., Gray, T., Rhodes, N., & Snow, M. (1985). Foreign language learning in the elementary schools: A comparison of three language programs. *Modern Language Journal, 69*(1), 44–54.

Canterfold, B. (1991). The "new" teacher: Participant and facilitator. *Language Arts, 68*, 286–291.

Cantoni-Harvey, G. (1987). *Content-area language instruction: Approaches and strategies*. Reading, MA: Addison-Wesley, 1987.

Caplan, D. (1976). Clause boundaries and recognition latencies for words in sentences. *Perception and Psychophysics, 12*, 73–76.

Carels, P. E. (1981). Pantomime in the foreign language classroom. *Foreign Language Annals, 14*, 407–411.

Carey, S. T. (1984). Reflections on a decade of French immersion. *Canadian Modern Language Review, 41*, 246–259.

Carpenter, J. A., & Torney, J. V. (1974). Beyond the melting pot. In P. M. Markun (Ed.), *Childhood and intercultural education: Overview and research* (pp. 14–23). Washington, DC: Association for Childhood Education International.

Carrell, P. L. (1981). Culture-specific schemata in L2 comprehension. In R. Orem & J. Haskell (Eds.), *Selected papers from the Ninth Illinois TESOL/BE Annual Convention, First Midwest TESOL Conference* (pp. 123–132). Chicago: Illinois TESOL/BE.

Carrell, P. L. (1983a). Some issues in studying the role of schemata, or background knowledge, in second language comprehension. *Reading in a Foreign Language, 33*, 183–207.

Carrell, P. L. (1983b). Three components of background knowledge in reading comprehension. *Language Learning, 33*, 183–207.

Carrell, P. L. (1983c, November). The effects of rhetorical organization on EFL/ESL readers. Paper presented at the Second Language Research Forum, at the University of Southern California, Los Angeles.

Carrell, P. L. (1984). The effects of rhetorical organization on ESL readers. *TESOL Quarterly, 18*(3), 441–489.

Carrell, P. L. (1985). Facilitating ESL reading by teaching text structure. *TESOL Quarterly, 19*(4), 727–752.

Carrell, P. L. (1987). Content and formal schemata in ESL reading. *TESOL Quarterly, 21*(3), 467–481.

Carrell, P. L., & Eisterhold, J. C. (1983). Schema theory and ESL reading pedagogy. *TESOL Quarterly, 17,* 535–552.

Carrell, P. L., & Wallace, B. (1983). Background knowledge: Context and familiarity in reading comprehension. In M. Clarke & J. Handscombe (Eds.), *On TESOL '82.* Washington, DC: TESOL.

Carroll, J. B. (1964). *Language and thought.* Englewood Cliffs, NJ: Prentice Hall.

Carroll, J. B. (1965). New directions in foreign language teaching. *Modern Language Journal, 49,* 273–280.

Carroll, J. B. (1967). Foreign language proficiency levels attained by language majors near graduation from college. *Foreign Language Annals, 1,* 131–151.

Carroll, J. B. (1970, February). Interview. *Modern English Teaching.* Kenkyusha, Tokyo.

Carroll, J. B. (1972). Defining language comprehension: Some speculations. In Freedle & Carroll (1972: 1–29).

Carroll, J. B. (1983). Psychometric theory and language testing. In Oller (1983: 80–107).

Carroll, J. B., & Bever, T. G. (1976). Sentence comprehension: A case study in the relation of knowledge and perception. In E. C. Carterette & M. P. Friedman (Eds.), *Handbook of perception. Volume 7, language and speech* (pp. 299–344). New York: Academic Press.

Carroll, J. B., Carton, A. S., & Wilds, C. P. (1959). An investigation of cloze items in the measurement of achievement in foreign languages. College Entrance Examination Board Research and Development Report. Cambridge, MA: Harvard University Laboratory for Research on Instruction. (ERIC Document Reproduction Service No. ED 106 749)

Casals, P. (1989). *Las aventuras de Héctor.* Barcelona: Editorial Planeta.

Cazden, C. B. (1977). Concentrated versus contrived encounters: Suggestions for language assessment in early childhood education. In A. Davies (Ed.), *Language learning in early childhood* (pp. 40–59). London: Heinemann.

Champagne, R. A. (1978). Responding to the challenge of survival: Multidisciplinary language courses. *Foreign Language Annals, 11,* 81–85.

Chan, K. (1983). Limited English speaking, handicapped, and poor: Triple threat in childhood. In M. Chu-Chang & V. Rodriguez (Eds.), *Asian- and Pacific-American perspectives in bilingual education* (pp. 153–171). New York: Teachers College Press.

Chapelle, C., & Jamieson, J. (1991). Internal and external validity issues in research on CALL effectiveness. In P. Dunkel (Ed.), *Computer-assisted language learning and testing: Research issues and practice* (pp. 37–60). New York: Newbury House.

Chapelle, C., & Roberts, O. (1986). Ambiguity tolerance and field independence as predictors of proficiency in English as a second language. *Language Learning, 36,* 27–45.

Chávez-Oller, M. A., Chihara, T., Weaver, K., & Oller, J. W., Jr. (1985). When are cloze items sensitive to constraints across sentences? *Language Learning, 35,* 281–206.

Cheng, L. (1987). Cross-cultural and linguistic considerations in working with Asian populations. *ASHA, 29,* 33–38.

Chihara, T., Sakurai, T., & Oller, J. W., Jr. (1989). Background and culture as factors in EFL reading comprehension. *Language Testing, 6*(2), 143–151.

Chihara, T., Weaver, K., Oller, J. W., Jr., Chávez-Oller, M. A. (1977). Are cloze items sensitive to constraints across sentences? *Language Learning, 27,* 63–73.

Chinn, P. (1979). The exceptional minority child: Issues and some answers. *Exceptional Children, 46,* 532–536.

Chomsky, N. A. (1982). *Some concepts of the theory of government and binding.* Cambridge, MA: MIT Press.

Chomsky, N. A. (1988). *Language and problems of knowledge: The Managua lectures.* Cambridge, MA: MIT Press.

Christensen, B. (1990). Teenage novels of adventure as a source of authentic material. *Foreign Language Annals, 23*(6), 531–537.

Christensen, K. (1986). Conceptual Sign Language acquisition by Spanish-speaking parents of hearing-impaired children. *American Annals of the Deaf, 131,* 285–287.

Christiansen, T., & Livermore, G. (1970). A comparison of Anglo-American and Spanish-American children on the WISC. *Journal of Social Psychology, 81,* 9–14.

Clark, H. H., & Clark, E. V. (1977). *Psychology and language: An introduction to psycholinguistics.* New York: Harcourt, Brace.

Clarke, D. F. (1989). Materials adaptation: Why leave it all to the teachers? *English Language Teaching Journal, 43*(2), 133–141.

Clarke, M. A. (1989). Negotiating agendas: Preliminary considerations. *Language Arts, 66*(4), 370–380.

Clarke, M. A. (1992, April). Professional development: Exploring alternatives. Paper presented at the Rocky Mountain TESOL Convention in Albuquerque, New Mexico.

Cohen, G., & Freeman, R. (1978). Individual differences in reading strategies in relation to handedness cerebral asymmetry. In J. Requin (Ed.), *Attention and Performance VII* (pp. 411–425). Hillsdale, NJ: Lawrence Erlbaum.

Cole, M., & Bruner, J. (1971). Cultural differences and inferences about psychological processes. *American Psychologist, 26,* 867–876.

Cole, N. (1981). Bias in testing. *American Psychologist, 36,* 1067–1077.

Coleman, E. B. (1963). Approximations to English: Some comments on the method. *American Journal of Psychology, 76,* 239–247.

Coles, G. (1978). The Learning Disabilities Test Battery: Empirical and social issues. *Harvard Educational Review, 48,* 313–340.

Collins, A., Brown, J. S., & Larkin, K. M. (1980). Inference in text understanding. In Spiro, Bruce, & Brewer (1980: 385–410).

Connor, U., & McCagg, P. (1983a). Text structure and ESL learner's reading comprehension. Revised version of a paper presented at the 1982 TESOL Convention, Honolulu.

Connor, U., & McCagg, P. (1983b). Cross-cultural differences and perceived quality in written paraphrases of English expository prose. *Applied Linguistics, 4,* 259–268.

Conti-Ramsden, G., & Friel-Patti, S. (1983). Mothers' discourse adjustments to language impaired and non-language-impaired children. *Journal of Speech and Hearing Disorders, 48,* 360–368.

Cooke, W. (Ed.) (1902). *The table talk and bon-mots of Samuel Foote.* London: Myers & Rogers.

Corder, S. P. (1978). Language-learner language. In Richards (1978: 71–93).

Corsini, R. (1966). *Roleplaying in psychotherapy: A manual.* Chicago: Aldine.

Courchêne, R. J., Glidden, J. I., St. John, J., & Thérien, C. (1992). *L'enseignement des langues secondes axé sur la compréhension.* Ottawa: Les Presses de L'Université d'Ottawa.

Cowper, E. A. (1992). *A concise introduction to syntactic theory: The government and binding approach.* Chicago: University of Chicago Press.

Cramblit, N., & Siegel, G. (1977). The verbal environment of a language-impaired child. *Journal of Speech and Hearing Disorders, 42,* 474–482.

Crandall, J. A. (Ed.) (1987). *ESL through content-area instruction.* Englewood Cliffs, NJ: Prentice Hall Regents.

Crandall, J. A., & Imel, S. (1991). Issues in adult literacy education. *The ERIC Review, 1*(2), 2–6.

Cratty, B. J. (1966). *The perceptual-motor attributes of mentally retarded children and youth.* Monograph. Los Angeles, CA: Mental Retardation Services Board of Los Angeles County.

Cratty, B. J. (1967). *Movement behavior and motor learning* (2nd ed.). Philadelphia: Lea & Febiger.

Cratty, B. J. (1969). *Perception, motion, and thought.* Palo Alto, California: Peek.

Cratty, B. J. (1970). *Perceptual and motor development in infants and children.* New York: Macmillan.

Cratty, B. J., & Martin, M. M. (1969). *Perceptual-motor efficiency in children.* Philadelphia: Lea & Febiger.Crawford, J. (1989). *Bilingual education: History, politics, theory, and practice.* Trenton, NJ: Crane.

Crawford, J. (1989). Bilingual education: History, politics, theory, and practice. Trenton, NJ: Crane

Creaghead, N. A. (1990). Mutual empowerment through collaboration: A new script for an old problem. *Best Practices in School Speech-Language Pathology, 1,* 109–116.

Crookall, D. (1978). The design and exploitation of a role-play/simulation. *Recherches et Échanges, 3*(1).

Crystal, D. (1987). *The Cambridge encyclopedia of language.* Cambridge: Cambridge University Press.

Cummins, J. (1977). Delaying native reading instruction in immersion programs: A cautionary note. *Canadian Modern Language Review, 34,* 46–49.

Cummins, J. (1980). The entry and exit fallacy in bilingual education. *NABE Journal, 4*(3), 25–60.

Cummins, J. (1981). The role of primary language development in promoting educational success for language minority students. In California State Department of Education (1981: 3–49).

Cummins, J. (1983). *Heritage language education: A literature review.* Toronto, Canada: Ministry of Education.

Cummins, J. (1984). *Bilingualism and special education: Issues in assessment and pedagogy.* Clevedon, England: Multilingual Matters.

Cummins, J. (1986). Empowering minority students: A framework for intervention. *Harvard Educational Review, 56,* 18–35.

Cummins, J. (1987). Bilingualism, language proficiency, and metalinguistic development. In P. Homel, M. Palij, & D. Aronson (Eds.), *Childhood bilingualism: Aspects of linguistic, cognitive, and social development* (pp. 57–74). Hillsdale, NJ: Lawrence Erlbaum.

Cummins, J. (1989). *Empowering language minority students.* Sacramento: California Association for Bilingual Education.

Cureton, G. O. (1973). *Action-reading.* Boston: Allyn & Bacon.

Curran, C. (1961). Counseling skills adapted to the learning of foreign languages. *Menninger Bulletin, 25*(2), 78–93.

Curran, C. (1976). *Counseling-learning in second languages.* Dubuque, IL: Counseling-Learning.

Curran, C. (1983). Counseling learning. In Oller & Richard-Amato (1983: 146–178).

Curtain, H. A. (1986). Integrating language and content instruction. *ERIC/CLL News Bulletin, 9*(2), 1, 10–11.

Curtain, H. A., & Pesola, C. A. (1988). *Languages and children—making the match.* New York: Addison-Wesley.

Cziko, G. A. (1978). Differences in first and second language reading: The use of syntactic, semantic, and discourse constraints. *Canadian Modern Language Review, 38,* 473–489.

Dalgish, G. (1987). Some uses of computers in teaching English as a second language: The issue of control. *Computers in the School, 4*(1), 81–93.

Damico, J. S. (1988). The lack of efficacy in language therapy: A case study. *Language, Speech and Hearing Services in Schools, 19,* 51–67.

Damico, J. S. (1992). *Whole language for special needs children.* Buffalo, NY: Educom Associates.

Damico, J. S., & Armstrong, M. B. (1990–1991). Empowerment in the clinical context: The speech-language pathologist as advocate. *NSSLHA Journal, 18,* 34–43.

Damico, J. S., & Oller, J. W., Jr. (1980). Pragmatic versus morphological/syntactic criteria for language referrals. *Language, Speech, and Hearing Services in Schools, 9,* 85–94.

Damico, J. S., Oller, J. W., Jr., & Storey, M. (1983). The diagnosis of language disorders in bilingual children: Surface-oriented and pragmatic criteria. *Journal of Speech and Hearing Disorders, 48,* 385–394.

Davey, B. (1983). Think aloud: Modeling the cognitive process of reading comprehension. *Journal of Reading, 37,* 104–112.

Davies, G., & Higgins, J. (1985). *Computers, language and language learning* (2nd ed.). London: Center for Information on Language Teaching (CILT).

Davies, N. F. (1976). Receptive versus productive skills in foreign language learning. *Modern Language Journal, 60,* 440–443.

Davis, A., & Wilcox, J. (1985). *Pragmatics and aphasia.* San Diego: College-Hill Press.

De Beaugrande, R. (1980). *Text, discourse, and process.* Norwood, NJ: Ablex.

Dease, B.C. (1982). The humanities and foreign languages: Analogous or anomalous. *ADFL Bulletin, 13*(3), 17–19.

DeAvila, E., Duncan, S., & Navarrete, C. (1987). *Finding out/descubrimiento: Teacher's resource guide.* Northvale, NJ: Santillana.

DeAvila, E., & Havassey, B. (1974). The testing of minority children: A neo-Piagetian approach. *Today's Education, 63,* 72–75.

Deely, J. N. (1983). Cognition from a semiotic point of view. In Deely & Lenhart (1983: 21–28).

Deely, J. N., & Lenhart, M. D. (Eds.) *Semiotics 1981*. New York: Plenum.

Delgado, G. (Ed.) (1984). *The Hispanic Deaf: Issues and challenges for bilingual special education*. Washington, DC: Gallaudet College Press.

Deuz, D. (1982). Silent and non-silent pauses in three speech styles. *Language and Speech, 25*(1), 11–28.

Dew, N. (1984). The exceptional bilingual child: Demography. In P. Chin (Ed.), *Education of culturally and linguistically different exceptional children* (pp. 1–41). Reston, VA: The Council for Exceptional Children.

Dewey, J. (1916). The existence of the world as a logical problem. In *Essays in experimental logic* (pp. 281–302). Chicago: University of Chicago. Also in Oller (1989: 37–52).

Dewey, J. (1926). *Experience and nature*. New York: Open Court. Excerpted in D. E. Hayden & E. P. Alworth (Eds.) (1965), *Classics in semantics* (pp. 265–296). New York: Philosophical Library.

Dirks, J. E. (1976). Strengthening foreign languages in humanities and in international studies. *ADFL Bulletin, 8*(2), 26–30.

Dixon, F. W. (1959). *The Hardy boys series*. New York: Grosset & Dunlap.

Dubin, F. (1974). Pop, rock and folk music: An overlooked resource. *English Teaching Forum, 12*(3), 1–5.

Dulay, H., & Burt, M. (1974). Natural sequences in child second language acquisition. *Language Learning, 24*, 37–53.

Dulay, H., Burt, M., & Krashen, S. D. (1982). *Language two*. New York: Oxford.

Dunkel, P. (1986). Developing listening fluency in L2: Theoretical principles and pedagogical considerations. *Modern Language Journal, 70*, 99–106.

Dunlea, A. (1984). The relationship between concept formation and semantic roles: Some evidence from the blind. In L. Feagens, C. Garvey, & R. Golinkof (Eds.), *The origin and growth of communication* (pp. 224–244). Norwood, NJ: Ablex.

Dykstra, G., & Nunes, S. S. (1970). The language skills program of the English project. *Educational Perspectives, 54*, 487–492.

Eagon, R., & Cashion, M. (1988). Second year report on a longitudinal study of spontaneous reading in English by students in early French immersion classes. *Canadian Modern Language Review, 44*, 523–526.

Early, P. B. (1977). *Postscript to games, simulations and role-playing*. London: ELT Documents, British Council.

Ebbinghaus, H. (1897). Über eine neue Methode sur Prüfung geistiger Fähigkeiten und ihre Anwendung bei Schulkindern. *Zeitschrift für angewandte Psychologie, 13*, 401–459.

Edelsky, C., Altwerger, B., & Flores, B. (1990). *Whole language: What's the difference?* Portsmouth, NH: Heinemann.

Edelsky, C., Draper, K., & Smith, K. (1983). Hookin' em in at the start of school in a "whole language classroom." *Anthropology and Education Quarterly, 14*, 257–281.

Edgerton, R. (1988, April). All roads lead to teaching. *AAHE Bulletin*, 3–9.

Edwards, H., Wesche, M., Krashen, S. D., Clément, R., & Kruidenier, B. (1984). Second language acquisition through subject-matter learning: A study of sheltered psychology classes at the University of Ottawa. *Canadian Modern Language Review, 41*, 268–282.

Ehrman, M., & Oxford, R. (1989). Effects of sex differences, career choices, and psychological type on adult language learning strategies. *Modern Language Journal, 73*, 1–12.

Einstein, A. (1936). Physics and reality. In Author, *Out of my later years* (pp. 59–97). Secaucus, NJ: Citadel; also in Oller (1989: 3–12).

Einstein, A. (1941). The common language of science. In Author, *Out of my later years* (pp. 111–113). Secaucus, NJ: Citadel; also in Oller (1989: 61–65).

Einstein, A. (1944). Remarks on Bertrand Russell's theory of knowledge. In P. A. Schilpp (Ed.), *The philosophy of Bertrand Russell* (pp. 277–291). New York: Tudor Library of Living Philosophers; also in Oller (1989: 21–29).

Eisele, C. (Ed.) (1979). *Studies in the scientific and mathematical philosophy of Charles S. Peirce*. Volumes 1–4. The Hague: Mouton.

Eisele, C. (1987). Peirce's pragmaticism. In Herbert Stachowiak, & Claus Baldus, *Pragmatik: Handbuch pragmatischen denkens* (pp. 83–98). Hamburg, Germany: Felix Meiner.

Eisele, C. (1988). Thomas S. Fiske and Charles S. Peirce. In American Mathematical Society, *A century of mathematics in America*, Part I (pp. 41–56). Providence, RI: American Mathematical Society.

El Paso Independent School District. (1987, July). *Interim report of the five-year bilingual education pilot, 1986–1987 school year*. El Paso, TX: El Paso Independent School District, Office for Research and Evaluation.

El Paso Independent School District. (1989a, January). *Bilingual education evaluation: The fourth year in a longitudinal study, 1987–1988 school year*. El Paso, TX: El Paso Independent School District, Office for Research and Evaluation.

El Paso Independent School District. (1989b, August). *Bilingual education evaluation: The fifth year in a longitudinal study*. El Paso, TX: El Paso Independent School District, Office for Research and Evaluation.

Elbow, P. (1986). *Embracing contraries: Explorations in learning and teaching*. New York: Oxford University Press.

Elenbaas, C. T. (1983). *Putting language acquisition theory to practice in the classroom*. (ERIC Document Reproduction Service No. ED 226 587)

Ely, C. M. (1986). An analysis of discomfort, risk-taking, sociability, and motivation in the L2 classroom. *Language Learning, 36*, 1–26.

Ely, C. M. (1988). Personality: Its impact on attitudes toward classroom activities. *Foreign Language Annals, 21*, 225–232.

Ely, C. M. (1989). Tolerance of ambiguity and use of second language strategies. *Foreign Language Annals, 22*, 437–445.

Enright, D. S. (1986). Use everything you have to teach English: Providing useful input to young language learners. In Rigg & Enright (1986: 113–162).

Enright, D. S., & McCloskey, M. L. (1988). *Integrating English: Developing English language and literacy in the multilingual classroom*. Reading, MA: Addison-Wesley.

Erickson, J., & Omark, D. (Eds.) (1981). *Communication assessment of the bilingual bicultural child*. Baltimore, MD: University Park Press.

Erickson, M. (1992). Hear together eyes: Write together heart. *The Ram's Horn, 6*, 8–14.

Ericsson, K. A., & Simon, H. A. (1980). Verbal reports as data. *Psychological Review, 87*, 215–251.

Faerch, C., & Kasper, G. (1983). Plans and strategies in foreign language communication. In C. Faerch &

G. Kasper (Eds.), *Strategies in interlanguage communication* (pp. 20–60). London: Longman.

Faerch, C., & Kasper, G. (1987). *Introspection in second language research*. Clevedon, UK: Multilingual Matters.

Feitelson, D., & Goldstein, Z. (1986). Patterns of book ownership and reading to young children in Israeli school-oriented and nonschool-oriented families. *The Reading Teacher, 39*, 924–930.

Ferreira, L. (1984). *Transitions: Intermediate student textbook*. Rowley, MA: Newbury House.

Fey, M. (1986). *Language intervention with young children*. San Diego: College Hill Press.

Fillmore, C. J. (1979). On fluency. In Fillmore et al. (1979: 85–101).

Fillmore, C. J. (1981). Ideal readers and real readers. In D. Tannen (Ed.), *Georgetown University Round Table on Languages and Linguistics*. Washington, DC: Georgetown University Press.

Fillmore, C. J. (1985). Linguistics as a tool for discourse analysis. In van Dijk (1985: 11–39).

Fillmore, C. J., Kempler, D., & Wang, W. S-J. (Eds.) (1979). *Individual differences in language ability and language behavior*. New York: Academic Press.

Finocchiaro, M. (1964). *English as a second language: From theory to practice*. New York: Regents.

Finocchiaro, M. (1973). *The foreign language learner: A guide for teachers*. New York: Regents.

Finocchiaro, M. (1984, March). I had a teacher once. Plenary address at the meeting of the International Teachers of English to Speakers of Other Languages Organization, Houston, Texas.

Finocchiaro, M., & Brumfit, C. (1983). *The functional-notional approach: From theory to practice*. New York: Oxford University Press.

Fisch, M., Kloesel, C. J. W., Moore, E. C., Roberts, D. D., Ziegler, L. A., & Atkinson, N. P. (Eds.) (1982). *Writings of C. S. Peirce: A chronological edition. Vol. 1*. Indianapolis, IN: Indiana University Press.

Fletcher, C. R., & Bloom, C. (1988). Causal reasoning in the comprehension of simple narrative texts. *Journal of Memory and Language, 27*, 235–244.

Floyd, P., & Carrell, P. L. (1987). Effects on ESL reading of teaching cultural content schemata. *Language Learning, 37*(1), 89–108.

Foss, K. A. & Reitzel, A. C. (1988). A relational model for managing second language anxiety. *TESOL Quarterly 22*, 437–454.

Fraser, B. (1983). The domain of pragmatics. In. J. C. Richards & R. W. Schmidt (Eds.), *Language and communication* (pp. 29–59). New York: Longman.

Fraser-Child, N. (1989, Summer). Should poor achievers transfer? *National Newsletter of Canadian Parents for French*, 46.

Freedle, R. O. (Ed.) (1979). *New directions in discourse processing*. Norwood, NJ: Ablex.

Freedle, R. O., & Carroll, J. B. (Eds.) (1972). *Language comprehension and the acquisition of knowledge*. New York: Wiley.

Freedle, R. O., & Hale, G. (1979). Acquisition of new comprehension schemata for expository prose by transfer of a narrative schema. In Freedle (1979: 121–136).

Fromkin, V. A. (1988). Sign languages: Evidence for language universals and the linguistic capacity of the human brain. In Wilcox (1988: 115–128).

Gallegos, J. C. (1992). Tele-classes: The way of the future, a report on a language exchange via satellite. *Foreign Language Annals, 25*(1), 51–58.

Gamel, M. K. (1984). Language and literature: Allies not enemies. *ADFL Bulletin, 15*(8), 8–11.

Gardner, R., & Lambert, W. E. (1959). Motivational variables in second language learning. *Canadian Journal of Psychology, 13*, 266–272.

Garrett, M. F., Bever, T. G., & Fodor, J. A. (1966). The active use of grammar in speech perception. *Perception and Psychophysics, 1*, 30–32.

Garrison, M., & Hammill, D. (1971). Who are the retarded? *Exceptional Children, 33*, 13–20.

Garrod, S., & Trabasso, T. (1973). A dual memory information processing interpretation of sentence comprehension. *Journal of Verbal Learning and Verbal Behavior, 12*, 155–167.

Gary, J. O. (1975). Delayed oral practice in initial stages of second language learning. In Burt & Dulay (1975: 89–95).

Gass, S. M., & Madden, C. G. (Eds.) (1985). *Input in second language acquisition*. Rowley, MA: Newbury House.

Genesee, F. (1981). *Evaluation of the Laurenval early partial and early total immersion programs.*

Montreal: Department of Psychology, McGill University.

Genesee, F. (1983). Bilingual education of majority-language children: The immersion experiments in review. *Applied Psycholinguistics, 4*, 1–46.

Genesee, F. (1984). Historical and theoretical foundations of immersion. In California State Department of Education (1984: 32–57).

Genesee, F. (1985). Second language learning through immersion: A review of U.S. programs. *Review of Educational Research, 55*, 541–561.

Genesee, F. (1987). *Learning through two languages*. Cambridge, MA: Newbury House.

Genesee, F. (1992). Second/foreign language immersion and at-risk English-speaking children. *Foreign Language Annals, 25*(3), 199–213.

Genesee, F., Holobow, N. E., Lambert, W. E., & Chartrand, L. (1989). Three elementary school alternatives for learning through a second language. *Modern Language Journal, 73*(3), 250–263.

Genesee, F., & Lambert, W. E. (1983). Trilingual education for majority language children. *Child Development, 54*, 105–114.

Genesee, F., Rogers, P., & Holobow, N. (1983). The social psychology of second language learning: Another point of view. *Language Learning, 33*, 209–24.

Genesee, F., Tucker, G. R., & Lambert, W. (1977). *An experiment in trilingual education: Report 3*. Unpublished manuscript, McGill University, Montreal.

Genesee, F., Tucker, G. R., & Lambert, W. (1978). An experiment in bilingual education: Report 3. *The Canadian Modern Language Review, 34*, 621–643.

Geoffrion, L. D., & Geoffrion, O. P. (1983). *Computers and reading instruction*. Reading, MA: Addison-Wesley.

Gerkein, K. (1978). Performance of Mexican-American children on intelligence tests. *Exceptional Children, 44*, 438–443.

Gersten, R. (1985). Structured immersion for language minority students: Results of a longitudinal evaluation. *Educational Evaluation and Policy Analysis, 7*, 187–196.

Gersten, R., & Woodward, J. (1985). A case for structured immersion. *Educational Leadership, 43*, 75–79.

Geva, E. (1983). Facilitating reading comprehension through flow charting. *Reading Research Quarterly, 28*, 384–405.

Giamatti, A. B. (1979). On behalf of the humanities. *ADFL Bulletin, 10*(4), 10–12.

Giordano, M. J. (1983). Icon and symbol: A reappraisal of the resemblance debate. In Deely (1983: 29–37).

Glenn, C. G. (1978). The role of episodic structure and of story length in children's recall of simple stories. *Journal of Verbal Learning and Verbal Behavior, 17*, 229–247.

Goldfield, J. D. (1990, March). CALL strategies and the production of a low-cost videodisc. CALICO Symposium, Baltimore, MD.

Goldfield, J. D. (1990, August). CALI familiarization: Authoring and video workshop. Dartmouth/Dana Collaborative, Dartmouth College, Hanover, NH.

Goldfield, J. D. (1991, April). The WinCALIS program: A new authoring tool. CALICO Symposium, Atlanta, GA.

Goldfield, J. D. (1992). Educational technology: Sharing the experience. *The Ram's Horn, 6*, 48–51.

Goldman-Eisler, F. (1961). The significance of changes in the rate of articulation. *Language and Speech, 4,* 171–174.

Goldman-Eisler, F. (1967). Sequential temporal patterns and cognitive processes in speech. *Language and Speech, 10*, 122–131.

Goldman-Eisler, F. (1968). *Psycholinguistics: Experiments in spontaneous speech.* New York: Academic Press.

Goodman, K. (1982). *The selected writings of Kenneth S. Goodman.* London: Routledge & Kegan Paul.

Goodman, K. (1986). *What's whole in whole language?* Portsmouth, NH: Heinemann.

Goodman, K., & Goodman, Y. (1983). Reading and writing relationships: Pragmatic functions. *Language Arts, 60,* 590–599.

Goodman, K. S. (1975). *Strategies for increasing reading comprehension.* Glenview, IL: Scott, Foresman.

Goodman, K. S. (1976). Reading: A psycholinguistic guessing game. In N. A. Johnson (Ed.), *Current topics in language* (pp. 370–383). Cambridge, MA: Winthrop.

Gorrell, R. M., Laird, C., & Freeman, R. E. (Eds.) (1970). *Modern English reader.* Englewood Cliffs, NJ: Prentice Hall.

Gough, P. B. (1972). One second of reading. In J. F. Kavanagh & I. A. Mattingly (Eds.), *Language by ear and by eye.* Cambridge, MA: MIT Press.

Gradman, H., & Hanania, E. (1991). Language learning background factors and ESL proficiency. *Modern Language Journal, 75*, 39–51.

Graesser, A. C., & Robertson, S. P. (1988). Incorporating inferences in narrative representations: A study of how and why. *Cognitive Psychology, 13*, 1–26.

Graman, Tomas. (1987). The gap between lower- and upper-division Spanish courses: A barrier to coming up through the ranks. *Hispania, 70*, 929–935.

Graves, D. H. (1983). *Writing: Teachers and children at work.* Portsmouth, NH: Heinemann.

Gray, B. (1980). Developing language and literacy with urban Aboriginal children. A first report on the Trager Park Project presented at Conference 80/2. Darwin, Australia: Northern Territory. Department of Education.

Gray, B. (1983, May). Helping children become language learners in the classroom. A paper presented at the Annual Conference of the Meanjin Reading Council, Brisbane, Australia.

Green, G. R. (1968). *A gesture inventory for the teaching of Spanish.* Philadelphia: Chilton.

Green, G. R. (1971). Kinesics in the foreign language classroom. *Foreign Language Annals, 5*, 62–68.

Green, J. (1990). Language understanding: A cognitive approach. In M. Nagamachi (Ed.), *Open guides to psychology* (Japanese edition Gengorikai). Tokyo: Kaibundo.

Grice, H. P. (1975). Logic and conversation. In P. Cole & J. Morgan (Eds.), *Syntax and semantics: Volume 3, speech acts* (pp. 41–58). New York: Academic Press.

Griffin, C. W. (1985). Program for writing across the curriculum: A report. *College Composition and Communication, 36*(4), 398–403.

Grosse, C. U. (1991). The TESOL methods course. *TESOL Quarterly, 25*(1), 29–49.

Grubb, E. (1974). The right to bilingual education. *California Journal of Educational Research, 25,* 240–244.

Guiora, A. (1972). Construct validity and transpositional research: Toward an empirical study of psychoanalytic concepts. *Comprehensive Psychiatry, 13,* 139–150.

Guiora, A., Hallahmi, B., Brannon, R., Dull, C., & Scovel, T. (1972). The effects of experimentally induced changes in ego status on pronunciation ability in a second language: An exploratory study. *Comprehensive Psychiatry, 13*, 421–428.

Gutkin T. (1979). Bannatyne patterns of Caucasian and Mexican-American learning-disabled children. *Psychology in the Schools, 16,* 178–183.

Haenicke, D. H. (1976). Foreign language study in international education. *ADFL Bulletin, 8*(2), 11–15.

Haenicke, D. H. (1979). Towards unity in the humanities. *ADFL Bulletin, 11,* 10–13.

Hakuta, K. (1986). *Mirror of language: The debate on bilingualism.* New York: Basic.

Hakuta, K., & Diaz, R. M. (1984). The relationship between bilingualism and cognitive ability: A critical discussion and some new longitudinal data. In K. E. Nelson (Ed.), *Children's language* (Vol. 5, pp. 319–344). Hillsdale, NJ: Lawrence Erlbaum.

Hall, E. T. (1959). *The silent language.* New York: Doubleday.

Hallahan, D., & Kauffman, J. (1977). Labels, categories, behaviors: ED, LD, EMR reconsidered. *Journal of Special Education, 11,* 139–149.

Halliday, M. A. K. (1973). *Language, context, and text: A social semiotic perspective.* Geelong, Australia: Deakin University Press.

Halliday, M. A. K., & Hasan, R. (1976). *Cohesion in English.* London: Longman.

Halliday, M. A. K., & Hasan, R. (1985). *Language, context, and text: A social semiotic perspective.* Geelong, Australia: Deakin University Press.

Hamayan, E. V., & Damico, J. S. (Eds.) (1991). *Limiting bias in the assessment of bilingual students.* Austin: PRO-ED.

Hammerly, H. (1982). *Synthesis in language teaching: An introduction to languistics [sic].* Blaine, WA: Second Language.

Hammerly, H. (1987). The immersion approach: Litmus test of second language acquisition through classroom communication. *Modern Language Journal, 71,* 395–401.

Hammond, R. (1989). Accuracy versus communicative competency: The acquisition of grammar in the second language classroom. *Hispania, 71,* 408–417.

Hansen-Krening, N. (1982). *Language experiences for all students.* Reading, MA: Addison-Wesley.

Harris, D. P. (1985). Some forerunners of cloze procedure. *Modern Language Journal, 69*(4), 367–376.

Hart, N. W. M., Walker, R. F., & Gray, B. (1977). *The language of children: A key to literacy.* Reading, MA: Addison-Wesley.

Hart, P. (1987). *The Spanish sleuth: The detective in Spanish fiction.* Cranbury, NJ: Farleigh Dickenson University Press.

Hartshorne, C., & Weiss, P. (Eds.) (1931–1935). *Collected writings of C. S. Peirce,* Volumes I–VI. Cambridge, MA: Harvard University Press.

Hatch, E. (1983). Simplified input and second language acquisition. In R. W. Andersen (Ed.), *Pidginization and creolization as language acquisition* (pp. 64–86). Rowley, MA: Newbury House.

Haugen, E. (1978). Bilingualism in retrospect. In Alatis (1978: 35–41).

Hauptman, P., Wesche, W., & Ready, D. (1988). Second language acquisition through subject matter learning: A follow-up study at the University of Ottawa. *Language Learning, 38,* 433–471.

Heald-Taylor, G. (1989). *Whole language strategies for ESL students.* San Diego: Dormac.

Hedges, W., & Turner, E. (1983). The cloze test becomes practical for use by the classroom teacher. *Computers, Reading and Language Arts, 1*(1), 1–13.

Heike, A. E. (1981a). A content processing view of hesitation phenomena. *Language and Speech, 8,* 207–216.

Heike, A. E. (1981b). Audio-lectal practice and fluency acquisition. *Foreign Language Annals, 14*(3), 189–194.

Henderson, A., Goldman-Eisler, F., & Skarbek, A. (1966). Sequential temporal patterns in spontaneous speech. *Language and Speech, 8,* 207–216.

Hendrickson, J. M. (1986). *Poco a Poco—Spanish for Proficiency.* Boston: Heinle & Heinle.

Henning, G. (Ed.) (1977). *Proceedings of the Second Language Research Forum.* University of California, Los Angeles.

Heyde, A. (1977). The relationship of self-esteem to the oral production of a second language. In Brown, Yorio, & Crymes (1977: 1–13).

Heyde, A. (1979). *The relationship between self-esteem and the oral production of a second language.* Unpublished doctoral dissertation, University of Michigan, Ann Arbor.

Higgins, J. (1988). *Language, learners, and computers.* New York: Longman.

Higgins, J., & Johns, T. (1984). *Computers in language learning.* Reading, MA: Addison-Wesley.

Higgs, T. V. (1985). The input hypothesis: An inside look. *Foreign Language Annals, 17,* 197–203.

Hillocks, G., Jr. (1986). *Research on written composition.* Urbana, IL: (ERIC Document Reproduction Service No. ED 265 552)

Hinds, J. L. (1979). Organizational patterns in discourse. In T. Givon (Ed.), *Syntax and semantics, Volume 12.* New York: Academic Press.

Hinds, J. L. (1982). *Ellipsis in Japanese.* Edmonton: Linguistic Research.

Hinds, J. L. (1983a). Contrastive rhetoric: Japanese and English. *Text, 3,* 183–195.

Hinds, J. L. (1983b). Retention of information using a Japanese style of presentation. Paper presented at the 1983 TESOL Convention, Toronto, Canada.

Hines, M. (1973). *Skits in English as a second language.* New York: Regents.

Hinofotis, F., & Bailey, K. (1978). Course development: Oral communication for advanced university ESL students. *UCLA Workpapers in TESL, 12,* 7–19.

Hirsch, E. D., Jr. (1987). *Cultural literacy: What every American needs to know.* Boston: Houghton Mifflin.

Ho, K. (1982a). Effect of language of instruction on physics achievement. *Journal of Research in Science Teaching, 19,* 761–767.

Ho, K. (1982b). Teaching physics through English. *Language Learning and Communication, 1,* 283–288.

Ho, K. (1985). The paradox of immersion in a second language. *NABE Journal, 10,* 51–6l.

Hoetker, J. (1969). *Dramatics and the teaching of literature.* NCTE/ERIC Studies in the Teaching of English. Champaign, IL: National Council of Teachers of English. (ERIC Documentaton and Reproduction Service No. ED 028 165)

Hoey, M. (1979). *Signalling in discourse.* Discourse Analysis Monographs, No. 6. English Language Research, University of Birmingham, United Kingdom.

Holmes, G. (1984). Of computers and other technologies. In G. A. Jarvis (Ed.), *The challenge for excellence in foreign language education. Report of the Northeast Conference on the Teaching of Foreign Languages* (pp. 93–105). Middlebury, VT: The Northeast Conference.

Holobow, N., Genesee, F., Lambert, W. E., & Chartrand, L. (1988). *The effectiveness of a partial immersion French program for students from different ethnic and social class backgrounds.* Unpublished report, McGill University, Department of Psychology, Montreal.

Holobow, N., Genesee, F., Lambert, W. E., Met, M., & Gastright, J. (1987). Effectiveness of partial French immersion for children from different social class and ethnic backgrounds. *Applied Psycholinguistics, 8,* 137–152.

Holt, V. (1973). *Curse of the kings.* New York: Doubleday (excerpted in *Reader's Digest Condensed Books, 3,* 324–466).

Hornby, P. A. (1980). Achieving second language fluency through immersion education. *Foreign Language Annals, 13,* 107–113.

Horwitz, E. K., & Young, D. (1990). *Language anxiety: From theory and research to classroom implications.* Englewood Cliffs, NJ: Prentice Hall.

Horwitz, E. K., Horwitz, M. B., & Cope, J. (1986). Foreign language classroom anxiety. *Modern Language Journal, 70,* 125–132.

Hoskins, B. (1990). Language and literacy: Participating in the conversation. *Topics in Language Disorders, 10,* 46–62.

Houghton, D. (1980). Contrastive rhetoric. *English Language Research Journal, 1,* 79–91.

Houghton, D., & Hoey, M. (1983). Linguistics and written discourse: Contrastive rhetorics. In R. B. Kaplan (Ed.), *Annual review of applied linguistics.* Rowley, MA: Newbury House.

Houser, N. (1986). Introduction. In Kloesel et al. (1986: xix–xx).

Hsu, V. (1975). *Play production as a medium of learning spoken Chinese.* Paper presented at the Asian Studies on the Pacific Coast Conference. (ERIC Document Reproduction Service No. ED 112 667)

Hudson, T. (1982). The effects of induced schemata on the "short-circuit" in L2 reading: Non-decoding factors in L2 reading performance. *Language Learning, 32,* 1–31.

Huey, E. B. (1908). *The psychology and pedagogy of reading.* Re-issued in 1968. Cambridge, MA: MIT Press.

Hug, W. (Ed.) (1985). *Unsere Geschichte.* Frankfurt am Main: Verlag Moritz Diesterweg.

Huggins, A. W. F., & Adams, M. J. (1980). Syntactic aspects of reading comprehension. In Spiro, Bruce, & Brewer (1980: 87–112).

Humphrey, J. H. (1960, March). Physical education and science concepts. *Elementary School Science Bulletin,* Issue No. 53, 1–2.

Humphrey, J. H. (1962, March). A pilot study of the use of physical education as a learning medium in the development of language arts concepts in third grade children. *American Association of Health Physical Education and Recreation Research Quarterly, 33,* 136–137.

Humphrey, J. H. (1965). Comparison of the use of active games and language workbook exercises as learning media in the development of language understandings with third grade children. *Perceptual and Motor Skills, 21,* 23–26.

Humphrey, J. H. (1967). The mathematics motor activity story. *Arithmetic Teacher, 14,* 14–16.

Humphrey, J. H. (1968). Use of the physical education learning medium in the development of certain arithmetical processes with second grade children. *American Association of Health Physical Education and Recreation Abstracts.*

Humphrey, J. H. (1970). Teaching slow learners science through active games. In J. H. Humphrey & D. D. Sullivan (Eds.), *Teaching slow learners through active games* (pp. 145–182). Springfield, IL: Charles C. Thomas.

Humphrey, J. H. (1972). The use of motor activity learning in the development of science concepts with slow learning fifth grade children. *Journal of Research in Science Teaching, 9,* 261–266.

Imhoff, G. (1990). The position of U.S. English on bilingual education. In C. Cazden & C. Snow (Eds.), *English plus: Issues in bilingual education. Annals of the American Academy of Political Science* (pp. 48–61). Newbury Park, CA: Sage Publications.

Incera, A. C. (1980). *Compendio de la civilización española e iberoamericana.* Miami, FL: Ediciones Universales.

Ingram, F., Nord, J. R., & Dragt, D. (1975). A program for listening comprehension. *Slavic and East European Journal, 19,* 1–10.

Inhelder, B., & Piaget, J. (1958). *The growth of logical thinking from childhood to adolescence.* New York: Basic.

Jackendoff, R. (1987). *Consciousness and the computational mind.* Cambridge, MA: MIT Press.

Jakobson, R. (1980). *The framework of language.* Ann Arbor: University of Michigan Press.

Jarvella, R. (1971). Syntactic process of connected speech. *Journal of Verbal Learning and Verbal Behavior, 10,* 409–416.

Jespersen, O. (1904). *How to teach a foreign language* (S. Y-O. Bertelsen, Trans.). London: George Allen & Unwin.

Johansson, Stig. (1973). *Partial dictation as a test of foreign language proficiency.* Contrastive Studies Report No. 3. Department of English, Lund University, Sweden.

Johnson, D., & Sikes, M. (1965). Rorschach and TA response of Negro, Mexican-American, and Anglo psychiatric patients. *Journal of Projective Techniques, 29,* 183–188.

Johnson, D. W., & Johnson, R. T. (1987). *Learning together and alone.* Englewood Cliffs, NJ: Prentice Hall.

Johnson, K. (1979). Communicative approaches and communicative processes. In Brumfit & Johnson (1979: 192–205).

Johnson, K. (1982). The deep end strategy in communicative language teaching. In K. Johnson (Ed.), *Communicative syllabus design and methodology* (pp. 192–200). Oxford: Pergamon.

Johnson, K. (1988). Mistake correction. *ELT Journal, 42*(2), 89–95.

Johnson, N. S., & Mandler, J. M. (1980). A tale of two structures: Underlying and surface forms in stories. *Poetics, 9,* 1–86.

Johnson, P. (1981). Effects on reading comprehension of language complexity and cultural background of a text. *TESOL Quarterly, 15,* 169–181.

Johnson, P. (1982). Effects on reading comprehension of building background knowledge. *TESOL Quarterly, 16,* 503–516.

Johnson, R. J., & Friedman, H. L. (1971). Some temporal factors in the listening behavior of second language students. In Pimsleur & Quinn (1971: 165–170).

Johnson-Laird, P. N. (1983). *Mental models.* Cambridge, MA: Harvard University Press.

Johnston, O. W. (1980). Implementing the intensive language model: An experiment in German at the University of Florida. *Foreign Language Annals, 13,* 99–106. Reprinted in Oller & Richard-Amato (1983: 348–362).

Johnston, O. W. (1983). Five years with the Rassias method in German: A follow-up report from the University of Florida. *Foreign Language Annals, 16*(5), 343–349.

Joiner, E. (1990). Choosing and using videotexts. *Foreign Language Annals, 23*(1), 53–64.

Jonz, J. (1976). Improving on the basic egg: The multiple choice cloze test. *Language Learning, 26,* 255–265.

Jorden, E. H. (1982). Language and area studies: In search of a meaningful relationship. *ADFL Bulletin, 14*(2), 25–30.

Jurasek, R. (1988). Integrating foreign language into the college curriculum. *Modern Language Journal, 72,* 52–58.

Kagan, S. (1985–1992). *Cooperative learning resources for teachers.* San Juan Capistrano, CA: Resources for Teachers.

Kagan, S. (1986). Cooperative learning and sociocultural factors in schooling. In California State Department of Education (1986: 231–298).

Kamil, M. L. (1978). Models of reading. In S. Pflaum-Connor (Ed.), *Aspects of Reading Education.* Berkeley, CA: McCutchan.

Kanoi, N. (1970). *The strategy of the total physical response for foreign language learning.* Unpublished manuscript. Hanover College, Hanover, IN.

Kany, C. E. (1960). *American Spanish euphemisms.* Berkeley: University of California Press.

Kaplan, R. B. (1966). Cultural thought patterns in inter-cultural education. *Language Learning, 16,* 1–20.

Kaplan, R. B. (1972). *The anatomy of rhetoric: Prolegomena to a functional theory of rhetoric.* Philadelphia: Center for Curriculum Development (distributed by Heinle & Heinle).

Kaplan, R. B., & Ostler, S. E. (1982). Contrastive rhetoric revisited. Paper presented at the 1982 TESOL Convention, Honolulu.

Kasper, G. (1984). Pragmatic comprehension in learner-native speaker discourse. *Language Learning, 34*(1), 1–20.

Katz, E. (1975). The mass communication of knowledge. In *Getting the message across* (pp. 93–114). Paris: UNESCO.

Keene, C. (1939). *The Nancy Drew series.* New York: Grosset & Dunlap.

Kekelis, L., & Andersen, E. (1984). Family communication style and language development. *Journal of Visual Impairment and Blindness, 78,* 254–265.

Kelly, L. G. (1969). *25 centuries of language teaching.* Rowley, MA: Newbury House.

Kemmis, S., & Taggart, R. (1982). *The action research planner.* Victoria, Australia: Deakin University Press.

Kenning, M. J., & M. M. Kenning. (1984). *An introduction to computer-assisted language teaching.* Oxford, England: Oxford University Press.

Kerka, S. (1989). *Women, work, and literacy.* ERIC Digest No. 92. Columbus: ERIC Clearinghouse on Adult, Career, and Vocational Education and Training for Employment, Ohio State University. (ERIC Document Reproduction Service No. ED 312 456)

Kestelman, R., & Maiztegui, S. (1980). *HILT-plus program in Spanish for educators.* Torrance, CA: MAIKEL Educational Services.

Kiddle, M. E., & Wegman, B. (1988). *Perspectivas: Temas de hoy y de siempre.* New York: Holt, Rinehart, and Winston.

Killian, I. (1971). WISC, Illinois Test of Psycholinguistic Abilities, and Bender Visual-Motor Gestalt test performance of Spanish-American kindergarten and first-grade school children. *Journal of Consulting and Clinical Psychology, 37,* 38–43.

Kintsch, W. (1974). *The representation of meaning in memory.* Hillsdale, NJ: Lawrence Erlbaum.

Kintsch, W. (1977). On comprehending stories. In M. A. Just & P. A. Carpenter (Eds.), *Cognitive processes in comprehension* (pp. 33–62). Hillsdale, NJ: Lawrence Erlbaum.

Kintsch, W., & Greene, E. (1978). The role of culture-specific schemata in the comprehension and recall of stories. *Discourse Processes, 1,* 1–13.

Kintsch, W., Mandel, T., & Kozminsky, E. (1977). Summarizing scrambled stories. *Memory and Cognition, 5,* 547–552.

Kintsch, W., & van Dijk, T. A. (1975). Comment on se rapelle et on résume des histoires. *Langages, 40,* 98–116.

Kintsch, W., & van Dijk, T. A. (1978). Toward a model of text comprehension and production. *Psychological Review, 85,* 363–394.

Kirch, M. (1979). Non-verbal communication across cultures. *Modern Language Journal, 63,* 416–423.

Kirsch, I. S., & Jungeblut, A. (1986). *Literacy: Profiles of America's young adults.* Princeton, NJ: National Assessment of Educational Progress, Educational

Testing Service. (ERIC Document Reproduction Service No. ED 275 701)

Klieman, G. M. (1975). Speech recording in reading. *Journal of Verbal Learning and Verbal Behavior, 14,* 323–339.

Klinck, P. A. (1985). French teacher training: A proposal for a new pedagogy. *Canadian Modern Language Review, 41,* 887–891.

Kloesel, C. J. W., Fisch, M. H., Houser, N., Niklas, U., Simon, M., Roberts, D. D., & Houser, A. (Eds.) (1986). *Writings of C. S. Peirce: A chronological edition. Vol. 4.* Bloomington, IN: Indiana University Press.

Knoll, S. B. (1976). Languages and international studies. *ADFL Bulletin, 8*(2), 22–25.

Krashen, S. D. (1981). *Second language acquisition and second language learning.* Oxford: Pergamon.

Krashen, S. D. (1982). *Principles and practice in second language acquisition.* Oxford: Pergamon.

Krashen, S. D. (1983). The input hypothesis. In Oller (1983a: 357–366).

Krashen, S. D. (1984a). Immersion: Why it works and what it has taught us. *Language in Society, 12,* 61–64.

Krashen, S. D. (1984b). *Writing: Research, theory and applications.* New York: Prentice Hall.

Krashen, S. D. (1985a). *Inquiries and insights.* Hayward, CA: Alemany Press.

Krashen, S. D. (1985b). *The input hypothesis: Issues and implications.* New York: Longman.

Krashen, S. D. (1985c). *Input in second language acquisition.* Oxford: Pergamon.

Krashen, S. D. (1987). Application of psycholinguistic research to the classroom. In Long & Richards (1987: 33–44).

Krashen, S. D. (1989a). We acquire vocabulary and spelling by reading: Additional evidence for the Input Hypothesis. *Modern Language Journal, 73,* 440–464.

Krashen, S. D. (1989b). Language teaching technology: A low-tech view. In Alatis (1989: 393–407).

Krashen, S. D. (1990). Reading, writing, form, and content. In Alatis (1990: 364–376).

Krashen, S. D. (1991, April). The input hypothesis: An update. Paper presented at the Georgetown Round Table for Languages and Linguistics. Washington, DC. In Alatis (1991).

Krashen, S. D. (1992). The input hypothesis and some competing hypotheses. In Courchêne et al. (1992: 19–38).

Krashen, S. D., & Biber, D. (1988). *On course: Bilingual education's success in California.* Sacramento, CA: California Association for Bilingual Education.

Krashen, S. D., & Terrell, T. (1983). *The natural approach.* San Francisco: Alemany Press.

Krashen, S. D., Terrell, T. D., Ehrman, M. D., & Herzog, M. (1984). A theoretical basis for teaching the receptive skills. *Foreign Language Annals, 17,* 261–275.

Kretschmer, R. R., & Kretschmer, L. W. (1989). Communication competence: Impact of the pragmatics revolution on education of hearing impaired individuals. *Topics in Language Disorders, 9*(4), 1–16.

Kunihira, S., & J. Asher. (1965). The strategy of the total physical response: An application to learning Japanese. *International Review of Applied Linguistics, 3,* 277–289.

Kuno, S. (1978). *Danwa no bunpoo.* Tokyo: Taishukan.

LaBerge, D., & Samuels, S. J. (1974). Toward a theory of automatic information processing in reading. *Cognitive Psychology, 6,* 203–223.

Labov, W., & Fanshel, D. (1977). Therapeutic discourse: Psychotherapy as conversations. New York: Academic Press.

Lafayette, R., & Buscaglia, M. (1985). Students learn language via a civilization course—a comparison of second language classroom environments. *Studies in Second Language Acquisition, 7,* 323–342.

Laforet, P. (1984). Vous n'avez jamais vu un "prof" de littérature comme ça. *Figaro du Samedi, 471*(12), 154–159.

Lamadrid, E. E., Bull, W. E., & Briscoe, L. A. (1974). *Communicating in Spanish, level 1.* Boston: Houghton Mifflin.

Lambert, W. E. (1967). A social psychology of bilingualism. *The Journal of Social Issues, 23,* 91–109.

Lambert, W. E. (1972). *Attitudes and motivation in second language learning.* Rowley, MA: Newbury House.

Lambert, W. E. (1974). A Canadian experiment in the development of bilingual competence. *Canadian Modern Language Review, 31,* 108–116.

Lambert, W. E. (1980). The social psychology of language: A perspective for the 1980s. In H. Giles, W. P. Robinson, & P. M. Smith (Eds.), *Language: Social psychological perspectives* (pp. 415–424). Oxford: Pergamon.

Lambert, W. E. (1987). The effect of bilingual and bicultural experience of children's attitudes and social perspectives. In P. Homel, M. Palij, & D. Aaronson (Eds), *Childhood bilingualism: Aspects of linguistic, cognitive, and social development* (pp. 197–222). Hillsdale, NJ: Lawrence Erlbaum.

Lambert, W. E., Just, M. A., & Segalowitz, N. (1970). Some cognitive consequences of following the curricula of the early grades in a foreign language. In J. E. Alatis (Ed.), *Monograph series on language and linguistics: 21st Annual Round Table*, No. 23 (pp. 229–262). Washington, DC: Georgetown University Press.

Lambert, W. E., & Tucker, G. R. (1972). *Bilingual education of children*. Rowley, MA: Newbury House.

Landry, R. G. (1973). The enhancement of figural creativity through second language learning at the elementary school level. *Foreign Language Annals, 7*(1), 111–115.

Lane, H. (1964). Programmed learning of a second language. *International Review of Applied Linguistics, 2,* 250.

Lane, H. (1984). *When the mind hears.* New York: Random House.

Lane, H. (1988). Educating the American Sign Language minority of the United States: In Wilcox (1988: 221–230).

Langer, J., & Applebee, N. (1986). Reading and writing instruction: Toward a theory of teaching and learning. In *Review of research in education.* Washington, DC: American Educational Research Association.

Lapkin, S. (1984). How well do immersion students speak and write French? *Canadian Modern Language Review, 40,* 574–585.

Lapkin, S., Swain, M., Kamin, J., & Hanna, G. (1984). Late immersion in perspective: The Peel study. *Canadian Modern Language Review, 39,* 182–206.

Larsen, S. F. (1983). Text processing and knowledge updating in memory for radio news. *Discourse Processes, 6,* 21–38.

Lasky, E., & Klopp, K. (1982). Parent-child interactions in normal and language-disordered children. *Journal of Speech and Hearing Disorders, 47,* 7–19.

Lawson, Joan. (1957). *Mime: Theory and practice of expressive gesture.* New York: Dance Horizons.

Layton, R. J. (1979). *The psychology of learning to read.* New York: Academic Press.

Lazier, G. (1969). Dramatic improvisation as English teaching methodology. *English Record, 20,* 46–51.

Leaver, B. L., & Stryker, S. B. (1989). Content-based instruction for foreign language classrooms. *Foreign Language Annals, 22,* 269–275.

Lee, J. F. (1987). Comprehending the Spanish subjunctive: An information processing perspective. *Modern Language Journal, 71,* 51–57.

Lee, V. (1983). A new interdisciplinary program. *ADFL Bulletin, 15*(1), 4–6.

Leech, C. N. (1983). *Principles of pragmatics.* London: Longman.

Leeson, R. (1975). *Fluency and language teaching.* London: Longman.

Legaretta, D. (1979). The effects of program models on language acquisition by Spanish speaking children. *TESOL Quarterly, 13,* 521–534.

Lein, J. D. (1992). *Eine kleine Rassiasmusik*: Using the Dartmouth intensive language model at Central Michigan University. *The Ram's Horn, 6,* 18–23.

Lennon, P. (1990). Investigating fluency in EFL: A quantitative approach. *Language Learning, 40,* 387–417.

Leonard, L., & Weiss, A. (1983). Application of non-standardized assessment procedures to diverse linguistic populations. *Topics in Language Disorders, 3,* 35–45.

Lerman, A., & Vila, C. (1985). A model for school services to Hispanic hearing-impaired children. In Delgado (1985: 167–181).

Lesser, G., Fifer, G., & Clark, D. (1965). *Mental abilities of children from different social-class and cultural groups.* Monographs of the Society for Research in Child Development, Serial No. 102, 30, No. 4, 1–115.

Lieberman, L. R., & Altschul, S. (1971). Memory for a list of commands: Imagining, seeing, doing. *Perceptual and Motor Skills, 33,* 530.

Lincoln, Y. S., & Guba, E. G. (1985). *Naturalistic inquiry.* Beverly Hills, CA: Sage Publications.

Lindholm, K. J. (1987). *Directory of bilingual immersion programs: Two-way bilingual education for language minority and majority students.*

Educational Report Series, No. 8. (ERIC Document Reproduction Service No. ED 291 241)

Lipiski, J. M. (1983). La norma culta y la norma radiofónica: /s/ y /n/ en español. *Language Problems and Language Planning, 7,* 239–262.

Little, G. D., & Sanders, S. L. (1989). Classroom community: A prerequisite for communication. *Foreign Language Annals, 22*(3), 277–281.

Littlewood, W. (1984). *Foreign and second language learning.* Cambridge: Cambridge University Press.

Loban, W. (1966). *Language ability.* Washington, DC: U.S. Government Printing Office.

Long, D. R., Pino, C., & Valdés, G. (1985). Building enrollment through curricular change: The implementation of a comprehension-based program in Spanish. *Foreign Language Annals, 5,* 413–425.

Long, M. H. (1981). Input, interaction, and second language acquisition. In Winitz (1981: 250–278).

Long, M. H. (1983). Does second language instruction make a difference? A review of research. *TESOL Quarterly, 17,* 359–382.

Long, M. H. (1985). *Bibliography of research on second language classroom processes and classroom second language acquisition.* Honolulu: Center for Second Language Classroom Research, Social Science Research Institute, University of Hawaii.

Long, M. H., & Porter, P. (1985). Group work, interlanguage talk, and second language acquisition. *TESOL Quarterly, 19,* 207–227.

Long, M. H., & Richards, J. (Eds.) (1987). *Methodology in TESOL: A book of readings.* New York: Newbury House.

Long, M. H., & Seliger, H. W. (1983). *Classroom oriented research in second language acquisition.* Rowley, MA: Newbury House.

Lozanov, G. (1978). *Suggestology and outlines of suggestopedy.* New York: Gordon and Breach.

Ludwig, C. (1955). *The effect of creative dramatics upon the articulation skills of kindergarten children.* Unpublished masters thesis, University of Pittsburgh.

Luetke-Stahlman, B., & Weiner, F. (1932). Assessing language and/or system preferences of Spanish-Deaf preschoolers. *American Annals of the Deaf, 127,* 789–796.

Lyster, R. (1987). Speaking immersion. *Canadian Modern Language Review, 43,* 701–717.

MacGinitie, W. H. (1961). Contextual constraints in English prose paragraphs. *Journal of Psychology, 51,* 121–130.

Mackie, J. L. (1973). *The cement of the universe.* Cambridge: Cambridge University Press.

Maclay, H., & Osgood, C. E. (1959). Hesitation phenomena in spontaneous English speech. *Word, 15,* 19–44.

Mahl, G. F. (1956). Disturbances and silences in the patient's speech in psychotherapy. *Journal of Abnormal and Social Psychology, 53,* 1–15.

Mahl, G. F., & Schulze, G. (1964). Psychological research in the extralinguistic area. In T. A. Sebeok, A. S. Hayes, & M. C. Bateson (Eds.), *Approaches to semiotics* (pp. 51–124). The Hague: Mouton.

Mandler, J. M. (1978a). A code in the node: The use of a story schema in retrieval. *Discourse Processes, 1,* 14–35.

Mandler, J. M. (1978b). *Categorical and schematic organization in memory.* CHIP Report No. 16. San Diego, CA: Center for Human Information Processing, University of California.

Mandler, J. M., & Johnson, N. S. (1977). Remembrance of things parsed: Story structure and recall. *Cognitive Psychology, 9,* 111–151.

Mandler, J. M., Scribner, S., Cole, M., & Deforest, M. (1980). Cross-cultural invariance in story recall. *Child Development, 51,* 19–26.

Mann, J. (1970). The present state of psychodramatic research. Paper presented at the American Psychological Association Convention, Miami Beach, Florida. (ERIC Document Reproduction Service No. ED 043 055)

Marbán, E. (1974). *El mundo iberoamericano: Hombres en su historia.* New York: Regents.

Marbén, E. (1983). *El mundo iberoamericano: Sus pueblos y sus tierras.* New York: Regents.

Markham, P., & Latham, M. (1987). The influence of religion-specific background on the listening comprehension of adult second-language students. *Language Learning, 37*(2), 157–170.

Markkanen, R. (1985). *Cross-language studies in pragmatics.* (ERIC Document Reproduction Service No. ED 259 581)

Marshall, W. A. (1970). Contextual constraint on deaf and hearing children. *American Annals of the Deaf, 115,* 682–689.

Martin, B. (1983). Brown bear, brown bear, what do you see? New York: Henry Holt.

Mattes, L., & Omark, D. (1984). *Speech and language assessment for the bilingual handicapped.* San Diego, CA: College-Hill Press.

Maurice, K. (1983). The fluency workshop. *TESOL Newsletter, 17*(4), 29.

Maxwell, S., & Delaney, H. (1990). *Designing experiments and analyzing data.* Belmont, CA: Wadsworth.

McCoy, I. (1979). Means to overcome the anxieties of second language learners. *Foreign Language Annals, 12,* 185–189.

McCreary, C., & Padilla, E. (1977). MMPI Differences among Black, Mexican-American and White male offenders. *Journal of Clinical Psychology, 33,* 171–177.

McCullough, C. M. (1976). What should the reading teacher know about language and thinking? In R. E. Hodges & E. H. Rudorf (Eds.), *Language and learning to read: What teachers should know about language* (pp. 2–7). Boston: Houghton Mifflin.

McDonald, D. (1984). Singing can break the conversation barrier. *English Teaching Forum, 22*(1), 35.

McDowell, J. (1979). *Evidence that demands a verdict* (revised ed.). San Bernardino: CA: Here's Life.

McDowell, J. (1981). *The resurrection factor.* San Bernardino, CA: Here's Life.

McIntyre, B. (1958). The effect of creative activities on the articulation skills of children. *Speech Monographs, 25*(1), 42–48.

McIntyre, B., & McWilliams, B. (1959). Creative dramatics in speech correction. *Journal of Speech and Hearing Disorders, 24,* 275–278.

McKay, S. L., & Wong, S-L. C. (Eds.) (1988). *Language diversity: Problem or resource?* New York: Newbury House.

McLaughlin, B. (1984a). Are immersion programs the answer for bilingual education in the United States? *The Bilingual Review, 11*(1), 3–11.

McLaughlin, B. (1984b). *Second-language acquisition in childhood: Vol. 1, Preschool children* (2nd ed.). Hillsdale, NJ: Lawrence Erlbaum.

McLeod, B., & McLaughlin, B. (1986). Restructuring or automaticity? Reading in a second language. *Language Learning, 36,* 109–123.

McMenamin, J. (1984). Language deficit in a bilingual child with cerebral cysticerosis. *The Bilingual Review, 11*(3), 25–30.

Mear, A. (1969). Experimental investigation of receptive language. Paper presented at the Second International Congress of Applied Linguistics, Cambridge University, Cambridge, England. In Pimsleur & Quinn (1971: 143–156).

Mehrabian, A., & Ferris, S. R. (1967). Inference of attitudes from non-verbal communication in two channels. *Journal of Consulting Psychology, 31,* 248–252.

Mercer, J. (1971). Sociocultural factors in labeling mental retardation. *Peabody Journal of Education, 48,* 188–203.

Mercer, J. (1973). *Labeling the mentally retarded.* Los Angeles, CA: University of California Press.

Mercer, J. (1983). Issues in the diagnosis of language disorders in students whose primary language is not English. *Topics in Language Disorders, 3,* 46–56.

Merino, B., & Faltis, C. (1986). Spanish for special purposes: Communication strategies for teachers in bilingual education. *Foreign Language Annals, 19*(1), 43–46.

Meyer, B. J. F. (1975). *The organization of prose and its effects on memory.* Amsterdam: North Holland.

Meyer, B. J. F. (1977). The structure of prose: Effects on learning and memory and implications for educational practice. In R. C. Anderson, R. J. Spiro, & W. E. Montague (Eds.), *Schooling and the acquisition of knowledge.* Hillsdale, NJ: Lawrence Erlbaum.

Meyer, B. J. F. (1979). Organizational patterns in prose and their use in reading. In M. L. Kamil & A. J. Moe (Eds.), *Reading research: Studies and applications* (pp. 109–117). Clemson, SC: National Reading Conference.

Meyer, B. J. F., Brandt, D. M., & Bluth, G. J. (1980). Use of top-level structure in text: Key for reading comprehension of ninth-grade students. *Reading Research Quarterly, 16,* 72–103.

Meyer, B. J. F., & Freedle, R. O. (1984). Effects of discourse types on recall. *American Educational Research Journal, 21*(1), 122–143.

Meyer, B. J. F., & Rice, G. E. (1982). The interaction of reader strategies and the organization of text. *Text, 2,* 155–192.

Meyer, R. M., & Tetrault, E. W. (1988). Getting started: Reading techniques that work from the very first day. *Foreign Language Annals, 21,* 423–431.

Mezynski, K. (1983). Issues concerning the acquisition of knowledge: Effects of vocabulary training on reading comprehension. *Review of Educational Research, 53,* 253–279.

Milk, R. D. (1990). Integrating language and content: Implications for language distribution in bilingual classrooms. In R. Jacobsen & C. Faltis (Eds.), *Language distribution issues in bilingual schooling* (pp. 32–44). Clevedon, England: Multilingual Matters.

Miller, G. A., Galanter, E., & Pribram, K. (1960). *Plans and the structure of behavior.* New York: Henry Holt.

Miller, G. A., & Selfridge, J. (1950). Verbal context and the recall of meaningful material. *American Journal of Psychology, 63,* 176–185.

Miller, N., & Abudarham, S. (1984). Management of communication problems in bilingual children. In N. Miller (Ed.), *Bilingualism and language disability* (pp. 177–198). San Diego, CA: College-Hill Press.

Mills, A. (Ed.) (1983). *Language acquisition in the blind child: Normal and deficient.* London: Croom Helm.

Modern Language Association of America. (1960). *Modern Spanish.* New York: Harcourt, Brace.

Moffett. J. (1967). *Drama: What is happening.* Champaign, IL: National Council of Teachers of English.

Mohan, B. A. (1986). *Language and content.* Reading, MA: Addison-Wesley.

Moline, J. (1990). On making foreign languages our own. *Humanities, 11,* 36–38.

Montgomery, J. (1984). Cloze procedures: A computer application. The *Computing Teacher, 11*(9), 16–17, 20.

Moore, E. C., Fisch, M. H., Kloesel, C. J. W., Roberts, D. D., & Ziegler, L. A. (Eds.) (1984). *Writings of Charles S. Peirce: A chronological edition (Vol. 2).* Bloomington, IN: Indiana University Press.

Morello, J. (1988). Attitudes of students of French toward required language study. *Foreign Language Annals, 21,* 435–442.

Morgan, J., & Rinvolucri, M. (1983). *Once upon a time: Using stories in the language classroom.* Cambridge: Cambridge University Press.

Morgan, J., & Sellner, M. B. (1980). Discourse and linguistic theory. In Spiro, Bruce, & Brewer (1980: 165–199).

Morrison, D. M. (1984). Gapper: A microcomputer-based learning game. *System, 12*(2), 169–180.

Moskowitz, G. (1978). *Caring and sharing in the foreign language classroom.* Rowley, MA: Newbury House.

Moulding, S. (1978). The development of appropriacy through drama techniques. *Recherches et Échanges, 3*(1).

Mowder, B. (1980). A strategy for the assessment of bilingual handicapped children. *Psychology in the Schools, 17,* 7–12.

Müller, K. E. (Ed.) (1989). *Languages in elementary schools.* New York: The American Forum.

Muma, J. R. (1978). *The language handbook.* Englewood Cliffs, NJ: Prentice Hall.

Munby, J. (1978). *Communicative syllabus design.* Cambridge: Cambridge University Press.

Murphy, E. (1974). The classroom: Meeting the needs of the culturally different child of the Navajo Nation. *Exceptional Children, 41,* 601–607.

Murphy, H. J. (1979). Book review of J. Asher, *Learning another language through actions: The complete teacher's guidebook. American Annals of the Deaf, 124,* 136.

Murray, J. H., Morgenstern, D., & Furstenberg, G. (1989). The Athena language-learning project: Design issues for the next generation of computer-based language-learning tools. In Smith (1989: 97–118).

Myers, J. L., Shinjo, M., & Duffy, S. A. (1987). Degree of causal relatedness and memory. *Journal of Memory and Language, 26,* 453–465.

Nagel, E. (1959). Charles Sanders Peirce: A prodigious but little known American philosopher. *Scientific American, 200,* 185–192.

Nation, P. (1989). Improving speaking fluency. *System, 17*(3), 377–387.

National Governors Association. (1989). *America in transition: The international frontier.* Report of the Task Force on International Education, Washington, DC.

Nelson, K. E. (1985). *Making sense: The acquisition of shared meaning.* New York: Academic Press.

Nelson, N. W. (1990). Only relevant practices can be best. *Best Practices in School Speech-Language Pathology, 1,* 15–28.

Nelson, R. J. (1972). Culture and culture: An integrated, multidisciplinary approach to foreign language requirements. *Modern Language Journal, 56,* 210–217.

Newmark, L. (1966). How not to interfere with language learning. *International Journal of American Linguistics, 32.* Also in E. W. Najam & C. T. Hodge (Eds.), *Language learning: The individual and the process.* Bloomington, IN: Indiana University Press. Reprinted in Oller & Richard-Amato (1983: 49–58).

Newmark, L. (1971). A minimal language-teaching program. In P. Pimsleur & T. Quinn (Eds.), *The psychology of second language learning* (pp. 11–18). New York: Cambridge University Press.

Nicola, M. (1990). Experimenting with the new methods. *Dialog on Language Instruction, 6,* 61–72.

Ninio, A., & Bruner, J. (1978). The achievement and antecedents of labeling. *Journal of Child Language, 5,* 1–15.

Nord, J. R. (1981). Three steps leading to listening fluency: A beginning. In Winitz (1981: 69–100).

Norris, J. A. (1989). Providing language remediation in the classroom: An integrated language-to-reading intervention model. *Language, Speech, and Hearing Services in Schools, 20,* 205–218.

Norris, J. A., & Damico, J. S. (1990). Whole language in theory and practice: Implications for language intervention. *Language, Speech, and Hearing Services in Schools, 21,* 212–220.

Norris, J. A., & Hoffman, P. R. (1990). Language intervention within naturalistic environments. *Language, Speech, and Hearing Services in Schools, 21,* 72–84.

Nuessel, F. (1985). Teaching kinesics through literature. *Canadian Modern Language Review, 41,* 1014–1019.

Nunan, D. (1985). Content familiarity and the perception of textual relations in second language reading. *RELC Journal, 16*(1). 42–51.

Nunan, D. (1988). *The learner-centered curriculum.* Cambridge: Cambridge University Press.

Nunan, D. (1989). *Designing tasks for the communicative classroom.* Cambridge: Cambridge University Press.

Nutell, E., Landurand, P., & Goldman, P. (1984). A critical look at testing and evaluation from a cross-cultural perspective. In P. Chin (Ed.), *Education of culturally and linguistically different exceptional children* (pp. 42–62). Reston, VA: The Council for Exceptional Children.

Oakland, S. (Ed.) (1977). *Psychological and educational assessment of minority children.* New York: Brunner/Mazel.

O'Brien, E. J., & Myers, J. L. (1987). The role of causal connections in the retrieval of text. *Memory and Cognition, 15,* 419–427.

Ogle, D. M. (1986). K-W-L: A teaching model that develops active reading of expository text. *Reading Teacher, 39*(6), 564–570.

Oller, J. W., Jr. (1970). Transformational theory and pragmatics. *Modern Language Journal, 54,* 504–507.

Oller, J. W., Jr. (1972). Scoring methods and difficulty levels for cloze tests of proficiency in EFL. *Modern Language Journal, 58,* 151–158.

Oller, J. W., Jr. (1974). Expectancy for successive elements: Key ingredient to language use. *Foreign Language Annals, 7,* 15–19.

Oller, J. W., Jr. (1975a). Cloze, discourse, and approximations to English. In Burt & Dulay (1975: 345–355).

Oller, J. W., Jr. (1975b). Pragmatic mappings. *Lingua, 35,* 333–344.

Oller, J. W., Jr. (1979). *Language tests at school.* London: Longman.

Oller, J. W., Jr. (1981). Language as intelligence? *Language Learning, 31,* 465–492.

Oller, J. W., Jr. (Ed.) (1983a). *Issues in language testing research.* Rowley, MA: Newbury House.

Oller, J. W., Jr. (1983b). Some working ideas for language teaching. In Oller & Richard-Amato (1983: 3–19).

Oller, J. W., Jr. (1988). Review of *The input hypothesis: Issues and implications, Language, 64,* 171–173.

Oller, J. W., Jr. (Ed.) (1989). *Language and experience: Classic pragmatism.* Lanham, MD: University Press of America.

Oller, J. W., Jr. (1990). Semiotic theory and L2 practice. In Alatis (1990: 65–89).

Oller, J. W., Jr., Bowen, J. D., Dien, T. T., & Mason, V. (1972). Cloze tests in English, Thai, and Vietnamese: Native and non-native performance. *Language Learning, 22,* 1–15.

Oller, J. W., Jr., Chesarek, S., & Scott, J. R. (1991). *Language and bilingualism: More tests of tests.* Cranbury, NJ: Bucknell University Press.

Oller, J. W., Jr., & Damico, J. S. (1991). Theoretical considerations in the assessment of LEP students. In Hamayan & Damico (1991: 77–110).

Oller, J. W., Jr., Hudson, A., & Liu, P. (1977). Attitudes and attained proficiency in ESL: A sociolinguistic study of native speakers of Chinese in the United States. *Language Learning, 27,* 1–27.

Oller, J. W., Jr., & Jonz, J. (Eds.) (in press). *Cloze and coherence.* Manuscript, Department of Linguistics, University of New Mexico.

Oller, J. W., Jr., & Obrecht, D. H. (1969). The psycholinguistic principle of informational sequence: An experiment in second language learning. *IRAL, 7,* 169–174.

Oller, J. W., Jr., & Richard-Amato, P. A. (1983). *Methods that work: A smorgasbord of ideas for language teachers.* Rowley, MA: Newbury House.

Oller, J. W., Jr., & Richards, J. C. (Eds.) (1973). *Focus on the learner: Pragmatic perspectives for the language teacher.* Rowley, MA: Newbury House.

Oller, J. W., Jr., & Taira, T. (in press). Cloze and episodic organization. In Oller and Jonz (in press: 345–369).

Oller, J. W., Jr., & Yü, G. K. S. (1986). Measuring gain from textual coherence with cloze. In Wangsotorn et al. (1986: 309–321).

Oller, J. W., Jr., Yü, G. K. S., Greenberg, L., & Hurtado de Vivas, R. (1986). The learning effect from textual coherence measured with cloze. In Oller & Jonz (in press: 247–268).

Oller, J. W., Sr. (1963). *Teacher's manual: El español por el mundo/primer nivel. La familia Fernández.* Chicago: Encyclopaedia Britannica Films.

Oller, J. W., Sr., & A. González. (1965). *El español por el mundo/segundo nivel: Emilio en España.* Chicago: Encyclopaedia Britannica Films.

Olmedo, E. (1981). Testing linguistic minorities. *American Psychologist, 36,* 1078–1085.

Olson, D. (1974). From utterance to text: The bias of language in speech and writing. Paper presented at the Epistemetics Meeting at Vanderbilt University in Nashville, Tennessee.

Olson, G. M., Duffy, S. A., & Mack, R. L. (1984). Thinking-out-loud as a method for studying real-time comprehension processes. In D. E. Kieras & M. A. Just (Eds.), *New methods in reading comprehension research* (pp. 253–286). Hillsdale, NJ: Lawrence Erlbaum.

Omaggio, A. (1986). *Teaching language in context: Proficiency-oriented instruction.* Boston: Heinle & Heinle.

Omark, D., & Erickson, J. (Eds.) (1983). *The bilingual exceptional child.* San Diego, CA: College-Hill Press.

Ortiz, A. A., & Yates, J. R. (1983). Incidence of exceptionality among Hispanics: Implications for manpower planning. *NABE Journal, 7,* 41–54.

Ostyn, P., & Godin, P. (1985). Ralex: An alternative approach to language teaching. *Modern Language Journal, 69,* 346–354.

Pacheco, R. (1983). Bilingual mentally retarded children: Language confusion or real deficit? In Omark & Erickson (1983: 233–254).

Palincsar, A. S. (1986). The role of dialogue in providing scaffolded instruction. *Educational Psychology, 21,* 73–98.

Palmer, H. E., & Palmer, D. (1970). *English through actions.* London: Longman.

Paradis, M., & Lebrun, Y. (Eds.) (1985). *Early bilingualism and child development.* Lisse, Netherlands: Swets & Zeitlinger.

Pardo, L., & Raphel, T. (1991). Classroom organization for instruction in content areas. *The Reading Teacher, 44,* 556–565.

Paris, S. G. (1989). *Reading and thinking strategies.* Lexington, MA: D. C. Heath.

Patrikis, P. C. (1987). Is there a culture in this language? *ADFL Bulletin, 18*(3), 3–8.

Patton, M. Q. (1980). *Qualitative evaluation.* Beverly Hills, CA: Sage Publications.

Paulson, D., Kintsch, E., Kintsch, W., & Premack, D. (1979). Children's comprehension and memory for stories. *Journal of Experimental Child Psychology, 28,* 379–403.

Pawley, C. (1981). How bilingual are French immersion students? *Modern Language Journal, 65,* 43–53.

Peck, B. (1987). Spanish for social workers—an intermediate-level communicative course with content lectures. *Modern Language Journal, 71,* 402–409.

Peck, J. (1989). Using storytelling to promote language and literacy development. *The Reading Teacher, 42,* 138–141.

Peck, R. N. (1980). *Secrets of successful fiction.* Cincinnati, OH: Writer's Digest.

Peck, S. (1977). Language play in child second language acquisition. In Henning (1977: 85–93).

Peirce, C. S. (1865a). Forms of induction and hypothesis. In Fisch et al. (1982: 256–271).

Peirce, C. S. (1865b). The logic notebook. In Fisch et al. (1982: 337–350).

Peirce, C. S. (1868). Consequences of four incapacities. *Journal of Speculative Philosophy, 2,* 140–157. Reprinted in Moore et al. (1984: 211–242).

Peirce, C. S. (1903a). The reality of thirdness. In Hartshorne & Weiss (1931: 173–178).

Peirce, C. S. (1903b). Scholastic realism. In Hartshorne & Weiss (1934: 64–67).

Pellerin, M., & Hammerly, H. (1986). L'éxpression orale aprés 13 ans d'immersion française. *Canadian Modern Language Review, 42,* 592–606.

Peña-Hughes, E., & Solís, J. (1980). *ABCs* (unpublished report). McAllen, TX: McAllen Independent School District.

Pequeño Larousse ilustrado. (1976). Paris: Larousse.

Perez, G. J. (1988). Review of Patricia Hart's *The Spanish sleuth: The detective in Spanish fiction. Hispania, 71,* 553–554.

Pesola, C. A. (1991). Culture in the elementary school foreign language classroom. *Foreign Language Annals, 24*(4), 331–346.

Peyton, J. K. (1987, April). *Dialogue journal writing with limited English proficient (LEP) students. ERIC/CLL Q & A.* Washington, DC: Center for Applied Linguistics.

Piaget, J. (1926). *The language and thought of the child.* New York: Harcourt Brace.

Piaget, J. (1947). *The psychology of intelligence.* Totowa, NJ: Littlefield Adams.

Piaget, J. (1981). *Intelligence and affectivity: Their relationship during child development* (Ed. and Trans. T. A. Brown & C. E. Kaegi). Palo Alto, CA: Annual Reviews.

Pica, T., & Doughty, C. (1985a). Input and interaction in the communicative language classroom: A comparison of teacher-fronted and group activities. In Gass & Madden (1985: 115–132).

Pica, T., & Doughty, C. (1985b). The role of group work in classroom second language acquisition. *Studies in Second Language Acquisition, 7,* 233–248.

Pica, T., Young, R., & Doughty, D. (1987). The impact of interaction on comprehension. *TESOL Quarterly, 21,* 737–758.

Pickering, M. (1976). Bilingual/bicultural education and the speech pathologist. *ASHA, 18,* 275–279.

Pimsleur, P. (1972, May 15). Children get pointed lesson in French. *Knickerbocker News.* Albany, New York.

Pimsleur, P., & Quinn, T. (Eds.) (1971). *The psychology of second language learning.* Cambridge: Cambridge University Press.

Plata, M. (1982). *Assessment, placement, and programming of bilingual exceptional pupils: A practical approach.* Reston, VA: The Council for Exceptional Children.

Plata, M., & Jones, M. (1982). Bilingual vocational education for handicapped students. *Exceptional Children, 49,* 538–540.

Porter, D. (1978). Cloze procedure and equivalence. *Language Learning, 28,* 333–341.

Porter, D. (1983). The effect of quantity of context on the ability to make linguistic prediction: A flaw in a measure of general proficiency. In A. Hughes & D. Porter (Eds.), *Current developments in language testing* (pp. 63–74). New York: Academic Press.

Porter, P. A. (1986). How learners talk to each other: Input and interaction in task-centered discussion. In Day, (1986: 200–222).

Porter, R. (1990a). *Forked tongue: The politics of bilingual education.* New York: Basic.

Porter, R. (1990b, April 30–May 6). Bilingual education has muted the future for minority children. *The Washington Post National Weekly Edition,* pp. 2–25.

Postovsky, V. (1974). Effects of delay in oral practice at the beginning of second language learning. *Modern Language Journal, 58,* 5–6.

Postovsky, V. (1975, August). The priority of aural comprehension in the language acquisition process. Paper presented at the 4th AILA World Conference, Defense Language Institute, Monterey, CA.

Postovsky, V. (1977). Why not start speaking later? In Burt, Dulay, & Finocchiaro (1977: 17–26).

Prabhu, N. S. (1987). *Second language pedagogy.* Oxford: Oxford University Press.

Prabhu, N. S. (1988, April). Materials for language learning and teaching: New trends and developments.

Paper presented at SEAMEO RELC 23rd Regional Seminar on Materials for Language Learning and Teaching: New Trends and Developments, Singapore.

Praninskas, J. (1959). *Rapid review of English grammar, for students of English as a second language.* Englewood Cliffs, NJ: Prentice Hall.

Propp, V. (1968). *Morphology of the folktale* (L. Scott, Trans.). Austin, TX: University of Texas Press.

Rafferty, E. A. (1986). *Second language study and basic skills in Louisiana.* Baton Rouge, LA: Department of Education.

Ragsdale, J. D. (1976). Relationships between hesitation phenomena, anxiety, and self-control in a normal communication situation. *Language and Speech, 19,* 257–265.

Ragsdale, J. D., & Silvia, C. F. (1982). Distribution on kinesic hesitation phenomena in spontaneous speech. *Language and Speech, 25*(2), 185–190.

Ragsdale, J. D., & Sisterhen, D. H. (1984). Hesitation phenomena in the spontaneous speech of normal and articulatory-defective children. *Language and Speech, 27*(3), 235–244.

Ramanauskas, S. (1972). The responsiveness of cloze readability measures to linguistic variables operating over segments of text longer than a sentence. *Reading Research Quarterly, 8,* 72–91.

Rattanavich, S. (1992). Classroom management. In Walker, Rattanavich, & Oller (1992: 12–32).

Rattanavich, S., & Walker, R. F. (1990). *The Rotary Literacy in Thailand Project: Education for all.* Report of the UNESCO South East Asia and South Pacific Regional Conference. Darwin, Australia: Northern Territory Department of Education.

Ratte, E. H. (1968). Foreign language and the elementary school language arts program. *French Review, 42,* 80–85.

Reschly, D. (1978). WISC-R factor structures among Anglos, Blacks, Chicanos, and Native-American Papagos. *Journal of Consulting and Clinical Psychology, 48,* 417–422.

Rhodes, L. K., & Dudley-Marling, C. (1988). *Readers and writers with a difference: A holistic approach to teaching learning disabled remedial students.* Portsmouth, NH: Heinemann.

Rhodes, N. (1987). *Total and partial immersion programs in U. S. elementary schools.* Los Angeles: Center for Language Education and Research, University of California, Los Angeles.

Richard-Amato, P. A. (1988). *Making it happen.* London: Longman.

Richard-Amato, P. A., & Snow, M. A. (1992). *The multicultural classroom.* London: Longman.

Richards, J. C. (1969). Songs in language learning. *TESOL Quarterly, 3*(2), 161–174.

Richards, J. C. (1974). *Error analysis: Perspectives on second language acquisition.* London: Longman.

Richards, J. C. (Ed.) (1978). *Understanding Second and Foreign Language Learning.* Rowley, MA: Newbury House.

Richards, J. C. (1983). Listening comprehension: Approach, design, procedure. *TESOL Quarterly, 17,* 219–240.

Richards, J. C., & Rodgers, T. (1982). Method: Approach, design, procedure. *TESOL Quarterly, 16,* 153–168.

Richards, J. C., & Rodgers, T. (1986). *Approaches and methods in language teaching.* New York: Cambridge University Press.

Richterich, R., & Chancerel, J. (1977). *Identifying the needs of adults learning a foreign language.* Strasbourg: Council for Cultural Co-operation of the Council of Europe.

Rigg, P., &, Enright, D. S. (Eds.) (1986). *Children and ESL: Integrating perspectives.* Washington, DC: TESOL.

Rivers, W. M. (1966). Listening comprehension. *Modern Language Journal, 50,* 196–204.

Rivers, W. M. (1981). *Teaching foreign language skills* (2nd ed.). Chicago: University of Chicago Press.

Rivers, W. M. (1983). *Communicating naturally in a second language: Theory and practice in language teaching.* London: Cambridge University Press.

Rivers, W. M. (1985). A new curriculum for new purposes. *Foreign Language Annals, 18,* 37–43.

Rivers, W. M. (1986). Comprehension and production in interactive language teaching. *Modern Language Journal, 70,* 1–7.

Rivers, W. M. (1987). Interaction as the key to teaching language for communication. In *Interactive Language Teaching.* Cambridge: Cambridge University Press.

Rivers, W. M., Azevedo, M. M., & Heflin, W. H., Jr. (1988). *Teaching Spanish: A practical guide*. Chicago: National Textbook.

Robinson, G. L. (1989). The CLCCS CALL study: Methods, error feedback, attitudes, and achievement. In Smith (1989: 119–134).

Rodari, G. (1973). *Grammatica della fantasia*. Einaudi.

Rodgers, T. (1988, April). Materials to support cooperative language learning: A classification and critique. Paper presented at SEAMEO RELC 23rd Regional Seminar on Materials for Language Learning and Teaching: New Trends and Developments, Singapore.

Rogers, C. V., & Medley, F. W., Jr. (1988). Language with a purpose: Using authentic materials in the foreign language classroom. *Foreign Language Annals, 21,* 467–476.

Rondal, J. (1984). Bilingualism and mental handicap: Some programmatic views. In Paradis & Lebrun (1984: 135–160).

Rosenblatt, L. (1978). *The reader, the text, and the poem*. Carbondale, IL: University of Southern Illinois Press.

Rossell, C. (1990). The effectiveness of educational alternatives for limited English proficient children. In G. Imhoff (Ed.), *Learning in two languages: From conflict to consensus in the reorganization of schools* (pp. 71–122). New Brunswick, NJ: Transaction.

Rossell, C., & Ross, J. M. (1986). The social science evidence on bilingual education. *Journal of Law and Education, 15,* 385–418.

Rucker, B. (1982). Magazines and teenage reading skills: Two controlled field experiments. *Journalism Quarterly, 59,* 28–33.

Rumelhart, D. (1975). Notes on a schema for stories. In Bobrow & Collins (1975: 211–236).

Rumelhart, D. (1980). Schemata: The building blocks of cognition. In Spiro, Bruce, & Brewer (1980: 33–58).

Sabatino, D., Hayden, D., & Kelling, K. (1972). Perceptual language and academic achievement of English, Spanish, and Navajo speaking children referred for special classes. *Journal of School Psychology, 10,* 39–46.

Saegert, J., Scott, M., Perkins, J., & Tucker, G. R. (1974). A note on the relationship between English proficiency, years of language study and medium of instruction. *Language Learning, 24,* 99–104.

Salisbury, D. F. (1990). Cognitive psychology and its implications for designing drill and practice programs for computers. *Journal of Computer-Based Instruction, 17*(1). 23–40.

Samuda, R., & Crawford, D. (1980). *Testing, assessment, counseling, and placement of ethnic minority students*. Toronto: Ministry of Education.

Samuels, S. J. (1977). Introduction to theoretical models of reading. In W. Otto (Ed.), *Reading problems* (pp. 7–41). Boston: Addison-Wesley.

Samway, K., Whang, G., Cade, C., Gamil, M., Lubandina, M. A., & Phommachanh, K. (1991). Reading the skeleton, the heart, and the brain of a book: Students' perspectives on literature study circles. *The Reading Teacher, 45,* 196–206.

Savage, K. L. (1984, January). Teaching strategies for developing literacy skills in non-native speakers of English. Paper presented at the National Adult Literacy Conference, Washington, DC. (ERIC Document Reproduction Service No. ED 240 296)

Savignon, S. (1972). *Communicative competence: An experiment in foreign language teaching*. Montreal, Canada: Marcel Didier.

Savignon, S. (1983). *Communicative competence: Theory and classroom practice*. Reading, MA: Addison-Wesley.

Saville-Troike, M. (1984). What *really* matters in second language learning for academic achievement? *TESOL Quarterly, 18*(2), 199–220.

Scarcella, R. (1983). Sociodrama for social interaction. In Oller & Richard-Amato (1983: 239–245).

Scarcella, R. (1990). *Teaching language minority students*. Englewood Cliffs, NJ: Prentice Hall Regents.

Schank, R. (1975). The structure of episodes in memory. In Bobrow & Collins (1975: 237–272).

Schank, R. (1980). Language and memory. *Cognitive Science, 4,* 243–282.

Schank, R., & Abelson, R. (1977). *Scripts, plans, goals, and understanding*. Hillsdale, NJ: Lawrence Erlbaum.

Schessler, E. (1985). *Spanish grammar through actions*. Los Gatos, CA: Sky Oaks Productions.

Schlanger, P., & Schlanger, B. (1971). Adapting role-playing activities with aphasic patients. *Journal of Speech and Hearing Disorders, 35,* 229–235.

Schleppegrell, M. (1984). Using input methods to improve writing skills. *System, 12,* 287–292.

Schlossman, S. L. (1983). Is there an American tradition of bilingual education? German in the public elementary schools, 1840–1919. *American Journal of Education, 91*(2), 139–186.

Schofer, P. (1990). Literature and communicative competence: A springboard for the development of critical thinking and esthetic appreciation of literature in the language. *Foreign Language Annals, 23,* 325–334.

Schorr, B. (1983, November 30). Grade school project helps Hispanic pupils learn English quickly. *The Wall Street Journal, 102* (106), 1, 24.

Schumann, J. (1975). Affective factors and the problem of age in second language acquisition. *Language Learning, 26,* 135–143.

Sebeok, T. A. (1991). *A sign is just a sign.* Bloomington, IN: Indiana University Press.

Segal, B. (1984). *Enseñando el español por medio de acción.* (ERIC Document Reproduction Service No. ED 235 686)

Seldin, P. (1990). *How administrators can improve teaching: Moving from talk to action in higher education.* San Francisco, CA: Josey-Bass.

Selinker, L. (1972). Interlanguage. *IRAL, 10, 209–231.*

Shaftel, F., & Shaftel, G. (1967). *Role-playing for social values.* Englewood Cliffs, NJ: Prentice Hall.

Shaftel, G., & Shaftel, F. (1952). *Role-playing and the problem story: An approach to human relations in the classroom.* New York: National Conference of Christians and Jews.

Shanahan, T., & Kamil, M. L. (1983). A further comparison of the sensitivity of cloze to passage organization. In J. Niles & L. Harris (Eds.), *New inquiries in reading research and instruction* (pp. 204–208). Rochester, NY: National Reading Conference.

Shanahan, T., Kamil, M. L., & Tobin, A. W. (1982). Cloze as a measure of intersentential comprehension. *Reading Research Quarterly, 17,* 229–255.

Shiffrin, R., & Schneider, W. (1977). Controlled and automatic human information processing: II, perceptual learning. In Bobrow & Collins (1975: 237–272).

Short, D. J. (1991). *Integrating language and content instruction: Strategies and techniques.* Washington, DC: National Clearinghouse for Bilingual Education, Program Information Guide Series.

Siegman, A. W., & Pope, B. (1965). Effects of question specificity and anxiety producing messages on verbal fluency in the initial interview. *Language and Speech, 2*(4), 522–530.

Silliman, E. R., & Wilkinson, L. C. (1991). *Communicating for learning: Classroom observation and collaboration.* Gaithersburg, MD: Aspen.

Silverstein, A. (1973). Factor structure of the Wechsler Intelligence Scale for Children for three ethnic groups. *Journal of Educational Psychology, 65,* 408–410.

Simmons, J. M. (Ed.) (1983). *The shortest distance to learning: A guidebook to writing across the curriculum.* Los Angeles: Los Angeles Community College District and University of California, Los Angeles.

Simon, P. (1980). *The tongue-tied American.* New York: Continuum Press.

Skinner, B. F. (1957). *Verbal behavior.* New York: Appleton, Century, Crofts.

Smith, F. (1978). *Reading without nonsense.* Cambridge: Cambridge University Press.

Smith, F. (1982). *Understanding reading.* Hillsdale, NJ: Lawrence Erlbaum.

Smith, F. (1988). *Joining the literacy club.* Portsmouth, NH: Heinemann.

Smith, R. J., & Johnson, D. D. (1976). *Teaching children to read.* Reading, MA: Addison Wesley.

Smith, W. F. (Ed.) (1989). *Modern technology in foreign language education: Applications and projects.* Chicago: National Textbook.

Snow, M. A., & Brinton, D. (1988). Content-based language instruction: Investigating the effectiveness of the adjunct model. *TESOL Quarterly, 22*(4), 553–574.

Snow, M. A., Met, M., & Genesee, F. (1989). A conceptual framework for the integration of language and content in second/foreign language instruction. *TESOL Quarterly, 23,* 201–217.

Snow, R. S., & Lohman, D. F. (1984). Toward a theory of cognitive aptitude for learning from instruction. *Journal of Educational Psychology, 76*(3), 347–376.

Sparks, R. L., Ganschow, L., Javorsky, J., Pohlman, J., & Patton, J. (1992). Test comparisons among students identified as high-risk, low-risk, and learning disabled in high school foreign language courses. *Modern Language Journal, 76*(2), 142–159.

Spilka, I. V. (1976). Assessment of second language performance in immersion programs. *Canadian Modern Language Review, 32,* 543–561.

Spiro, R. J., Bruce, B. C., & Brewer, W. F. (Eds.) (1980). *Theoretical issues in reading comprehension.* Hillsdale, NJ: Lawrence Erlbaum.

Spolsky, B. (1973). What does it mean to know a language, or how do you get someone to perform his competence? In Oller & Richards (1973: 164–176).

Spolsky, B. (1985). A critical review of Krashen. Lecture presented at the University of New Mexico.

Spolsky, B. (1989). *Conditions for second language learning: Introduction to a general theory*. Oxford: Oxford University Press.

Stabb, C. (1990). Teacher mediation in one whole literacy classroom. *The Reading Teacher, 43*, 548–552.

Stansfield, C., & Horner, J. (1987). The Dartmouth-Rassias model of teaching foreign languages: A modification of the Dartmouth intensive language model. *ADFL Bulletin, 19*(1), 18–21.

Staton, J. (1983). Dialogue journals: A new tool for teaching communication. *ERIC/CLL News Bulletin*. ERIC, March.

Stauffer, R. (1981). *Directing the reading-thinking process*. New York: Harper & Row.

Steffensen, M. (1986). Register, cohesion, and cross-cultural reading comprehension. *Applied Linguistics, 7*(1), 71–85.

Steffensen, M. S., Joag-Dev, C., & Anderson, R. C. (1979). A cross-cultural perspective on reading comprehension. *Reading Research Quarterly, 15*, 10–29.

Stein, N. L., & Glenn, C. G. (1979). An analysis of story comprehension in elementary school children. In Freedle (1979: 53–120).

Stern, H. H. (1978). Bilingual schooling and foreign language education: Some implications of the Canadian experiments in French. In Alatis (1978: 165–188).

Stern, H. H. (1992). *Issues and options in language teaching*. Oxford: Oxford University Press.

Sternfeld, S. (1988). The applicability of the immersion approach to beginning college foreign language instruction. *Foreign Language Annals, 21*, 221–226.

Stevick, E. W. (1974). Language instruction must do an about-face. *Modern Language Journal, 58*, 379–384.

Stevick, E. W. (1976). *Memory, meaning, and method*. Rowley, MA: Newbury House.

Stevick, E. W. (1980). *A way and ways*. Rowley, MA: Newbury House.

Stevick, E. W. (1982). *Teaching and learning languages*. London: Cambridge University Press.

Stevick, E. W. (1986). *Images and options in the language classroom*. London: Cambridge University Press.

Stevick, E. W. (1990). *Humanism in language teaching*. Oxford: Oxford University Press.

Stewart, R. F. (1980). *. . . And always a detective*. Vermont: David & Charles.

Stokes, J. (1988). Some factors in the acquisition of the present subjunctive in Spanish. *Hispania, 71*, 705–710.

Stokes, J., & Krashen, S. D. (1990). Some factors in the acquisition of the present subjunctive in Spanish: A re-analysis. *Hispania, 73*, 805–806.

Straight, H. S. (1990, March). Languages must be taught "across the curriculum" to insure that students develop functional skills. *The Chronicle of Higher Education, 7*, B2.

Strain, J. (1986). Method: Design-procedure versus method-technique. *System, 14*(3), 287–294.

Strevens, P. (1980). *Teaching English as an international language*. Oxford: Pergamon.

Strong, M. (1984). Integrative motivation: Cause or result of successful second language acquisition? *Language Learning, 34*, 1–14.

Stubbs, J. B., & Tucker, G. R. (1974). The cloze test as a measure of English proficiency. *Modern Language Journal, 58*, 239–241.

Suozzo, A. G., Jr. (1981). Once more with content: Shifting emphasis in intermediate French. *French Review, 54*, 405–411.

Swaffar, J. K. (1985). Reading authentic texts in a foreigh langauge: A cognitive model. *Modern Language Journal, 69*, 15–34.

Swaffar, J. K., Arens, K. M., & Byrnes, H. (1991). *Reading for meaning: An integrated approach to language learning*. Englewood Cliffs, NJ: Prentice Hall.

Swaffar, J. K., & Woodruff, M. S. (1978). Language for comprehension: Focus on reading. A report on the University of Texas German program. *Modern Language Journal, 62*, 27–32.

Swain, D. V. (1973). *Techniques of the selling writer*. Norman, OK: University of Oklahoma Press.

Swain, M. (1973). *Bilingual Schooling: Some Experiences in Canada and the United States*. Toronto: The Ontario Institute for Studies in Education.

Swain, M. (1978). Immersion: Early, late, or partial? *Canadian Modern Language Review, 43,* 577–585.

Swain, M. (1982). Immersion education: Applicability for non-vernacular teaching to vernacular speakers. In B. Hartford, A. Valdman, & C. R. Foster (Eds.), *Issues in international bilingual education: The role of the vernacular* (pp. 81–97). New York: Plenum.

Swain, M. (1985). Communicative competence: Some roles of comprehensible input and comprehensible output in its development. In Gass & Madden (1985: 235–253).

Swain, M. (1988). Manipulating and complementing content teaching to maximize second language learning. *TESL Canada, 6,* 68–83.

Swain, M., & Lapkin, S. (1982). *Evaluating bilingual education: A Canadian case study.* Clevedon, England: Multilingual Matters.

Swain, M., & Lapkin, S. (1989). Canadian immersion and adult second language teaching: What's the connection? *Modern Language Journal, 73,* 150–159.

Taglieber, L. K., Johnson, L. L., & Yarbrough, D. B. (1988). Effects of pre-reading activities on EFL reading by Brazilian college students. *TESOL Quarterly, 22*(3), 455–472.

Taira, T. (1986). The prospect of CAI in English teaching in Japan. *Ryudai Review of Language & Literature, 31,* 49–71.

Taira, T. (1987). Computer-assisted language learning in diverse situations: An introduction to a new program. *Ryudai Review of Language & Literature, 32,* 135–152.

Taira, T. (1989). Situational English learning through CAI: An introduction of flow charts of a newly developed computer program. *Ryudai Review of Language & Literature, 34,* 75–94.

Taira, T. (1991). Pragmatic strategies for inferences and interepretations. *Ryudai Review of Language & Literature, 36,* 17–32.

Taira, T. (1993). *Episodic organization and CALL: A pragmatic approach.* Unpublished doctoral dissertation, University of New Mexico, Albuquerque.

Tardif, C., & Weber, S. (1987). French immersion research: A call for new perspectives. *Canadian Modern Language Review, 44,* 67–77.

Taylor, B. (1987). Teaching ESL: Incorporating a communicative student-centered component. In Long & Richards (1987: 45–60).

Taylor, W. L. (1953). "Cloze procedure": A new tool for measuring readability. *Journalism Quarterly, 30,* 415–433.

Taylor, W. L. (1954). *Application of "cloze" and entropy measures to the study of contextual constraints in samples of continuous prose.* Unpublished doctoral dissertation, University of Illinois, Urbana-Champaign.

Taylor, W. L. (1956). Recent developments in the use of "cloze procedure." *Journalism Quarterly, 33,* 42–48, 99.

Taylor, W. L. (1957). Cloze readability scores as indices of individual differences in comprehension and aptitude. *Journal of Applied Psychology, 41,* 19–26.

Teeter, A., Moore, C., & Petersen, J. (1982). WISC-R verbal and performance abilities of Native American student referred for school learning problems. *Psychology in the Schools, 19,* 39–44.

Temple, L. (1985). He who hesitates is not lost: Fluency and the language learner. *Révue de Phonétique Appliquée, 73–75,* 293–302.

Terrell, S., & T. Terrell. (1983). Distinguishing linguistic differences from disorders: The past, present, and future of non-biased assessment. *Topics in Language Disorders, 3,* 1–7.

Terrell, T. (1986). Acquisition in the natural approach: The binding/access framework. *Modern Language Journal, 70,* 213–227.

Terrell, T. D. (1986). Recent trends in research and practice: Teaching Spanish. *Hispania, 68,* 193–202.

Thaiss, C. (1987). Writing across the curriculum: The state of the art. *Quarterly of the Material Writing Project and Center for the Study of Writing, 9*(1), 14–17.

The Australian. (1991, June 29–30). Illiteracy may be inherited.

Thorndyke, P. W. (1977). Cognitive structures in comprehension and memory of narrative discourse. *Cognitive Psychology, 9,* 77–110.

Tonkin, H. (1985). Foreign language and the humanities. *ADFL Bulletin, 17*(2), 5–8.

Toth, Carolyn R. (1990). *German-English bilingual schools in America: The Cincinnati tradition in historical context.* New York: Peter Lang.

Trabasso, T., Secco, T., & van den Broek, P. (1984). Causal cohesion and story coherence. In H. Mandl, N. L. Stein, & T. Trabasso (Eds.), *Learning and comprehension of text* (pp. 1–25). Hillsdale, NJ: Lawrence Erlbaum.

Trabasso, T., & Sperry, L. L. (1985). The causal basis for deciding importance of story events. *Journal of Memory and Language, 24,* 595–611.

Trabasso, T., & van de Broek, P. (1985). Causal thinking and the representation of narrative events. *Journal of Memory and Language, 24,* 612–630.

Trabasso, T., van den Broek, P., & Suh, S. Y. (1989). Logical necessity and transitivity of causal relations in stories. *Discourse Processes, 12,* 1–25.

Traven, B. (1971). *Marcario.* Boston: Houghton Mifflin.

Tucker, J. (1980). Ethnic proportion in classes for the learning disabled: Issues in non-biased assessment. *Journal of Special Education, 14,* 93–105.

Tudor, I. (1990). Pre-reading format and learner proficiency level in L2 reading comprehension. *Journal of Research in Reading, 13*(2), 43–106.

Tuffs, R. J., & Tudor, I. (1990). What the eye doesn't see: Cross-cultural problems in the comprehension of video materials. *RELC Journal, 21*(2), 29–44.

Umemoto, T. (1987). *Ninchi to pafomansu* (Cognition and performance). Tokyo: Tokyo University Press.

Underwood, J. H. (1984). *Linguistics computers and the language teacher.* Rowley, MA: Newbury House.

Ur, P. (1981). *Discussions that work.* Cambridge: Cambridge University Press.

Urwin, C. (1978). The development of communication between blind infants and their parents. In A. Loc (Ed.), *Action, gesture, and symbol* (79–108). New York: Academic Press.

Urwin, C. (1979). Pre-verbal communication and early language development in blind children. *Papers and Reports of Child Language Development, 17,* 119–127.

Van Dijk, T. A. (1983). Discourse analysis: Its development and application to the structure of news. *Journal of Communication, 33,* 20–43.

Van Dijk, T. A. (1985). *Handbook of discourse analysis.* London: Academic Press.

Van Lier, L. (1988). *The classroom and the language learner.* New York: Longman.

VanPatten, B. (1985). The acquisition of *ser* and *estar* by adult learners of Spanish: A preliminary investigation of transitional stages. *Hispania, 68,* 399–406.

VanPatten, B. (1987). On babies and bathwater: Input in foreign language learning. *Modern Language Journal, 71,* 156–164.

VanPatten, B., LeMieux, T., & Wenmen, F. (in progress). The acquisition of complex syntax in Spanish: The case of *gustar.*

Vetter, E. B. (1983). TPR-plus. Paper presented at the meeting of the California Association of Teachers of English to Speakers of Other Languages, Los Angeles, CA. (ERIC Document Reproduction Service No. ED 230 035)

Via, R. (1976). *English in three acts.* Honolulu, Hawaii: East-West Center, University of Hawaii.

Vigil, N., & Oller, J. W., Jr. (1976). Rule fossilization: A tentative model. *Language Learning, 26,* 281–295.

Von Raffler-Engel, W. (1980). Kinesics and paralinguistics: A neglected factor in second language research and teaching. *Canadian Modern Language Review, 36,* 225–237.

Voss, J. F., Vesander, G. T., & Spilich, G. J. (1980). Text generation and recall by high and low knowledge individuals. *Journal of Verbal Learning and Verbal Behavior, 19,* 651–667.

Vygotsky, L. S. (1934). *Language and thought.* Cambridge, MA: Harvard University Press.

Vygotsky, L. S. (1978). *Mind in society.* Cambridge, MA: Harvard University Press.

Wade, S. (1990). Using think alouds to assess comprehension. *The Reading Teacher, 43,* 442–451.

Walker, K. S. (1969). *Eyes on mime: Language without speech.* New York: The John Day Co.

Walker, R. F. (1981). *The language of entering children at Traeger Park School.* Occasional Paper No. 11. Canberra, Australia: The Australian Curriculum Development Center.

Walker, R. F., Rattanavich, S., & Oller, J. W., Jr. (1992). *Teaching all the children to read.* Buckingham, England: Open University Press.

Wallace, N., & Fischgrund, J. (1985). Minority Deaf students: An overview. *ASHA, 27,* 28.

Walters, J., & Wolf, Y. (1986). Language proficiency, text content, and order effects in narrative recall. *Language Learning, 36,* 47–63.

Walz, J. (1989). Context and contextualized language practice in foreign language teaching. *Modern Language Journal, 73*(2), 160–168.

Walz, J. A. (1936). *German influence in American education and culture.* Philadelphia: Carl Schurz Memorial Foundation.

Wangsotorn, A., Maurice, A., Prapphal, K., & Kenny, B. (Eds.) (1986). *Trends in language program evaluation*. Papers Presented at CULI's First International Conference on Trends in Language Program Evaluation, December 9–11, 1986. Bangkok, Thailand: Chulalongkorn University Language Institute.

Watkins, B. T. (1990). Program at St. Olaf College offers students incentives to make foreign languages more than a requirement. *The Chronicle of Higher Education*, November 28, A19, A21.

Watzlawick, P., Beavin, J., & Jackson, K. (1967). *Pragmatics of human communication*. New York: Norton.

Weaver, C. (1972). *Human listening: Processes and behavior*. Indianapolis: Bobbs-Merrill.

Weaver, C. (1980). *Psycholinguistics and reading: From process to practice*. Boston: Little Brown.

Webb, N. M., & Kenderski, C. M. (1984). Student interaction and learning in small-group and whole-class settings. In P. Peterson, L. Wilkinson, & M. Hallinan (Eds.), *Social context of instruction group organization and group processes*. Orlando, FL: Academic Press.

Webber, B. L. (1980). Syntax beyond the sentence. In Spiro, Bruce, & Brewer (1980: 141–164).

Weinreich, U. (1953). *Languages in Contact*. New York: Publications of the Linguistics Circle of New York.

Weissenrieder, M. (1987). Listening to the news in Spanish. *Modern Language Journal, 71*(1), 18–26.

Wells, G. (1981). *Learning through interaction: The study of language development*. Cambridge: Cambridge University Press.

Wells, G. (1986). *The meaning-makers: Children learning language and using language to learn*. Portsmouth, NH: Heinemann.

Wesche, M. (1977). Learning behaviors of successful adult students in intensive language training. In Henning (1977: 355–370).

Wessels, C. (1987). *Drama*. Oxford: Oxford University Press.

Wessels, C. et al. (1991). *Soap opera*. London: Macmillan Bookshelf Readers.

Westby, C. (1989). Assessing and facilitating text comprehension. In A. Kamhi & H. Catts (Eds.), *Reading disabilities: A developmental perspective* (pp. 199–259). Boston: College-Hill.

Westby, C., & Rouse, L. (1985). Culture in education and the instruction of language learning-disabled students. *Topics in Language Disorders, 6*, 15–28.

Whitaker, B. T., Schwartz, E., & Vockell, E. L. (1989). *The computer in the reading curriculum*. Watsonville, CA: Mitchell.

Wickert, R. (1989). *No single measure: A survey of Australian adult literacy*. Canberra: Commonwealth Department of Employment, Education, and Training.

Widdowson, H. G. (1979). Directions in the teaching of discourse. In Brumfit & Johnson (1979: 49–60).

Widdowson, H. G. (1983). *Learning purpose and language use*. New York: Oxford University Press.

Wilbur, R. (1987). *American Sign Language*. Boston: College-Hill Press.

Wilcox, S. (Ed.) (1988). *Academic acceptance of American Sign Language: Sign Language Studies, Special Issue*, 59. Silver Spring, MD: Linstok.

Wilcox, S., & Wilcox, P. (1991). *Learning to see: American Sign Language as a second language*. Englewood Cliffs, NJ: Prentice Hall.

Wiley, P. D. (1985). A model FLEX (foreign language experience) program for the elementary school. Paper presented at the International Conference on Second Language Acquisition by Children, Oklahoma City, OK. (ERIC Document Reproduction Service No. ED 256 171)

Wilkins, D. A. (1976). *Notional syllabuses*. London: Oxford University Press.

Willets, K. F. (Ed.). (1986). *Integrating language and content instruction*. Los Angeles: University of California, Center for Language Education and Research. (ERIC Document Reproduction Service No. ED 278 262)

Willig, A. C. (1985). A meta-analysis of selected studies on the effectiveness of bilingual education. *Review of Educational Research, 55*, 269–317.

Willig, A. C. (1987). Reply to Baker. *Review of Educational Research, 57*, 363–376.

Willig, A. C., & Ortiz, A. A. (1991). The non-biased individualized educational program: Linking assessment to instruction. In Hamayan & Damico (1991: 241–302).

Wilson, D., & Sperber, D. (1986). *Pragmatics: An overview*. (ERIC Document Reproduction Service No. ED 268 840)

Winitz, H. (Ed.) (1981). *The comprehension approach to foreign language instruction*. Rowley, MA: Newbury House.

Winitz, H., & Reeds, J. (1973a). *Comprehension and problem solving as a strategy for language training—the OHR method*. Prepublication monograph, University of Missouri. Kansas City, Missouri.

Winitz, H., & Reeds, J. (1973b). Rapid acquisition of a foreign language by the avoidance of speaking. *International Review of Applied Linguistics, 11*, 295–317.

Winitz, H., & Reeds, J. (1975). *Comprehension and problem solving as strategies for language training*. The Hague: Mouton.

Winks, R. W. (1980). *Detective fiction*. Englewood Cliffs, NJ: Prentice Hall.

Wipf, J. A. (1984). Strategies for teaching second language comprehension. *Foreign Language Annals, 17*, 345–348.

Wittrock, M. C. (1977). The generative process of memory. In M. C. Wittrock, J. Beatty, J. E. Bogen, M. S. Gazzaniga, H. J. Jerison, S. D. Krashen, R. D. Nebes, & T. J. Teyler, *The human brain*. Englewood Cliffs, NJ: Prentice Hall.

Wolkomir, R. (1980, May). A manic professor tries to close up the language gap. *The Smithsonian, 11*, 80–86. In Oller & Richard-Amato (1983: 89–100).

Wollman-Bonilla, J. (1989). Reading journals: Invitations to participate in literature. *The Reading Teacher, 42*, 112–119.

Wong-Fillmore, L. (1976). *The second time around: Cognitive and social strategies in second language acquisition*. Unpublished doctoral dissertation, Stanford University, Palo Alto, CA.

Wong-Fillmore, L. (1982). Instructional language as linguistic input: Second-language learning in classrooms. In L. C. Wilkinson (Ed.), *Communicating in the classroom* (pp. 283–296). New York: Academic Press.

Wong-Fillmore, L. (1985). When does teacher talk work as input? In Gass & Madden (1985: 17–50).

Woodruff, M. (1976). Integration of the TPR strategy into a first-year German program: From obeying commands to creative writing. Paper presented at the Spring Conference of Texas Chapters of the American Association of Teachers of German, North Texas State University, Denton, TX. (ERIC Document Reproduction Service No. ED 126 688)

Wright, A. W., Barrett, R. P., & Van Syoc, W. B. (1968). *Let's learn English: Intermediate course*. New York: American Book.

Wyatt, D. H. (1983). Computer-assisted language instruction: Present state and future prospects. *System, 11*(1), 3–11.

Wylie, L. (1977). *Beaux gestes: A guide to French body talk*. Cambridge, MA: Undergraduate Press.

Yudkovitz, E., Lewison, N., & Rottersman, J. (1976). *Communication therapy in children's schizophrenia: An auditory monitoring approach*. New York: Grune & Straton.

INDEX

Smith, W. F.   320, 324, 328, 408, 412, 413

Snow, C.   401

Snow, M. A.   xii, xiv, 85, 86, 125, 126, 134, 136, 142, 146, 150, 181, 255, 305, 306, 326, 390, 391, 411, 413

Snow, R. S.   255, 413

soap opera   310, 368, 370–372, 417

sociocultural background   2, 98, 108, 164, 181, 208, 220, 334, 337, 341, 343, 381, 384, 402, 406

sociodrama   74, 413

Solís, J.   95, 410

Songkla, Thailand   216, 218

songs   5, 115, 118, 120, 122, 124, 175, 180, 333–338, 358, 360, 361, 411

Sparks, R. L.   320, 413

special populations   320–324, 328–330

spelling   89, 134, 171, 177, 263, 273, 277, 278, 403

Sperber, D.   417

Sperry, L. L.   232, 416

Spilich, G. J.   365, 416

Spilka, I. V.   130, 413

spiral (the learning curve)   174, 269–271, 316

Spiro, R. J.   387, 393, 401, 407, 412, 413, 417

Spolsky, B.   3, 271, 383, 414

spontaneity   29, 46, 71, 75, 76, 80–82, 403

Srinakharinwirot University, Bangkok   163

SSMT   143, 144, 146–148

St. John, J.   125, 393

Stabb, C.   324, 325, 414

stabilization   135

Stachowiak, Herbert   395

Stanislavski   73

Stansfield, C.   x, 9, 414

Stapleton, Shirley   x

Staton, J.   324, 414

Stauffer, R.   327, 414

Steffensen, M. S.   192, 202, 231, 243, 248, 414

Stein, N. L.   192, 414, 415

Steinbeck, Robert   320, 321

Stern, H. H.   x, xi, xiv, 10, 11, 70, 83, 141, 326, 327, 368, 414

Sternfeld, S.   x, xiv, 93, 127, 145, 147, 160, 181–183, 190, 414

Stevick, E. W.   x, xvi, xvii, 182, 190, 310, 311, 346, 351, 414

Stewart, R. F.   291, 414

Stokes, J.   145, 414

Storey, M.   394

storytelling   5, 63, 113–115, 120, 121, 352, 354, 355, 357, 410

Straight, H. S.   2, 7, 9, 43, 132, 157, 414

Strain, J.   2, 414

strategic competence   283, 284

    abandonment   304, 305

    editing   31, 123, 177, 292, 303

    elaboration   8, 209, 269, 305

    humor   9, 24, 29, 44, 45, 49, 287, 339

    negotiating   136, 143, 148, 168, 173, 175, 176, 273, 278, 279, 288, 358, 362, 384, 393

    rejection   71, 72, 74, 76, 80, 82, 83

    scaffolding   1, 3–5, 7, 118, 126, 159–161, 168–171, 173, 175, 180, 181, 190, 247, 264, 265, 280, 320, 322, 324, 326–329, 342

    searching (as a monitoring editorial procedure)   22, 165, 188, 303–305, 321, 356

    thematic understanding   33, 120, 132, 249

    translating   3, 107, 174, 286, 384

Strevens, P.   2, 414

Strong, M.   110, 414

structural competence   16, 27, 29, 38, 48, 50–52, 58, 104, 133, 146, 194, 242, 252, 310, 314, 337, 350, 352, 363

structure drills   53, 55, 56, 62

Stryker, S. B.   150, 151, 181, 404

Stubbs, J. B.   316, 414

styles of storytelling   357

subject-matter   132–134, 143, 145, 147, 148, 183, 184, 189, 395

submersion   4, 86, 90, 91, 93, 97, 98, 126

subtractive bilingualism   86, 126

suggestopedia   32, 346, 351, 391

Suh, S. Y.   232, 416

Sullivan, D. D.   401

Suozzo, A. G., Jr.   182, 190, 414

Sussex, R.   309, 387

Swaffar, J. K.   32, 125, 182, 190, 414

Swain, D. V.   366, 414

Swain, M.   1, 95, 125, 129, 130, 138, 144–147, 173, 182, 263, 264, 375, 383, 387–389, 404, 414, 415

syntax   57, 62, 115, 135, 241, 242, 281, 304, 314, 341, 347, 364, 398, 400, 416, 417

Tada, Minoru   216, 228

Taggart, R.   402

Taglieber, L. K.   248, 415

Taira, T.   xiv, 5, 10, 161, 206, 207, 217, 224, 264, 265, 309–312, 315, 317–319, 409, 415

Tannen, D.   396

Tardif, C.   130, 415

target language   2–4, 7–10, 13, 15, 20–22, 31, 33, 34, 39, 49–55, 58, 61–63, 70, 71, 73, 83, 85, 86, 88, 99, 110, 117–120, 122, 124–126, 130, 136–141, 143, 147–149, 157, 160, 175, 176, 181, 182, 223, 263, 269, 281, 290, 295, 297, 304, 308, 310, 334, 339, 343, 354, 362, 366, 383, 384

Taylor, B.   110, 415

Taylor, W. L.   208, 216, 399, 415

TBE (see transitional bilingual education)

teacher-centered classrooms   133, 184

Teeter, A.   105, 415

Temple, L.   302, 415

temporal arrangement of discourse   52, 75, 160, 191, 194, 198, 199, 201, 364, 376, 398, 399, 402

Terrell, T.   ix, 31, 33, 105, 110, · 114, 119, 121, 306, 403, 415

Terrell, S.   415

TESL   72, 281, 335, 400, 415

TESOL   216, 220, 228, 334, 387–393, 398, 400–402, 404–406, 410–415

testing and tests (see also evluation and elicitation procedures)   2, 3, 7, 15, 17, 19, 20, 24, 32, 44, 48, 52, 58, 67, 69,